Making History

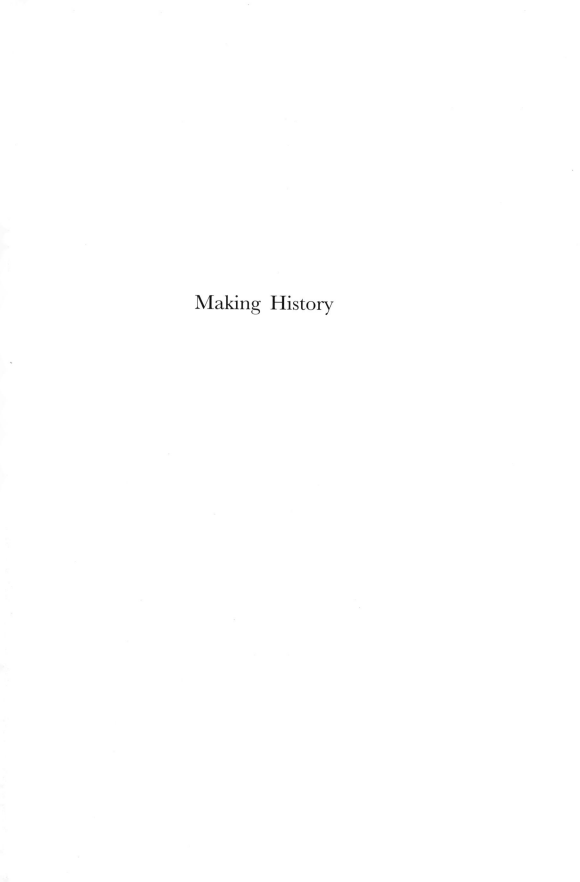

Supplements
to the
Journal for the Study
of Judaism

Editor
John J. Collins
The Divinity School, Yale University

Associate Editor
Florentino García Martínez
Qumran Institute, University of Groningen

Advisory Board

J. DUHAIME — A. HILHORST — P. W. VAN DER HORST
A. KLOSTERGAARD PETERSEN — M. A. KNIBB — H. NAJMAN
J. T. A. G. M. VAN RUITEN — J. SIEVERS — G. STEMBERGER
E. J. C. TIGCHELAAR — J. TROMP

VOLUME 110

Making History

Josephus and Historical Method

Edited by

Zuleika Rodgers

BRILL

LEIDEN • BOSTON

2007

This book is printed on acid-free paper.

Library of Congress Cataloging-in-Publication Data

Making history : Josephus and historical method / edited by Zuleika Rodgers.
 p. cm. — (Supplements to the Journal for the study of Judaism, ISSN 1384-2161 ;
 v. 110)
 Includes bibliographical references and index.
 ISBN 90-04-15008-0 (alk. paper)
 1. Josephus, Flavius—Congresses. 2. Jews—History—586 B.C.–70
A.D.—Historiography—Congresses. I. Rodgers, Zuleika. II. Series.

DS115.9.J6M35 2006
933'.05092—dc22

2005058245

ISSN 1384-2161
ISBN 10: 90 04 15008 0
ISBN 13: 978 900415 0089

CONTENTS

PART ONE

CONCEPTUAL FRAMEWORKS:
ANCIENT AND MODERN

PART TWO

JOSEPHUS' USE OF SOURCES

CONTRIBUTORS

Kenneth Atkinson, University of Northern Iowa, Cedar Falls, USA

Mordechai Aviam, Institute for Galilean Archaeology, University of Rochester, USA

Honora Howell Chapman, California State University, Fresno, USA

Niclas Förster, Georg-August-Universität, Göttingen, Germany

Alessandro Galimberti, Università Cattolica del Sacro Cuore, Milan, Italy

Gunnar Haaland, Norwegian Lutheran School of Theology, Norway

Gohei Hata, Tama Bijyutsu University, Tokyo, Japan

Jan Willem van Henten, University of Amsterdam, The Netherlands

Morten Hørning Jensen, University of Aarhus, Denmark

Steve Mason, York University, Toronto, Canada

James S. McLaren, School of Theology (Victoria), Australian Catholic University, Australia

Etienne Nodet, École Biblique et Archéologique Française de Jérusalem, Israel

Jack Pastor, Oranim, Academic College of Education, Israel

Uriel Rappaport, Jordan Valley College and University of Haifa, Israel

Samuel Rocca, Bar Ilan University, Israel

Daniel R. Schwartz, The Hebrew University of Jerusalem, Israel

Folker Siegert, Institutum Judaicum Delitzschianum, Münster University, Germany

Zeev Weiss, Hebrew University of Jerusalem, Israel

LIST OF ILLUSTRATIONS

ABBREVIATIONS

We have generally adopted the abbreviations of the *SBL Handbook of Style: For Ancient Near Eastern, Biblical, and Early Christian Studies*, ed. Patrick H. Alexander et al. Peabody. 1999. Additional abbreviations are as follows:

ABR	*Australian Biblical Review*
DOP	*Dumbarton Oaks Papers*
ESI	*Excavations and Surveys in Israel*
HH	*Historikà Hypomnemata*
INJ	*Israel Numismatic Journal*
JRA	*Journal of Roman Archaeology*
JRMES	*Journal of Roman Military Equipment Studies*
Plu.	Plutarch
QUCC	*Quaderni urbinati di cultura classica*
RH	*Revue Historique*
RRJ	*Review of Rabbinic Judaism*
RSA	*Rivista storica dell'antichità*
SCI	*Scripta Classica Israelica*
Xen.	Xenophon
FJTC	Flavius Josephus Translation and Commentary Brill Series, Edited by Steve Mason
War	*Jewish/Judean War*
Ant.	*Jewish/Judean Antiquities*
Apion	*Against Apion*

PREFACE

A volume such as this is made possible by the generosity of many people and institutions. The scholars who contributed took time out of their busy schedules to travel to Dublin to participate in the International Josephus Colloquium at Trinity College, and to prepare their articles for publication, a process with innumerable tedious stages. I am very grateful to them for their willingness to be involved; their goodwill and hard work made my job as editor significantly easier. I would also like to thank the other scholars, and also the students who participated in the Colloquium.

The International Josephus Colloquium, which took place in Trinity College Dublin in September 2004, was hosted by the Centre for Mediterranean and Near Eastern Studies. This project is funded by the Government of Ireland's National Development Plan, under the auspices of the Higher Education Authority's Programme for Research in Third Level Institutions. I would like to mention Prof. Seán Freyne and Prof. Brian McGing who, as directors of the Centre for Mediterranean and Near Eastern Studies, granted funding for the Colloquium, and I am grateful to them for their practical advice and encouragement. They also allowed me to focus on the Colloquium and this publication as part of my Post-Doctoral Fellowship in the Centre for Mediterranean and Near Eastern Studies.

I received further financial support for the Colloquium from the Project on Ancient Cultural Engagement at York University Toronto and as Post-Doctoral Fellow there in 2004–2005, I had access to their fine resources and a stimulating work environment. In particular I am indebted to Prof. Steve Mason for his sage advice, persistent encouragement, and generous support for both the Colloquium and the preparation of the manuscript.

The Herzog Centre for Jewish and Near Eastern Religion, Trinity College Dublin and the Irish School of Ecumenics also provided financial assistance for the Colloquium, while undergraduate and graduate students from the School of Religions and Theology and the School of Classics energetically and enthusiastically prepared and organised many aspects of the Colloquium. I am most grateful to them and cannot imagine how we would have managed the smooth

running of the Colloquium without their dedicated efforts. The staff
of the Chester Beatty Library, Dublin made us most welcome and
willingly facilitated our technical needs.

The editorial staff at Brill have been most efficient and helpful, and
in particular I would like to thank Mattie Kuiper and Anita Roodnat.
As editor of the Supplement Series to the *Journal for the Study of
Judaism*, Prof. John Collins' support has been central to the production of this volume. For his guidance and encouragement, I am
particularly grateful. My thanks also go to Conor Trainor for his
dedicated work on the indices. In preparing the material for publication I have tried to correct errors and misprints; I hope that I
have not done a disservice to all those who contributed to this volume, and responsibility for all errors remains with me.

INTRODUCTION

"Josephus's report was accurate," declared a headline in the "New Worlds" section of the Jerusalem Post. The article noted that "Josephus Flavius' abilities as an accurate 'reporter' have been confirmed by the Weizmann Institute researchers," whose study on the environmental conditions atop Masada in the Roman period corroborated Josephus' notice that some sort of cultivation was possible there. These scientists concluded that "the reliability of the famous historian has thus far remained unshaken." Q.E.D.! The idea of scientists "proving" Josephus' reliability is enticing but it reflects a simplistic approach to historical reconstruction. Yet traditionally scholarship using Josephus focused on the accuracy of certain vignettes or topics and was content to criticize Josephus' historical credentials rather than employing the sort of critical methodologies to which other ancient authors were subjected. Irresistible as a potential source, Josephus' works were approached as if they offered discrete pieces of historical information on Judea in the early Roman period. Underlying this approach was a belief that Josephus had simply collected, organized, and added editorial comments to his material, so that once his biases were identified, a sort of clean version of events could be reconstructed from his less subjective sources.

During the 1990s Josephan studies underwent a shift that produced a strong reaction against this arguably positivistic tradition.[1] More recent studies and projects devoted to Josephus, in many languages, tend to proceed from the assumption that his works are true compositions, requiring ever more sophisticated modes of analysis with full consideration of literary context, characteristic language, and rhetorical artifice.[2] New questions have also arisen about the

---

[1] For summaries on the development of Josephan studies, see Bilde 1988, 123–71 and Mason 2003, 145–50.

[2] The International Josephus Colloquium, which began in Muenster a decade ago, its papers (most recently, Sievers and Lembi 2005), the Josephus seminar in the Society of Biblical Literature, and other international meeting, such as the 2001 conference on Josephus in Flavian Rome (Edmondson, Mason, and Rives, 2005) have contributed much to this renaissance in Josephan studies. Translation and commentary projects in English, German, French, and Italian, as well as a growing list of web-based resources (e.g., http://pace.cns.yorku.ca) will continue to encourage new approaches in the field.

critical use of Josephus for contemporary archaeology, and the use of archaeology in understanding Josephus. While the ultimate goal for most scholars of Josephus remains historical reconstruction, how does the shift in perspective affect the way in which Josephus may now be used for that purpose?

This question of method provided the thematic framework for the International Josephus Colloquium at Trinity College Dublin in September 2004, where scholars were invited to address the method-ological encounter between interpretation and history. This dialectic provides the conceptual framework and organizing principle for the papers in this volume. It is divided thematically into four parts and an appendix. Although approaches, methods, and conclusions vary considerably, the interplay between narrative and history remains a central focus. As will become clear, the contributors represent a variety of subdisciplines in the study of Jewish antiquity. But each one has been conscious of the need to argue clearly before the others. This effort to communicate beyond one's academic comfort zone has generated, we hope, the qualities required of a useful book for the general educated reader.

The contributions to Part One, "Conceptual Frameworks: Ancient and Modern" focus both on Josephus' and the modern critical reader's historical methods. In the opening essay Folker Siegert sets out some fundamental questions of historical method, especially with regard to the language of historical discourse. While historians look to depict events in the past they must take account of the means by which the information is transmitted to them. For example, when reading Josephus, the question arises as to how we can distinguish between "Josephus' experiences, and those related by him, from his after-thoughts, interpretations, distortions, or even inventions." Siegert reminds us that, "the historian's raw material is not facts as such, but representations of facts, linguistic ones and others; it is these that give the facts their names and their contours." Since "facts" come to us as representations (texts, coins, and other artefacts), which must be interpreted, it is imperative that we do not confuse the language we use for facts with that which we use for words and texts (object language and meta-language). While there are no false facts (only untrue statements, distortions, and fictions) the content of a statement and the fact behind that statement must be distinguished.

Siegert asks, what is truth for historians? While a fact is related to an event or an object, truth is concerned with meaning. Meaning is validated by its reference to human experience, which includes critical investigation. He notes that, "... a statement is called true if both its references and its content can be verified by appropriate means. In this respect, and generally speaking, archaeology is about references, and historiography is about meanings. Both are concerned with truth." Siegert concludes that in the discipline of history, truth is an issue of interpersonal acceptance, which underlines the importance of discourse in such settings as colloquia.

A critical point of Siegert's contribution for the focus of this volume is his drawing out the complex process of historical method: this must include both an understanding of the nature of the evidence we use, including an awareness of Josephus' own methods, and the recognition that language profoundly complicates critical methodologies.

Siegert's reflections on the complexities involved in distinguishing fact from its representation and motive from reason are echoed by James McLaren, who examines the role of hindsight in Josephus' account of the war against Rome. Since Josephus wrote about the events from a post-70 C.E. perspective, and in light of his own experience in Rome, surely hindsight influenced his conceptual framework. What was Josephus' historical method: was he remembering, revising, rewriting? McLaren's focus is the dissonance he detects between Josephus' relatively rare explicit commentary and his recording of events, which makes up the body of the *Jewish War* and *Life*. In his explicit reflections, Josephus stresses that he was aware of the outcome of the war, and his acceptance of the futility of the rebellion was shared by other aristocrats (e.g., Ananus b. Ananus) who, at the outset of hostilities, were pro-Roman. McLaren understands Josephus to claim that responsibility for the war then lay with a small group of rebels, though this position was difficult to maintain since it implicitly suggested that the aristocrats failed to implement their pro-peace programme.

On the other hand, in spite of the different version of events in *War* and *Life*, the actions recorded by Josephus unequivocally reveal that he, like the Jerusalem authorities, was bellicose in his attitude towards Rome. Josephus' involvement in the course of events demonstrates his full participation in the war. McLaren finds this conflict between recorded actions and commentary particularly evident in the Iotapata episode. Here, when one would most expect a reflection on the view of the futility of the war and the need to submit to Rome, instead Josephus' explanation for his surrender is informed by his belief that divine will was behind Roman success and his defeat. This sentiment is further expressed with regard to the siege and fall of Jerusalem.

Scholarship has been traditionally dominated by two defining positions: those who find the "facts" in the commentary and those who see the recorded actions as revealing them. Where scholars have detected a lack of consistency between commentary and reported action, they have drawn negative conclusions regarding Josephus' integrity, accusing him of attempting to cover up his actions during the war. In contrast, those scholars who give precedence to his commentary find ways to reconcile the seeming contradictions by focusing on the complex role of this provincial aristocrat. McLaren proposes that understanding the role of hindsight in Josephus' narrative method can simultaneously reconcile these positions that the reported actions are preferable with the view that Josephus retained a consistent ideological stand and did not suddenly transfer his allegiances to Rome.

McLaren recognises that Josephus' works are crafted literary constructions comprised of episodes Josephus chose to narrate, and so we inherit his "interpretative framework." Yet he proposes that Josephus' reported actions can reveal his behaviour and attitudes during the war period for, "At the very core of *Jewish War* and *Life* lie historical realities: some Jews did go to war against the Romans, the Jewish forces opposed to Rome were defeated, Jerusalem was besieged, with much of the city destroyed in the process. Whatever Josephus may have decided to add, delete and/or alter regarding these events, they are not fiction." In spite of Josephus' agenda as divulged in his explicit commentary, he cannot cover up the fact that he did pursue the war against Rome. Living everyday with the consequences of the war, Josephus needed to provide an explanation as to why and how it happened. Hindsight established a causation paradigm for Josephus who attempted to explain motivations and intentions, as well as ascribe reasons for the disastrous outcome. To modern historians of first-century Judea, McLaren recommends that the causation paradigm not direct the focus of research since, "Much as we tend to ignore the question, "*what if*," it does play an integral part of the way history is formed, and reformed. The certainty of the outcome should not negate consideration of exploring the various possibilities at any given moment in the war. At the extreme end of such exploration, it would be intriguing to consider the type of narrative Josephus would construct if the revolt had concluded with increased Jewish autonomy."

Focusing on Josephus' hindsight not only distinguishes his actions from his commentary but also explains how he understood the events and outcome of the war. Belief in an all-powerful God informed Josephus' understanding of the war and so when he took up the sword, he did so because he believed that this was divine will. In this way, McLaren proposes that Josephus did not change sides, betray his people, or adopt a politically expedient aristocratic position. Rather hindsight brought him to the realization that his defeat at Iotapata and that of his compatriots in Jerusalem revealed that a victory was not part of the divine plan.

Such a focus on the controlling nature of hindsight in both ancient and modern historical methods provides a means of discerning the facts behind the representations (actions and commentary) and of distinguishing between reason and motive. Whereas McLaren finds that Josephus' stated reasons contrast with and expose his actual actions and motives, Uriel Rappaport examines Josephus' reported actions so as to reveal his motives. He proposes that the claims Josephus makes about his achievements during the war, as well as the personal qualities he ascribes to himself, are unsubstantiated and outlandish. *Life* and *War* are particularly open to distortion since they were written under various pressures: to impress the Romans and especially the Flavians, to depict his people in a positive way to the Gentile world, and to justify his own behaviour in the face of charges of being both an insurgent as well as a traitor. Rappaport wonders why the recreant Josephus, who had little military expertise or success, and was certainly neither a *hacham* nor an accomplished historian, would construct the personality we meet in his works. Psychohistory, the science of historical motivation, provides Rappaport with a way to understand the emotional origins of Josephus' claims, and he puts the historian on the psychologist's "couch."

Rappaport proposes that ambitious as Josephus was, he was hindered from fulfilling his personal expectations. Unable to reconcile this conflict between ambition and achievement, he created an imaginary personality or "Ideal Ego." "An 'Ideal Ego' has such virtues that are recognized by the subject himself (in this case Josephus) as affirmative and desirable and incorporated in the totality of values and attitudes of the society to which he belongs." Josephus dissembled his failings by creating an "Ideal Ego" and the components of this personality provided a response to the pressures he faced.

Pro-Roman but pretending otherwise, Josephus had to resort to *legerdemain* to avoid confrontation with enemy forces. The Iotapata story for Rappaport is replete with inventions, as Josephus constructs his imaginary personality: he uses tricks or stratagems that must have been copied from military handbooks. In contrast with McLaren, Rappaport links Josephus' view on the futility of the war against Rome with the Iotapata episode and rejects the possibility that Josephus was involved with the defense of the town. Likewise Josephus' account of his survival lacks any historical value, except perhaps to reveal that Josephus was secretly working for the Romans. The story reflects the sort of heroism Josephus respects in others, for example the Sicarii, and it resembles his account of Eleazar's leadership at Masada. Since military accomplishment was highly valued in Rome, but not in Jewish society, Rappaport proposes that ". . . his [Josephus'] purported generalship served two needs: to compensate for his unachieved accomplishments in Galilee and to gain appreciation and respect for him in his new surroundings. To a certain measure it reflects Josephus' double life between Rome and the Jewish nation."

Both McLaren's and Rappaport's essays call for an appreciation of the literary nature of these texts, and present us with the challenge of distinguishing Josephus the man from an image arising from his narrative choices.

The importance of the literary context is further highlighted by Honora Howell Chapman, who focuses on the Masada episode in *War* 7 and its relationship with the Masada "myth." The site at Masada was designated as a UNESCO "cultural property," chiefly because of its symbolic value for Jewish cultural identity and the struggle for freedom from oppression. Chapman points out that the material remains at Masada could not have engendered this perception; it could only be established by a particular reading of Josephus' *War* 7, where the Sicarii are interpreted as freedom fighters against Roman oppressors. Yet for Chapman, Josephus' narrative presents a more complex picture than that perpetuated by the ideology that led to its UNESCO designation (and its former place in the IDF induction ceremony). She notes that, "the desire to appropriate the text for modern political, military, and cultural agendas has driven archaeological efforts and has affected modern scholarly interpretations, thereby testifying strongly to Josephus's power as a narrator. Francis Cornford may have called Thucydides 'Mythistoricus,' but this epithet is certainly applicable to Josephus as well."

Chapman examines the Masada episode against the thematic concerns of the last two-thirds of *War* 7 and observes that Josephus presents "... a study of how the Romans exercise their *imperium* and how their weaker opponents make choices in the face of this greater power. The historian clearly is trying to explain through a series of examples that the Romans simply do not lose in their game of imperialism." Chapman illustrates that the theme of salvation by submission to Rome, so prevalent throughout *War*, is central to the narrative in the episodes at Herodium, Machaerus, and the forest of Jardes, as well as the story of the Commagene affair. In the "game of imperialism" those who chose to resist faced death, whereas submission saved lives; the ideal of passive resistance ("ὑπομονή") does not find support. Rather the insurgents encountered a choice in the face of Roman invincibility. At Masada the option of suicide presented itself. Parallels between *War* 7 and Julius Caesar's *Gallic War* further complete the argument that Josephus condemns the actions of Eleazar and the Sicarii.

By highlighting the role our own socio-political needs play in our reading of the Masada story, Chapman raises again the problem of distinguishing facts from representations—Josephus' and ours. The interpretation guiding the UNESCO designation explores neither the nuances of Josephus' narrative portrait nor the historicity of the episode as narrated. Further questions about Josephus' historical method arise: were Josephus' views on Roman imperialism a result of hindsight? How did these views affect the narration of his own story at Iotapata?

Providing a unifying motivation for Josephus' *oeuvre* is the subject taken up by Etienne Nodet. He identifies Josephus' ambition to reorganize Judaism from Rome as the all-informing conceptual framework within which Josephus approaches his literary endeavor. Evidence for this can be found both in Josephus' own works and personal statements as well as the way in which he was omitted from rabbinic sources. Josephus' Jewish credentials are provided by the *Life*, which functioned as a sort of résumé, explicitly stating his qualifications as a teacher of Judaism while also revealing his Galilean connections. The Galilean portion of his career is given disproportionate attention because, according to Nodet, "... Galilee (let us say on both sides of the lake) was a highly significant province, allowing very concrete ties with the land of Israel (peasants). But its historical and cultural connection with Babylon entailed problems, from a Roman point of view, for Babylonian Jewry was on the side of the

Parthian enemies, while many Jews were living within the Roman
Empire." The Pharisees were an important component of the Galilean-
Babylonian connection, and so Josephus wished to be seen as an
influential member of this group who had experience in Galilee, but
was now based in Rome. In *War* he had claimed that God now
resided in Rome, and *Antiquities* was written as a kind of Pharisaic
teaching tool for a Jewish audience in the Roman Empire. In this
way, Josephus places himself strategically between the Jews and Rome
for his ambitious restructuring programme: the priest Pharisee backed
by the Romans who has influence with a potentially unstable Jewish
Galilee. For the Romans, *War* provided further evidence of his loyalty.

Nodet suggests that Josephus may have intended to establish the
ritual of the paschal lamb in Rome as part of this programme.
Rabbinic tradition alludes to an influential Jewish scholar who was
censured by the community at Yavneh for attempting just this, and
the Mishnah determines that the sacrifice only be performed in
Jerusalem. Further traces of a rivalry between the leaders at Yavneh
and Josephus are traced by Nodet: he notes that while Josephus
emphasizes his links with the Pharisees, he does not hesitate to show
his strained relationship with Gamaliel II's father, Simon; and rabbinic tradition recasts Johanan ben Zakkai as the one who predicts
Vespasian's succession and consequently saves Judaism, rather than
Josephus. Nodet proposes that Josephus' exclusion from rabbinic
sources may have been due to his notice about the Jesus movement:
in the Slavonic version of *War*, which Nodet regards as preserving
an early Greek draft, the Jerusalem authorities are condemned for
putting Jesus to death. This text may reveal his interest in a very
Jewish Jesus movement in Judea, different from the Christianity he
encountered only in Rome.

Proposing such ambitions for Josephus reminds us of the uncer-
tainty of the post-70 c.e. period, in which the ascendancy of the
Yavneh community was by no means assured. Our hindsight should
not exclude the fact that there may have been a number of possibilities for the development of Jewish identity and authority, in which
Josephus himself may have played a role.[3]

Part Two focuses on Josephus' use of sources, and Daniel Schwartz

---

[3] For a different sort of effort to reconstruct Josephus' role after 70 c.e., see
Schwartz 1990.

opens with a reflection on methods of identifying sources in the text. Schwartz responds to an article by Steve Mason that calls for a greater appreciation of the literary nature of Josephus' works.[4] Mason observes that an awareness of the literary nature of the works has consequences for using the text for historical reconstruction. The fundamental questions of the aims and the themes of these works must be addressed before claiming that a contradiction or an inconsistency reveals Josephus' use of sources or points to an external historical reality. Where Josephus is our only source, we cannot propose probable solutions to historical problems. Schwartz is concerned, however, that Mason's focus on the literary devalues the historical and he takes up again the question of contradictions as indicators of Josephus' use of sources.

Contradictions in toponyms and chronology alone are not necessarily a sign of a source, Schwartz concedes, but the context in which they are found may confirm a larger problem with the text. If one finds a discrepancy in the storyline then one can only assume that Josephus was relying on a source, and Schwartz proposes that we can get behind the text to this source: "For when we acknowledge that we can recognize within Josephus' writings the products of more than one mind, we must take into account the possibility that they will contradict one another. It seems, in other words, that we are back where we started: If Josephus used sources, and if at least sometimes we can discern which parts of Josephus' account are based on which sources, then we can hope to compare what Josephus put into his narrative when his mind was fully engaged and what he put in only as an excerpt, more or less edited, from someone else's work."

To demonstrate his case, Schwartz examines the episodes in which Pontius Pilate comes into conflict with the Jewish population in *War* 2.169–177 and *Ant.* 18.55–62. The stories in *Antiquities* function as a diptych that complement each other, share a leitmotif, and belong to a larger narrative concern in *Ant.* 18. These present a version that is different from the parallel accounts in *War*, and composition criticism can explain this due to the degree that it highlights Josephus' changed perspective on Jewish land and law between *War* and *Antiquities*.

---

[4] Mason 2003.

This does not preclude the possibility that Josephus used a source or sources for these episodes, however, since two different points of view may indicate someone else's opinion—perhaps edited to fit Josephus' agenda. A detailed comparison of the accounts reveals that in *War*'s aqueduct episode in particular, Pilate is presented in a positive light, unlike the Jews, who appear as a generic mob working against their own interests. Schwartz proposes that Josephus used a source here, perhaps written by Pilate or one of his officials, which he lightly edited. A major theme in *War* is the incompetence and insensitivity of the Roman governors, and since this Pilate episode seems to contradict the larger narrative interests of the work, it must reflect the viewpoint of his source. Schwartz concludes that, "while examination of *Ant.* 18.55–62 shows that Josephus was very much at work as a successful author, turning his sources into much more than a sum of their parts, this does not preclude the possibility of reasonably recovering something of those sources."

Examining how and why Josephus used the sources that we are to a greater degree certain about is the focus of the following two papers. Analysing Josephus' use of Strabo's *Historikà Hypomnemata*, Alessandro Galimberti reveals the depth of Josephus' authorial control over his material. The *Historikà Hypomnemata* seems to have taken the form of a universal history and included Strabo's interest in events in the East. Although it included some information on the Jews and their culture, it did not reserve any special place for them. While Strabo praises Moses, he condemns the subsequent direction of Jewish history, which he viewed as descending into decadence under the tyrannical leadership of the priesthood. A survey of the fragments in *Ant.* 13 and 14 shows that Josephus had a direct knowledge of the *Historikà Hypomnemata* and used it a number of different ways, without always referring explicitly to Strabo. But why would Josephus turn to this text when Strabo's attitude towards the Jews is not particularly benevolent?

According to Galimberti's analysis, Josephus uses Strabo as a counterpoint to Nicolaus of Damascus for the Hasmonean and Herodian periods: "In his effort to be objective, as clearly stated throughout his work—suffice to mention the *proems* to the *War* and *Antiquities*—Josephus feels the need to balance Nicolaus' partiality by using other sources, and one of them is certainly Strabo." Josephus' use of Strabo indicates that the historian is concerned with presenting his audience with a valid account—and Strabo seemed to be authoritative on Jewish history—underlined by his objectivity and documentary accuracy.

Josephus could have chosen Posidonius as a source but did not, according to Galimberti, because he shared with Strabo an ideological understanding of Roman domination as an indisputable fact. Often the context of a fragment seems to be ignored and Josephus carefully uses Strabo to support his own views, but the similarities between these two historians is striking: "Strabo, who belonged to one of those pro-Roman, eastern élites that supported Rome enthusiastically, was a sort of model for Josephus (especially after the catastrophe of the war) as part of a group of intellectuals and, in particular, of historians whose status was completely established within the reality of the empire.

It appears that Josephus paid a great deal of attention when choosing and using Strabo as a source, and Niclas Förster's analysis of the way in which he employed non-Greek historians in the *Against Apion* confirms the historian's critical approach to certain source material. In developing his apologetic regarding the antiquity of the Jews and the Exodus from Egypt, Josephus displays a great deal of critical awareness, drawing on legal-rhetorical traditions and cross-examining his literary sources as if they were witnesses in a trial. Förster proposes that: "Die Schrift *Contra Apionem* stellt überdies ein hervorragendes Beispiel für das quellenkritische Vorgehen des Josephus dar und belegt dessen Bedingtheit durch die polemisch zugespitzte Verteidigung der jüdischen Religion."

Josephus' use of Egyptian sources, and particularly Manetho, reveals that he was aware of the perception among Greek writers that these were reliable material for the history of the near east (and the Jews). Herodotus and Dio Chrysostom, for example, cited Egyptian sources to critique the Homeric version of Greek history beginning with the Trojan war. While Herodotus relied on oral traditions, Dio noted internal inconsistencies in the Homeric tale and seemed to have no actual knowledge of Egypt. Josephus' method differed radically for he subjected his sources to rigorous examination. His presentation of evidence differentiates between the chronological framework of king lists and legends based on oral traditions, sources are quoted, their credibility examined for internal consistency, and their conclusiveness evaluated.

In his desire to defend the biblical version of events against Greek detractors, Josephus turns to the very sources they used to correct the Homeric version of Greek history. Apion even claims to have learnt about Moses from the old men of Egypt. Unlike his Greek counterparts, Josephus' apologetic needs forced him to ignore the customs of historiography and to spell out his critical approach to his sources. By the standards of modern critical research his methods fall short, but they must be viewed as a genuine attempt to evaluate his sources.

That Josephus used sources is indisputable. For historians, however, the issues are whether we can identify and recover these, and how Josephus chose and employed them within his narrative. Schwartz has challenged those who focus on composition criticism to provide an explanation for contradictions and inconsistencies, especially when they contradict the larger narrative interest. Galimberti and Förster have analyzed Josephus' use of readily identifiable sources, arguing that he judiciously chose these, using them with care and control. In attempting historical reconstruction, what role might the recovery and delineation of his sources play?

In the third part of this volume, the papers address the problem of using Josephus as a source for historical reconstruction, given the ways in which his literary and rhetorical concerns shape his narrative. Jan Willem van Henten identifies and analyses the "noble death" passages in Josephus' works to see if we get past the ancient writer's perspective on this subject to more "reliable traditions." Josephus employs the theme and language of noble death numerous times, and these texts have become important for identity constructions: Masada is a symbol for modern Israelis, and an understanding of Judaism as a religion characterised by martyrdom became an essential part of the Christian *praeparatio evangelica*.

While van Henten can identify parallels between Jewish martyr texts and Josephus' presentation of the fate of those willing to die for the law, when it comes to the matter of suicide, he finds conflicting views. This ambiguity is underlined by Josephus' use of both negative and positive assessments of self-killing. Scholars note the similarities between the Iotapata and Masada stories yet van Henten observes that while they share motifs, Josephus presents opposing arguments with regard to suicide.

In Josephus' works the Jewish people are characterized by their contempt for punishment and death, and this is explicitly articulated in the *Apion* as preferring death to transgressing ancestral customs. But can any of these passages provide us with external historical information? Van Henten recognizes that the noble death passages serve Josephus' literary and rhetorical needs, but by checking parallel passages in external sources, and by applying a criterion of plausibility, one can make historical claims. He takes the Masada episode as an example: the description of events functions within a larger theme of the *War* and reflects an historiographical motif; yet Josephus' ambiguous attitude towards suicide and his practice of diminishing the honorable aspects suggest that a plausible case can be made for a collective suicide—perhaps not as Josephus relates it—at Masada. The rebels' preference for obedience to God and death over capture by the enemy appears numerous times in *War* and corresponds to Josephus' Masada narrative. Thus "If one would follow this line of argument, Josephus' description of the Masada suicide would have a historical plausibility, and the ambiguity that may be illuminated by certain details in the report (above) would indicate Josephus' own restrained criticism of such a display of self-sacrifice."

Steve Mason examines the interaction between literary analysis and historical reconstruction with regard to the Essenes, against the background of the dominant Essene-Qumran hypothesis. The initial identification of the Dead Sea Scrolls as Essene texts did not give equal value to the Greek and Latin sources, but interpreted them through observed parallels in the Scrolls. The Essene passages in Josephus were not examined in their own right because scholarship at the time had little interest in the compositional aspects of the texts. Mason's treatment of *War* 2.119–161 "*in situ*" attempts to redress the situation in part, and also to consider the historical implications of such analysis.

In the ancient world the character of a society determined its worth. For the Romans, manliness (*virtus*) defined the national character and was the essential component of their *imperium*: Roman men wielded control over foreigners, women, and their own passions. The Spartans, with their renowned contempt for both pleasure and suffering, furnished a model for Roman self-understanding, while foreigners, especially vanquished enemies, were often depicted as effeminate and slaves to their passions. In Flavian Rome, the Judean victory functioned as propaganda for this fledgling dynasty, and coins depicted an emasculated Judea subjugated by a powerful and essentially male Rome. Mason demonstrates how Josephus meets this perception by depicting the excellent character of the Judean nation (and its individuals) in each of his works. The Judeans deserve respect;

during the war in Judea, their fighters were courageous and stal-
wart, in contrast with the disorganized and disheartened Romans.
Josephus' admiration for the virtues of the Judean nation, which he
makes superior even to the Spartans, reaches a high point with the
Essenes: "These are 'men's men,' legionaries of the soul, engaged in
the serious pursuit of the virtuous life: disciplined, courageous, perfectly just, and contemptuous of the pleasures as much as the fears
that drive ordinary people."

Many correspondences between items in *War*'s Essene passage and
the Dead Sea Scrolls have been proposed, and Mason analyzes a
number of these in light of Josephus' narrative interests. He concludes: "The specific agreements between Essenes and Qumraners
are *not* more extensive as those between Essenes and other utopian
groups of the Greco-Roman world—Hyperboreans or Pythagoreans—
and nowhere near as extensive as evocations of Sparta, though no
one would suggest that Essenes were Spartans." Given Josephus'
interest in the Essenes, on the one hand, and his proud enlargement
upon his own priestly caste elsewhere in his narratives, Mason argues
that his failure to develop the priestly character of the Essenes would
be particularly strange if they were the people of the Scrolls—which
do indeed give priests a leading role.

But in the end it is the very different and conflicting worldview
of the Scrolls that convinces Mason of the inherent flaw in the
Qumran-Essene hypothesis: Josephus, the proud priest is a "world-
affirming Jerusalem aristocrat and statesman . . ., whose elegant *War*
is imbued with the spirit of Greek *paideia*," whereas the Scrolls suggest a "world-denying" perspective and "their core beliefs involved
rejection of the priestly establishment in Jerusalem and anticipation
of a conflict that would destroy *those* sons of darkness along with the
wicked foreign rulers." Mason's paper urges us to reevaluate how
we move from Josephus' narrative to historical reconstruction, particularly in cases where we have potentially relevant sources such as
the Scrolls.

Gunnar Haaland also focuses on the literary and historiographical context of the excursuses concerning the three "schools" in
Josephus' works, and observes that these groups represent "model
Jews." Halaand examines the way these digressions function within
the narrative so as to reveal Josephus' concerns and strategies of persuasion: "These excursuses provide not just information and explanation, but also embellishment and rhetorical amplification."

The excursuses, according to Haaland, reflect the larger themes and concerns of Josephus' work in terms both of their content and their position within the narrative. In *War* 2.119–166 the schools provide a counterpoint to Judas' discord: the Essenes, for example, resemble barbarian sages whose values are universal, and consequently the nation as a whole cannot be responsible for the type of conflict that led to the rebellion. In contrast, the excursus in *Ant.* 18.11–22 is relatively more positive towards Judas, but the Pharisees are portrayed in a less favorable light, while the Essenes are not promoted as *the* model Jews. The persuasive elements of the excursuses are similar, though, as both try to demonstrate that Jewish factionality *per se* is not dangerous. The excursus at *Ant.* 13.171–173 is somewhat more puzzling with regard to its position in the narrative, but it represents Josephus' ethnographical reflections, and the Jews' image as barbarian sages appears here too. The excursuses play an essential role in directing and controlling the narrative.

In the presentation of the Jewish constitution in *Apion*, the schools are not included and Josephus avoids using explicit philosophical language. The virtues of the Jewish character are described in admiring terms but harmony and unity are emphasized: "He [Josephus] has become a common citizen—an active member of society, not an ascetic and not a philosopher. The ideal community of the few has been replaced by the ideal society of the many." How can we explain this apparent change in Josephus' portrayal of the Jewish nation? Haaland proposes that the historical context provides an explanation: employing philosophical language may have been perilous under Domitian because of his expulsion of certain philosophers from the city, while the model Jew of the *Apion*, "a respectable citizen, clearly and thoroughly romanized . . . reflects a development in the way Josephus perceived himself as a Jew in Rome."

Josephus' narrative control and the consequences of literary analysis for historical reconstruction are central also to Morten Hørning Jensen's examination of the figure of Herod Antipas. Antipas is especially important in the context of Galilean studies, which are polarized with regard to his impact on first-century Galilee. Where sources are so scarce, a clear evaluation of the Antipas material in Josephus' narrative is all the more necessary.

Jensen examines the Antipas descriptions within the larger narratives of the Herodian house. King Herod receives the most extensive treatment, and his relations with Romans and Jews provide the

criteria for Josephus' assessment of his reign. The influence of Rome
leads Herod to introduce innovations into Judea and his behavior is
characterized by tyranny and impiety. He is contrasted with the
Hasmoneans and the ultimate consequence of his transgressions will
be the destruction of Jerusalem and the temple. Archelaus fares no
better: he too is accused of impiety and tyranny. While the emergence of the "fourth philosophy" heralds his downfall, there is an
implicit comparison drawn between this group and the Herodian
house: both introduce innovations that lead to the downfall of the
nation.

Philip and Agrippa I, however, escape Josephus' censure. There
is scant material on Philip, but he is contrasted with an impious
Antipas while Agrippa achieves the right balance in his relations with
Rome and the Jews. As for Antipas: his close relationship with the
emperor Tiberius could be evaluated in either a negative (like Herod)
or a positive (like Agrippa) way, but his relations with Jewish tradition dominate Josephus' portrait. The location of his new city Tiberias,
John the Baptist's execution, and his marriage to Herodias demonstrate that he is "another example of bad Herodian rule, who was
not able to safeguard the ancient and stable Jewish way of life."
Some chinks appear in this picture as Josephus includes episodes
that reveal a sensitivity toward the Jews and their traditions, but the
general impression remains very much in line with Josephus' judgment on Herod and Archelaus.

Balancing Josephus' narrative interests with these other nuggets of
information, Jensen proposes that the only conclusion we can reach
in using this material is that Antipas was unremarkable. Reconstructing
the economic situation of Galilee is severely restricted methodologi-
cally, since Josephus does not ask our questions and is generally not
interested in the welfare of the lower classes. Until further evidence
is available, Jensen suggests that ". . . a picture of Galilee on the
brink of meltdown in the first half of the first century can hardly
be substantiated by the narratives of Josephus."

Samuel Rocca also tries to look through the narrative interest of
Josephus' depiction to see if it reveals anything of King Herod's
actual ideology. He finds that there is no explicit treatment of this
subject because of Josephus' negative estimation of Herod's character and reign. Nevertheless there are a number of links between
Herod and Solomon in Josephus' account of these kings.

Rocca notes that Solomon was an obvious choice as a model for

Herod since he represented the glorious days of the Israelite monarchy. Like David, Herod expanded his kingdom and like Solomon, his reign was peaceful and prosperous. His rebuilding of the Temple further highlighted the Solomon link. Unlike the Hasmoneans, Herod was not a priest and so a connection with Solomon could legitimize his reign while his temple-building gave him control over this institution, along with his appointment of the high priest. The messianic tradition that grew up around the House of David and Solomon would naturally have attracted Herod to Solomon.

External evidence of this messianic aspect of Herod's ideology can be found in the *Psalms of Solomon*, according to Rocca. In this text written by one of Herod's subjects, Solomon becomes the archetype for Herod's reign and *Pss.* 17 in particular reflects Herod's deeds. Herod's awareness of this messianic identification is supported by numismatic evidence. If one looks to the Hellenistic east, it becomes apparent that Herod is very much following the practice of other kingdoms: "Herod thus tries to imitate a very ancient tradition of kingship, common to most peoples of the ancient Near East. It must be clearly understood that what Herod is doing is nothing new. The only difference between Herod and the Macedonian kings is that Herod was a native."

Although economic history, like so much else, lay outside the scope of Josephus' interest, in this area too we must examine his writings because they are often our sole source of information. Jack Pastor therefore focuses on Josephus as a source for economic history. This involves the study of "that part of human society that describes the way which society produces goods and services and how it distributes them. It is the way resources are managed. Economic history or economic historical facts include agriculture, manufacturing, construction, settlement, prices, taxes, and markets, to mention only a few general topics." For some later periods, historians have extensive documentation, but for first-century Judea we must try to make optimal use of Josephus' often anecdotal material. To use it to reconstruct the economic history of Judea, Pastor observes that we must employ a rigorous methodological process, using both internal and external analysis. It is a worthwhile endeavor, however, since it can shed light on other historical questions.

The famine under Herod as described in *Ant.* 15.299–316 provides a test case for Pastor. He examines a number of details in the account and checks them against our knowledge from other disciplines, such as climate studies, anthropology, archaeology, and famine studies. The details that can be verified by external evidence strongly suggest that Josephus' account to a large extent is authentic.

If the ultimate goal is to reconstruct history, using external sources and placing the evidence from Josephus squarely within its historical context is crucial, and Rocca's and Pastor's studies confirm this. To illuminate Herod's reign Rocca looks to numismatic and textual evidence as well as to the political and cultural conventions of monarchies in the Hellenistic east, whereas Pastor complements the ancient sources with data from modern studies in various disciplines to create a picture of the economic history.

External archaeological evidence for episodes described by Josephus provides the methodological approach of Part Four. The subject of noble death is revisited by Kenneth Atkinson, but now with a focus on how we can use archaeology to evaluate Josephus' accounts of Masada and Gamala. Both of these stories hold an important place in *War*'s narrative but without them we would have a rather different idea about how the besieged met their deaths. At Masada there are no mass graves to suggest a collective suicide, and the evidence from the site does not support the numbers indicated by Josephus. The Romans only committed a single legionary force, and Atkinson agrees with Jonathan Roth that the siege itself did not take as long as assumed.[5] The rebels had no artillery and did not seriously challenge the Roman force. Atkinson finds Josephus' description of Masada wanting and suggests that he was never actually atop the fortress. Not only is Josephus' story of noble death on a mass scale unsupported by the archaeology, but Atkinson also proposes that the archaeological evidence reveals aspects of the siege that Josephus tries to conceal: priests were involved in the siege, not only the irresponsible Sicarii of Josephus' narrative. As a priest living in Rome, he was not willing to divulge this information. Concluding his evaluation of the data, Atkinson suggests that, "based on archaeology alone, we would simply conclude that the defenders of Masada succumbed to the same fate as their fellow countrymen who opposed the Romans, namely slavery and, if they were unfortunate, death in the arena."

Since Josephus was present at the siege of Gamala, it may well yield more information than the Masada episode, but Atkinson finds

---

[5] Roth 1995.

that while Josephus' account of Vespasian's siege is a valuable source
for Roman warfare, his descriptions of the topography and fortifications
of the site are not accurate. The number of victims at Gamala is
exaggerated, as is the description of their jumping from the peak to
their death. It is physically impossible for a large number to commit suicide in that way, and while some could have been caught in
the panic and died on the steep slopes it seems that many fighters
simply ran away. Atkinson suggests two reasons for Josephus' mis-
representation of the Gamala siege: he may have betrayed his people by revealing the vulnerable part of the wall, and as a general,
if he had fortified the town, he must not have done a thorough job
since it could not withstand the Roman siege for any length of time.

The similarities between the Masada and Gamala accounts of
noble death suggest that these stories function on a literary level to
illustrate the virtues of both the Jews and the Romans: "By presenting his readers with fictional stories of noble deaths at Gamala
and Masada, Josephus demonstrates the bravery and obstinacy of
the Jewish population to account for difficulties that the Romans
experienced in ending this revolt. At the same time, he highlights
the superiority of the Roman legions, who had to overcome formidable military and typographical obstacles to crush this rebellion."
Suicide is not unequivocally praised and for Josephus, the victims at
Masada and Gamala were misguided for they indulged in internecine
strife, bringing God's judgment upon themselves. For Atkinson, archaeology challenges Josephus' account and underscores the importance
of a thorough appreciation of the literary nature of Josephus' works.

The siege sites of Gamala and Iotapata were abandoned in antiquity but then excavated extensively in modern times, and Mordechai
Aviam suggests that archaeology provides a unique perspective on
Josephus' accounts. Although the siege of Iotapata receives a fuller
description in Josephus, the briefer Gamala episode includes valuable details. Aviam finds Josephus' geographical descriptions of both
sites to be accurate, and excavations also reveal that the fortifications
generally correspond with Josephus' descriptions: they were of a
makeshift nature, hastily constructed with reused material lacking
adequate foundations.

In comparing Josephus' battle descriptions with the archaeological data Aviam again finds that a similar picture emerges. For example, remains of Roman army equipment were discovered at Gamala
confirming Josephus' account of the death of Roman soldiers there,

while the lack of such finds at Iotapata corroborates his report that there were few Roman casualties. The descriptions of the wall breaches by battering rams can be confirmed by the site, while the face-to-face battles as depicted by Josephus are plausible in light of the topography of the towns. Although the human remains at Iotapata are witness to the massacre as it appears in the *War*, the single human jawbone found at Gamala suggests that if a massacre took place at all, it must have happened at the summit of the town, which is not well preserved and has not been fully excavated. For Aviam it is unlikely that Josephus commanded the forces in Galilee or erected all the fortifications that he claims responsibility for, "but his very detailed narrative of the battle at Yodefat, illuminated by the archaeological finds, strongly suggest that he was there, and probably commanded the battle."

The papers by Atkinson and Aviam demonstrate that if we wish to reconstruct a plausible account of the sieges described by Josephus, it is imperative that the evidence provided by archaeology be seriously assessed. But neither the narrative nor the archaeology is self-explanatory, and the use of both together in reconstructing scenarios presents an ongoing challenge.

The cities of Tiberias and Sepphoris are of particular interest to scholars concerned with the impact of Hellenism and Roman culture on Galilee. It has generally been assumed that these cities were similar in many ways, both undergoing radical development under Herod Antipas. Using both the literary sources and the archaeological material from the recent excavations, Zeev Weiss focuses on the urban topography of these two cities. Josephus' descriptions of Tiberias are full and detailed, he notes, whereas Josephus gives little attention to the physical appearance or administrative organization of Sepphoris. Although one might explain this in light of Tiberias' larger role in Josephus' story of the revolt, the archaeological data suggest a different reason.

In Weiss' analysis, the archaeological material reveals that these cities were very different both in terms of government and physical appearance on the eve of the revolt. Tiberias was constructed by Herod Antipas in a monumental style with buildings and institutions characteristic of a Greek or Roman city: it enjoyed the political and administrative independence of a *polis*. Sepphoris, however, was not established as a capital by Antipas and lacked Roman-style buildings. It was only after the revolt that we see Sepphoris undergoing

a transformation. Evaluating Josephus' account against the archaeological evidence, Weiss suggests that "the author neither ignores the
buildings in Sepphoris nor refrains from mentioning them, but rather
faithfully describes the reality of his era, wherein the city lacked a
monumental appearance—in contrast to its counterpart Tiberias."

Notwithstanding the degree to which Josephus' literary concerns
have shaped his accounts, Weiss highlights how important his testimony can be for complementing the archaeological record.

The Josephus Colloquium in 2004 took place in Trinity College
Dublin, and the final essay in this volume was a special paper commemorating a graduate of this university who was also a translator
of Josephus—Robert Traill. The idea for this lecture came from
Gohei Hata, whose work is at the forefront of scholarship on the
history of the English translations of Josephus. Of particular interest
in Hata's paper is Traill's role as the first critic of William Whiston's
translation of Josephus' works. Whiston's eighteenth-century translation has remained influential into the twenty-first century. Yet, as
Hata observes, it was "was full of errors, erratic Christian interpretations, as well as anti-Jewish sentiments." Although Hata does not
consider Traill to have improved on this translation, it seems that
he was the first to challenge many of the assumptions about Josephus
and the Jews that accompanied it.

What unites the essays in this collection, then, is not a single view
of Josephus—as historical figure or author. Rather all of the contributors have taken up aspects of a problem basic to all researchers
who would use Josephus for historical purposes, namely: What is the
relationship between narratives and history? Underlying this, of course,
is the surprisingly difficult question: What is history?

This collection includes efforts to tackle the theoretical issues, but
most essays work through such questions in concrete engagement
with the texts of Josephus, other literary texts, case studies of particular events, and material remains. None of these categories is
unproblematic. Simply seeking to understand Josephus raises larger
questions about what exactly is to be understood: his actual thoughts?
His sources? His first audience's plausible perception? At what point
are we reading him: with the fundamental reshaping of post-70 hindsight? Or in keeping with deeply ingrained perspectives of long standing? Or can we discover sources lightly edited?

The archaeological evidence, though free of authorial manipulation, is not necessarily easier to read: this collection provides a

sufficient range of opinion as to what evidence tells us about what really happened—at Iotapata, Gamala, and Masada. By presenting such a wide range of scenarios—for understanding texts in historical context and material remains in literary context—we hope to have contributed substantially to sustained reflection on the problem of "Josephus and history."

Zuleika Rodgers

BIBLIOGRAPHY

Bilde, P.
    1988   *Flavius Josephus between Jerusalem and Rome: His Life, His Works, and Their Importance.* Sheffield.
Edmondson, J., S. Mason, and J. Rives, eds.
    2005   *Flavius Josephus and Flavian Rome.* Oxford.
Mason, S.
    2003   Contradiction or Counterpoint? Josephus and Historical Method. *RRJ* 6:145–88.
Roth, J.
    1995   The Length of the Siege of Masada. *SCI* 14:87–109.
Schwartz, S.
    1990   *Josephus and Judaean Politics.* Leiden.
Sievers J. and G. Lembi, eds.
    2005   *Josephus and Jewish History in Flavian Rome and Beyond.* Leiden.

PART ONE

CONCEPTUAL FRAMEWORKS: ANCIENT AND MODERN

ON REFERRING TO SOMETHING, MEANING
SOMETHING, AND TRUTH:
A TERMINOLOGICAL PROPOSAL

Folker Siegert

Introductory Questions

How does human speech refer to non-linguistic reality? To put the
question this way may lead to something of an irony, because we
do not know what we mean, or what we are referring to, when we
speak of "reality."[1] Nobody knows it all, and there are many means
of access, all very partial. This shortcoming has been much exploited
by idealistic philosophers who say that the only reality you may be
sure of is the one you think of.

As historians rather than philosophers, we may re-state our question. *How does human language refer to human experience, present or past?*
Putting the question this way, we may avoid metaphysical problems
about what is not given to human experience.

History, taken in a sober sense, is about facts related to humans.
Even revelation is related to humans, and it has its fixed points in
time and space. History—as told or written history—may be defined
as an account of the past, with the corollary that it is always somebody's (or some group's) past. In a more sophisticated sense of the
term, history aims at the positioning of an individual or of a group
vis-à-vis facts or supposed facts; but we shall not go far in this direction here. There are good hermeneutics to help us and, again, we
need not risk metaphysical assumptions. The important thing is not
to overlook a witness' or a commentator's point of view.

If history is about facts related to humans, as we have defined it,
our next question will be: "Whose experience are we looking for?"
If it is not ours, how can we be sure about it? This question does

---

[1] As this paper repeats commonplaces of English ordinary language philosophy,
no detailed bibliography seems necessary. The following notes, instead, will illustrate certain points from this Colloquium's papers and discussions.

not create an *aporia* either, because, happily, experiences may be shared, even across distances of time. Nearly all of the disciplines called "humanities" are about building bridges across distances in time and place, including changes of language and of lifestyle. If the human being may be defined as an animal speaking a language, its very difference over against other species capable of using sounds and even symbols lies in the very fact that only human language is capable of transmitting a knowledge of the past.

Turning to Josephus as a historical writer belonging himself to the past, we may now proceed to ask: Who was he, what sort of life was his, and what experiences does he refer to? No historian will ever be content with a structuralist approach to his sources, as useful as it may be. We rather ask: What means do we have to distinguish Josephus' experiences, and those related by him, from his afterthoughts, interpretations,[2] distortions[3] or even inventions?[4]

Experience is not truth, but it is not a complete illusion either. The problem is that in experiencing something, we always experience our own feelings and thoughts along with the input of our senses. There is much spontaneous interpretation in what we perceive. We should be aware of the inaccuracies of sense perception,[5] which are as great as those of memory. In this article, however, my only aim is to present the language, ancient and modern, that helps historians to know better what they deal with and not to get lost in

[2] See the accounts of "noble death" during the Judean war as discussed in this volume by van Henten, Atkinson, and Chapman. A case in point is Gamla (Gamala): speaking of the events there, it may well be that Josephus, being an eye-witness, sees mere panic as voluntary mass suicide. There never was a pit under the town wall such as "seen" by Josephus.

[3] One kind of distortion—a very conventional one in antiquity—consists of exaggerations. In a number of papers in this volume it may be seen how Josephus found it easier to exaggerate the more the objects described were out of the Romans' supposed horizon.

[4] After reading Josephus' story about how he was saved at Jotafat (*War* 3.145–306), and on reading Rappaport's article in this volume, one might suspect that it is a wholesale invention by Josephus, destined to attract the Romans' curiosity and to save his life. Invented or not, it did save his life, and later on he *had* to repeat it and stick to it. There may be even less truth in the rabbinic re-telling of Josephus' stories as tales about Rabbi Johanan ben Zakkai, as hinted at by Nodet in this volume.

[5] Weiss' article in this volume may prompt one to wonder how Josephus' eye mistook well-made columns for columns made from one piece, and refined plasterwork as carved stone. If he knew the refinement behind the appearances, this assumption would lead us to conclude that he wanted his readers to believe what the objects' makers had wanted visitors to believe.

pseudo-problems, by which I mean problems created by inappropriate language.

Leaving the problem of lying to the methods of ordinary inquiry, especially cross-questioning of witnesses, and admitting a fringe of incertitude in all we get to know of other's thoughts and acts, we can avoid self-illusions by means of a clear terminology related to past events.

1. *Facts and Words*

History is about facts of the past. So we need a distinction between *facts* (a semi-abstract term to be defined in what follows), and *words* or other signs or systems of signs representing facts.

As regards words and other signs, those representing facts may be further distinguished from those representing something else, e.g., thoughts and beliefs. Both, again, are different from *objects* that are neither facts nor words, for example pieces coming from an archaeological excavation.

If facts are counted as level 1 and words etc. as level 2 (with a possible level 3 of methodological meta-language, as in this paper), archaeological objects lie, so to speak, on level 0. They are "mute" at first hand. Mixed cases are possible and even frequent, e.g., an archaeological find bearing an inscription.

What are abundantly given are words not relating, or not directly relating, to facts. This is the historian's daily problem. Yet it may be useful to know whether some opinion expressed in a source, e.g., Josephus, is his own opinion or someone else's who is nearer to the events.

But what are "events" in history, what are "facts?" As you may all agree, there are no "mere" facts, no *bruta facta*. You may be run over by a car, yet there will be questions about what happened. Facts need to be "established." The historian's raw material is not facts as such, but *representations* of facts, linguistic ones and others; it is these that give the facts their names and their contours. We may be sure that many humans died during the Roman Civil War, but where did it begin and where did it end, and who participated in it?

This is at least a problem of exactness. Mountains, to take an analogy, may be known according to their exact height (compared with sea level), but no one can tell where they "begin" on the ground.

(In a similar way, the length of the coast of Ireland is not determinable—a matter depending on methods of measuring—, whereas
its surface is determinable.) Yet we are sure that there are mountains and do not fail to identify them by their proper names. In history, contours and coherences are even less visible. The Civil War
in ancient Rome is a matter of mental reconstruction and naming,
and the exact contours of the object so named depend on our analyses and finally on conventions. Those conventions may be sufficient,
or they may be in need of revision or refining. In the case of a
traffic accident, a report will be made, and it will tell, more or less
accurately, "what happened." In this way history—I mean written
history—makes the past "readable," so to speak (and French intellectuals very much like to speak in such terms).

To give an example from Josephus: The Judean war has no clear
beginning if you count with it its determining factors—as does
Josephus, who writes one book and a half on Hasmonean rule,
Roman provincial administration, and so on, before he comes to the
events which are considered as belonging to the Judean war "proper."
Josephus' account also has an open end. We may hesitate whether
we assign it the dates "66–70 c.e." or "66–74 c.e.," the latter of
which includes the waiting for the fall of Masada. Most historians
opt for the first delimitation, and rightly so, as nobody thinks that
Masada was the place where the war was finally decided. We rather
say that it "ended" with the fall of Jerusalem, even though we know
that there were four more years of warfare; an analysis of factors
shows that they were of no consequence. Even today, they are only
given a symbolic meaning.[6]

The capture of Jerusalem, again, is not an event that ended on
one day. You know that even the "exact" day of the temple's being
burnt is given differently in Josephus and in rabbinic sources. It is
a bit like the "chaos" of fractals in mathematics; the more exact you
want to be, the more details will surprise you. But these problems
are of no metaphysical dignity; they are simply limitations of accuracy in our statements, depending on a lack of contours on the side
of the events. In the case I have chosen, the difference between the
9th of Av (so the Rabbis) and the 10th of Av (Josephus) is not alarm-

---

[6] See the article by Chapman in this volume.

ing, and there may have been material enough in the *naos* at Jerusalem to burn for even more than two days.

Thus "facts" like the Judean war or, as part and end of it, the capture of Jerusalem may pose problems of accuracy in our speaking of them. Yet the tried-and-tested inaccuracies of ordinary human language are very appropriate for speaking of the "flow" or the "stream" of history.

2. *Signs, Tokens, Symbols, Images*

In some sense, thus, facts are artificial or conventional, at least in our speaking of them. Now somebody may claim that he or she has access to pieces coming from the time and the place we are interested in, and which are, so to speak, "silent witnesses" of what we want to know.[7] Let us take the lots found at Masada and presumably used for the last time in order to determine who should kill whom. These pieces are not *signs*, just as words or phrases are signs, but they are *tokens* (Fr. *indices*, Germ. *Indizien*). There must be someone to "interpret" them. In our case, "interpreting" means to say which use has been made of the piece, to describe the circumstances of its use and so on, which presupposes a lot of "interpreting" in different senses of the word, including the interpretation of texts. As regards the latter, I admit that interpretation may and must be more than just an answer to questions about facts of the past. We need not go, however, into the details of hermeneutics: There is much sophistication possible, and historians will keep aloof from such hermeneutics as consist in a mere interplay between words. Our questions in this paper are on a more elementary, and factual, level.

Between signs and tokens there are *symbols*. To the defenders of Masada, this place may have "meant" Judean independence even when this was not achieved after the fall of Jerusalem. Coins are symbols *par excellence*, at least as far as they bear symbols (e.g., the front of the temple with its two columns which never were visible that way). They may also bear signs—words written in Hebrew or in Greek, telling "something"; but these signs may have an extra symbolic value in that they are Hebrew characters (as a symbol of

---

[7] For a recent attempt, see Jeska 2003, 110–34, a paper focussing on cross-inferences of different means of investigation, textual and archaeological.

cultural, or even political, independence)—let alone ancient Hebrew
characters, which are a symbol of non-compromise with other cultures and of protest against age-long compromises of that kind, if I
am not mistaken. One problem about symbols is that they may be
ambiguous; another, and more serious, problem is that their meaning may get lost.[8]

But let us come back to the normal use of coins. Originally, they
were minted for payment in the marketplace, which includes the job
market (and the military). Their stamp guaranteed their weight and
their alloy. These seem to be material and, so to speak, "objective"
facts, and, true, you may weigh a coin and determine its material
content. Yet this does not tell its exact value on earlier markets. In
order to know this, one must again resort to all kinds of information or evidence, including texts. Thus, pieces are not facts; there
must be some effort to relate them to facts.

Now it may be that Josephus himself helps us in relating pieces
to facts. For example, we can read his description of the Roman
triumph of Vespasian and Titus along with some kind of "reading"
of the plastic representations, or material *images*, on the Titus Arch.[9]
Images representing facts are a kind of link between them and our
own perception of the past. Of course, they are the more valuable
the nearer in time they are to the facts.

"Time" in this context does not only mean the difference in date
between the material objects. Images may keep up an iconographi-
cal tradition for centuries and may be its authentic reproductions
even if their date of fabrication is late, whereas others, designed on
other bases of information or of interpretation, may be older in date,
but more recent in design. This leads to our next point.

---

[8] The "chi" on the coins described in the article by Rocca are a case in point.
Christos ("anointed one," king or priest) would be somewhat paradoxical since outside the Septuagint and the New Testament this meaning of the Greek word is
nearly unknown.

[9] Other examples are passages in Josephus' *War* and *Life* that correspond exactly
to archaeological finds in Galilean towns (see Weiss, Aviam, and Atkinson in this
volume), so that a find gives the object, and the text tells the event (e.g., fortification
or destruction) that happened to it.

3. *Causes and Ends*

Aristotles's Four "Causes"

Each time we spoke of "determining factors" or the like, we used a notion, which, in Greek, is *aitia*. Aristotle distinguished four kinds of "causes," the material one, the formal one, the efficient one, and the final one. Thus a Hasmonean coin may be described—

- as to its *material* "cause," by an analysis of its alloy,
- as to its *formal* "cause," by a description of its stamps, *recto* and *verso*,
- as to its *efficient* "cause," by the identification of the workshop or the persons that made it or, rather, the person who had it made (the latter normally being named on the piece), and also of the tools and method of coining, and,
- as to its *final* "cause," by giving an account of its intended use or uses, which may not only be for paying, but also for making political claims.

A complete description of such a piece would also include an account of the *circumstances* of its use, i.e., of the market on which it had its value, and also of the contemporaneous economic and political powers, including their conflicts.

Part of the "form" of the coin, speaking with Aristotle, is its inscription. It may *refer* to some king or high priest, and it may *mean* (express, convey) his claims of being in such-and-such a position. Here we may, and should, make a distinction between two different levels of meaning:

1. on the intentional level (which is that of production) we may distinguish between what is plainly said or clearly signified, and what is only alluded to or intimated;
2. on the non-intentional level (which is the level of reception) there may be losses of meaning as well as surpluses of meaning created, e.g., by linguistic change or by changing circumstances.

To give an example for the former: Those Hasmonean monarchs who were kings as well as high priests and who used the two sides of their coins to express both did so in Greek for presenting themselves as kings, and in Hebrew for presenting themselves as high

priests. This alludes to different ideologies of legitimacy.[10] On the
level of reception, there may be a loss or a change of finality, for
example, by soldering a hook on it and using it as a button. There
may also be mistakes of interpretation of its legend, or difficulties in
reading it.[11] The constrained symbolism of coins excludes meanings
other than what their makers intended—as may happen with literary texts such as Josephus' *Life*, in which the Dortmund Josephus
conference of 2002 found traces of its author's aspiration to a high
priestly or royal dignity.[12] The longer a text is, the more you can
read "between the lines," i.e., interpret what is not explicitly said.
Normally, Josephus is well aware of what he tells his readers and
what he does not tell; so even his silences may be significant.[13]
Hermeneutics will help to follow his allusions, at least as far as they
are voluntary. Furthermore, his text may even be involuntarily transparent for its author's hidden thoughts and aspirations.[14] From *War*
1.3 and 6 it may be gathered that one of the purposes for which
the Roman emperors charged Josephus to write his account of the
Great Revolt was to dissuade his Babylonian fellow Jews, who lived
in the country of Rome's most feared enemy, from engaging in any
subsequent attack or rebellion.[15]

Cause vs. Occasion

Since Thucydides, serious historians take care not only to narrate
events, but also to tell their causes—mainly their "efficient causes,"

---

[10] Cf. Jensen and Mason in this volume.

[11] An extreme case, which consists of an obelisk inscribed with hieroglyphs is discussed in the article by Förster in this volume: Here only a parallel transmission
of a Greek translation helped the Romans understand it.

[12] Kalms and Siegert 2003. Previous colloquia, see vol. 2, 4, 6, 10, and 12 of
the same series. There will be a summary review by Tessa Rajak in the *Journal of
Roman Studies*. In the present volume, cf. Nodet.

[13] For example, leaving the last high priest unmentioned in his list in *Ant.* 20.251
amounts to annulling his legitimacy and opens the list possibly for Josephus himself (see Gussmann 2003, 124–29). For an intra-textual analysis, the (dis-)qualification
asêmos for this high priest Panhas (Pinhas) b. Shamuel (Shemuel) contrasts with *Life*
1 where Josephus claims that he himself came from an important (*ouk asêmos*) family.

[14] Mason studies a case in point in showing for what silent purposes the (otherwise inexplicably broad) accounts of the Essenes have been inserted in most of
Josephus' writings. Each "sect" of Judaism is called upon in each of Josephus' writings to present the ideal Jew—if possible, in Josephus' own person: see the role (it
is not a historical, but an interpretive role) of the Essenes in *War*, the Pharisees in
Antiquities and *Life*, and the (Sadducean) priesthood in *Apion* 2:164–167 (the "theo-
cracy" passage). There can be no archaeological confirmation for such statements.

[15] See Aviam in this volume.

as Aristotle would say. Now Thucydides expressly distinguishes causes properly (*aitiai*), mostly in the plural, from a pretense (*prophasis*) to act in such-and-such a way, e.g., acting aggressively towards one's neighbour. Such a *prophasis* may be some kind of excuse, in words, but it may also be the "occasion" as part of a given situation.

Thus since Thucydides and Polybius the account of a war is bound to be the account also of its causes, and not only of a series of events. Thus pre-history belongs to history.

Josephus stuck to this rule when he began his *Judean War* with the Hasmonean epoch while in contrast, the neglect of pre-history makes 1 Maccabees so highly misleading. As to 2 Maccabees, it only superficially overcomes this lack by prefixing some documents, including a forgery.

Cause vs. Reason

Coming back to Aristotle's distinction of "causes," I now want to remove the inverted commas from the word "causes" by telling what they are in modern terminology. Today, by saying "cause," we rarely mean anything else but efficient causes, or "factors." The "material cause," for us, is just the "material," whereas the "formal cause" is much more than we call a "form": In the case of a coin it is its shape plus everything distinguishable on it—images, symbols, inscription and all that belongs to a "formal" description, e.g., in a catalogue.

Let us turn now to the "final" cause. For modern sensibility, it goes in the opposite direction from what we call "cause," because it is not about what lies behind an object (temporally speaking), but before it. So we no more speak of a "cause" of that kind, rather slightly but importantly changing Aristotle's terminology, of the "finality" of the object. It is the openness for the future that makes it particularly interesting and which justifies us in putting it aside from Aristotle's list. Again, for modern feeling the finality of an object is not a part of it. It is rather some kind of thought, or a complex of intentions and choices that played their part in its coming-to-be. When we speak of "what a thing is for," we mostly draw conclusions from an object's "formal" to its "final" cause, to speak again with Aristotle; but this also says those two "causes" are not situated on the same level. Finalities are less material and less visible than are "forms." Thus any description of a coin, for example, changes at some point from what is materially given to what can only be expressed in words. What Aristotle called an object's "cause" turns out to be some person's "reason," or "reasons."

Reasons can only be given in words. These, in turn, can be translated from one language to another. They represent the human factor in history; some may say, even the divine one, sharing Josephus' own belief. Reasons are what link archaeological objects to written histories. A good historian is one who tells why humans acted the way they did; and this is giving reasons.

In a better case, the acting persons tell their reasons themselves, and in the best of cases they tell them all. Politicians seldom do. Nor does Josephus, who is as much a politician as he is a historian. He always gives some reasons, but rarely, or perhaps never, gives them all. This would be too much of a laying bare of Jewish feelings over against Rome. Why and for what purpose did he lead around his Galilean army from place to place—forty-two times, as did Moses with Israel in the wilderness? He would never tell us, because he would never tell it to the Romans who defeated his initial cause.

Now, in speaking of feelings, we leave the realm of reasons, or conscious reflections, and come to something barely conscious, or even sub-conscious, which is rather found someway up on Aristotle's list: It belongs to his efficient causes, or factors. One more distinction in our modern vocabulary is now called for.

Reason vs. Motive

The "reason" lying behind some action may be defined as something clearly thought and expressed, or that can be clearly expressed, by the acting person(s) or by others who know and understand them sufficiently. By contrast, an acting person or group may be motivated by something unconscious, by instincts and feelings; this is normal. In the latter case we better speak of a "motive" or a set of motives. Motives, too, are something immaterial, and they may be brought to consciousness, which sometimes creates a conflict with reason (in the singular).

You may be conscious of your feelings, yet they are not reasons. Feelings as well as reasons may be told in words,[16] just as they may

---

[16] These words may be welcome with regard to the interpretation of Josephus'

be hidden with words. In historiography, as in political debate, motives may be hidden in order not to reveal too much of a political actor.[17] Correspondingly, motives that are declared overtly may be intentionally misleading.[18]

With reasons, of course, there is less interpretative effort necessary. The richer a given language is—the sources' language and also the historian's language—the fuller his or her account will be. In this respect we may be grateful that Josephus wrote in Greek, the very richest language of his day, comparable with today's English. Biblical Hebrew (or Aramaic) provide means of expressing a person's motives, which may be expressed in charmingly naive or indirect ways, but the result is rarely as clear as what Josephus may give us if he wants.

Giving motives and telling reasons can also be overdone. Such seems the case of the *clementia* of Titus. Surely the Romans had great respect for foreign gods, especially at places where those gods where at home (so to speak), and they used to preserve their sanctuaries, feeling somewhat dependent even on those gods' good will. In the case of the Great Revolt, however, such sympathy must have considerably suffered, as the course of events also shows. Here a modern historian must take into account Josephus' own motives in writing, and also the emperor's very own command of that work as its *causa efficiens*. But here I am speaking of trivialities of interpretation of historical texts. Let us return to our problem of exact terminology.

4. *Theory of Language*

Reference vs. Meaning

Coming back to our initial question of how words can refer to something other than words, I want to stress an important distinction that has not been sufficiently clear in our Greek or Latin heritage.

---

text, but also misleading for questions concerning historical factors and facts. Hence the opening passage of McLaren's paper in this volume.

[17] Thus Roman witnesses of the Great Revolt must have been as misled about the Zealot's motives—as are Josephus' readers on this point. *Pleonexia* clearly was not the prime motive for their *guerilla*, but rather messianic aspirations—not to be told to non-Jews.

[18] See again the paper by McLaren.

"Meaning" something—Gr. *legein ti*—may again be placed on two fundamentally different levels. *Meaning something* may be giving one symbol (or set of symbols) for another, conveying ideas, thoughts, or the like; *referring to something* is a way of pointing to it by linguistic means. Thus, meaning things is a different activity from referring to things (French: *se référer à*, German: *sich beziehen auf*; noun: *Bezug*). They may be found together, yet distinctly, as in the Greek formula *legein ti peri tinos* (John 6:71; meaning bound to reference). Philology is about meanings, whereas archaeology is about references, and it is very apt to correct them.

To give an example from everyday life: a speaker may *refer to* an Irish stew which has just been served in a restaurant in a phrase *meaning*, e.g., that it is not well prepared, or that it has fallen from one's dish, or that one is not willing to pay for it—to take examples from the three perspectives in time Aristotle has distinguished, i.e., present, past, and future. References to the future are of a special kind, though not impossible, for example, in making appointments. Prophecies are more problematic. Mostly so was the *chrêsmos amphibolos* (*War* 6.312) that contributed to the audacity of the warfaring party. In any case, such references should not be called references to "facts" (Latin *factum* is a past participle, and wisely so). However, one may refer to future moments and to anticipated events.

As regards given texts, a proper analysis will not only distinguish "meanings" of words and phrases; it also will distinguish "uses" of the phrases[19] as such and inquire into their "pragmatic" force. On the level of so-called speech acts, it is of crucial importance to see whether a given text, or a phrase, is intended to inform an audience, to praise something before an audience, to recommend it to an audience, to call it into question or into doubt, and so on.

Illusions of "Reality" Language

As has been said, a phrase may have sense—a "meaning"—, and it may refer to things. We shall speak of them in the plural, because the singular "reality" is one of the illusions inherent in that expres-

---

[19] A very subtle problem is illustrated by Pastor (in this volume) when he speaks of measures and indications of quantity in Josephus. Here, some very exact control may be possibly by means of archaeology. His main question, however, is: How much is "much," "a lot," "myriads" and so on.

sion. "Meaning" reality is not an efficient way of referring to it. So, paradoxically, the best way of losing reality is using "reality" language.

Immanuel Kant rightly said that 100 "real" shillings are no more than 100 shillings. You cannot change them by words, you cannot even assure their existence or presence anywhere by what you say of them. Thus in order to make a valid reference, "reality" language is of no use. You must say, for example, *whose* 100 shillings you mean, *where* they may be found, and so on. In doing so, you make a reference—to a person in this case, or to a place. References may go to all sorts of things, living or not, as long as they are accessible to human experience. This latter restriction may not be valid in every branch of philosophy, but it is so in the art, or science, of history.

Instead of defining "reality," which is not possible, philosophers and linguists of the twentieth century have defined terms that help against illusions. Meaning something is a mental effort, expressed in signs, whereas referring *to* something is an act of pointing to it. Any statement that something is "real" remains on the semantic level. It cannot replace the effort of a concrete reference.

Now the speech act of reference may be done by a variety of means that may even cross borderlines of time and space. With respect to Kant's 100 shillings, there is no difference whether you say: "I have got them" or "I have really got them." There is only a change of emphasis between the two phrases, a change that can as well be expressed by saying: "I *have* got them," or: "It's me who has got them."

Is there a link between reality and truth? In answer to this I should say that, first, truth is best defined on the level of meaning. Secondly, there are two important terms belonging to modern speech-act theory that Aristotle did not know and which are useful here. The terms are these: The reference of a phrase to a thing or to things may be *successful*; the content of this phrase may be *true*. Thus two different requirements must be fulfilled before a phrase, or a text, may, as we say, "correspond to reality."

Whether this is the case and the *adaequatio rei et intellectus* has succeeded, depends on different sets of conditions concerning references as well as meanings, on which there are elaborate philosophies. Here Aristotelian vocabulary shows up again; but I shall not go into the details.

The Plurality of Perspectives: An Aside on Polybius

An extraordinary reading with respect to our question is Polybius'
12th book. Here Polybius gives a magisterial lesson on how to perceive facts of the past and on how to distinguish misleading evidence
from good, or "true" evidence. He is able to do this without using
the vocabulary of metaphysics. He never speaks abstractly of concrete things. So he does an admirably good job in describing the
professional skills of a historian; and he does so without resorting to
any metaphysics or any ideology. Polybius demonstrates by examples that an intelligent evaluation of a given piece of evidence, including its enlargement where it is possible, can lead to a better account
of facts of the past than could even one's own participation in them,
or one's presence in the place, or at the time. Today we use the
term *perspective*: The best perspective of a historian is being not too
near, but not too far either.

Secondly, a historian should try to see the events from more than
one angle. This is a thing Josephus fails to appreciate. According to
Apion 1.28–43 he prefers the unique witness of a prophet-priest to
any plurality, at least as regards the history of Israel.

There is no such ideology in ancient historiography outside
Josephus.[20] In modern times, changing one's perspective in perceiv-
ing the past has become an obligatory task of any historian.[21] In
fact, this is the only advantage the historian has over the eyewitness.

Name and Notion

Another couple of terms, frequently blurred in ancient thought and
even in modern times, are contained in the Greek word *onoma*,
"noun." *Onoma* means both a particular *name* and a general *term* (or
notion). A Greek who wanted to make this distinction could speak of

---

[20] The fact must be noted, however, that the manuscript transmission of ancient
history tends to cling to one report on one series of events and shuns the pain of
transmitting alternative accounts and/or of correcting one report by means of
another. In last year's colloquium, Doron Mendels pointed to this phenomenon,
which does not seem to be supported by an ideology, though, but by simple economy.

[21] It may be applied with good results to Josephus' own parallel reports; see
Schwartz in this volume. On Josephus and Strabo, see Galimberti, also in this
volume.

onoma idion vs. *onoma koinon*, but this rarely happens. So until now we speak of the "names" of plants or animals, which are no names at all, but terms, or—to give a formula of compromise—names of species. Much confusion could be avoided by being conscious and making clear whether an *onoma* we use in a phrase refers to one single thing (animate or not) or to a class of things.

Here the English language has some advantage over German in putting a capital letter to every name, whereas German orthography sticks to a metaphysical and largely useless distinction between nouns and other kinds of words—as if nouns were more appropriate to speak of something real. This is one of the illusions of "reality" language.

Names—proper names—may also refer to peoples or groups, and thus to a plurality of persons within one unity of geographic, ethnic, or religious character. Yet they are names. To know this will help us to make a better use of the term—excuse me: of the name— "Jew," "Jews," "Jewish."

Qualifying these words as "names" automatically entails that there will be no definition of such an object. There is no "Judaism" or "Jewishness" without reference to a unique people, the "Judeans" (in antiquity) or "Jews." Scholars in Jewish studies therefore should refuse to define what they mean by "Jew." This is an old trap, as you know, but it can be avoided *a priori* by avowing that such a word is not capable of being used—and defined—as a notion. You can only *refer to* Jewish personal or collective identity or identities, a very complex thing indeed.

Language vs. Meta-language

The most important distinction to be mentioned in this survey on terminology is that between a language used for speaking of facts and a language used for speaking of words and texts. Both are necessary, but mingling them quickly becomes misleading. I am speaking of "object language" versus "meta-language." The terms are modern, but in ancient Greek you could already say: *to logos*, which would mean: "the (word) logos." All I am exposing in this paper is meta-language; only for the sake of illustration have I sometimes changed to object language. "Objects" in this sense are objects of inquiry; this may be the Judean War, it may also be Josephus' account of it. A commentary on a text is meta-language with respect to the text, but it may be object language with respect to the references it makes besides.

One more definition: A statement found in a text normally has got its *context*. I mean the literary context or, with another term, the *syntagma*. The world in which things happen or in which records are written recently came to be called "context" as well, but this is to blur the difference between texts and what they speak of. As for myself, I prefer not to call something extra-textual a "context."

The distinction between object language and meta-language has often been blurred, even programmatically so, in idealistic philosophy. But for most uses of human language, there is a fundamental difference between speaking of words and speaking of things outside the would-be self-sufficiency of language. For Josephus scholars, Josephus speaks of facts—hopefully so—, whereas a commentary on a text of his may be pure meta-language (as long as it is a purely text-critical and philological one), but it may also endeavour to clarify the facts Josephus is speaking of; in this case a fresh attempt at using object language is being made. In our editions of the *Life* and *Against Apion*, we did both, and we were always conscious of what we were doing.

Now there is a long-standing discussion, mainly nourished by French intellectuals, that language is unable to speak of anything "outside" language. There is no "outside" of language, we are told by the school of Jacques Derrida and others. There may be some scientific sense in which this is true. Those of us who have read de Saussure's *Cours de linguistique générale* (1915) may have wondered why in his chapter on semantics he excludes any use of language to refer to something that is not language. He seems to think that scientifically he is not able to speak of such a use. I am sure, however, that on ordering an Irish stew in a restaurant he did not content himself with swallowing words, but waited for the thing itself.

Now de Saussure's modern followers want us to believe that the whole world is a "text," as far as it is comprehensible to us. But here they speak metaphorically. Again our applause should go to the Greeks who were able to distinguish a *kyrion onoma* (a word in its principal meaning, Germ. *Grundbedeutung*) from a *metaphora* (metaphor).

Returning to the definition of "object" language, we may restrict our metaphysics concerning this point to the statement I have already made: That facts need to be "established" or "assessed" or whatever you would call this procedure which, true, is bound to language and even to society, i.e., to the collaboration of competent persons. Yet language is not identifiable with the things it is about. As a prisoner of his own flawless, well-functioning theory, Ferdinand de Saussure fails to tell us what language is for—a very academic shortcoming indeed.

The greatest problem of object language arises with objects remote by time or space, or both, as in the case, for example, of the Judean war. Today, one may overcome the distance of space, as did one of our collaborators in the edition of the *Life* when he flew to Israel and went to Galilee in order to see some excavation sites, including Gamla (ancient Gamala), that had come to light since 1968. There he was shown a town wall in which an ancient opening has been closed by the middle of the first century, as Josephus affirms to have done with this very town in his *Life* 185.[22] Yet the problem of temporal distance remains, and every affirmation that it was Josephus who did the repair of the wall—i.e., who had it done by some of his contemporaries—remains dependent on interpretations. These are interpretations of texts as well as of archaeological objects.

I already said that "*interpreting*" in such a case means a very different activity. Again I am not going into details of hermeneutics. Suffice it to say that "*understanding*" in its full sense involves also the reader of the texts concerned; it establishes a relationship between human persons of different times and/or places and their ways of mastering their lives, and so on: This has been well discussed from Wilhelm Dilthey to Paul Ricoeur, and it need not be re-examined here. We all know that Josephus not only informs us about things past; he also wants us to share certain values (most clearly expressed in *Apion* 2:165–189), and so on.

5. *On Facts and Truth*

Facts and Contents (of statements); Facts and Fictions

In historical texts, but also in everyday speech, much confusion arises from a failure to distinguish between the *content* of a statement and

---

[22] Vogel, 1999. The same has also provided a new map of Galilee's towns and villages as mentioned by Josephus and ascertained by archaeology; see Siegert, Schreckenberg and Vogel 2001, 218; for an alphabetical description, 208–17.

the *fact* that statement is about. Meaning is not reference, and vice versa. There may be *true* statements on *known* (or accessible) objects. In any Western language, different terms are available in speaking of utterances and in speaking of objects. There are not many terms applicable to both. A statement may be *proven*, as may be the existence of an object—but the latter, again, comes very close to a statement, viz. the statement that it exists. The content of a phrase, its "propositional content" (as linguists say), fictional or not, is one thing; its accuracy as to the things referred to—facts, causes, etc., concrete or abstract—is another.

Now facts, especially historical facts, depend on statements or other symbolic procedures in order to be identified, separated, and linked again. Yet there is a fundamental difference between a statement demonstrably linked to a fact and another statement purely narrating or depicting something, which requires only appealing to your imagination. Happily, the Greek (and Latin) *historia* has been differentiated, in English, between "history" on one hand, and "story" on the other. There are many stories in the Bible, in Josephus and so on, but the difficulty of determining their "historical" value or content is the very problem this Colloquium is about.

The Greeks were already aware of it in defining the adjective *historikos* in the sense of "historical" and "historian." But also *historia*, in an emphatic sense, may be opposed to such notions as *terpsis* (*divertissement*), as it is in Josephus, *Ant.* 8.56 (here, he has the Hiram correspondence to his credit). We may compare his opposition of *logos* and *alētheia* in *Ant.* 14.68, a passage very reminiscent of Thucydides 1.21.1. Josephus' language in *Apion* 2.217, however, is less appropriate, as if there were truth in the facts themselves.[23]

Even in antiquity, intelligent people (cf. "Cause vs. Occasion" above) never doubted that the content of a phrase is one thing, and that the facts or things corresponding to it (if there are any) are another. There are no "true" facts as opposed to "wrong" or "false" ones. Only the word "thing," vague as it is, may be used to refer to anything we may speak about, without *a priori* discrimination. Thus, things represented in a statement can be distinguished from things that happen or happened in any verifiable way. You may

---

[23] This latter opinion prevailed in philosophical, especially "logical" writings until Kant.

even speak of things that lie in the future, but not of facts of the future (as theological fundamentalism does in depicting eschatology). In German, there is a juridical offence called *Vorspiegelung falscher Tatsachen*, which is misleading language indeed. One should rather say: *Vorspiegelung falscher Sachverhalte*. There are no "wrong facts," but only untrue statements, and there are, of course, distortions of facts, and wholesale fictions.

In much of Second Temple Jewish literature the historian has the painful choice of distinguishing between the latter two. There is a very faint perception and a distorted rendering of what actually happened or had happened in books such as *3 Maccabees*, and there is only an indirect or symbolical representation of facts in a romance like *Joseph and Asenath*. It seems to me that Jewish minds of the Second Temple period were particularly overcharged with representations of what had never happened (e.g., the coming about of a homogeneous Judaic society) or of what should happen, but never did (this means the whole of Israel's apocalyptic aspirations).

A Problem of English Syntax

In co-editing some papers of last year's conference, I met with a curious problem of English syntax that arises in paraphrases of historical or would-be historical texts. Texts speaking in the past tense and referring to the past are normally paraphrased[24] in the past. This seems simple; but inadvertently, it turns a text's affirmations into its user's ones, implying the latter's convictions (see "Statements and Performative Utterances" below), whether he or she likes it or not. Paraphrasing in the present tense, as would be done in other languages, seems to be against good style.

Thus, in order to avoid confusion, some explicit provision always will be necessary, e.g.: "According to Josephus' report, Saul was a good king"; "as Josephus tells us, Saul did such-and-such," etc.

Fact vs. Myth—An Ancient, but Much Neglected, Distinction

There are no "false facts," we said, but there are phrases wrongly purporting to refer to facts. Furthermore, there are texts not directly

---

[24] Paraphrasing may not be the best way of dealing with source texts, but it is sometimes indispensable for the sake of brevity.

referring to anything, but only indirectly representing, say, human experiences. This may be one definition of "poetry," it is also a definition of myth. Sallustius' definition (4th century C.E.) was: "It never happened, but always is" (*egeneto men oudepote, esti de aei,* 4.9). Such texts do not purport to speak about facts, even though they are normally formulated in the aorist tense, the tense used for all kinds of narration including reports and historical accounts.

Ancient discussions of myth, e.g., in the writings of Alexandrian scholars like Callimachus or Eratosthenes, often are very critical of the texts' more or less fictional character. Eratosthenes is reported to have said, "you will find the route of Odysseus' wandering as soon as you find the cobbler who sewed together the bag of the winds" (Strabo 1.2.15). Thus Greek and Roman intellectuals, including Jews like Philo and Josephus, had learned to be suspicious of what they called *mythōn plasmata,* "fictions of myth."[25] In a world dominated by the Romans only concrete knowledge counted, be it historical, be it empirical.

Now it is one of Josephus' mistakes to presume—as did Philo—that everything written in the Hebrew Bible is history (as far as it is about some past), whereas everything contradicting it outside the Bible must be myth (see his *Apion* 1:154 and throughout). In this sense, Jewish interpreters took their national traditions much more seriously than the participants of Greco-Roman culture took theirs.[26] This was the birth of modern fundamentalism. Since then, this pseudo-intellectual attitude never ceased. It has been mistaken as an example or as a part of what we call religious faith.

The Notion of Truth

We now may proceed to make a proposal about the notion of "truth", especially historical truth. Ancient authors sometimes speak of an *alētheia tōn pragmatōn* (Josephus, *Apion* 2.217) as if there was a truth in the facts, but this may be a misunderstanding. There are no "true"

---

[25] For Josephus, cf. *mythos* at *Apion* 1.287; 2.256. His use of *mytheuein, mythologein,* and *mythologia,* too, is rather pejorative.

[26] Josephus included such obvious storytelling as found in the books of Jonah and Daniel in his *Antiquities,* and there has been more "scientific" effort to identify Jonah's "fish" as there ever was in order to find the cobbler of Homer's bag of winds.

facts as opposed to "false" ones, as we have already stated (be it by way of definition). We rather should explain Josephus' phrase as an abbreviation, speaking of a "truth *about* facts," a "truth *relating to* the facts." This is one sense of the Greek genitive. I insist on this because truth, as we defined it, is on the level of meaning, and reference to facts (events, objects) is another thing. There will be no question of truth if a phrase or a text fails to make a valid reference.

There may be kinds of philosophy that are independent from references, as idealism purports to be, and surely the objects of mathematics and of logic are different in kind from those of human experience. They may be treated as "formal" or "necessary" truths (as far as they are not pure definitions). In history, however, references must go to things experienced; and the historians' proper concern is sharing—and describing—experiences of the past.

For historians' use, "*truth*" may be defined as the content (or, meaning) of a statement that is confirmed by human experience, including proper inquiry. In order to be "understood," historical truths need some link with actual experiences of the person who deals with them, which is the proper domain of hermeneutics.

As opposed to "formal" truth of pure logic, "material" truth is not demonstrable in a statement itself, but only after a successful procedure of communicating an experience. Thus, a statement is called "true" if both its references and its content can be verified by appropriate means. In this respect, and generally speaking, archaeology is about references, and historiography is about meanings. Both are concerned with truth.

In every science, definitions of truth are linked to procedures of verification. These procedures change from one domain to another, philosophy being a link between them all. So there is no resignation necessary, as in saying: "This is *my* truth, and that is *yours*," or: "This was Josephus' truth, and that was somebody else's." In the science of history, as in many others, truth is a matter of *interpersonal acceptance*. This is why colloquia and other means of intellectual exchange always will precede good books.

Statements and Performative Utterances

One further definition must be put in place. When I said that *speaking of* reality is not *referring to* reality, I did not yet mention a particular way of *creating* reality. There is a curious link between language and reality, the nature of which has escaped the ancient grammarians' notice. There is a difference between a statement that such-and-such is the case, on one hand, and other uses of language made to bring about a change in the realm of facts, on the other. John Austin spoke of this phenomenon in his lectures on *How to Do Things with Words*.[27]

Let us come back to Kant's 100 shillings. There is not only the question whether you have them or not, or who has them. Someone may happen to say, "Take these 100 shillings," or "I hereby make you a gift of 100 shillings," or "I acknowledge my debt of 100 shillings to N.N." or the like. These are *performative* utterances. By such utterances, spoken or written, one can do a lot of things. I may give something to someone else, I may receive something into my property, I may give names to a child, a group may appoint a chairperson, and so on. The differences consist in the formulas used, notably in the verbs, so-called "performative" verbs—"I declare . . .," "I hereby give . . .," "I hereby take possession of . . .," etc. The adverb "hereby" often underscores the performative character of the utterance. Performative utterances cannot be "wrong," but they can be void, invalid, without effect. There are kinds of them that do not bring about a major turn in the state of affairs (e.g., greeting someone, giving thanks to someone); others do. And even those that do not seem to be of much influence are necessary and useful in order to maintain social coherence.

The counterpart to performative utterances is *statements*. Statements, however, are not the same thing as propositional contents of phrases. They may be performative in turn, and they will be so as soon as it matters who made them. In certain situations—which are not rare at all—a statement may imply a speaker's responsibility. He or she (or a group) may be held responsible for what they say—all the more so if the speaker's social position lends itself to it. Such, then, is the case of any historian, e.g., Josephus, insofar as he is deemed to be more than a storyteller.

We may extend this statement by saying that the historian as a writer is also responsible for his or her sources, independently of whether he or she names or quotes them explicitly or not. The latter case implies an even greater responsibility, because citation is a

---

[27] Austin, 1962.

means of distance, at least for the reader, whereas quoting or repeating someone's statements without saying so shifts the responsibility
to the one who quotes. Source analysis[28] is about *who* speaks, i.e.,
whose "testimony" (taken a performative utterance) is present. In this
sense Josephus himself takes his sources, e.g., Polybius and Strabo,
as "testimonies" (*Ant.* 12.135; 13.286, 319; 14.114, 138).[29]

Likewise, in reading "king of Israel" on some coin, we are entitled to ask the question whether this is a simple affirmation of something every user knew at that time, or whether it is a claim that
never came true, or only partially, as may be the case of the Bar
Kokhba coins. Numismatists, I presume, will say that any legend on
a coin is not a statement, but a claim—because the very spot on
which it appears was conventionally and juridically reserved for making claims.

To conclude, the historian cannot avoid taking the responsibility
of what he or she purports in their analyses or accounts. Happily,
our modern means of communication in print allow us to present
our sources, be they texts or objects, in an unprecedented com-
pleteness.

In doing so, language philosophy will be an efficient means of
ascertaining the "reality" (we should rather say, the truth, as regards
facts) of what we say, including ancient claims. Our effort in reading ancient sources will not be much different from what we believe
we see at the sites. Josephus was not the last to be mistaken by his
own eyes . . . and afterthoughts.[30] The service language philosophy
performs for modern scholars consists in helping them not to be misled by their own language.

BIBLIOGRAPHY

Austin, J. L.
    1962   *How To Do Things With Words: The William James Lectures Delivered at
        Harvard University in 1955.* Oxford.
Gussman, O.
    2003   Der Bedeutung der hohepriesterlichen Genealogie und Sukzession nach
        Josephus, A 20:224–251. Pages 119–31 in *Internationales Josephus-Kolloquium,
        Dortmund 2002.* Edited by J. U. Kalms and F. Siegert. Munster.

---

[28] See mainly the article by Jensen in this volume.
[29] Cf. *Life* 361–367 on external testimonies to the reliability of Josephus' *War.*
[30] See again McLaren.

Jeska, J.
    2003   Josephus und die Archäologie. Pages 110–34 in *Zeichen aus Text und Stein.
            Studien auf dem Weg zu einer Archäologie des Neuen testaments.* Edited by
            S. Alkier and J. Zangenberg. Tübingen.
Kalms J. U. and F. Siegert, eds.
    2003   *Internationales Josephus-Kolloquium Dortmund 2002.* Münster 2003.
Mendels, D.
    2005   The Formation of an Historical Canon of the Greco-Roman Period:
            From the Beginnings to Josephus. Pages 3–19 in *Josephus and Jewish
            History in Flavian Rome and Beyond.* Edited by J. Sievers and G. Lembi.
            Leiden.
Siegert, F., H. Schreckenberg, and M. Vogel, eds.
    2001   *Flavius Josephus: Aus meinem Leben <Vita>. Kritische Ausgabe, Übersetzung und
            Kommentar.* F. Siegert and H. Schreckenberg. Tübingen.
Vogel, M.
    1999   "Bericht über eine archäologische Erkundung Galiläas auf den Spuren
            des Josephus." Online: http://www.bibfor.de/archiv/99–1.vogel.htm

DELVING INTO THE DARK SIDE:
JOSEPHUS' FORESIGHT AS HINDSIGHT

James S. McLaren

The bulk of the content of *Jewish War*, and all the content in *Life*, relate to events that took place while Josephus was alive. It is little wonder that for much of what Josephus narrated he willingly claimed to be either a participant and/or an eyewitness.[1] It is also understandable that such immediate contact with the subject matter has triggered ongoing comment and debate about the exact nature of the authorial bias. A curious oversight in much of the existing discussion, however, is the impact of hindsight on what Josephus wrote.[2] Although a contemporary of the subject matter, Josephus constructed his narratives *ex eventu*.

Constructing an account of the war in Rome that openly supported the rebel cause would have been foolhardy, to say the least. It is no surprise, therefore, that what Josephus wrote is regularly regarded as being critical of the war against Rome. The challenge comes when our focus is an exploration of questions about attitudes and actions at the time of the war. Here it is necessary to address the extent to which the narrative of Josephus is primarily remembering, or revising and/or rewriting what happened. This investigation centres on the crucial issue of Josephus' own involvement in the war. How did knowing the outcome impact on what Josephus says about his activities before 70 c.e.? Was he primarily trying to remember and describe what happened? Was he providing a revision of what happened, altering certain details in the light of the outcome? Alternatively, was Josephus using hindsight to write an entirely new version of what he did during the war?

---

[1] Josephus was eager to make known his direct contact with the subject matter (*War* 1.3, 13–16; *Apion* 1.47–48 50–52, 55; *Life* 359–637).

[2] Note the general comments of Rajak (2002, 4, 65, 78–79) about how writing after the event has influenced what Josephus wrote.

The Approved Version, Part One:
The Explicit Comments regarding Josephus' Attitude

An obvious starting point for exploring Josephus' account about his participation in the war is the commentary he provides. There are four occasions where Josephus speaks directly about his supposed understanding of what was happening.[3] Chronologically the first occasion is in Jerusalem before the war began. Josephus claims he already knew the war against Rome was bound to end in disaster for the Jews (*Life* 19). The next reference occurs during the resolution of a hazardous situation for himself at Tiberias (*Life* 155–174). While dining with the leaders of the people who had just tried to oust him, Josephus declared that he knew the Romans were too powerful to defeat (*Life* 175). The two final occasions coincide with the arrival of Vespasian in Galilee. In the context of the panic and fear displayed by some of his troops, Josephus claims that he was well aware that the war was a doomed cause (*War* 3.131). Next, when Josephus arrived in Tiberias his comprehension of the situation is made even more apparent: "for he [Josephus] foresaw the final catastrophe for which the fortunes of the Jews were heading, and recognized that their only hope of salvation lay in submission" (*War* 3.136 [Thackeray, LCL]).[4]

These four brief statements ascribe to Josephus, as a participant, foresight regarding the outcome of the war. The war was futile and the only sensible course of action was to avoid hostilities and to accept Roman rule. It is interesting that Josephus is not consistent about precisely when he acquired this level of understanding of the likely outcome. In *Jewish War* Josephus first makes an appearance in the narrative after the revolt began (*War* 2.568) and the first reference to his comprehension of the situation occurs shortly before he engages Roman troops. In *Life* Josephus makes a few brief remarks about his activity before the revolt, and, in particular, about what he was doing during the machinations in Jerusalem in 66 C.E. In

---

[3] The small number of statements is not particularly significant. Josephus was sparing in his explanation of how most people behaved. Far more energy was placed in attacking the motivation of those deemed responsible for the disaster than in defending those whom he excused of any responsibility for what happened.

[4] Note that Josephus goes on to declare that he would have preferred to die rather than surrender to the Romans (*War* 3.137).

that context, he claims knowledge that going to war against Rome was doomed before hostilities had commenced.[5] In other words, the greater the chronological break from the event, the more detail Josephus provides about what he allegedly thought at the time the war commenced.

Caution is required regarding the level of credence allocated to these four comments. For instance, there are several tensions in the *War* 3 narrative. Josephus claims to have successfully trained his troops (*War* 2.577–582; *Life* 77) only for a number of them now to contemplate surrender and to flee at the first sight of the Romans (*War* 3.129). In what could be an ironic twist, Vespasian allegedly delayed attacking the Jews on the basis that it would allow them time to surrender (*War* 3.127). Therefore, the Jewish troops did have the opportunity they had been hoping for, the chance to surrender (*War* 3.129). In particular, the naming of Justus and his father complicates the level of historical credence allocated to the comment in *Life* 175. The banquet is part of a larger reply to claims made by Justus (*Life* 336–367). At first glance, it is puzzling that Josephus allegedly decided to make a frank declaration about the war to the very people who had been conspiring to oust him. Read in terms of replying to the claims of Justus, however, the alleged declaration has a significant part to play. In the process of narrating what happened in Galilee during the war, Josephus asserts that he informed Justus of his true thoughts and intentions. By implication, when it came to writing their accounts of what happened it must have been Justus who had lied, not Josephus. The focus here is on countering Justus, not informing the reader of what Josephus actually thought about the situation back in 66–67 c.e.

Josephus portrays other Jews as understanding the gravity of the situation. In particular, Ananus b. Ananus is a prominent Jew involved in the war who apparently recognized that the conflict would end in disaster for the Jews. Ananus hoped to persuade those favouring war to abandon the preparations for conflict (*War* 2.651). A second, more extensive, reference to Ananus occurs in the eulogy after his death (*War* 4.320–321). Ananus always placed communal interests first and he was motivated by a desire to maintain peace. Once the

---

[5] Note also that in *Life* 208–209 Josephus claims he received insight regarding his immediate future through a dream.

war commenced Ananus committed himself to ensuring it was well commanded. Although he always hoped to bring about a peaceful resolution through negotiations, he did not intend to provide the Romans with an easy victory if a battle was to ensue. Josephus adds, with great confidence, that the war would have been resolved in quite a different way had Ananus lived.[6]

As with the references to Josephus' level of self-understanding, there is reason to be cautious regarding the validity of these comments about Ananus. Of particular concern is the manner in which Ananus' alleged outlook appears in the narrative. In *War* 2 Ananus apparently hopes to find a means to bring about a peaceful resolution, at some point in the future. In *War* 4, after he is dead, Josephus claims Ananus would have found a way to achieve an appropriate end to the conflict but for his early death. Josephus' most detailed praise for Ananus is for what "might" have been achieved and, even in the flow of the narrative, it occurs after the event. This failed desire for peace is probably a deliberate ploy by Josephus. Given the outcome of the war it was not appropriate to present any Jews in favour of peace as still holding effective authority as the war progressed. However, he could readily allocate a pro-peace attitude to appropriate Jews in the early stages of the war. Indeed, it was crucial that Josephus did identify such people in order to deflect responsibility for the war from the majority of the Jewish community. As such, Ananus is a role model of appropriate thinking in a larger agenda. What Ananus actually thought at the time of the war is not relevant.[7]

Even with the two references to Ananus Josephus is very economical regarding the number of explicit statements about how he and other possible likeminded Jews understood the state of affairs in Judea before and during the war.[8] Such reluctance on the part of

---

[6] Other Jews apparently held a similar view to Ananus (*War* 4.322). Note also *Life* 60, where Philip is described as managing to persuade the people of Gamala to remain loyal to Agrippa II and, therefore, to Rome. Philip dwelt on the power of Rome and Agrippa's generous benefaction toward the town.

[7] There is a significant complication in the description of the situation in the *War* 2 passage. Ananus wanted to stop the preparations for war, but did not do so. By implication, other people held more sway than Ananus in Jerusalem when he was the commander. A similar problem exists in the *War* 4 eulogy. Ananus was allegedly an accomplished public speaker but he and his colleagues had recently failed to dissuade the Idumeans from attacking Jerusalem.

[8] It is important to note that Josephus never explicitly links himself with Ananus

Josephus was probably deliberate. The more Josephus dwelt on how prominent, sensible Jews realised that a war against Rome was wrong, the more those people would be open to criticism for having failed to win over the community. Josephus walks a fine line, claiming that he and other Jews apparently understood what was going to happen and that they tried to prevent the disaster. At the same time, he places on centre stage various rogue Jews seizing control, whose ruthless pursuit for power drove the Jews to utter destruction.

The Approved Version, Part Two: The Recorded Actions of Josephus

Josephus was careful to locate the few explicit comments about his supposed attitude at the time of the war within the broader narrative of the events. They are brief asides made in the context of telling the story. As such, the activities of Josephus are important to examine for what they offer regarding the nature of his involvement in the war. The eight actions will be examined in chronological sequence.

Public Oration in Jerusalem during 66 c.e. (Life *17–23*)

Here Josephus explicitly displays opposition to the prospect of going to war against Rome. He engages in public discourse, advocating the cause of not taking up arms (*Life* 17–19). Josephus goes on to describe such a course of action as being fraught with danger (*Life* 20). He also claims that he sought refuge from the danger in the inner court of the temple (*Life* 20) only to reappear in the public arena with other likeminded aristocrats to again urge restraint (*Life* 22–23).

There is a clear connection between the described action and the alleged understanding of the situation made explicit in the *Life* narrative. There are, however, a number of problems. The most important of these concerns the lack of correspondence with the account of the same period in *War* 2.408–432. The two accounts do agree that aristocrats and others spoke against the war in order to restore peace. However, even here the match is not complete. In *Jewish War*

---

in *Jewish War*. In *Life*, Josephus is linked with unnamed leaders of the community who are opposed to the war.

those people go on to either fight the rebels or flee the city after
the defeat of Cestius (*War* 2.418–419, 422–424, 556). In *Life*, there
is no reference to any such course of action taken by the advocates
of peace. In other aspects of detail, the two accounts contradict one
another. A key example is the reference to Josephus being in the
inner court of the temple. In *War* this area was always in the hands
of the rebel group while in *Life* Josephus went there to escape from
the rebels.[9]

The Appointment of Josephus as Commander in Galilee (War 2.562–568; Life 28–29)[10]

The two accounts of Josephus' appointment in Galilee have been
the cause of much discussion. Rebels are responsible for fostering
war in both accounts (*Life* 28, *War* 2.562) and Josephus, along with
likeminded Jews, responds to the circumstances. However, the nature
of Josephus' commission is markedly different in the two texts. It is
not surprising that the *Life* version reinforces the preceding account
of how he and other elements of the Jewish aristocratic leadership
tried to curtail the spread of the war. Josephus' task was to bring
order to Galilee and to prevent the situation from becoming any
worse (*Life* 28–29). Restraint was the principle objective. The com-
missioning of Josephus is an *ad hoc* decision, made in the light of
news that Galilee was not yet fully committed to the war (*Life* 28).
In *War* 2.566–568 no such restraint is evident. The defeat of Cestius
marked the end of the hope for the quick restoration of peace. The
appointment of the "additional generals" is a co-ordinated, deliber-

---

[9] Cf. Mason 2001, 30–31. A further reason for caution, especially regarding the
Life 19 reference, is its positioning in the text. Josephus had travelled to Rome and
when he returned to Jerusalem the move to war had already commenced (*Life*
16–17). By implication, Josephus had nothing to do with the beginning of the
conflict. This information worked well for Josephus' larger agenda. Justus had accused
Josephus of being a promoter of war, especially in terms of what happened in
Galilee. In response, the account in *Life* helped close a major gap in *Jewish War*
that had made Josephus vulnerable to criticism, namely, his activities at the outbreak of the war.

[10] The number of commanders appointed for Galilee is unclear. If any credence
is given to the list of generals named in *War* 2.566–568 it would make sense that
more than one person was appointed to command Galilee. However, the *Life* reference to fellow commanders serves Josephus well by showing him to be the most
diligent of those appointed and by helping to counter the idea that Josephus alone
was responsible for the Galilee going to war.

ate action to help oversee the war effort (*War* 2.562). The location of the account in *Jewish War* primarily reflects a concern of Josephus to separate the named people, including himself, from the beginning of the war. Even allowing for such manipulation the implication is that the revolt, started in Jerusalem, spread well beyond the city limits in a co-ordinated manner (*War* 2.563–568). In that setting Josephus makes his first appearance as a character in the narrative: a general commissioned to oversee the war effort in Galilee (*War* 2.569).

Josephus as Commander in Galilee: Preparations for Conflict (War *2.569–584*; Life *77–79, 186–188*)

In both accounts there are three main areas of activity. Josephus helps organize the construction of walls for many towns (*War* 2.572–573, *Life* 77, 186–188). Josephus also forms, trains and supplies an army (*War* 2.576–578; *Life* 77). Part of this process appears to have involved negotiating a deal with local bandits (*Life* 77–78). The third aspect of the preparations undertaken by Josephus was the appointment of local aristocrats to act as judges (*War* 2.570; *Life* 79). The primary function of the two summary accounts of what Josephus did by way of preparation is to promote his supposed ability. The accounts extol Josephus' prowess as a highly skilled and diligent commander and they have probably exaggerated what he was able to achieve. However, there is no doubt that Josephus readily asserts he undertook preparations to defend Galilee against an anticipated Roman attack.[11]

Josephus as Commander in Galilee: Disputes with Other Jews (War *2.585–594, 610–646, 3.61–62*; Life *70–76, 84–113, 122–125, 132–178, 189–335, 373–380, 399–406*)

The various details of the machinations and the specific nature of differences between the two accounts are not of concern here. The key point to note is that Josephus claims he tried to assert control over the Jews in Galilee. This type of action dominates Josephus' account of affairs in Galilee, especially in *Life*. Again, with a clear concern to appear in the best possible light, Josephus repeatedly manages to avoid the adverse intentions of his rivals. In *Life*, particular

---

[11] On the fortification and siege of Jotapata see Aviam 2004.

emphasis is placed on showing how Josephus continually worked to
maintain peace and order in the region, reinforcing the portrait of
a person commissioned to control the spread of conflict. However,
there is an important shared aspect of the two accounts that points
toward a pro-war stance. Josephus readily describes his opposition
to those Jews who sided with the Romans. Hence, Josephus justifies
an attack on Sepphoris in terms of the desertion of the town to the
Romans (*War* 3.61–62, *Life* 373–380) and relates an encounter with
the troops of Agrippa II (*Life* 399–406). Such action makes little
sense for someone trying to look for a quick, peaceful resolution to
the war and who understood the futility of the conflict.

*Josephus as Commander in Galilee: Destruction of the Royal Palace at
Tiberias* (Life *64–69*)

The decision to include this incident in *Life* is probably due to some
comment made by Justus in his account of the war in Galilee. In
other words, Josephus is responding to Justus with his own version
of what happened. Throughout the account, Josephus devolves himself of responsibility for the destruction of the palace. The original
order came from Jerusalem (*Life* 65) and certain locals moved before
Josephus (*Life* 66) could put his plan into action. Josephus was then
quick to restore order, bringing an end to the looting (*Life* 67–68)
and then placing the retrieved goods in the trust of aristocrats from
Tiberias (*Life* 68–69).

Although it is not possible to categorically confirm the action was
initiated in Jerusalem, the fact that Josephus does not write it off as
a local issue suggests it was the result of an order from the capital.
Having devolved himself of blame, Josephus diligently fulfils instruc-
tions provided by a central command that was working to principles about the way the Jewish state should look. By implication, the
Jerusalem-based administration that Josephus was working for did
not see the conflict with Rome as a short-term one nor was it one
that they were trying to quell at the earliest possible moment.[12]

---

[12] On this incident see Vogel 1999, 65–79.

Josephus as Commander in Galilee: Seizure of Royal Baggage
(War *2.595–610*; Life *126–131, 139–144*)

Young men from Dabaritta seize a baggage train that belonged to the wife of Ptolemy, an official in the service of Agrippa II. In effect, their decision to take the booty to Josephus affirms his status as commander. What Josephus does with the booty is the cause of much trouble in the narrative. He claims to have kept the booty with the intention of returning it to Ptolemy (*War* 2.597; *Life* 131). Understandably, the men who captured the goods felt aggrieved at the lack of any reward. In turn, it provides Josephus with a further opportunity to display his prowess for being able to avoid a perilous situation (*War* 2.598–607; *Life* 136–144). It also indicates that Josephus did not seek to gain financially from his post as a commander. However, the incident is of little help in determining how Josephus regarded the war and the nature of his involvement in the conflict, especially given the absence of an explanation about why the booty was presented to him.[13]

Josephus as Commander in Galilee: Fighting against the Romans
(War *3.135–339*; Life *398–404, 412*)

There is a major imbalance here between the two accounts. In *Jewish War* Josephus' engagement against Roman forces was the centrepiece of the Galilee narrative while in *Life* it was merely a brief afterthought. The main topic covered in *Jewish War*, the siege of Jotapata, is full of self-adulation. As a general Josephus exceeds the skill and determination of Vespasian, his defeat is the result of treachery and fatigue (*War* 3.317–322, 327).

Of particular relevance is the account of how Josephus initially came into contact with Vespasian's forces. Hearing Vespasian had arrived, Josephus wrote to Jerusalem for advice: should he sue for peace or fight (*War* 3.139)? There is no reference to Josephus receiving an answer. What we hear next is that he goes from Tiberias to Jotapata (*War* 3.142; *Life* 412). This move is crucial. Vespasian captured Gabara (*War* 3.132) and Jotapata is listed as his next object. In the vicinity of Garis (*War* 3.129), Josephus is deserted by troops

---

[13] It is even possible that the action of the young men was the result of an order issued by Josephus regarding the seizure of booty.

who fear the presence of the Romans and he goes to Tiberias. From there Josephus could have sent messengers to Vespasian, suing for peace. Instead, Josephus goes to Jotapata. This move placed him in the front line of the Roman attack. The most plausible explanation of this action is that Josephus was actively preparing to fight Vespasian.[14]

Josephus as Commander in Galilee: the Surrender of Josephus (War *3.340–408*)

This incident remains one of the most intriguing aspects of Josephus' narratives. That Josephus did not die indicates he was not a fanatical fighter like some of the rebels he describes. However, it does put him in the same situation as a number of the people he openly criticises, like Simon b. Gorias and John of Gischala. They all surrendered after apparently actively resisting the Romans (*War* 6.433; 7.26–36). What makes Josephus different is that he went to the Romans as a messenger. It is likely, therefore, that when he wrote of his surrender Josephus did not view his action in such terms.

The key point to note here is what is missing from the explanation Josephus provides for his decision to surrender. At no stage does Josephus try to connect his surrender with what he claimed was the most appropriate course of action in his explicit comments about the war—the need to submit to Rome. Rather, Josephus cites divine providence as the explanation for his survival (*War* 3.341, 387). Furthermore, during the siege of Jotapata, Josephus apparently contemplated flight when he realized the town was going to be captured by the Romans (*War* 3.193). After much pleading by the townspeople for him to stay, Josephus agrees to fight on with renewed vigour (*War* 3.195–204). At no stage in the siege does Josephus suggest he was acting on the basis that fighting was futile or that he wanted to surrender.

The decision of Josephus to explain his surrender within the confines of established Jewish thinking is important to note. It resonates well

---

[14] As a further complication, Josephus adds the comment that he preferred to die rather than surrender (*War* 3.137). It is important to note that this marks the first occasion in the *Jewish War* that Josephus adds commentary about his motivation and awareness of the situation. Note that the contributions of Atkinson and Rappaport in this volume advocate a different reading of Josephus' intentions at Jotapata.

with speeches attributed to Josephus during the siege of Jerusalem, in which he acts as a spokesperson for submission to Rome (*War* 5.362–419, 6.96–110). Although the main speech, in *War* 5, strongly asserts the importance of accepting the reality and legitimacy of Roman power (*War* 5.364), it is the belief that God has favoured Rome that makes submission particularly appropriate (*War* 5.366–367). Josephus goes on to outline how God has always protected the faithful (*War* 5.376–390, 406–412) and that past defeats, including the capturing of Jerusalem, were expressions of divine punishment for taking up arms (*War* 5.391–398).[15]

Two observations stand out regarding the actions of Josephus. One is their rather potted nature, in the sequencing and number. Josephus does provide an extensive account of some of his activity in Galilee, against the Romans in *Jewish War* and against other Jews in *Life*. There are, however, a number of major gaps in the account. A key example is what Josephus does not reveal about his activity in *Jewish War* during the summer of 66 C.E. There is a significant imbalance in what Josephus does describe. In *Jewish War* the siege at Jotapata and his subsequent capture is prominent. In *Life*, the nature of Josephus' appointment in Galilee dominates the narrative. Josephus is clearly choosing to be selective when reflecting on his involvement in the conflict. In this context, it is notable that the commission, as recorded in *Life*, and the surrender, as recorded in *Jewish War* stand out as key events. The two actions are allocated a privileged position in the narrative by the decision to provide detail regarding Josephus' supposed motivation at the time.

The other observation is the lack of correlation between the actions described and the explicit commentary regarding the involvement of Josephus. It is legitimate to expect that the general tenor of the description of actions associated with Josephus would concur with the way he allegedly thought about the war. Some restraint in the way Josephus behaved may have been necessary if the community at large favoured war, and/or, that radical proponents of war were dominant at the time. Indeed, Josephus suggests that open opposition to the war had to turn into a more subtle line of action (*War*

---

[15] Josephus' claim that taking up arms was an inappropriate action for Jews (*War* 5.399) is most curious given that the first event recounted in *Jewish War* is the success of the Maccabean uprising.

3.136; *Life* 19, 175–176).[16] However, any caution required at the time of the war did not necessarily apply when Josephus came to write about the conflict. If anything, it would make a stronger line of argument for Josephus to be able to show how he and other Jews supposedly opposed to the war actively went about doing their best to bring about a negotiated settlement. At no stage does Josephus present himself as undertaking such a course of action.[17]

There is no doubt that Josephus was concerned to present himself in the best possible light. He was, apparently, an intelligent, able commander who turned many dangerous situations to his advantage and never allowed personal safety to control his decisions. Even allowing for such self-promotion, the actions Josephus attributes to himself do not suggest that he was an advocate of peace before his capture. Instead, the actions indicate that Josephus accepted a commission to command the Jewish forces in Galilee. This command placed Josephus at the front line. There he oversaw preparations for the expected Roman counter attack. When the Romans did march on Galilee Josephus was quick to meet the challenge. He readily went into battle, taking command of the defence of Jotapata.[18]

This tension between the supposed comprehension of the situation and the actions undertaken has drawn much attention within scholarly assessment of Josephus' works. Two broad schools of thought dominate discussion. One school of thought rejects the tenor of the explicit commentary, giving preference to the actions. Josephus was a willing rebel, readily involved in the process of opposing Rome.[19]

---

[16] Note the story of Ananus b. Jonathan (*War* 2.533–534) and that of Judes b. Judes (*War* 5.534–540). Both men wanted to surrender but they were prevented from so doing.

[17] Several of the actions undertaken by Josephus are also attributed to Ananus and his colleagues. Preparing for conflict (*War* 2.647–650) Ananus oversees the provision of arms (*War* 2.648–649), the training of men (*War* 2.649) and the extension of the city walls in Jerusalem (*War* 2.648). He is also engaged in disputes with fellow Jews (*War* 2.652–653; 4.158–325). Note the irony in the dispute narrated in *Jewish War* 4. Ananus apparently wanted to negotiate terms with Rome. Indeed, this is the charge levelled against him by the Idumeans and yet he, and Jesus, vehemently reject those charges (*War* 4.252–253, 268–269). The attack on Ascalon (*War* 3.9–28) also suggests that negotiating peace was not the primary objective of the Jerusalem administration.

[18] If anything, the decision to make a stand at Jotapata indicates Josephus' lack of strategic and tactical ability. He had no military experience to draw upon.

[19] For example, see Drexler 1925, 277–312 and Price 1992, esp. 32, 34–35 regarding the contradiction between the actions and the commentary.

The commentary was part of an attempt by Josephus to re-write why he was a participant in the war. This approach has been the impetus of much criticism levelled at Josephus. It has opened the way for negative judgements about Josephus' lack of personal integrity. In particular, it has paved the way for charges of manipulating details about what happened in the war to suit Josephus' own interests.[20]

By way of contrast, the second school of thought places credence in the explicit commentary provided by Josephus and seeks ways to explain away any supposed contradictions between the commentary and the actions. The claims to foresight and understanding regarding how the war would end are deemed to be genuine. Like most other aristocrats, Josephus was opposed to the war and he was part of a moderate group of leading Jews that took on the task of commanding the war effort once the die had been cast and the revolt had commenced.[21] These men, however, were never serious about resisting Rome at all costs: they always wanted to find a peaceful solution. Josephus was remembering and revising what happened.[22] As such, he is an excellent example of a provincial aristocrat trying to come to terms with the reality of Roman rule, acting as an intermediary between the conquering power and his own community.

Focusing attention on the role of hindsight for the way Josephus has presented his own contribution to the war provides a way to navigate through the battle lines of the two well-established schools of thought. It confirms that Josephus' description of actions and events, however distorted it may be, should take precedence over any statements in the narrative that ascribe motivation and intention to his character. Equally important, it also allows scope for attributing to Josephus a consistent line of thought about how he could undertake what looks like an abrupt change of allegiance, turning from actively rebelling against Rome to finding a way of living with Roman rule without changing his principles.

---

[20] For example, see Cohen 1979. The papers presented by Rappaport and Atkinson also operate from the premise that Josephus was lying to cover up what he did and to deal with his own guilt about what happened.

[21] For example, Rajak 1983, esp. 4, 42, 128–31, 158, 167.

[22] An off-shoot of this second school of thought has been proposed recently by Mason 2003, 145–88. He argues that attention should focus on understanding what is happening in the narrative, that the events underlying the text are beyond recovery given the level of dependence on Josephus for information. From such a perspective, Mason proposes that Josephus presents a consistent portrait of the aristocracy working for peace.

Hindsight and History in Josephus

The ability to look back and review events after they have reached a known outcome is integral to what we understand as the activity of an historian. A fundamental impact of working from hindsight is the inherent tendency to operate within a causation paradigm. The focus of attention revolves around establishing the cause and effect connection that leads us to a certain known endpoint.

In the case of Josephus, the key issue was to explain how and why the disaster of 70 C.E. occurred, especially in terms of deciding who was to blame for what happened. The general outline of his explanation is well known. Faced with an increasing number of abuses from poor Roman administration, an unrepresentative minority of radical Jews launched the war against Rome. Their criminal activities and evil desires for power at all costs continued unabated until God decided to use the Romans as instruments of divine punishment. So hideous were the crimes of these radicals that God allowed the city and the temple to be destroyed. The vast majority of the Jews, especially the leaders of the community, were opposed to the revolt and they did everything they could to prevent its outbreak. Most Jews recognized that peaceful co-operation with Rome was the sensible course of action. Constructed after 70 C.E., there was no advantage in presenting oneself as an active participant in the war who advocated the cause. Opposing the war, and/or counselling for peace were the only sensible options.

Clearly, Josephus had a personal interest in ensuring that his explanation of the war enhanced his standing among those who were concerned to know what happened. We are not reading the work of an abstract or neutral observer, let alone someone long since removed from the consequences of what happened. Rather, every day of Josephus' life after 70 C.E. was a direct result of what had happened during the war. The numerous references to defending himself against the charge of being a traitor (*War* 2.598, 599, 3.354, 359, 381, 439; *Life* 133, 140) indicate the extent to which he was still living in the shadow of the war. In a similar vein, Josephus expends substantial effort in *Life* explaining that he was not responsible for the bellicose state of affairs in Galilee, as alleged by Justus (*Life* 29, 30, 43, 46, 185, 340–341, 349).[23] In these circumstances,

---

[23] Cf. Mason (2001, 29–33) regarding the extent to which *Life* was constructed

Josephus decided to provide a Jewish explanation of what occurred. The account of the war and its outcome had to accommodate a core principle of his religious heritage, the one God was all powerful.

One possible way of comprehending the extent to which hindsight has influenced the structure and content of Josephus' works is to consider the impact of him writing at a different time. If the account had been constructed in early 67 C.E. what would it have looked like? Would Josephus have viewed the situation as one of impending disaster, even though the specific outcome was unknown, and what events would he have included in the account? Did he really believe in 66 C.E. that a Roman victory was the likely outcome, and so act accordingly? An obvious difficulty with adopting such an approach is that we are entering into a realm of speculation where possibilities abound.

Another, more tangible and direct way of recognizing the central role of hindsight in what Josephus chose to write is to acknowledge the implications of the fact that his accounts of the war are clearly crafted constructions. The choice of subject matter and the way it is presented are what has been elsewhere labelled as his "interpretative framework."[24] It is not simply a case of being able to separate Josephus' authorial input from the data by identifying imposed explicit commentary on the events described. Instead, even the very choice and location of subject matter is an integral part of Josephus shaping and controlling his explanation of what happened in 70 C.E. It is, therefore, not a coincidence that the claim to foresight about the outcome of the war and his supposed intentions are contained in authorial commentary attached to the events described. Allocating

---

as a response to the work of Justus. The dominance of Josephus needing to defend himself is apparent from the disproportionate use of the word "traitor" in his writings. Of the eighteen times the word appears in *Jewish War* and *Life*, eight relate to Josephus. For no other person is the term used on multiple occasions. The twenty-one accusations of treacherous behaviour in *Jewish War* and *Life* are also significant. Four relate to Josephus (*War* 2.602, 3.361, 439; *Life* 140), three to Zacharias (*War* 4.336, 347, 352) and five to Ananus and Jesus (*War* 4.211, 245, 246, 257, 280). Together they indicate a concern to defend and justify the actions of Josephus and fellow aristocrats.

[24] McLaren 1998, 48–67. It is, therefore, an artificial divide which is being made in distinguishing between actions and commentary in what follows. However, such a divide is important to make in order to establish how the framework is constructed. What may hold most significance in terms of understanding the approved interpretation, constructed after the event, does not necessarily also apply when the focus is on what actually happened at the time the events took place.

motivation to participants and explaining their attitude in given situations provides Josephus with the opportunity to convey his intended
message. Like speeches, they represent the views Josephus has chosen to attach to the characters in the narrative. Because the accounts
are constructed with hindsight, this explicit commentary cannot stand
on its own right as evidence of how people actually thought at the
time the events were unfolding.

   Josephus' choice of subject matter is also an integral part of his
interpretative framework. As much as his skills allow, we should
expect Josephus to choose incidents that concur with his explanation of how and why the disaster of 70 C.E. occurred. In this context, it is likely that some events have been left out of the narrative
and that others have been heavily edited. Similarly, people's actions
have been distorted and/or extra details have been provided in an
effort to ensure the event conforms to the broad requirements of
Josephus' viewpoint. Two significant examples of this approach are
his silence regarding the capture of the Roman standards in 66 C.E.,
and his silence regarding the argument in favour of ceasing to offer
sacrifices on behalf of the Romans.

   Even with these difficulties in mind, actions remain the best way
to assess Josephus' behaviour during the war, and his understanding of the situation at the time. At the very core of *Jewish War* and
Life lie historical realities: some Jews did go to war against the
Romans, the Jewish forces opposed to Rome were defeated, Jerusalem
was besieged, with much of the city destroyed in the process. Whatever
Josephus may have decided to add, delete and/or alter regarding
these events, they are not fiction. There was a war. A brief aside in
Life 348 makes clear the nature of the situation in 66 C.E. and, for
that matter, throughout the war. Josephus describes the actions of
the people of Sepphoris: "Even while our greatest city, Jerusalem,
was under siege and the common temple of all was at risk of coming
under the authority of the enemy, they did not send an allied force—
not wanting to appear to take up weapons against the Romans."[25]
(Mason, FJTC)

---

[25] Agrippa II also provides a further example of how to respond to the war. The
king's open support for Rome means a legitimate course of action for the leaders
of the community was to oppose the war.

To take up arms against Rome was not an option for an advocate of peace. Given the chosen subject matter, no matter how Josephus tried to dress-up his account of what he did during the war he could not rewrite the reality of having actively resisted Roman invasion.

Conclusion

Although contrived and potted in their presentation, the few actions that Josephus allows his audience to view display a person who willingly went to war against Rome. After glossing over the details of his activity when the war actually began, Josephus became a commander of forces in Galilee, a likely target for the initial assault by the Romans. He helped prepare the region for the upcoming Roman attack and, when the advance came, he readily went to encounter the Romans. No match for the strength of the attacking army, Josephus was quickly defeated. A moment of crisis confronted Josephus. His ability to survive the war, as well as the circumstances he encountered in Rome, made it necessary to provide some explanation for what had happened. The outcome of the war, therefore, had a massive impact on what Josephus wrote about his involvement in the war.

In the process of narrating his capture the following claim is made: "... he [Josephus] would have preferred to suffer a thousand deaths rather than betray his country and disgracefully abandon the command which had been entrusted to him ..." (*War* 3.137). In the light of subsequent actions, this commentary is readily dismissed as being absurd. Without any hesitation, Josephus' claim is subject to the scrutiny of actions recorded in the narrative. This principle should run for the whole narrative. The comments about intentions and motivation cloth the account to meet the issues and concerns of Josephus' post 70 C.E. circumstances. They are part of an effort to rewrite the nature of his involvement in the war.[26]

---

[26] Source material independent of Josephus confirms that the war was undertaken with much vigour, right from the outset. The coinage produced by Jews from as early as 66 C.E. was the work of people committed to the removal of Roman control. Silver coinage was minted in Jerusalem almost immediately after the war began, with the purpose of allowing Jews to use their own coins for the payment of the upcoming Temple Tax. See McLaren 2003, 135–52.

We conclude with two suggestions that take us into "dark" crevices of Josephus' world not yet thoroughly explored. The first one relates to our use of Josephus for interpreting the first century, especially in terms of the war against Rome. It is time that we let go of the control exerted by the causation paradigm of the known endpoint, the devastating defeat of the Jews. Rather than reflecting back on the war as a foolish and forlorn cause, attention can be directed toward exploring it in terms of the aspirations and hopes associated with its beginning. Much as we tend to ignore the question, "*what if*," it does play an integral part of the way history is formed, and reformed.[27] The certainty of the outcome should not negate consideration of exploring the various possibilities at any given moment in the war. At the extreme end of such exploration, it would be intriguing to consider the type of narrative Josephus would construct if the revolt had concluded with increased Jewish autonomy.

The second suggestion pertains to our understanding of Josephus. We need to ponder further the ramifications of the idea that the most fundamental, ongoing concern for Josephus was making sense of his world vis-à-vis God. Along with many other Jews in 66 C.E., Josephus thought he was working for God in trying to remove the Romans. By 70 C.E. Josephus realised he had been wrong. This error had resulted in a terrible disaster. At no stage, however, was Rome or Jerusalem ever the central point of reference for Josephus. He was not a rebel who became a Roman servant. Nor was he an aristocrat who carried out the duty incumbent on such a position in society, deciding to serve the public interest, even though he recognized that Roman power was unstoppable. There was no change of allegiance. Josephus always upheld the principle that God was in control of what was happening. The underlying ethos remained the same. What experience and hindsight did was dramatically change the way Josephus understood how divine control was articulated. The decision to find a means of surviving the siege at Jotapata became a major turning point in the life of Josephus. He boldly

---

[27] Acknowledging Josephus as trying to rewrite what happened encourages an analysis of his rhetorical activity. In this context, a flaw is immediately apparent. Attributing the war to the persistence of fanatical revolutionaries implies that the aristocracy failed in one of their primary tasks, maintaining peace. It is notable that this flaw has been widely accepted in scholarship as reflecting the actual situation before the war.

opposed Vespasian, confident that his God would help bring victory. The reality of defeat and the likelihood of death meant that a new understanding of how God viewed the situation was required. It is time our reading of Josephus gave due recognition to the profound ramifications of this dramatic moment in his life.

BIBLIOGRAPHY

Aviam, M.
    2004   *Jews, Pagans and Christians in the Galilee*. Rochester.
Cohen, S. J. D.
    1979   *Josephus in Galilee and Rome: His Vita and Development as Historian*. Leiden.
Drexler, H.
    1925   Untersuchungen zu Josephus und zur Geschichte des jüdischen Aufstandes. *Klio* 19:277–312.
McLaren, J. S.
    1998   *Turbulent Times? Josephus and Scholarship on Judaea in the First Century C.E.* Sheffield.
    2003   The Coinage of the First Year as a Point of Reference for the Jewish Revolt (66–70 C.E.). *SCI* 22:135–52.
Mason, S.
    2001   *Life of Josephus*. Vol. 9 of *Flavius Josephus: Translation and Commentary*. Edited by S. Mason.
Price, J. J.
    1992   *Jerusalem under Siege: The Collapse of the Jewish State, 66–70 C.E.* Leiden.
Rajak, T.
    2002   *Josephus: The Historian and his Society* (Second Edition). London.
Thackarey, H. St. J.
    1927   *Josephus II* (LCL; Cambridge, Mass.).
Vogel, M.
    1999   Vita 64–69, das Bilderverbot und die Galileapolitik des Josephus. *JSJ* 30:65–79.

JOSEPHUS' PERSONALITY AND THE CREDIBILITY OF HIS NARRATIVE

Uriel Rappaport

Every narrative should be scrutinized carefully and critically, without going to extremes, by reading it in accordance with what the reader understands, wishes or judges as right. The same approach is agreed upon among historians about historic texts, both ancient and modern. Primarily it should be clarified to whom it is useful, i.e., whose interests it serves, or as it is said in Latin *cui bono* (to whom is it good). Likewise the personal, social, and political situation of the writer within his own society and his attitude towards the subjects about which he writes should be clarified.

What is necessary in relation to all historical writings is vital in the case of Flavius Josephus, a noble Jewish priest, a war captive, and a Roman citizen (*libertinus*). Josephus' writings are a notable case of a narrative that was written under various "pressures" which make Josephus' writings in general, and *Jewish War* and *Life* in particular, notorious for doubtful credibility. There is a wide consensus that Josephus served his patrons, the Flavian family and especially Titus, by depicting them usually in a favorable light. At the same time, he tried to present his own people in a positive way to Gentile readers by placing the responsibility for the revolt with the rebels, whom he claims were a minority who brought disaster on an innocent people. Moreover, he had to defend himself against contradictory attacks, either accusing him of being a rebel, or of being a traitor.

In this paper I will try to present an additional aspect that may shed some light on Josephus' tortuous way of telling the history of the Jewish revolt of 66–73 C.E. I also intend to discuss Josephus' personality, though I am aware of the deficiencies of such an approach. Psychohistory was fashionable some decades ago,[1] but was also

---

[1] The peak of publication activity in the field of psychohistory seems to be in the 1970s. It includes various subjects such as history of childhood, individual psycho-historical investigation, and collective-social phenomena (concerning revolutions, aggression etc.). See for example Friedlander (1975) and the bibliography there.

criticized on various grounds, mainly because of the inability of the historian to treat his "patient" personally, on the psychologist's sofa so to speak.

This criticism may be justified from the psychologist's point of view, but not necessarily from that of the historian. The historian is not obliged to achieve a full psychological portrait and complete analysis of the personality of the individual who interests him or her. We can be satisfied with a partial analysis of the subject, if it helps us to understand certain behavioral patterns of the person who is central to our research; as in the case under discussion, if it explains or answers questions like why did Josephus tell incredible and unacceptable facts and events in his report about his participation in the Great Revolt? These will be dealt with below in greater detail. Here they will be listed briefly: Did Josephus fortify ten places in Galilee? Did he organize a huge army, structured in line with the Roman military model? Was he really a military expert and an efficient commander? Was he the commander of Yodefat when the Romans besieged it? Is it credible that he survived the siege of Yodefat by casting lots and divine help?

Had all these have been told only in the *Life* it could have been argued that these stories were fabricated in accordance with literary conventions of the autobiographical genre, but since some are found not only there but also in *War*, this explanation is not satisfactory. We will try to explain the distortions of the story of Josephus' role in the history of the Great Revolt as (among other causes) a result of a personal irresistible impulse.

To the writings of Josephus, the prolific Jewish historian, we owe almost all of our knowledge of important chapters in the history of the Jewish people in the period of the Second Temple, or "im Zeitalter Jesu Christi," as Schürer defined it. Josephus had a complex personality about which different and opposing opinions have been expressed.[2] For our enquiry it is not important to make a value

---

Our investigation of Josephus' personality is extremely limited because of the paucity of the evidence available.

[2] Various historians describe Josephus in differing ways, some as a traitor, coward, crook etc., others as dedicated to the welfare of his people and champion of Judaism etc. Various polar opinions are listed in Klausner (1954, 170–71). Josephus also has a place in literature and among many novelists who wrote about Josephus: probably L. Feuchtwanger's *Josephus*, a trilogy, published 1932, 1934, 1952 (in German), which was translated into many languages and appeared in various forms

judgment about Josephus,[3] but to try to delve into the inner work-
ings of his mind and soul and acquaint ourselves with the many
facets of his personality (what the psychologist may call empathy). It
may help us to understand better his writings, his motivations for
writing, what he wrote and the manner in which he wrote it, and
to elucidate his amazing stories. Perhaps we can find a comprehensive
explanation to queries that can also be explained separately. So we
are not trying to invalidate other explanations of various actions and
events in his life, but to offer an additional common denominator
and understanding of his complex personality and its influence on
certain passages in his writings.

In his activity as a public figure he clearly lacks some virtues, such
as personal courage, real military talent and expertise, "learning"
(i.e., being an expert in the Jewish *halakah* and being considered
a "sage"), fidelity (either national or personal), and as a historian
he lacks the analytical and critical sense needed for good historical
writing.[4]

Nevertheless Josephus surely was an ambitious person, but he could
not reconcile his limited achievements (whether because of ability
and/or circumstances) with his heart's desire. This gap between what
is attainable and what is desired, between what a man really is and
what he aspires to be (and to be recognized as such), may cause the
development of a kind of an additional imaginary personality, which
contains those traits that are missing in the real person himself. This
second imaginary person is characterized by those virtues, which
Josephus lacks, but associates with himself.

In Josephus' writings there is a tension, which stems from this gap
between Josephus, the real man, and his "Ideal Ego." An "Ideal
Ego" has such virtues that are recognized by the subject himself (in
this case Josephus) as affirmative and desirable and incorporated in

---

is the best known. A most recent novel in Hebrew is Y. Zafrir's *Josephus' Life: The
Book that Disappeared*. See also, Shoham 1990, 180–90.

[3] See for example, Cohen 1979, 229.

[4] It may sound too harsh an evaluation of Josephus, the man and the historian
(as is the name of Thackeray's famous monograph on Josephus), and surely it
depends to whom he is compared. Obviously he is not even equal to the three
great historians of antiquity: Thucydides, Polybius, and Tacitus, neither as a critical and analytical historian nor by his deep understanding of historical processes.
Yet he may fare well with Diodorus Siculus or Dionysius of Halicarnassus and other
historians of the Greco-Roman period.

the totality of values and attitudes of the society to which he belongs. Josephus had good reason to be dissatisfied with his accomplishments (probably both from the Jewish and the Roman point of view),[5] and therefore presents, or rather identifies himself with, the virtues and the achievements of his "Ideal Ego," as a way to compensate and to satisfy his own self-esteem. In this way, unconsciously, Josephus identifies himself with his better self, the ideal one, which in various junctions he presented to his readers.

In relation to the "Ideal Ego" it should be emphasized that we are not dealing with a split personality (i.e., a schizophrenic one), but with an energetic and ambitious Josephus, whose destiny made it impossible for him to fulfill his aspirations. Unable to reconcile himself with this reality, of being a failure as a commander and as a leader, one who achieved very little to be proud of, he "embraced" an "Ideal Ego,"[6] that contained those characteristics, which were complete opposites from the deficiencies of his real self. This phenomenon may clarify some of the questions that pop up when reading Josephus' writings. Let us examine some of them.

The Courageous Coward

Josephus does not seem to have been a brave man. He refrained from openly expressing his opinions about the revolt against Rome because it was too dangerous (*Life* 20–23). He often resorted to cunning and avoided confrontation, which shows that he neither excelled in moral, nor in physical bravery. The story of his command of Galilee, despite its pretensions, does not show any meaningful achievements by him. Nevertheless he did not refrain from describing himself as a distinguished governor and commander: Skillful, popular, loyal and noble. According to Josephus' own words he was the general

---

[5] See Cohen 1979, 228–29 esp. n. 98.

[6] For the sake of clarity we have chosen the term "Ideal Ego," taken from psychology. This term describes a system of values and attitudes, which one admires and sees as a model for imitation, which is different from one's self-image. See Hilgard 1996, 449; 465–66; Freud 1960, 52–53. For our needs we may skip questions that concern childhood, imitation of parental figures (we know too little about Josephus' childhood and parents) etc. Probably we may assume that by identifying himself with his self-ideal Josephus was in a way actualizing his self, or filling the incongruence between his self and his self-ideal.

who fortified Galilee, recruited a huge army and prepared it to withstand the Roman attack.[7] All these assertions are baseless.

That Josephus did not fortify about ten towns and villages in the
Galilee[8] is evident. The places he mentions were either fortified
against him (like Gush Halav, which was held by his arch-enemy
John, and also probably Sepphoris, which was consistently pro-
Roman), or were already fortified before without any connection to
his activity or initiative. It seems that Josephus appropriated to his
own credit the fortification of places in Galilee, no matter when or
by whom they were fortified. It also should be noticed that of all
these places only two actually stood against a real Roman siege—
Yodefat and Gamala.[9]

It is also impossible that Josephus recruited and drilled about
100,000 young men in the Roman fashion (*War* 2.576 and cf. *War*
2.583). He had neither the knowledge nor the arms to do it,[10] and
lacked the authority to force the Galileans to enlist.[11] In addition the
demographic potential of Galilee was insufficient to raise such a large
number of soldiers ("young men" as Josephus put it), or even a
smaller group.

Josephus also pretended that he was a great general, who mas-
tered military skills (*War* 2.577–582), as can be seen by his becoming, for example, an advisor to the Romans on military matters (*Life*
420) and being at the side of Titus when he besieged Jerusalem (*War*
5.261, 361, 541). But, more than any other event in Josephus' life,
it is his command in Yodefat, that is an example of an imaginative

---

[7] As is related in both *War* (2.573–575) and *Life* (187–188) it cannot be treated
as a literary convention, typical to the autobiographic genre.

[8] We skip here the textual and geographical problems in these lists, but see
Mason 2001, 95–97.

[9] In both places the archaeological findings testify that a Roman siege took place
there and ended with their destruction. The excavations in Gamala confirm that a
wall was built there shortly before the Roman siege, but it neither confirms nor
contradicts Josephus' pretension to be involved with its building. See also the papers
by Aviam and Weiss in this volume. In any case no visit of Josephus in Gamala
is recorded and this makes it even less probable that he participated in the fortification
of the place.

[10] And he himself admits more than once that the Jewish warriors were fighting
differently from the Roman soldiers (e.g., *War* 3.207 [Yodefat]; *War* 5.285).

[11] Even if he had such an authority it is evident that he could not force it on
the inhabitants of the Galilee, who were enlisted to the service of others, who
opposed Josephus, or were "paid" or "bribed" to cooperate with him (*Life* 77–78).

story which reveals a Josephus, who exists only in Josephus' mind, a Josephus who never really existed, but with whom the real Josephus identified himself.

It may be argued against our contention that Josephus did not have military knowledge, that indeed he may have had some know-how in military matters, or alternatively that one could command an army at that period without any military experience or preparation.[12] Yet it should be stated that Jewish education did not include military education unlike that which non-Jewish nobility might acquire.[13] According to the Babylonian Talmud, (b. Qiddushin 29a) a Jewish father should teach his son Torah (the Jewish holy scriptures), a profession and swimming. As for Josephus himself no military education or experience is mentioned, neither in *Life*, where he enlarges on his education (*Life* 8–12), nor in his other writings. It is nevertheless probable that young Jewish aristocrats, like the princes of the Herodian house, had some kind of military and/or physical training (even through hunting or sporting activity), but Josephus came from a priestly family, which though aristocratic was not supposed to prepare its youngsters for a military career. The absence of any mention of Josephus' military experience in *Life* is even more conspicuous, when we take account of its autobiographic style, which follows Roman conventions and was written for Roman readers, who would appreciate such information.[14]

Another argument that can be raised against the assumption that Josephus did not have any military expertise is that we cannot evaluate his military performance differently from that of the other commanders of the Jewish rebels of this same period. Did John of Gush Halav or other rebel leaders have a better military knowledge than Josephus? I think the answer to this question is—yes, they were either local leaders, older and more experienced than he was or dedicated to the war against the Roman occupation, that was in itself a

---

[12] Steve Mason put this possibility to me at the Dublin Colloquium—Is it possible that Josephus, a young Jewish aristocrat, had some military education, like many aristocrats in Greco-Roman society? I thank him for the question, which I will try to respond to below.

[13] On education in Greek and Roman society, see Marrou 1948.

[14] See Stern 2004 and cf. Mason 2001, xli–xliii; Shatzman, to be published, ch. 4, 1 (I thank Professor Israel Shatzman for letting me read and refer to his manuscript).

military activity. Josephus did not have either the motivation to fight the Romans, or the opportunity to be involved in armed conflicts with them before his appointment as governor of the Galilee (whatever this meant).

If we compare Josephus' career to that of John of Gush Halav, though we have no information about any military experience or training he had, we can follow John's public activity in a town bordering on Tyrian territory. There he was involved in local violent conflicts with irregular fighters from Tyrian Kadesh, both in defense of his town and in reprisals against its enemies. Only four years later, after being involved in armed clashes, he came to show a real military ability in the defense of Jerusalem against its Roman besiegers. As for Simon Bar Giora his "brigand" like career no doubt made him a natural commander.

Summing up this topic it seems that Josephus did not have even slight military knowledge or experience on his arrival in Galilee. Though he might have been involved in some violent confrontations in Galilee he could use only his personal intelligence to manage these, but nothing that can explain the stratagems executed in Yodefat or his being admired by an old experienced Roman commander like Vespasian.

There is also no reason to suppose that there was an ephebic institution in Jerusalem during this period or that Josephus took part in such organization even if there was such in the Holy City. As for young Roman aristocrats, they received their training either through some degree of preparation and physical training or during their career (*cursus honorum*), in which they usually and gradually advanced in their military grades, acquiring experience in its course.

The case of Yodefat, mentioned above, demonstrates the way in which one Josephus is describing another Josephus. The story of Josephus in Yodefat is inconceivable and cannot be real either in its whole or in its details. The absurdity of the story comes out in many details: Josephus deserted by his army goes to Tiberias (*War* 3.130–131): he leaves Tiberias and enters Yodefat (*War* 3.142). This move is inexplicable both logically and according to Josephus' narrative.[15]

---

[15] The only explanation I consider possible is that he came back to Yodefat to surrender it to Vespasian but was taken prisoner by the rebels there or, at least, was kept there under guard against his will.

Josephus tells that he saw no chance to stand against the Romans.[16] Leaving aside for a moment the exploits of the war, he admits that he planned to desert the town, but was hindered by the inhabitants, and, according to Josephus, it could have led to his imprisonment there (*War* 3.203). In itself this event casts doubt regarding Josephus being the commander of Yodefat either before or after this incident. As a commander Josephus tells us that he made use of extraordinary military feats and trickery, yet many of them are to be found in *strategemata* writings of the Hellenistic and Roman era.[17] The report of the siege of Yodefat is full of such military devices and tricks (*strategemata*), which Josephus ascribes to himself. Scholars found that many of these stratagems are described in military handbooks of antiquity, and considering Josephus' lack of military expertise and experience, think that all or most of those stratagems were copied by Josephus from books of this genre. It is evident that in Josephus' life up to 67 C.E., barely at the age of thirty and without any military experience, it was impossible that he had even the minimal know-how to perform all those "tricks" in the defense of Yodefat, purportedly under his command. Either nothing of the kind happened in Yodefat or, if they took place, it was not under Josephus command.[18]

Josephus' deliverance from the cave in which he found refuge with forty of his men, after the Romans took the town, is also both incredible and pretentious (*War* 3.340–391). Josephus tells that he was directed by a divine message to stay alive, which depicts him on the one hand as a holy man while on the other hand presents him, not as a traitor, but as God's messenger. At the same time his generalship is extolled since, as he tells us, Vespasian is deeply concerned to take him captive: "A search for Josephus was then instituted by the Romans to satisfy both their own resentment and the keen desire of the general [Vespasian], who considered that the issue of the war

---

[16] *War* 3.131: "Already he had fears for the ultimate issue of the war," and also 3.135–136.

[17] See Wheeler 1988, *passim*; Mason (2001, xlvi–xlvii) refers to Caesar's *Gallic War* and *Civil War* and to Frontinus' *Strategemata* as possible sources for direct, or indirect, influence on Josephus' *Life*; Cohen 1979, 195–96.

[18] Cohen (1979, 91–97) is aware of this fact, but hesitates to draw the conclusion that Josephus is bluffing in ascribing all these tricks to himself.

depended largely on his [Josephus] capture" (*War* 3.340).[19] The end
of the cave story is also illuminating. After his comrades killed each
other by drawing lots (*War* 3.387–391),[20] he came out of the cave
on the condition that an officer in the Roman army, Nicanor by
name, whom he knew before, would come to negotiate his surrender.[21] If any conclusion can be drawn from this story it is only that
Josephus served as a "fifth column" in the service of Rome and
insisted that his "connection" come to rescue him for his own safety.

Are these stories about the stratagems against the Roman besiegers
in Yodefat credible? I think that they depict a siege of Yodefat in
which another Josephus is playing the role of its commander, the
ideal Josephus who never existed in real life. The story of his deliverance after the fall of Yodefat is simply a sheer fantasy.

It is also interesting to note whom the models for Josephus' ideal
ego were. In a way it reminds us of some of the real leaders of the
revolt. The defense of Yodefat was not less courageous then that of
Jerusalem and the feats of valor performed in Yodefat go surely,
according to Josephus' story, to his own credit. The resemblance of
the siege of Yodefat with that of Masada is even more striking. A
short time before the fall of Yodefat, Josephus gave a speech to his
soldiers on the topic of suicide and in Masada, Eleazar, the son of
Yair, gave his famous speech, from a different standpoint but on the
same topic.[22] In both cases the speech was followed, although not
fully alike and not under the same circumstances, by an act of common suicide.

It seems that in spite of the defects in his own behavior Josephus
admired heroism. He was glorifying the heroic death of the Sicarii
and other rebels.[23] He emphasized the bravery of these people and
stressed their ability to suffer all kinds of hardship and torture and
his admiration is evident from the way he describes them as being
completely fearless of any kind of corporal suffering. All these point

---

[19] This unsubstantiated pretension is already put forward at the beginning of the
siege (*War* 3.143–144).
[20] See Thackeray 1927, 687 n.a.
[21] *War* 3.346. Nicanor is mentioned only once more in *War* 5.261 and see
Thackeray 1927, 673 n.a.
[22] See Josephus' speech in Yodefat in *War* 3.362–382 and cf. also another case
of suicide there *War* 3.331. For Eleazar's two speeches see *War* 7.323–336, 341–388.
[23] See *War* 7.418–419.

to Josephus' desire to acquire for himself some heroic semblance on account of the admiration shown by him for those heroes.

Yet it may be seminal to consider a connection between Josephus' pretended generalship and the Roman attitude towards the martial arts and his being a newcomer in Rome. As a new arrival in a new environment he must have been concerned to adapt to certain values of the society of which he became a member. What could have been more respectable in the eyes of his Roman patrons and his new Roman acquaintances than bravery on the battle field? So he supposedly tried hard to adapt himself to these attitudes and values of his new environment. After all martial arts were not highly appreciated in Jewish society and so his purported generalship served two needs: To compensate for his unachieved accomplishments in Galilee and to gain appreciation and respect for him in his new surroundings.[24] To a certain measure it reflects Josephus' double life between Rome and the Jewish nation.

That Josephus liked to play the role of a military expert is shown also in the *Antiquities*, which were written in Rome some years after he settled there. Feldman points to the length of Josephus' discussion about the war with Amalek and its military aspects, a discussion which is far beyond the scope of the account in the biblical source.[25]

Summing up this section we can either treat Josephus as a liar (which he was indeed more than once)[26] or understand this story as an unconscious psychological impulse, necessary to compensate Josephus, through his ideal ego, for what he really was.

The Sage

The virtuous person cannot be only a warrior and general, at least not within the parameters of Jewish society, which admires wisdom, erudition, education, manners, and descent too. The last virtue Josephus had, the rest he had to a certain measure, but surely not

---

[24] This point came out in discussions with Dr. Gadi Rappaport, a psychiatrist and my son.

[25] See Feldman 2004, 28 and for other examples page 39, n. 60, 75, and 184.

[26] See Rappaport 1994; Jossa (1994) arrives at the same conclusion, that Josephus was pro-Roman all along, though by different arguments.

enough for the ideal person, who was called *hacham* (sage) and was expected to be an expert on the Jewish law and the holy scriptures, able to serve as a judge, excellent in ethical conduct in public and private life, and much more. The introduction to Josephus' *Life* tells us about Josephus' genealogy and education as well as his being a *wunderkind*: "I won universal applause for my love of letters (*to philo-grammaton*); insomuch that the chief priests and the leading men of the city used constantly to come to me for precise information on some particulars in our ordinances." (*Life* 9 [Thackeray, LCL])

But the introduction to *Life*, it must be admitted, is a personal encomium conventional in autobiographical writings and should not be taken at face value. Nevertheless Josephus repeats this act of glorifying himself as erudite in Jewish law elsewhere too, as in *Ant.* 20.263; "For my compatriots admit that in our Jewish learning I far excelled them." With all due respect to Josephus' learning (which was quite impressive) this is a pretentious statement, and to say the least, there is not a shred of evidence, that the "them" ever knew about the erudition of Josephus or considered him as a sage.

So far the depicted ideal figure bears two laurels on his head: the general and the sage. But the real Josephus was not satisfied with his wishful person. He also thought of himself, or actually of his ideal ego, not as a traitor, but rather as a patriot.[27]

The Patriot

Josephus' patriotism is not only a reflection of his ideal ego, it also results from his national outlook as a supporter of the pro-Roman party, under the leadership of Hanan and his colleagues, such as Joshua son of Gamala and Simeon son of Gamaliel. His mission to Galilee, as I understand it, was to pacify it in expectation of an imminent Roman invasion. Yet the conduct of this government was two-faced. Its declared position was to lead a war for independence,

---

[27] By traitor we are not judging Josephus' anti-revolt view, which was as legitimate (and probably more reasonable) as other views among Jews at that time, but his betrayal of those who were under his command or believed his declared position as one who supports the rebellion against Rome. For my opinion about the policy of the Jerusalem government under Hanan son of Hanan, see Rappaport 1983, 34–61 and Rappaport 1992, 133–42.

whereas its real aim was to reach a settlement with Rome. Josephus, as the commander of Galilee, adhered to this policy, which demanded on the one hand showing outward support for the revolt, and on the other hand trying to limit the power of the rebels and to cherish the good will of the Romans, mainly (in Galilee at least) through Agrippa II.[28]

Such conduct was open to criticism as a betrayal of the people who had confidence in him, as hypocrisy and treachery.[29] Josephus tried hard to discredit such views of himself and to justify his conduct (God ordered him to stay alive in the cave at Yodefat), to blame his opponents, and indeed to serve his people in various ways through his writings, the most impressive among them, in this vein, is *Against Apion*.

It is difficult to form an opinion of this side of Josephus' personality. Is it simply an apologetic effort, a continuity of ideological argument, or a kind of psychological compensation for the low or negative appreciation of him by many Jews (and probably also Romans)?

An Immaculate Historian

Josephus was very proud of himself as an historian. He wrote "for lovers of the truth and not to gratify my readers" (*War* 1.30). This phrase recalls Thucydides' formulation of his task as an historian.[30] Yet it is well known that the only similarity between Josephus and Thucydides is in the outward framework of *Jewish War* and the *Peloponnesian War*, and that both are *autopsia* (written by an eyewitness). Apart from these similarities Josephus is an historian who was motivated by various aims and wrote under pressure from different directions: From his Roman benefactors and patrons to whom he owed his life and the comfort he enjoyed in Rome, from his people whom he tried to serve in his own way, and from himself, criticized (and probably also hated) by many.

His proficiency as an historian is also inadequate; he does not show analytic and critical talents in the treatment of source material,

---

[28] See for example the affair of Dabaritta in *Life* 126–131 and *War* 2.595–597.
[29] Strangely enough this polemic is going on to this day. See n. 2 above.
[30] See Thucydides 1.22 (at the end). In any case the similarity is superficial.

or know how to simultaneously utilize more than one source at a time.[31]

Yet it is difficult to estimate how much his pretension to be a trustworthy and excellent historian is only his vainglory, a simple boasting of an immodest person, or also the *alter*, ideal ego, of his suffering dissatisfied soul.

Conclusion

Who is the Josephus that Josephus wishes us to have in mind? Surely it is the distinguished general, the erudite man (the sage, *hacham*), the prophet (or at least one with whom the divinity made contact), an excellent historian and a patriotic leader from any point of view.

To understand this portrait of a man who did not exist we have of course to take account of Josephus' motives in depicting himself in this way. It is clear that vanity[32] and apologetics, as well as personal considerations and interests, play a part in the picture that Josephus draws of himself in his writings, but I think that these are not enough to explain Josephus' pretensions, some of which are incredible. Foremost among them is the portrait of a commander with military expertise, a general highly appreciated by Vespasian, a builder of fortresses (which clearly were not built by him), an inventor of stratagems, which surprised and baffled the Roman army, and perhaps also a figure that resembles a sage and a prophet. These claims should be attributed to a psychological problem caused by frustration, the failure to achieve certain wishes, and to fulfill some aspirations. These in turn were compensated by the appearance at his side of an *alter ego*, who pretends to be Joseph son of Matthias.

---

[31] Though he used, almost exclusively, 1 Maccabees, on which he based his narrative, and had, or could acquire easily, also 2 Maccabees, he never used it in his work. Even when he had at his disposal more than one source (e.g., Nicolaus and Strabo) he used these sources more in a "cut and paste" way, than by integrating them into one and his own version. See Shatzman, forthcoming.

[32] Cohen (1979, 229) explains Josephus' story about the siege of Yodefat as a result of his vanity. I would concur with him but I think that it crossed the bounds of sheer vanity and became a psychological, personal (even pathological) defect. Cf. also idem 91–93, concerning Josephus' depiction of himself as a great historian and a second Moses.

BIBLIOGRAPHY

Feldman, L. H.
    2004   *"Remember Amalek!" Vengeance, Zealotry, and Group Destruction in the Bible according to Philo, Pseudo-Philo, and Josephus.* Cincinnati.
Freud, S.
    1960   *Group Psychology and the Analysis of the Ego.* New York.
Friedlander, S.
    1977   *Histoire et psychoanalyse.* Paris.
    1996   *Hilgard's Introduction to Psychology.* London.
Jossa, G.
    1994   Josephus' Action in Galilee During the Jewish War. Pages 265–78 in *Josephus and the History of the Greco-Roman Period: Essays in Memory of Morton Smith.* Edited by F. Parente and J. Sievers. Leiden.
Klausner, J.
    1952   *History of the Second Temple.* Vol. 5. Jerusalem. [Hebrew]
Marrou, H. I.
    1948   *Histoire de l'éducation dans l'antiquité.* Paris.
Mason, S.
    2001   *Life of Josephus.* Vol. 9 of *Flavius Josephus: Translation and Commentary.* Edited by S. Mason. Leiden.
Rappaport, U.
    1983   *Judea and Rome.* Jerusalem. [Hebrew]
    1992   The Jewish Leadership in Jerusalem in the First Half of the Great Rebellion. Pages 133–42 in *Leaders and Leadership.* Edited by I. Malkin and Z. Tsahor. Jerusalem. [Hebrew]
    1994   Where Was Josephus Lying—In his *Life* or in the *War*? Pages 279–89 in *Josephus and the History of the Greco-Roman Period: Essays in Memory of Morton Smith.* Edited by F. Parente and J. Sievers. Leiden.
Shoham, C.
    1990   Der Jude als Vermittler zwischen Orient und Okzident. *IVG* 8:180–90.
Stern, P.
    2004   *Josephus'* Life. PhD Thesis. University of Haifa.
Thackeray, H. St. J.
    1929   *Josephus. The Man and the Historian.* New York.
Wheeler, E. L.
    1988   *Strategem and the Vocabulary of Military Trickery.* Leiden.

MASADA IN THE 1ST AND 21ST CENTURIES

Honora Howell Chapman

Introduction

What do the Historic Center of Vienna, Villa d'Este at Tivoli, and
the Alto Douro Wine Region in Portugal all have in common, besides
being nice places to visit on vacation? What links them to Tsodilo
in Botswana, the Yungang Grottoes in China, the Zollverein Coal
Mine Industrial Complex in Germany, and Samarkand in Uzbekistan?
And what in the world do any of them have to do with Masada in
Israel? The answer is found in the report of the 25th session of the
World Heritage Committee of the UNESCO Convention Concerning
The Protection Of The World Cultural And Natural Heritage, held
in Helsinki in December 2001.[1] Here we discover that Masada
became inscribed as a "Cultural Property" on the World Heritage
List[2] along with 24 other places, including the ones named above.[3]
UNESCO asks that the "State Party" proposing a particular site for
the World Heritage List "should provide all the information to demonstrate that the property nominated is truly of 'outstanding universal
value.'"[4] The guidelines further state: "With regard to cultural properties, States Parties are invited to attach to the nomination forms
a brief analysis of references in world literature (e.g. reference works
such as general or specialized encyclopaedias, histories of art or architecture, records of voyages and explorations, scientific reports, guide-
books, etc.), along with a comprehensive bibliography." Though I

---

[1] Report of the 25th session of the World Heritage Committee of Helsinki,
Finland, 11–16 December 2001 UNESCO (United Nations Educational, Scientific,
and Cultural Organization) Convention Concerning the Protection of the World
Cultural and Natural Heritage, found at: http://whc.unesco.org/archive/repcom01.htm.

[2] For the List, see http://www.thesalmons.org/lynn/world.heritage.html. According
to this source, there were 788 sites on the List as of July 2004.

[3] This designation is beneficial as it encourages more government oversight and
concern for Masada's maintenance.

[4] From http://whc.unesco.org/opgulist.htm, "Establishment of the World Heritage
List."

have not seen the original Israeli documentation for the nomination of Masada, I assume it included reference to or even quotation from Josephus's *War* Book 7, along with the multi-volume final archaeological reports from the 1963–1965 excavations[5] and Yigael Yadin's influential book.[6]

UNESCO has established clear criteria by which it judges a site worthy, including:

> A monument, group of buildings or site—as defined above—which is nominated for inclusion in the World Heritage List will be considered to be of outstanding universal value for the purposes of the Convention when the Committee finds that it meets one or more of the following criteria and the test of authenticity. Each property nominated should therefore:
>
> a.
> i. represent a masterpiece of human creative genius; or
> ii. exhibit an important interchange of human values, over a span of time or within a cultural area of the world, on developments in architecture or technology, monumental arts, town-planning or landscape design; or
> iii. bear a unique or at least exceptional testimony to a cultural tradition or to a civilization which is living or which has disappeared; or
> iv. be an outstanding example of a type of building or architectural or technological ensemble or landscape which illustrates (a) significant stage(s) in human history; or
> v. be an outstanding example of a traditional human settlement or land-use which is representative of a culture (or cultures), especially when it has become vulnerable under the impact of irreversible change; or
> vi. be directly or tangibly associated with events or living traditions, with ideas, or with beliefs, with artistic and literary works of outstanding universal significance (the Committee considers that this criterion should justify inclusion in the List only in exceptional circumstances and in conjunction with other criteria cultural or natural).[7]

Masada qualified for the List as follows:

Property: Masada
Id. N°: 1040

---

[5] Yadin et al., 1989–.
[6] Yadin 1966; the proposal probably did not include the ideas of critical studies such as: Ben-Yehuda 1995 and 2002; Zerubavel 1995; Silberman 1989 and 2002.
[7] From http://whc.unesco.org/opgulist.htm, section 24.

State Party: Israel
Criteria: C (iii) (iv) (vi)
The Committee inscribed the Masada National Park on the World Heritage List under criteria (iii), (iv), and (vi):
Criterion (iii): Masada is a symbol of the ancient Jewish Kingdom of Israel, of its violent destruction in the later 1st century C.E., and of the subsequent Diaspora.
Criterion (iv): The Palace of Herod the Great at Masada is an outstanding example of a luxurious villa of the early Roman Empire, whilst the camps and other fortifications that encircle the monument constitute the finest and most complete Roman siege works to have survived to the present day.
Criterion (vi): The tragic events during the last days of the Jewish refugees who occupied the fortress and palace of Masada make it a symbol both of Jewish cultural identity and, more universally, of the continuing human struggle between oppression and liberty.
Although the site was originally nominated as a mixed property, the Committee did not inscribe Masada National Park under natural criteria.
The Chairperson congratulated Israel on the inscription of its first site on the World Heritage List. In agreement with the State Party, the name of the property was changed to Masada.[8]

As we see, UNESCO chose to inscribe Masada in 2001 as the "first" Israeli site on its World Heritage List, to which it then added also in 2001 the Old City of Acre. Why did they not go with the Old City of Acre as the first designated Israeli site? (We should note that the Old City of Jerusalem and its Walls were enrolled in 1981 with Jerusalem being its own State Party, akin to the Holy See, and thus it was not the "first" Israeli site.) Furthermore, the Romans did not destroy "the ancient Jewish Kingdom of Israel" at Masada, as given under criterion iii (unless one takes Eleazar, Manaemos, et al. as messiah king-figures). I have no objection to the points raised in criterion iv, but the case for Masada, at least under criterion vi, seems to be predicated upon a particular reading of Josephus's *War* Book 7, one which I would like to reconsider now with you. The archaeological record alone would never have elicited such a description.

Though UNESCO has labeled Masada a place that speaks "of the continuing human struggle between oppression and liberty" (following the logic that the Roman army was oppressive and that the

---

[8] From http://whc.unesco.org/archive/repcom01.htm, 139–40.

cause of the "refugees" on Masada was a fight for "liberty"), I shall show that as we examine the latter part of Book 7 systematically, we shall find that the literary accompaniment that Josephus provides to the archaeological site itself offers a much more complex and layered portrait than UNESCO's well-intentioned picture of victimized freedom fighters does. None of this, however, detracts from the fact that it is marvelous that after over two decades of having a World Heritage List, the UN could decide to honor Israel in this way.

As in so many other cases in Josephan studies, we should turn first to Louis Feldman for his insight into the role of Masada in the modern imagination, which explains in part the depiction found above in the UNESCO justification:

> No single event in the history of the Second Jewish Commonwealth has occasioned more discussion in recent years than the fall of Masada, the mausoleum of martyrs, as it has been called. This has given rise to a term 'Masada complex', in discussions of the attitude of the government of the present-day State of Israel toward negotiations with the Arabs. Our age, which has seen the sprouting of radicals and terrorists in so many nations, is understandably more interested in the radical terrorists who held out for so long at Masada against the mighty forces of Rome. The spectacular discoveries in the excavations by Yadin in a nation where digging is a veritable form of prayer have made Masada a shrine for the Jewish people.[9]

Josephus's *War*, though so focused upon the temple in Jerusalem as *the* shrine,[10] has provided a very different kind of "shrine," as Feldman calls it, at Masada for the modern State of Israel. (Interestingly, the majority of the other UNESCO sites that qualified in 2001 under the same criteria iii, iv, and vi are religious in nature.[11]) Feldman sees a Masada occupied during the Jewish War by terrorists.[12] The Israeli government and now UNESCO, however, apply the textual and archaeological symbols differently.[13] One great irony is that the

---

[9] Feldman 1984, 764–65; cf. Feldman 1975, 229–30.
[10] See Chapman 2005.
[11] The others that qualified under criteria iii, iv, and vi were: Vat Phou in Lao People's Democratic Republic; the Royal Hill of Ambohimanga in Madagascar; Churches of Peace in Jawor and Swidnica, Poland; and the Tombs of Buganda Kings at Kasubi, Uganda; and Villa d'Este at Tivoli, Italy.
[12] Laqueur (2004, 76) places the Sicarii first on his timeline of "History of Terror" running from the first to the twenty-first century.
[13] Zerubavel (1995, 195) describes "activist [based on Zionism] and the tragic [linked to the Holocaust] commemorative narratives of Masada" that are chosen

very soldiers who *used to* be initiated into the Israeli Defense Forces at Masada[14] to be "freedom fighters" are perceived by the Palestinians to be the oppressors. I emphasize "used to" because I have learned recently from a spokesman with the rank of Major in the reserves of the IDF that: "There are no longer any military swearing in ceremonies conducted up there but there are what we call 'seeyum maslool' ceremonies which are kind of course completion meetings that are held there. Apparently the military does not look to Masada as it once did."[15] One does have to wonder what motivated this change. It makes sense, in any case, that they did re-evaluate their ideological use of Masada, because this juxtaposition of the IDF with the Sicarii[16] of the First Jewish Revolt was a bizarre one, especially given the negative tenor of Josephus's presentation of the Sicarii both before and after the Masada episode in the *War*.[17] The desire to appropriate the text for modern political, military, and cultural agendas has driven archaeological efforts and has affected modern scholarly interpretations, thereby testifying strongly to Josephus's power as a narrator. Francis Cornford may have called Thucydides "Mythistoricus,"[18] but this epithet is certainly applicable to Josephus as well.[19]

---

for Israeli as opposed to foreign tourist audiences at Masada, adding: "Moreover, various military, national, and religious ceremonies that have been performed at Masada (such as the youth pilgrimage, the soldiers' oath-taking rituals, and the bar mitzvah rituals) have perpetuated the emphasis on heroism, patriotic sacrifice, and renewal promoted by the activist narrative."

[14] Shargel (1979, 363) comments: "For the military establishment, the ceremony provided legitimation in historical terms, as indicated by the wording of the formula recited by the recruits: 'Because of the bravery of the Masada fighters, we stand here today.'" Also, in Yadin (1966, 202–3) see under "Masada and Israel Today" the photographs of the oath-swearing by the armored unit of the IDF and of the Israeli stamps and medal commemorating Yadin's excavations. The medal bears the following inscriptions in Hebrew and English: "We shall remain free men," and (on reverse) "Masada shall not fall again." The view of Masada on the medal does not include, naturally, the Roman ramp on the west side of the rock.

[15] David Fishbein, e-mail correspondence, 7/7/04. I do not know when the IDF stopped the ceremonies. Also, see Whitelam 1996, 16–18.

[16] Feldman (1975, 228–29) discusses the scholarly debate over the identity of the Jews at Masada. As he points out, "Josephus (*Bell. Jud.* 4.400 and 7.253) clearly identifies them as Sicarii."

[17] Ladouceur (1980, 245–260; 1987, 95–113) argues that Josephus is presenting the Sicarii at Masada in a generally negative light, in keeping with the rest of the *War*.

[18] Cornford 1907, vii.

[19] See Chapman (1998, 58–121; Chapman 2000) on Josephus's creation of the "myth" of Mary who eats her baby during the siege of Jerusalem in *War* 6.

Josephus's tale of the mass murder-suicide at Masada emotionally affects the participants within the story, the internal audience who were Roman soldiers, and readers today who make the pilgrimage to Masada to see where this tragedy unfolded. The power of Josephus's narrative to move audiences almost two thousand years later to care about and to identify with the final moments of a resilient band of rebels and their families and even to argue in scholarly guise whether or not they were heroes[20] is a remarkable feat. It is not only the facts[21] that Josephus transmits which compel an audience to read and commemorate the deeds in his text, but it is also *how* he tells the tale. Had Josephus not created this lengthy narrative of Masada with its two set speeches, we would know nothing from literature of the deaths of supposedly 960 men, women, and children.[22] Instead, we would have the magnificent remains of Herodian palaces, with other structures, high on a plateau in the desert overlooking the Dead Sea. We would also have the physical testimony of a Roman siege against it, spanning from the Roman camps below and the gigantic ramp on the rock's western flank to the tiniest bronze and silver coins dating to the years of the Jewish rebellion found scattered and in hoards among the ashes on top of Masada.[23]

The Masada episode looms over *War* 7 like the big rock itself. Because of this, the rest of Book 7 after the Roman triumph scene, as Seth Schwartz says, "has been neglected by modern scholarship."[24] The content of Book 7 does appear disparate and the style inelegant,[25] but I do perceive an overall coherence to its message. The first third of Book 7 is a celebration of Flavian ascendancy and power, as the triumph scene vividly makes clear; it also accords a special place to the objects taken from the temple at Jerusalem, which makes sense since Josephus was a priest.[26] With regard to the prominence of the Masada episode in the latter part of Book 7, Tessa

---

[20] Consider, however, Zeitlin 1964/5 and 1966/7, 269: "The surrender of Masada to Rome was not heroic to say the least. The Jews cannot be proud of it. Neither can they be proud of the Sicarii."

[21] Broshi (1982) assesses the reliability of measurements in Josephus, including those at Masada, and believes that Josephus must have gotten these figures from the imperial commentaries, since he seems never to have visited the place himself.

[22] There is no other literary source from antiquity telling this story.

[23] Yadin 1966, 108–9.

[24] Schwartz 1986, 373.

[25] Schwartz 1986, 373–75.

[26] See Chapman 2005.

Rajak has suggested that "it was not aesthetic considerations but a serious uneasiness on Josephus's part about his handling of the triumph which drew him to provide a counterweight."[27] I do not doubt that Josephus was emotionally uneasy when thinking and writing about the triumph, but I would like to concentrate here instead upon the thematic logic of his text in Book 7.

Back in Book 2, Josephus describes how he fortified the area under his command and then trained his troops directly in response to "the unconquerable strength of the Romans that derived especially from their discipline and military training" (*War* 2.577). The historian outlines his training regimen for the Jewish troops, which addressed both the body and the soul in battle (*War* 2.580). He concludes by saying that he warned them that "if they were bad deep down not only would they deal with personal enemies coming against them but also with God as an enemy in war" (*War* 2.582). Success and failure, therefore, are a direct result of one's choices. And in Josephus's opinion, God ultimately chooses the winners, as he states so bluntly in his speech at the wall of Jerusalem (*War* 5.367). Yahweh will finally join forces with Rome, and the results will be tragic and cataclysmic for Jews who have not accepted this as fact and for the innocent victims as well.

I shall argue that in the last two-thirds of *War* 7 Josephus shapes his material into a study of how the Romans exercise their *imperium* and how their weaker opponents make choices in the face of this greater power.[28] The historian clearly is trying to explain through a series of examples that the Romans simply do not lose in their game of imperialism.[29] Masada appears *within this context* as by far the most developed and dramatic example of the choice the Jewish opposition makes when confronting Rome's onslaught. Josephus fashions Eleazar's speeches at Masada and recounts the mass murder-suicide not simply to glorify it, but ultimately to underline the futility of resisting Rome. I agree with Vidal-Naquet that "for Josephus, Masada . . . was an episode almost at the end of the revolt, which in his eyes was an appalling error, perhaps heroic, but above all

---

[27] Rajak 1983, 221.
[28] Shaw (1993) examines several scenes from the *War* (especially on Herod the Great), but he does not discuss Masada or the rest of Book 7.
[29] See Mattern 1999 and Eckstein 1990.

contrary to the will of God and to that of the prominent people."[30] Overall, through this investigation of Book 7 we can see Josephus's particular interpretation of Roman imperial policy and of the Flavian ideology playing out on the international stage.[31]

An Outline of Book 7

I. *Activities of the Flavians*

1–4: Titus's final command for Jerusalem's razing
5–20: Titus's awards ceremony for his army
21–22: Vespasian's return to Italy
23–62: Titus's victory tour in the Middle East (with special emphasis on Jews in Antioch)
63–74: Vespasian greeted warmly at Rome
75–95: revolts quelled in Germany, Gaul (by Domitian), and Moesia
96–120: Titus's travels and return to Rome
121–162: the Flavian triumph

II. *Activities of the Roman army in Judea under Lucilius Bassus*

163: capture of fortress of Herodium
164–209: capture of fortress of Machaerus
210–215: successful attack on forest of Jardes
216–218: Vespasian orders Bassus and procurator Laberius Maximus to sell all Jewish land and impose tax of two drachmas on all Jews

III. *Seemingly Random Events in the Fourth Year of Vespasian's Rule (72/3 C.E.)*

219–243: story of Antiochus of Commagene
244–251: raids of the Scythian Alani in Media

---

[30] Vidal-Naquet 1978, 5.
[31] See Levick 1999, 65–78; Millar 1993, 366.

IV. *"Meanwhile, back in Judea . . ." under Flavius Silva*

252–406: Masada
    252–274: background on Sicarii and other major dissident Jewish factions during the war
    275–303: Roman preparations for siege; topography, buildings, and stockpiles at Masada
    304–319: Roman siege: construction of ramp, tower, successful breach of first wall, burning of second wooden wall
    320–336: Eleazar's reaction: first speech urging death over slavery
    337–338: mixed audience response
    339–388: Eleazar's reaction: second speech, philosophical and practical, urging suicide
    389–401: the mass murder-suicide, dated to Passover
    402–406: the Roman response upon entering the fortress
407–408: all Judea completely subjugated

V. *The subsequent "Madness of the Sicarii" in Egypt and Libya and the Attack on Josephus's Reputation in Rome*

409–436: affairs in Egypt under Lupus:
    409–419: punishment of Sicarii at Alexandria
    420–436: closure of the Jewish temple at Leontopolis, with explanation of its founding and its final depredation under Lupus's successor, Paulinus
437–453: affairs in Libya under Catullus and the aftermath in Rome
    437–442: Romans put down band of "poor folk" led by Jonathan, who after being captured informs on "richest of the Jews" at Alexandria
    443–449: Catullus urges Jonathan, and others, to inform on Jews in Alexandria and Rome, *including Josephus*
        450: Vespasian has Jonathan tortured and killed
    451–453: God tortures and kills Catullus

VI. *Conclusion of Jewish War*

454: accuracy
455: style and truth

The latter two-thirds of Book 7 (starting with Roman numeral II in my outline) presents a series of encounters displaying Roman power and a variety of responses. Josephus himself in his speech in Book 5 has already transformed the Vergilian art of Roman *imperium* (*Aeneid* 6.852–853) into a natural law that one must "yield to the stronger, and rulership is for those who have supremacy of arms" (*War* 5.367). Now in Book 7 he shows that some reactions to the Roman army are submissive, recognize Roman superiority, and result in people saving their lives and prospering, whereas others involve resistance, both active and passive, to Roman rule, which leads to the loss of life. Most of the events described are a series of power plays between the Romans and the Jews carried out over an undetermined number of years—perhaps over two decades.[32] Furthermore, the sphere of activity has broadened considerably beyond Judea to distant locales such as Alexandria, Rome (in Roman numeral V), and even Media (in Roman numeral III). Masada is clearly Josephus's centerpiece example of the greater Roman power encountering the weaker Jewish opponent. Starting with the Masada episode, he identifies the Jewish resistance as composed specifically of Sicarii, a splinter group he has previously indicated that he particularly detests.

Activities of the Roman Army in Judea under Lucilius Bassus (II on outline)

This portion of *Jewish War* 7 is crucial for our understanding of the Masada episode since it offers several brief examples of different power exchanges between the Romans and the Jews after the fall of Jerusalem and before the siege of Masada. These events are: the Roman capture of the fortress of Herodium, the capture of the fortress at Machaerus, and the slaughter of the Jews at the forest of Jardes. These military scenes prepare the reader to evaluate the historian's major example of Jewish resistance to Rome at Masada.

Josephus's presentation of the capture of the fortress at Herodium reminds us how the historian can expand or contract his material, depending on his narrative aims. The fall of this fortress appears as a mere statement: "Meanwhile, Lucilius Bassus had been sent out to Judea as legate, and after he got the army from Cerealis Vetilianus, he took over the fortress at Herodium with its garrison." (*War* 7.163)

---

[32] Schwartz 1986.

The telegraphic nature of this notice emphasizes one stark, possible narrative outcome in a power game involving Roman supremacy: Rome attacks and wins, end of story. And without a good Josephan tale attached, Herodium, despite its grandeur, does not really stand a chance of making the UNESCO list, unless perhaps they find King Herod's body there, and it then becomes a major tourist attraction.

The next example, the capture of the fortress at Machaerus (*War* 7.164–209), is much deeper in its coverage and vivid description. Josephus dwells upon the topography and the buildings at Machaerus and delivers a dramatic account of the siege and capture of a certain Eleazar, who, unlike the one at Masada, urges submission to Rome. After Eleazar is captured, Bassus orders the Jewish captive to be stripped naked and placed in the spot most visible from the city so that when the residents looked out, they see Eleazar being scourged (*War* 7.200). This move in the Roman power game, using Eleazar's body[33] to assert authority, produces a tremendous emotional, even tragic response: the onlookers are so stricken by Eleazar's "πάθος" that the entire city breaks into cries of "οἴμοι" and lamentation (*War* 7.200). Josephus editorializes here that the reaction is beyond the pale, given that only one man is suffering, and he offers no explanation for why the "foreigners" in the town below would care about Eleazar, especially since he and the other defenders had relegated them, "the mob," to stay in the town outside the protection of the fortress.

Josephus's account is a true "play-by-play" commentary on the Roman game of imperialism. The historian reports that Bassus "seeing" this emotional instability decides to put into play a "trick" to force the defenders to hand over the fortress. The Roman general orders a spectacle, more dramatic and life-threatening: the erection of a cross. Bassus does not even have to have Eleazar placed upon the cross (a standard form of Roman capital punishment); the threat of such is enough to inflict the viewers with "greater pain, wailing and crying that the suffering was immense and unendurable" (*War* 7.202).

Eleazar then delivers Josephus's central message for this episode *and* Book 7 in general. The Jewish captive begs the spectators in the fortress:

---

[33] See Gleason 2001.

And then, moreover, Eleazar begged them not to watch him having submitted to the most pitiful of deaths, and to furnish deliverance for themselves by yielding to the might and the fortune of the Romans, after everyone else had already been subdued.

This advice is striking for several reasons. First of all, this is a variation on the theme of salvation through submission to Rome running throughout the *War*. For instance, in Book 3, Josephus admits the same realization as a general in Galilee facing Vespasian: "for he saw where the outcome of the Jews was headed, and he knew that their one salvation would be if they would change their minds [i.e., submit]" (*War* 3.136).

Secondly, here in Book 7 Eleazar characterizes his own possible suffering, should he be hung on the cross, as a form of "endurance" and "most pitiful." The participle "ὑπομείναντα" is vital here. As Brent Shaw has shown, the strategy of passive resistance or endurance ("ὑπομονή") was gaining currency in the later first century among those facing yet defying punishment by the Roman State. Unlike the martyrs in *4 Maccabees* or the early Christian martyrs, who so prized ὑπομονή as their weapon against greater imperial powers,[34] Josephus's character Eleazar denies that this is an effective or desirable strategy and instead begs the people to *accept* Roman power as a fact and to *live* with it. His friends and family support this move, and beseech the defenders in the same vein to submit. Josephus bitingly reports that the remaining defenders, "against their own nature give in to pity" (*War* 7.204)[35] and decide to negotiate a surrender, whereby they and Eleazar are allowed to go free. Tragedy, therefore, is averted for the defenders. The townsfolk, however, do not fare so well. The "bravest" of them escape, but the remaining 1,700 men are killed; the women and children are sold into slavery. Josephus delivers no pathetic eulogy over them. He has met the aims of this particular narrative, and there is hardly any gain in bewailing the fate of this "mob" as a tragedy.

In Josephus's account of the capture of Machaerus, therefore, we see the economy of imperialism[36] in action: choices are made, prices

---

[34] Shaw 1996, 289; *contra* Shaw, see Moore and Anderson 1998, 257, n. 22.

[35] Josephus has not specifically labeled these Jewish defenders as Sicarii, but this negative description points to this as a possibility.

[36] See Plass 1996, 126 on the "economy of violence" at Rome, and Shaw 1996, 285 on the "economy of the body"; combining the two, we have the economy of Roman imperialism.

are paid for these choices, and benefits are reaped for the prices paid.[37] An element of chance comes into play, but the Romans capitalize upon it. Under Roman rules (to which Josephus adheres), this is as close to a win-win outcome as any group initially opposing Rome could hope to experience. Josephus presents this episode at Machaerus precisely to explore these rules of Roman *imperium*. But since Machaerus does not attest to "the continuing human struggle between oppression and liberty"[38] with the victims dying tragically and a modern nation rallying around it as a symbol, and since Machaerus was in Perea across the Dead Sea in modern day Jordan, it, unlike Masada, certainly will not make the World Heritage List, unless they find the head of John the Baptist there.

The final military encounter between the Romans under Bassus and the Jews occurs at a forest called Jardes (*War* 7.210–215). The Romans have learned that refugees from Jerusalem and Machaerus are gathering in the forest. Bassus, therefore, surrounds the place, and orders his infantry to cut down the trees. The historian speculates that the Jews are driven "to the necessity of doing something noble, to fight out of recklessness so that they might even escape" (*War* 7.212). Despite the stricture of necessity and the possibility of nobility, "ἐκ παραβόλου,"[39] their recklessness quickly undermines the reputation of the Jews here as well,[40] a point which Josephus emphasizes by having them rush from the forest as barbarians would: "μετὰ βοῆς" (*War* 7.212).[41] Josephus conveys the contrasting battle mentalities of the Romans and the Jews with a neatly balanced genitive absolute: "while they [the Jews] were employing much madness, the others [the Romans] were using a love of competition" (*War* 7.213). This attitude results in twelve casualties on the Roman side, while all the Jewish fugitives, numbering over three thousand, die. The latter do at least die fighting, but one cannot help seeing the futility of their effort given the Roman war machine that Josephus has

---

[37] Josephus uses economic vocabulary himself as the final word on Machaerus when introducing Bassus' next military move at *War* 7.210: "Ταῦτα δὲ διοικησάμενος ἠπείγετο τὴν στρατιὰν . . ."

[38] See Masada criterion vi above in the UNESCO description.

[39] There is an alternate reading in MS P, "ἐκ παραλόγου."

[40] Again, Josephus does not identify these Jews with any specific group, but he does connect them with the rebels at Machaerus, whom he has generally scorned.

[41] *War* 3.92–93 has the Romans advancing in silence; cf. Briton behavior: Tacitus, *Agricola* 33.1.

been describing. The historian does not praise the Jews' courage in the face of a hopeless situation; instead, he concludes the scene by mentioning that one of the slain was their general Judas, son of Ari (*War* 7.215). As at Herodium and Machaerus, Rome wins again. Unlike the game at Machaerus, however, *all* the Jews here lose because they do not consider submission to Rome. Josephus does not grant the Jewish fugitives even a moral victory at the forest of Jardes. This is sober and telling preparation for his account of the resistance at Masada. And since scholars cannot decide where the forest is located, it will not make the UNESCO list either.

Seemingly Random Events (III on outline)

After detailing Bassus' administrative efforts on behalf of the emperor, Josephus now presents events occurring in the fourth year of Vespasian's reign: the reported insurrection in Commagene and the movements of the Alani, a Scythian tribe, beyond the edges of the Roman Empire. Seth Schwartz has commented that "the introduction of the story of the Commagenic war and the invasion of Media by the Alani (219–51) . . . are apparently irrelevant to Jewish history."[42] Schwartz has proposed that this portion of the *Jewish War* is a late addition reflecting the prominence of the Commagene royal family in the 90s and early second century.

I would, however, also add that the Commagene affair fits neatly into Josephus's overall narrative scheme in the last two-thirds of Book 7 of showing how the game of Roman imperialism plays out. Josephus portrays the Roman invasion of Commagene as a well-considered response to a report of possible rebellion, which would also invite trouble from Parthia. The historian apologetically remarks that King Antiochus of Commagene had no intention of going to war with Rome (*War* 7.228), and that "the king surely could not be induced by necessity to do anything hostile against the Romans, but lamenting his fortune, he was enduring whatever he might have to suffer" (*War* 7.231). Though ἀνάγχη presses upon him, Antiochus chooses not to act against Rome. This example offers a counterpart to Eleazar's upcoming arguments at Masada in favor of suicide predicated on

---

[42] Schwartz 1986, 374.

the goads of necessity. Josephus clearly is showing his audience in advance an alternate response to the approach of Roman troops. Josephus underlines the correctness of Antiochus's choice by consistently presenting the royal family in a positive light, whether in battle or in flight (*War* 7.232–233). Antiochus is apprehended in Tarsus, but Vespasian then orders the prisoner on the road to Rome released from his chains, considering their "ancient friendship" stronger than his "inexorable wrath" (*War* 7.239).[43] The emperor exercises his power by extending his clemency to the obviously subdued opponent. Josephus, however, does not present this as a loss for the royal family of Commagene; in fact, it becomes a win-win situation within the narrative.[44]

This story has a very happy ending. Antiochus settles in Lacedaemon on a generous stipend; his faithful sons, Epiphanes and Callinicus, learn this, are greatly relieved, and apply for amnesty from Rome through the Parthian king Bologeses. Josephus provides their reason for this move: "for they would not be happy enduring life outside the Roman Empire" (*War* 7.242). Josephus has outdone himself here, using the *complete* opposite of the typical first-century meaning of ὑπομονή when facing Roman imperialism! The royal family reunites in Rome under the gracious auspices of the emperor, and presumably they all live happily ever after, as Josephus says, "deemed worthy of every honor" (*War* 7.243).

Masada (IV on outline)

All attention now shifts to Masada, where Josephus will show that another major choice is available to the opposition in the Roman game of imperialism: preemptive suicide, a tactic known and practiced by the Romans themselves.[45]

Given that Josephus did not write in a literary vacuum, I would like to examine a compelling parallel between Book 7 of the *Judean*

---

[43] See Shaw 1993 and 1995 on personal power.

[44] This is not a possible outcome in the "payoff matrix" which Plass (1995, 123) presents for political suicide at Rome. Josephus is trying to show that accepting clemency does not equal a loss of status, as literature supporting the opposition would lead one to believe. Instead, acquiescence translates into the best possible outcome of peace and prosperity, given the reality of Roman power.

[45] Plass (1995, 123) charts this as one of the two main ways (the other being martyrdom) for the opposition at Rome to score a "win" against the emperor.

War and Book 7 of Julius Caesar's *Gallic War*: people after being conquered by the Romans now seek the freedom that their ancestors once enjoyed, preferring "death over dishonour, and liberty instead of subjection."[46] Caesar relates how Vercingetorix, an Arvernian whose father Celtillus had been a king, is himself proclaimed king (*Bell. gall.* 7.4). Book 7 of the *Gallic War* culminates in the great siege of Alesia, which surely was on Josephus's mind when he composed his own great siege scene in his Book 7 of the *Judean War*.[47] Steve Mason has observed that "Josephus's *Life* contains many echoes of Iulius Caesar's *commentarii*"; Mason continues that "this need not mean that Josephus had read Caesar in Latin, though that is entirely possible. Caesar's exploits were famous enough for Josephus to have known them."[48] We have also noted in our Brill translation and commentary that when Josephus begins his digression on three main groups within Judaism at *War* 2.119, he seems also to be using the opening of the *Gallic War* as a template.[49]

Caesar heightens the drama of the siege of Alesia by providing a version of a speech given by another "Arvernian of highest birth and considered to be a man of great influence" named Critognatus; Caesar calls the speech worthy of recording "because of its unique and abominable cruelty" (*Bell. gall.* 7.77). In it, Critognatus recommends that the defenders resort to cannibalism in order to preserve their freedom based on historical precedent. Josephus works from this model, among others already noted by scholars, and provides his freedom-fighting leader Eleazar with two speeches involving much more expatiation and philosophizing while urging suicide. Unlike the scene at Masada where the defenders actually perform the mass murder-suicide, at Alesia they will never need to resort to cannibalism because the end comes too quickly for them. After the Gauls lose in battle, the king Vercingetorix, just as Eleazar will at Masada, gives his men options about how to proceed, while claiming that "he had undertaken this war not in his own interests but for the liberty of all" (*Bell. gall.* 7.89). Vercingetorix will surrender, and Book 7 of the

---

[46] Hammond 1996, 237.

[47] Roth (1995, 104) compares the building of the siege ramp at Avaricum in Caesar, *Bell. gall.* 7.24 (in 25 days) with that at Masada, but Roth never suggests that Josephus derived inspiration for the writing of his text from Caesar's account.

[48] Mason 2001, xlvi–xlvii.

[49] Chapman et al. 2006; *War* 2.119 and *Bell. gall.* 1.1.

Gallic War ends with a twenty-day thanksgiving decreed at Rome
(*Bell. gall.* 7.90). Aulus Hirtius continues the account with a Book 8
that tells the rest of the story of the pacification of the Gauls, just
as Josephus will do in the rest of Book 7 about the Romans rounding up remaining Sicarii after the fall of Masada. I do not think
these parallels are coincidental.

Jonathan and Daniel Boyarin comment on the Masada account
as a "myth":

> We would argue that far from being a conscience-ridden return to
> and valorization of 'his' people, the account of the honorable suicide
> to avoid surrender at Masada was another step in Josephus's self-
> Romanization. It was, accordingly, a further betrayal (or, alternatively,
> another step in the self-justification of his betrayal). Similarly, the adop-
> tion of this myth by Yadin was a maneuver in the modern transfor-
> mation of 'sheep-like effeminate' Jews into real Israeli men.[50]

I have to ask: Why is it necessarily "betrayal" to survive enslave-
ment and then to learn how another culture operates and to try to
communicate to people within that culture in an intelligible fashion?
Betrayal, like freedom fighting, is in the eye of the beholder. The
Boyarins do concede in a footnote the possibility that "Josephus's
story is to be read as critical of the Masadans, in which case it is
only Yadin and his fellows who have bought the 'Roman' value system."[51] What I sense in the Boyarins' commentary is a real dis-
comfort with militaristic machismo whether in the first or twenty-first
century, which tells us as much about them as it does about the text
they are analyzing.

But the Boyarins are not alone in this. Neil Asher Silberman concludes a recent essay:

> The Roman determination to obliterate any people who refused to
> worship the emperor or prize imperial allegiance over every other value
> paved the way for the birth over many centuries—for good and for
> bad, for righteousness and continuing evil—of the interconnected world
> and imperial civilization in which we all live today.[52]

We cannot pretend that our own experiences with and opinions
about warfare and imperialism do not color our judgment of the

---

[50] Boyarin and Boyarin 2002, 49.
[51] Boyarin and Boyarin 2002, 137, n. 19
[52] Silberman 2002, 250.

Josephan text or the First Jewish Revolt in general. Even the IDF has reexamined its own relationship with Masada as an idea in just the past few years.

The Masada scene represents the most dramatically narrated choice made in response to a Roman attack in Book 7. Eleazar chooses death as the "best of the available [choices]" (*War* 7.322), and then convinces the others after delivering two speeches. This choice hardly occurs in a void, but against the entire backdrop of the history that Josephus has recounted. Yes, the mass murder-suicide may have looked noble to a Roman or a Jew, but the narrative context prompts one to consider the negative side of this action as well. Furthermore, two women, one of whom Josephus praises (*War* 7.399, 404), decided on a different course of action and saved themselves along with five children. I would like to imagine that one of the Roman officers who heard their harrowing tale shared with these women Vergil's *Aeneid* Book 4, where a strong woman Dido faced a horrible decision at night also, as preserved in one of the earliest existing manuscripts of the *Aeneid*, a papyrus scrap found at Masada: "An]na [s]or[o]r quae me susp[ensam insomnia terrent" (*Aen.* 4.9).[53] In any case, why don't modern audiences consider these surviving women as heroic or even more heroic than the men who killed their families and themselves?

Given the inevitability of invincible Roman rule as delineated in Book 7, does it *really* pay to hold out against the Romans and then to kill your loved ones and yourself? No, not if one considers the lessons from the siege of Machaerus and the happy ending for the ruling house of Commagene. True deliverance does not come from self-annihilation—or so Josephus's text seems to be saying.[54]

Conclusion

Book 7 of the *War* offers a concentrated selection of several case studies of Roman imperialism in action. Josephus describes the encounters between Roman commanders with their armies and the Jewish

---

[53] Cotton et al., 31–35, no. 721.
[54] See Chapman 1998, 122–93 for a more complete analysis of this passage and the rest of Book 7.

rebels in various locations to show how choosing to resist Rome, no matter how nobly, leads to self-destruction. The Jewish rebels are the opponent in this history, and in Book 7, Masada is the paradigmatic case of the utter futility of opposing Roman imperialism; the lesson is there for all to read and understand (unless one is a "rebel" and refuses to accept such logic). The historian also highlights the positive outcomes for those who submit and live, just as he himself chose to do at Jotapata.

Those who proposed that Masada be added to UNESCO's World Heritage List might not agree with this interpretation of Josephus's account of Masada, but the beauty of Josephus's text is that it opens the door to a variety of responses, replete as it is with powerful descriptive passages and irony.[55] Considering the IDF's recent downplaying of its use of Masada, I would predict that the presentation of the "Masada myth" is going to continue to evolve as Israel's self-definition changes and as the use of imperial force continues to play out on the world stage.

BIBLIOGRAPHY

Ben-Yehuda, N.
    1995   *The Masada Myth: Collective Memory and Mythmaking in Israel.* Madison.
    2002   *Sacrificing Truth: Archaeology and the Myth of Masada.* Amherst.
Broshi, M.
    1982   The Credibility of Josephus. *JJS* 33:379–84.
Caesar
    1996   *The Gallic War.* Translated by C. Hammond. Oxford.
Chapman, H. H.
    1998   *Spectacle and Theater in Josephus's Bellum Judaicum.* Ph.D. Diss. Stanford University.
    2000   "A Myth for the World": Early Christian Reception of Cannibalism in Josephus, *Bellum Judaicum* 6.199–219. *SBL 2000 Seminar Papers.* Atlanta.
    2005   Spectacle in Josephus' *Jewish War.* Pages 289–313 in *Flavius Josephus and Flavian Rome.* Edited by J. Edmondson, S. Mason, and J. Rives. Oxford.
Chapman, H., A. Forte, S. Mason, and J. Sievers
    2006   *Judean War 1–2.* Vol. 1 of *Flavius Josephus: Translation and Commentary.* Edited by S. Mason. Leiden.
Cornford, F.
    1907   *Thucydides Mythistoricus.* London.
Cotton, H. and J. Geiger, with J. D. Thomas.
    1989   *Masada II.* Jerusalem.

---

[55] See Mason 2005.

Eckstein, A.
    1990   Josephus and Polybius: A Reconsideration. *Classical Antiquity* 9:175–208.
Edmondson, J., S. Mason, and J. Rives
    2005   *Flavius Josephus and Flavian Rome*. Oxford.
Feldman, L. H.
    1975   Masada: A Critique of Recent Scholarship. Pages 218–48 in *Christianity,
            Judaism and Other Greco-Roman Cults, Studies for Morton Smith at Sixty*. Edited
            by J. Neusner. Leiden.
    1984   *Josephus and Modern Scholarship* (1937–1980). Berlin.
Gleason, M.
    2001   Mutilated Messengers: Body Language in Josephus. Chapter 2 in *Being
            Greek under Rome: Cultural Identity, the Second Sophistic and the Development of
            Empire*. Edited by S. Goldhill. Cambridge.
Ladouceur, D.
    1980   Masada: A Consideration of the Literary Evidence. *GRBS* 21:245–60.
    1987   Josephus and Masada. Pages 95–113 in *Josephus, Judaism, and Christianity*.
            Edited by L. Feldman and G. Hata. Detroit.
Laqueur, W.
    2004   World of Terror. *National Geographic*. 206.5:72–81.
Levick, B.
    1999   *Vespasian*. London.
Mason, S.
    2001   *Life of Josephus*. Vol. 9 of *Flavius Josephus: Translation and Commentary*. Edited
            by S. Mason. Leiden.
    2005   Figured Speech and Irony in T. Flavius Josephus, Pages 243–88 in
            Flavius Josephus and Flavian Rome. Edited by J. Edmondson, S. Mason,
            and J. Rives. Oxford.
Mattern, S. P.
    1999   *Rome and the Enemy: Imperial Strategy in the Principate*. Berkeley.
Millar, F.
    1993   *The Roman Near East, 31 BC–AD 337*. Cambridge, MA.
Moore, S. and J. Anderson
    1998   Taking it Like a Man: Masculinity in *4 Maccabees*. *JBL* 117.2:249–73.
Plass, P.
    1995   *The Game of Death in Ancient Rome: Arena Sport and Political Suicide*. Madison.
Rajak, T.
    1983   *Josephus: The Historian and his Society*. London.
Roth, J.
    1995   The Length of the Siege of Masada. *SCI* 14:87–110.
Schwartz, S.
    1986   The Composition and Publication of Josephus's *Bellum Judaicum* Book
            7. *HTR* 7:373–386.
Shargel, B.
    1979   The Evolution of the Masada Myth. *Judaism* 28:357–71.
Shaw, B.
    1993   Tyrants, Bandits and Kings: Personal Power in Josephus. *JJS* 44:176–204.
    1995   Josephus: Roman Power and Responses to It. *Athenaeum* 83:357–90.
    1996   Body/Power/Identity: Passions of the Martyrs. *JECS* 4.3:269–12.
Silberman, N.
    1989   The Fall of Masada. Pages 87–101 in *Between Past and Present*. New York.
    2002   The First Revolt and its afterlife. Pages 237–52 in A. Berlin and J. A.
            Overman, *The First Jewish Revolt*. London.
Vidal-Naquet, P.
    1978   Flavius Josèphe et Masada. *RH* 102:3–21.

Whitelam, K.
    1996   *The Invention of Ancient Israel: The Silencing of Palestinian History.* London.
Yadin, Y.
    1966   *Masada: Herod's Fortress and the Zealots' Last Stand.* Translated by
                M. Pearlman. New York.
Yadin, Y. et al.
    1989–.   *Masada I–VI: The Yigael Yadin Excavations 1963–1965 Final Reports.*
                Jerusalem.
Zeitlin, S.
    1964/5   Masada and the Sicarii. *JQR* 55:299–317.
    1966/67   The Sicarii and Masada. *JQR* 57:251–70.
Zerubavel, Y.
    1995   *Recovered Roots: Collective Memory and the Making of Israeli National Tradition.*
                Chicago.

JOSEPHUS' ATTEMPT TO REORGANIZE
JUDAISM FROM ROME

Etienne Nodet

Josephus wrote a great deal, but his works have quite different scopes. Let us first consider them briefly in order to summarize his attitudes toward the Jews and Rome.

The *Jewish War* is mainly an account of the wars leading to the capture of Judea by the Romans. Josephus claims to be a faithful eyewitness, but, interestingly enough, he begins with the Maccabean crisis. In any case, this work was granted authorization by Titus; thus it should fit the Roman point of view. In the introduction, Josephus explains that his nation is a great ancient one, but the destruction of Jerusalem was caused by the divisions among the Jewish parties. Within the history itself, he ventures to say "God now dwells in Italy" (*War* 5.367), which he states in his speech to the besieged Jerusalemites; in *War* 6.290–299, he quotes some traditions about signs showing that God wants to leave Jerusalem and the temple.[1] This fits the Roman custom of *evocatio*: the gods of the conquered nations are invited to the Capitol. But there were many Jews outside the Roman Empire, beyond any Romanization. In this perspective, the settlement of priests at Gophna by Titus, to prepare, just in case, for a future cult under Roman control, can be understood as a wise measure (*War* 6.114–116).

The *Jewish Antiquities* is a lengthy story of the Jews, from Adam through 66 C.E., just before the wars. The context is different, for Josephus assumes that the Jerusalem institutions function to some extent. Well after 70 C.E., Josephus speaks of the laws concerning the marriage of priests, which require a study of genealogies in order to avoid any mismatch (*Apion* 1.31); he explains that a copy of all documents concerning personal status drawn up in the Diaspora is sent to the archives at Jerusalem, which have been restored after the

---

[1] So Tacitus, *Historiae*, 5.13.3 *audita maior humana vox: excedere deos; simul ingens motus excedentium*; see Saulnier 1989, 545–62. The topic occurs in the Bible (Isa 49:14 and elsewhere).

war of 70 C.E. In *Apion* 2.193–195, he recalls, still in the present, that there is one sole temple for one God, that the priests are constantly occupied in its service, and he even mentions the daily sacrifices offered by the Jews for the emperors and the Roman people (2.77–80).[2]

The autobiography or *Life* of Josephus is a strange little book, which claims to be the conclusion of the *Antiquities*, written or at least published in 93 C.E. The overwhelming portion of the book is an account of the short time he spent in Galilee in 66–67, in which he restates what he has already said in the *War*. But he deals only with Jewish matters: his relationship with the Jerusalem authorities, his problems with Galilean factions, his controversies with Justus of Tiberias, another historian, and so on. When the actual war with the Romans begins, he simply refers to his previous work. Thus, one may ask, from Rome: who can have been interested in such a parochial account in a remote sub-province, some twenty-five years after the events? Hardly the Gentiles. Now we can give a perspective to the way he introduces himself: he was a priest of very prominent descent and boasts to have been an outstanding young scholar, knowing the teaching of the three main schools. These are his credentials as a teacher of Judaism, but not as an historian, for the true historian is not the compiler of previous accounts, but the eye-witness, as he says himself, following Thucydides. Thus it would seem that the *Antiquities* was a book written for the Jews, whilst Josephus states in the prologue that he addresses the general Greek-speaking reader, paralleling himself to the high priest Eleazar of the *Letter of Aristeas*, who agreed to have the Pentateuch translated into Greek for the Egyptian king and people, and protected in the best library of the time.

We can move a step further by considering Josephus' last work, improperly called *Against Apion*, in which he deals with two main topics: first, to show the antiquity of Judaism, by quoting a significant number of proof-texts from Greek historical works; and second, to

---

[2] According to Philo, *Legat.* 157, these sacrifices had been instituted by Caesar at his own expense, but a change of custom after 70 C.E. is likely, since the poll tax was confiscated, which implies the Roman authority's control of the cult as with the rest of the administration. Previously, the half-*sheqel* served also for maintenance of the city, aqueducts, etc. cf. *m. Sheqalim* 4:2 and Alon 1980, 46–47 (the sums in question could have been considerable, cf. *Ant.* 18.313). Until Domitian's death (96 C.E.), there appears not to have been any major conflicts, which would tend to show that a *modus vivendi* was found, at least for the time being.

refute the attacks against the Jews, mainly by the sophist Apion, by expounding the superiority of Judaism over Greek philosophy. The work has the style of a well-educated polemicist, at home in Greek culture. In the historical part, he mentions the Bible, but never quotes it, for it is no authority for the intended readers. Moreover, when he summarizes the main tenets of Judaism, he does not cite or quote it either, as if oral tradition were superseding Scripture. Indeed, he has stated in the *Life* that after his experience in the three schools, he chose to act as a Pharisee. To sum up, the contrast with the *Antiquities* is striking, for its main authority there was the Bible.

These remarks lead us to some questions:

1. Why is the Galilean portion of Josephus' credentials so important?
2. Why did he bother to paraphrase the Bible, when the Greek speaking Jews already had the Septuagint?
3. Can we say something about Josephus' relationship with early rabbinic traditions?
4. He seems to have been banned by rabbinic tradition. Why?

I. *Josephus and Galilee*

The aim of this section is to show that Galilee was—at least since Herod's time—the most significant province in Eretz-Israel for main-stream Diaspora Judaism.

The famous expression "Galilee of the nations (or of the Gentiles)" comes from Isa 8:23 (in the LXX), quoted by Matt 4:15. In the finale of Matt 28:16–20 the risen Christ summons his disciples to Galilee to send them out to all nations, so that Galilee appears to be the gateway to the Gentiles. This is, however, a play on words since the original meaning of Isaiah is simply "ring of the nations," with an overtone of enemy encirclement.[3]

It is obvious that the Galilean Jews cannot have been the rem-nants of ancient Israelites of Issachar, Zebulun, Asher, and Naphtali,

---

[3] In 1 Macc 5:15 (the original of which is Hebrew), the "Galilee of the for-eigners" is a ring of enemies, which Josephus understands as "the foreigners of Galilee" (*Ant.* 12.331). In the expression גליל הגוים, גליל can mean either "ring, cir-cle" (cf. גלגל, Deut 11:30; Josh 4:19, etc.), or "rolls, waves" (cf. גלול Lev 26:30; Ezek 6:4, etc.).

for they would have been Samaritans.[4] A common view[5] holds that these Jews were circumcised by Aristobulus, but this is connected with a Christian liberal theology, which argues that the Galileans were prepared to get rid of the Laws of Moses and to rush into Christianity.

The proof-text of this view is Josephus' statement that about 104 B.C.E. King Aristobulus annexed a part of Iturean territory and circumcised the inhabitants by force (*Ant.* 13.319). Josephus has no direct source for this and has to cite Strabo who quotes Timagenes, but his way of presenting it suggests that this "part of Iturea" is none other than Galilee. In other words, he is insinuating that the Galileans had been Judaized by force and so were only second-class Israelites, without pedigree, of more recent extraction than even the Idumeans. These Itureans are known elsewhere as mountain folk, and sometimes described as Syrians or Arabs, and they are supposed to have originated in the mountains of Lebanon. Josephus, sheltering behind Strabo, appears not to know where this territory was to be found, otherwise he would have clearly designated it as Galilee. We may add that he hated the Galileans, because of his failure to unite them during the revolt, i.e., to take control of the Zealots. Moreover, Strabo explains that the Judean king, whom he does not name, was an outstanding ruler. However, this cannot fit the appalling reign of Aristobulus, which lasted only one year and was marred by family conflicts, as Josephus himself said in the *War*, and repeated in the *Antiquities*, before quoting Strabo. But a simple solution pre-

---

[4] For the opposite view, see among others Freyne (1980, 1–44) who holds that the loyalty of Galilee to Jerusalem, from which it was separated by Samaria, came from the success of the "deuteronomistic" reform of Josiah, along with the small scale deportations at the time of the fall of the kingdom of Israel, at least according to Assyrian sources. However, this view is too "Judean" and gives rise to more problems than it solves: 1. The historical substance of this reform is far from clear, since 2 Macc 6:1–5 shows that even at the time of redaction of this book, the existence of two temples for a single nation posed no major problem, while the uniqueness of the temple is a major tenet of Deuteronomy. 2. According to 2 Kgs 15:29, Galilee and the surrounding cities were taken and their inhabitants deported by Tiglath-Pilesar more than ten years before the capture of Samaria by Sargon; even if the information is exaggerated, it implies that the social (and religious) coherence of the region was destroyed. More recently, Horsley (1995) tries a more nuanced approach to Jewish Galilee, but does not succeed in giving a good explanation of the bases of its traditional culture.

[5] See Schürer 1973–1987, I:141, 562, and II:8.

sents itself: the successful king was John Hyrcanus, described by Josephus as king, high priest, and prophet, and the word "Itureans" was just a misspelling for "Idumeans," whom Hyrcanus actually conquered and circumcised. We cannot exclude the possibility that Josephus purposely inserted Strabo's notice—with its misspelling—into Aristobulus' reign.

The origin of the Galilean Jews is not very clear. We learn from 1 Macc 5:23 how Simon, during the Seleucid persecutions, brought the Galilean Jews with their families and goods to Judea, which indicates that they were peasants dwelling in scattered settlements, without strongholds. Their presence may have been connected with the policy of a beneficent Antiochus III, who restored Jerusalem and was very much interested in the faithfulness of the Jewish *ethnos*, who were very numerous in his kingdom.

As for the identity of the Galileans, Herod's career provides us with some outlines. As a young man, he was put "in charge" of Galilee, in somewhat obscure circumstances. Among other feats, which he accomplished there, he crushed a certain "brigand" Ezekias and his band, who were at large on the Syrian border (*Ant.* 14.159–162). But a lawsuit followed, which was tried before the Sanhedrin at Jerusalem. The trial comes as a surprise; if it had been only a question of putting robbers out of action, there would hardly have been cause for a lawsuit.[6] Finally this Ezekias is not just an ordinary bandit, since he is regarded as the ancestor of the Galilean movement (*War* 2.56). So there is something more at stake, which is both political[7] and religious. Politically, Herod's victims cannot be associated with the partisans of Aristobulus, the adversary of Rome

---

[6] The parallel account in *War* 1.209 says simply that the plotters forced Hyrcanus to summon Herod, the rising star, to answer charges of not acting in accordance with "Jewish law" and the "national customs," by putting many people to death without trial. This formulation, which avoids saying that the plotters were partisans of Ezekias, draws attention to the monopoly of the Jerusalem tribunal and away from the brigands. This faction was clearly seeking to make political capital out of their demand for legality. The conclusion reached by Schäfer (1983, 98), that the issue at stake was a monopoly of the death penalty for the Jerusalem Sanhedrin, in which the Pharisees were influential (only according to *Antiquities*), goes well beyond the texts by attributing to the Sanhedrin more substance than it can be shown to have had, and by giving insufficient attention to the nature of the "brigands."

[7] Cf. Freyne (1988, 50–68), who emphaises the socio-political situation. Schwier (1989, 145–48) discusses various opinions about these bandits.

in Pompey's time, since their sorrowing mothers laid their grievances before Hyrcanus, who was entirely a vassal of the Romans. It could be argued that Herod was trying to carve out a fief in opposition to Hyrcanus, and so earned the jealousy of the court, but his actions won the favor of the governor Sextus Caesar, who would certainly not have put himself against Hyrcanus, a protégé of Julius Caesar, and was even less likely to look kindly on a sedition compromising the *pax romana*. In the end, Herod was appointed by Sextus as governor of Coele-Syria and Samaria, thus already giving proof of that exceptional flair for politics. Only one conclusion is possible: these "brigands" were anti-Roman Jews. The lawsuit was brought against Herod by Jews, and especially the Pharisees, who were defending the Law without the slightest thought for Roman allegiance.

In 40 B.C.E., Herod had himself appointed king of Judea by the Roman senate (*Ant.* 14.381–386), but he only obtained this promotion thanks to a war in which Rome needed local allies: Antigonus, the last Hasmonean king, had just obtained the throne with the help of the Parthians, who pushed the Romans out of Syria and captured Hyrcanus. In 39 B.C.E., Herod, with the support of the Romans who were still fighting against the Parthians, landed at Ptolemais in order to re-conquer Judea. Josephus affirms that the whole of Galilee rapidly rallied to him "with some exceptions" (*Ant.* 14.395), but later, he had to go back to Galilee, where Antigonus still had some strongholds. He entered Sepphoris without striking a blow, but was soon obliged to commit considerable forces in a difficult struggle against "brigands living in caves." In other words, the resistance put up by Antigonus' partisans was negligible, but once again, Herod was up against "brigands," who formed a distinct party and were strong enough to cause him trouble. Some incidents show that these "brigands" could not accept him as a king, for he was a "half-Jew" (*Ant.* 14.403), while Herod strove for recognition. For them, circumcision on the eighth day was not enough to make a Jew. In any case, it is noteworthy that Herod sought the backing of Galileans, as Josephus himself was to do in somewhat similar circumstances.

When Herod died in 4 B.C.E., the situation became confused, with succession disputes around Archelaus, abuse of power by the Roman army, and various uprisings, especially on the occasion of the pilgrimages to Jerusalem at Passover and Pentecost. In Galilee, Sepphoris was at the center of a rebellion led by Judas of Gamala, called in Judea Judas the Galilean. He was the founder *together with a Pharisee* of the "madness" which Josephus is constrained to call a "fourth party" (18.4).[8] Judas is represented as the "son of Ezekias," the one whom Herod had overcome more than 40 years previously. But Judas was his successor rather than his own son.[9] But the closeness of the "brigands" to the Pharisaic school is very instructive.

For Josephus, the Pharisees were the first school (*War* 2.162–164), the Sadducees forming the second. If we accept as a definition that the most typical tenet of the Pharisaic doctrine was the importance of ancestral tradition over Scripture, we can see that Nehemiah acted as a pure Pharisee, especially in his second trip to Judea: he brought in and enforced unscriptural customs and put them under the umbrella of the Law of Moses, proclaimed in Jerusalem. Now Ezra and Nehemiah came from Babylon, and built up the group known in rabbinic sources as *anshei knesset ha-gedolah*,[10] "The Men of the Great Congregation." Thus there was a significant connection between Babylon and the Pharisean trend.

Now we can mention another piece of Herod's policy. Josephus tells us (*Ant.* 17.23–31) how, at a period that is not well defined,[11] Herod wanted protection from raiders operating out of Trachonitis. They could once again have been Jewish "brigands." In order to set up a buffer zone in Batanea (Golan), he created a peaceful Jewish settlement, which could protect the pilgrimage route as well as the district. He installed a group of Babylonian Jews who were already in Syria and well regarded by the Romans. He gave them lands to

---

[8] Cf. Hengel 1985, 62–66, 331.

[9] Similarly, about 65 C.E., there appears "a certain" Menahem, "son" of Judas the Galilean (*War* 2.433); here too, it is a question of a successor rather than of a son, not only because of the distance between the dates, which makes direct sonship unlikely, but also because of the contradiction between "a certain," which supposes the lack of a known genealogy, and the "son of," which expresses the contrary. Cf. Nodet (1998, 136–41), where I follow others in showing that the duplication between Judas the "brigand" and Judas the founder is created by a system of doublets, in which the same episodes, after Herod's death, are told twice over and combined according to two different perspectives.

[10] Bickerman 1948, 397–402.

[11] Josephus places the call of Zamaris after he had been installed at Daphne, near Antioch, by Saturninus, governor of Syria at the end of Herod's reign (9–6 B.C.E.), so at the time when the latter was already mired in domestic difficulties; cf. Schürer 1973–1987, I:257. That is improbable. It is better to look to the period when he was consolidating his own authority (37–25 B.C.E.). There was a governor Calpurnius in 34–33 B.C.E.: the date is better, and the names could have been confused. Again, this error on the part of Josephus, who often seeks to cover the traces, may not be accidental.

cultivate and exempted them from taxes. Their leader, called Zamaris, built a town, Bathyra, and several strongholds. He summoned from everywhere "people faithful to the Jewish customs"; tax-free status and a remote situation were very attractive, especially for folk who had a high degree of religious motivation but were not interested in furthering political ambition. Herod's choice of Babylonian Jews who were not interested in politics was certainly clever, especially in view of the nearby Galileans on the other shore of the lake who had resisted him; they too had some connection with Babylon. Rabbinic tradition has it that Hillel the Elder, the most prominent of its founders, came from Babylon by Herod's time and became the head of the Bathyra school (*b. Bava Metzi'a* 85a). Much later, after very difficult wars, the *Mishnah*, published in Galilee, was immediately received in Babylon, at least by some scholars, after a struggle about the primacy of Galilee over Babylonian Jewry.

To sum up, it appears that Galilee (let us say on both sides of the lake) was a highly significant province, allowing very concrete ties with the land of Israel (peasants). But its historical and cultural connection with Babylon entailed problems, from a Roman point of view, for Babylonian Jewry was on the side of the Parthian enemies, while many Jews were living within the Roman Empire. This may explain the privileges granted to the Jews in major Roman cities from the time of Julius Caesar, therefore some time before Herod's reign: they were allowed to hold meetings, to observe the Sabbath idleness, to have a financial organization, and above all to be free from military service, so that they could hardly rebel against Roman dominion. It is not far-fetched to imagine that the Romans helped build Herod's temple, in order to have more control over the eastern pilgrims. Thus we can understand Herod's fear of the Pharisean influence over the whole Jewish people, the focus being in Babylon. We can understand, too, the context of Josephus' purpose to look like a leading Pharisee in Rome.

II. *Josephus' Teaching and the Bible*

This section aims to show that Josephus wrote the *Antiquities* mainly for the Jews of the Roman Empire, with a purpose to teach them, or at least to provide them with a written tool, if we accept his Pharisean affiliation. Since he relies upon Roman dominion, he is not afraid to be isolated among the Jews.

Besides his credentials, we may observe that when he paraphrases and comments on the books of Jeremiah and Daniel, and also in other places, he has some illusions that he sees himself as a new Jeremiah (hated and/or suspected by his countrymen) and a new Daniel (isolated in a foreign court). Even Feldman admits that Josephus was thinking of Jewish readers, for in *Ant.* 4.197 he apologizes for his reorganizing the laws in order to expound them more clearly. He admits, too, that Josephus addresses the Jews to warn them against foreign wives when, in the Zimri affair, he lets the Moabite seducers (he calls them Madianites, *Ant.* 4.134–155) utter attractive speeches, with Zimri himself ridiculing Jewish separatism and the burden of Moses' laws (4.145–149).

As for the Bible, Josephus himself tells us that he has "translated" (μεθηρμηνευμένην) from the Hebrew Scriptures, as stated in the prologue of the *Antiquities* (1.5). The same claim is sometimes made within the narrative, even more clearly. About Jonas, he feels compelled to tell of the miracles as written "in the Hebrew books" (*Ant.* 9.208). Later he insists (*Ant.* 10.218): "In the beginning of this history, I have said that I intended to do no more than translate (or 'paraphrase' μεταφράζειν) the Hebrew books into the Greek language . . . without adding to, or removing from, them anything of my own."[12] In *Apion* 1.54 he states: "I have translated (μεθηρμήνευκα) the *Archaeology* from the holy books." It is obvious, however, that he has many contacts with the LXX against the MT: therefore many commentators have not taken these statements seriously, on the assumption that the only Hebrew Bible extant in his time was the MT, supposed to have been fixed at the Yavneh academy and immediately diffused everywhere. But things have not been that simple. From a careful study of Books 1–9, I conclude that the best hypothesis to explain the peculiarities of Josephus' text is that he did not use a Greek Bible, but paraphrased a much altered Hebrew source including marginal glosses or variant readings. In other words, this *Vorlage* was a perused reference copy, most probably the one taken by Titus when he plundered the temple archives in 70 c.e. This is

---

[12] About the Book of Daniel, which Josephus uses extensively, he warns his reader that should he want to know the secrets of the future, he must scrutinize the text by himself, a difficult task that he has done privately (*Ant.* 10.210). We may surmise that he does not refer to a Greek book, which suggests that he addresses the Jews.

suggested by Josephus in *Life* 417, but unfortunately the passage is corrupted.[13]

Now, in the same prologue of the *Antiquities*, he alludes, as a precedent to his own work, to the story of the Greek translation of the Pentateuch made in Alexandria upon a request of King Ptolemy II. Then he adds (1.12–13): "But [the king] did not obtain all our writing at that time: those who were sent to Alexandria as translators gave him only the books of the Laws, while there are a vast number of other matters in our sacred books, for they contain the history of five thousand years."

So Josephus has three statements: 1. He translated or paraphrased from the Hebrew 2. He is the first to render into Greek the historical books (former Prophets), at least in connection with an official request, which implies some protection of the works in public libraries. 3. He adds or omits nothing. The third point is easy to check: unlike what he did to the Pentateuch, he follows faithfully the historical books, only adding some speeches and personal comments and removing some inconsistencies in detail. As for the first claim, the way he transcribes the proper names as well as some peculiar readings or interpretations indicate that his *Vorlage* was in Hebrew.

What about the LXX? It is generally accepted that after the Pentateuch, the other books of the Bible were translated into Greek. But there is no evidence available of any official translations. On the contrary, Josephus dedicates his *Antiquities* to Epaphroditus, who had a renowned library, and later Eusebius tells us that Josephus' works were protected in public libraries.

But some additional remarks are in place here. First, it is interesting to observe that the New Testament, which frequently cites biblical history, quotes only two passages from the historical books (besides pieces of poetry which may come from the Psalms): 2 Sam 7:8, 12, 14 (Nathan's prophecy) and 1 Kings 19:14–18 (Elijah at Horeb). These well-known, short passages may have been a kind of *ad hoc* translation or come from *testimonia*. In other words, this does not imply that an approved translation of all the historical books was available. Philo's testimony is interesting too: for him, David was only a poet (Psalms), Solomon a sage (Proverbs, Wisdom); moreover, there was no exile, but voluntary Jewish emigration in order

---

[13] See Nodet 1997, 154–94; see the introduction of Nodet 2005.

that Moses' Law be known everywhere, for only it had the power to overcome wars. So we may wonder what was his authoritative Greek Bible.

Secondly, we cannot conclude that there was nothing. Some fragments of the Prophets in Greek were found in the Qumran caves. In his prologue dated 132 B.C.E., Ben Sira's translator complains that the (Greek) translations of the Law and Prophets seriously differ from the Hebrew original. These were not approved translations.[14] The same way, the *Letter of Aristeas* explains (30) that Demetrius, the Alexandrian librarian, was complaining that he had inaccurate copies of the Jewish laws; they were marked, in other words they did not meet the standard requirements of the royal library. As a result, the king launched the project of an official translation of the Pentateuch by the seventy-two experts. The story tells us that this was done with an outstanding accuracy. In other words, there may have been some partial, private translations of portions of books; in fact, the Greek Bible as we know it is not homogeneous; it looks like a collection of partial translations, for there is no consistency in the rendering of the Hebrew words, even within a book.

III. *Josephus and Rabbinic Traditions*

We may observe some signs of rivalry between Josephus and the founders of the Tannaitic schools. We will show it in three instances.

Eating the Passover Lamb

The total absence of any Christian tradition regarding the paschal lamb at Rome does, however, raise a curious question, since Josephus, writing around 90 C.E. at Rome, gives two hints that the rite of the paschal lamb was still practiced. Retelling the story of the deliverance from Egypt following Exod 12:1–36, he speaks of sacrifices made by clans or groups of families, of purification by blood, and of a meal; he does not explicitly mention the paschal lamb, but he concludes (*Ant.* 2.313): "Whence it comes that even today we sacrifice according to the custom." Further on (*Ant.* 3.248), he recalls what he has already said while explaining that these sacrifices made by

---

[14] See Harl, Dorival, and Munnich 1988, 100–111.

clans are called "Passover" and continues to speak in the present, but without any reference to Joshua's Passover.[15] As so often, Josephus' language is imprecise, or more exactly he generally tries to place himself above all controversy; here, it is not clear whether he is speaking of the Passover at Jerusalem, in the setting of a more or less restored cult, or at Rome, that is, anywhere at all, which would bring him fairly close to Philo.[16]

There is a rabbinic tradition that throws light on Josephus' hesitation (*b. Pesahim* 53a–b). A certain Theodosius (or Theodore),[17] at Rome, wanted to institute (or restore) the paschal lamb,[18] and they sent from Yavneh to tell him that, if he had been a less important person, he would have been excommunicated. As to why he was important, some say that he was a scholar, others that he possessed power that could be dangerous, so should not be too openly opposed. Both opinions suit Josephus quite well, in his position as a recognized writer and high-ranking imperial freedman. The name of Theodosius ("gift of God") is obviously not the same as Joseph, but it could be the translation of the Hebrew Mattathias (*mattat-yahu*, "gift of Yhwh"), which was precisely the name of Josephus' father (*Life* 3).[19] Whatever the truth of that, this initiative left no trace that can be identified, except perhaps for the rabbinic Passover *Seder*, which also focuses on the Exodus and may have been an indirect response to an initiative that was judged too hasty. At any rate, there is no paschal lamb in this *Seder*, but there are traces of it in the sketch given in the *Mishnah* (*m. Pesahim* 10:3). According to this source,

---

[15] However, he mentions this (*Ant.* 5.20–22), but without any particular significance other than a simple accident of the calendar; so for him, Passover is only the commemoration of the departure from Egypt, and not the celebration of the entry into the Promised Land.

[16] Philo, *Spec.* 2.146 is also imprecise, probably for similar reasons (he never refers to a legal controversy): he emphasizes (well before 70 C.E.) that for the paschal sacrifice the whole people is a priest, as in the time of Moses; this could mean either "the whole people assembled," that is on pilgrimage, or each one at home, that is outside the "metropolitan area." Behind the ambiguity, there may have been two concurrent customs.

[17] Theodosius (or Theodore) is transcribed תודוס or תוד וס.

[18] A lamb roasted whole (הגדי המקולס), that is with its inwards exposed to the fire; cf. *t. Kifshutah* 5:958 (on *t. Betzah* 2:15).

[19] The use of this sort of code is not rare in the rabbinic tradition; the fact of giving a Greek, rather than a Hebrew name could also be significant (Josephus wrote in Greek); finally, the name Mattathias lends itself to such a translation, since it has a Greek equivalent, whereas Joseph does not.

the roasted lamb was brought from the temple between the parsley dipped in salted water and the children's questions. In other words, the rite could not be performed outside Jerusalem.

Now we can identify some signs of a rivalry between Josephus and the dynasty of Gamaliel II son of Simon, the second founder of the Yavneh academy, who strove to provide the whole Jewish people with a point of reference.

Let us note first the relationship between John of Gischala and the notable Pharisees of Jerusalem, in particular Simon b. Gamaliel (*Life* 190–194), father of Gamaliel II, against Josephus: although not Zealots, as good Pharisees they were akin in views, and perhaps in origin. Josephus is not afraid to show himself in opposition to this Simon, while at the same time affirming that he is close to the Pharisean current. There seems to be a contradiction. On the one hand he is a priest, and expresses his readiness to accept the dispersion of Jews throughout the Empire, provided that Jerusalem remains accessible to pilgrims. On the other hand, surely a more pressing reason, there was certainly rivalry between him and the house of Simon in putting forward, under "Pharisaic" auspices, a future for Judaism. John and Simon had other options, in the name of another conception of Judaism and even of the Pharisaic spirit, for which residence in the land of Israel was a major value. From Josephus' precautions, we can deduce that these other options had serious backers in Rome, whose censure he had to elude. A probable inference is that in the meantime he got wind of the rise in influence of Yavneh after its second foundation, under the patronage of Gamaliel II son of Simon.

The Heirs of Shemaya and Abtalion

The famous *m. Avot* 1:1–4 states briefly how the Torah received by Moses was transmitted down to the Tannaitic sages. At some point, by Herod's time, Shemaya and Abtalion transmitted it to Hillel and Shammai. In fact, there was a gap between these two pairs, for we learn in the passage mentioned above that Hillel, a disciple of Shemaya and Abtalion, became the head of the Bathyra school in peculiar circumstances; in any case, he was not enthroned by them.

But Josephus knew of them, for he gives a few points that are not particularly coherent but provide a perspective. According to *Ant.* 15.3, "the Pharisee Pollion and his disciple Sameas" were held

in honor by Herod, for they had advised the inhabitants of Jerusalem
to open the gates to him when he finally arrived as king in 37 B.C.E.
If Pollion is a (Latin) equivalent for Abtalion,[20] the transcription
"Sameas" is ambiguous: it may come from his colleague Shemaya,
or else from Shammai, his disciple and the inseparable opponent of
Hillel, which looks more likely here. However, *Ant.* 14.172 reports
that a certain Sameas, a member of the Sanhedrin, "a just man and
therefore above all fear," reproached the court and King Hyrcanus
for their cowardice in the face of Herod's crimes, during his trial,
already mentioned, for the murder of the "brigand" Ezekias. Later,
Josephus attributes this intervention to Pollion (15.4), who recom-
mended to the Sanhedrin that they get rid of Herod. So he mixes
them up, which would rather suggest that they belonged to the same
generation, that is, that Sameas was really Shemaya. Josephus' information appears imprecise, and his carelessness is proverbial, but in
any case the question is largely artificial, for Shemaya and Shammai
are two forms of the same name, which can both be transcribed as
"Sameas."[21] Besides, we can easily guess that Josephus is ill at ease
with his sources: Herod represses the Pharisees, who were not afraid
to oppose the king (17.41–45), but, whereas he puts the entire
Sanhedrin to death, he spares Sameas, the only one who dared to
speak up. Josephus later tries to find an explanation (14.176), but in
reality it applies to Pollion (15.370), and not to Sameas. So confusion reigns, but the speech that Josephus places on the lips of Sameas
during Herod's trial gives a clue. Addressing Herod, he does not
charge him with acting illegally, but attacks only the sanhedrists and
King Hyrcanus II for not daring to resist him, and predicts that
when Herod becomes king he will kill them all. And so he did, continues Josephus, when he came to power ten years later, in 37 B.C.E.,
but Sameas and/or Pollion were spared. Sameas' speech is clever,
but purely that of a courtier and impossible on the lips of an incor-
ruptible judge: he brings off the remarkable feat of flaunting his freedom of speech while at the same time attracting the favor of Herod,

---

[20] Cf. Feldman 1958, 53–62.

[21] שמאי being an abbreviation of שמעיה, as Yanay/Jannaeus (ינאי) is of Johanan/John
(יוחנן), etc.; cf. discussion and examples in Dérenbourg 1867, 95, n. 1. It is even
possible that Shammai is a duplication of Shemaya-Sameas, deliberately put at the
time of Hillel; cf. Neusner (1971, 158–59), who prefers to remain critical of the
rabbinic sources, rather than to look for an historical context.

to which he later owed his survival. In fact, it is not Sameas speaking, but Josephus, trying to reconcile his admiration for Herod with his pro-Pharisee choice,[22] whereas in reality the two camps were at war. To sum up, Josephus introduces Shemaya and Abtalion as prominent Pharisees in Herod's time, who were able to escape persecutions. Thus he obliquely suggests: follow them, even in Rome.

Johanan ben Zakkai and Josephus

There are two rabbinic versions of Johanan founding the Yavneh school. According to one, he gave himself up to Vespasian, foretold that he would become emperor, and obtained permission to settle at Yavneh with some teachers. The other tells how, having tried in vain, in Jerusalem under siege, to persuade his fellow citizens to give up a hopeless war, he fled the city hidden in a coffin in order to give himself up to Vespasian and obtain concessions.[23] These accounts, which recall what Josephus writes about himself, have long been subjected to analysis because of the difficulty of reconciling them. The escape from Jerusalem is comprehensible under Titus but not under Vespasian, whereas the prediction can only fit Vespasian and not Titus. Modern historians mostly discuss the question, under which of the two generals to place this episode, even if it means interpreting it as an act of treason, but it is always taken for granted that Johanan ben Zakkai came from Jerusalem. However, this all important point is questionable.[24] First, Josephus, who never fails to mention anything or anyone of social consequence, does not speak of Johanan, whereas he knows Simon b. Gamaliel, the father of Gamaliel II. Secondly, Johanan's active life before Yavneh, known only from rabbinic sources, consists in having kept a school for twenty

---

[22] He declares this (tardily) in *Life* 12. The introduction of Pollion and Sameas into the second redaction of the narrative in *Antiquities* is a bit clumsy, but it has to be seen in the context of the development of Josephus, who began by praising the Essenes.

[23] Cf. *Avot of Rabbi Nathan* A.4; these accounts have been transmitted in several versions, presented with commentary by Neusner 1970, 152–56. We adopt different conclusions, except for the date of Johanan's arrival at Yavneh.

[24] Despite legends in which Johanan witnesses the burning of the temple (*Avot of Rabbi Nathan* B.7). In order to console a colleague, he declares that there is a mode of expiation which is just as effective as the cult i.e., charity (*Avot of Rabbi Nathan* A.4), but that is really a way of *bypassing* the temple, for this precept already existed well before the destruction, cf. *m. Avot* 1:2, which attributes it to Simon the Just.

years at Arab, near Sepphoris, so in Galilee proper (not Batanea), but with only moderate success (*j. Shabbat* 16:8). Further, a curious Christian legend tells how, still in Galilee, his father (Zakkai-Zachaeus) had to bow before the knowledge of the child Jesus (*Inf. Gos. Thom.* 6–8).[25] So, even beyond Tannaitic circles there was talk of the Galilean background of Johanan b. Zakkai, perhaps in certain Jewish-Christian groups in Galilee.[26] Finally, he is given as the last disciple of Hillel the Elder (*m. Megillah* 13a). As we have seen, the latter, a Babylonian, had rather narrowly succeeded in being promoted by "the elders of Bathyra," an event which is to be situated in Galilee, taken in a broad sense to include Batanea.

There is no indication that either Hillel or Johanan ben Zakkai ever settled permanently at Jerusalem, but that does not, of course, mean that they never went there on pilgrimage; they may even have taught on such occasions and had disciples there.[27] On the other hand, they have clear associations with Galilee, against a background of Babylonian Judaism. They are also politically somewhat unsophisticated, in a way that recalls that of the Hasideans mentioned in 1 Macc 7:13 whose authority was, nonetheless, feared by the high priest.[28] In these conditions, the foundation of the school of Yavneh can be explained by a very simple hypothesis, in the setting of the campaign in 68 C.E.: Johanan, a person from the provinces, unknown or little known in Jerusalem, was one of the submissive (or non-polit-

---

[25] This legend went around, as it is known to Irenaeus, *Haer.* 1.20.1. There are also some features in common between Jesus' parables (of the kingdom) and those of Johanan ben Zakkai; cf. Matt 22:1–14 par. and *b. Shabbat* 153a.

[26] See the discussion by Neusner 1970, 53–56.

[27] According to *b. Pesahim* 26a, he used to teach in the temple precincts. *T. Hagigah* 2:11 testifies to Hillel's presence in Jerusalem, but it was precisely on the occasion of a pilgrimage. *Midrash Tan'anit* 26:13 reports that, on a legal question, Simon b. Gamaliel and Johanan ben Zakkai were seen together in Jerusalem (in the vicinity of the Dung Gate) writing officially to the people of Upper and Lower Galilee and to those of the "South," Upper and Lower. However, the effect of symmetry is fictitious, as the "South" designates not Idumea but Judea, Upper and Lower, to the west of Jerusalem (cf. *b. Zevahim* 22b), i.e., to the south of Galilee; so the redaction has been made from a Galilean perspective. The account is important from two points of view: 1. It indicates a harmony (at least momentary) between the Galilean Johanan and the Jerusalemite Simon; notably, this same Simon was in touch with John of Gischala, another witness to rural Galilee, although politically more active. 2. The episode of these common letters is nothing out of the ordinary in the case of regular authorities, and the fact that it was noted shows that it was exceptional; without going into the nature of this non-sacerdotal authority, we can at least conclude that Jerusalem was not Johanan's usual home.

[28] Cf. Kampen 1988, 85–93.

ical) Galileans settled by Vespasian at Yavneh, a Judean town not subject to the jurisdiction of Jerusalem.[29] His prediction to Vespasian took place in Galilee, like that of Josephus at Jotapata (*War* 3:401), in circumstances so similar that we may well ask whether they were really two different events; the account featuring Johanan might even be secondary, with the underlying idea of showing that he, and not Josephus, is the real savior of Judaism.

On our hypothesis, the first version of Johanan's story is the more reliable. The second version, mainly Johanan's escape from a Jerusalem besieged *by Vespasian*, would then have resulted from a fusion of two themes: Johanan's escape under Vespasian from an unknown place that was besieged, and the escape of unknown persons from Jerusalem under Titus. This latter theme could itself be a deliberate reinterpretation of the deportation of priests to Gophna by Titus, so as to show that the school of Yavneh, though independent of properly sacerdotal influence, was nevertheless heir to traditions relating to the temple; various testimonies show precisely that there were tensions between Johanan b. Zakkai, who was always opposed to the Sadducees, and certain priests.[30]

This conclusion, which assigns to the school at Yavneh a modest beginning *before* the downfall of Jerusalem, throws light on other points. First, Johanan never cites his master Hillel (or any other), but numerous decisions are attributed to him concerning the calendar[31] or rites, sometimes involving discussions with "the people of

---

[29] In *b. Rosh HaShanah* 29b, "people of Bathyra" (בני בתירה) are also to be found at Yavneh from the beginning, with a notable rank; later, a Judah b. Bathyra was a contemporary of Akiba (*m. Kelim* 2:4), but left to found (or resume) a school at Nisibis in Mesopotamia (*Sifre Deut.* 80).

[30] *M. Eduyyot* 8:3, *m. Sheqalim* 1:4, etc., cf. Guttman (1967, 137–48) who, although maintaining traditional views on the patriarchal authority at Jerusalem of the Hillelites (Gamaliel, Simon, etc.), insists, with support of sources, on the opposition of Johanan to war against the Romans, also to the Sadducees, the priests, and temple worship. It has also been noted that of the fourteen doctors who report memories of the temple in the Talmud, only one (Yehoshua b. Hanania) was a disciple of Johanan b. Zakkai; see Büchler 1895, 16. In another order of ideas, the rabbinic tradition shows little interest in the twenty-four priestly courses who assured the service of the temple; cf. Trifon 1989, 77–93; *t. Taanit* 3:9–11 explains that each destruction of the temple took place when the course of Yoyarib was on duty (that of Mattathias and his sons, high priests after the Maccabean crisis); it was indeed the first of the courses, but afterwards lost its rank; cf. *Tosefta Kifshutah* 5:1075, l. 5.

[31] Fixing the authority to establish the calendar, it is noteworthy that he defines a place to receive testimony of the new moon (בית הועד), even if the one in charge of this place (president of the tribunal, patriarch) is absent (*m. Rosh HaShanah* 4:4);

Bathyra," that is to say with the circles of Babylonian origin which had promoted Hillel.[32] So he was not principally a transmitter but in circumstances that required it, an organizer, who encountered a certain amount of opposition. Perhaps his school was originally a brotherhood, without statutory authority over others. Eventually, he had notable disciples (*m. Avot* 2:8), among whom was a priest, and also Eliezer and Yehoshua who praised Aquila's translation of the Bible. Finally, we can note that he was aware of the growing authority of scriptural reference.[33]

IV. *Conclusion.* Damnatio Memoriae *of Josephus*

In conclusion, we may ask why Josephus was banned by rabbinic tradition. Some explanations come to mind?

---

m. Eduyyot 7:7 recounts a fact indicating that such was the custom at Yavneh (Gamaliel being absent). *M. Rosh HaShanah* 3:1 even says that a tribunal of three suffices, whence later controversies on the role of the Jerusalem Sanhedrin when it existed (cf. Maimonides, *Sefer HaMitzvot* 153), for another saying affirms that it alone had power to intercalate a month (*Mekilta Bo* 2). Is this a case of succession or of competition?

[32] As we have seen, these "people of Bathyra" are situated at Yavneh (*b. Rosh HaShanah* 29b). Their controversy with Johanan, already mentioned, concerned the relative importance of New Year and the Sabbath. This narrative is at the origin of the decree attributed to Johanan b. Zakkai, after the downfall of the temple (*m. Rosh HaShanah* 4:1), to sound the *shofar* even outside the sanctuary if New Year fell on a Sabbath. However, the rest of this decree (4:2) explains that Jerusalem (including the sanctuary) is more important than Yavneh in terms that suppose the two cities and their institutions to be contemporaneous, as Epstein (1964, 652) concludes on the basis of *j. Rosh HaShanah* 4:2, 49b (cf. the discussion of *Tosefta Kifshutah* 5:1048). In other words, if the episode really took place *before* the downfall (but after the foundation of Yavneh), the final normative decision appears to have been reworked by adding the words "after the downfall of the temple" (משׁח ב בהיימ); in that case it was a question originally of an *ad hoc* decision taken locally and proper to the school (or brotherhood) of Johanan. In the last analysis, it cannot be excluded that, as in the case of a Passover on the Sabbath, the concurrence of New Year and the Sabbath was a new phenomenon, since in the calendar of the *Jubilees* New Year, 1 Tishri (like 1 Nisan), is always a Wednesday, and we have seen this calendar problem arising in connection with the Passover at Bathyra, in the time of Hillel. Finally, it cannot be excluded either, that the *ad hoc* decision in question, then the decree in its normative form, was made *after* 70 C.E., if some cult had been restored; in this case, the words "after the downfall of the temple" can be taken as originally a chronological indication.

[33] According to *m. Sotah* 5:2, he forecasts that in the future the category of third-degree impurity will be abolished, for want of scriptural basis, but Akiba eventually finds one, based on a detail of the Hebrew text; for Johanan, therefore, the laws on impurity are traditional, but the problem of their being abolished for want of a scriptural basis is *new*.

The first one would be that he was reproached for his defection to the Romans, but we have seen that Johanan ben Zakkai did the same, and was credited with Josephus' deeds. Johanan was a good representative of the Bathyra trend: submissiveness to the political authority, provided that the Torah can be observed in Eretz Israel. Later on, R. Gamaliel did the same on a larger scale, under the Roman umbrella.

A second explanation is more relevant: Josephus left Eretz Israel and moved to Greek-speaking Judaism, while the Tannaites remained faithful to Hebrew and Aramaic, and kept strong ties with Babylonian Jewry. According to a saying (*b. Menahot* 110a), "Westward from Tyre, they know neither Israel nor their father in Heaven."

A third explanation, maybe more controversial, would be that he spoke too much of the Jesus movement, a Jewish element which was to become Christianity. In the short notice of *Ant.* 18.63–64 the *Testimonium de Jesu*, his cautious wording indicates that the denunciation of Jesus to Pilate by the Jewish rulers was not unjustified, for he had founded a school mixing up Jews and Gentiles in the name of the Bible. Thus, he was referring to Christianity, not to a Jewish Jesus movement. But if we consider the Slavonic version of the *War*, which in my view was the first Greek draft given by Josephus to his educated assistants, we hear of several characters mentioned in the New Testament, including a powerful wonderworker stupidly put to death by the Jewish rulers, out of fear and jealousy. Thus he hinted at an interesting Jewish Jesus movement in Judea, but not at Christianity, which he may have discovered only in Rome.

BIBLIOGRAPHY

Alon, G.
    1980   *The Jews in their Land in the Talmudic Age (70–640 C.E.).* Jerusalem.
Bickerman, E.
    1948   Viri magnae congregationis. *RB* 55:397–402.
Büchler, A.
    1895   *Die Priester und der Cultus.* Vienna.
Dérenbourg, J. N.
    1867   *Essai sur l'histoire et la géographie de la Palestine*, Paris.
Epstein, J. N.
    1964   Mavo' L-Nusach haMishnah, 2 vols. Jerusalem.
Feldman, L. H.
    1958   The Identity of Pollio, the Pharisee, in Josephus. *JQR* 49:53–62.
Freyne, S.
    1980   *Galilee from Alexander to Hadrian: A Study of Second Temple Judaism.* Delaware.
    1988   Bandits in Galilee: A Contribution to the Study of Social Conditions in

First-Century Palestine. Pages 50–68 in *The Social World of Formative Christianity and Judaism*. Edited by J. Neusner et al. Philadelphia.

Guttman, A.
1967   The End of the Jewish Sacrificial Cult. *HUCA* 38:137–48.

Harl, M., G. Dorival and O. Munnich
1988   *La Bible grecque des Septante*. Paris.

Hengel, M.
1985   *The Zealots. Investigations into the Jewish Freedom Movement in the Period from Herod I until 70 A.D.* Edinburgh.

Horsley, R. A.
1995   *Galilee. History, Politics, People*. Valley Forge.

Kampen, J.
1988   *The Hasideans and the Origin of Pharisaism. A Study in 1 and 2 Maccabees*. Atlanta.

Neusner, J.
1970   *A Life of Johanan ben Zakkai, Ca. 1–80 C.E.* Leiden.
1971   *The Rabbinic Traditions about the Pharisees Before 70*. Leiden.

Nodet, E.
1997   Josephus and the Pentateuch. *JSJ* 28:154–94.
1998   *Baptême et résurrection. Le témoignage de Josèphe*. Paris.
2001   *Flavius Josèphe. Les Antiquités juives: Livres VI et VII*. Paris.
2005   *Flavius Josèphe. Les Antiquités juives: Livres VIII et IX*. Paris.

Saulnier, C.
1989   Flavius Josèphe et la propagande flavienne. *RB* 96:545–62.

Schäfer, P.
1983   *Geschichte der Juden in der Antike. Die Juden Palëstinas von Alexander dem Großen bis zur arabischen Eroberung*. Stuttgart.

Schürer, E.
1973–1987   *The History of the Jewish People in the Age of Jesus Christ (175 B.C.–A.D. 135): A New English Version*. Revised and edited by G. Vermes, F. Millar, and M. Goodman. 3 vols. in 4. Edinburgh.

Schwier, H.
1989   *Tempel und Tempelzerstörung*. Fribourg/Göttingen.

Trifon, D.
1989   Did the Priestly Courses Transfer in Galilee? *Tarbiz* 59:77–93.

PART TWO

JOSEPHUS' USE OF SOURCES

COMPOSITION AND SOURCES IN *ANTIQUITIES* 18: THE CASE OF PONTIUS PILATE

Daniel R. Schwartz

I. *Introduction*

"The whole question of investigation of sources, what the Germans call *Quellenkritik*, though a necessary and sometimes fascinating task for the historian, is apt perhaps to appear somewhat repellent."[1] So wrote the dean of Josephus scholars, three quarters of a century ago, and not much has changed; indeed, if anything has changed it is that the post-modernist attack on the study of history now devalues even the begrudged concession that source-criticism, although repellent, is nevertheless necessary for historical study. Thus, by 1999 one of the relevant handbooks found it necessary to begin its discussion of the topic with the pronouncement that "*Quellenforschung* should not be a dirty word."[2] The persistent use of German terminology contributes, of course, to the tendency to marginalize this pursuit.[3]

At the opposite pole from source-criticism there is composition criticism, which insists that we read Josephus' writings as his own work. Although all admit that Josephus used various sources, according to the composition-critical approach problems and inconsistencies within Josephus' writings should be taken to indicate that he himself, or the reality he described (as he understood it), was problematic and inconsistent, not that his narrative reflects his use of sources with differing points of view. Moreover, such an approach encourages a disposition not to see many problems and inconsistencies—and when we do see them, we should prefer to consider

---

[1] Thackeray 1929, 62.

[2] Potter 1999, 90.

[3] On western scorn for German scholarship, as early as 1922, see Housman 1972, 3.1061. See also, for example, S. J. D. Cohen's comment that "only a German source critic could claim that *AJ* 18–20 is a paraphrase of a single source—anonymous, of course" (1979, 59). For a brief review of the Josephan source criticism that similarly focuses on its German origins, see S. Mason 's introduction to *Judean Antiquities 1–4* (FJTC, 2000) xiv; cf. below, at n. 7.

them low-key; as a recent article by Steve Mason puts it, we should see them merely as "counterpoints," not "contradictions."[4] After all, if we focus upon Josephus himself we would rather he be worth our time.

What is really at stake here, however, may be seen clearly in Mason's opening statement (p. 146), where he comments that "the movement toward reading *Josephus through*, not merely reading *through Josephus* to external realities, now provides the dominant agenda." To my mind, the operative word in this sentence is "merely." For it bespeaks the conviction that the external realities, be they Josephus' sources or the events he describes, are less important than Josephus himself; this goes hand in hand with Mason's conclusions, at the end of the article, that "the consequence of this for historical argumentation is that, where Josephus' narrative is the only evidence to be explained, we have no way of making a hypothesis probable" (p. 185), so all historians can and should do, on the basis of Josephus, at least in those many cases where his is the only evidence, is either "construct hypotheses for heuristic purposes only, abandoning any claims to probability" (which is fine because "there is indeed 'no harm in asking'") or else "shift our sights from the events behind Josephus' accounts to the compositions themselves as historical phenomena" (p. 187). The latter alternative is, of course, a type of history (studying questions of composition, audiences, reception and the like), but the former amounts to a denial that we can study, with any probability, the events Josephus describes (if, indeed, such events really occurred).

Whether or not this approach, and such corresponding restrictions upon the use of Josephus' writings for the study of history, really "provide the dominant agenda," they do constitute a challenge. Josephus wrote his compositions in order to tell us what happened, and now we are being told that when he is the only witness we cannot use him. Before we go that far, we should reconsider. Since Mason focuses on a single case in order to show how groundless source-critical work can be, I will first discuss that case. After showing why I believe it can still serve as a model of the validity and usefulness of the source-critical approach, I will turn to another section in the same book (*Ant.* 18) and show how, in my opinion, both composition criticism and source criticism have their uses.

---

[4] Mason 2003, 145–88.

II. *Acceptable Counterpoint or Intolerable Contradiction? On Puteoli,
Dicaearcheia, and Agrippa's Finances*

On p. 153 of his article, referring to the preface of my book on
Agrippa I,[5] Mason writes that

> Schwartz allows that he first became aware of the different sources for
> Agrippa [scil. in *Ant.* 18–19] when he observed the sudden switch from
> the Greek city name Dicaearcheia to the Latin Puteoli at *AJ* 18.160–161,
> where the switch accompanies a difference of perspective—from Cypros'
> to Agrippa's. This difference of nomenclature for the Italian port comes
> up repeatedly in his argument.

To which Mason responds, as an instance of this part of his general case that "it is an uncomfortable fact for the more ambitious
varieties of source-criticism that Josephus himself has the authorial
habit of repeating and contradicting himself, and of varying his
terminology" (p. 156), as follows (155–6):

> As for the distinction between Dicaearcheia and Puteoli at *AJ* 18.160–161:
> in his autobiography (*V*16) Josephus himself juxtaposes the two names.
> Since he writes from personal experience, it is not plausible to posit
> sources there. Elsewhere too, and commonly in *AJ* 18–19, he alter-
> nates the names of peoples and places, evidently for the sake of vari-
> ety. Why, then, should the shift at *AJ* 18.160–161 imply different
> sources?

Here, then, we have an exemplary case of the "counterpoint" vs.
"contradiction" issue: Mason claims that Josephus' procedure here
is contrapuntal, as is typical for him, not contradictory in a way that
would imply the survival of something in a source he had used.
Three responses:

1. In *Life* 16 Josephus does not merely "juxtapose" the two toponyms.
   Rather, when he writes "When having arrived safely in Dicaearcheia, which the Italians call Puteoli" he makes it clear not only
   that the two names refer to one and the same city, but also that
   he does not assume his readers know that. In *Ant.* 18.160–161
   the situation is totally different; as I can testify both concerning
   myself, and many other readers I have used as guinea pigs, those
   who do not know the two names refer to the same city do not

---

[5] Schwartz 1990, xv.

suspect that is the case, and instead wonder why Agrippa did not go to Dicaearcheia. But we see from *Life* 16 that Josephus supposed there were many similar ancient readers, so his procedure at *Ant.* 18.160–161 is mystifying.[6] I would say it contradicts his procedure in *Life* 16, and while it is going too far to say that that, in and of itself, *requires* an explanation, it should encourage us to look for one.

2. At the end of the sentence beginning "Elsewhere, too, and commonly in *AJ* 18–19," Mason appends his long n. 57. But all the examples given there pertain to the endings of names alone: Parthos as opposed to Parthuaios, Peraios as opposed to Peraites for Perean; Galadenos and Galaadites for Gileadite; Essaios and Essenos for Essene. These hardly compare with the difference between Dicaearcheia and Puteoli. To adduce a comparison with which I am familiar, I would say that the cases Mason assembled are like hearing English-speakers resident in Germany alternating between references to "Munich" and references to "München," or English-speaking Israelis alternating "Jerusalem" and "Yerushalayyim;" both are very common and require no special explanation. But if we were to encounter a written text which did that, *and certainly if we encountered a written text which at times referred to "Jerusalem" and at times to "Al-Quds,"* without any evident explanation, I assume we would suspect the use of a source or the interference of a copyist, and that we would then look for other problems that could be solved by that same hypothesis, or for other evidence that it is indeed true.

Until now we have responded to Mason's argument with mine as if the latter derived, as he represented it, merely from the switch from "Dicaearcheia" to "Puteoli" between 18.160 and 18.161. Our response has been to say, first of all, that the switch is indeed quite a striking one, more striking than those adduced as putative parallels, and so does urge us to seek an explanation. Nevertheless, as noted above I would agree that this switch does not force us to assume that Josephus could not have written it all without sources; as Mason put

---

[6] Note, by way of contrast, that Feldman saw a need to solve the problem, in his LCL translation, by adding a note on 18.160 explaining that Dicaearcheia is the Greek name for Puteoli. Jones (1967, 188), in retelling our story made life even easier by silently replacing "Dicaearcheia" with "Puteoli." These are both equivalent to Josephus' procedure in *Life* 16, and point up what is lacking in *Ant.* 18.160–161.

is (with another dig at those villainous Germans), oddities in Josephan style "do not *ohne weiteres* imply incompatible sources."[7] In this case, however, there is *etwas weiteres*, namely:

3. My argument did not, in fact, depend upon the switch from the Greek toponym to the Latin one. Rather, the main consideration here, as I indicated in my *Agrippa I* (pp. 6–7), was something else entirely, namely, the fact that the *contents* (not the terminology) of the story that begins in 18.161 are radically different, in a very specific and even quantifiable way, from what preceded it. Namely, in *Ant.* 18.159–160 Josephus reports that when Agrippa—soon to be King Agrippa I—was once way over his head in debt, Alexander the Alabarch—a rich Alexandrian Jew—agreed to lend him 200,000 drachmas (denarii). Of these, Josephus reports, Alexander gave Agrippa five talents—that is, around 30,000 drachmas—in Alexandria, along with a draft for the remainder to be paid when Agrippa reached Dicaearcheia. However, we never hear anything more about that draft, and when Agrippa gets to Italy (18.161) he has to raise the full sum of his debt—300,000 drachmas—by borrowing it from Antonia Minor, who had been close to his family for years (18.164; see also 18.167, where Agrippa repays Antonia). At this point, I believe that readers—even those who only raised their eyebrows at the move from "Dicaearcheia" to "Puteoli," but were willing to shrug it off as merely contrapuntal, should be jolted out of their chairs[8] by the question: what happened to the first 200,000 drachmas, or, at least, to the 170,000 Agrippa would presumably have been careful to collect in Dicaearcheia?

In grappling with this problem, some twenty years ago, my first point of departure was that no one should tell a story this way. So if the story is told this way, it is a *prima facie* indication that the story was produced not by someone, but, rather, by more than one person; which suggestion constitutes, in practical terms, an impetus to find proof of such use of a source, or additional problems that would be resolved by that same hypothesis. And that suggestion immediately brought results: once I was open for the notion that more than one

---

[7] Mason 2003, 156.
[8] To borrow a phrase from Housman (1972, 3.903).

hand, or mind, had produced the story, another problem immediately presented itself: the switch from Dicaearcheia to Puteoli in *Ant.* 18.160–161. That is, here there is not only discontinuity in the realm of banking; there is also a glaring inconsistency in the use of geographical nomenclature as well. And while it might be true that consistency is the humbug of small minds, it is also the case that inconsistency—certainly with regard to things so basic as the name we use to refer to a city—can point to more than one mind being at work.

Of course, theoretically it is possible that Agrippa got two different loans. That, however, would not solve our problem regarding Josephus; and I should emphasize that what we have here is a problem about Josephus, just as much as, if not more than, one about Agrippa's finances. Indeed, we can imagine any number of historical explanations for what happened to the first loan; perhaps, for example, Agrippa lost the money at cards during the sea voyage from Alexandria to Rome, perhaps at a homecoming party in Rome. For Agrippa's skill at losing money, see *Ant.* 18.144–145. But however we imagine answering the historical question (admittedly, not a very important one) about what happened to Alexander's loan, it will do nothing to alleviate the difficulty of accepting the notion, that one hand, of a sane man, uninfluenced by any sources, created Josephus' narrative. Moreover, in fact there is—by some lucky chance—a datum which makes it very easy for us to assume that there was in fact only one loan: *Ant.* 19.276 mentions that Alexander the Alabarch was the manager of Antonia Minor's properties. That makes it very easy for us to understand how the lender could be described once as Alexander and once as Antonia: probably what happened (or what someone thought happened) is that Alexander lent Agrippa some of Antonia's money, and *Ant.* 159–160 and 164 simply view the same transaction from different points of view. But different points of view imply different sets of eyes.

This, then, was the point of departure for my working hypothesis that Josephus was using two sources here. And the latter, in turn, became the heuristic basis for a further analysis of Josephus' account of Agrippa I, in *Ant.* 18–19, to see if further use of such sources could be observed.[9]

---

[9] This is the topic of the first chapter of my *Agrippa I*.

Thus, to revert to Mason's terminology, what the reader must decide is whether the gap between *Ant.* 18.160 and 161—now seen to be not only one of nomenclature but also of story line—is merely a "counterpoint" which we may ascribe to a single writer, or, rather, the type of contradiction which points either to an imbecile or to the use of sources. Although Mason concludes his discussion with the verdict that "we have no traction for getting behind Josephus" (p. 187), it seems to me that in a case like this[10] the choice must be precisely between getting behind him or concluding he was an idiot. And that he definitely was not.[11]

This being the case, it follows that the premise of Mason's second thesis, namely, that we cannot discover contradictions between what Josephus wanted to tell us, on the one hand, and what slipped into his account, on the other, is also undercut. For when we acknowledge that we can recognize within Josephus' writings the products of more than one mind, we must take into account the possibility that they will contradict one another. It seems, in other words, that we are back where we started: if Josephus used sources, and if at least sometimes we can discern which parts of Josephus' account are based on which sources, then we can hope to compare what Josephus put into his narrative when his mind was fully engaged and what he put in only as an excerpt, more or less edited, from someone else's work.

However, a *plaidoyer* for the continued validity of source criticism need not deny the validity of composition criticism. If Josephus used *sources*, it is also the case that he *used* sources, edited them. First,

---

[10] That is, especially in cases like this, where the contradiction is blatant and between two adjacent passages. For discussion of another striking example, *Ant.* 14.74–78, where the point of view and grammatical person change just where the nature of the narrative changes from detail to overview, see my 2002 article, 65–70. Obviously, the further the passages are one from another, and the less blatant the contradiction is, the inference from contradiction to use of source will be less cogent, require more corroboratory evidence, and probably remain more debatable.

[11] True, when a narrative is contradictory we might wonder about the writer's capabilities even if we recognize that he or she was writing on the basis of disparate sources. Nevertheless, since we see our students doing it all the time, maybe ourselves as well, we are more prepared to accept that explanation, either because we realize that the mind is less engaged when copying than when creating, or because we suspect the writer viewed his or her work as something of an anthology. For thoughts about this, see my 1989/90 article, 127–29.

even if all he did were cutting and pasting, he still had to decide
where, and to what extent, to do that. Moreover, it seems that he
did not merely cut and paste. In what follows, I would like to remain
in *Antiquities* 18 and see, on the basis of a few soundings, how to
strike a balance between the two poles. We will focus on two adjacent passages in Josephus' account of Pontius Pilate, of which, for
convenience, my English translation—along with that of the parallel narrative in *War* 2.169–177—appears as an appendix at the end
of this essay. In the first passage, *Ant.* 18.55–59, Josephus reports
that Pilate introduced busts of Tiberius Caesar into Jerusalem, and
that due to the tenacious passive resistance of Jews—who viewed the
busts as an infringement of their religion—he removed them to
Caesarea. In the second passage, *Ant.* 18.60–62, Josephus reports
that Pilate took money from the temple treasury to build an aqueduct to Jerusalem, and that when the Jews protested he had his soldiers attack them, killing some and wounding others.

III. Ant. *18.55–62: A Josephan Composition*

There is no reason to deny that Josephus actively composed these
two adjacent accounts. For together they form a balanced diptych:
the first has a happy ending, the second has a tragic ending, and
the way Josephus tells the story explains the difference. Namely,
whereas in the first story the Jews have a legitimate complaint, a
point that Josephus demonstrates by pointing out that previous governors had avoided doing what Pilate had done, in the second story
Josephus makes no effort to justify the complaint and leaves the Jews
protesting the actions of their governor who seems to be doing his
job and looking out for their benefit: he is said to have used Jewish
public funds to do public works—build an aqueduct—for the Jews.
Furthermore, whereas in the first story Josephus has the Jews entreat
and supplicate Pilate to remove the busts from Jerusalem, and has
them honorably ready to die rather than tolerate the busts, in the
second story the Jews as a whole "cry out against" (καταβοάω) Pilate
and some also "employed insults and abuse of the man, as a crowd
will tend to do." It is all *ad hominem*. The contrast, between those
who argue respectably for a legitimate cause, and those who argue
in an unrespectable manner and for an unjustified cause, could not
be sharper, and we have no reason to deny Josephus the title "author."

Moreover, as already Eduard Norden noted, Josephus used *thory-bos* language in both of these stories, as in all the other episodes of his chapter on Pontius Pilate in *Antiquities*.[12] In *Ant.* 18.58, in the first story, he has Pilate demand that the Jews stop θορυβεῖν, just as in 18.62, in the second story, Pilate orders his soldiers to kill those Jews who θορυβοῦντας. This prepares us for ἐθορύβει in 18.65 and θορύβου in 18.85, 88. That is, our two stories are not only part of a diptych; they are part of a much larger series of stories, linked together by a *Leitmotif.*

And, finally, these two stories also bespeak a general case being argued by Josephus in *Antiquities* 18: that Jews are devoted to their laws and willing to die rather than consent to violation of them. This is the theme of the Pilate stories (especially the first one), it is again intimated in the story at *Ant.* 120–121 about how the Jews requested that Vitellius not enter Judea with his iconic standards and he graciously agreed, and it is the central theme of the long story, the centerpiece of *Ant.* 18, of the Jews' opposition to Gaius' plan to have a statue erected in the temple of Jerusalem. No reader of Book 18 can fail to see the similarity of the Jews' demonstrations in 18.55–59 and 18.263–268, 271–272.

Indeed, the two stories are linked together insofar as they are both premised on the same bit of illogic, the same inconcinnity. Namely, in *Ant.* 18.55 Josephus says that what was wrong with Pilate's standards is that "the making of images is forbidden to us by the law" (εἰκόνων ποίησιν ἀπαγορεύοντος ἡμῖν τοῦ νόμου), just as in *Ant.* 18.264 the Jews tell Petronius, who had been sent by Gaius to erect the statue in the temple, that he should kill them first, for "it is impossible for us to survive and see things which are forbidden to us by the lawgiver and by our forefathers"; here too Josephus refers to things forbidden to us (πράγματα ἡμῖν ἀπηγορευμένα). The inconcinnity is, of course, in the fact that in both cases Josephus says it was forbidden for Jews to make such images, but in both cases it was a Gentile—here Pilate, there Petronius—who was making them.

Now this inconcinnity is not just a slip on Josephus' part, a piece of sloppy formulation. It is not very likely that he would simply slip up twice the same way, in such sensitive contexts. Rather, it is—as emerges from a comparison of these stories to their counterparts in

---

[12] Norden 1913, 640–41 = idem 1966, 244–46 = 1973, 31–33.

Josephus' earlier work, the *War*—a case of deliberate obfuscation. For when we look up these stories in the *War* we find that in both cases Josephus makes clear that what the Jews claimed was not that *they* were not allowed to make such images but, rather, that such images were not allowed in the Holy City. Namely, in the Pilate story Josephus, as narrator, explains that the Jews viewed the standards as if they trampled the Jews' *nomoi* underfoot, for those *nomoi* do not allow the erection of any image in the city (*War* 2.170), and in the Gaius story the Jews tell Petronius that their law and ancestral custom forbade the erection of any image, whether of God or of any man, not only in their temple but even in any place at all in their country (*War* 2.195); for the same contrast compare *War* 1.650 to *Ant.* 17.151. That is, in the *War* Josephus made it very clear that what motivated the Jews was a notion of there being such a thing as a Jewish capital city and (accordingly) a Jewish land and the concomitant notion that Jewish law—the law of the Jewish sovereign—should govern what happened in that land. By the time he wrote *Antiquities*, Josephus was getting used to the rules of the game in the Diaspora, in which land and religion do not go together, and accordingly he rewrote the Jews' claims in such a way as to eliminate or at least attenuate the notions of Holy Land and Holy City— even if this resulted in a lack of logic in his narratives.

Without getting into any details now, I can add that similar cases can be found elsewhere in Josephus, as for example in his refusal in *Antiquities* 20.167–172, as opposed to *War* 2.258–265, to reveal that first-century Jewish prophets were involved in anti-Roman violence; the result is that *Antiquities* leaves us wondering why the Roman governors moved against the prophets.[13] That is just like the way *Antiquities*, in the Pilate and Gaius cases discussed here, leaves us wondering why the Jews complained about pagans doing pagan things. Of course, our understanding and imagination suggest explanations and let us fill in the blanks. The question is why Josephus would leave his narratives this way, especially given the fact that in his earlier work, the *War*, he told stories that made sense. And the answer is, as explained above, a composition-critical one: by the time he was writing *Antiquities*, Josephus was shaping his narratives according to the needs of diasporan Jews.

---

[13] For this and similar cases, see my article from 1992, 29–34.

So to summarize until now, we can say that the two stories Josephus tells in *Ant.* 18.55–62 are built in such a way that they (1) correspond antithetically one to another; (2) fit into the larger thematics of Josephus' chapter on Pilate and the *thoryboi* of his years; and (3) correspond to a broader and overarching case made by *Ant.* 18–20, as opposed to the *War*, namely, that being Jewish requires devotion to Jewish law but not a special status for Judea or Jerusalem. If these stories fit so well together with other parts of his work there is no reason to deny that Josephus composed them.

IV. Ant. *18.55–62: Josephus' Sources*

However, to say Josephus composed this page is not to say he wrote it without sources, nor that inquiry into his sources will not lead to some important deductions about what really happened in the first century. Already at the outset we began, for example, with the way Josephus' use of both "Dicaearcheia" and "Puteoli" could point the way to resolving a conundrum about Agrippa's finances, a relatively insignificant issue which, however, turned into the foundation for a much larger analysis of Agrippa's career. For another case, we could point to the way the separation of priestly material from Herod Antipas material, between *Ant.* 18.90 and 125, can allow us to determine that two Josephan accounts of visits to Jerusalem by Lucius Vitellius (18.90–95, 120–125), the Roman governor of Syria, report one and the same visit from different points of view.[14] This source-critical conclusion allows us to resolve an old and well-known chronological conundrum, for scholars who thought that Vitellius had in fact made two such visits had been forced to make one or another desperate assumption, such as that it took Pontius Pilate more than a year to go from Judea to Rome (although Josephus says Pilate hurried [18.89] and indeed he had reason to do so) or that it took news of Tiberius' death several months to reach Vitellius (although he was the senior Roman official in the East). Neither of those is at all palatable, and realization that Josephus in fact juxtaposed two accounts of the same event eliminated the need to maintain them.

Both of those cases regarded hard and fast contradictions (and not just "counterpoints")—money that did not add up or crass chrono-

---

[14] See Schwartz 1992, 202–17 (on the chronological conundrum and attempts to resolve it within the assumption of two visits, see pp. 203–5).

logical problems. Some sort of resolution was needed, and source criticism could step in and let us understand what happened; indeed, as an added bonus, it also broadened the ancient points of view accessible to us, for now we can look at Agrippa's loans, or at Vitellius' visit to Jerusalem, through a few pairs of eyes and not only through Josephus'. But sometimes the problems which source criticism might resolve are less clear-cut; not numbers, but attitudes. In what follows, we will focus again on the first two Pilate episodes—his introduction of standards into Jerusalem and his use of temple funds for an aqueduct—and ask if we can, with any conviction, characterize Josephus' source or sources, if any, for these episodes.

To give us a focus, let us concentrate, to begin with, on one single question. At the end of the aqueduct story, in *Ant.* 18.62, Josephus reports that in the face of the soldiers' blows the Jews "displayed no cowardice" and that "many of them were killed there while others, wounded, withdrew (ἀνεχώρησαν)." In the parallel in the *War* 2.177, in contrast, Josephus says nothing about the Jews showing no faintheartedness, writing instead that "when the Jews were beaten, many perished: many under the blows and many others—trampled by other Jews in their flight"—quite an unrespectable sight. Correspondingly, the last line of this account is "Stricken by the suffering of those killed, the mob kept silent"; Thackeray, in his somewhat freer LCL translation, captures the nuance of καταπλαγέν better with "cowed by the fate of victims, the multitude was reduced to silence." Hence, we have two historical questions here. The fairly trivial one, of the same order of magnitude as Agrippa's finances and Vitellius' visits, is how, in fact, the Jewish demonstrators behaved when attacked by Pilate's men. The more interesting historical question is why Josephus' two accounts tell the story in so radically different ways. Is this because Josephus changed his mind between his two books, or rather because one or both of the stories reflects someone else's mind? Or are, perhaps, both explanations correct, that is, did Josephus perhaps use a source or sources and edit it (or them) according to his own agenda?

In order to answer this question, we should undertake a detailed comparison of the stories in *War* with those in *Antiquities*.[15] There are several differences, and some seem to point in the same direction:

---

[15] For a brief comparison of the two narratives, see Hölscher 1904, 62; he sup-

1. In *War* Pilate has no reason to bring his troops to Jerusalem; in *Antiquities* he was bringing them there for quartering for the winter. While the *War* account does not have to mean Pilate is a troublemaker, the *Antiquities* version definitely portrays him as a governor carrying out his normal responsibilities.

2. According to the first line of the account in *War*, Pilate knew he was being provocative, and therefore brought the busts in by night and under cover so as to create a *fait accompli*. According to *Antiquities*, he may not have known of the problem; although it is noted that he brought them in at night, this is mentioned not at the outset, as in *War*, but only in the midst of the story (18.56b), and without the amplification "under cover." Here too, more clearly than in our first comparison, the Pilate of *War* is a troublemaker; the Pilate of *Antiquities* may merely have blundered into the confrontation.

3. In *War* (2.171) Pilate simply refuses to give in to the Jews' entreaties concerning the standards, whereas in the parallel in *Antiquities* (18.57) Josephus explains that he refused so as not to be guilty of hubris vis à vis the emperor. Thus, as in our first comparison, while *War* does not clearly portray Pilate as a troublemaker, *Antiquities* makes it clear that he in fact had good reason for his behavior.

4. Moving to the second story, about the aqueduct, in *War* Pilate is right at the opening said to have "provoked another disorder" by spending money. This again implies, as does our second comparison (which too pertained to an opening line), that Pilate was to blame for the first clash. According to the parallel opening in *Antiquities*, in contrast, Pilate spent the money and the Jews became upset; Pilate is not the author of the disorder.

5. Similarly, according to the *Antiquities* Pilate ordered the Jews to disperse and had his soldiers attack them only when they persisted and, indeed, increased their abusive protesting. In the *War*, no

---

poses that some differences in detail indicate that, apart from *War*, the narrative in *Antiquities* depends upon some additional source as well. But he makes no attempt to characterize that other source, and the few details he notes could easily be Josephus' own contribution. For a synoptic table of Josephus' parallel narratives, see Lémonon, 1981, 140–46, 160–64. But in his discussions Lémonon says next to nothing about the differences between the two narratives.

such warning is given, and the Jews gave no additional provocation. Again, in other words, as in the first and third comparisons, Pilate of the *War* is not condemned, while in *Antiquities*
Josephus makes him come off well.

6. Indeed, in the aqueduct story the Jews are much worse in *Antiquities*
than they are in *War*: while the *Antiquities* has the Jews employing insult (λοιδορία) and personal abuse (ὕβριζον εἰς τὸν ἄνδρα),
there is none of either in the account in *War*, which uses only
καταβοάω—"cry out against"—of the Jews' protest. But if the Jews
are worse in *Antiquities*' version of the story, then Pilate—who
reacts to their provocation—comes off better.

Thus, while Pilate is not presented badly in *War*, apart from the
opening lines of each story (our second and fourth comparisons, to
which we shall return), in *Antiquities* his image is much better. In
Antiquities he comes off well in both stories, thus leaving the difference
with the Jews: when they are good they are very very good, elicit
respect from good people like Pilate, and get what good people
deserve; and when they are bad they are awful and get—even from
good people like Pilate—what bad people deserve. To make this
point, Pilate had to be good in both stories, and in the second story
the Jews have to be portrayed much worse than in the first story,
and they are; but only in *Antiquities*. Only in *Antiquities* does Josephus
have the Jews not only angry but also "employ[ing] insults and abuse
of the man," behaving like a "mob," and then again "intensify[ing]
their insulting." As we have seen, this all makes the second story
into the antithesis of the first, and there is no reason to deny Josephus
authorial responsibility for creating this well-balanced diptych. In the
War, in contrast, as we saw, at least the opening lines of the stories
present Pilate as the troublemaker while the Jews are good in the
first story and not so bad in the second, so the contrast is not so
clear and the point about the Jews is easily missed (or, rather, no
particular point is made about them). The only clear statement made
by these stories, taken together, in terms of who was good and who
was bad, is the one made by the opening line of each episode: Pilate
was a troublemaker.

Now, just as we viewed the narratives in *Antiquities* as part and
parcel of general cases made by Josephus about law rather than territory and the proper way to deal with Rome, so too we could, and
should, view *War*'s narrative here as part of Josephus' general case

in that book, that bad and troublemaking Roman governors were
to blame for the deterioration of the situation which eventually led
to the final catastrophe. This is a widespread theme of *War*; note
especially the deterioration from one governor to the next portrayed
in 2.272–279 and Agrippa II's speech at 2.348–354.[16]

However, a further examination of Josephus' two Pilate narratives
in *War*, and especially of the aqueduct story, reveals a number of
additional points that in fact point away from Josephus:

1. The account in *War* refers to the temple treasury as if it were
   called *Korbonas*, which is—as any Jerusalem priest should have
   known—a mistake; indeed, elsewhere Josephus quite properly inter-
   prets this word as meaning "gift" to God (*Ant.* 4.73; *Apion* 1.167).
   In the *Antiquities*' version of our aqueduct story, Josephus simply
   says that Pilate took sacred money (τῶν ἱερῶν χρημάτων).
2. *War* has Pilate arming his soldiers in advance whereas *Antiquities*
   has him doing so only in response to abusive and threatening
   Jews, and the *War* account calls Pilate's move not "looking for
   trouble" but, rather, "foresight" (προῄδει – 2.176). This is a very
   friendly way of depicting Pilate; if I were a Roman governor I
   would like people to think that I foresee danger and am proac-
   tive, not only—as in *Antiquities*—reactive.[17] But Josephus, in the
   War, is not friendly to Roman governors.
3. Where *Antiquities* (18.62) has Pilate's soldiers going far beyond his
   orders, *War* does not: they were ordered to use their cudgels and
   nothing indicates that they did more than that or gave blows
   stronger than warranted. As above, if I were a Roman governor
   I would like people to think my soldiers follow my orders; I would
   not like it said that they violated them.[18]
4. In the *War* account of the second affair the Jews are consistently
   called a *plēthos* (2.175, 176, 177), whereas the account in *Antiquities*—

---

[16] See Bilde 1979, esp. 188–89.
[17] Cf. Felix's anticipation of rebellion in *War* 2.260; Moses' anticipation of *thory-
bos* in *Ant.* 4.63; David's foresight of ruses in *Ant.* 7.217; etc.
[18] Here I disagree with Hölscher 1904, 62, who interpreted *Antiquities*' claim that
Pilate's soldiers went beyond their orders as a way of exculpating him from responsibility for the bloodshed. If a Roman governor had to defend himself in connection with such bloodshed (cf. 18.88–89), the way to do it would be—as Josephus
knew (*War* 2.282–283)—to play up the Jews' guilt, not to argue that he could not
control his own soldiers.

where we have seen much evidence of Josephan editing—consistently avoids it; the only time the term appears is of the Roman soldiers sent against the Jews (18.61). We would expect a Roman official to term the Jews a mob.

5. Correspondingly, the *War* account consistently portrays the Jews as one unified mass of opponents, whereas the one in *Antiquities* features the distinction between the Jews who protested and those who went even further, crossing the line to insult and abuse (18.60, 62). If I were a Roman official I would tend to generalize about the Jews, while Jews, especially apologetic Jews, would find it more important to distinguish between the good respectable ones and the bad apples. And Josephus himself makes such distinctions frequently in *War* 2.[19]

6. While both accounts agree the Roman soldiers were ordered to attack the Jews with cudgels, the account in *War* takes the trouble to indicate explicitly that Pilate ordered his soldiers to do so *rather than attacking the Jews with their swords*, a point which goes together with the fact that the *War* explains that many of the Jews were killed by being trampled by their fellows. That is, Pilate was not responsible for the bloodshed; he tried to minimize it. If I were Pilate I would like to hear that too; it testifies to my moderation and self-restraint. But that, of course, is not what is indicated by the opening lines of these episodes in *War*, where Josephus underlines Pilate's culpability.

Above we emphasized that when Josephus set to work as an author in these passages, in *Antiquities*, the result was a very clear and expressive diptych, as opposed to the picture in *War*, in which the contrasts were not at all so clear. Now we may add that all six of the points we just adduced indicate not only that Josephus was not working very hard on these passages in *War*, apart from their opening lines (where editorial work is most to be expected),[20] but also that

---

[19] See *inter alia*, *War* 2.316, 320, 411, 417–418, 556. Discussion of this Josephan theme, and the question whether conflicting Josephan statements are his own counterpoints or, rather, represent non-Josephan reality that shows his claim is untrue, is the main topic of the second part of Mason 2003, 158–83.

[20] For this natural assumption, see e.g., my following studies: 1992, 211 (on *Ant.* 18.90); 1990a, 14 (on *Ant.* 19.292), 103 (on *Ant.* 19.279), and 120, n. 53 (on Acts 12:1); 1990b, 187 (on *Ant.* 11.326). For an example in the material discussed in the present article, note that the *thorybos* language that unifies the chapter on Pilate (see above, n. 12) appears at the beginning of two episodes: *Ant.* 18.65, 85.

he was not their original author. Rather, all six points suggest this text began as one friendly to Pilate, one bespeaking Pilate's point of view; perhaps it was a report composed by the governor, or by someone on his staff.[21] And the same may now be said of yet a seventh point, namely, the one with which we began—the *War* portrays the Jews as cowards who flee, who trample one another in their panic, and who are cowed into silence. That too is something we can well understand as bespeaking the arrogance and disgust of Pilate vis à vis his Jewish subjects; "look at the cowards run."

So it seems that the *War's* version of the aqueduct story began as a story from Pilate's point of view. Josephus took it and very lightly edited it. The only essential he seems to have done is to add, at the very outset, the seam—what those German *Quellenkritiker* would call a *Flickvers*—connecting this story to the preceding one; it is only in this seam that Josephus blames Pilate for the affair, saying that it was he who set this tumult into motion (ἐκίνει). Apart from this, there is nothing in the story that Pilate would not like to hear.

Our suggestion, that *War* 2.175–177 is based on a Roman source, gets further support from the fact that the whole point of departure makes fools of the Jews, for it has them protesting Pilate's initiation of useful public works for them. In this way, it reminds us of the way the *Historia Augusta* (*Hadrian* 14.2) will later poke fun at the Jews for rebelling when they were prohibited to continue mutilating their genitals.[22] Just as anyone who insists on the right to mutilate his genitals is obviously ludicrous, so is anyone who protests the use of sacred funds for the construction of something so useful as an aqueduct.[23] Here, I suggest, we hear something of the frustration of a

---

[21] For the assumption that the stories we have studied depend upon "some sort of a chronicle, or annals," we need look no further than our standard handbook: Schürer, 1973–1987, 1.438. Here, I have tried to characterize such a source. For the suggestion that *Ant.* 20.173–178 should be traced to a source similarly positive about another governor and negative about the Jews, see my article from 1992/3, esp. 274–79.

[22] See Isaac 1996, 113–14.

[23] Note that Feldman, in order to make the Jews sound reasonable, is forced to explain (LCL, Feldman, 9.46–47, n. b) they were "outraged because Pilate was expropriating for his own secular purposes the shekalim which had been contributed by Jews everywhere for the purchase of sacrificial animals (see *m. Sheqalim* 3:2)." But there is no justification for Feldman's "his own." Moreover, note that the Mishnah (ibid. 4:2) rules that it is fine to use available *sheqalim* money for the needs of the city of Jerusalem, including its water supply (although, presumably, its authors would not be happy about a non-Jewish governor deciding upon such things).

Roman governor who finds that with these subjects he cannot do anything right.

What about the first story, about the standards Pilate introduced into the city? Here we note that, *a priori*, we tend to assume it comes from the same source. The account is so short, and the two events are so exceptional in this part of the *War* (the only stories about pre-Agrippan governors), that something of a presumption like this exists.[24] Moreover, note the stories are closely linked in *War*: both are called ταραχή (but not in *Antiquities*), both use πατέω (of laws in 2.170 and of trampled Jews in 2.177), both have ἀγανάκτησις (2.170, 175); the soldiers who "ring" the Jews in 2.173 (περιστάσης) are echoed by the Jews who "ring" (περιστάντες) Pilate in 2.175; both have Pilate on his βῆμα (2.172, 175), and reference to swords in 2.173 explains the reference to them in 2.176.

But if this is so, then given what we have just seen about 2.175–177 the implication would be that 2.169–174 is, as 175–177, based upon a report from Pilate's point of view. Indeed, inspection of this story too reveals that, just as with the aqueduct story, it is only the very first sentence that says anything he would not like to hear. Only here does Josephus blame Pilate, saying that he introduced the standards at night and in secret, the implication being, as we have seen, that he was a troublemaker. Otherwise there is nothing to indicate that it did not all begin simply due to Pilate's unfamiliarity with the Jews' sensitivities, and, as we have noted, the general tone of the story is one that portrays the confrontation of Jews who take their religion seriously with a conscientious Roman governor who insists upon law and order and respect for the emperor but who, when made to understand that his opponents too are serious men of conscience, knows how to respect such tenacity. Pilate would have been happy with such a story, especially given the fact that the next episode proved he was no pushover.

We conclude, therefore, that while examination of *Ant.* 18.55–62 shows that Josephus was very much at work as a successful author,[25] turning his sources into much more than a sum of their parts, this

---

[24] For a similar assumption about two other adjacent passages in *War* 2, and an argument that bolsters it, see my Schwartz 1990a, 5–11.

[25] Thackeray (1929, 107) sensed a certain Josephan "weariness" in last six books of *Antiquities*. Be that as it may, in the present case Josephus seems to have been on his toes.

does not preclude the possibility of reasonably recovering something of those sources. This, we argue, can be done to a high degree of probability not only when that which forces us to dissect Josephus' narrative is something as unequivocal as discrepancies about money or chronology, but also when the issue is one of points of view. For while sometimes changed points of view indicate that Josephus' point of view had changed, other times, when we find Josephus saying things that do not serve any usual Josephan point of view, the most reasonable thing to say is that Josephus has used sources written from other points of view. Which is not very revolutionary; we all know historians use sources, and there is no reason why we may not hope to recover some of them. Of course, it can be risky. But so can the interpretation of texts even when we know they were authored on a *tabula rasa*. And if there are risks, there are also benefits, for discovery of sources means discovery of other points of view. How much wouldn't we be happy to find some authentic *Acta Pilati*?[26] Perhaps we will, someday; you never know what might turn up here or there. But if there is a good chance we can come close to such by reading Josephus carefully, it would still seem to be a good idea to try.

APPENDIX

The Two Pilate Passages in English Translation (by D.R.S.)

War 2.169–177	*Ant.* 18.55–62
(169) Having been sent to Judea as procurator, by Tiberius, Pilate brought into Jerusalem—at night and under cover—images of Caesar called *semaiai*. (170) With daylight this aroused very great commotion among the Jews: those who were nearby were stricken by the sight, as if their laws had been trampled, for they do not allow the erection of any image in the city, while at the indignation of those in the city the population from the country too streamed together *en masse*. (171) After they set out ener-	(55) Pilate, the governor of Judea, in bringing his army from Caesarea and transferring it to winter quarters in Jerusalem, thought to abrogate Jewish customs by bringing into the city busts of Caesar, which were attached to the *semaiai*, although the law forbids us to make images. (56) And it was for this reason that former governors had made their entry into the city with *semaiai* without such ornaments; Pilate was the first who, without the people knowing it for his entry was at night, having brought

[26] On such *Acta*, see Schwartz 1992, 184–85.

getically after Pilate, to Caesarea, they beseeched him to take the *sema-iai* out of Jerusalem and preserve their ancestral laws. When Pilate refused they threw themselves prostrate around his residence, and for five days and as many nights they persisted without a budge.

(172) On the next day Pilate, having seated himself upon a tribunal in the great stadium and summoned the mob as if he wanted to give it an answer, gave the soldiers a pre-arranged sign to encircle the Jews, armed. (173) The Jews, surrounded by a line of battle three ranks thick, were stricken speechless by the unexpected sight, and Pilate—saying that he would cut them down if they did not accept the images of Caesar—signaled to the soldiers to bare their swords. (174) The Jews, as if by prearrangement, threw themselves down *en masse* and—stretching out their necks—cried out that they were willing to be killed rather than transgress the law. Pilate, overcome with amazement at the purity of their religious reverence, ordered (his men) to remove the *semaiai* from Jerusalem immediately.

(175) After these things he touched off another commotion by expending the sacred treasure, called Corbonas, for an aqueduct—which brought the water down from a distance of 400 furlongs. The mob was upset at that, and when Pilate came to Jerusalem they encircled his tribunal, crying out in protest. (176) He, since he had foreseen their commotion, had hidden the soldiers amidst the mob, mixing them in armed but in civilian clothes; having ordered them not to use swords but,

the images to Jerusalem set them up. (57) When they knew of it, they went *en masse* to Caesarea and pleaded, for several days, for the removal of the images. When he didn't agree for it would lead to hubris vis à vis Caesar, but they did not desist from entreating him, on the sixth day he stationed his armed force unseen and himself got up on his tribunal. This had been set up in the stadium, where the ambushing force hid. (58) When again the Jews beseeched him, at a given signal he surrounded them with his soldiers and threatened to pronounce a death penalty immediately if they did not cease their tumult and return to their homes.

(59) But they threw themselves prostrate, and baring their throats said they would gladly accept death rather than dare transgress the wisdom of the laws. And Pilate, amazed by their fortitude in the observance of the laws, immediately removed the images from Jerusalem and brought them back to Caesarea.

(60) He also made an aqueduct to bring water from Jerusalem, at the expense of the sacred money, taking the stream from about two hundred furlongs. But they did not like the works concerning the water, and many myriads of people assembled and cried out against him to stop that which he planned; some of them also employed insults and abuse of the man, as a crowd will tend to do. (61) He stationed around himself a large multitude of soldiers in their (the Jews') garments, carrying clubs under their garments, and sent them off to surround the Jews, ordering them to withdraw. When they, however, intensified their insulting he

rather, to beat the protestors with wooden clubs, from the tribunal he gave them a codeword.

(177) When the Jews were beaten, many perished: many under the blows and many others—trampled by other Jews in their flight. Stricken by the suffering of those killed, the mob kept silent.

gave the soldiers the prearranged sign. (62) But they beat (the Jews) much more than Pilate had ordered them to do, punishing both those who rioted and those who did not. But they displayed no cowardice, the result being that—taken as they were unarmed by men who were attacking them well-prepared—many of them were killed there while others, wounded, withdrew. Thus ended the stasis.

BIBLIOGRAPHY

Bilde, P.
    1979   The Causes of the Jewish War According to Josephus. *JSJ* 10:79–202.
Cohen, S. J. D.
    1979   *Josephus in Galilee and Rome: His Vita and Development as a Historian.* Leiden.
Hölscher, G.
    1904   *Die Quellen des Josephus für die Zeit vom Exil bis zum jüdischen Krieg.* Leipzig.
Housman, A. E.
    1972   *The Classical Papers of A. E. Housman.* 3 vols. Edited by J. Diggle and F. R. D. Goodyear. Cambridge.
Isaac, B.
    1996   Orientals and Jews in the Historia Augusta: Fourth-Century Prejudice and Stereotypes. Pages 101–18 in *The Jews in the Hellenistic-Roman World: Studies in Memory of Menahem Stern.* Edited by I. M. Gafni, A. Oppenheimer, and D. R. Schwartz. Jerusalem.
Jones, A. H. M.
    1967   *The Herods of Judea.* Oxford.
Josephus
    1965   Translated by L. H. Feldman. Vol. 9. LCL. Cambridge, Mass.
Lémonon, J. P.
    1981   *Pilate et le gouvernement de la Judée: Textes et monuments.* Paris.
Mason, S.
    2003   Contradiction or Counterpoint? Josephus and Historical Method. *RRJ* 6:145–88.
    2000   Introduction to the *Judean Antiquities.* Pages xiii–xxxvi in *Judean Antiquities 1–4.* Vol. 3 of *Flavius Josephus: Translation and Commentary.* Translation and Commentary by L. H. Feldman. Edited by S. Mason. Leiden.
Norden, E.
    1913   Josephus und Tacitus über Jesus Chrstus und eine messianische Prophetie. Pages 637–66 in *Neue Jahrbücher für das klassische Altertum, Geschichte und deutsche Literatur* 31 = Pages 241–75 in *Kleine Schriften zum klassischen Altertum.* Edited by B. Kytzler. Berlin, 1966 = Pages 27–69 in *Zur Josephus-Forschung.* Edited by A. Schalit; Darmstadt, 1973.
Potter, D. S.
    1999   *Literary Texts and the Roman Historian.* London.

Schürer, E.
  1973–1987   *The History of the Jewish People in the Age of Jesus Christ (175 B.C.–A.D. 135): A New English Version.* Revised and edited by G. Vermes, F. Millar, and M. Goodman. 3 vols. in 4. Edinburgh.
Schwartz, D. R.
  1989/90   On Drama and Authenticity in Philo and Josephus. *SCI* 10:113–29.
  1990a   *Agrippa I: The Last King of Judea.* Tübingen.
  1990b   On Some Papyri and Josephus' Sources and Chronology for the Persian Period. *JSJ* 21:175–99.
  1992   *Studies in the Jewish Background of Christianity.* Tübingen.
  1992/93   Felix and *Isopoliteia,* Josephus and Tacitus. *Zion* 58:265–86. [Hebrew].
  2002   Rome and the Jews: Josephus on 'Freedom' and 'Autonomy.' Pages 65–81 in *Representations of Empire: Rome and the Mediterranean World.* Edited by A. K. Bowman et al. Oxford.
Thackeray, H. St. J.
  1929   *Josephus: The Man and the Historian.* New York.

Alessandro Galimberti

Status Quaestionis

As is known, there are 10 fragments of Strabo's *Historikà Hypomnemata* in Stern's collection that depend on Josephus' express reference, all included in Books 13, 14, and 15 of the *Antiquities*.[1] However, in 1976, Stern wrote (p. 262): "There is much more in books thirteen and fourteen of the *Antiquities* that depends on Strabo's *Historikà Hypomnemata* than Josephus' express references to Strabo." Feldman's reviews (that stop at 1984) as well as his bibliography (that starts from 1985)[2] include four works, which however do not dwell upon the relation between Josephus and Strabo and do not question the validity of Stern's statement: I am referring to the works by L. Prandi, D. Ambaglio, J. Bellemore, and J. Engels.[3]

Prandi analyses the relationship between Ephorus and Strabo and puts forward a hypothesis on the starting point of Strabo's work: divided into forty-seven books, it must have started from 340 B.C.E. (i.e., the end of Ephorus' *Histories*) and continued until 264 B.C.E. (the beginning of Polybius' *Histories*), which marks the end of Book 4 (known as προκατασκευή). Book 5 was the beginning of the actual *continuatio Polybii* that reached the reign of Augustus. Ambaglio's interesting work allows the orderly consultation of fragments and their

---

[1] *GLAJJ* 98–108 = *FGH* 91 F 4, 6–7, 10–18; frg. 16–17 are correctly unified by Stern (1976, 107) in one single fragment. Stern's Strabonian collection is not limited to the *Historikà Hypomnemata* (this only covers the fragments that Josephus quoted), because it includes all Strabonian fragments relating to Judean themes (passages from Books 16 and 17 of the *Geography* are also included). Therefore, I shall quote the *Historikà Hypomnemata* and the *Testimonia* according to Jacoby's numeration (also adopted by Ambaglio 1990), and the other Strabonian quotations, not included by Jacoby in his collection, according to Stern's edition.

[2] Feldman 1984a; 1984b II 21.2:763–862; 1989. Up to 1978, Biraschi et al. (1981) is useful.

[3] Prandi 1988, 50–60; Ambaglio 1990, 377–424; Bellemore 1999, 94–118; Engels 1999, 269–72.

correct historical and chronological contextualisation. Bellemore's work, which analyses the different versions of the *War* and of the *Antiquities* with respect to the events of 63 B.C.E., deals with the issue of the relationship between Strabo and Josephus using as a starting point a hypothesis proposed by Stern about the date of the taking of Jerusalem by Pompey in the same year, 63 B.C.E. With reference to Engels' impressive work, although a whole chapter is devoted to the *Historikà Hypomnemata*, the author only writes a few pages on the topic of relations between Josephus and Strabo, and affirms that Strabo is a secondary source in comparison to Nicolaus of Damascus with regard to the Hasmonean and Herodian period.

In the light of these remarks, I would like to propose a new approach to Strabo's fragments in Books 13 and 14 of the *Antiquities*, in order to investigate the reasons why Josephus preferred Strabo and to identify further possible relations between Strabo's work and *Antiquities* 13–14.

On a superficial reading, the first thing that catches one's attention is that more than half of the nineteen available fragments of the *Historikà Hypomnemata*—ten to be precise—depend on Josephus: nine are documented in the *Antiquities* and belong to the *continuatio*, therefore, chronologically, they come after 146/5 B.C.E. The oldest fragment, however (frg. 10 in the *Apion*), makes reference to the plunder of the temple of Jerusalem by Antiochus IV, in 170 B.C.E., whereas the most recent one, dated 37 B.C.E., describes Herod's coming to the throne of Judea for Antony's will, in order to replace Antigonus. But the chronological framework of the *Historikà Hypomnemata* is wider, as can be inferred from the other available fragments (Strabo himself in the *Geography*, Plutarch in some of his *Lives* [*Sulla, Lucullus, Caesar*], a papyrus fragment [P. Mil. Vogl. 46.40]), based on which one could presume[4] that Strabo started from Alexander to cover at least the period up to 27 B.C.E., according to the most cautious hypothesis, or to 23 C.E. (the date of the papyrus fragment on the battle of Pselchis fought against the Ethiopians by the Romans under the command of C. Petronius, who was Aelius Gallus' successor as Prefect of Egypt).[5]

[4] Cf. Prandi 1988, 50–60.
[5] Engels (1999, 77, 80–84 with *status quaestionis*) sets the end of the *HH* at 27 B.C.E. The date 23 C.E. emerges from the analysis of the papyrus fragment by Manganaro (1974, 157–71). Most recently, Stickler 2002, 85–101.

According to Paul Pédech and in line with an old but still useful study by Otto,[6] Strabo's historical work can be recovered not only from the nineteen fragments known indirectly, but also from several passages of the *Geography* (not included in current collections of the *Historikà Hypomnemata*) that were composed after the *Historikà Hypomnemata*: these are mostly reminiscences of the *Historikà Hypomnemata* that Strabo mentions, sometimes in an inaccurate or even erroneous way.

What is even more interesting is the characterisation of the *Historikà Hypomnemata* in their historical-narrative structure, outlined by Pédech on the basis of his working hypothesis, i.e., that the *Historikà Hypomnemata* were a work of universal history, in which events were arranged annalistically. Moreover, Strabo must have possessed a sensitivity towards economic themes in his analysis of events and may well have devoted special attention to the history and administrative organisation of the different territories of the empire. Furthermore, he must have had a good knowledge of eastern events, although his work, in line with the Polybian model, is fundamentally Romanocentric and the history of other regions is always seen against the background of the history of Rome. The *Historikà Hypomnemata* must have paid a "biographic" attention to some important personalities (as can be inferred from frg. 2),[7] and Pédech hypothesises that Strabo must have known well the period of the Mithridatic wars (since one of his ancestors had been among Lucullus' supporters), and in particular Pompey's administrative activity that revolutionised the eastern order, as well as the dynastic events of the different reigns. His thorough knowledge of eastern events must have been the core of the *Historikà Hypomnemata*, to such an extent that Pédech states, without hesitation, that "aussi peut-on affirmer que l'histoire de l'orient formait la plus grande partie de son ouvrage, et la plus détaillée."[8]

In light of this methodological proposal, which is certainly valid and productive—though not always verifiable—I think we should

---

[6] Pédech 1972, 395–408; cf. Otto (1889), who thought he had reconstructed as many as 257 fragments from Strabo's work by analysing the *Geography*. See detailed critical remarks by Engels 1999, 76–80 on the subject.

[7] ἔτι δὲ τὸν αὐτὸν τρόπον, ὅνπερ ἐκεῖ τὰ περὶ τοὺς ἐπιφανεῖς ἄνδρας καὶ βίους τυγχάνει μνήμης, τὰ δὲ μικρὰ καὶ ἄδοξα παραλείπεται.

[8] Pédech 1972, 399.

proceed to an analysis of the fragments of the *Historikà Hypomnemata* (taking into consideration also the fragments "drawn" from the *Geography*) with regard to both those expressly quoted by Flavius Josephus and to some significant passages Josephus wrote, in order to try and identify the nature of relations existing between Strabo's material and Josephus' use of it.

Strabo's Quotations in Josephus

First of all, I shall try to find an answer to the following question: did Josephus know Strabo's work directly or did he only quote it indirectly? From a point of view we may call "formal," I think there are at least three ways in which Josephus quotes the *Historikà Hypomnemata*:

a. *Quotation of significant passages*

In frg. 4 (*Ant.* 13.284–287), when speaking of the dynastic conflict between Cleopatra III and her son Ptolemy Lathyrus in 108/7 B.C.E., Josephus quotes a passage from Strabo concerning Cleopatra's choice to entrust the command of her armies to Chelkias and Ananias, two Judean commanders. In frg. 6 (*Ant.* 14.111–113), dated to about 88 B.C.E., Josephus quotes Strabo in relation to the huge treasure in the temple of Jerusalem: it is worth noting that frg. 4 and frg. 6 are connected to each other because the riches that Mithridates VI took in 88 B.C.E. belonged to Cleopatra III (cf. *Ant.* 13.349).[9] We can infer from this that Josephus read *directly* at least one coherent section of the Strabonian text. In frg. 7, Josephus quotes Strabo in relation to Judean expansion to Cyrene, to Egypt and from there to the whole *ecumene*. The way in which Josephus makes reference to Strabo is significant because in this case not only does Josephus quote the largest Strabonian extract, but he also claims that Strabo had described Judean expansion all over the world "in another passage as well," thereby revealing that, very likely, he had examined the *Historikà Hypomnemata* at length. In frg. 8, another Strabonian passage is quoted

---

[9] Despite Jacoby's clear opposition (293) "das zusammentreffen F6–*AJ* XIII 349 ist ohne Bedeutung," even though the author does not provide any explanation of his position.

concerning the episode of Herod's appointment as king of Judea by Antony in 37 B.C.E.

b. *Quotation with other historians*

In frg. 10, Strabo is included in a list after Polybius and before Nicolaus of Damascus, Timagenes, Castor, and Apollodorus, in relation to the episode of the plunder of the temple of Jerusalem by Antiochus IV in 170 B.C.E.

In frg. 13, Josephus draws a very short, but extremely significant parallel between Strabo and Nicolaus that shows that he had read both of them, when he states that "Nicolaus of Damascus and Strabo of Cappadocia give the same account of the campaigns organised by Pompey and Gabinius against Judeans." In frg. 14 reference is made to Aristobulus' gift to Pompey that "Strabo also mentions." In frg. 15, with reference to the fall of Jerusalem, Strabo is included in the small circle of those who "gave an account of events in the age of Pompey," together with Nicolaus and Livy.

c. *Quotation of indirect sources mentioned by Strabo*

In frg. 11 Josephus mentions a short passage in which Strabo expresses a judgement on Aristobulus I based on Timagenes (ὡς μαρτυρεῖ τούτωι καὶ Στράβων, ἐκ τοῦ Τιμαγένους ὀνόματος λέγων οὕτως). In frg. 16 a reference is made to Hyrcanus' participation in the expedition to Egypt in support of Caesar, narrated by Strabo who used Asinius Pollio as his source. In frg.17 Strabo is quoted when he speaks of Mithridates of Pergamos basing his account on Hypsicrates.

In addition to the fact that Josephus mentions Strabo as many as ten times in Books 13–14 of the *Antiquities* (this is already a significant indication *per se* that corroborates the hypothesis that Josephus read Strabo's work directly), Josephus reveals his direct knowledge of the *Historikà Hypomnemata* when he makes reference to different passages relating to the same subjects or to topics that are linked to each other (this is the case in frg. 4 and frg. 6), when he refers to other passages of Strabo's work by simply summarising them (frg. 7), when he compares Strabo to other historians (Nicolaus of Damascus in frg. 13), or when he quotes the same sources that Strabo himself said he had used (frg. 11, 16, 17).

Strabo's Point of View on Judaic History and Judaism

Having said that, we can now try and investigate the relation between these two authors from a content viewpoint, along two directions: first by assessing whether it is possible to reconstruct Strabo's point of view on Judaic history and Judaism, and then by analysing the reasons that led Josephus to use the *Historikà Hypomnemata*.

Judging by the fragments handed down by Josephus, in the *Historikà Hypomnemata* Strabo took into consideration the period of Judaic history included between 170 B.C.E. and the beginning of Herod's reign (37 B.C.E.). Although in frg. 10 Strabo's name appears in a list together with the names of other historians—the first of whom is Polybius—which may lead us to think that Strabo only made an isolated reference to the plunder of the temple by Antiochus IV, strictly speaking we cannot exclude that he also dealt with Judean issues before 146/5 B.C.E., since the first books of the *Historikà Hypomnemata*, gave an account of the "history of Alexander" (frg. 3).[10] In that case—but we shall come back to this topic with reference to Book 13 of the *Antiquities*—one might even think that he also dealt with the conflicts involving the Syrian kings during the Maccabean and Hasmonean periods. Indeed, the available fragment that immediately follows (frg. 4) brings us to 108/7 B.C.E., the peak of the Hasmonean age. In any case, Strabo dealt with both the history of the Judeans of Palestine, and with Diaspora Judaism, as revealed by frg. 4, which makes reference to the Judeans of Alexandria and Cyprus, as well as by frg. 7, concerning the community of Cyrene.

If we wanted to reconstruct Strabo's viewpoint on Judaic history by reading Josephus' fragments, we would find ourselves in serious difficulty, because very little can be inferred from them. One gets the impression that in Strabo's work, no special place is reserved for Judaic history: indeed, Judeans are only mentioned in connection with single episodes of Roman and Hellenistic history that our author narrates from time to time. In my opinion, this is understandable in the light of the fact that before the war against Rome, Judeans had neither played a prominent role on the international scene nor caused any concern to Rome. In the eyes of a "Roman" historian, though of eastern origin, Judaic history must have only seemed subsidiary—

---

[10] Jacoby (295) succinctly writes, "möglicherweise aus προκατασκευή."

though significant at times—to the larger history of moribund Hellenistic monarchies and to the interests of Rome in the East. This does not mean that Strabo's accounts are irrelevant, but I believe that their correct contextualisation in Josephus' work can help clarify the reasons why the Judean historian chose to use the *Historikà Hypomnemata* as a source.

One reason can be found in the fact that in the eyes of Josephus, his source—among those who, like Nicolaus, continued Polybius' tradition, was also used from Book 13 of the *Antiquities*—must have definitely seemed authoritative in the field of Judaic history. Therefore Strabo was a precious source for Josephus, who wanted to use his work to inform his readers in a scrupulous and authentic way, as can be seen several times both in the *War* and the *Antiquities*.[11] This is testified, once again, by the fact that Josephus quotes Strabo together with other eminent historians (frg. 10, 13, 15) and in particular in frg. 10, *after* Polybius and *before* Nicolaus (*multi et digni conscriptores*). As a consequence, it is not surprising that Josephus quotes Strabo to confirm the versions of the events he narrates, or better, exclusively to *justify* his theses. There are at least four cases that I consider illuminating and that clearly show Josephus' attempts to force the meaning of the Strabonian text:[12]

1. In frg. 4, regarding Cleopatra's appointment of Chelkias and Ananias—sons of Onias IV, founder of the Egyptian temple in Leontopolis[13]—at the head of her armies, which were to attack her son Ptolemy Lathyrus, Josephus makes reference to Strabo to justify his thesis that in this period the Judeans had achieved remarkable power and prestige in Egypt and Cyprus. However, the connection between the fortunes of the Judeans and Strabo's fragment is made by Josephus by means of a short introduction to *Ant.* 13.284, and if we analyse what Strabo says, it seems to me that the only thing we can infer is that some Judeans and their valiant commanders enjoyed the respect of Cleopatra, but

---

[11] Suffice to mention here the two *proems*. Evidently, on one hand we have Josephus' intentions and on the other hand we have their fulfilment: in fact, all Strabonian works are marked by a solid apologetic core.

[12] Cf. Ambaglio 1990, 405–416 *passim*.

[13] Josephus quotes it in *Ant.* 13.69–72. As far as Chelchias and Ananias are concerned, cf. *Ant.* 13.348 (see *infra*).

not that, as Josephus says, "Cleopatra did nothing without their approval."

2. In frg. 6,[14] which is connected, as already said, to frg. 4, when Josephus writes about the plunder of the temple treasure by Crassus (55 B.C.E.), he quotes a passage by Strabo in which mention is made of eight hundred talents—deposited in Cos by Judeans— that Mithridates took in 88 B.C.E. Josephus himself comments on this and notes that the talents had been deposited there by the Judeans of Asia, therefore assuming that the sum had not been collected by the Judeans of Judea or by the Judeans of Alexandria, because the former lived in a fortified city that was sufficiently protected and had the temple while the latter had no fear of Mithridates VI.

   In this case, however, Strabo only mentions the wealth of the Judeans, without specifying if it had been accumulated thanks to the contribution made by the Judeans of Asia. Moreover, his quotation of Strabo's account seems anachronistic when it comes to Crassus' plunder, which took place more than 30 years after the episode of Mithridates VI.

3. In frg. 7, which immediately follows frg. 6 in the *Antiquities*, Josephus quotes Strabo to provide evidence of the high number of Judeans who populated the whole *ecumene*: although the context seems consistent with Josephus' assumption, i.e., the massive expansion of Judaism, Strabo's passage does not seem to justify Josephus' enthusiasm towards his fellow countrymen. On the contrary, it seems to me that in Strabo's words one may even detect a hint of irritation for the high-handedness shown by diaspora Judeans.

4. In frg. 18, Josephus quotes a Strabonian passage relating to the beheading of Antigonus, son of Aristobulus II, ordered by Antony in Antioch in 37 B.C.E. In this case, Josephus makes reference to Strabo to underline the heroic resistance of Judeans, who even faced torture because they did not want to accept Herod's sovereignty. In addition to that, the detail concerning Anthony's original plan, i.e., that Antigonus had to be captured and held in custody until the time of triumph, can only be found in the lines (*Ant.* 15.8) that Josephus writes to introduce the quotation and there is no reference to it in Strabo's testimony.

---

[14] This account is also found in Appian, *Mithr.* 23.92.

If we now compare some fragments from the *Historikà Hypomnemata* and some pages from the *Geography*—written after the *Historikà Hypomnemata*—we can see that Strabo's attitude towards Judeans and Judaism is heterogeneous, to say the least.

In a passage of Book 16 of the *Geography* (16.2.34–46 = *GLAJJ* 115), Strabo speaks at length of Judea and of the historical origins of Judaism. After a brief introduction on the geographical position of Judea, there is an account of the historical origins of Judaism and of the Jerusalem temple, which he traces back to Egypt, based on what he believes to be the most reliable account. Moses was an Egyptian priest who controlled a region of Lower Egypt. Since he disapproved of idolatrous and anthropomorphic polytheism, he moved to Judea together with several loyal worshippers of God (τὸ Θεῖον). He settled in Jerusalem, which had been built in an abandoned and unfavourable area, and there he founded the cult and the priesthood, although in a few generations unworthy people became priests and promoted superstition, despotism, circumcision, and abstinence from pork, and subdued large areas of Syria and Phoenicia (the allusion is to the Hasmoneans).

Nevertheless, Judeans were praiseworthy because they aspired to a "positive" law of divine inspiration, as the Greeks did, since Moses, like the mythical Greek legislators, drew his inspiration from the divine to define the rules according to which Judeans lived together. After this *excursus* (*Geogr.* 16.2.38–39), Strabo provides a brief account of Alexander Jannaeus—who was the first king—and of the conflict that erupted between his sons Hyrcanus II and Aristobulus II, of Pompey's subsequent intervention, and of the siege and taking of Jerusalem in 63 B.C.E. The account ends with a series of geographical descriptions of Jericho, the Dead Sea, Gadara, and Tarichaea, followed by a short mention of Herod and his successors.

This account offers plenty of food for thought, but I shall only dwell on the parts that, in my opinion, are more relevant to the topic I am dealing with.

This long account can be divided into at least two parts: the first part concerns the Egyptian origin of the Judeans and the practices connected to their religious activity, whereas the second part deals with more recent Judaic history, within the framework of the Roman-Hellenistic world. Therefore, the whole passage seems to draw inspiration from material of different origins:

a. With reference to the Egyptian origins of Judeans, Strabo himself says that he had based his account on the most authoritative
   version.[15] It is worth noting that this version has several elements
   in common with the better-known version by Hecataeus of Abdera
   (*GLAJJ* 11). Both in Hecataeus and in Strabo, Moses fights against
   the worship of anthropomorphous gods. The sky (Hecataeus) and
   the sea (Strabo) that embrace the earth are identified with God.
   For both Hecataeus and Strabo, Judea was completely deserted
   when Moses arrived.

b. The first part of the passage, which combines an historical account
   with remarks on Judean practices, contains two important elements: on the one hand it proposes a much more benevolent version of the Judaising carried out by the Idumeans. For Strabo,
   in fact, the Idumeans (of Nabatean origin), were sent away from
   their lands after an insurrection and "joined up with the Judeans
   and shared their customs." Then we learn from Josephus (*Ant.*
   13.357) that the Idumeans were subdued by Hyrcanus I soon
   after 130 B.C.E. and their Judaising was pursued with the use of
   force. On the other hand, we have Strabo's (or his source's?)
   extremely negative judgement, in which a comparison is made
   between ancient Judaic religion and the current situation, and
   criticism is expressed for the progressive degeneration of priesthood after Moses, when priests first became superstitious and then
   tyrannical. First they established superstitious customs that Judeans
   "still follow today," then they became marauders who spread
   chaos in their country, robbed neighbouring territories, and subdued "most of Syria and Palestine." The interesting fact that
   emerges from Strabo's passage is that in very few lines we can
   see two opposing tendencies: on the one hand there is the version of the integration between Idumeans and Judeans, which is
   perfectly in line with the peaceful Judaising promoted by Moses
   on his arrival to Palestine and that, in my opinion, looks more
   pro-Herodian than pro-Hasmonean.[16] It was indeed in the interest of the Idumean Herod, who was considered a half-Judean by

---

[15] On the Egyptian tradition, see Stern (1976, 305). Suffice to mention, among
the most famous exponents, Hecataeus of Abdera and Artapanus, see Troiani 2000,
99–105; Cheremon in *Apion* 1.288–292, see Barzanò 1985, II 36.2:1981–2001. Other
Strabonian passages on the Egyptian origins of Jews are 16.4.9; 17.2.5.

[16] Stern 1976, 305.

his opponents, to depict Idumea as a Judaic *naturaliter*. On the other hand, the blame for the degeneration of priesthood and for the tyrannical drift seems to be a clear allusion[17] to Hasmonean expansionism in Syria and Palestine supported by Hyrcanus I, Aristobulus I, and Alexander Jannaeus during the first half of the first century B.C.E. (*Geogr.* 16.2.37).[18] It seems to me that this is also confirmed by the fact that after the *excursus* on legislators, Strabo (or his source) introduces the episode where Alexander Jannaeus adopts the title of king in a way that is evidently hostile when he says that, during this time, Judea was ruled by a tyrannical regime. The link between the onset of tyranny and the superstitious practices "that are still typical of Judeans nowadays" looks like an unrelated element, introduced by Strabo, which reveals he had little sympathy for Judaism.[19] In another passage of the *Geography* (17.1.15 = *GLAJJ* 121), Strabo again seems to manifest his not totally benevolent attitude towards the Jews when, between the lines, he accuses them of greed.

c. Statements concerning the political co-existence of Judeans of Palestine can be attributed to a Greek viewpoint or to a Greek source. This is revealed by at least two circumstances: the fact that in *Geogr.* 16.2.37, it is said that despite tyranny, the acropolis was respected and honoured as a sacred place, and the fact that Judeans, like Greeks, obeyed a "πρόσταγμα."[20]

d. Among Strabo's sources, we can certainly number Posidonius, who is expressly mentioned (*Geogr.* 16.2.43) with reference to the extraction of asphalt from the Dead Sea. Although some scholars[21] share the view that Strabo used Posidonius as a source for the whole account, in particular for Moses and the Egyptian origin of Judaism, it is certainly more prudent to admit a partial use for this anecdote only. Moreover, we can infer from Josephus'

---

[17] Cf. Stern 1976, 306. Decadence after Moses is reaffirmed in 16.2.39.
[18] The same hostile attitude towards marauders is also found in *Geogr.* 16.2.28.
[19] About the traditional lack of understanding—or rather intentional lack of understanding—of Judaism and its rites by the Romans, see the recent work by Schäfer (1999) *passim*.
[20] The long *excursus* on legislators, too, seems consistent with the expressed viewpoint, because it aims at showing that laws "either come from Gods or from men."
[21] *Status quaestionis* in Stern (1976, 263–67 [*in primis* K. Reinhardt]). The quotation of Posidonius seems also isolated from any specific problem, like the quotation of Erathostenes.

    pages (*Apion* 2.79) that Posidonius was hostile to Judeans, while
    Strabo uses words of praise for Moses.

e. The account of the taking of Jerusalem by Pompey reveals a
    significant coincidence with *Ant.* 14.66 (we shall go back to this
    later).

f. The recurrent allusions to the Herodian age contained in the
    account do not allow the formulation of a clear judgement about
    his tendency, but clearly show the good quality of information
    (*Geogr.* 16.2.34, 41). The striking fact is that in the final part of
    the account we can see a *unicum* according to which apparently
    Herod had even become the high priest. Since we learn from
    Josephus (*Ant.* 14.403–404)[22] that the controversy concerning
    Herod's unworthiness to assume the rank of king, to which the
    supreme priesthood was inherent, because he was a "half-Judean,"
    was still alive at the end of the first century C.E., one can pre-
    sume that Strabo's source created a fake to demonstrate Herod's
    full legitimacy to be a priest. In any case, Strabo must not have
    disliked the role played by Herod as guarantor of Roman inter-
    ests in Palestine.

I think that from this schematic analysis, which combines a variety
of different remarks each of which would deserve further consideration, several elements emerge that might better define Strabo's attitude towards Judeans and Judaism. Strabo believed that the most
reliable source on Moses and the exodus was the Egyptian one,
according to which Moses, like the mythical Greek legislators, is seen
as a wise prophet who fights against idolatry to peacefully establish
a monotheistic cult. Judaic history after Moses is marked by a progressive decline that culminates in the decadence of priesthood and
in the tyrannical policy adopted during the Hasmonean age. Nevertheless, the attitude towards the Hasmoneans is not always hostile.
Judaism looks to Strabo like a cult with which superstitious practices
are associated. From an historiographic point of view, Strabo seems
to combine Egyptian traditions with sources of different origin (anti-
Hasmonean and pro-Herodian).[23]

---

[22] Josephus' sharp polemical attitude derives from the fact that he was very proud
to belong to the Hasmonean family (*Ant.* 16.183–187; *Life* 2).

[23] I think it is unlikely that a condemnation of Hasmonean expansionism can be
inferred from the Herodian source, because such a topic was dangerous for Herod
himself.

Therefore, given Strabo's "lack of interest" in Judaic history shown in the *Historikà Hypomnemata* and his not always benevolent attitude towards Judaism in the *Geography*, though mitigated by some positive comments that can be derived from a few passages of the above-mentioned work, one might conclude that in Josephus' works, the use of Strabo was limited and functioned exclusively for his apologetic interests, which often led him to force the literal meaning of Strabo's text (Josephus, as already said, nearly always uses a paraphrase to introduce the *verbatim* quotation of Strabonian passages). But I believe that it is important to stress that, as Josephus tells us, Strabo was a source Josephus had consulted, in addition to Nicolaus of Damascus (frg. 10, 12, 13, 15), to reconstruct the *same* events of Judaic history. I think that the parallel use of Strabo and Nicolaus can be explained, first of all, in the light of the objections made by Josephus to Nicolaus in Book 16 of the *Antiquities* where (*Ant.* 16.183–187), as is known, Josephus does not condone Nicolaus' encomiastic attitude towards Herod. In his effort to be objective, as clearly stated throughout his work—suffice to mention the *proems* to the *War* and *Antiquities*—Josephus feels the need to balance Nicolaus' partiality by using other sources, and one of them is certainly Strabo. The characteristics of the *Historikà Hypomnemata* so far identified on the basis of fragment analysis (Romano centric perspective, the interest in diaspora Judaism, especially the Hellenistic dynasties of Syria and Egypt, and in particular in the community of Alexandria, and anti-Hasmonean and moderate pro-Herodian tendencies) certainly permit us to say that Strabo expressed a viewpoint that differed from Nicolaus' yet complemented it. That is, it seems to me to be very likely Josephus found in Strabo a valid alternative to Nicolaus even if in one case (frg. 12, concerning the cruelties committed by the Ptolemaic armies after the battle of Asophon) he is pleased to point out that Strabo's and Nicolaus' versions coincide.[24]

The Reasons for a Choice

At this point, one may wonder why Josephus chose Strabo as an alternative source and not Posidonius—Strabo knew Posidonius at

---

[24] As already seen in that case, like in frg. 10, Strabo's name precedes Nicolaus'. As is known, Strabo quotes Nicolaus in *Geogr.* 15.1.73 with reference to the Indian embassy to Augustus in Antioch.

the time of the *Historikà Hypomnemata* as shown by frg. 1—who, like
Strabo, was among those who continued the traditions of Polybius:
a first hint can be found in *Apion* 2.79 where Posidonius is mentioned by Josephus together with Apollonius Molon as one of Apion's
sources for slanders about the Judeans and the temple of Jerusalem.[25]
I believe that one of the basic reasons can be found in the different
historiographical and political approach that Strabo offered for the
political situation of the time in comparison to Posidonius: Strabo
differs radically from Posidonius, since he fully adhered to Augustus'
viewpoint that Roman domination was indisputable and the notion
of decadence could not be entertained. Posidonius dwells on the reasons that led to Roman conquests and especially on the methods,
sometimes reproachable, adopted by Rome during its domination,
against the background of a wider philosophical-moral framework.
Strabo, however, believes that the only way to provide an explanation is by illustrating why the Romans had reached such a level of
prosperity, equilibrium, and peace throughout the empire. It seems
to me that from this point of view, there is an ideological affinity
between Josephus and Strabo: it is sufficient to read the famous
speech by Agrippa II, or the speech by Josephus himself in *War*[26]
to realise that Josephus, too, believed that the empire was an indisputable fact. From this perspective, Strabo offers a very good "dis-
guise" for Josephus who is committed, especially in the *Antiquities* (for
example, the series of documents that the Roman authorities issued
to guarantee privileges to Judean communities throughout the Mediterranean area),[27] to finding the means, including the cultural ones,
to justify the need for peaceful co-existence between himself and
his fellow countrymen and the Roman empire.

Further Relationships

Indeed, if we start from this point and follow the remarks made by
Stern, which I mentioned at the beginning, perhaps it is possible to

---

[25] With reference to this subject, it is worth noting that Polybius must have
had words of praise for the temple, if he intended to treat specifically this topic
(*GLAJJ* 32).
[26] Gabba 1976–1977, 189–94.
[27] Troiani 1984, 39–50 and 2003, 467–78.

hypothesise that Strabo's work provides the basis for some of the accounts in Books 13 and 14 of the *Antiquities*—where Strabo's name is not mentioned—and modify the view on the relations between Josephus and Strabo that we have analysed so far.

In Book 13 of the *Antiquities*, the account goes from 160 to 57 B.C.E. and includes the events relating to the Maccabeans/Hasmoneans from Jonathan to Salome Alexandra: up to *Ant.* 13.214 Josephus essentially follows 1 Macc, then he uses other sources.[28] In particular, a hypothesis has been put forward that Josephus already used a Judean source different from 1 Macc (Eupolemus?)[29] in *Ant.* 13.62–79, for the events relating to Onias IV, son of Onias III and the foundation of the temple of Leontopolis in Egypt at the time of Ptolemy VI.[30] However, it should be noted that the events concerning Chelkias and Ananias, sons of Onias IV, are mentioned again in *Ant.* 13.284–287 where Strabo's testimony is provided (frg. 4). Chelkias and Ananias appear again both in *Ant.* 13.349 (very briefly) and in *Ant.* 13.358 with reference to the conflict that opposed Ptolemy Lathyrus to his mother Cleopatra III in Cyprus. Since in *Ant.* 13.287 it is said that Cleopatra sent the Egyptians to Cyprus "at a later time" and the account only starts again there (13.358), the impression is that Josephus put together a single account using different parts of his work. Given Strabo's interest in Egyptian Judaism (which can also be seen in frg. 7 and *GLAJJ* 115) and in the dynastic episodes of Hellenistic monarchies,[31] one might assume that Strabo must have also been consulted by Josephus with reference to the events of the Lagid dynasty in the second half of the second century B.C.E.

In *Ant.* 13.344, when speaking about the battle of Asophon, Josephus provides the number of casualties: "It was said that 30,000 Judeans were killed, as many as 50,000 according to Timagenes; the others were captured as prisoners, or managed to find a refuge in their lands."

Since Josephus' mention of Timagenes in frg. 11 (= *Ant.* 13.319) depends on Strabo's quotation referring to the judgement on Aristobulus,

---

[28] This can also be noticed if a comparison is made between *War* 1.54 and *Ant.* 13.228 for the account of the same events starting from the death of Simon Maccabee, see Gafni 1989, 116–31.

[29] Garbini 2000, 367–82.

[30] The account of these events is introduced already in *Ant.* 12.387–388.

[31] Cf. mainly Pédech (1972, *passim*); for the Attalids, see Virgilio (1984, 21–37).

I think it is not unlikely that Josephus took the number mentioned by Timagenes once again from Strabo, so much so that in *Ant.* 13.347 Josephus says he had consulted both Nicolaus and Strabo to gather information on the battle of Asophon. It can be added that Timagenes is quoted by Josephus in the *Antiquities* only in the two above-mentioned passages, i.e., *Ant.* 13.319 and 344. To conclude: references to Timagenes are derived from Strabo and Josephus apparently used Strabo-Timagenes for the account of the battle of Asophon. If this is true, I think it is particularly interesting to stress once again that this confirms the fact that Strabo very likely dealt predominantly with issues concerning Judeans and Judaism in relation to Egyptian events (at Asophon, Ptolemy fought against Aristobulus, Hyrcanus' son). The most striking fact, however, is that Josephus used Timagenes, who was probably an anti-Augustan historian, although he is mediated by Strabo. However, it seems to me that based on the very few fragments that can be reconstructed here—nothing more than quotations from Strabo—it is not possible to go beyond a judgement based on impressions: in the first case (the positive judgement on Aristobulus), the episode suits well an evidently pro-Hellenic historian,[32] since Aristobulus favoured Hellenisation and was the first (according to Strabo, *GLAJJ* 115) to assume the role of king in the Hellenistic way. In the second case, in addition to the huge discrepancy in the figure of dead Judeans (30,000, for one source, probably Nicolaus, and 50,000 according to Timagenes) it seems to me that we can only venture the hypothesis that Timagenes tended to exaggerate figures in order to favour King Lagid. These two examples seem to suggest that Josephus, as usual, put together two different sources in order to document his special attention towards objectivity: in the first case, indeed, his judgement on Aristobulus seems to be rather contradictory because Strabo-Timagenes' words of praise are preceded by a judgement which is not benevolent at all. In the second case, we see a discrepancy in figures that, in the final analysis, is used to show Josephus' particular attention towards documentary accuracy.

The history of the Herodians begins in Book 14, where Antipater the Idumean appears for the first time, and continues up to Book

---

[32] Hellenocentrism is emphasised by Sordi (1982, II 30.1:775–97); with reference to the relation between Timagenes-Strabo, see Engels 1999, 240–42.

17. At first it combines with the account of the end of the Hasmoneans: Book 14 begins with the succession of Salome Alexandra's sons, Hyrcanus (II) and Aristobulus (II), in 67 B.C.E., and ends with the violent death of Antigonus (37 B.C.E.), Aristobulus' son.[33]

Nicolaus of Damascus is Josephus' main source, especially for events relating to Antipater and the Herodians: he served Herod for many years and became one of his closest friends. Therefore his accounts exalt his friend and protector and, consequently, Herod's father Antipater as well, whereas the last Hasmoneans are presented in an unfavourable light. Apparently, Josephus tried to mitigate this tendency in Nicolaus' accounts by resorting to one or more anti-Herodian sources.[34]

Where do we see Strabo in this book? In addition to explicit uses of Strabo (frg. 6, 7.13–17) Stern, and more recently Bellemore, have highlighted that the *Historikà Hypomnemata* must have been at the basis of the (inaccurate) dating of the fall of Jerusalem in 63 B.C.E., as also shown by the unusual coincidence between the dating in *Ant.* 14.66 (mentioned again in 14.487) and in *Geogr.* 16.2.40 (*GLAJJ* 115).[35] Moreover, consular dates, together with the dates of Olympic years, are only found in *Antiquities* 14.

First of all, I would like to point out that Book 14 of the *Antiquities* contains almost all of the Strabonian quotations in Josephus (as many as seven out of ten) and therefore the use of Strabo does not seem to be of minor importance. Moreover, I think we can cautiously

---

[33] A separate section of the book includes paragraphs from 186 to 267, which reproduce a series of Roman decrees issued by the Romans in favour of Judeans, see Pucci Ben Zeev 1998 and, most recently, Troiani 2003, 467–78.

[34] Unlike the *War* 1.120–124 where Josephus seems to have drawn upon Nicolaus alone: on the whole, the presentation of Herodians found in the *Antiquities* is, in fact, less favourable than that in *War*. For example, in *Ant.* 14.41–48 with reference to the embassy of notable Judeans to Pompey, soon before his intervention in Jerusalem, the rejection of monarchy (Herod was *amicus et rex populi Romani*) as well as the priesthood polemic (since Herod was a "semi-Judean," he had always been judged unworthy to be a priest by traditionalists) clearly indicate an anti-Herodian source. On Josephus and Nicolaus see Wacholder 1989, 147–72.

[35] A hint can be found in the fact that both in Josephus' and Strabo's passages, Saturday is called "fasting day," which is not true at all: it is likely that, as Stern (1976, 276, 307) suggests (quoted by Bellemore 1999, 112) Strabo saw Saturday, the day when Jews abstained from any activity, as a fasting day; indeed, the same confusion is also found in Dio 37.16.2–4. In fact, we learn from Josephus himself (14.63) that Pompey carried out the works of fortification needed for the siege of Jerusalem on Saturdays: the city was conquered in the summer of 63 B.C.E.

speculate that the historian from Amasea was used as a reference for some other episodes:

1. In *Ant.* 14.29–34 concerning Pompey's decision to intervene in Judea, Josephus quotes two judgements on Hyrcanus and Aristobulus that reveal the attitude of his source: Hyrcanus is defined as "poor and quibbling," whereas Aristobulus is defined as "generous and moderate": if the attitude in favour of Aristobulus is Strabonian, as already seen with reference to *Ant.* 13.319, in this case we could also hypothesise the same relationship, even more so given that in the paragraphs that immediately follow (*Ant.* 14.35–36) Strabo is expressly mentioned (frg. 14) with reference to the present sent by Aristobulus to Pompey in Damascus. Therefore in these paragraphs, Josephus shows that he had used another source in addition to Strabo (very likely it was Nicolaus, given that the two historians are quoted together by Josephus in *Ant.* 14.68 [= frg. 15]) since, for example, he provides an account of Pompey's arrival in Damascus twice in the span of a few paragraphs: in *Ant.* 14.34 ("soon afterwards, Pompey arrived in Damascus") and in *Ant.* 14.38 and 40: "after ordering that the rival parties should appear before him, in early spring Pompey moved with his army from the winter quarters to Damascus . . . and once he crossed the mountains that separate Coele-Syria from the rest of Syria, he arrived in Damascus." From this we could infer that the Roman general went to Damascus twice, in 64 and 63 B.C.E. Instead, Pompey only went to Damascus once, in the spring of 63 B.C.E.: in my opinion the duplicate can only be explained by the fact that in *Ant.* 14.34–40 Josephus first uses Strabo (14.34–36) and then Nicolaus (14.37–40).[36] In *Ant.* 14.36 Alexander (Jannaeus) is called king of Judeans, a piece of information that is only found in Strabo (*GLAJJ* 115: the traditional and univocal opinion is that the title of king of Judea was assumed for the first time by Aristobulus and not by his father Alexander).

2. In *Ant.* 14.98 it is said that Gabinius, while fighting against the Parthians and when he had already crossed the Euphrates, changed his mind and decided to go back to Egypt to bring Ptolemy back

---

[36] In *Ant.* 14.37 the account resumes and moves back to the date of the embassy by Hyrcanus and Aristobulus that marks the end of *Ant.* 14.36 to 64 B.C.E., when Pompey was still in Aspis (cf. Dio 37.7).

to the throne "as already mentioned elsewhere": who is Josephus alluding to here? It is worth noting that in *Ant.* 14.104 Josephus says that "both Nicolaus of Damascus and Strabo of Cappadocia speak of the campaigns of Pompey and Gabinius against the Judeans, and they are in agreement." It is not easy to say exactly which parts are derived from either Nicolaus or Strabo, but a comparison with *Geogr.* 17.1.11, where in a summary of Egyptian-Hellenistic history relating to the Lagids Strabo focuses his attention on Auletes and his relation with Gabinius ("who, at that time, was engaged in the war against the Parthians"), might suggest that in this case Josephus is alluding to Strabo's work.[37]

3. Both in *Ant.* 14.137 and 144 mention is made again of the fact that Caesar confirmed Hyrcanus as high priest (the priesthood had been conferred on him by Pompey): the duplicate raises suspicion that this episode may be the awkward combination, made by Josephus, of two different sources, one of which could certainly be Strabo (if the other one is Nicolaus).

4. In *Ant.* 14.334 the δρυμός at Mount Carmel is mentioned and the same reference is also found in *Geogr.* 16.2.27–28 (= *GLAJJ* 114).

Conclusions

If we consider plausible our reconstruction of the facts so far, we must conclude that Josephus knew and consulted Strabo's *Historikà Hypomnemata* directly, especially with reference to Books 13 and 14 of the *Antiquities*, even when no express reference to Strabo is made. The way he uses this work is clear: first, Josephus reads the work instrumentally, because Strabo is only quoted by Josephus to support his reconstruction of events and sometimes even by forcing the meaning of words. Apparently, Josephus is not interested in the context of Strabonian episodes and tends to use them in his accounts to support his own views. Strabo's interest in Judaic history is sporadic: to him, Judaic history matters only in that it is part of the larger history of the empire. It is not by chance that the presence

---

[37] Strabo might also be drawn upon for *Ant.* 14.89–91, where the administrative structure of Gabinius' Judea is mentioned.

of Strabo, together with Nicolaus of Damascus, can be found mainly in Book 14 of the *Antiquities*, where Josephus writes about Pompey, Gabinius and Crassus, who had experienced their successes and failures on the eastern front. In addition to that, Josephus does not seem to dislike Strabo's attitude towards Judaism: despite his inevitable Roman prejudices, Strabo seems to be an observer not completely hostile to Judaism, on the contrary, he gives a positive assessment of its origins. Given the efforts Josephus makes in the *Apion* (where Strabo is also mentioned), immediately after the *Antiquities*, to demonstrate that Judaism is a historical and rational religion, Strabo's attitude is acceptable to him.

However, perhaps the main reason why Josephus prefers Strabo's historical work, which could explain, at least in part, why Josephus did not consult Posidonius, lies in the fact that Josephus found in Strabo a historian in line with the Augustan regime and therefore sufficiently authoritative and appreciated by Josephus' readers. We can see a sort of basic ideological agreement between Strabo and Josephus that can also be explained, among other things, by the *status* of the two historians. What I mean is that Strabo, who belonged to one of those pro-Roman, eastern élites that supported Rome enthusiastically, was a sort of model for Josephus (especially after the catastrophe of the war) as part of a group of intellectuals and, in particular, of historians whose status was completely established within the reality of the empire. This seems to be repeatedly confirmed by several references that Josephus makes in the *Life* to the "official" recognition of his work by the Flavian emperors.

BIBLIOGRAPHY

Ambaglio, D.
  1990   Gli Historikà Hypomnemata di Strabone. Introduzione, traduzione italiana e commento dei frammenti. *Memorie dell'Istituto Lombardo* 39.
Barzanò, A.
  1985   Cheremone di Alessandria. *ANRW* II.36.2:1981–2001. Edited by W. Haase. New York.
Bellemore, J.
  1999   Josephus, Pompey and the Jews. *Historia* 48:94–118.
Biraschi, A. et al.
  1981   *Strabone. Saggio di bibliografia 1469–1978*. Perugia.
Engels, J.
  1999   *Augusteische Oikumenegeographie und Universaltheorie im Werk Strabons von Amaseia*. Stuttgart.

Feldman, L. H.
1984a   *Josephus and Modern Scholarship (1937–1980)*. Berlin.
1984b   Flavius Josephus Revisited: the Man, his Writings, and his Signi-
            ficance. *ANRW* II.21.2:763–862. Edited by W. Haase. New York.
1989   A Selective Critical Bibliography of Josephus. Pages 330–448
            in *Josephus, the Bible and History*. Edited by L. H. Feldman and
            G. Hata. Leiden.

Gabba, E.
1976–77   L'impero romano nel discorso di Agrippa (Ioseph., B.I., II, 345–401).
            RSA 6–7:189–94.

Gafni, I. M.
1989   *Josephus and I Maccabees*. Leiden.

Jacoby, F.
1923–1958   *Die Fragmente der griechischen Historiker*. Leiden.

Manganaro, G.
1974   Il Pap. Vogl. 46 (40) di Milano e la battaglia di Pselchis. *QUCC*
            18:157–71.

Otto, P.
1889   *Strabonis Ἱστορικὰ Ὑπομνήματα Fragmenta collegit et enarravit adiectis
            quaestionibus strabonianis Paulus Otto*. Leipzig.

Pédech, P.
1972   Strabon historien. Pages 395–408 in *Studi Classici in onore di Q.
            Cataudella*. II. Catania.

Prandi, L.
1988   Ipotesi sugli Historikà Hypomnemata. *Aevum* 62:50–60.

Pucci, Ben Zeev M.
1998   *Jewish Rights in the Roman World. The Greek and Roman Documents
            Quoted by Josephus Flavius*. Tübingen.

Sordi, M.
1982   Timagene di Alessandria: uno storico ellenocentrico e filobarbarico.
            ANRW II.30.1:775–97. Edited by W. Haase. New York.

Stern, M.
1974–1984   *Greek and Latin Authors on Jews and Judaism: Edited with Introductions,
            Translations and Commentary*. 3 vols. Jerusalem.

Stickler, T.
2002   *Gallus amore peribat? Cornelius Gallus und die Anfänge der augusteische
            Herschaft in Ägypten*. Rahden.

Troiani, L.
2000   *Apocrifi dell'Antico Testamento*. V. Brescia. (ed.)
1984   Per un'interpretazione della storia ellenistica e romana contenuta
            nelle «Antichità Giudaiche di Giuseppe» (libri XII–XX). Pages
            39–50 in *Studi Ellenistici I*. Edited by B. Virgilio. Pisa.
2003   Il dossier prodotto da Giuseppe nel libro XIV delle Antichità
            Giudaiche. Pages 467–78 in *L'uso dei documenti nella storiografia antica*.
            Edited by A. M. Biraschi et al. Naples.

Virgilio, B.
1984   Strabone e la storia di Pergamo e degli Attalidi. Pages 21–37 in
            Studi Ellenistici I. Edited by B. Virgilio. Pisa.

Wacholder, B. Z.
1989   Josephus and Nicolaus of Damscus. Pages 147–72 in *Josephus, the
            Bible and History*. Edited by L. H. Feldman and G. Hata. Leiden.

GESCHICHTSFORSCHUNG ALS APOLOGIE: JOSEPHUS UND DIE NICHT-GRIECHISCHEN HISTORIKER IN *CONTRA APIONEM*

Niclas Förster

Die apologetische Schrift des Josephus *Contra Apionem* zeichnet sich durch zahlreiche Zitate aus den Werken antiker Historiker des alten Orients aus, die nicht-griechischer Herkunft waren, ihre Texte aber in griechischer Sprache verfaßten. Das literarische Panorama dieser Autoren ist weit gespannt und umfaßt Nachrichten über die Geschichte der Reiche der Ägypter, Babylonier und der phönikischen Stadtstaaten. Zu diesen griechisch-römischen Schriftstellern zählen u.a. der ägyptische Priester Manetho, der babylonische Mardukpriester Berossos aber auch phönikische Geschichtsschreiber wie Dion und Menander. So ist die Apologie des Josephus durch diese ausführlichen Zitate eine unentbehrliche Testimoniensammlung dieser Historiker und durch ihre vergleichsweise langen und teils wörtlichen Exzerpte eine Fundgrube wertvoller, historischer Informationen, die die wechselhafte Geschichte der altorientalischen Völker betreffen.

Das apologetische Anliegen des Josephus in Contra Apionem

Josephus selbst ging es, als er diese Nachrichten, die beispielsweise den Exodus der Juden aus Ägypten, König Salomos Kontakte zum tyrischen Stadtkönig Hiram oder das babylonische Exil betrafen, in seine Verteidigungsschrift aufnahm, um zwei für seine apologetische Argumentation zentrale Gesichtspunkte:

– Er bemühte sich, einen über alle Zweifel erhabenen Beweis für das hohe Alter seines Volkes zu führen, wobei er durch die Berichterstattung der genannten Historiker die in der griechischen Historiographie fehlende Erwähnung der Juden zu ergänzen suchte. Dieser Altersnachweis war für den jüdischen Historiker ein Fixpunkt seines Denkens, weil im Altertum das hohe Alter, z.B. eines Volkes oder einer Religion, als besondere Auszeichnung angesehen wurde, denn wer als Epigone nur überkommene Vorbilder nachahmt, galt als minderwertig.[1]

– Ferner wollte Josephus gewisse gegen sein Volk gerichtete historische Überlieferungen widerlegen und als haltlos entlarven, die die Juden in ein wenig vorteilhaftes Licht rückten. Beispielsweise konnte man in der Antike bei verschiedenen Historikern eine ganz und gar nicht schmeichelhafte Schilderung des jüdischen Exodus aus Ägypten lesen, nach der die von Moses geführte Schar eine Gruppe von Aussätzigen und Unreinen war, die auf göttlichen Befehl vom ägyptischen Pharao aus dem Land vertrieben wurde.

Besonders wichtig für die vorliegende Studie ist nun, daß Josephus es für notwendig erachtete, seine Verteidigung der historischen Tradition vom hohen Alter des jüdischen Volkes sowie den Nachweis der Zuverlässigkeit der biblischen Nachrichten über den Auszug aus Ägypten in die Form einer regelrechten quellenkundlichen Untersuchung zu kleiden.[2] Er unternahm es dabei, den Wert und die Richtigkeit der einzelnen, bei nicht-jüdischen Autoren erhaltenen Informationen zu erhärten oder zu falsifizieren, indem er die verschiedenen Quellen gegeneinander abwog und in seiner Beweisführung miteinander verglich, wobei er an lange Zitate der relevanten Quellenpassagen anknüpfte. Es muß in diesem Zusammenhang betont werden, daß Josephus seine Gedanken ausdrücklich in das sprachliche Gewand einer Gerichtsrede hüllte, wie sie von Rhetoren für Prozesse vor griechischen Gerichtshöfen entwickelt worden war und zu der u.a. das Abwägen, Hinterfragen oder Widerlegen von Zeugenaussagen gehörten. Auf der Folie solcher Prozeßreden gestaltete Josephus dann seine Auseinandersetzung mit den historischen Quellen,[3] weswegen man in seiner Schrift unbestreitbare Parallelen zu einer gerichtlichen Verteidigungsrede wahrnehmen kann.[4] Daher werden

---

[1] Schäublin 1982, 318; Cancik 1986, 53; Pilhofer 1990, 193–200.

[2] Vgl. hierzu die Bemerkungen von Cohen (1988, 1–11), der zu der Schrift *Contra Apionem* bemerkt "that the work is basically an extended essay on historiography," ebd. 3 s. ferner 4–5.

[3] Kasher 1996, 170–72; Barclay 1998, 196–97.

[4] Gerber 1997, 80. Die kritische Zeugenbefragung gehörte zum Repertoire des Gerichtsredners. Sie wurde in den einschlägigen Handbüchern als wichtiges Hilfsmittel für die Prozeßpsychologie gelehrt, nicht aber als Methode zur kritischen Würdigung literarischer Quellen, s. Apsines 11 (Spengel 1894, 296,1–12); Quintilian *Inst.* 5.7 (Russel 2001, 340–45).

die Quellentexte von Josephus auch wie bei Gericht aufgerufene
Zeugen behandelt und wie bei einer Beweisaufnahme ins Kreuzverhör
genommen. Die Schrift *Contra Apionem* stellt überdies ein hervorragendes Beispiel für das quellenkritische Vorgehen des Josephus dar
und belegt dessen Bedingtheit durch die polemisch zugespitzte
Verteidigung der jüdischen Religion. Es soll an dieser Stelle nicht
unerwähnt bleiben, daß der jüdische Historiker in seinen *Jüdischen
Altertümern* teilweise dieselben nicht-jüdischen Geschichtsschreiber
des alten Orients als zusätzliche, glaubwürdige Zeugen zitierte, in
deren Werken sich bestimmte, in der Bibel bezeugte Ereignisse in
Parallelüberlieferungen belegen lassen. Seine Auseinandersetzung
unterscheidet sich jedoch erheblich von der Argumentation in
Contra Apionem, wo er Autoren wie Manetho, Berossos oder die phönikischen Geschichtsschreiber ausdrücklich als seine Zeugen (μάρτυς) anführt und auf ihren Wahrheitsgehalt befragt.[5] So fügt Josephus in
seine Schrift sogar expressis verbis die Bemerkung ein, daß er den
Geschichtsschreiber Manetho gleichsam wie einen lebendigen Men-
schen in den Zeugenstand aufrufe, um dessen Darstellung zu analy-
sieren (*Apion* 1.74). In dieser Formulierung zeigt sich deutlich die
Vorgehensweise des Josephus, die auf eine kritische Befragung und
Überprüfung des Quellenmaterials abzielte. In den bisherigen Ausführungen dürfte bereits deutlich geworden sein, daß Josephus sein
Plädoyer für das Judentum und dessen religiöse Überzeugungen mit
einer eingehenden und methodisch wohlüberlegten Analyse bestimmter
Mitteilungen der betreffenden Historiker des alten Orients unter-
mauerte, was nun am Beispiel der Texte, die das alte Ägypten
betreffen, untersucht werden soll. Die obengenannten Autoren und
ihre Erörterung durch Josephus eignen sich in ausgezeichneter Weise
als Grundlage für unsere Untersuchung, da sich mit ihrer Hilfe der
eigentümliche, methodische Umgang des Josephus mit diesen Geschichts-
dokumenten zeigen läßt. Ferner werden die Gemeinsamkeiten und
Unterschiede zu einigen paganen Schriftstellern augenfällig, die ebenfalls ein großes Interesse an der ägyptischen Geschichtsüberlieferung
und ihren Urkunden wie z.B. den beeindruckenden Steininschriften

---

[5] *Apion* 1.4 "χρήσομαι ... μάρτυσι"; 1.59 "μαρτυρίας ... παρέξω"; 1.70 "μάλιστα
δὴ χρήσομαι μάρτυσιν"; 1.112 "παραθήσομαι μάρτυρα" 1.115 und 1.116; vgl. zu dieser
Methode Schäublin 1982, 322; Conzelmann 1981, 207; Cancik 1986, 48 Anm. 38;
Gerber 1997, 79–82. Auch Plutarch kennt die Formulierung, sich mit Hilfe von
Plato als seinem "Zeugen" (μάρτυρα) zu verteidigen, Mor. 435F (Babbitt 1969, 486).

auf den Wänden der Tempelanlagen hatten, sich aber in ihrem Umgang mit dem überlieferten Material signifikant von Josephus unterscheiden. Demnach handelt es sich bei dieser Beschränkung unserer Untersuchung auf die Auseinandersetzung des Josephus mit der ägyptischen Geschichtsliteratur in griechischer Sprache um eine heuristische Zuspitzung, denn auf diesem Weg läßt sich gerade im Vergleich mit paganen Autoren das methodische Bewußtsein des Josephus erhellen und in seiner polemischen Verwurzelung zum Vorschein bringen.

Josephus Auseinandersetzung mit der griechisch-römischen Historiographie über Ägypten

Befassen wir uns also zuerst mit den Erörterungen der Geschichtsschreiber des alten Ägyptens in *Contra Apionem*:

– Josephus betont in den Passagen, in denen er auf den Altersbeweis für das Judentum zu sprechen kommt, zuerst das hohe Alter der nicht-griechischen, historischen Quellen, wobei er sich an eine unter den Griechen verbreitete Hochschätzung der ununterbrochenen und bis in frühe Zeit zurückreichenden Geschichtsschreibung der Ägypter anlehnt.[6] Nach Josephus legten auch die Juden ebenso wie andere orientalische Völker großen Wert auf eine genaue Dokumentation ihrer Geschichte (*Apion* 1.29).[7]
– Des weiteren erhebt Josephus den übereinstimmenden Gehalt der ihm vorliegenden Nachrichten über dieselben Ereignisse zum Wahrheitskriterium und führt mit Hilfe dieser inhaltlichen Konvergenz seinen Beweis. Deshalb bemüht er sich, seine Quellen sorgfältig aufzuführen und miteinander zu vergleichen, wobei er die divergierenden Darstellungen derselben Begebenheiten bei seinen griechischen Zeitgenossen kritisiert (*Apion* 1.26). Nach seiner Ansicht bestätigen die Nachrichten Manethos über den Einfall der Hyksos und ihre Herrschaft über Ägypten den biblischen Exodusbericht und verhelfen zu einer genauen zeitlichen Einordnung dieses Ereignisses im Rahmen der ägyptischen Geschichte.[8]

---

[6] Vgl. z.B. Plato *Tim.* 22b–c; s. dazu Cancik 1986, 47 und Feldman 1993, 179.
[7] Vgl. Hay 1979, 94; O'Neill 1999, 272.
[8] Aziza 1987, 42, 48, 50.

– Josephus bemüht sich überdies um eine Bewertung und Klassifikation
  seiner Quellen. Besonders hoch schätzte er, entsprechend der
  Gepflogenheit zeitgenössischer, griechischer Historiker,[9] die Aufzeichnungen von Augenzeugen (*Apion* 1.45–47, 54–55). Außerdem
  erwähnt er die judenfeindliche Haltung der Ägypter, weil deren
  Vorurteile jede projüdische Voreingenommenheit ausschlössen und
  ihre historischen Erinnerungen besonders vertrauenswürdig machen
  (*Apion* 1.70–71).
– Von Bedeutung ist auch, daß der jüdische Historiker seine Vorlagen
  mit genauer Stellenangabe zitiert. Für die ägyptischen Geschichtsschreiber bildet der Priester Manetho seine Hauptquelle (*Apion*
  1.73), wobei er ausdrücklich hervorhebt, die ägyptischen Original-
  dokumente nur in der Übersetzung dieses Autors gelesen zu haben.[10]
– Josephus beschäftigt sich gleichfalls mit der inneren Wahrschein-
  lichkeit der Berichte (*Apion* 1.83) und führt im Werk des Manetho
  eine Quellenscheidung zwischen dem chronologischen Gerüst alt-
  ägyptischer Königslisten und den von Manetho in diesen Rahmen
  eingefügten Erzählungen unklarer Herkunft durch. Dabei gelangt
  er zu dem Ergebnis, daß diese sagenhaften Überlieferungen in vielen Fällen weit weniger glaubwürdig als die chronologischen Notizen
  sind (*Apion* 1.105).[11]
– Darüber hinaus ist Josephus bemüht, auf der Basis der ägyptischen Quellen eine möglichst exakte Chronologie der altorientalischen Geschichte zu erarbeiten und versucht, die griechische
  Geschichte, beginnend mit dem troianischen Krieg, darin einzuord-
  nen, um dann über diesen Umweg außerbiblischer Quellen seine
  Behauptung vom hohen Alter des jüdischen Volkes zu erhärten
  (*Apion* 1.103).

Mit derselben Zielsetzung, wie er sie im Bezug auf die ägyptischen
Historiker verfolgte, bearbeitete Josephus auch die phönikischen
Chroniken (*Apion* 1.106, 116–127) sowie die Nachrichten des baby-

---

[9] Polybius kritisierte z.B. die Büchergelehrsamkeit eines *Timaios*, Polybius 12.27
(Dindorf, Buettner-Wobst 1962, 228 / Drexler 1979, 825): "Wer aus Büchern
schöpft, braucht keine Strapazen auf sich zu nehmen, setzt sich keiner Gefahr aus";
dazu Pédech 1961, 145; Avenarius 1956, 37, 78; Meister 1975, 44, 47.
[10] Josephus nennt die ägyptischen Quellen Manethos "ἐκ δέλτων ἱερῶν," *Apion*
1.73, "ἱεραῖς . . . βίβλοις," *Apion* 1.91 oder "ἱερῶν γραμμάτων," *Apion* 1.228 vgl 1.105.
[11] s. auch Verbrugghe, Wickersham 1996, 106.

Ionischen Mardukpriesters Berossos (*Apion* 1.128),[12] um das hohe Alter seines Volkes zu beweisen. Den Erörterungen des Josephus, die die phönikische und babylonische Geschichte betreffen, kann aber in dieser Untersuchung nicht weiter nachgegangen werden. Ebenso würde die Analyse der langen Liste griechischer Schriftsteller und ihrer Zeugnisse über das Judentum, die Josephus sodann anführt (*Apion* 1.161–218), über das Thema der vorliegenden Studie weit hinausgehen.

Josephus Widerlegung der ägyptischen Berichte über den jüdischen Exodus aus Ägypten

Blicken wir nun auf diejenigen Abschnitte von *Contra Apionem*, in denen Josephus sich kritisch mit der ägyptischen Darstellung des jüdischen Exodus auseinandersetzt. Aus diesen Teilen seiner Verteidigungsschrift lassen sich nämlich mehrere Gesichtspunkte erheben, die für die Darlegungen des Josephus in inhaltlich-methodischer Hinsicht leitend waren und eine deutliche Parallele zu seiner Beweisführung bilden, mit der er das hohe Alter des jüdischen Volkes belegen wollte:

– Um seine Leser zu überzeugen, führt Josephus wiederum lange Zitate insbesondere aus dem Geschichtswerk Manethos an und widerlegt dann eingehend dessen ägyptische Version des Exodus, nach der Moses und die ihn begleitenden Israeliten Unreine und Leprakranke waren, die vom ägyptischen Pharao auf göttliches Geheiß des Landes verwiesen wurden.[13] Diese Angaben Manethos, die wie ein polemisch verzerrtes Gegenbild der biblischen Überlieferung wirken, weist Josephus als haltlos zurück, dadurch daß er seinen Lesern detailliert ihre mangelnde inhaltliche Stringenz vor Augen führt (*Apion* 1.252). Auch in diesem Fall muß es unterbleiben, die zahlreichen Belege, mit deren Hilfe Josephus diesen Nachweis erbringt, ausführlich zu diskutieren.

---

[12] Wieder hebt Josephus den wörtlichen Charakter seiner Zitate hervor, *Apion* 1.134 und macht genaue Angaben über deren Herkunft z.B. "ἐν τῇ τρίτῃ βίβλῳ τῶν Χαλδαϊκῶν," *Apion* 1.142; zur Person des Berossos s. Schnabel 1923, 1–9; Sterling 1992, 104–9; Verbrugghe, Wickersham 1996, 13–34; vgl. ferner auch Stern 1976, I.55.

[13] Aziza 1987, 47.

– Es soll aber noch einmal hervorgehoben werden, daß Josephus
  zwischen dem chronologischen Rahmen im Geschichtswerk Manethos, dem er historische Zuverlässigkeit zubilligt, und den legendären
  Erzählungen wie der von der Vertreibung der Unreinen und
  Leprakranken unterschieden hat und nur diese sagenhafte Geschichte
  entschieden bekämpft. Die Strategie des Josephus bestand also
  darin, seinem griechisch-römischen Publikum vor Augen zu führen,
  daß eben diese Erzählungen ungenau oder sogar frei erfunden
  seien. Josephus ist bei seiner Bewertung der erzählerischen Einschübe
  im Werk des Manetho allerdings nicht ganz konsequent, denn er
  akzeptiert Manethos Schilderung der Invasion und Fremdherrschaft
  der Hyksos als vertrauenswürdigen Beleg für die Zuverlässigkeit
  der biblischen Berichte über den Aufenthalt des Volkes Israel in
  Ägypten, ohne in diesem Vorgehen einen Widerspruch zu seiner
  Kritik an der ägyptischen Exodustradition zu sehen.
– Abschließend sei noch darauf hingewiesen, daß Josephus noch
  weitere Autoren kritisch hinterfragte, die eine ähnliche Exo-
  dusüberlieferung wie Manetho in ihre Werke aufgenommen hatten.[14] Er nennt in diesem Zusammenhang ausdrücklich den
  ägyptischen Priester und stoischen Philosophen Chaeremon (*Apion*
  1.288–303),[15] den Geschichtsschreiber Lysimachus[16] sowie den
  alexandrinischen Grammatiker und Homerforscher Apion,[17] gegen
  den sich seine Streitschrift in besonderem Maße richtete. Auch
  diese Berichte weist Josephus entschieden zurück, indem er ihre
  Ungereimtheiten und gegenseitigen Widersprüche ausführlich nach-
  zeichnet.

---

[14] Zur Biographie Manethos und der historischen Situation, in der er unter den
Königen Ptolemaius I Soter und Ptolemaius Philadelphos (308–246 v.Chr.) seine
Werke verfaßte, s. Kind 1930, insbes. 1060–62; Thissen 1980, 1180–81; Müller
1877, 120–25; Momigliano 1931, 491–92; Sterling 1992, 117–35; Troiani 1977, 87;
Schürer 1986, 595–97; Aziza 1987, 48; Verbrugghe, Wickersham 1996, 95–102.
[15] Vgl. Frg. 1 bei Schwyzer 1932, 26–27; Frg. 1 bei van der Horst 1984, 8–9;
Nr. 178 bei Stern 1976, I.417–21; zu Chaeremon s. Schwyzer 1932, 9–12; Aziza
1987, 60; Frede 1989, 2068–69. Zur Person Chaeremons und seiner Karriere vgl.
Schwartz 1899, 2026–27; van der Horst 1984, IX–X; Barzanò 1985, 1981–92.
[16] *Apion* 1.304–319 (= Stern 1976, Nr. 158, I.382–86); zu Lysimachus s. Gudeman
1930, 35; Schürer 1986, 600–601; Aziza 1987, 56; Feldman 1993, 140, 193.
[17] Schürer 1986, 604–7.

Die historische Methode des Josephus

Betrachtet man nun die bisher skizzierte Arbeitsweise des Josephus und seine Auswertung der historischen Quellen in der Schrift *Contra Apionem*, so zeigt sich, wie er durch überlegtes methodisches Vorgehen einem heidnischen Leserkreis die Geschichte seines Volkes auf biblischer Grundlage zu vermitteln und dabei sein Urteil sowohl durch eine transparente Beweisführung als auch durch eine nachvollziehbare Quellenkritik zu bekräftigen suchte.

- In seiner Apologie machte Josephus wohl aus diesem Grund seine Vorlagen namhaft, zitierte die von ihm besprochenen Texte der Geschichtswerke und überprüfte mit Hilfe seiner quellenkritischen Überlegungen deren Glaubwürdigkeit.
- Ferner bewertete er die Inhalte dieser Texte, befaßte sich mit der Beweiskraft und Schlüssigkeit ihrer Überlieferungen und verglich sie nicht nur miteinander, sondern gerade auch mit möglichen Parallelen in den heiligen Schriften der Juden, um so deren Glaubwürdigkeit mit Hilfe der altorientalischen Geschichtsüberlieferung über jeden Zweifel erhaben zu machen.

Die griechisch-römische Auseinandersetzung mit der Ägyptischen Geschichte im vergleich mit Contra Apionem

Vergleicht man die Arbeitsweise des Josephus und seine Quellenanalyse mit den Zeugnissen paganer Autoren der griechisch-römischen Zeit, die sich ebenfalls mit der ägyptischen Geschichte beschäftigt haben, dann lassen sich evidente Divergenzen wohl kaum bestreiten, die jedoch höchst aufschlußreich sind, um das Vorgehen des Josephus zu verstehen. Darum ist nun diesen Schriftstellern unsere Aufmerksamkeit zuzuwenden, denn sie interessierten sich durchaus für die altägyptische Geschichte und waren sich des hohen Wertes der ununterbrochenen und lange Zeiträume umfassenden, historischen Überlieferung dieses Landes wohl bewußt. Sie billigten den Ägyptern sogar eine längere Geschichtstradition als den Griechen selbst zu und waren z.B. durchaus bereit, die in den homerischen Epen überlieferten Geschehnisse mit Hilfe der ägyptischen Geschichtsdarstellung zu korrigieren. Untersucht man jedoch diese literarischen Zeugnisse genauer, die sich mit der ägyptischen Geschichte befassen, so reflektieren sie eindeutig eine andere Gewichtung und Bewertung der

Quellen und weichen deutlich vom methodischen Vorgehen des
Josephus und der ihn auszeichnenden Arbeitsweise ab. Ein auf-
schlußreiches Beispiel, das die Unterschiede zu Josephus transparent
werden läßt, stellen m.E. die Nachrichten Herodots dar, der ausführlich über den angeblichen Ägyptenaufenthalt der von Paris ent-
führten Helena erzählt. Auch aus der Homerkritik in der 11. Rede
des Dio Chrysostomus lassen sich wichtige Erkenntnisse gewinnen.

Herodots Darstellung der Rolle Ägyptens im troianischen Krieg

Beginnen wir also mit Herodot: Der griechische Geschichtsschreiber,
der weite Reisen durch die damals bekannte Welt unternahm, berich-
tete in seinen berühmten Historien eingehend über die Geogra-
phie Ägyptens, dessen fremde Kultur und Religion sowie über die
ägyptische Geschichte. In diesem Zusammenhang bemühte er sich
bewußt um eine Einordnung der von ihm geschilderten Ereignisse
im Rahmen der griechischen, historischen Tradition und schenkte
darum dem Verhältnis ägyptischer, historischer Erinnerungen zu den
homerischen Epen und zur Geschichte des troianischen Kriegs besondere Beachtung.[18] In dem Ägypten behandelnden Teil seines Werks
beruft sich Herodot neben eigenen Beobachtungen mehrfach auf
seine Gespräche mit ägyptischen Priestern.[19] Sie vermittelten ihm
nach seinem Bekunden eine bemerkenswerte Variante der Geschichte
von der Entführung der Helena, die von der Darstellung Homers
wesentlich abweicht.[20] So berichteten seine ägyptischen Gewährsleute,
daß Paris, nachdem er Helena entführt hatte, auf der Rückreise von
Sparta nach Troia durch ungünstige Winde nach Ägypten verschlagen
wurde. Dort entkamen einige seiner Sklaven in ein nahes Tempelasyl
und denunzierten Paris wegen seiner Tat. Auf diesem Weg habe der
Pharao erfahren, daß ein Fremder das Gastrecht in Griechenland
verletzt habe, die Frau seines dortigen Gastfreundes Menelaos und
dessen Schätze geraubt habe und nun nach Ägypten gekommen sei.
Dieser Pharao mit Namen Proteus[21] habe daraufhin Paris befohlen,
Helena und das geraubte Gut in Ägypten zurückzulassen, und Paris

---

[18] Szarmach 1978, 195; Bichler 2000, 188.
[19] z.B. *Hist.* 2.116 (Legrand 1948, 142); 118 (Legrand 1948, 143).
[20] *Hist.* 2.112–119 (Legrand 1948, 139–44).
[21] Herter 1957, 953–55.

sei allein nach Troia zurückgekehrt. Dort belagerten und eroberten die Griechen die Stadt, denn sie schenkten den Beteuerungen der Troianer, daß Helena nicht bei ihnen sei, keinen Glauben.[22] Erst nach der Einnahme der Stadt hätten die Griechen erkannt, daß die Troianer die Wahrheit gesagt hätten, und daraufhin sei Menelaos nach Ägypten gesegelt und habe vom Pharao Helena mit seinem geraubten Vermögen zurückerhalten. Menelaos dankte seinem ägyptischen Gastgeber diese großmütige Geste aber schlecht, denn als günstige Winde für die Heimreise ausblieben, habe er zwei ägyptische Kinder geopfert und sei nach diesem Verbrechen nur knapp nach Libyen entkommen. An diese Erzählung, die ihm, wie Herodot hervorhob, von ägyptischen Priestern übermittelt wurde, knüpft er die erste uns bekannte Homerkritik in der griechischen Literatur an.[23] In dieser Kritik plädiert er dafür, daß Homer, "diese Historien wohl gekannt hat, aber weil sie in sein Epos nicht so gut paßt wie die andere Sage von der Helena, hat er sie absichtlich übergangen. Trotzdem verrät er, daß sie ihm bekannt ist."[24] Diese These versuchte Herodot mit Hilfe einiger Stellen aus der Ilias zu stützen, die einen Ägyptenbesuch Helenas vorauszusetzen scheinen.

Diese Nachrichten Herodots sind, wie von verschiedenen Forschern angenommen wird, in ihrem Kern durchaus vertrauenswürdig und könnten in der Tat auf seine Gespräche mit ägyptischen Priestern zurückgehen.[25] Die Ägypter waren nämlich, als Herodot das Land bereiste, schon seit Generationen mit griechischen Händlern, Söldnern und Siedlern in Kontakt gekommen, die in der Hafenstadt Naukratis wohnten, die ihnen unter dem Pharao Amasis ca. 560 v. Chr. als Handelsplatz bestimmt worden war.[26] Durch die Anwesenheit der

---

[22] Kaiser 1969, 257–58.

[23] Lloyd 1988, 50.

[24] *Hist.* 2.116 (Legrand 1948, 142): "Δοκέει δέ μοι καὶ Ὅμηρος τὸν λόγον τοῦτον πυθέσθαι· ἀλλ', οὐ γὰρ ὁμοίως ἐς τὴν ἐποποιίην εὐπρεπὴς ἦν τῷ ἑτέρῳ τῷ περ ἐχρήσατο, [ἐς δ'] μετῆκε αὐτόν, δηλώσας ὡς καὶ τοῦτον ἐπίσταιτο τὸν λόγον."

[25] Herodot schöpfte keineswegs nur aus griechischen Quellen wie Hekataios, vgl. Diels 1887, 443–44; Fehling 1971, 62–64; Lloyd 1988, 47, dessen Ausführungen über Ägypten ohnehin nur höchst fragmentarisch überliefert sind, Kannicht 1969, 43–44. Herodot kombinierte wohl sagenhafte und volkstümliche Überlieferungen, die in der ägyptischen Literatur tatsächlich vorhanden waren, durch Papyrusfunde bezeugt sind und von den Priestern allerdings mündlich wiedergegeben wurden, Evans 1991, 137–38; Erbse 1991, 134–36; vgl. auch Mendels 1990, 91, 101, 110. Beispiele solcher Erzählungen in demotischen Papyri aus griechisch-römischer Zeit analysiert Hoffmann 2000, 205–7; vgl. ferner Verbrugghe, Wickersham 1996, 103–15.

[26] Helck 1975, 10; s. ferner Spiegelberg 1926, 12–15; Froidefond 1971, 179–81.

Griechen könnte die Geschichte des troianischen Kriegs nach Ägypten
gelangt sein, und es ist nicht verwunderlich, daß sie der Priesterschaft
bekannt war,[27] die sie ihrerseits mit deutlich antigriechischer Spitze
umformulierte,[28] wie das Kinderopfer des Menelaos zeigt[29] und an
Herodot weitergaben. Es ist überdies mit einer gründlichen Redaktion
dieser mündlichen Mitteilungen durch Herodot zu rechnen.[30]

Die Homerkritik des Dio Chrysostomus und die ägyptische
Geschichtsüberlieferung

Wichtig für unsere Untersuchung ist aber, daß Herodot nicht der
einzige griechische Autor war, der die ägyptische Geschichtstradition
als Korrektiv der eigenen, historischen Überlieferung und speziell der
homerischen Epen benutzte. Unter seinen zahlreichen Nachfolgern
ist vor allem der Redner Dio Chrysostomus zu erwähnen. Er kannte
zweifellos den Bericht des Herodot und orientierte sich an ihm als
seinem literarischen Vorbild. Es war wohl sein Ziel, die Homerkritik
Herodots an Umfang und Grundsätzlichkeit noch zu übertreffen,
denn er bemühte sich um eine systematische Widerlegung von Homers
Schilderung des troianischen Kriegs und präsentierte seinen Lesern
einen ganz anderen, alternativen Kriegsverlauf.[31] Nach Dio wurde
Helena nie von Paris entführt, sondern wurde ihm von ihrem Vater
zur Frau gegeben. Der griechische Angriff auf Troia war demnach
nicht gerechtfertigt. Auch wollten die Troianer Helena natürlich nicht
an die Griechen ausliefern. Der Schlachtverlauf war ebenfalls ein
ganz anderer als ihn Homer darstellte: So wurde Achill von Hektor
getötet und nicht umgekehrt, wie in der Ilias geschildert. Die Gestalt
von Achills besten Freund, Patroklos, sei eine pure Erfindung Homers.

---

[27] Lloyd 1975, 109; Kendrick Pritchett 1993, 68.
[28] Plutarch polemisierte später gegen Herodot, der an dieser Stelle seine Voreingenommenheit gegenüber den Ägyptern offenbare, Mor. 857A–B (Cuvigny/ Lachenaud
1981, 146), s. Froidefond 1971, 179; Smelik, Hemelrijk 1984, 1873–74. Plutarchs
Kritik an Herodot, die zahlreiche Widersprüche nachzuweisen versucht, ist dabei
aber oft "ungerecht, mangelhaft," s. Ziegler 1952, 871; Kaiser 1969, 254.
[29] Herter 1957, 954; Legrand 1948, 33; Froidefond 1971, 181. Sie bemühten
sich möglicherweise bewußt, eine Verbindung zwischen griechischen Sagen und ihrer
historischen Erinnerung und mythischen Tradition herzustellen, Mortley 1978, 321.
[30] s. dazu Evans 1991, 138–39.
[31] *Troj.* 11.43–124. Eine Gegenüberstellung von Ausführungen Dios und Herodots
mit einer Diskussion ihrer Abhängigkeit enthält Hagen 1887, 47–49.

Im Gegensatz zu Ilias brachen die Griechen nach Dio die Belagerung Troias erfolglos ab und erreichten nach blutigen und verlustreichen Kämpfen einzig und allein einen Friedensvertrag mit den Troianern. Das hölzerne Pferd war demzufolge keine Kriegslist sondern ein Versöhnungsopfer für Athene. Die ganze Beweisführung Dios zielt also auf die Darlegung der Unwahrheit der homerischen Dichtung und auf ihre Richtigstellung durch die wahre Geschichte des troianischen Kriegs.[32]

Der für uns wichtige Punkt ist aber, daß Dio den Kern der Rede, d.h. die Schilderung des tatsächlichen Kriegsverlaufs, wie Herodot einem ägyptischen Priester in den Mund legt:

> Ich will nun berichten, was ich bei den ägyptischen Priestern von einem hochbetagten Greis in Onuphis erfahren habe. Er machte sich unter vielem anderen darüber lustig, daß die Griechen in den meisten Dingen nicht Bescheid wüßten, und als schlagenden Beweis führte er an, daß sie davon überzeugt seien, Agamemnon habe Troia eingenommen und Helena habe sich noch als Gattin des Menelaos in Paris verliebt. Und davon seien sie getäuscht durch einen einzigen Mann, so fest überzeugt, daß sie einzeln darauf schwören würden.[33]

Als Beweis für seine Behauptungen habe sich dieser Priester aus dem Gau Onuphis auf Inschriften in ägyptischen Tempeln berufen,[34] die die Zeiten überdauert und wichtige historische Ereignisse für die Nachwelt bezeugt hätten:

> Er erzählte mir, daß die ganze Vergangenheit bei ihnen aufgeschrieben sei, zum Teil in den Tempeln, zum Teil auf gewissen Säulen. Manches habe sich auch nur im Gedächtnis weniger Leute gehalten, wenn die Säulen zerstört worden seien, und vieles von dem, was auf den Säulen verzeichnet sei, finde aus Unkenntnis und Gleichgültigkeit der Nachwelt keinen Glauben mehr. Unter den jüngsten Eintragungen befänden sich auch die Ereignisse um Troia. Menelaos sei nämlich zu ihnen gekommen und habe berichtet, wie sich alles zugetragen habe.[35]

---

[32] Desideri 1978, 431; Jones 1978, 17; Bolonyai 2001, 29.

[33] *Troj.* 11.37 (Cohoon 1971, 474): "Ἐγὼ οὖν ὡς ἐπυθόμην παρὰ τῶν ἐν Αἰγύπτῳ ἱερέων ἑνὸς εὖ μάλα γέροντος ἐν τῇ Ὀνούφι, ἄλλα τε πολλὰ τῶν Ἑλλήνων καταγελῶντος ὡς οὐθὲν εἰδότων ἀληθὲς περὶ τῶν πλείστων, καὶ μάλιστα δὴ τεκμηρίῳ τούτῳ χρωμένου ὅτι Τροίαν τέ εἰσι πεπεισμένοι ὡς ἁλοῦσαν ὑπὸ Ἀγαμέμνονος καὶ ὅτι Ἑλένη συνοικοῦσα Μενελάῳ ἠράσθη Ἀλεξάνδρου· καὶ ταῦτα οὕτως ἄγαν πεπεισμένοι εἰσὶν ὑφ᾽ ἑνὸς ἀνδρὸς ἐξαπατηθέντες ὥστε καὶ ὀμόσαι ἕκαστος." Übersetzung: Elliger 1967, 184.

[34] Kees 1939, 529–30.

[35] *Troj.* 11.38 (Cohoon 1971, 474): "Ἔφη δὲ πᾶσαν τὴν πρότερον ἱστορίαν γεγράφθαι παρ᾽ αὐτοῖς, τὴν μὲν ἐν τοῖς ἱεροῖς, τὴν δ᾽ ἐν στήλαις τισί, τὰ δὲ μνημονεύεσθαι

Diese inschriftlich aufgezeichneten Erzählungen des Menelaos habe
der Priester nach Dio dann mit einer nachdrücklichen Kritik an
Homer verbunden, wobei seine Bemerkung, Helena sei "zwar von
Paris entführt, dann aber hierher zu uns nach Ägypten gekommen,"[36]
wohl auf Herodot anspielt. Vermutlich ist die Begegnung des Dio
mit dem Priester nur eine literarische Fiktion des Redners,[37] der sich
dabei an den in der Antike verbreiteten Topos des weisen, ägyptischen Priesters anlehnte und sich von Vorbildern wie Herodots
Geschichtswerk leiten ließ. Im Gegensatz zu Herodot dürfte sich Dio
nämlich wohl kaum die Mühe gemacht haben, für seine Rede in
ägyptischen Tempeln Erkundigungen einzuholen, sondern er stützte
sich eher auf das in der griechischen Literatur im Gefolge Herodots
bereits verbreitete Bild von der gelehrten, ägyptischen Priesterschaft
und ihren historischen Aufzeichnungen.[38] Diesen Topos setzte er
geschickt ein, um seine eigene Homerkritik durch das uralte Geschichts-
wissen der Ägypter zu rechtfertigen und seine Sicht der Ereignisse
gegen jeden Zweifel erhaben zu machen.[39] Überprüft man nämlich
seine alternative Version des troianischen Kriegs, was in dieser Studie
allerdings nicht umfassend geleistet werden kann, so zeigen sich in
ihr keine Beziehungen zu Ägypten und der dortigen Tempelgelehr-
samkeit.[40] Dio schöpfte vielmehr allein aus den homerischen Epen

---

μόνον ὑπ' ὀλίγων, τῶν στηλῶν διαφθαρεισῶν, πολλὰ δὲ καὶ ἀπιστεῖσθαι τῶν ἐν ταῖς
στήλαις γεγραμμένων διὰ τὴν ἀμαθίαν τε καὶ ἀμέλειαν τῶν ἐπιγιγνομένων· εἶναι δὲ
καὶ ταῦτα ἐν τοῖς νεωτάτοις τὰ περὶ τὴν Τροίαν· τὸν γὰρ Μεινέλαον ἀφικέσθαι παρ'
αὐτοὺς καὶ διηγήσασθαι ἅπαντα ὡς ἐγένετο." Übersetzung: Elliger 1967, 184.

[36] *Troj.* 11.41 (Cohoon 1971, 476): "ἄλλοι δέ τινες, ὡς ἁρπασθείη μὲν Ἑλένη ὑπὸ
τοῦ Ἀλεξάνδρου, δεῦρο δὲ παρ' ἡμᾶς εἰς Αἴγυπτον ἀφίκοιτο." Übersetzung: Elliger
1967, 185.

[37] Vgl. v. Arnim (1898, 184) der bemerkt: "Anfänglich wird die Fiction durchge-
führt, daß der Priester dem Dio die Geschichte erzählt. (. . .) Im weiteren Verlauf
der Rede tritt diese Einkleidung mehr in den Hintergrund. Es wird nicht mehr
zwischen der Person des Priesters und Dios unterschieden." Kindstrand (1973, 142)
konstatiert, daß durch die Einführung des Priesters, "die Darstellung teils von einer
scheinbaren Objektivität, teils von einer alten unwiderlegbaren Weisheit geprägt ist."

[38] Fuchs (1996, 133) die von einem "fiktiven" Gewährsmann spricht. Die These
von Fuchs, die gesamte Rede "nicht als ernstgemeint, sondern im ursprünglichen
Sinne des Wortes als ironisch aufzufassen", ebd. 135, erscheint hingegen als wenig
fundiert. Es bleibt aber festzuhalten, daß Dio sich wohl bewußt an Herodots
Darstellung als seinem Vorbild orientierte, ebd. 134–35.

[39] Kindstrand 1973, 141 Anm. 104 mit Hinweis auf Plato, *Tim.* 21e; vgl. Mesk
1920/21, 122.

[40] Bolonyai 2001, 33: ". . . what he offers is not the product of a historian's investigation . . . ."

und erschloß aus den Ungereimtheiten und Widersprüchen des homerischen Textes den seiner Meinung nach tatsächlichen, von Homer
aber verschwiegenen Ablauf der Ereignisse.[41]

Josephus und die homerkritische Adaptation der ägyptischen
Geschichtsschreibung durch Herodot und Dio Chrysostomus

Vergleichen wir nun die zuvor analysierten Notizen Herodots und
auch die Rede des Dio Chrysostomus mit der apologetisch ausgerichteten Argumentation des Josephus in seiner Schrift *Contra Apionem*,
so sind aufschlußreiche und in der Forschung kaum beachtete Über-
einstimmungen und Unterschiede festzustellen:

– Zunächst ist darauf hinzuweisen, daß Josephus die homerkriti-
  schen Stimmen in der griechischen Literatur sehr genau kannte
  und sogar mitzuteilen wußte, daß Homer seine Dichtung zuerst
  nur mündlich tradiert habe und die verstreuten Lieder erst später
  zu einem Werk vereint worden seien: "Und deswegen habe es
  zahlreiche Ungereimtheiten in sich."[42] Mit der Erwähnung dieser
  Widersprüche (διαφωνίαι) macht Josephus auf dieselben inhaltlichen
  Divergenzen innerhalb der homerischen Epen aufmerksam, auf die
  auch Dio Chrysostomus das Augenmerk seiner Leser gerichtet
  hatte und die er mit seiner radikalen Theorie zu beheben suchte.
– Das Geschichtswerk Herodots war Josephus ebenfalls vertraut,
  denn er erwähnt nicht nur Manethos Kritik an Herodots Ägyp-
  tendarstellung (*Apion* 1.73), sondern setzt sich auch eingehend mit
  einem Abschnitt auseinander, in dem Herodot die Sitte der
  Beschneidung in Syrien beschrieb, was Josephus als Anspielung
  auf die Juden wertete (*Apion* 1.168–171).
– Josephus war ferner mit dem in der griechischen Literatur verbreiteten Motiv bekannt, bestimmte weise Ägypter wie die Tempel-
  priester als Quelle historischer Informationen über die Geschichte
  des alten Orients wie u.a. des Judentums anzuführen, und er
  setzte sich mit dieser Form der Legitimation von geschicht-
  lichem Wissen kritisch auseinander. Der Judengegner Apion, den
  Josephus vor allem im zweiten Buch seiner Verteidigungsschrift

---

[41] Kindstrand 1973, 142; Bolonyai 2001, 33; vgl. auch del Cerro Calderón 1997,
104–5.
[42] *Apion* 1.12: "καὶ διὰ τοῦτο πολλὰς ἐν αὐτῇ σχεῖν τὰς διαφωνίας."

bekämpfte, beruft sich in seiner Kritik der Juden und ihrer Religion gleichfalls auf die Alten der Ägypter als seine Gewährsleute.[43] Bei Apion konnte man beispielsweise lesen, die alten Ägypter hätten ihm erzählt, daß Moses aus Heliopolis stamme und Gebetshäuser mit Sonnenuhren errichtet habe. Möglicherweise handelte es sich dabei genauso wie bei dem Priester aus Onuphis, den Dio als seinen wichtigsten Zeugen anführte, nicht um die Wiedergabe historischer Wirklichkeit sondern um eine vorgeschobene Quellenangabe, die Apions Behauptungen mehr Glaubwürdigkeit verleihen sollte. Josephus jedenfalls machte sich über diese Informanten Apions lustig, denn Berichte von alten Männern aus Ägypten waren für ihn keine zuverlässige Quelle (*Apion* 2.13). Dann verweist Josephus explizit auf die Homerexegese und -kritik, für die Apion als Fachmann bekannt war und wirft ihm indirekt vor, diese kritischen Maßstäbe, die er gegenüber Homer anlegte, bei den jüdischen Überlieferungen aus Voreingenommenheit nicht anzuwenden.

– Um dieser judenfeindlichen Polemik entgegenzutreten, die ja auch ein Angriff auf Josephus' Geschichte des jüdischen Volkes, die Jüdischen Altertümer, war, weil sie indirekt die Zuverlässigkeit dieser geschichtlichen Darstellung infrage stellt, mußte Josephus einen Gegenbeweis antreten. Er konnte sich dabei nicht auf Autopsie berufen, denn für die ganze jüdische Geschichte, die sich nach Josephus eigenen Worten auf über 5000 Jahre erstreckte (*Apion* 1.1), mußte der jüdische Historiker sich zu einem großen Teil auf die Bibel als seine Hauptquelle verlassen. Aus diesem Grund führte Josephus als Beleg für die Zuverlässigkeit der jüdischen Tradition zunächst das junge Alter der griechischen, historischen Überlieferung an, die "von gestern und dem Tag davor, wie einer sagen könnte"[44] datieren. Als zusätzliches Argument verweist Josephus darauf, daß die Griechen erst vergleichsweise spät das Alphabet von den Phöniziern übernommen hätten und begonnen hätten, Aufzeichnungen der eigenen Geschichte anzulegen.[45] Außerdem hebt Josephus hervor, daß die griechisch schreibenden Historiker

---

[43] *Apion* 2.10 "παρὰ τῶν πρεσβυτέρων τῶν Αἰγυπτίων"; s. dazu Sperling 1886, III–XXII, XIX.

[44] *Apion* 1.7 "καὶ χθὲς καὶ πρῴην, ὡς ἄν εἴποι τις."

[45] Cancik 1986, 45; vgl. auch Droge 1996, 116–17.

der Geschichte des alten Orients, die er als seine Kronzeugen
anführt, damals das Vertrauen der griechisch-römischen Öffentlichkeit
besaßen (*Apion* 1.28). Deshalb wollte er mit ihrer Hilfe, wie bereits dargelegt wurde, das hohe Alter des jüdischen Volkes belegen.
– So kommt es bei Josephus also bedingt durch die apologetischen
Ziele, die ihn beim Schreiben leiteten, zu einer methodisch
reflektierten, an den Quellen orientierten, historischen Arbeit. Dabei hat er seine Auswertung, Sichtung und kritische Analyse der
literarischen Hinterlassenschaft der orientalischen Völker, die für
viele griechische Geschichtsschreiber zu den Vorarbeiten ihrer
Forschungen gehörte und keineswegs vor dem Leser ausgebreitet
wurde, explizit gemacht, um so sein apologetisches Anliegen zu
erreichen. Damit setzte sich Josephus in seinem Bemühen, die
Überzeugungskraft seiner Argumente und somit der biblischen
Überlieferung zu erhöhen, über die Gepflogenheiten antiker
Historiographie hinweg. Im Hinblick auf die Ergebnisse, zu denen
Josephus kam, melden sich jedoch aus der Sicht der modernen,
historischen Forschung Bedenken, denn seine Ausführungen sind
in vieler Hinsicht als durchaus einseitig zu bezeichnen und bleiben
klar vom Standpunkt jüdischer Glaubensüberzeugungen geprägt.
Josephus ließ auch keine kritische Exegese biblischer Texte zu, die
er als prophetische Geschichtsschreibung als schlechthin wahr
betrachtete. Dennoch trugen seine apologetischen Motive indirekt
zu einer Vertiefung des Umgangs mit dem Material bei, das ihm
als Historiker zur Verfügung stand. Bezeichnend ist hierfür, daß
Josephus sich um eine Auswertung schriftlicher Dokumente über
die Geschichte des alten Ägyptens bemühte. Dies ist ein wichtiger
Unterschied zwischen dem jüdischen Historiker und vielen nicht-
jüdischen Autoren, die sich mit der Geschichtstradition des alten
Ägyptens beschäftigten und sich dabei im Gefolge Herodots aus-
schließlich auf mündliche Mitteilungen ihrer Gewährsleute verließen.

Josephus und das Interesse der griechisch-römischen Öffentlichkeit an
altägyptischen Hieroglypheninschriften

Das besondere quellenkundliche Interesse des Josephus läßt sich noch
klarer beleuchten, wenn man sich bewußt macht, aus welchen Gründen
die griechisch-römische Öffentlichkeit an pharaonischen Original-
dokumenten interessiert war: Wenn sich nicht-jüdische Autoren aus

den Kreisen der gebildeten, römischen Oberschicht den steinernen
Zeugen der pharaonischen Vergangenheit zuwandten und die schrift-
lichen Dokumente des alten Ägyptens heranzogen, dann leitete
sie nämlich keineswegs historischer Forschungsdrang oder auch nur
ein genuines historisches Interesse. Dies läßt sich besonders ein-
prägsam anhand der griechischen Übersetzung einer pharaonischen
Obeliskeninschrift demonstrieren, die auf dem von Kaiser Augustus
im Jahr 10 v. Chr. von Heliopolis nach Rom transportierten Obelisken
im Circus Maximus angebracht war. Diese Inschrift dürfte Ammianus
Marcellinus im Auge gehabt haben, der in seiner Römischen Geschichte
ein Zitat daraus anführt, das in der Forschung weitgehend unbeach-
tet blieb. Dieser römische Historiker beschreibt am Ende des 4. Jh.
n. Chr., wie Kaiser Constantius 357 n. Chr. einen Obelisken von
Ägypten nach Rom bringen und ihn in Circus Maximus aufstellen
ließ.[46] In diesem Zusammenhang berichtet er auch über andere
Obelisken Roms und erwähnt dabei u.a. das von Augustus nach
Rom geschaffte Exemplar. Dieser Obelisk wurde im Jahr 1587 im
Circus Maximus wiederentdeckt und von Papst Sixtus V auf der
Piazza del Popolo aufgerichtet, wo er heute noch steht.[47] Es handelt
sich dabei ursprünglich um ein Monument, das von einem der bedeu-
tendsten Pharaonen des Neuen Reichs, Sethos I, in Auftrag gegeben
worden war und nach seinem Tod von seinem berühmten Sohn
Ramses II vollendet wurde.[48]

Wie wir durch Ammianus wissen, wurde die Widmungsinschrift
dieses Obelisken in der für Römer unverständlichen Hieroglyphenschrift
durch einen gewissen Hermapion übersetzt. Hermapion war wohl
ein in Rom lebender Gelehrter ägyptischer Herkunft, der die Zeichen
der Hieroglyphen lesen und pharaonische Dokumente ins Griechische
übertragen konnte.[49] Weil diese Übersetzung von einigen Irrtümern

[46] S. dazu Dondelinger 1977, 83; vgl. Coarelli 1986, 292.
[47] Seyfarth 1968, 306 Anm. 50; Sabbah 1970, 171 Anm. 39; Coarelli 1986,
76–83, insbes. 81.
[48] Ramses II bestieg 1304 v. Chr. den ägyptischen Thron. Zu diesem Datum
und den Bauaktivitäten des Pharaos und seines Vaters Sethos I in Heliopolis s.
Faulkner 1975, 223–5.
[49] Plaumann 1918, 1124; Norden 1924, 120; Iversen 1961, 50; de Jonge 1977,
120; Cancik 1986, 51. Cancik gibt weitere Beispiele für in Rom lebende, gelehrte
Ägypter. Hermapion gehörte damit zu den letzten Gelehrten, die die Hieroglyphenschrift noch beherrschten, denn im Laufe der römischen Kaiserzeit nahmen
etwa ab Ende des 2. Jh. n. Chr. die Schriftkenntnisse der ägyptischen Priesterschaft rapide ab, s. Sternberg–El Hotabi 1994, 219–20.

behaftet ist und überdies nicht den vollständigen Text der Inschrift wiedergibt, läßt sich nur vermuten, daß Hermapion die Inschrift dieses Obelisken als Vorlage hatte.[50] Seine Übersetzung gibt aber dennoch ein im großen und ganzen zutreffendes Bild des pharaonischen Originals wieder.[51] Der Anfang der Inschrift lautet in Hermapions Übertragung: "Helios spricht zu König Ramses: Ich habe dir gegeben, über die ganze Welt mit Freude zu herrschen, dir, den Helios liebt.— Und Apollon, der Mächtige, der die Wahrheit liebt, der Sohn Herons, der gottgeborene Gründer der Welt, den Helios erwähnt hat, der tapfere Sohn des Ares, König Ramses."[52] Bei diesen Zeilen handelt es sich um die Übersetzung der Beischrift zu den Bildern am oberen Teil des Obelisken, wo die Gottheit zum König redet.[53] Die Tatsache, daß Ammianus diesen Text zitierte, dokumentiert uns deutlich die Motive für das Interesse, das gebildete Römer solchen monumentalen Inschriften aus dem alten Ägypten entgegenbrachten. Man wußte demnach von ihrem geschichtsträchtigen Inhalt, wie auch Dio Chrysostomus im Hinblick auf die Säulen der alten Tempelanlagen Ägyptens voraussetzt. Ferner darf man wohl annehmen, daß Ammianus die Übersetzung Hermapions als Zeichen seiner eigenen Gelehrsamkeit in sein Werk aufnahm.[54] Die Neugier der Römer wurde darüber hinaus sicherlich auch dadurch geweckt, daß Tausende von ihnen den Obelisken bei den regelmäßigen Wagenrennen im Circus Maximus betrachten konnten und sich gefragt haben mögen, was die rätselhaften Zeichen auf ihm wohl bedeuten könnten.[55] Dies war aber eher ein durch die Umstände und den Ort der Aufstellung motiviertes Interesse und es richtete sich sicher nicht auf die Inschrift als Geschichtsquelle, sondern auf ein merkwürdiges Zeugnis aus der

---

[50] Vgl. die Diskussion dieser Frage bei Erman 1986, 160–61; Iversen 1961, 50 sowie Daumas 1972, 43.

[51] Iversen 1961, 50. E. Winter (199, 89) gibt allerdings zu bedenken, "daß kein antiker Schriftsteller mit den floskelhaften Wendungen einer ramessidischen Königsinschrift etwas anfangen konnte."

[52] Amm. Marc. 17.4.18 (Seyfarth 1978, 110, 10–13): "Ἥλιος βασιλεῖ Ῥαμέστῃ· δεδώρημαί σοι ἀνὰ πᾶσιν οἰκουμένην μετὰ χαρᾶς βασιλεύειν, ὃν Ἥλιος φιλεῖ.—καὶ Ἀπόλλων κρατερὸς φιλαλήθης υἱὸς Ἥρωνος θεογέννητος κτίστης τῆς οἰκουμένης, ὃν Ἥλιος προέκρινεν, ἄλκιμος Ἄρεως βασιλεὺς Ῥαμέστης." Übersetzung: Seyfarth 1968, 219.

[53] Erman 1986, 154.

[54] Barnes 1998, 169 vgl. auch Brandt 1999, 104.

[55] Zur Faszination der Römer durch die ihnen unverständliche Hieroglyphenschrift s. van der Horst 1982, 115–23, 116–18.

uralten Vergangenheit Ägyptens. Josephus dagegen wurde durch seine
Arbeit an der apologetischen Verteidigung seines Volkes und d. h.
vor allem an dem Nachweis der Wahrheit der biblischen Überlieferung zu historischen Nachforschungen angespornt. Hierbei macht
er über seinen Gebrauch der Quellen eine bemerkenswerte Aussage,
die in diesem Zusammenhang nicht übergangen werden darf: Er
bedauerte es nämlich, keinen Zugang zu ägyptischen Original-
dokumenten zu haben und sich auf den aus ihnen schöpfenden
Historiker Manetho beschränken zu müssen (*Apion* 1.73), um, wie er
sich ausdrückte seine Gegner „von ihrer beabsichtigten Verdrehung"
(τὴν ἑκούσιον ψευδολογίαν) überzeugen zu können.[56] Aus dem Ziel,
die eigene biblische Tradition gegen alle Angriffe zu verteidigen,
resultierte also ein auf die Quellen und die ägyptische Geschichte
als solche gerichtetes wissenschaftliches Bemühen, das sich signifikant
von der nicht-jüdischen Umwelt unterscheidet.

Resümmee

Als Resultat dieser Untersuchung ist festzuhalten, daß Josephus sich
durch die spezielle apologetische Situation, in der er seine Schrift
Contra Apionem verfaßte, im Hinblick auf die ägyptischen Geschichts-
quellen zu einer vertieften und an einer kritischen Auseinandersetzung
mit den Quellen ausgerichteten Geschichtsforschung herausgefordert
sah, die sich in ihrer quellenbezogenen und von den Lesern daher
überprüfbaren Analyse deutlich von nicht-jüdischen Autoren unterscheidet und Aspekte einer methodenbewußten und kritischen, historischen Forschung zeigt.

QUELLEN

Ammien Marcellin
    1970   *Histoire tome II (livres XVII–XIX)*. Texte établi, traduit et annoté par
            G. Sabbah. Paris.
Ammianus Marcellinus
    1986   *Römische Geschichte*. Lateinisch und Deutsch und mit einem Kommentar
            versehen von W. Seyfarth. Erster Teil Buch 14–17. Darmstadt.
    1978   *Rerum Gestarum libri qui supersunt*. Edidit W. Seyfarth adiuvantibus
            L. Jacob, K. et I. Ulman, Vol. 1 libri 14–25. Leipzig.

---

[56] *Apion* 1.3.

Apsines
    1894   Τέχνη ῥητορική. Pages 217–329 in Rhetores Graeci ex recognitione L. Spengel. Vol. 1 Part 2. Edited by C. Hammer. Leipzig.
Dio Chrysostomus
    1967   *Sämtliche Reden.* Eingeleitet, übersetzt und erläutert von W. Elliger. Zürich.
Dio Chrysostom
    1971   Translation by J. W. Cohoon vol. 1. LCL. Cambridge, Mass.
Hérodote
    1948   *Histoires livre II Euterpe.* 1948. Texte établi et traduit Ph.-E. Legrand. Paris.
Josephus
    1976   *The Life. Against Apion.* Translated by H. St. J. Thackeray. Vol 1. LCL. Cambridge, Mass.
Plutarch
    1969   *Moralia in Sixteen Volumes.* Vol. V 351c–438e with an English translation by F. C. Babbitt. LCL. Cambridge, Mass.
Plutarque
    1981   *Œuvres morales tome XII.* Il ne faut pas s'endetter. Vies des dix orateurs. Texte établi et traduit par M. Cuvigny. Comparaison d'Aristophane et de Ménandre. De la malignité d'Hérodote. Texte établi et traduit par G. Lachenaud. Paris.
Polybios
    1979   *Geschichte. Gesamtausgabe in zwei Bänden.* Vol. 2. Eingleitet und übertragen von H. Drexler. Zürich.
Polybe
    1961   *Histoires livre XII.* Texte établi, traduit et commenté par P. Pédech. Paris
Polybius
    1962   *Historiae.* Vol III, libri IX–XIX. Editionem a L. Dindorfio curatam retractavit Th. Buettner-Wobst. Editio steriotypa editionis prioris (1893). Stuttgart.
Quintilian
    2001   *The Orator's Education Books 3–5.* Edited and translated by D. A. Russell. Vol. 2. LCL. Cambridge, Mass.

LITERATUR

Arnim, H. v.
    1898   *Leben und Werke des Dio von Prusa. Mit einer Einleitung: Sophistik, Rhetorik, Philosophie in ihrem Kampf um die Jugendbildung.* Berlin.
Avenarius, G.
    1956   *Lukians Schrift zur Geschichtsschreibung.* Meisenheim/Glan.
Aziza, C.
    1987   L'utilisation polémique du récit de l'Exode chez les écrivains alexandrins (IVème siècle av. J.-C.–Ier siècle ap. J.-C.). *ANRW* II.20.1:41–65. Edited by W. Haase. New York.
Barclay, J. M. G.
    1998   Josephus v. Apion: Analysis of an Argument. Pages 194–221 in *Understanding Josephus. Seven Perspectives.* Edited by S. Mason. Sheffield.
Barnes, T. D.
    1998   *Ammianus Marcellinus and the Representation of Historical Reality.* Ithaca.
Barzanò, A.
    1985   Cheremone di Alessandria. *ANRW* II.32.3:1981–2001 Edited by W. Haase. New York.

Batta, E.
    1986   *Obelisken. Ägyptische Obelisken und ihre Geschichte in Rom.* Frankfurt a.M.
Bichler, R.
    2000   *Herodots Welt. Der Aufbau der Historie am Bild der fremden Länder und Völker ihrer Zivilisation und ihrer Geschichte.* Mit Beilagen v. D. Feil u. W. Siebner. Berlin.
Bolonyai, G.
    2001   The Uses of Progymnasmata: The Case of "Refutations" and Dio's Trojan Oration. *Acta antiqua academiae scientiarum Hungaricae. Acta antiqua Hungarica* 41:25–34.
Brandt, A.
    1999   *Moralische Werte in den Res gestae des Ammianus Marcellinus.* Göttingen.
Cancik, H.
    1986   Geschichtsschreibung und Priestertum. Zum Vergleich von orientalischer und hellenischer Historiographie bei Flavius Josephus, contra Apionem, Buch I. Pages 41–62 in *"Wie gut sind deine Zelte, Jaakow . . ."* Edited by E. L. Ehrlich and B. Klappert in Zusamenarbeit mit Ast, U. Gerlingen.
Cerro Calderón, G. del
    1997   Las claves del discurso troyano de Dión de Prusa. *Habis* 28:95–106.
Coarelli, F.
    1975   *Rom. Ein archäologischer Führer.* Freiburg.
Cohen, S. J. D.
    1988   History and Historiography in the *Against Apion* of Josephus. Pages 1–11 in *Essays in Jewish Historiograph: History and Theory* 27. Middletown.
Conzelmann, H.
    1981   *Heiden—Juden—Christen. Auseinandersetzungen in der Literatur der hellenistisch-römischen Zeit.* Tübingen.
Daumas, F.
    1972   Les textes bilingues ou trilingues. Pages 41–45 in *Textes et Langages de l'Égypte pharaonique. Cent cinquante années de recherches 1822–1972, hommage à J.-F. Champollion.* Cairo.
De Jonge, P.
    1977   *Philological and Historical Commentary on Ammianus Marcellinus XVII.* Groningen.
Desideri, P.
    1978   *Dione di Prusa. Un intellettuale greco nell'imperio romano.* Messina-Florenz.
Diels, H.
    1887   Herodot und Hekataios, *Hermes* 22:411–44.
Dondelinger, E.
    1977   *Der Obelisk. Ein Steinmal ägyptischer Weltanschauung.* Graz.
Droge, A. J.
    1996   Josephus Between Greeks and Barbarians. Pages 115–42 in *Josephus' Contra Apionem: Studies in its Character and Context with a Latin Concordance to the Portion Missing in Greek.* Edited by L. H. Feldman and J. R. Levison. Leiden.
Erbse, H.
    1991   Fiktion und Wahrheit im Werke Herodots. *NAWG* 4. Göttingen.
Erman, A.
    1986   Die Obeliskenübersetzung des Hermapion. Pages 133–61 in *Akademieschriften (1880–1928).* Mit einem Vorwort von Burkhardt, A., und W. F. Reineke. Leipzig. Repr. of Sitzungsberichte 1914. Pages 245–73.
Evans, J. A. S.
    1991   Oral Tradition in Herodotus. Pages 89–146 in *Herodotus, Explorer of the Past: Three Essays.* Princeton.

Faulkner, O.
1975 Egypt. From the Inception of the Nineteenth Dynasty to the Death of Ramesses III. Pages 217–51 in *The Cambridge Ancient History. Third Edition, Vol. II part 2, History of the Middle East and the Aegean Region c. 1380–1000 B.C.* Edited by Edwards, I. E. S. et al. Cambridge.

Fehling, D.
1971 *Die Quellenangaben bei Herodot. Studien zur Erzählkunst Herodots.* Berlin.

Feldman, L. H.
1993 *Jew and Gentile in the Ancient World: Attitudes and Interactions from Alexander to Justinian.* Princeton.

Frede, M.
1989 Chaeremon der Stoiker. *ANRW* II.36.3: 2067–103. Edited by W. Haase. New York.

Froidefond, C.
1971 *Le mirage égyptien dans la littérature grecque d'Homère a Aristote.* Aix-en-Provence.

Fuchs, E.
1996 Die 11. Rede des Dion Chrysostomos als Lügenerzählung. *Lexis* 14:125–36.

Gerber, C.
1997 *Ein Bild des Judentums für Nichtjuden von Flavius Josephus, Untersuchungen zu seiner Schrift Contra Apionem.* Leiden.

Gudeman, A.
1930 Lysimachos. Pages 32–39 in vol. 14 of PW.

Hagen, P.
1887 *Quaestiones Dioneae.* Kiel.

Hay, D. M.
1979 What is Proof?—Rhetorical Verification in Philo, Josephus, and Quintilian. SBLSP 2:87–100. 2 vols. Missoula.

Helck, W.
1975 Art. Naukratis. Page 10 in vol. 4 of *KlPauly.*

Herter, H.
1957 Proteus. Pages 940–75 in vol. 23 of PW.

Hoffmann, F.
2000 *Ägypten. Kultur und Lebenswelt in griechisch-römischer Zeit, eine Darstellung nach den demotischen Quellen.* Berlin.

Horst, P. W. van der
1982 The Secret Hieroglyphs in Classical Literature. Pages 115–23 in *Actus: Studies in Honour of E. L. W. Nelson.* Utrecht.
1984 Chaeremon. Egyptian Priest and Stoic Philosopher: The Fragments Collected and Translated with Explanatory Notes. Leiden.

Iversen, E.
1961 *The Myth of Egypt and its Hieroglyphs in European Tradition.* Copenhagen.

Jones, C. P.
1978 *The Roman World of Dio Chrysostom.* Cambridge, Mass.

Kaiser, M.
1969 Herodots Begegnung mit Ägypten in Morenz, S. *Die Begegnung Europas mit Ägypten mit einem Beitrag von M. Kaiser.* Zürich.

Kannicht, R., ed.
1969 *Einleitung u. Text.* Vol. 1 of *Euripides Helena.* Heidelberg.

Kasher, A.
1996 Polemic and Apologetic Methods of Writing in *Contra Apionem.* Pages 143–86 in *Josephus' Contra Apionem: Studies in its Character and Context with a Latin Concordance to the Portion Missing in Greek.* Edited by Feldman, L. H. and J. R. Levison. Leiden.

Kees, H.
1939   Onuphis. Pages 529–30 in vol. 18 of PW.
Kendrick Pritchett, W.
1993   *The Liar School of Herodotos.* Amsterdam.
Kind
1930   Manethon. Pages 1060–102 in vol. 14 of PW.
Kindstrand, J. F.
1973   *Homer in der Zweiten Sophistik. Studien zu der Homerlektüre und dem Homerbild bei Dion von Prusa, Maximos von Tyros und Ailios Aristeides.* Uppsala.
Lloyd, A. B.
1975   *Herodotus Book II. Introduction.* Leiden.
1988   *Herodotus Book II Commentary 99–182.* Leiden.
Meister, K.
1975.   *Historische Kritik bei Polybios.* Paligenesia 9. Wiesbaden.
Mendels, D.
1990   The Polemical Character of Manetho's Aegyptiaca. Pages 91–110 in *Purposes of History. Studies in Greek Historiography from the 4th to the 2nd Centuries B.C. Proceedings of the International Colloquium Leuven, 24–26 May 1988.* Edited by H. Verdin, G. Schepens, and E. De Keyser. Leuven.
Mesk, J.
1920/21   Zur elften Rede des Dio von Prusa. *Wiener Studien* 42:115–24.
Momigliano, A.
1931   Intorno al Contro Apione. *RFIC* 59:485–503.
Mortley, R.
1978   L'historiographie profane et les pères. Pages 315–27 in *Paganisme, Judaïsme, Christianisme. Influences et affrontements dans le monde antique. Mélanges offerts à M. Simon.* Paris.
Müller, J. G.
1969   *Des Flavius Josephus Schrift gegen den Apion. Text und Erklärung.* Edited by C. Riggenbach, J. Von Orelli, and C. Basel. 1877. Repr. New York.
Norden, E.
1924   *Die Geburt des Kindes. Geschichte einer religiösen Idee.* Leipzig.
O'Neill, J. C.
1999   Who Wrote What in Josephus' *Contra Apionem?* Pages 270–77 in *Internationales Josephus-Kolloquium Brüssel 1998.* Edited by J. U. Kalms and F. Siegert. Münster.
Pilhofer, P.
1990   *Presbyteron Kreitton. Der Altersbeweis der jüdischen und christlichen Apologeten und seine Vorgeschichte.* Tübingen.
Plaumann, X.
1918   Hermapion. Page 1124 in vol. 3 PWSup.
Schäublin, C.
1982   Josephus und die Griechen. *Hermes* 110:316–341.
Schnabel, P.
1923   *Berossos und die babylonisch-hellenistische Literatur.* Leipzig, Berlin.
Schürer, E.
1973–1987   *The History of the Jewish People in the Age of Jesus Christ (175 B.C.–A.D. 135): A New English Version* by E. Schürer. Revised and edited by G. Vermes, F. Millar, and M. Goodman. 3 vols. in 4. Edinburgh.

Schwartz
   1899   Chairemon. Pages 2025–7 in vol. 3 of PW.
Schwyzer, H. R.
   1932   *Chairemon.* Leipzig.
Smelik, K. A. D. and E. A. Hemelrijk
   1984   "Who knows not what monsters demented Egypt worships?"
                 Opinions on Egyptian Animal Worship in Antiquity as Part of
                 the Ancient Conception of Egypt. *ANRW* II 17:4:1853–2000.
                 Edited by W. Haase. New York.
Sperling, A. G.
   1886   *Apion der Grammatiker und sein Verhältnis zum Judentum.* Dresden.
Spiegelberg, W.
   1926   *Die Glaubwürdigkeit von Herodots Bericht über Ägypten im Lichte der ägyp-
                 tischen Denkmäler.* Heidelberg.
Sterling, G. E.
   1992   *Historiography and Self-Definition. Josephus, Luke-Acts and Apologetic
                 Historiography.* Leiden.
Stern, M.
   1974–1984   *Greek and Latin Authors on Jews and Judaism: Edited with Introductions,
                 Translations and Commentary.* 3 vols. Jerusalem.
Sternberg – El Hotabi, H.
   1994   Der Untergang der Hieroglyphenschrift. Schriftverfall und Schrifttod
                 im Ägypten der griechisch-römischen Zeit. *ChrEg* 69:218–45.
Szarmach, M.
   1978   Le "Discours Troyen" de Dion de Pruse. *Eos* 66:195–202.
Thissen, H.-J.
   1980   Manetho. Pages 1180–1 in vol. 3 of LÄ.
Troiani, L.
   1977   *Commento storico al "Contro Apione" di Giuseppe. Introduzione, Commento
                 storico, traduzione e indici.* Pisa.
Verbrugghe, G. P., and J. M. Wickersham
   1996   *Berossos and Manetho, Introduced and Translated. Native Traditions in
                 Ancient Mesopotamia and Egypt.* Ann Arbor.
Winter, E.
   1991   Hieroglyphen. Pages 83–103 in vol. 15 of *RAC*.
Ziegler, K.
   1952   Plutarchos von Chaironeia. Pages 636–962 in vol. 21 of PW.

PART THREE

JOSEPHUS AS A SOURCE

NOBLE DEATH IN JOSEPHUS: JUST RHETORIC?

Jan Willem van Henten

Introduction

Josephus is an important source for noble death in Second Temple Judaism. I counted fifty-one relevant passages by following a rather minimal definition of noble death as a literary phenomenon based on three criteria: 1) focus on a violent death, sometimes self-inflicted but in any case forced by the circumstances, 2) a positive assessment of this death, and 3) vocabulary and/or motifs typical for noble death passages. Thirty-eight passages match one or two of these criteria or can be considered as relevant because they clearly contrast specific noble death passages in Josephus. Thirteen passages seem to match all three criteria (see nos. 6, 7, 19, 20, 25, 27, 30, 31, 33, 36, 38, 39, 40 in the checklist below). My first and third criteria should be obvious, but the second may need some illustration. A clear example of such a positive assessment of someone's end of life as a noble death is the brief description of Samson's suicide, with which he killed three thousand Philistines (Judg 16:23–31; *Ant.* 5.314–317): "And it is but right to admire the man for his valour, his strength, and the grandeur of his end (τοῦ περὶ τὴν τελευτὴν μεγαλόφρονος), as also for the wrath which he cherished to the last against his enemies" (5.317 [Thackeray-Marcus, LCL]; cf. 6.343–344, 348 concerning Saul, below). Most of the noble death passages in Josephus are brief, but all in all they contain much more material than the two chapters on martyrdom in 2 Maccabees that became so famous in early Christian literature. There are at least three reasons to have a fresh look at the noble death passages in Josephus.

First, Josephus' noble death passages are important sources about constructions of Jewish identity and some have an impact up to the present time. Israel's world-famous archaeological site at Masada ("Masada shall never fall again," with Yitzhak Lambdan), one of the great icons of Israeli national identity since the thirties of the twentieth century and boosted by Yigael Yadin's preliminary publication of the excavations in 1966, would probably not have existed without Josephus'

description of the collective suicide (*War* 7.320–406) at this place in
the aftermath of the war against Rome (66–70 C.E.).[1] A very different
identity construction sprouted from German sociology and theology
in the first decades of the last century and was most clearly articulated in Wilhelm Bousset and Hugo Gressmann's handbook about
Jewish religion in the late Hellenistic period. They characterized
Jewish religion as a religion of martyrdom ("eine Religion des
Martyriums"), which originated in the martyrdom of the pious ones
in the Maccabean times and came to full bloom in Christian religion.[2]
Part of the key passages for Bousset-Gressmann's view, which is, of
course, a clear case of presenting Hellenistic Judaism as *praeparatio
evangelica*, are Josephus' passages about the noble death of the "Essenes."

Second, Josephus' noble death passages deserve further study also
because some of them seem to be ambiguous about Jewish noble
death itself, as I briefly suggested a few years ago in connection with
the Masada episode in the *Jewish War*. Josephus' vocabulary concerning
noble death in this passage is not consistently positive, the two women
who survive deconstruct, perhaps, the glorifying presentation of the
suicide, and the striking parallels with the suicide episode at Yodefat
(*War* 3.361–382), with the opposite outcome, also enhance the reader's
doubt whether this suicide was so glorious.[3] If other noble death passages would appear to be ambiguous as well, Josephus' presentation
of noble death may show a significant similarity with some of the
rabbinic martyrdom passages, which also seem to offer ambiguous
assessments of such deaths.[4]

Third, apart from the relevance of Josephus' noble death passages
for identity constructions, whether ancient or contemporary, and the
issue of Josephus' possible ambiguity about noble death, there is the
important question whether these passages, or at least some of them,
reflect reliable traditions, or to put it differently, whether the deaths
depicted as noble death by a positive assessment and noble death
vocabulary and/or motifs in these passages are Josephus' own interpretation or go back to older and, perhaps, more reliable traditions.

---

[1] Yadin 1966. Zerubavel (1995, 60–76, 114–37 and 192–213) and Ben-Yehuda
(1995) offer fascinating discussions of recent Israeli interpretations of the Masada
episode. See also Chapman's contribution to this volume.

[2] Bousset and Gressmann 1926, 374 and 190.

[3] Van Henten and Avemarie 2002, 83–87. See further Atkinson's contribution
to this volume.

[4] Van Henten 2004b.

This complicated question will be briefly addressed at the end of my paper. I will start with a survey of all noble death passages, attempting to point out some trends in them and shamelessly simplifying Josephus' materials.

Noble Death Passages in Josephus

The full list of relevant passages in Josephus' works with brief descriptions of their content is as follows,[5] with the numbers of passages that match all three criteria of my noble death definition (above) given in italics.

Relevant Passages

Jewish War
(1) 1.41–45 (heroic self-killing of Eleazar; cf. *Ant.* 12.373–374)
(2) 1.57–60 (torture and execution of John Hyrcanus' mother and brothers; cf. *Ant.* 13.230–235)
(3) 1.150 (death of priests in the temple)
(4) 1.271–272 (heroic self-killing of Phasael; cf. *Ant.* 14.367–369; 15.13)
(5) 1.309–313 (self-killing of a father, his wife and seven children; cf. *Ant.* 14.420–430)
(6) 1.648–655; 2.5–7 (Herod's interrogation and execution of the young men who removed the golden eagle from the temple; cf. Ant. 17.148–164)
(7) 2.151–153 (contempt of death of the Essenes)
(8) 2.169–717 (provocations by Pilate; Jews ready to die for their faithfulness to Jewish practices; cf. *Ant.* 18.55–62)
(9) 2.184–203 (Gaius' statue; Jews ready to die for their faithfulness to Jewish practices; cf. *Ant.* 18.261–288)

---

[5] There are, of course, many other passages that refer to a violent death (e.g., *War* 4.314–325, murder of Ananus and Jesus by Idumaeans; 5.446–451, execution of Jewish prisoners, but they omit positive assessments and noble death vocabulary or motifs. *War* 4.357–362 about the murder of Gourion and Niger from Peraea emphasizes, for example, that these were fine and brave men, but noble death vocabulary and a positive assessment of their death are missing. This is also true for passages that belong to the traditional forms of prophets murdered by their own people (*Ant.* 9.167–169, violent death of Zechariah ben Jehoiada; 9.265, Israel's murdering of the prophets; 10.37–39, murdering of the prophets by Manasseh; 18.116–120, execution of John the Baptist) or suffering righteous (cf. *Ant.* 14.22–24, the stoning of Honi-Onias; 20.200 (stoning of James, Jesus' brother, and certain others).

(10) 2.469–476 (heroic self-killing of the Jewish traitor Simon)
(11) 3.320–321 (torture and execution of a prisoner of Yodefat)
(12) 3.331–332 (self-killing of Josephus' soldiers)
(13) 3.361–391 (self-killing in Josephus' speech at Yodefat and self-killing of Josephus' fellow-soldiers)
(14) 3.475 (bravery and contempt of death of Jews)
(15) 4.326–333 (torture and murder of noble and young Jews by Idumeans and Zealots)
(16) 5.88 (contempt of death of Jews)
(17) 5.315 (bravery and contempt of death of Jews)
(18) 5.458 (bravery and contempt of death of Jews)
(19) 6.54–67 (self-sacrifice of the Roman soldier Sabinus for Titus)
(20) 6.81–90 (death of the centurion Julianus)
(21) 6.186–187 (heroic self-killing of the Roman soldier Longus)
(22) 6.280 (self-killing of Meirus the son of Belga and Josephus the son of Dalaeus)
(23) 7.320–336 (self-killing in Eleazar's first speech at Masada)
(24) 7.341–388 (self-killing in Eleazar's second speech at Masada)
(25) 7.389–401 (self-killing of Jews at Masada)
(26) 7.406 (contempt of death of the Jews)
(27) 7.416–419 (execution of the *Sicarii*).

Antiquities
(28) 1.223–236 (binding of Isaac)
(29) 5.263–266 (Jephthah's daughter's sacrifice)
(30) 5.314–317 (heroic self-killing of Samson)
(31) 6.343–350; 368–372; 7.1–4 (death of Saul and his sons on the battlefield)
(32) 7.228–230 (self-killing of Ahitophel)
(33) 12.373–374 (heroic self-killing of Eleazar; cf. *War* 1.41–45)
(34) 13.230–235 (torture and execution of John Hyrcanus' mother and brothers; cf. *War* 1.57–60)
(35) 14.69–71 (self-killing of priests after Pompeius' capture of Jerusalem; cf. *War* 1.50)
(36) 14.367–369; 15.13 (heroic self-killing of Phasael; cf. *War* 1.271–272)
(37) 14.420–430 (self-killing of a father, his wife and seven children; cf. *War* 1.309–313)
(38) 15.231–237 (execution of Mariamme)
(39) 15.280–91 (execution of the conspirators against Herod)

(40) 17.148–164 (Herod's interrogation and execution of the young men who removed the golden eagle from the temple; cf. *War* 1.648–655; 2.5–7)
(41) 17.256 (contempt of death of the Jews)
(42) 18.23–24 (contempt of death of the fourth philosophy)
(43) 18.55–62 (provocations by Pilate; Jews ready to die for their faithfulness to Jewish practices; cf. *War* 2.169–177)
(44) 18.261–309 (Gaius' statue; Jews ready to die for their faithfulness to Jewish practices; cf. *War* 2.184–203)
(45) 19.198–200 (murder of Gaius' wife and daughter)

Life
(46) 137–138 (Josephus disregards Simon's advice to kill himself)

Against Apion
(47) 1.42–43 (dying for the laws and contempt of death of the Jews)
(48) 1.190–193 (dying for the laws and contempt of death of the Jews)
(49) 2.146 (contempt of death of the Jews)
(50) 2.218–220, 225–235 (Jewish obedience to the laws and contempt of death)
(51) 2.293–294 (contempt of death of the Jews)

Most of the noble death passages are included in the list but not all concern Jews. The exceptions are nos. 19, 20, 21 and 45.[6] No. 19 about the soldier Sabinus' self-sacrifice for Titus comes close to a *devotio pro imperatore*,[7] Sabinus expresses his willingness to die for the benefit of Titus[8] and Josephus seems to assess his military death positively at first glance, with his references to the soldier's courage (ἀνδρεία, 6.66; cf. 54, 59), but his concluding remarks are ambiguous, he notes that the man deserved a better fate (τύχη) and that he "'he had fallen in accordance with his enterprise'" (πεσὼν δὲ τῆς ἐπιβολῆς ἀναλόγως 6.66), which is an implicit criticism of his over-boldness.[9]

---

[6] The Galilean brigands of nos. 4 and 30 might be Jews, but this is not explicit in the texts.
[7] Cf. Dio Cassius 53.20; 59.8.3–4; 69.11; Suetonius, *Cal.* 27; *Nero* 36; *Aug. Hadr.* 14.5–7. See Versnel 1980, 571–72.
[8] *War* 6.57: ἐπιδίδωμί σοι, Καῖσαρ, ἔφη προθύμως ἐμαυτόν ... ἀλλ᾽ ὑπὲρ σοῦ κρίσει τὸν θάνατον ᾑρημένον.
[9] With Michel and Bauernfeind 1962–1969, 2.2:13 with n. 17 on p. 163.

Correspondences with Martyrdom

As indicated already, I intend to discuss three trends here, which in my view can be observed in the noble death passages of the check-list. The first observation concerns the significant formal correspondences between some of Josephus' noble death passages and early Jewish martyr texts like 2 Macc 6:18–31 and 7. None of Josephus' passages should be considered martyr texts themselves, though, because the Jewish heroes in these passages are not forced to participate in practices that counter Jewish religion and culture.[10] Yet, the similarities between some of Josephus' passages and early Jewish martyr texts in form, motifs and vocabulary are striking (see especially nos. 6, 7, 9, 27, 39, 40 and 44).

Space allows me to illustrate this point with only one or two examples. The two descriptions of the suicidal removal of the golden eagle from the temple roof during Herod the Great's rule (nos. 6 and 40), report that the young men who took care of the removal of this despicable symbol of Herod's power were inspired by two famous scholars, Judas the son of Sariphaeus (or Sepheraeus) and Mathias the son of Margolothus (*War* 1.648; *Ant.* 17.149).[11] These scholars' motivation for the eagle's removal matches in vocabulary and content statements of the voluntary noble death of the Maccabean martyrs:

> Therefore, the experts ordered them to pull down the eagle. For, (they said), even if there would be some danger of a death penalty being reserved for them, the virtue gained by death would appear much more advantageous than the pleasure of life for those about to die for the safety and observance of the ancestral customs. (τοῖς ἐπὶ σωτηρίᾳ καὶ φυλακῇ τοῦ πατρίου μελλήσουσι τελευτᾶν). For they would have arranged the eternal fame of being praised: they would be praised among those in the present and leave behind their lives as an ever-lasting memory (ἀειμνημόνευτον καταλιπεῖν τὸν βίον) for those in the future. (*Ant.* 17.152)

The willingness to die for God's laws, identical with the Jewish ancestral laws, or die for the ancestral way of life that is implied by these laws is the crucial motivation here, as it is for the Maccabaean martyrs according to 2 and 4 Maccabees.[12] And indeed other issues in

---

[10] Cf. the definition of a martyr text and a formal paradigm of such a text in van Henten and Avemarie 2002, 2–6.

[11] The names vary in the textual traditions. See van Henten forthcoming.

[12] Van Henten 1997, 125–269. Cf. faithfulness to ancestral laws and/or practices as an important motive in *War* 2.171, 174; *Ant.* 18.59 (context: Pilate's provocations,

the sages' order, like the voluntary dimension of the youngsters' death, their dying for piety (εὐσέβεια), their posthumous vindication and the glorious remembrance by those staying behind recall the Maccabean martyrs as presented in 2 and 4 Maccabees.[13]

Moreover, Josephus' reports and the Maccabean martyrdoms share the formal element of a dialogue scene that opposes the wicked ruler and the Jewish heroes who remain steadfast in resisting him as well as several motifs that come with such a scene (*War* 1.652–655; *Ant.* 17.158–160). Herod is characterized as a tyrant (*War* 1.654; *Ant.* 17.148–164; also *War* 2.84, 88) and acts during the interrogation as the foreign ruler in martyrdoms.[14] He asks the youngsters after their arrest whether it was they who had dared to take down the golden eagle. The boys not only confess,[15] but elaborately explain the motivatation for their deeds in a way that recalls one of the Maccabaean martyrs' refusal to give in to Antiochus IV.[16] In line with the view of the two scholars who instigated their act they tell Herod that "the ancestral law" (ὁ πατρίος νόμος) ordered them to remove the eagle.[17] In the version in *Jewish War* Herod asks them also why they were so cheerful even though they faced execution. They answer him that they would enjoy even greater happiness after death, a hint at their posthumous vindication (1.653). In *War* 1.650 the sages already refer to the immortality of the soul as a reward for those who die such a noble death. This Greek articulation of the young men's reward for their noble deed differs from the recreation that 2 Maccabees seems to ascribe to the seven sons of the Maccabean mother, but closely corresponds to one of the concepts that *4 Maccabees*

War 2.169–177; *Ant.* 18.55–62); *War* 2.192, 196; 4.328–329; *Ant.* 18.263, 266, 270–271 (context: Gaius' statue, *War* 2.184–203; *Ant.* 18.261–288); *Apion* 1.42–43 (every Jew if necessary dies for the laws). *Apion* 2.146, 218–219, 225–235; cf. 2.293–294 and 1.191–193.

[13] Van Henten forthcoming.

[14] Cf. the father who killed his seven sons and his wife and reproached Herod because of his humble descent or lowness of spirit (ταπεινότης) *War* 1.311 and *Ant.* 14.429.

[15] About confessions in martyr texts, see Buschmann 1994, 113–14, 117–19, 193–95, 205, 229–32, 251–53; van Henten 1997, 89–90; 237–38.

[16] *War* 1.652–653; cf. *Ant.* 17.158–160. Cf. 2 Macc 6:19; 7:2, 30; *4 Macc.* 5; 8:1–9:9; 12:1–19.

[17] *War* 1.653; *Ant.* 17.149, 150, 151, 152 and 159. Cf. *War* 1.649. In *Ant.* 17.159 the sages' followers contrast the king's decrees with Moses' laws, which echoes the stories in Dan 3 and 6 as well as the martyr stories in 2 Maccabees and *4 Maccabees* (2 Macc 7:30); cf. van Henten 1997, 10–14.

uses in its description of the martyrs' afterlife.[18] Thus, besides a similar narrative pattern with a prominent dialogue between ruler and heroes before their execution we find in Josephus' golden eagle passages at least three motifs that are important in martyr texts: dying for the Jewish ancestral/God's laws, dying for piety's sake, and posthumous vindication.

Josephus' description of the execution of those *Sicarii* (the "daggerpeople") who had fled to Egypt in the aftermath of the war against Rome (*War* 7.416–419) also shows motifs current in martyrdoms. The passage implies that the *Sicarii*, probably one of the Jewish groups that rebelled against Rome,[19] held death in contempt, a motif that Josephus frequently mentions in passing with respect to Jews (below). It also includes motifs which are typical for stories of martyrdom: steadfastness during torture (7.417–418), ignoring or even enjoying the sufferings,[20] and the admiration of the onlookers, impressed by the heroes' young age (7.419).[21] The double reference to these *Sicarii*'s refusal to confess that the emperor was their Lord (7.418, 419) presupposes a dialogue between them and a Roman official, but there is no trace of such a dialogue in Josephus.[22]

---

[18] *4 Macc.* 18:23; cf. 13:13 and 14:6. Van Henten 1997, 172–84.

[19] Hayward 1979, 598–606; Stern 1982–1983. Yadin (1966) and several other scholars assume that the *Sicarii* is a name indicating all participants in the war against Rome.

[20] *War* 7.418 suggests that the *Sicarii*'s soul was happy under the sufferings. Cf. *War* 7.344 and *Ant.* 17.152, and see Cavallin, 143–44. On joy about sufferings in the context of martyrdom, see 2 Macc 6:28, 30; 7:10; *4 Macc.* 9:29, 31; 10:20; *y. Berakhot* 9:5, van Henten 1997, 128–29; for Christian passages, see van Henten and Avemarie 2002, 130. Cf. also the prisoner from Yodefat who laughed about his execution by crucifixion (*War* 3.321).

[21] Cf. 2 Macc 7:12, which lacks a reference to the age of the martyr, and *4 Macc.* 8:10, 20. Cf. also the Roman reaction to the Masada suicide (*War* 7.406).

[22] See also *War* 4.326–333, reporting that the Zealots and the multitude of the Idumeans, after murdering the high priest Ananus, slaughtered the common people of Jerusalem as if they were unclean animals but kept the elite and youngsters (εὐγενεῖς καὶ νέους) alive in the hope that they would join their force. But all of them refused this and were tortured terribly until they died. Josephus introduces this report with a formula that indicates their preference to die rather than do something against the fatherland, which recalls the decision of martyrs to die rather than violate their ancestral customs: "Not one, however, listened to their overtures, all preferring to die rather than side with these criminals against their country, notwithstanding the fearful agonies which they underwent for their refusal: they were scourged and racked, and only when their bodies could no longer sustain these tortures were they grudgingly consigned to the sword" (*War* 4.328–329 [Thackeray, LCL]). Cf. *War* 7.337; *Ant.* 17.152 and 18.59. See van Henten forthcoming. Josephus also describes in horrific scenes how their bodies were thrown on

Self-Killings

A lot of Josephus' noble death passages concern self-killings (nos. 1, 4, 5, 10, 12, 13, 21, 22, 23, 24, 25, 30, 32, 33, 35, 36, 37, 46), and these passages, especially, show conflicting views about noble death in Josephus, sometimes perhaps reflecting his own hesitations about such deaths. Some passages only hint at noble death and an assessment of the self-killing is missing, as, for example, in the passage about the ostentatious self-killings of Josephus' soldiers (*War* 3.331–332) as well as *War* 6.280 about Meirus the son of Belga and Josephus the son of Dalaeus. A related passage is *War* 1.150, which refers to the death of priests when the Romans entered the sanctuary after Pompeius' capture of Jerusalem. These priests continued to fulfil their sacrificial duties while being slaughtered, because "they considered their deliverance secondary to the service for the divine." *Ant.* 14.69–71 (no. 35) reports the self-killing of some Jews who hurled themselves down the precipices (κατὰ κρημνῶν ἑαυτοὺς ἐρρίπτουν) and burned themselves within their houses, "because they could not bear to endure what happened" (τὰ γινόμενα καρτερεῖν οὐχ ὑπομένοντες, 14.70). Josephus' restrained positive assessment of this self-killing is apparent from a remark in 14.71, where he indicates, taking side with those who killed themselves, that the Romans' entering the sanctuary was a severe sin.

Sometimes, however, killing oneself ostentatiously in a hopeless situation is explicitly praised with noble death vocabulary, and assessed positively because it was a means to avoid being killed shamefully by the enemy. Samson's self-killing with Josephus' positive assessment

---

the streets and concludes that 12,000 of them were murdered in this way (*War* 4.333). If this number is exaggerated, that might be explained by Josephus' tendency elsewhere to suggest that most or even all Jews were ready to die for the ancestral laws. Cf. *War* 4.357–362 and the reference to Gourion's παρρησία (*War* 4.358). Josephus' retelling of Zechariah ben Jehoiada's, violent death (2 Chron 24:20–22; *Ant.* 9.167–169) reminds one of the Maccabaean martyrs who predict God's punishment of Antiochus IV for his evil deeds (2 Macc 7:35–36) as well as the reaction of the righteous in the wilderness attacked on the Sabbath (1 Macc 2:29–38). Zechariah also called for divine retribution in his last moments (2 Chron 24:22) and Josephus adds to the biblical narrative that he called upon the Lord as witness (*martys*) and judge: "As he died, however, Zechariah made God the witness and judge of what he had suffered in being so cruelly and violently put to death in return for his good counsel and for all that his father had done for Joash" (*Ant.* 9.169 [Marcus, LCL] cf. 1 Macc 2:37).

204 JAN WILLEM VAN HENTEN

of it as a noble death is a case in point (*Ant.* 5.317).²³ Another case is Herod's brother Phasael, who being imprisoned by Antigonus killed himself by dashing his head against a rock (*War* 1.271–272; *Ant.* 14.367–369; 15.13).²⁴ *Ant.* 14.367 describes this clearly with noble death vocabulary:²⁵

> As for Phasael, one must admire his courage (εὐψυχία), for though he knew he was marked for slaughter, he did not look upon death as terrible in itself (οὐχὶ τὸν θάνατον ἡγήσατο δεινόν) but believed it was a most bitter and shameful thing to suffer at the hands of a foe (τὸ δ' ὑπ' ἐχθροῦ τοῦτο παθεῖν πικρότατον καὶ αἴσχιστον ὑπολαβών); and so, not having his hands free to destroy himself because of his chains, he dashed his head against a rock and removed himself from the world of the living, which he thought was the best thing to do in view of his helpless position, and *thus he deprived the enemy of the power of killing him as they pleased.*²⁶ (Marcus, LCL; my emphasis)

Josephus repeats this motivation in his cross-reference to Phasael's death in *Ant.* 15.13, with, perhaps, a critical note by his choice of the word "murderer" and taking more distance as narrator by ascribing the decision for noble death to Phasael himself: "But Phasael could not bear the disgrace (τὴν αἰσχύνην) of being in bonds and considered a glorious death better than all life (πάσης δὲ ζωῆς κρείττονα τὸν μετὰ δόξης ἡγούμενος θάνατον). So he became his own murderer (φονεύς), as I have told earlier."²⁷

In some cases it looks as if Josephus really sat on the fence with respect to these self-killings. On the one extreme side of the spectrum Josephus emphasizes with powerful rhetoric that suicide was stupid and contrary to God's will, as he obviously does in his Yodefat speech (below),²⁸ but on the other side some of his descriptions of

---

²³ Cf. above about the Masada suicide, which is presented as a necessity in Eleazar's speech, because of the hopelessness of the situation and the fact that suicide would be the only way to avoid the Romans from harming their wives and children and making them slaves, *War* 7.321. Cf. 7.324, 334, 336, 364–366, 372–379, 381–385, 388. Cf. also the motivation of the Astapaeans to commit suicide given in Livy 28.22–23 and discussed by Cohen 1982, 388.
²⁴ See also below pp. 213–14.
²⁵ Cf. 14.369, σφόδρα τὴν τελευτὴν εὐθύμως ὑπέμεινε; *War* 1.371, ἀρετή; ἀνδρειότατα θνήσκει; 1.372, τὴν ἀρχὴν ἔχει λαμπράν.
²⁶ Cf. *War* 1.311 and *Ant.* 14.429; *War* 2.475; 5.458; 6.186–187; 6.280. For the opposite view in *War* 3.380; *Life* 137–138. See about the Masada suicide also below (pp. 214–15).
²⁷ Cf. *War* 3.362.
²⁸ The contrasting presentations of suicide in the speeches at Yodefat and Masada complicate the view of several scholars that the speeches in Josephus are tools for expressing Josephus' own opinion.

self-killings do read like noble death reports. And in some of those Josephus' own ambiguity about self-killings seems to shine through.

As is well known, Josephus' own speech at Yodefat (*War* 3.361–382) contains motifs that are strikingly similar to those in Eleazar's two speeches at Masada (*War* 7.320–336, 341–388), but Josephus argues exactly the opposite to Eleazar.[29] To mention just a few points: first, freedom is a crucial goal, but has to be fought for during battle (*War* 3.365; cf. 7.334, 336, 341, 372, 386).[30] Second, suicide is associated with divine punishment, as in Eleazar's Masada speeches,[31] but in a very different way. Suicide is the most ignoble thing and a crime against God as humankind's creator, which will not be left unpunished (3.369–379).[32] Third, dying during war is glorious, Josephus says in 3.363, but only by the hand of the enemy! Although David's councillor Ahithophel's self-killing as presented in *Ant.* 7.228–230 might hint at a noble death, Josephus' reading of it is negative nevertheless. Having sided with Absalom in his conspiracy against David and ended up in a desperate situation, Ahithophel decided to hang himself (2 Sam 17:23). Josephus does present the motivation for Ahithophel's suicide with noble death vocabulary: "Therefore, he said, it was better for him to remove himself from the world in a free and noble spirit (ἐλευθέρως καὶ μεγαλοφρόνως) than surrender himself to David to be punished for having in all ways helped Absalom against him" (*Ant.* 7.229). But Josephus adds a brief negative comment; Ahithophel had become his own judge (δικαστὴν αὑτῷ γενόμενον, 229), which is explained by the context, indicating that Ahithophel did not wait for David's punishment. Perhaps the comment also suggests that Ahitophel disregarded God's judgment (cf. *War* 3.369–379).

In connection to Josephus' criticism of some of the self-killings in his works it is fascinating to see what he makes of the death of Saul

---

[29] Cohen (1982, 396) notes these parallels. See Atkinson's contribution to this volume.

[30] Cf. *War* 5.315, suggesting that Jewish fighters took dying most lightly if it happened after killing one of the enemies. Also *War* 5.458.

[31] Eleazar's repeated conviction that suicide was a necessity (*War* 7.330, 358, 380, 387; cf. 392) goes hand-in-hand with the idea that God had destined that this was their fate (7.324–325, 330–336; cf. 7.358–359). Apparently they were punished for their misdeeds and did not receive God's support as the core group of the chosen people (7.329; cf. 7.327 and 359).

[32] In *War* 3.377 Josephus connects suicide with the command not to leave the corpse of an executed criminal unburied during the night (Deut 21:23), which also implies that suicide is a crime in his view.

(and his sons), one of the four self-killings in the Hebrew Bible (*Ant.* 6.343–350, 368–372; 7.1–4, no. 31). Josephus' sources, the biblical reports in 1 Sam 31 and 2 Sam 1:1–16, are ambiguous because Saul's death is described twice and the two versions are not identical. In 1 Sam 31:4 Saul's self-killing by falling upon his sword in his hopeless situation in the battle with the Philistines seems justified, the text provides two reasons for it. It prevented the Philistines from making sport of him and he had to kill himself because his armour-bearer refused to do it. But 2 Sam 1:1–16 suggests that the Amalekite who reported to David killed Saul. Josephus' introduction to the panegyric section that precedes the description of Saul's death itself (*Ant.* 6.343–350) sets the tone and presents this death as glorious and patriotic:

> But now I shall touch on a subject profitable to states, peoples and nations, and of interest to all good men—one whereby all should be induced to pursue virtue and to aspire to those things which may procure them glory and eternal renown (δόξαν καὶ μνήμην αἰώνιον),[33] one, moreover, that should instil into the hearts of kings and rulers of cities a great desire and zeal for noble deeds, should stimulate them to face dangers and death for their country's sake (τὸν ὑπὲρ τῶν πατρίδων θάνατον), and teach them to despise all terrors (καὶ πάντων καταφρονεῖν διδάξοντα τῶν δεινῶν). (*Ant.* 6.343 [Thackeray-Marcus, LCL])

Saul is characterized very positively by important Greek virtues (δίκαιος, ἀνδρεῖος and σώφρων, 6.345; εὔψυχοι δὲ καὶ μεγαλότολμοι καὶ τῶν δεινῶν καταφρονηταί, 6.347), and his death is assessed positively, because he did not flee and escape the danger but fell for his subjects while fighting (6.344, 348). Josephus' description of Saul's death (6.368–373) repeatedly notes that Saul and his sons fought magnificently (γενναίως ἀγωνιζόμενοι . . . καλῶς ἀποθανεῖν, 6.368; λαμπρῶς ἀγωνισά-μενος, 6.370). The point at issue, whether Saul killed himself or not, has been resolved by Josephus by harmonizing the two biblical versions. Saul tries to kill himself with his own sword as in 1 Sam 31, which is turned into a dramatic scene by Josephus. Saul lacks the physical strength to push the sword or put it through him and asks the Amalekite to do that (cf. 2 Sam 1). Josephus' section consistently presents Saul's death as a noble death, and not as a suicide. The section ends in *Ant.* 7.1–6 with the reference to David composing laments and eulogies (θρήνους καὶ ἐπιταφίους ἐπαίνους) for Saul and Jonathan's funeral (7.6).

---

[33] Cf. *Ant.* 6.345, τὸν ἔπαινον καὶ τὴν ἀγήρω μνήμην ἕξειν; 349 εὐφημία.

Another self-killing concerns Josephus' two versions of the self-sacrifice of Eleazar Avaran (*Ant.* 12.373–374; *War* 1.41–45), one of the five Maccabean brothers. Eleazar tried to kill the Seleucid king on his elephant in the Battle of Beth-Zechariah (162 B.C.E.), south of Jerusalem. Josephus' source, 1 Macc 6:43–47, probably presents this self-sacrifice as a noble death, although Eleazar's attempt failed and the battle did not end well for the Jews: "He gave his life to save his people and to achieve for himself an everlasting name (περιποιῆσαι ἑαυτῷ ὄνομα αἰώνιον)" (1 Macc 6:44).[34] *Ant.* 12.373–374 states that Eleazar risked his life by rushing upon it most stout-heartedly (σφόδρα εὐκαρδίως) and is mildly positive about the attempt in its concluding remark: "And destroying so[35] many of the enemies with good courage, he met his end in this manner" (12.374). The version in the *War* is longer and more critical about Eleazar's attempt, there is still noble death vocabulary (θέμενος εὐκλείας ἐν δευτέρῳ τὸ ζῆν, 1.43; λαμπροῦ κατορθώματος, 1.44), but the negative result of the audacious attempt gets more emphasis through several nuances than in the parallel passage in *Antiquities*, as is particularly apparent from 1.44: "In fact, the elephant driver was a commoner; yet even if he had happened to be Antiochus, the daring fighter would have accomplished nothing more than to appear to have chosen death for the single prospect of a brilliant heroic action" (Sievers-Forte, FJTC).[36]

Noble Death and the Jewish People

Josephus frequently applies noble death motifs to the entire Jewish people, depicting the people in this way in a particular light. A considerable number of the passages on my checklist, especially passages in the *Jewish War* and *Against Apion*, concern brief references about brave ways of dying and contempt of death of Jews in general, sometimes explicitly connected with an absolute obedience to the Jewish laws (nos. 8, 9, 11, 14, 16, 17, 18, 26, 41, 43, 44, 47, 48,

---

[34] See van Henten and Avemarie 2002, 62–63. Adinolfi (1969, 103–22) questions the interpretation of 1 Macc 6:43–46 as a noble death story.

[35] Reading οὕτως with most MSS.

[36] See about the ambiguity in the description of the Masada suicide p. 196. See also *War* 2.469–476 about the traitor Simon's self-killing.

49, 50, 51).[37] The *Jewish War* has several brief statements about the bravery and contempt of death of Jews without offering much comment (*War* 3.320–321, 475; 5.315; 5.458; 7.406; cf. 5.88; and *Ant.* 17.256).[38] One example is the Jewish rebels' abuse of Titus and Vespasian after Titus' call on Simon and John to surrender, emphasizing that they did hold death in contempt (τοῦ μὲν θανάτου καταφρονεῖν), for they rightly preferred it to slavery and intended to harm the Romans as much as possible as long as they were alive (*War* 5.458). For the reader the repetition of such references slowly but steadily helps to construct an image of the Jews as a people who were famous for their contempt of death. Little hints support this image, like the brief remark about Gourion, who was executed by the Zealots: "He was full of love for freedom, *as any other of the Jews* (φρονήματος ἐλευθερίου μεστός, εἰ καί τις ἕτερος Ἰουδαίων)" (*War* 4.358).[39] A similar hint is put in the mouth of Vespasian when Josephus notes in connection to a defector during Yodefat's siege that Vespasian knew about the mutual loyalty of the Jews and their contempt of punishments (τῷ ... τό τε πρὸς ἀλλήλους πιστὸν εἰδότι τῶν Ἰουδαίων καὶ τὴν πρὸς τὰς κολάσεις ὑπεροψίαν, *War* 3.320).[40] Josephus proves this point by reporting that a prisoner from Yodefat caught earlier had remained steadfast during torture and revealed nothing about the situation in the city: "For on a former occasion a man of Yodefat who had been taken prisoner had held out under every variety of torture, and, without betraying to the enemy a word about the state of the town, even under the ordeal of fire, was finally crucified, meeting death with a smile." (*War* 3.321 [Thackeray, LCL]).

In *Against Apion*, however, Josephus makes this topic explicit by emphasizing several times that, if necessary, every Jew gladly died for the ancestral laws (*Apion* 1.42–43; 1.190–193 quoting Hecataeus;

---

[37] Cf. *War* 2.151–153. About the Essenes, see Toki 1981; *War* 7.416–419 about the *Sicarii* and *Ant.* 18.23–24 about the "fourth philosophy."

[38] *War* 3.475: καὶ διότι Ἰουδαῖοι μέν, εἰ καὶ σφόδρα τολμηταὶ καὶ θανάτου καταφρονοῦντες, ἀλλ' ἀσύντακτοί ...; 5.315: καὶ Ἰουδαῖοι μὲν ἀμελοῦντες τοῦ παθεῖν ... ὅ τε θάνατος αὐτοῖς ἐδόκει κουφότατος εἰ μετὰ τοῦ κτεῖναι τινα τῶν πολεμίων προσπέσοι·; 5.458: καὶ τοῦ μὲν θανάτου καταφρονεῖν ἐβόων, ᾑρῆσθαι γὰρ αὐτὸν πρὸ δουλείας καλῶς ...

[39] Michel and Bauernfeind 1962–1969, 2.1:59: "von einer Freiheitsliebe durchdrungen, wie nur irgendein Jude."

[40] Josephus' report of the Jewish petition to Petronius at Tiberias in connection with Gaius' statue (below) suggests that the entire Jewish people were ready to be slaughtered if the statue was erected (*War* 2.197).

2.146, 218–235; 293–294).⁴¹ Elaborating a contrast between Jews and Greeks, Josephus notes in *Apion* 1.42–44 with respect to the Jews' treatment of their own sacred Scriptures identified as God's decrees: "... and it is natural *for all Jews, right from the day of their birth*, to consider them as God's decrees, abide by them, and, if necessary, *gladly die for them* (καὶ ὑπὲρ αὐτῶν, εἰ δέοι, θνήσκειν ἡδέως)" (*Apion* 1.42 [Thackeray, LCL; my emphasis]). The continuation of this brief passage suggests that Jewish history had shown many examples of this attitude: "Indeed, many times already many prisoners were seen enduring tortures and manifold kinds of death in the theatres while uttering not a single word against the laws and the documents that go with it" (1.43). One of the quotations in *Against Apion*, which Josephus is said to have taken from Hecataeus of Abdera's work about the Jews, makes a similar point about not transgressing the Jewish laws (1.190–193):⁴² "And so (he says), neither the slander of their neighbours and of foreign visitors, *to which all of them are exposed*, nor the frequent outrages of Persian kings and satraps can shake their determination; for these laws they face, defenceless, tortures and death in its most terrible form, not repudiating the ancestral commands" (*War* 1.191 [Thackeray, LCL; slightly altered, my emphasis]). Next Josephus offers, basing himself again on Hecataeus, not very specific proof of this attitude to the laws (1.192–193),⁴³ which he characterizes as ἰσχυρογνωμοσύνη. Thackeray translates this phrase pejoratively with "obstinacy,"⁴⁴ but the word may have the neutral or even positive meaning "strict attitude."⁴⁵ This meaning would suit the context better. Both examples concern situations of idolatry; one is set in the time of Alexander the Great in Babylon and the other in the homeland of the Jews. Josephus concludes this passage with another reference to Hecataeus implying that it is right to admire the Jews for this attitude (1.193).

---

⁴¹ For various views concerning genre and composition of *Against Apion*, see Mason 1996, 187–228; van Henten and Abusch 1996, 296–98; Gerber 1997, esp. 28–42, 78–88, 189–90; Barclay 1998.

⁴² *Apion* 1.190: ... τοὺς νόμους, ὅτι πάντα πάσχειν ὑπὲρ τοῦ μὴ παραβῆναι τούτους ... See for references about the authenticity debate concerning this work Stern 1976–1984, 1:21–24; Bar-Kochva 1996, 54–121; Mittmann-Richert 2000, 205–06.

⁴³ For comments on *Apion* 1.190–193, see Stern 1976–1984, 1:42–43; Holladay 1980–1996, 1:328–29; Bar-Kochva 1996.

⁴⁴ Thackeray, LCL, with *LSJ* s.v. 843.

⁴⁵ Cf. Philo, *Somn.* 1.218.

At the beginning of the extensive laudatory section about the
Jewish constitution in *Against Apion*'s second book (2.145–286),[46]
Josephus turns around the argument of 1.42–43 and 1.190–193.
Here the laws bring about the excellent behaviour of the Jews, mostly
in line with Greek virtues:

> From this, I think, it will be apparent that we possess a code (ἔχομεν
> τοὺς νόμους) excellently designed to promote piety (εὐσέβειαν), friendly
> relations (κοινωνίαν) with each other, and humanity (φιλανθρωπίαν) towards
> the world at large, besides justice (δικαιοσύνην), hardihood (τὴν ἐν τοῖς
> πόνοις καρτερίαν), and contempt of death (θανάτου περιφρόνησιν). (*Apion*
> 2.146 [Thackeray, LCL]).[47]

The most elaborate passage that depicts such a positive view of the
Jewish people with emphasis on its contempt of sufferings is *Apion*
2.218–235. Josephus adds an important argument, which probably
intrigued Greeks and Romans alike, by comparing the Jews with the
Spartans, who had such an outstanding military reputation. The
Spartans were famous in the ancient world for their contempt of
death, obedience to the laws, and particular system of education.
Others used them as models time and again.[48] Josephus takes advantage
of this comparison by arguing that the Spartans' excellence had
become history, while the Jewish faithfulness to the laws and their
attitude towards sufferings remained unchanged, no matter what the
circumstances were. He notes that the Spartans remained faithful to
their laws *only as long as they were independent*, while the Jews had never
betrayed their laws, not even during the most extreme sufferings
(*Apion* 2.226–228):

> Let them [i.e., the admirers of the Lacedaemonians vH] further reflect
> that the Lacedaemonians thought good strictly to observe their laws
> only so long as they retained their liberty and independence, but when
> they met with reverses of fortune forgot well-nigh all of them. We, on

---

[46] Gerber 1997.

[47] In the concluding passage of Book 2 Josephus repeats this ideal picture in a
summary that also emphasizes the contempt of death during war (2.293–294).

[48] Simonides' famous epigram for Leonidas and his soldiers who sacrificed themselves in 480 B.C.E. at Thermopylae (*Anthologia Graeca* 7.249; Herodotus 7.228) has
been cited by several authors: Lycurgus, *Contra Leocratem* 109; Cicero, *Tusc.* 1.101.
More references in Lycurgus, *Contra Leocratem*, 106–107; Cicero, *Tusc.* 1.100–102.
About the Spartans as models in Stoic and Cynic diatribes: Oltramare 1926, 20,
27, 55, 78, 121, 169, 170 n. 5; 180, 188, 199, 212, 224, 241 n. 6, 274 n. 4 and
279. See also Mason's contribution to this volume.

the contrary notwithstanding the countless calamities in which changes of rulers in Asia have involved us, never even in the direst extremity proved traitors to our laws . . . (*Apion* 2.227–228 [Thackeray, LCL]).[49]

Josephus emphasises that the Jews were forced to undergo the most difficult way of dying: "death accompanied by physical torture, which is thought to be the hardest of all." He refers here to the Jewish refusal to do or say something in the presence of foreign rulers that would contravene their laws (*Apion* 2.233).[50] He almost offers an excuse to these foreign rulers and stresses at the same time the spectacular dimension of Jewish noble death, by suggesting that these rulers were not driven by hatred against the Jews, but by "a curiosity to witness the astonishing spectacle (θέαμα) of humans who believe that the only evil which can befall them is to be compelled to do any act or utter any word contrary to their laws" (2:233). This echoes the earlier reference to heroic behaviour of Jews under suffering in the theatres in *Against Apion* (1.43), and is close to Jewish and early Christian presentations of martyrdom as a public spectacle.[51]

In short, Josephus makes scattered hints in the *War* and the *Antiquities* to the willingness of Jews to die for their laws if necessary as well as to their contempt of tortures and death much more explicit in *Against Apion*. In *Against Apion*, especially, he seems to portray them collectively and consistently as a special people because of their unsurpassed willingness to die for their laws and endurance of suffering. This eulogy of his own people remaining faithful to the laws even under greatest distress is striking because it is a generalisation that evokes a stereotype that is extremely positive in the perspective of Greco-Roman noble death traditions, but could easily evolve in its opposite, making the Jews look ridiculous because of their obstinate and stupid acceptance of suffering and violent death.[52]

---

[49] Cf. Ps.-Plutarch's summary of Sparta's history at the end of his *Spartan Customs* (Plutarch, *Mor.* 239F–240A), which also implies that Sparta's pre-eminence had come to an end after abandoning Lycurgus' laws. I thank Prof. Robert Doran (Amherst College) for this reference.

[50] Cf. above, pp. 201–02. Cf. also Philo's description of Petronius' motivation for his policy after Gaius' order to put a statue of him in the Jerusalem temple (*Legat.* 215).

[51] *4 Macc.* 17:11–16; *Passio Perpetuae* 20 and *Martyrium Lugdunensium* 5.1.17.20– 3.24.37–40. Cf. 2 Macc 7:12, 20; Salisbury 1997, 119–48; Frilingos 2004, 96–102 and 118–20.

[52] Cf. Max Weber's characterization of the Jews as a "Pariavolk," among other reasons because of their penchant for martyrdom, Weber 1923, 232.

Noble Death and Josephus' Rhetoric

Twenty years ago Arnaldo Momigliano published his essay "The
Rhetoric of History and the History of Rhetoric," a fundamental
attack on Hayden White's approach of history writing as a literary
construct.[53] Historians should base themselves, in Momigliano's view,
on evidence and "are supposed to be discoverers of truth."[54] The
problem with Josephus' noble death passages is, however, that archives
are missing and ancient criteria of autopsy and experience (Polybius)
are not very helpful in most cases. The deaths referred to in these
passages are undisputed, of course—everybody dies—, but who turned
the ends of life of these people into noble deaths? With Hayden
White I think that it is impossible to go, as it were, behind the
sources, reconstruct a noble death, and prove, for example, that it
was intended as such by the person who died. Jan Assmann's distinction
between figures of history and figures of memory makes us aware
of the fact that we are always looking at such a death through the
lens of the survivors, through the perspective of their and others'
memory.[55] Moreover, Josephus has integrated these deaths in a story
told with the help of many literary and rhetorical conventions. These
noble death traditions, therefore, have become part of an intricate
process of interpretation that did not end with Josephus but continues up to our own readings of these passages. This implies not
only that it is impossible to say something about the truth of these
deaths, but also that it is simplistic or even misleading to consider
them just rhetoric or Josephus' invention. Many acknowledge these
days that history and fiction are always complementary in some
way;[56] but one should not stop at this point. It is possible, in my
opinion, to make claims about Josephus as a historical source concerning noble death by using two tools: 1) a comparison with parallel
versions of the same death, within or outside Josephus, and 2) the
application of the criterion of plausibility.

    In several cases we are able to compare a noble death passage in
Josephus with a parallel version. Some of these may have functioned

---

[53] Momigliano 1984.
[54] Momigliano 1984, 50; cf. 51–52.
[55] Assmann 1997, 1–54. Martyrs illustrate this point well, they are only martyrs
because others commemorate them as such, Cohen 2004; van Henten 2004a.
[56] Going against a famous passage in Aristotle that opposes the two, *Poet.* 9.1415b.
See Rüsen 1982, 14–35; Lorenz 1997.

as Josephus' source. The comparison of the various versions offers us the opportunity to analyse Josephus' adaptations, which are clues for his re-interpretations of these deaths. Some of Josephus' renderings of biblical passages, for example, show embellishments with noble death motifs and vocabulary. Isaac's sacrifice (Gen 22; *Ant.* 1.223–236), for example, is first presented as a test for Abraham (1.223, 233), who intends to be fully obedient to God's will (1.225). Next, Josephus focuses upon Isaac, emphasizes his noble spirit (γενναῖον τὸ φρόνημα) and also refers to Isaac's joy about his father's announcement that he would be sacrificed to God (δέχεται πρὸς ἡδονὴν τοὺς λόγους, 1.232). Stating that he submitted himself to God and his father's will, Isaac rushes to the altar, which reminds one of some of Euripides' heroes of voluntary death.[57] Another well-known case from the Hebrew Bible is the sacrifice of Jephthah's daughter (Judg 11:34–40; *Ant.* 5.263–266). Josephus' criticism of Jephthah's vow is obvious; the sacrifice was neither according to the law nor pleasing to God (5.266). Yet, his version presents the anonymous daughter's response to her fate as a patriotic death, not unfamiliar to the death for the fatherland of some of Euripides' heroes: "But she without displeasure learnt her destiny, to wit that she must die in return for her father's victory and the liberation of her fellow-citizens, and therefore he should do in accordance with his vow" (*War* 5.262 [Thackeray-Marcus, LCL]).[58] As we have seen already, Josephus presents Saul's death in an elaborate passage consistently as a noble death, turning Saul also into a model of Greek virtues. At the same time he seems to re-interpret this death by downplaying references to Saul's self-killing. Thus, in comparison to the biblical reports, Josephus clearly adds noble death motifs and lines the biblical figures of these passages up with Greek heroes of self-sacrifice.

On the other hand, Josephus' versions of Eleazar Avaran's death under a Seleucid elephant, which the brief report in 1 Macc 6:43–46 seems to present in the light of noble death, are ambiguous about Eleazar' attempt that results in his being crushed by the elephant. The longer version in *Jewish War* especially is rather sceptical about Eleazar's initiative, and downplays the noble death motifs of his self-sacrifice (above). In connection to Phasael's death Josephus himself

---

[57] E.g. Menoeceus, see van Henten 1997, 146–49.
[58] Cf., e.g., Euripides, *Iph. aul.* 1368–1401; Erechtheus fragment 50 lines 18; 34–35; 51–52 (Austin ed. 1968, 25–28).

refers to two traditions, one implying Phasael's suicide and the other contradicting it (*War* 1.271–272; *Ant.* 14.367–369; 15.13).[59] Josephus concludes that it was a heroic death in any case. In the version in the *Jewish War* the motif of escaping a shameful punishment by the enemy (see above) is not explicit, as in *Ant.* 14.367; 15.13, but *War* notes that both versions of Phasael's death imply that he died nobly (τὴν ἀρχὴν ἔχει λαμπράν, *War* 1.272).[60]

The criterion of plausibility can be applied in several ways. One can focus on the coherence, consistency and plausibility of Josephus' description of a certain event in relation to others, with or without a comparison with other reports,[61] but also use it in a broader way by checking the plausibility with what we know about a historical or a literary context;[62] in the latter case the effect of the description may be taken into account as well. I can illustrate its use here only by giving one brief example concerning the Masada episode at the end of Book 7 of the *Jewish War*, which is in agreement with Josephus' tendency to highlight the noble death of Jews at least in some cases, but shows, in my opinion, also the ambiguity that he felt about some of these deaths (above). From a literary perspective Josephus reports the Masada suicide as part of a coherent chain of events. First, he describes the site and Masada's siege by the Roman governor Flavius Silva, in the spring of 73 or 74,[63] in great detail (*War* 7.275–319).[64] Next, Eleazar's two

---

[59] Cf. in connection to the additional motif of revenge on the enemy (*War* 1.372; *Ant.* 14.369) *War* 5.317 (Samson), *Ant.* 9.169 (Zechariah ben Jehoiada, above) and *War* 4.361–362.

[60] Josephus' report of Gaius' attempt to erect his own statue in the Jerusalem temple in the *Jewish War* is much shorter than its parallel passage in *Antiquities* (*War* 2.184–203//*Ant.* 18.261–309), but the depictions of Jewish determination to die rather than accept this transgression of their laws are similar in both versions, which also have a parallel in Philo's extensive description in his *Legatio ad Gaium* (*War* 2.192, 195–198, *Ant.* 18.263–264, 266–268, 270–271; Philo, *Legat.* 208–10; 215; 233–236; 265; 308). Both passages present the Jews as being ready to be slaughtered (*War* 2.197; *Ant.* 18.271) and Petronius as considering sacrificing his own life for the Jews' benefit (*War* 2.201; *Ant.* 18.278, 280, 282). Perhaps all three reports exaggerate the Jewish responses to the statue, but the correspondences between them render it probable that at least a section of the Jewish population was determined to sacrifice its life instead of living on with Gaius' statue in the temple.

[61] Cf. Schwartz 1989–1990.

[62] Cf. Theissen and Winter 1997, 175–232.

[63] The traditional date of Masada's fall in the spring of 73 c.e. has been questioned by Eck (1970, 93–111), who argues on the basis of two inscriptions that the Roman governor Flavius Silva could only have arrived in Judea in the spring of 74 c.e. Cotton (1989) offers a discussion of the old and the new date and more references.

[64] Roth (1995) discusses Josephus as well as archaeological data and argues that the siege lasted only about seven weeks.

elaborate speeches incite his fellows to collective suicide (7.320–336; 340–388),[65] followed by the suicide report itself and the brief reference to the Roman capture of the fortress (7.389–406).[66] In a well-known article Shaye Cohen has questioned the credibility of Josephus' transmission of Eleazar's speeches and the suicide report. He points at significant discrepancies between the archaeological data and Josephus' report and argues that the chain of events according to Josephus' description is highly implausible.[67] After gaining access to the fortress the Romans must have been rather stupid to let Eleazar first deliver two grand speeches and next allow him and his fellows to commit suicide in subgroups and burn their possessions. This argument inevitably leads to the question whether Josephus invented his Masada report with the famous suicide, perhaps because he was inspired by the convention in ancient histories to combine a report of the capture of a city with a dramatic description of a collective suicide of its inhabitants.[68] On the other hand, Josephus' own ambiguity about ostentatious self-killings and his tendency to downplay the glorious portrait of those who killed themselves in such a way seems to plead for the plausibility of some sort of collective suicide at Masada. Such a suicide also matches Josephus' presentation of Jewish radical groups like the Zealots, *Sicarii* and Essenes, who all showed a determination to remain obedient to God, no matter what the circumstances were, and to kill themselves rather than fall into the hands of the enemy.[69] If one would follow this line of argument, Josephus' description of the Masada suicide would have a historical plausibility, and the ambiguity that may be illuminated by certain details in the report (above) would indicate Josephus' own restrained criticism of such a display of self-sacrifice.

---

[65] Morel 1926, 106–14. Bünker 1981; Luz 1983.

[66] Nikiprowetzky 1971; Ladouceur 1980; Ladouceur 1987; Cohen 1982; Stern (1982–1983), Roth (1995), and Eshel (1999) among others, discuss the Masada episode.

[67] Josephus mentions only one of the two palaces excavated, refers to just one fire while many buildings show severe damage because of fire, refers to 960 people who were killed while only 28 bodily remains of people have been found etc., Cohen 1982, 394–95. On Masada's buildings, see Netzer 1991. Carbon 14 research confirms a date around that of the fall of Masada for the 25 skeletons found in a cave; cf. Zias, Segal & Carmi 1994. See also Atkinson's contribution to this volume.

[68] Cohen (1982, 386–92) emphasizes that Josephus' report was not unique in the ancient world by discussing sixteen Graeco-Roman reports about collective suicide that show many correspondences with Josephus' passage. See also Stern 1982–1983.

[69] Eleazar's motivation of the suicide at Masada fits in with the *Sicarii*'s strong belief that they should not accept any other authority than that of God; cf. Stern 1982–1983, 385–86.

BIBLIOGRAPHY

Adinolfi, A.
    1962   Eloquenza e patetismo nel secondo libro dei Maccabei. *RivB* 10:18–31.
Assmann, J.
    1997   *Moses the Egyptian: The Memory of Egypt in Western Monotheism.* Cambridge, Mass.
Bar-Kochva, B.
    1996   *Pseudo-Hecataeus 'On the Jews': Legitimizing the Jewish Diaspora.* Berkeley.
Barclay, J. M. G.
    1998   Josephus v. Apion: Analysis of an Argument. Pages 194–221 in *Understanding Josephus: Seven Perspectives.* Edited by S. Mason. Sheffield.
Ben-Yehuda, N.
    1995   *The Masada Myth: Collective Memory and Mythmaking in Israel.* Madison.
Bousset, W. and H. Gressmann
    1926   *Die Religion des Judentums im Späthellenistischen Zeitalter.* Tübingen.
Bünker, M.
    1981   Die rhetorische Disposition der Eleazarreden (Josephus, *Bell.* 7,323–388). *Kairos* 23:100–107.
Buschmann, G.
    1994   *Martyrium Polycarpi—Eine formkritische Studie: Ein Beitrag zur Frage nach der Entstehung der Gattung Märtyrerakte.* Berlin.
Cavallin, H. C. C.
    1974   *Life after Death: Paul's Argument for the Resurrection of the Dead in 1 Cor. 15, Part I: An Enquiry into the Jewish Background.* Lund.
Cohen, J.
    2004   *Sanctifying the Name of God: Jewish Martyrs and Jewish Memories of the First Crusades.* Philadelphia.
Cohen, S. J. D.
    1982   Masada: Literary Tradition, Archaeological Remains and the Credibility of Josephus. *JJS* 28:385–405. [= *Essays in Honour of Yigael Yadin.* Edited by G. Vermes and J. Neusner]
Cotton, H. M.
    1989   The Date of the Fall of Masada: the Evidence of the Masada Papyri. *ZPE* 78:157–62.
Eck, W.
    1970   *Senatoren von Vespasian bis Hadrian: prosopographische Untersuchungen mit Einschluss der Jahres- und Provinzialfasten der Statthalter.* München.
Eshel, H.
    1999   Josephus' View on Judaism without the Temple in Light of the Discoveries at Masada and Murabba'at. Pages 229–38 in *Gemeinde ohne Tempel/ Community without Temple: Zur Substituierung und Transformation des Jerusalemer Tempels und seines Kults im Alten Testament, antiken Judentum und frühen Christentum.* Edited by B. Ego et al. Tübingen.
Frilingos, C. A.
    2004   *Spectacles of Empire: Monsters, Martyrs, and the Book of Revelation.* Philadelphia.
Gerber, C.
    1997   *Ein Bild des Judentums für Nichtjuden von Flavius Josephus: Untersuchungen zu seiner Schrift Contra Apionem.* Leiden.
Hayward, C. T. R.
    1979   Appendix B: The Fourth Philosophy: *Sicarii* and Zealots. Pages 598–606 in vol. 2 of *The History of the Jewish People in the Age of Jesus Christ (175 B.C.–A.D. 135): A New English Version* by E. Schürer. Revised and edited by G. Vermes, F. Millar, and M. Goodman. 3 vols. in 4. Edinburgh.

Henten, J. W. van
1997   *The Maccabean Martyrs as Saviours of the Jewish People: A Study of
                2 and 4 Maccabees.* Leiden.
2004a   Internet Martyrs and Violence: Victims and/or Perpetrators?
                Pages 193–212 in *Sanctified Aggression: Legacies of Biblical and Post-
                Biblical Vocabularies of Violence.* Edited by J. Bekkenkamp & Y.
                Sherwood. London.
2004b   Jewish and Christian Martyrs. Pages 163–81 in *Saints and Role
                Models in Judaism and Christianity.* Edited by M. Poorthuis and
                J. Schwartz. Leiden.
   Forthcoming Ruler of God: The Demolition of Herod's Eagle.
Henten, J. W. van, and R. Abusch
1996   The Depiction of the Jews as Typhonians and Josephus' Strategy
                of Refutation in Contra Apionem. Pages 271–309 in *Josephus'
                Contra Apionem: Studies in its Character and Context with a Latin
                Concordance to the Portion Missing in Greek.* Edited by L. H. Feldman
                and J. R. Levison. Leiden.
Henten, J. W. van, and F. Avemarie
2002   *Martyrdom and Noble Death: Selected Texts from Graeco-Roman, Jewish,
                and Christian Antiquity.* London.
Ladouceur, D. J.
1980   Masada: Consideration of the Literary Evidence. *GRBS* 21:245–60.
1987   Josephus and Masada. Pages 95–113 in *Josephus, Judaism and
                Christianity.* Edited by L. H. Feldman and G. Hata. Detroit.
Lorenz, C.
1997   *Konstruktion der Vergangenheit: Eine Einführung in die Geschichtstheorie.*
                Cologne.
Luz, M.
1983   Eleazar's Second Speech on Masada and Its Literary Precedents.
                Rheinisches Museum für Philologie NS 126:25–43.
Mason, S.
1996   The *Contra Apionem* in Social and Literary Context: An Invitation
                to Judean Philosophy. Pages 187–228 in *Josephus' Contra Apionem:
                Studies in Character and Context with a Latin Concordance to the Portion
                Missing in Greek.* Edited by L. H. Feldman and J. R. Levison. Leiden.
Michel, O., and O. Bauernfeind
1962–1969   *Flavius Josephus* De bello judaico: der jüdische Krieg *Griechisch
                und Deutsch.* Vols 1–3.2. München.
Mittmann-Richert, U.
2002   *Einführung zu den historischen und legendarischen Erzählungen. JSHRZ*
                6.1.1. Gütersloh.
Momigliano, A.
1984   The Rhetoric of History and the History of Rhetoric: on Hayden
                White's Tropes. Pages 49–59 in *Settimo contributo all storia degli
                studi classici e del mondo antico.* Rome.
Morel, W.
1926   Eine Rede bei Josephus (Bell. Iud. VII 341 sqq.). *Rheinisches
                Museum für Philologie* 75:106–14.
Netzer, E.
1991   *Masada.* Vol. 3 of *Masada I–VI: The Yigael Yadin Excavations
                1963–1965: Final Reports.* Edited by Y. Yadin, J. Naveh, H. M.
                Cotton, et al. Jerusalem.
Nikiprowetzky, V.
1971   La mort d'Éléazar fils de Jaïre et les courants apologétiques dans
                le *De bello judaico* de Flavius Josèphe. Pages 461–90 in *Hommages
                à André Dupont-Sommer.* Paris.

Oltramare, A.
    1926   *Les origines de la diatribe romaine.* Lausanne.
Roth, J.
    1995   The Length of the Siege of Masada. *SCI* 14:87–110.
Rüsen, J.
    1982   Geschichtsschreibung als Theorieproblem der Geschichtswissenschaft:
                    Skizze zum historischen Hintergrund der gegenwärtige Diskussion.
                    Pages 14–35 in *Formen der Geschichtsschreibung.* Edited by R. Koselleck,
                    H. Lutz and J. Rüsen. München.
Salisbury, E.
    1997   *Perpetua's Passion: The Death and Memory of a Young Roman Woman.*
                    New York-London.
Stern, M.
    1974–1984   *Greek and Latin Authors on Jews and Judaism: Edited with Introductions,*
                    Translations and Commentary. 3 vols. Jerusalem.
Schwartz, D. R.
    1982–1983   The Suicide of Eleazar Ben Jair and his Men at Masada and the
                    "Fourth Philosophy." *Zion* 47:367–98. [Hebrew]
    1989–1990   On Drama and Authenticity in Philo and Josephus. *SCI* 10:113–29.
Theissen, G., and D. Winter
    1997   *Die Kriterienfrage in der Jesusforschung: vom Differenzkriterium zum Plausibi-*
                    litätskriterium. Freiburg.
Toki, K.
    1981   Der literarische Charakter des Bell.Jud. II 151b–153. *Annual of the*
                    Japanese Biblical Institute 7:53–69.
Versnel, H. S.
    1980   Destruction, *Devotio* and Despair in a Situation of Anomy: The
                    Mourning for Germanicus in Triple Perspective. Pages 541–618
                    in *Perennitas: Studi in onore di A. Brelich.* Rome.
Weber, M.
    1923   *Das antike Judentum.* Vol. 3 of *Gesammelte Aufsätze zur Religionssoziologie.*
                    Tübingen.
Yadin, Y.
    1966   *Masada: Herod's Fortress and the Zealots' Last Stand.* London.
Zerubavel, Y.
    1995   *Recovered Roots: Collective Memory and the Making of Israeli National*
                    Tradition. Chicago.
Zias, J., D. Segal, and I. Carmi
    1994   Addendum: The Human Skeletal Remains from the Northern
                    Cave at Masada—A Second Look. Pages 366–67 in vol. 4 of
                    Masada I–VI: The Yigael Yadin Excavations 1963–1965: Final Reports.
                    Edited by Y. Yadin, J. Naveh, H. M. Cotton, et al. Jerusalem.

ESSENES AND LURKING SPARTANS IN JOSEPHUS' *JUDEAN WAR*: FROM STORY TO HISTORY[1]

Steve Mason

Recent vigorous disagreement about the identity of the Qumran community[2] exposes in part the faulty method by which conclusions were initially drawn and permitted to ossify. Once the site of Qumran had been identified as an Essene installation and the Dead Sea Scrolls declared Essene productions, this nexus imposed constraints upon interpreters of both the DSS and the Greek and Latin texts that describe Essenes. Exegesis had now to fit the theory. And since the Scrolls had become *primary sources for the Essenes*, those texts that actually mention the *Essenoi/Esseni*[3] suffered the greater violence. Difficulties in aligning these very different kinds of texts could be explained as resulting from the misunderstandings of outsiders.[4] Still today, the main print resources for the "Qumran Essenes," whether comprehensive studies[5] or specific treatments of Josephus' Essenes,[6] substitute an item-by-item accommodation to the Scrolls for a contextual reading of the Essene passages.

---

[1] The heart of this paper was presented at the 2004 International Josephus Colloquium in Dublin. I wish to thank Dr. Zuleika Rodgers for the opportunity to gain feedback from so many specialists, and the specialists themselves for helpful critique. The material will appear in full in my commentary to *War* 2, volume 1a of *Flavius Josephus: Translation and Commentary* (Brill, expected 2006).

[2] Stegemann 1992; Golb 1995; Cansdale 1997; Donceel 1997; Hirschfeld 2004.

[3] Various attempts have been made to find a Semitic root for the Essenes' name in the DSS. But all face the same liability: unless there is a compelling reason in the Scrolls themselves to think that the term was a primary group label (rather than an *ad hoc* characterization) *and* unless it is naturally rendered in Greek as *Essaioi*, conditions far from satisfied thus far, any proposal for a Semitic root must lean upon the Qumran-Essene hypothesis; so, its use as proof of the same hypothesis would entail a circular argument.

[4] Cross (1961, 70): the Essene descriptions reveal an "exterior view or Hellenizing tendency"; cf. 76, 78; Sanders (1992, 379): "Certainly his description does not convey adequately the flavour of the Scrolls."

[5] E.g., Black 1956; Dupont-Sommer 1961; Adam 1972; Goodman and Vermes 1989; VanderKam 1994.

[6] Beall 1988, 3; Gray 1993, 5, but 81; Bergmeier 1993, 9, 51–52; Rajak 1994, 143.

Such a circular method[7]—we interpret Josephus' Essenes (for instance) in light of the DSS and then use the alleged parallels to prove identity[8]—could not generate stable results. A historical hypothesis identifying the DSS authors with Josephus' Essenes should have been required to show how adequately the posited Qumran-Essene phenomenon would explain Josephus' treatment of the group. But in the 1950s, when the Authorized View was becoming established, there were no interpretations of Josephus' Essene portrait, or of much else in his *oeuvre*, to be explained.[9] In the near absence of any appreciation of his works as compositions—of their structures, major and minor themes, language, or rhetorical devices—scholars were not in a position to demand that the new hypothesis explain Josephus' portrait, and this crucial requirement of historical hypotheses was overlooked.

Now that the Qumran-Essene hypothesis is creaking under other pressures, while many students of Josephus' works have at last begun to attend to their compositional traits, it seems an appropriate time to re-evaluate Josephus' Essenes *in situ*—without assuming a DSS referent. How would we understand his accounts if we examined them solely in light of his larger narratives and first audiences, the way we are beginning to analyze this corpus in general? Available space does not permit complete coverage of Josephus' Essenes here. It must suffice to consider the main passage, *War* 2.119–161, which Josephus characterizes as his definitive statement (*Ant.* 13.173; 18.11; *Life* 10). My thesis has two sides, namely: that *War*'s Essene passage is an integral part of the larger story, and that understanding the way in which the *War* uses the Essenes makes the Qumran-Essene hypothesis even more implausible than one might have feared. The first claim may seem obvious or even trite to readers unfamiliar with the state of Josephus studies. Since the Essene passage along with much else

---

[7] Opponents of the Qumran-Essene hypothesis often find a similarly vicious circle in the assumed connection between Khirbet Qumran and the Scrolls from the nearby caves. See Hirschfeld 2004, 4–6.

[8] Put clearly by VanderKam (1994, 89): "It is reasonable to interpret the evidence in such a way that the sources [e.g., Josephus and the DSS] do not conflict." I cannot see the reason in this approach, which seems to borrow more from systematic theology than from history.

[9] Bilde 1988, 71, 92, 102, 118. Even at his time of writing he could find little or no scholarship on the structures, aims, and audiences of Josephus' major compositions.

in Josephus has long been cheerfully consigned to other hands,[10] however, it is still necessary to ground one's interpretation of almost anything in this author with a defense of the proposition that he actually wrote it. Still, that task is incidental to our main goal of understanding the Essenes of Josephus' *War*.

Before turning to our main subject, I must address what might otherwise prove a distraction. It is commonly proposed in the still-dominant literature advocating the Qumran-Essene hypothesis that (a) remarkable parallels between the communities of the DSS and the Essenes of Josephus (and Philo) almost require the connection, but (b) what really seals it is the elder Pliny's notice in *Natural History* 5.73 concerning the Essenes' location. The allegedly striking parallels will come up incidentally in what follows (they are neither extensive nor striking, if only Josephus is read on his own terms). As for Pliny's notice, readers will be familiar with the debate over his meaning in locating the *Esseni* on the west side of the Dead Sea, with En Gedi *below them* (*infra hos*).[11] I for one take the view that *infra* cannot plausibly mean either "south of" or "down the coast from" the Essenes (i.e., at Qumran to the north). Irrespective of his intended meaning, however, the use of Pliny faces two other serious obstacles.

First, no matter what he intended with *infra*, Pliny displays no sound knowledge of relative locations in Judea and around the Dead Sea.[12] Even if we could be certain of his meaning, as we are sure about the meaning of "south" in his erroneous location of Machaerus and Callirhoe (*Nat.* 5.72), we would have no reason to trust him.

More importantly, no matter what he meant, the scholarly use of Pliny in support of the Qumran-Essene hypothesis produces yet another circular argument. From the middle of the nineteenth century, Dead Sea explorers both tried to locate Pliny's Essenes along the western shore and observed the intriguing surface remains at Qumran

---

[10] For example, Black 1956; Smith 1998; Bergmeier 1993; Gray 1993, 82. Different sorts of challenge or partial refutation are in Burchard 1977; Baumgarten 1984; Williams 1994. But the dates of these clusters indicate that the problem is ongoing.

[11] See already Audet 1961; Burchard 1962.

[12] Pliny locates Bethsaida-Iulias with Hippos *east* of the Kinneret, though Bethsaida is to the north (*Nat.* 5.71). He places Tarichea on the south and Tiberias on the west of the same lake, whereas Tarichea is north of Tiberias on the west (5.71). And in his description of the Dead Sea region he locates both Machaerus and Callirhoe, which lie to the east, to the *south* (5.72).

to the north.[13] Yet it seems never to have occurred to them to connect the two—so little did Pliny's language appear suited to an Essene
settlement at the north end. The possibility that he might have
intended to put Essenes at Qumran emerged only after 1947 and
the discovery of the Scrolls. Scholars did not yet commit a logical
fallacy as long as they viewed Pliny's notice as something that would
find a new—albeit counter-intuitive—explanation *if* the Essene identification of the Scrolls were valid on other grounds. The logical cir-
cuit was shorted, however, when they used Pliny's notice *as if it
independently located the Essenes at Qumran*, apparently forgetting that this
link itself depended upon the proposition that the DSS were Essene
products and now insisting that Pliny's indication of Qumran established the hypothesis.[14] To assert that we know what Pliny means
about the Essenes because of the Qumran discoveries *and* that we
know what the Qumran scrolls mean (i.e., they are Essene) because
of Pliny is to beg the question.

We may therefore disregard Pliny's notice for present purposes
and focus on understanding the Essenes of Josephus' *Judean War*.

I. *The* Judean War *and its Essene Passage: Context, Aims, and Themes*

In the opening sentences of the *War*, Josephus justifies his work by
complaining that other writers either lack reliable information or, if
they have it, distort it in order to flatter the Romans and diminish
the conquered Judeans (1.1–2). Those other accounts have not survived, but Josephus' assessment is perfectly plausible. Writing after
the Parthian war of Lucius Verus a century later, the Syrian-Greek

---

[13] For pre-DSS efforts to identify Pliny's site, see Kohler 1905, 5.231–32; Bauer
1924, 4.390; and the explorers' reports summarized by Cansdale 1997, 20, 26–27.
For early exploration of Qumran, see Hirschfeld 2004, 14–16.

[14] So Burchard (1962, 534): *given the disparity between the Greek portraits of the Essenes
and the Scrolls*, the statement of Pliny is crucial for identifying the two groups ("Étant
donné la disparité des récits de Philon et de Josèphe comparés entre eux et avec
l'ensemble des manuscrits de Qumran, l'argument géographique est toujours le
meilleur support de l'identification des anciens habitants de Kh. Qumran avec les
Esséniens ou une branche du mouvement essénien."). Cf. Grabbe (1992, 2.494),
"The statement of Pliny... seems incompatible with any interpretation other than
Qumran"; VanderKam 1994, 71–75; Vermes (1995, xxv), "the remarkable coincidence between the geographical setting of Qumran and Pliny the Elder's description of an Essene settlement near the Dead Sea *between Jericho and Engedi*" [emphasis
added because Pliny does *not* place the Essenes between Jericho and En-Gedi].

Lucian makes a similar complaint: "most of them neglect to investigate what actually happened, but elevate their own leaders and generals to the sky while disparaging (καταρρίπτω) those of the enemy beyond all proportion" (*Hist. conscr.* 7). Josephus, for his part, accuses contemporary authors of bullying (καταβάλλω) and humiliating (ταπεινόω) the Judeans (*War* 1.7). An abundance of material evidence from Flavian Rome, indications in literary texts,[15] and standard Roman attitudes toward enemies and troublemakers[16] render it antecedently probable that in Josephus' post-war Rome, the Flavians' much celebrated defeat of the Judeans meant the humiliation of the Judean ἔθνος.

Scholars have proposed many themes—or slogans—to account for the *War*'s "biases." Throughout the twentieth century the work was most often considered Flavian propaganda directed primarily at the Parthians.[17] Recently, critics have argued that the *War* attempts to protect Josephus and his aristocratic peers from war guilt, by insisting that they opposed the revolt,[18] or even to advance the claims of the surviving priesthood as a potential Judean government.[19] Yet it is difficult to see how these interpretations, which more or less ignore Josephus' own stated reasons for writing, are adequate to the complexity of the *War*. A comprehensive interpretation would need to take account of the values shared by Josephus and his Roman audience, the extra-textual resources that give coherence to the text. But even sketching the rudiments of an adequate interpretation would require a study of its own. For the sake of economy I offer some thoughts on crucial features of the *War* that help to situate the Essene passage.

1. With respect to both individuals and peoples, many ancient analysts assumed that character or nature (ἦθος, φύσις, *natura, ingenium*) determined behavior. In the case of nations (ἔθνη) or at least their aristocracies, this character was also reflected in the chosen constitution (πολιτεία).

---

[15] On the material and literary evidence, see the *Iudaea Capta* coins, the inscription from the lost arch of Titus (*CIL* 6.994), and the triumphal friezes of the current restored arch; for standard Roman attitudes to the enemy, Ziolkowski 1993; for scholarly analysis of the Judean war as Flavian legitimization, Levick 1999, 53–54; the introduction and relevant essays in Boyle and Dominik 2003; Edmondson, Mason, and Rives 2005.

[16] Mattern 1999, 1–23, 163–210.

[17] Laqueur (1920, 126–27) and Thackeray (1929, 27–31) set this durable theory in motion. The decisive challenges are Rajak 1983 and Bilde 1988.

[18] Goodman 1987, 167; Price 1992, xi; Mader 2000.

[19] S. Schwartz 1990, 81, 87.

Plato famously links national characters with distinctive constitutions (*Resp.* 544d–591) and Xenophon opens his work on Athenian administration with the remark: "I have always thought along this line: that whatever the leaders of a state are like, so also is their constitution" (*Vect.* 1.1).[20] Ethnographers typically attributed distinct ethnic characters to disparate environmental conditions.[21] Polybius, Josephus' principal Greek model for the *War*, regularly passes comment on the characters of whole peoples: morality, anger, treachery, jealousy, or love of freedom and piety (1.13.12; 3.3.3 7.1; 4.1.1–8, 53.5; 5.106). With the neo-Platonists, this deeply entrenched theory of regional diversity would be subsumed under a sort of divine workflow chart, with tutelary deities governing each nation according to its distinctive character (cf. Celsus in Origen, *C. Cels.* 5.25). The emperor Julian would speak eloquently of such diversity (*C. Gal.* 138a), holding that the codes of discipline developed by lawgivers merely reflect the innate dispositions of their various peoples (*C. Gal.* 131c).

If individuals and nations acted according to their characters, then to understand that character was already to know why they behaved as they did—for they *would* do that, wouldn't they? This principle was reflected at the personal level in the ubiquitous appeal to "probability" in court trials—the argument that it was not in a man's character (proven, for example, by ancestry and ancestors' achievements) to have done what he stands accused of doing.[22] The personal and the national are artfully combined by Polybius, when he claims that Hasdrubal's character, which was marked by ambition and love of power and was mirrored in his brother-in-law Hannibal, furnished the *real* cause of Carthage's war with Rome (3.8). Whereas Fabius Pictor had sharply distinguished the personal character of these leaders from the national character of the Carthaginians, Polybius binds the two together. The more sophisticated authors, among whom we should include Josephus, were capable of such reflection on personal and national character.

---

[20] Within the context of Roman affairs, Tacitus observes (*Ann.* 4.33) that those who wish to understand the different states of the constitution during periods of plebeian or patrician ascendancy need to understand the nature of the masses (*vulgi natura*) and of the senate and aristocracy (*senatusque et optimatium ingenia*), respectively.
[21] Isaac 2004, 56–74.
[22] E.g., Aristotle, *Rhet.* 1.2.1–15.1356a; 2.1.2–3.1377b; Cicero, *De or.* 2.182; Quintilian, *Inst.* 5.12.10; Aulus Gellius, *Noct. att.* 4.18.3–5; May 1988, 6–8; Kennedy 1994, 102–27.

There is no need to rehearse here the many attempts at depicting the character of the Judean *ethnos* through the four centuries (300 B.C.E.–100 C.E.) that separated Megasthenes and Clearchus from Plutarch, Tacitus, and Juvenal—also Josephus.[23] It is enough to observe that when war with Rome erupted, many Greeks and Romans naturally linked its causes with their suppositions about the Judean character. This inference-chain was anticipated by Cicero when he attributed the devastated condition of the Judeans in 59 B.C.E., after Pompey's subjection of Jerusalem, with their putative alien and abhorrent nature (*Flac.* 69)—after equally convenient assessments of the Greek and Asiatic characters (*Flac.* 62–66). Strikingly similar is the extant section of Tacitus' build-up to his lost account of the war of 66–73 C.E.: the Judeans embrace customs and rites that are both reprehensible in themselves and at sharp variance with the Romans' *mos maiorum* (*Hist.* 5.4–5). That character, in Tacitus' eyes, presumably went some way toward explaining the Judean defeat at Roman hands (*Hist.* 5.2).[24]

This fundamental issue of the Judean character is Josephus' beginning point in the *War*. Notice that his complaint about other writers, in keeping with the general principles of ancient historiography, is not as much about their factual inaccuracies as about their moral assessments: these so-called histories are filled with invective against the Judean people (*War* 1.2, 7–8). Redress will come not from factual accuracy in any modern sense, but from the correction of such partiality. Recognizing the centrality of the character question helps us to see the coherence of Josephus' entire corpus. It lays the groundwork for *Antiquities*' elaboration of the Judean constitution (1.5, 10) and Josephus' autobiographical treatment of his personal character (*Life* 430), and all of this reaches a summit in *Apion*'s vigorous defense of the Judean character along with advocacy of the Mosaic constitution.

2. In Greco-Roman usage, good character or virtue (ἀρετή, *virtus*) was in the first instance about *manliness*: toughness, physical courage, endurance, and practical wisdom. Because it is so often observed

---

[23] The first volume of Stern 1974–1984 contains the essential material, which has been extensively analyzed, by him and many others.

[24] Bloch 2002.

that Socrates sublimated the category of ἀρετή, it needs to be stressed that the word nevertheless retained its deep associations with masculinity. Ancient philosophy was largely about toughening oneself to become a real man—something that Josephus, among others, discusses (*Life* 10; Seneca, *Ep.* 108.14; Lucian, *Nigr.* 28). Well-trained soldiers achieved by another route what philosophers pursued: they cultivated an equal contempt for pain and death, on the one hand, and for luxury and pleasure on the other. Plato indeed requires that the Guardians (φύλακες) of his ideal *polis* be both soldiers and philosophers (*Resp.* 7.525b).

This close connection between virtue and masculinity becomes clear in what we might call the Spartanization of political and moral philosophy (e.g., Aristotle, *Pol.* 1270a–b, 1333b).[25] We catch a glimpse of this process already in Xenophon's encomiastic descriptions of the Spartan warrior-king Agesilaus (*Ages.* 8.8; 9.5; 10.1–2) and of the philosopher Socrates (*Mem.* 1.2.1–4, 2.5–15; cf. 2.1.20; 3.1.6), which are remarkably similar. The king was a model for those wishing to train in manly excellence (τοῖς ἀνδραγαθίαν ἀσκεῖν βουλομένοις) because he made a fortress *of his soul* and became a master of endurance (καρτερία). But the philosopher receives very similar praise for his tough regimen (δίαιτα [*Mem.* 1.3.5])—a word often associated with Spartan practice, and used by Josephus of Judeans and Essenes. Both men cultivated a steadfast imperviousness to external conditions: changes in weather, hardships, pleasures, and things feared by other men.

Cynics, Stoics, and other philosophers found in the Spartiates' rigorous training, simplicity of diet and lifestyle, displacement of marriage and family, communal masculine solidarity, rugged adaptability to all hardships, disdain for convention, keen sense of personal honor at all costs, and unflinching courage in the face of pain and death—albeit stripped of objectionably bellicose traits (Plato, *Leg.* 626c–d)—the realization of their own philosophical aspirations (Plutarch, *Lyc.* 31.1–2).[26] Indeed, the simple rough cloak that continued to mark out philosophers through Roman times was in origin the coarse τρίβων of the Spartans.[27]

---

[25] Tigerstedt 1974, 1.228–309.
[26] Tigerstedt 1974, 1.228–2.30–48.
[27] Cf. Hadot 1998, 7–8.

Roman moralists found the Spartan model singularly appealing, exempting the city from their typical characterization of Greeks as effeminate, preening windbags. Irrespective of its recent woes, old Sparta seemed a model of Cato's virtues enacted through a whole society:[28] neither the attractions of money and sex nor the ultimate evil of death could turn the head of a man who had passed through the Spartan ἀγωγή or a true Roman. Polybius adduced crucial constitutional parallels between Rome and Sparta (6.10–11, 51), evidently regarding Sparta as the benchmark of wise government (6.50). The city remained largely decoupled from Greece's general fortunes, prospering as a Roman ally after the destruction of Corinth in 146 B.C.E. and, from Augustus to Nero, enjoying special favor and native rule under a *de facto* monarchy.[29] Although Nero's fondness for the other Greece temporarily reversed this trend, it seems that the Flavian period marked the beginning of a second recovery for the storied city.[30]

In Rome, masculine virtue had its own distinctive language. A burgeoning library of modern studies on conceptions of barbarians, women, and sexuality has exposed a deep vein in the Roman male psyche, according to which men exercised *imperium*—both the right to control others, especially foreigners or women, and the obligation to control themselves—because of their superior *virtus* or maleness. So a variety of writers from Cornelius Nepos to Pliny the elder connect the Romans' matchless *virtus* with their consequent *imperium*.[31] The logical consequence was that Rome's enemies, indeed all other nations and especially easterners—Greeks, Asians, Cypriots, Egyptians, and Parthians—, were at best diminished specimens of masculinity, at worst outright effeminate. Ever since Crassus' disastrous campaign in Parthia in 53 B.C.E., the Parthians were often portrayed in effeminate terms: assumed to indulge in oriental luxury, they appeared on the leg carvings of Roman household tables as Ganymede-Peter Pan types.[32] After Trajan's later successes against the Parthians, his PARTHIA CAPTA coins personified the neighboring empire as cowering barbarians, sometimes in the form of a kneeling woman.[33]

---

[28] Wardman 1976, 90–93.
[29] Cartledge and Spawforth 2002, 97–103.
[30] Cartledge and Spawforth 2002, 103. An inscription mentions Vespasian's donation to the city (*IG* v. 1. 691, *SEG* xi. 848).
[31] Williams 1999, 135.
[32] Schneider 1998, 106–10.
[33] Schneider 1998, 100.

Even formerly virile Roman men could become effeminate if they spent too much time among the eastern barbarians, as we see most strikingly in the propaganda against Marc Antony—portrayed as a slave at once to his passions, to Queen Cleopatra, and to eastern luxury. Freedom from the passions and from the fear of pain and death were not simply part of the enlightened life; they were *masculine* ideals. Valerius Maximus considers the craving for life, *cupiditas vitae*, a feminine trait (9.13.pr.) and contrasts those who faced death like men with those who were "spineless and effeminate" at the end.[34]

It seems that many Roman males lived in dread of being considered feminine in dress, deportment, gait, voice, gestures, or especially sexual behavior;[35] so it was perhaps inevitable that they should project these traits on rivals. Making defeated enemies appear womanish is probably a near-universal tendency, as the jailing of a Malaysian opposition leader on sodomy charges and the sexually charged outrages at Abu Ghraib prison in Iraq suggest. But Romans appear to have had a special interest in this sort of vilification, and to have discussed it more openly. Because *virtus* and *imperium* implied the control of others, one man's claim necessarily came at the expense of others.

The Flavian revival of Augustus' barbarian CAPTA coinage rendered Judea the latest manifestation of the eastern menace, the recent counterpart to Egypt and Parthia whose subjection had been so important to the foundation of the principate.[36] Just as Octavian had transformed his defeat of an Egypt allied with his Roman rival Marc Antony as a victory over barbarians, the Flavian forces treated Vitellius' redoubt at Cremona as a foreign stronghold, sacking it, and Vespasian and Titus portrayed their quelling of a provincial rebellion into victory in a foreign war.[37] It merited a quasi-Augustan dynastic triumph, celebratory coins, and a monumental building campaign that would reshape the city center (*forum pacis*, Flavian amphitheatre, arches honoring Titus).[38] Judeans were portrayed on Vespasian's IUDAEA CAPTA (provincial ΙΟΥΔΑΙΑΣ ΕΙΑΛΩΚΥΙΑΣ) coins as

---

[34] Williams 1999, 138–39.
[35] Gleason 1995; Corbeill 2004, 122, 134.
[36] Cody 2003, 107–13.
[37] Mattern 1999, 151, 168, 193; cf. Cody 2003, 109.
[38] Boyle (2003, 4–5) and Mellor (2003, 80–84), e.g., chart some signal Augustan-Flavian parallels.

cowering in submission, often as a seated mourning woman with the powerful Roman male conqueror—in the pose of a Greek god—standing nearby in proud victory.[39]

3. In Judean culture the fullest paradigm of manly virtue, at both political and personal levels, was furnished by the "greatest generation": the leaders of the Hasmonean resistance against Antiochus IV, who had laid the foundation of the last independent state. The Hasmonean uprising was a prime source of inspiration for those who prosecuted the revolt of 66 C.E.[40] It produced vivid and heart-rending stories of heroism, toughness, endurance, and contempt for torture and death—on the part of women as well as men (2 Macc 7; *4 Macc.* 5).[41] The Hasmonean literature also preserves intriguing claims to genetic links with Sparta (1 Macc 12:7). These associations help to explain Josephus' otherwise puzzling decision to begin his account of the war of 66–73 C.E. nearly a quarter of a millennium earlier, with the Hasmonean revolt (1.31). A proud priest who cherishes his own Hasmonean ancestry (*Life* 1–6), he will exploit that glorious heritage to depict the manly Judean character, while at the same time displaying the Hasmoneans' wise political leadership and the meaning of political "freedom" in relation to foreign powers.

4. Josephus wrote the *Judean War*, as also his later works, to defend the Judean character after the failed revolt, when it was being widely abused as weak and womanish. There are many things one can and should say about the *War* and its connected themes—*stasis* and tyranny; gubernatorial malfeasance; Judean governance and relations with Rome; debts to the Prophets, Thucydides, and Polybius; its place among Second Sophistic literature; literary and rhetorical devices—but what lies underneath all of this and gives it coherence is Josephus' claim that the Judeans deserve respect as real men. The language of the *War* is surprisingly often about being a man, and Josephus compares the Roman and Judean claims on this score. He promises not to counter the chauvinist-Roman accounts with an equally jingoistic Judean statement, but to give due credit to both

---

[39] Meshorer 1982, 2.77–78, 288–89, plate 35; Cody 2003, 109 figs. 1, 3.
[40] Especially Farmer 1973; Hengel 1989.
[41] Droge 1992; van Henten 2002.

sides (*War* 1.9). Nevertheless, his exploration of Judean virtues comes at some cost to the current Roman image.

We have often been misled, I think, by Josephus' famous description of legionary training early in Book 3, which Laqueur and Thackeray seized upon as evidence of the Roman propaganda alleged to define the work (see n. 17 above). This excursus claims in superlative language that because of their unbelievably strict and constant preparation, Roman soldiers *never* act impulsively and their commanders *never* leave anything to chance (3.98–101), with the result that they have *never* been beaten, whether by superior numbers or by stratagem, by difficult terrain or even by fortune (3.106–7). But this is the purest nonsense, as any Roman familiar with the disasters of Crassus (53 B.C.E.) and Varus (9 C.E.) knows. In Josephus' story itself, this excursus comes shortly after the shameful defeat of Cestius Gallus and his Twelfth Legion (τὸ Κεστίου πταῖσμα, *War* 1.21; *Life* 21; ἡ Κεστίου συμφορά, *War* 2.556) by Judean irregulars (*War* 2.507–555), and it is an ironic setup for the rest of the narrative, which systematically undermines any notion that the Romans were masters of warfare.

The remarkable thing is that Josephus' habit of singling out Judean soldiers for honorable mention, as if in military dispatches, is not limited to his own campaign at Iotapata (3.229–230) or to some presumed period of the war's legitimacy under aristocratic direction. It continues right to the end of the narrative, even increasing in his account of the siege of Jerusalem, though he plainly has no sympathy for the "tyrant" commanders at that point: at *War* 6.147–148 he will list the Judean heroes by the faction to which they belonged: Simon's, John's, or the Idumeans'.

When Titus arrives on Mt. Scopus and the Mount of Olives with his four imposing legions in glistening battle array, rather than being intimidated the Judeans unite their forces and rush out against the renowned *legio X fretensis* (*War* 3.65), formerly commanded by M. Ulpianus Traianus (*War* 3.289), one of Vespasian's closest associates and among those honored by a consulship already in 70,[42] the father of a future emperor;[43] now led by A. Larcius Lepidus (*War* 6.237),

---

[42] Gallivan 1981, 187.
[43] Isaac and Roll (1976) describe a milestone on the Caesarea-Scythopolis road from 69 C.E., established by Traianus as *legatus* of *legio X* and honoring Vespasian.

another favorite of Vespasian's and future governor of Pontus-Bithynia. Josephus emphasizes, however, the confusion and disorder of this legion, which is driven from its new camp before Titus restores order by his personal courage (5.71–84). Yet even when the Judeans are driven down the slope they renew their attack, prompting most of the Tenth to flee up the hill—in spite of the ostensible advantage of terrain—so that even the men who are guarding Titus advise him to retreat (5.85–97).

As the story continues, one clever ploy after another gives the Judeans time and temporary advantage (e.g., 5.305–306). Josephus' ongoing comparisons frequently favor the Judeans, as when we read (5.315–16):

> The Judeans, for their part, careless of their sufferings, were intent solely on the damage they could inflict, and death itself seemed to them trivial if it meant attacking and killing one of the enemy. Titus, by contrast, took as much care for the security of his soldiers as for success. Saying that the reckless charge was foolish, and that it was only valor if accompanied by forethought and avoiding the risk of casualty, he directed his side to be manly (ἀνδρίζεσθαι) in ways that posed no risk to themselves.

In one characteristic passage the Judean fighters make a rush through a concealed gate and, carrying firebrands, resolve to reach the Roman trenches. Though the legionaries turn to face them, Josephus recounts, "the *daring of the Judeans overmatched the discipline of the Romans*, and having routed those whom they first encountered, they pressed ahead against the troops who were gathering up" (6.285). In the ensuing chaos, Judean desperation was proving superior and would probably have won the day, had not an élite Alexandrian force appeared to hold the ground ("for the most part") until Titus arrived (5.287–288).

Josephus even claims that when the Romans completed a new set of earthworks after losing previous efforts to Judean counterstrikes, they were dejected in spite of their achievement. For they feared that if the Judeans destroyed these as well, they would run out of the necessary materials and energy to repeat the task. Josephus remarks that "among the [Roman] soldiers: their bodies were by now falling beneath their labors, their souls in the face of repeated reverses" (6.11). In particular, they despaired at the Judeans' determination and daring (6.13–14):

> Worst of all was the discovery that the *Judeans possessed a fortitude of soul superior to faction, famine, war, and such disasters.* They began to suppose that the attacks of these men were irresistible, that their *cheerfulness in*

distress was invincible. For if they were inspired to valor by disasters, what would they not endure if they should be favored by fortune?

The Romans' despondency resulting from the Judeans' efforts is reinforced by the several speeches that Vespasian and Titus must make to rally the dejected legions. After suffering a setback in Gamala, Vespasian consoles his troops with thoughts about fortune's reversals, while also gently reminding them of good Roman military tactics against this "barbarian" enemy (4.39–48). And as soon as he concludes the Galilean campaign, he sends his troops to Caesarea for rest and training, because he sees what lies ahead: "He reckoned that even without walls, the determination of the [Judean] men and their daring actions would be difficult to cope with. So he trained his soldiers just like athletes for contests" (4.91).

Titus' first such speech, even before the battle for Tarichea in Galilee, is filled with references to the Judeans' refusal to accept defeat, their courage and intrepidity (3.472–484); his best hope is to reassure his troops that reinforcements are on the way (3.481). But even *with* massive reinforcements, including 2,000 archers, Josephus notes that the Judeans inside Tarichea continued fighting until they were actually pierced by lances and run over by horses (3.487–488). Again, after a rout in Jerusalem Titus must harshly reprimand his troops for breaking discipline (5.120–124).

Most interesting is Titus' speech when his troops discover, after exhausting themselves to destroy the wall protecting the fortress Antonia, that the defenders have built another behind it (6.33–53). Here we see deep despondency on the Roman side. The main part of Titus' oration, accordingly, has to do with the glory that comes from death on the battlefield. Abandoning his earlier risk-aversion policy, he lambastes his soldiers for failing to dare, like the Judeans, who do so without hope of victory but only to make a raw display of their manly courage (διὰ ψιλὴν ἐπίδειξιν ἀνδρείας, 6.42). He offers the consolation that one who dies in battle is instantly released from life's miseries and suffering to come. Near the end, he adds the qualification (6.50):

> I have said all this as if it were not possible for those who undertake this mission [attacking Antonia] to be saved; but indeed *those who show themselves to be men* (τοῖς ἀνδριζομένοις) *may be saved* from even the most hazardous operations.

In the event, only twelve of Titus' men are stirred by the pep talk, one of whom leads the charge in a spirit that Josephus admires

(6.46–52), though unfortunately he slips and is killed; the others die or return to the Roman side wounded.

Recent interpretation of the *War* has held that Josephus wrote to absolve the ruling class of complicity in the revolt. In view of the foregoing survey, I find this an untenable position. The very first sentence (*War* 1.1–3) establishes Josephus' role as a general in the war, which was in any case well known in Rome, and which he greatly elaborates in Books 2–3. The many dignitaries who fled Jerusalem after the Cestian disaster he describes in the most unflattering terms: they deserted the city like those abandoning a sinking ship (2.556), thus forsaking the most basic responsibilities of statesmen.[44] Tellingly, the deserters did not include either Josephus himself or the leaders he admires most, the chief priests Ananus and Jesus (4.326–365; cf. 7.267). Rather than trying to avoid all responsibility for the war, Josephus demands respect for his people and their rightful aristocratic leaders, who made life exceedingly difficult for the Romans and would have done so even more had the brilliant chief priests lived—or they would have come to honorable terms (4.320–321).

The narrative tendencies outlined here are considerably more prominent and structurally important than his occasional (and *de rigueur*) flattery of the Roman rulers, which has received disproportionate attention. Moreover, what might at first seem obsequious groveling may turn out to be something else entirely.[45]

5. Some of the *War*'s characteristic language reinforces the ethos of Judean manly virtue, for example: contempt for death and terror (καταφρόνησις θανάτου, τῶν δεινῶν), endurance (καρτερία), and "in close order" (ἀθρόος). The collocation of καταφρόνησις or περιφρόνησις with θάνατος or τὰ δεινά is well attested in historians and moral philosophers of the Roman period.[46] But the author with the heaviest investment in this language is Josephus, for whom the disdain for terrors or death itself is a singular Judean virtue. The *War* introduces

---

[44] See Plutarch's contemporary essay on *Precepts of Statecraft*.

[45] Mason 2003, 2005.

[46] Diodorus Siculus 5.29.2; 15.86.3; 17.43.6, 107.6; Dionysius of Halicarnassus, *Ant. rom.* 5.46.4; Philo, *Prob.* 30; *Abr.* 183; Musonius Rufus, *Diss.* 10; Epictetus, *Diatr.* 4.1.70, 71; Plutarch, *Brut.* 12.2; Lucian, *Peregr.* 13, 23, 33; Aristides, *Plat.* 171.10 [Jebb]; *Periphth.* 382.30 [Jebb]; Marcus Aurelius, *Med.* 4.50.1; 9.3.1; 12.34.1; Polyaenus, *Strat.* 5.14.1; Diogenes Laertius 1.6; Phalaris, *Ep.* 103.3; Appian, *Celt.* 1.9; *Bell. civ.* 5.4.36; Cassius Dio 43.38.1; 46.26.2, 28.5; 62.25.1.

the theme in the person of Athrongeus, the rebel of 4 B.C.E. (2.60). Thereafter it becomes the chief characteristic of all Judean fighters (3.357, 475; 5.88, 458; 6.42; 7.406), which the Roman generals can only *try* to inculcate in their legions (6.33). Throughout the *Antiquities* too Josephus features this Judean quality, beginning with an encomium on King Saul (*Ant.* 6.344–347). There we meet the other example in Josephus outside the Essene passage of the rare agent-noun κατα-φρονητής: other would-be "despisers of terrors" will learn from Saul's example. Most compelling are Josephus' remarks in the *Against Apion*: that the Judean constitution inculcates contempt for death (θανάτου περιφρόνησις), among other virtues (*Apion* 2.146), and that precisely in wartime Judeans despise death (θανάτου καταφρονεῖν, 2.294). Josephus' description of the Essenes thus embodies his vision of the entire Judean tradition.

Josephus' phrase καταφρονηταὶ τῶν δεινῶν, which he uses twice of the Essenes and once of Saul, is striking because this *nomen agentis* form ("despiser") hardly appears before his time,[47] though his con-temporaries Epictetus (*Diatr.* 4.7.33) and Plutarch (*Brut.* 12.2; *Mor.* 84a, 1044a) begin to use it. Yet Josephus has it twice within the Essene passage, predicated of wealth (2.122) and terrors (2.151). Both Josephus and Plutarch characterize *good* men as despisers—of death and pleasures, the two conventional human motivators—, shedding the usually negative associations of "disdain" (for the laws, gods, etc.). Plutarch also uses the cognate verb καταφρονέω, like Josephus, to portray those who despise the pleasures (*Mor.* 210a) and death (210f, 216c, 219e)—in Plutarch's case, the Spartans.

Endurance (καρτερία) was the most conspicuous trait of the Spartans and the whole focus of their training,[48] emulated by philosophers (Xenophon, *Mem.* 1.2.1; 2.1.20; 3.1.6). This is an important word group for Josephus, who uses it about 134 times, nearly half of these (63) in the *War*—usually in relation to the endurance of the Judean fighters or the "steadfastness" of their defenses. In the *Apion*, again, Josephus makes this a distinctive Judean trait (1.182; 2.146, 170, [225], 228, 273, 284), and three times (*Apion* 2.225, 228, 273) he contrasts the Spartans' mere *reputation* for endurance with the unde-niable Judean display of this virtue in the recent war. On Essene

---

[47] LXX Hab. 1:5; 2:5; Soph. 3:4; Philo, *Leg.* 322.
[48] Xenophon, *Ages.* 5.3; 10.1; 11.9; Plutarch, *Mor.* 208c, 210a, 237a; *Lyc.* 2.2; 16.5–6; 18.1; 29.5; *Ages.* 11.7; 30.3.

endurance during the war, which is another important theme binding the Essene passage to the larger narrative, see *War* 2.151–158, which unfortunately we lack the space to discuss here.

As for ἀθρόος, it occurs 45 times in *War*, only 12 times in Josephus' later works. Often he seems to employ the term to suggest that what the Roman legions must train themselves in, disciplined marching in columns, the Judeans achieve spontaneously when their laws are threatened (*War* 1.81, 84; 2.170, 174; 6.80, 82, 86).

6. The parallels we have already seen between *War*'s Essene passage and *Apion*'s portrait of the Judean nation could be developed at some length. Space limitations here mandate brevity, but the crucial point is that these parallels confirm Josephus' use of the Essenes to exemplify larger currents in the *War* and in his larger world-view. They are an integral part of his ongoing effort to explain the Judean character.

Some parallels may be seen efficiently by a glance at the final sections of the *Apion* (2.293–294), where Josephus idealizes Judean culture. Italicized phrases below match those that he applies to the Essenes in *War* 2.119–161:

> What greater beauty than inviolable *piety* (εὐσέβεια)? What greater *justice* (δικαιότερον) than obedience to the laws? What more beneficial than to *be in harmony* with one another (πρὸς ἀλλήλους ὁμονοεῖν), to be a *prey neither to disunion* (διίστασθαι) in adversity, *nor to arrogance* (ὑβρίζοντας) and *faction* (στασιάζειν) in prosperity; in war *to hold death in contempt* (θανάτου καταφρονεῖν), in peace *to devote oneself to crafts or agriculture* (τέχναις ἢ γεωργίαις); and to be convinced that *everything in the whole universe* (πάντα δὲ καὶ πανταχοῦ) is under the eye and direction of God?

Just as harmony becomes a national characteristic in the *Apion* (cf. *War* 2.122–123, 134, 145 on the Essenes), so also the solemnity, gravity, or dignity (Greek σεμνότης) that Josephus identifies as the outstanding Judean trait (*Apion* 1.225; 2.223), most conspicuously exhibited by his good self (*Life* 258) but very few others,[49] happens to be the first general point he makes about the Essenes: they certainly are known for cultivating *gravitas* (*War* 2.119). In *Apion* 2.193–196, 199–202, 205, similarly, Josephus attributes other fundamental Essene characteristics to all Judeans, including simplicity of life and an insistence that marital sex be exclusively for procreation.

---

[49] Cf. *War* 7.65 on Vespasian; *Ant.* 12.24 on the Tobiad Joseph.

Again, Josephus introduces his "non-panegyric" on Judean culture in the *Apion* (2.145–146) thus:

> For I think it will become clear that we have laws optimally oriented towards piety (εὐσέβεια), towards community (κοινωνία) with one another, and towards humanity (φιλανθρωπία) among the world at large; yet further, towards justice (δικαιοσύνη), towards endurance in the course of struggles (ἡ ἐν τοῖς πόνοις καρτερία), and towards contempt for death (θανάτου περιφρόνησιν).

All of these qualities figure prominently in *War*'s Essene digression.

Lurking behind Josephus' implied connections between Essenes and all Judeans is the ghost of Sparta. He displays great interest in the moral-philosophical aspects of the Spartan legend. In the *War*, Sparta appears incidentally as a fallen power from the past (1.425, 513, 532; 2.359, 381; 7.240–243). In the *Antiquities*, Josephus reproduces the letters from 1 Maccabees (12:5–23) that asserted an ancestral bond (ὡς ἐξ ἑνὸς εἶεν γένους, *Ant.* 12.26) between Judeans and Spartans (12.225–228; 13.164–171). Louis Feldman has recently itemized the remarkable parallels between Josephus' life of Moses and Plutarch's biography of the Spartan Lycurgus.[50]

In the *Apion*, most tellingly, Josephus reconciles the positive and negative sides of his Spartan interest. Whereas Xenophon had enthused that everyone praised Spartan customs but no other city was willing to emulate them (*Lac.* 10.8), Josephus concedes that "everyone eulogizes Sparta" (*Apion* 2.225) but insists that Judeans have the better of them on every score. Although the Spartans are universally admired as the most courageous and disciplined people ever (*Apion* 2.130), he says, their reputation is not entirely deserved. The Spartans have long since abandoned their noble traditions and therefore lost their sheen (*Apion* 2.273), as Plutarch (*Mor.* 240a–b) also allows, so that the Judeans have a much longer and more impressive record of rigorous training (*Apion* 2.172), discipline, endurance, and courage—as witnessed by the recent war (*Apion* 2.225–231, 272–273). The Spartan constitution was defective in significant ways, among these its military preoccupation and hostility toward others (hence Judean superiority in φιλανθρωπία), and it was therefore unsustainable (2.172, 226–230, 259; cf. Aristotle, *Pol.* 1333b). At the end of the day, the world-renowned Spartans are for Josephus only a benchmark (*Apion* 2.259;

50 Feldman 2005.

compare Polybius' use above), in the same genetic line as, but inferior to, their Judean relations.

This three-way connection among all Judeans, Spartans, and Essenes in Josephus' thought receives confirmation from an unexpected quarter. Early in the fourth volume of Porphyry's third-century work *On Abstinence*, he examines the Spartans as a model of the regimented diet (*Abst.* 4.3.1–5.2). Shortly thereafter he turns to the Judeans and their famous food restrictions. For Porphyry, however, the Essenes are the best examples of the Judean way. Between brief introductory and concluding remarks on all Judeans (*Abst.* 4.11.1–2, 14.1–4), therefore, he portrays the Essenes in great detail, borrowing nearly verbatim the passage that we are considering from *War* 2 (*Abst.* 4.11.3–13.10). Curiously, Porphyry gives his sources for the Essenes as not only *War 2* and the parallel in *Antiquities* 18, but also the second book of Josephus' work against the Greeks: i.e., *Against Apion*. Since the *Apion* does not mention Essenes, Porphyry seems to have recognized the sorts of parallels that we have explored and inferred that Josephus' description of *all* Judeans in *Apion* 2.151–196 was really or especially about the Essenes. Perhaps he pragmatically assumed that an entire *ethnos* was incapable of living in such a disciplined way. Josephus himself, however, presents the Essenes as embodying the virtues of the entire nation.

7. The *War* has a symmetrical structure, which enfolds the Essene passage, confirming in another way that it belongs fully to the narrative. At the beginning of the *Antiquities* (1.7) Josephus reflects that he tried hard to "measure off" (συμμετρέω) the beginning and ending sections of the *War*, symmetrically, and analysis of the *War* shows that he did just that. The central panel or fulcrum is occupied by the fateful murder of Ananus and Jesus (4.326–365; cf. 7.267), which marked the beginning of the tyranny, irredeemable *stasis*, and catastrophe. At the beginning and end of the work are its only discussions of the temple at Leontopolis (1.33; 7.421), and there are many parallel stops along the way. Here I observe only that the Essene passage contributes to the symmetry. At *War* 2.154 Josephus describes the ascetics' view that at death the souls of the good return up to "the most refined ether" (ἐκ τοῦ λεπτοτάτου αἰθέρος). The only other occurrence of "ether" in Josephus, except for a quotation at *Apion* 2.11, comes in Titus' pep talk at 6.47—a roughly symmetrical location in the seven-volume work: he encourages his troops with the

thought that souls released on the battlefield are welcome "into the purest element, ether" (τὸ καθαρώτατον στοιχεῖον αἰθήρ).

II. *Essenes in the* Judean War: *General Considerations*

The foregoing analysis already suggests important ways in which *War*'s Essene passage functions in that narrative and expresses Josephus' larger concerns. Before discussing a few specific points within the passage, we briefly consider its tenor and situation in *War* 2.

A. *Context in* War *2*

The Essene passage is bound securely to its immediate context both fore and aft. I formerly thought that the orderly and obedient philosophers were included chiefly as a foil for Judas the Galilean and his "school": whereas Judas rejected any recognition of mortal rulers and fomented revolt (2.118), the Essenes take an oath to maintain loyalty to those in charge (τοῖς κρατοῦσιν), because no one comes into leadership without God (2.140). But it seems from the context that the leaders intended there are Judean officials or the sect's own governors, rather than *world* rulers.[51] At any rate, many other connections with the narrative deserve mention.

The preceding material in Book 2 (2.1–118) highlights the serious shortcomings of the later Herodians, whose long and bitter succession struggle ends with the egregious Archelaus as ethnarch of Judea, probationary to possible appointment as king should he prove worthy (2.93). Worthy he is not, and so he finds himself ignominiously exiled (2.111). Josephus' interests are, typically, with moral questions. In his concluding remarks, he describes the lust that drove Archelaus to abandon his wife and take up with Glaphyra, widow of both Herod's son Alexander and the "Libyan" King Juba II. He also alleges this woman's wantonness, exposed in a dream by Alexander's ghost, which presages her death (2.114–116). It can hardly be a coincidence that the Essene passage provides immediate and sharp contrasts on all fronts. The first points Josephus stresses about the group are connected with their mastery of the passions, their awareness

---

[51] The counterpart to the same oath commits the Essene, should *he* come into a position of governance, not to distinguish himself by outward signs of power. The government in question must be local at most, possibly sectarian.

of women's wantonness, and their utter lack of concern about natural succession (2.119–121). He goes on to emphasize their community of goods, opposition to personal distinction, and perspicuity when in positions of power (2.122–123, 140).

Josephus' association of vice and submission to the passions with women's influence, both in the Archelaus episode and in the opening lines of the Essene passage, is typical of his narrative tendencies. One small but clear example is the phrase "wanton ways of women" at *War* 2.121 (ἀσελγείαι γυναικῶν), which is hardly found before him,[52] though he uses it formulaically—of Herod's wife Mariamme (*War* 1.439), Jezebel (*Ant.* 8.3180), Cleopatra (*Ant.* 15.98), and transvestite Galilean Zealots in Jerusalem during the war (*War* 4.562). The portrayal of women as "faithless" and fickle in these two contiguous passages likewise matches his tendencies perfectly.[53]

At the end of the story, the heroic endurance of the Essenes, to the point of death if necessary (2.151–158), prepares for several examples of endurance in defense of the laws on the part of the Judean populace as a whole: under Pontius Pilate (2.169–177) and then in the face of Gaius Caligula's hubristic demands (2.184–205). Although the Essenes adopt a peculiar lifestyle, they embody Judean virtue in a concentrated form.

B. *"Despisers of wealth and terrors": the Structure of the Essene Passage*

We have noted the conspicuous use of "despiser" (καταφρονητής) in this passage. As it happens, the two occurrences fall near the beginning (predicated of wealth) and near the end (of terrors) of the passage, prompting one to ask whether the excursus like the *War* itself has a symmetrical or "concentric" arrangement. It does. The symmetry is established at the beginning and end by mention of the Pharisees and Sadducees (2.119, 162), and by discussion of women, marriage, and succession (2.119–121, 160–161). In this architecture, the central panel comprises the twelve oaths taken by initiates (2.139–142). The pivotal function of the central panel is emphasized by the matching verbs "reckon in" (ἐνκρίνω) and "reckon out" (ἐκκρίνω), which sit as

---

[52] Philo, *Vit. Mos.* 1.305; Dio Chrysostom, *Or.* 2.56; and fragments of some astrological writers. Otherwise, wantonness was often attributed to *men* under the influence of drink and women (Polybius 10.38.2; 25.3.7).

[53] For the language, cf. *Ant.* 4.219; 13.430–431; 17.352; *Apion* 2.201. On women in Josephus: Mayer-Schärtel 1995; Ilan 1999, 85–125; Matthews 2001.

gateways before and after the oaths (2.138, 143)—and appear only
here in Josephus. Similarly, the reverence for the sun as a deity
emerges in roughly parallel places (2.128, 148), as does the rare phrase
"they make it a point of honor" (ἐν καλῷ τίθνται) at 2.123, 146.

C. *Men at Work: the Tone of the Essene Excursus*

In keeping with the *War*'s ethos, the Essenes appear above all as
tough, hard, and supremely courageous men. Modern readers may
be predisposed to see such philosophers as meek pacifists, but that
is not what Josephus says. They lead quiet lives, to be sure, free of
what are characterized as feminine emotions and pleasures, but that
only contributes to their image of seriousness or *gravitas* (the first
point made about them: 2.119).

1. The passage is filled with the language of martial order, reminiscent of the Spartans: τάγμα, προστάσσω, τάξις, εὐταξία, ἄσκησις,
and δίαιτα. Only in the *War* context does Josephus call the Essenes
a τάγμα. This is the word that he normally use for Latin *legio*, the
legion—by far his most common use in the *War* also, where the
word occurs roughly 128 times. Although he calls all the schools by
various other names (αἵρεσις, φιλοσοφία, μοῖρα, etc.), however, he
uses τάγμα of the Essenes *five times* in this passage, and once of the
Sadducees immediately afterward (2.122, 125, 143, 160, 161). Although
he has the phrase ἐν τάξει only four times in all his writings, two
of these are near each other in *War*'s Essene passage (2.130, 133):
the Essenes do things in an orderly way. More generally, Josephus
claims that they only take action when *ordered* to do so, using the
cognates προστάσσω and ἐπίταγμα (2.134, 139). Other terms related
to martial virtues that are conspicuously prominent in this passage
are δίαιτα ("regimen")—five of *War*'s eleven occurrences are in this
passage (this is a characteristic term elsewhere for Spartan life)—and
ἄσκησις or ἀσκέω ("discipline," "training"—2.119, 150, 166 [cf. *Ant.*
1.6 and *Apion* 2.192, where Josephus claims that Moses perfected
training in virtue, ἄσκησις ἀρετῆς]). Since this usage is only in *War*,
not in the Essene passages of *Antiquities*, it appears that Josephus has
shaped his account to fit *War*'s overall martial outlook.

2. We have noted the importance of "endurance" (καρτερία) in
Josephus' lexicon and the word's Spartan associations. At *War* 2.138
he says that endurance was the goal of the tough three-year Essene

initiation. Then in 2.151–153 he gives (symmetrically) a vivid portrait of the results. Exhibiting a genuine contempt for death, during
the war Essenes endured every kind of torture, and "smiled in their
agonies." Although Josephus dwells on this physical and mental toughness, it tends to get ignored in assumptions about Essenes as pacifists.
This section has particularly strong verbal associations with the famous
Hasmonean accounts, and it reinforces the *War*'s general ethos of
masculine courage.

3. Finally, analysis of Josephus' Essene passage reveals a concentra-
tion of words and phrases that most often appear elsewhere, in such
proximity, in descriptions of the Spartans. By making this connection I do *not* mean to suggest that Josephus presents Essenes as would-
be Spartans or Spartan imitators. To the contrary, as we have seen,
he considers the Judeans superior to the Spartan reputation. The
Spartan legend had profoundly shaped the discourse of masculine
ideals, and Josephus, fully aware of this, draws from this same repertoire in describing the Essenes. See Table 1 (pp. 255–57) for examples.

III. *Specific Items in Josephus' Description of the Essenes*

It remains to survey a few particulars of the Essene passage in context, before drawing historical conclusions.

1. Essenes Avoid Oil

> **123** They consider olive oil a stain, and should anyone be acciden-
> tally smeared with it he scrubs his body, for they make it a point of
> honor to remain hard and dry, and to wear white always.

Since olive oil was considered indispensable in ordinary life, and
presses have been found even in small towns of Galilee,[54] Josephus'
claim that the Essenes avoided it and bathed only in cold water (*War*
2.129) would make them seem remarkable ascetics to a Roman audience. The stative verb αὐχμέω ("be parched, hard and dry") normally
has negative connotations ("be unwashed, squalid"), indicating a
condition to be relieved through rain or washing,[55] but Josephus

---

[54] Garnsey 1999, 12–14; Tyree and Stefanoudaki 1996.
[55] *War* 4.457; *Ant.* 7.297; Plato, *Resp.* 606d; Plutarch, *Numa* 13.6–7; *Ages.* 30.3;
Mor. 193a, 365d.

inverts this usage by making dryness a point of honor. In light of our investigation thus far it is noteworthy that the Spartans were also remembered for considering their dry—and unwashed—skin a mark of toughness (Plutarch, *Lyc.* 16.6; *Mor.* 237b: αὐχμηροὶ τὰ σώματα). Both groups thus invert conventional standards of comfort, grooming, and the luxury of gymnasium-baths. The same general theme is continued in the Essenes' wearing threadbare clothes (*War* 2.126; cf. the Spartans' and philosophers' τρίβων, above) and above all in their Spartan-like rejection of private ownership in favor of communal sharing and exchange as needed (2.122, 127; see Table 1).

There is more. Although Romans used oil for the necessities of life, some associated liberal use with Greek effeminacy. Tacitus characterizes Nero's distribution of oil to the equestrian and senatorial orders as "a Greek predilection (*Graeca facilitate*)" (*Ann.* 14.47), and Silius Italicus has a Roman commander encourage his troops to destroy the Greek soldiers of Sicily because they are effeminate: they practice the lazy pursuit of wrestling in the shade, where they love to gleam with oil (*Pun.* 14.134–138).[56] Similarly, in Josephus' *War*, men who have no shred of self-control indulge the use of oil. At 5.565–566, John of Gischala impiously distributes the sacred supplies of oil and wine from the temple to his men, who anoint themselves and drink heartily. This same rebel group, Josephus claims (4.561–562), went so far as to adopt women's ways: plaiting their hair, wearing women's clothes (but cf. *Ant.* 4.301), drenching themselves in perfume, applying make-up, giving in to "the passions of women" and indulging a "surfeit of wantonness." As surely as the tyrants' degeneracy produces a disgraceful demeanor, the Essenes' Spartan- and Roman-like discipline in physical appearance reflects their moral perspicuity.

Though Josephus features the Essene avoidance of oil, there is no known parallel in the DSS. The arguments of J. M. Baumgarten and Todd Beall for making this an issue of the oil's purity, which require a particular manuscript reading of CD 12.15–17,[57] illustrate the methodological problem I seek to address. Josephus' account says nothing about purity concerns, but plainly links avoidance of oil with a preference for dry, hard skin.

---

[56] Cf. Williams 1999, 136.
[57] Baumgarten 1967, 183 and Beall 1988, 45, 142 n. 56; note the very different reading in Vermes 1995, 111.

2. Election of Leaders

> **122** Hand-elected are the curators of the communal affairs, and indivisible are they, each and every one, [in pursuing] their functions to the advantage of all.

The adjective "hand-elected" (χειροτονητός) occurs only here in Josephus (cf. the participle χειροτονοῦντες at *Ant.* 18.22) and is rare elsewhere. The main alternative to being elected by show of hands was to be "lot-elected" (κληρωτός: Aeschines, *Tim.* 21; *Ctes.* 29; Aristotle, *Ath. pol.* 55.2), as were some early Christian leaders (Acts 1:26). Election by show of hands implies the conscious preference of one's peers rather than the choice of Fate (Aristotle, *Ath. pol.* 54.3; Lucian, *Nav.* 29).

It is unclear how this system of elected officials relates to the four-phase seniority system ("according to the duration of their training") indicated at the symmetrical counterpart, 2.150. Did the senior members take direction from elected officials of lesser seniority? The tension is resolvable if Josephus describes here the practices of full members only—a status achieved only after the three years of initiation (cf. 2.138)—whereas the four grades of 2.150 refer to those in the various phases of initiation. At *Ant.* 18.22 the text seems to imply that both the community's financial administrators and its priests—whose tasks appear confined to food preparation—are elected.

Contrast the DSS, which feature (a) an individual community leader known as the מבקר ("guardian": 1QS 6.12, 20; CD 9.18–22; 13.11, 16; 15.8–14) or פקיד ("official": 1QS 6.14; CD 14.6)[58] and (b) group-rankings dependent upon caste (priests, Levites, and others, possibly Israelites and proselytes, CD 14.3–6).[59] Among Josephus' Essenes, neither the elected officials (plural, also at 2.129, 134) nor the four grades *according to time in the order* (at 2.150) have any connection with caste. He mentions priests only in connection with blessings over food in this passage (*War* 2.131), more generally in connection with food preparation at *Ant.* 18.22. Although Josephus himself was an immensely proud priest, who shaped his biblical and other source material to enhance priestly roles, the priests do not figure among either the ranks by seniority or the elected offices of his Essenes.

---

[58] Beall 1988, 46–47.
[59] Beall 1988, 99–100.

3. Essenes Have No Centre

124 No one city is theirs, but they settle amply in each.

One of the biggest casualties of the Qumran-Essene hypothesis is
Josephus' plain statement here. The context enhances this claim by
continuing to speak about the Essenes' lack of possessions, their easy
and frequent travel from one city to another, and their provisions
for such constant movement, with each community appointing a special officer for visitors (2.124–125). Josephus' portrait creates the
impression that a visitor to Judea should expect to see these (celibate) Essenes frequently traveling the roads with worn-out clothes
and shoes, sticks for protection, and little else. Qumran interference
has created the common picture of celibate Essenes at Qumran (1QS)
and married ones living in communities elsewhere (CD). Such a proposal, however, in no way harmonizes Josephus with the Scrolls, but
rather stands him on his head. This passage is all about *celibate*
Essenes (he will not mention the marrying kind until the end,
2.160–161), and it is they who are easily mobile, lacking any particular base.

4. Essenes Revere the Sun as God

128 Toward the Deity, at least: uniquely pious [ways]. Before the sun
rises, they utter nothing of the mundane things, but only certain ancestral prayers to him, as if begging him to come up ... **148** On the other
days they dig a hole of a foot's depth with a trowel—this is what that
small hatchet given by them to the neophytes is for—and wrapping
their cloak around them completely, so as not to outrage the rays of
God, they relieve themselves into it [the hole].

Essene reverence for the sun, emphasized and even celebrated by
Josephus, is another awkward item for the Qumran-Essene hypothesis. The vivid phrase "the rays of God" (τὰς αὐγὰς τοῦ θεοῦ) recalls
Euripides (*Heracl.* 749–750), where the Chorus calls upon the "lumi-
nous *rays of the God* who brings light to mortals," and it anticipates
Julian's *Hymn to King Helios* (1.9), which also gives a vivid sense of
the piety that might be associated with sun-reverence.[60] Josephus'

---

[60] Cf. *Hymn. homer. cer.* 35, 280; Nicander, frg. 74.39 (Gow and Scholfield);
Athenaeus, *Deipn.* 15.31.42 (Kaibel). Philo of Alexandria speaks frequently, though
metaphorically, of God as "the purest ray" or as rays of sun: *Fug.* 136; *Mut.* 6; *Somn.*
1.72, 116 ("the rays of God"), 239; *Praem.* 25; *Mos.* 1.66.

verb ἱκετεύω ("entreat, approach as supplicant") is common in his narratives, but its more than one 100 occurrences commonly have God as predicate. Taken together with "the rays of God" this is a strong statement of something approaching worship.

Josephus' comments on this matter have long puzzled interpreters who must read this passage in light of the DSS. His words are either neutralized to match the Scrolls' "prayers at dawn"[61] or they encourage arbitrary source theories,[62] on the ground that no observant Jew could speak thus. Indeed, the Temple Scroll from Qumran only intensifies the biblical prohibition of sun-worship—on pain of death by stoning (11QTemple 55.15–21; cf. Deut 17:2–5; Ezek 8:16–19). We need, however, to read this passage in light of Josephus' narrative themes and audience values.

Elsewhere, Josephus also tends to personify the sun and to see it as a representation of God. Later in the *War* he claims that the Zealots "polluted the Deity" when they left corpses unburied beneath the sun (*War* 4.382–383; cf. 3.377; 4.317). His Titus vows to bury the memory of Jerusalem's cannibalism in rubble, so that "the sun cannot look upon it" (*War* 6.217). In *Ant.* 1.282–283 God synonymously parallels His watching over the earth with the sun's: Abraham's children "shall fill *all that the sun beholds* of earth and sea... *for it is I* who am watching over all..." Moses positions the tabernacle, the special house of God (3.100), so as to catch the sun's first rays (3.115). He also directs the Israelites, once in Canaan, to create an altar oriented toward the sun (4.305). The high priest's upper garment is woven with gold to represent the ever-present rays of the sun (3.184). God has made the Judeans the happiest people under the sun, says Balaam (4.114). Saul promises victory to allies, such that "the ascending sun should see them already victors" (6.76; cf. 216; 8.49; 9.225). It is telling that, while otherwise intensifying the biblical portrait of King Josiah's reforms (*Ant.* 10.268–270; cf. 2 Kgs 23:19–20), Josephus entirely omits the biblical reference to Josiah's destruction of horses and chariots *dedicated to the sun* by Menasseh and Amon (2 Kgs 23:11). In his paraphrase of 1 Maccabees, Josephus changes the phrase "Far be it from me to do this deed!" (1 Macc 9:10) into "May the sun not look upon such a thing" (*Ant.* 12.424). And he has Marc Antony

---

[61] Beall 1988, 52–54.
[62] Bergmeier 1993, 84.

speak of the sun's looking away from the murder of Julius Caesar
(14.309; cf. 16.99, 108; 18.46; *Apion* 1.306). Josephus' portrayal of
the Essenes thus matches his demonstrable narrative tendencies, and
it should neither be attributed to his sources, as if it were "non-
Jewish," nor explained as his misunderstanding.

For Josephus' Roman audience, Essene reverence for the sun would
have been highly resonant. Sun-worship was widespread through the
near and far east, already from the emergence of Akhenaten ("glory
of the [sun-disk] Aten") in the 18th Dynasty (14th cent. B.C.E.). In
early Greece, the informal worship of Helios was commonplace,
reflected also in the popularity of Heliodorus ("gift of the sun") as
a name. Anaxagoras' claim that the sun was merely a red-hot mass
reportedly caused outrage (Diogenes Laertius 2.12). Hesiod (*Op.* 339)
mentions offering sacrifices at both the rising and the setting of the
sun (the "holy light"), and Plato speaks of Socrates' prayers to the
sun (*Sym.* 220d; cf. *Leg.* 887d–e and Albinus, *Epit. doctr. Plat.* 14.6).
The prestige of the sun for philosophers was helped along by the
Stoic Cleanthes' (early third-century B.C.E.) identification of it as the
driving principle of the world (Diogenes Laertius 7.139; cf. Philo,
Opif. 116; *Somn.* 187). In utopian literature after Alexander, sun-worship continued to have a prominent role, inspired partly by Plato's
Atlantis (*Criti.* 113b–121c, esp. 115b), the travel narrative of Iambulus
to an Island of the Sun (Diodorus Siculus 2.55–60), and the *Sacred
Inscription* of Euhemerus, in which the Sacred Isle (Panchaia) was
associated with the sun (Diodorus Siculus 5.41.4–6; cf. Ferguson
1975, 104–6). Worship of the sun was further catalyzed by its
identification with Apollo (Euripides, *Phaethon* 225; Horace, *Saec.* 9)—
incidentally, one of Sparta's chief deities[63]—a constant reminder of
which in Josephus' Rome was the statue of Helios driving his chariot atop the Palatine temple of Apollo.[64] The native Roman god Sol
Indiges would eventually be eclipsed by the Syrian import Sol Invictus
(the Unconquered Sun), who remained dominant from the third century C.E. until the rise of Christianity (temporarily reversed by Julian's
sun worship).

---

[63] Cartledge and Spawforth 2002, 193–94.
[64] Incidentally, Lycurgus is said to have established his constitution under the
tutelage of Delphic Apollo, and reverence for Apollo remained customary among
the Spartans (Herodotus 1.65; Plato, *Leg.* 674d; Xenophon, *Ages.* 1.34; 2.15, 17;
Lac. 8.5).

For Josephus, his audience, and his Essenes, reverence for the sun was an assumed component of respectable piety. We have no right to interpret Josephus in ways that render his Essenes more congenial to the DSS or any other writings.

5. Essenes are Devoted to the Compositions of the Ancients

> **136** They are extraordinarily keen about the compositions of the ancients, selecting especially those [oriented] toward the benefit of soul and body. On the basis of these and for the treatment of diseases, roots, apotropaic materials, and the special properties of stones are investigated.

As others have noted,[65] this passage has a close parallel in *Ant.* 8.44–49. There Josephus credits King Solomon with thousands of "compositions" (συντάσσω, 8.44–45). Those volumes recorded Solomon's comprehensive study of nature and the various properties (ἰδιώματα) of each form (8.44). In particular, they described the craft (τέχνη) of exorcism, "for the benefit and treatment" (εἰς ὠφέλειαν καὶ θεραπείαν) of humanity (8.55). Josephus even describes an instance of such *therapeia* (8.46) that he witnessed. The exorcist used a root (ῥίζα) prescribed by Solomon for the purpose (8.47). So again, Josephus' Essenes are admirable examples of the traits he claims for himself and for Judean culture as a whole.

Beall makes a good case for including among "the ancients" the pseudepigraphous *1 Enoch* and *Jubilees*, which mention cures through herbs and roots (*Jub.* 10.10–14; *1 Enoch* 7.1; 8.3; 10.4–8), and which were widely read by Judeans in the first century.[66] But there seems no reason to limit these ancients to Judeans. The study of roots for curative purposes had a long history in the Greco-Roman world. Aristotle's prolific student Theophrastus (fourth century B.C.E.) observes (*Hist. plant.* 9.8.1): "The powers of roots are many and for many [purposes], but the medicinal ones are especially sought out as being the most useful." The same Theophrastus devoted a work to stones and their "special properties" (*Lap.* 3.5; 41.1; 48.1; cf. Galen, *Simpl. med. temp.* 12.207.2). The combination of roots and stones (the stones were typically broken and the fragments applied to certain roots) is found frequently in the medical and magical writers of antiquity, not

---

[65] See Thackeray's LCL note on this passage.
[66] Beall 1988, 70–73.

248 STEVE MASON

least among Josephus' near contemporaries Dioscorides Pedanius,[67] Cyranides,[68] and Galen.[69] Another contemporary, Pliny the Elder, included in his *Natural History* detailed studies of plants and roots (*radices*) as remedies (*Nat.* 24–28). The "virtues of roots" were among the things of which King Solomon was alleged by some Judean authors to have had deep knowledge (Wis 7:20).

6. Essenes Protect the Name of the Lawgiver

145 There is a great reverence among them for—next to God—the name of the lawgiver, and if anyone defames him he is disciplined by death.

The word "lawgiver" (νομοθέτης) is Josephus' characteristic term for Moses (e.g., *Ant.* 1.6, 15, 18; *Apion* 2.156, 161). Notwithstanding the relentless effort to read this passage in light of the DSS, the term cannot be a reference to the Righteous Teacher of Qumran.[70] The extraordinary rank that Josephus implies here for Moses, in relation to God, such that defamation of his name amounts to a capital charge akin to misusing the divine name, is supported by his account of Moses, the divine man (θεῖον ἄνδρα) in the *Antiquities* (3.180). He speaks of Moses' "super-human power" (τῆς ὑπὲρ ἄνθρωπον . . . δυνάμεως, 3.318). Because Moses' laws clearly originate with God, he is "esteemed higher than his own nature" (τῆς αὐτοῦ φύσεως κρείττονα νομίζεσθαι, 3.320). Moses surpassed all other men (4.328), and in his words one seemed to hear the very speech of God (4.329). Although Josephus does not exactly divinize Moses, he does leave his special status ambiguous in much the same way as Josephus' Essenes do. Note that the Spartans regarded their lawgiver as a demi-god, granting Lycurgus a temple in Sparta after his death, where he received annual sacrifices "as to a god" (Xenophon, *Lac.* 15.2, 9; Plutarch, *Lyc.* 5.3; 31.3).

In the roughly symmetrical parallel to this notice (2.152), Josephus claims that Essenes could not be compelled to "defame the lawgiver" (βλασφημεῖν τὸν νομοθέτην—the same phrase as here), even under inventive torture and the threat of death.

---

[67] Pedanius, *Eup. simpl. med.* 1.133.1; 2.36.4, 118.2, 119.4; *Mat. med.* 1.78.2; 4.91.1; esp. 5.126.3.
[68] Cyranides 1.7.19, 8.26, 10.95, 17.16.
[69] *Simpl. med. temp.* 11.811.4; 12.41.13, 68.7.
[70] Correctly Beall 1988, 92–93, with discussion.

7. Essenes Avoid Spitting—Middles and Right

> **147** They guard against spitting into [their?] middles or to the right side and, even more than all other Judeans. . . .

The somewhat peculiar prepositional phrase, "into middles" (εἰς μέσους) is a favorite of Josephus'. Before his time, the heaviest user of this phrase was Dionysius of Halicarnassus,[71] outside of whom it appears only once or twice in each of four authors. Josephus has it a remarkable fifteen times.[72] If the meaning were "into the middle," we should have expected the neuter singular substantive εἰς τὸ μέσον, which is far more evenly distributed among ancient authors and across genres, though Josephus uses it only twice (*Ant.* 9.149; 17.177). It is odd that he should prefer the masculine adjective without definite article. Moreover, Josephus departs even from the established usage of εἰς μέσους. Those few writers who had employed the phrase earlier did so in a nearly formulaic way: with a verb of aggressive motion (βιάζω, ὠθέω, ῥίπτω, ἵημι) and a complementary direct object explaining whose "middles" were in question—usually πολεμίους (combatants) or ἐχθρούς (enemies, adversaries). Thus, it was usually a case of someone's charging bravely into the enemy's distributed middle. Josephus, however, has these combinations in only three of the phrase's fifteen occurrences (*Ant.* 5.206; 9.56; 12.429). In his narratives the accompanying verb is usually neutral (χωρέω, πάρειμι, προ/παρέρχομαι, παράγω, φέρω) and the "middles" are left without a noun-object complement (*War* 4.216; *Ant.* 3.308; 5.54; 17.130–131; 19.261; *Life* 37, 251, 255). Often, accordingly, the group comprises one's own compatriots. The oddity of the plural masculine adjective without article and Josephus' vague application of it render its precise meaning less than immediately obvious to us.

Although it is possible that the Essene prohibition of spitting into middles has to do with simple politeness, the larger construction (τὸ πτύσαι εἰς μέσους ἢ τὸ δεξιὸν μέρος) makes another explanation more likely. Spitting in general, but particularly into the middle area *of one's body* (Theophrastus, *Char.* 16.14; Pliny, *Nat.* 28.36)—the chest or torso (εἰς κόλπον πτύσαι; *in sinum spuendo*)—or to the right side—e.g., into the right shoe before dressing (Pliny, *Nat.* 24.172; 28.38;

---

[71] *Ant. rom.* 1.87.2; 5.46.4; 6.12.2, 5; 7.35.5; 8.65.5; 9.11.4, 48.3; 10.41.4.
[72] Here and *War* 4.216; 6.42; *Ant.* 3.13, 308; 5.54, 206; 9.56; 12.429; 17.130, 131; 19.261; *Life* 37, 251, 255.

cf. Petronius, *Sat.* 74.13)—were behaviors popularly thought to prevent or cure illness. The custom of spitting for luck or health was grounded in a belief in the curative powers of human saliva (Pliny, *Nat.* 38.35–39). Because of the very specific alternative provided by Josephus ("into the right side/part"), it seems more likely that his μέσους ("middles") refers to the centres *of bodies*—equivalent to κόλπους,[73] rather than to a singular *group middle* as normally assumed. If this interpretation is valid, then Josephus' Essenes, like the philosophical observers of such practices, reject spitting for good luck or to ward off disease, but not to clear one's throat. The right-side restriction apparently precludes the meaning "into the group."

It is commonly asserted that Josephus' remarks on Essene avoidance of spitting (albeit in two directions) is "strong evidence" for the Qumran-Essene hypothesis,[74] because the *Community Rule* (1QS 7.13–15) prescribes a month's penance for anyone who has spat *in an assembly*. But the superficially similar expression, "spat into the middle" (ירוק אל תוך), in the *Community Rule* appears to be *un faux ami*. First, 1QS 7 is listing a number of gauche behaviors liable to punishment: insulting companions, treating communal property recklessly, speaking foolishly, falling asleep during an assembly, going naked without good reason, *spitting into the assembly*, dressing shabbily, guffawing stupidly, and so forth. In such a context, refraining from spitting at the group seems perfectly sensible. If we had detailed community rules for other groups (Jesus' followers, Pharisees, Baptists, trade guilds, philosophical schools), we might expect them also to prohibit spitting during meetings. The Talmud, with characteristic vividness, confronts the problem of spittle build-up during prayer, and what to do about it—along with belching, yawning, and sneezing—and recommends ways to avoid spitting (*b. Ber.* 24a–b). In Josephus, however, there is no such list. Both his directional indicators (middles and right) and his coupling of the spitting prohibition with scrupulous observance of the Sabbath (2.147) suggest a purpose like that suggested above. In spite of common assumptions under the influence of the DSS, there is nothing to indicate that the spitting in question is in a communal context at all, any more than the toilet practices of the same paragraph (2.148).

---

[73] For this literal sense, cf. *Life* 326, where Josephus seizes an opponent wrestler-style, around the μέσος; cf. Herodotus 9.107; Aristophanes, *Eq.* 387; *Nub.* 1047.
[74] Beall 1988, 96; cf. Grabbe 1992, 2.495; VanderKam 1994, 87.

These few examples must suffice as a base for at least preliminary conclusions. Of the remainder—Josephus' treatments of women, marriage, and children in the Essene context, their community of goods, initiation, courage under torture, and sublime views of the afterlife (2.151–158), much more could be said. But all such analysis would confirm that the Essenes of *War* 2 represent in concentrated form many characteristic features of Josephus' outlook. The passage is remarkable for its combination of parallels and evocations: of material elsewhere in Josephus, of the Hasmonean literature, and of Greek and Roman myth.

One small matter is typically revealing for the source-critical question. The phrase ἔμοιγε δοκεῖν ("to seem to me, at least"), with which Josephus moves from Essene longevity to regimen and courage at 2.151, is an almost unique stylistic trait of the *War*. Contrast the more expected finite ἔμοιγε δοκεῖ ("it seems to me, at least"), which is attested dozens of times in earlier authors. Josephus' phrase with the infinitive appears, outside the *War*, only a couple of times before the second century C.E.[75] Yet he has it here and at *War* 2.479; 3.302; 4.312; 6.4. Again, the Essene passage is deeply embedded in the *Judean War*.

Conclusions and Historical Implications

1. *War*'s Essenes contribute both to this narrative and to Josephus' larger program in countless ways. His later works will describe a very few individuals—Moses, Solomon, and of course himself—as the embodiment of Judean virtues. But no group other than the Essenes, not even the priesthood as a body, so perfectly illustrates the characteristics of the nation. These are "men's men," legionaries of the soul, engaged in the serious pursuit of the virtuous life: disciplined, courageous, perfectly just, and contemptuous of the pleasures as much as the fears that drive ordinary people. It is no accident that the great Essene digression comes in the *War*, a work targeted precisely at improving the post-war image of the Judean national character. The Essenes carry the torch lit by the Hasmoneans in the story's opening paragraphs.

---

[75] Plato *Meno* (81a) and *Hippias Maior* (291a); it is also in the Orphic *Testimonia*, frag, 5.6, and Stobaeus, *Anth.* 4.1.114—both of the latter difficult to date.

2. Given that Josephus offers the Essenes as exemplary Judeans, to what extent has he manipulated the real group, or whatever he had in mind as the real group, to serve his aims? Clearly the language is his. Even the many *hapax legomena* in this passage, created by the unique nature of the subject matter, fit the patterns of his *hapax legomena* elsewhere: they serve the purposes of variation and showing off; they tend to be sparsely attested before his time, but well paralleled from Plutarch onward; and so they do not likely come from a source, but show Josephus' strenuous efforts to latch onto the new Atticism of the Second Sophistic.

Given Josephus' thorough working over of this school for his literary purposes, however, may we suppose that he has (or could have) taken almost any group, even one of an entirely different character, and beaten them into this image without respect for their actual nature? We have two strong indicators that he did not do this. First, he did not impose upon the Essenes a priestly identity, in spite of his demonstrable willingness to enhance priestly themes elsewhere in his narratives. Given his evident love for both Essenes and the priesthood, the temptation to color them as priests would presumably have been strong if he felt able to portray them however he wished.

Second, Josephus could not have reshaped the Essenes in radical ways because two independent authors, Philo (*Prob.* 75–91; fragments in Eusebius, *Praep.* 8.11.1–8) and Pliny the Elder, give much the same impression of them, even without Josephus' distinctive language and themes. It also occurred to Philo to use them as exemplary Judeans (*Prob.* 75). In historical work it is a rare luxury to be able get behind one ancient author's bias by consulting independent accounts of the same phenomenon. In the case of the Essenes we have that luxury, and since all accounts point to the same sort of historical phenomenon, we should take this agreement seriously.

3. Did the people behind the DSS belong to the Essene order? This is exceedingly difficult to imagine, for reasons that I hope will now be clear. We have seen that the case for identity is made on two grounds: allegedly extensive agreements in detail (initiation, holy meals, not spitting, etc.) and the persistent belief that Pliny's location of the Essenes indicates Qumran. But these are not good reasons. The specific agreements between Essenes and Qumraners are *not* more extensive than those between Essenes and other utopian groups of the Greco-Roman world—Hyperboreans or Pythagoreans—

and nowhere near as extensive as evocations of Sparta, though no one would suggest that Essenes were Spartans. Further, the *differences* between Josephus' Essenes and the DSS authors are substantial and intransigent, if Josephus is taken seriously as a source for the Essenes and not dismissed by *petitio principii*. Since the use of Pliny's notice to place Essenes at Qumran makes a fully circular argument, we should relinquish that appeal forthwith.

I am aware that the foregoing study, preliminary as it is, may tempt readers to consider an inference opposite to my intention, namely: if Josephus had such strong authorial tendencies as I argue, then perhaps even if he did have in mind the people of the DSS when he wrote of the Essenes, he might have had a motive to bend them completely out of shape. This would return us in essence to the argument of Cross and many others (above) that Josephus has skewed and "Hellenized" the Essene phenomenon. Leaving aside the circularity of this potential objection—it bypasses the methodological problem as to why scholars make the connection in the first place, and rushes headlong toward the safe haven of unfalsifiability—, there is a deeper problem.

Perhaps I can make the point most easily made by analogy. For decades now, American presidents have made it a habit in their annual State of the Union speech to plant in the balcony audience citizens who in some way or other embody American values: military personnel, educators, civil servants, and ordinary heroes who have distinguished themselves in the past year. Let us say that this custom is somewhat like Josephus' use of the Essenes to illustrate Judean virtues. In April 1993, U.S. federal agents stormed the compound of a religious sect called the Branch Davidians near Waco, Texas. This was an apocalyptic group gathered around a prophetic teacher-figure, David Koresh, which exhibited many parallels to the world-view developed in the DSS. Those parallels have been explored in detail by prominent scholars of ancient apocalypticism.[76]

We should all have been shocked if President Bill Clinton had, in his State of the Union Address of January 1994, singled out the Waco survivors as praiseworthy Americans. It would not have lessened the shock if he had focused on the Branch Davidians' remarkable sense of community, sharing of property, devotion to study, and good personal hygiene—say, their care not to spit. Implying that these

---

[76] Tabor and Gallagher 1995; Schaefer and Cohen 1998.

were the Branch Davidians' fundamental characteristics, while ignoring the apocalyptic-eschatological, dualistic, world-denying, anti-governmental animus that defined them, would be a psychological impossibility. We could not explain the President's choice by saying that of course he had his biases: he misinterpreted some of their beliefs and put his own Americanizing slant on others, even if we all agreed that the language was characteristically his. Such an explanation would be absurd because it would fail to answer the question, *Why?* Why would the President choose a group so fundamentally opposed to everything he valued: his inclusive, liberal-progressive, outward-looking agenda?

The people of the Scrolls were about as far as one could get from Josephus' view of the world. Their core beliefs involved rejection of the priestly establishment in Jerusalem and anticipation of a conflict that would destroy *those* sons of darkness along with the wicked foreign rulers. They were a world-denying sect, in the language of William James, who espoused every kind of dualism: cosmic, anthropological, and temporal. The world-affirming Jerusalem aristocrat and statesman Josephus, whose elegant *War* is imbued with the spirit of Greek *paideia*, embraced (as author) none of these perspectives. He vehemently rejected futile messianic hopes, "pseudo-prophets," and popular charismatic leaders. His heroes were the slain chief priests and other figures of the Jerusalem establishment.

It seems to me no less improbable that Flavius Josephus promoted the sect(s) behind the DSS and remade them as ideal Essene philosophers than that President Clinton should have promoted the Branch Davidians as model Americans.

Table 1: Essenes and Spartans

Essenes	*Spartans*
The Essenes follow a prescribed *regimen* (δίαιτα), a word used in this philosophical sense conspicuously in the Essene passage (5 of 11 times in *War*); otherwise, it is used sparingly: of all Judeans in *Apion* (1.182; 2.173–174, 235, 240) and of the Pharisees (*Ant.* 18.12, 15).	Lycurgus laid down a comprehensive regimen (δίαιτα) for all Spartiates to follow (Xen., *Lac.* 5.1; 7.3; Plu., *Lyc.* 24.1; *Mor.* 209f, 210a, 225f, 226f, 227b), a discipline that Josephus elsewhere claims they were unable to maintain in spite of military prowess; contrast the Judeans (*Apion* 2.235).
"Whereas these men shun the pleasures as vice, they consider self-control and not succumbing to the passions virtue" (2.120).	King Agesilaus, asked what benefit the laws of Lycurgus had brought Sparta, alleged replied, "contempt for the pleasures" (Plu., *Mor.* 210a).
As a sign of their immunity to the appeal of pleasures, Essenes avoid marriage and women altogether (2.120)—or (in the case of one group) minimize their implications by marrying only women of proven fertility, for the sole purpose of procreation (2.160–161).	The best indicator of the Spartan king Agesilaus' self-control is shown by his remarkable refusal to touch the one he loved (Xen. *Ages.* 5.4–6); Lycurgus' laws treat the indulgence of sexual feelings as very shameful (Xen., *Lac.* 2.12–14).
Marrying Essenes prove by their abstinence during pregnancy that they are coupled solely for the purpose of bearing children (τέκνων χρείαν, 2.161).	The Spartan constitution is radically oriented toward procreation: women's chief task is procreation (τεκνοποιία; Xen., *Lac.* 1.4). Although young men must marry, this is not for pleasure. They visit their wives only for brief conjugal visits, while still living with their male peers; wives and husbands can also be shared for maximum productivity (Xen., *Lac.* 1.5–10; Aristotle, *Pol.* 1270b).
Boys are adopted and raised with a rigorous training in the group's principles of character (2.120).	Boys are removed from their parents and raised by the community, to inculcate the values of simplicity and endurance (Xen., *Lac.* 2.2–6).
They are despisers of wealth (2.122). They practice community of goods (2.122).	Lycurgus forbade free Spartans from pursuing material gain; anyone found possessing gold or silver was fined (Xen., *Lac.* 7.1–6). He made wealth unenviable and dishonored (Plu., *Mor.* 239e).
Keeping their skin hard and dry (τὸ αὐχμεῖν), they make it a point of honor to avoid the use of oil (2.123).	Plutarch says that Spartiates kept their bodies hard and dry (αὐχμηροὶ τὰ σώματα), avoiding ointments and baths (Plu., *Mor.* 237a; *Lyc.* 16.6; *Ages.* 30.3).

Table 1 (cont.)

Essenes	Spartans
They dress with extreme simplicity, wearing as few clothes as practicable and replacing them only when absolutely worn out (2.126).	Spartiates go without the customary Greek tunic and receive only one cloak each year (Plu., *Mor.* 237a). They punished a man who put a border on his sack coat (*Mor.* 239c).
They do not buy and sell, but take from each other and from the common store as needed (2.127).	Spartiates are forbidden to sell anything. If they need something, they freely take it from their neighbors (Plu., *Mor.* 238f).
They have a special reverence for the sun as divine, addressing prayers to it (him) in the morning and avoiding offense to the sun's rays (2.128, 148).	Spartans continue to revere Apollo—widely identified with the sun—who is the guarantor of their constitution (Herodotus 1.65; Plato, *Leg.* 674d; Xen., *Ages.* 1.34; 2.15, 17; *Lac.* 8.5).
Almost everything in their lives is ordered by their freely-chosen leaders (2.134).	Even the most important Spartans live under obedience to their leaders: for example, they run when called (Xen., *Lac.* 8.1–4)
The 3-year Essene probation aims at producing endurance (καρτερία) and resistance to all hardship in its members (2.138; cf. 2.150–153). In the *Apion* Josephus makes καρτερία a distinctive Judean trait, in explicit contrast to the *undeserved* Spartan reputation for this quality (*Apion* 2.225, 228, 273).	Καρτερία was a renowned Spartan trait, the goal of their whole system of training (Xen., *Ages.* 5.3; 10.1; 11.9 Plu., *Mor.* 208c, 210a, 237a; *Lyc.* 2.2; 16.5–6; 18.1; 29.5; *Ages.* 11.7; 30.3)
Essenes practice complete equality, never surpassing another in dress or other signs of advantage when in positions of authority (2.122, 140).	Lycurgus banished wealth and poverty, persuading the citizens to live together in equality (Plu., *Lyc.* 8.1–9.2). King Agesilaus insisted on using the worst bed and wearing simple dress (Xen., *Ages.* 4.2; 10.2; 11.11).
They share a special communal meal of simple food, admission to which is permitted only to full members, after probation and initiation (2.129–132, 137–142).	Lycurgus instituted communal meals, the most distinctive trait of Spartiate life (Plu., *Lyc.* 10–12); at these meals, candidates were assessed for initiation (*Lyc.* 12.5–6).
Their meals are free of unseemly noise (2.132).	Spartan communal meals are free of outrage, drunken uproar, shameful behavior or speech (Xen., *Lac.* 5.6).

Table 1 (*cont.*)

Essenes	*Spartans*
They practice rare moderation in consuming food and drink, taking in only as much as necessary (2.133; cf. *Apion* 2.195).	Lycurgus ordered that Spartiates receive just enough food and drink, not too much or too little (Xen., *Lac.* 5.3–4).
They swear to keep their internal affairs secret and they are closed to the outside world (2.129, 141).	Spartiates neither travel abroad nor accept foreign visitors (unless willing to adopt their constitution); what is said at their meetings remains secret (Plu., *Mor.* 236f, 238e).
They have an extremely high and severe standard of justice, including expulsion from the order (2.143–145).	Whereas other states punish only crimes against others, Lycurgus inflicted severe penalties on anyone failing to live the most virtuous life possible; those who fail to meet the standards of the νόμιμα are no longer included among the peers (Xen., *Lac.* 10.4–7).
They especially honor the lawgiver, as next in rank to God (2.145), in keeping with Josephus' claims elsewhere about Moses' super-human status (*Ant.* 3.180, 318–320; 4.329).	All Spartan kings have divine ancestry and are treated as demi-gods at death (Xen., *Lac.* 15.2, 9), but the lawgiver Lycurgus was honored above all, partly through a temple in his honor and annual sacrifices "as to a god" (Plu., *Lyc.* 5.3; 30.3).
They submit to the elders and to a majority (2.146).	Lycurgus, by making elders the ultimate judges over life and death, enhanced their prestige beyond that of all others (Xen., *Lac.* 10.1–3).
They are long-lived (2.151).	The only lawgiver listed in Lucian's essay on the long-lived (*Macr.* 28) is Lycurgus the Spartan.
They have trained themselves to be contemptuous of pain, suffering, and death itself (2.151–153). For Essenes, death with honor (τὸν θάνατον, εἰ μετ᾽ εὐκλείας) is better even than deathlessness (2.151).	Lycurgus' most admirable achievement: causing the Spartans to regard noble death (τὸν καλὸν θάνατον) as better than a life in shame (Xen., *Lac.* 9.1)
They study "apophthegms of prophets" (2.159). "Apophthegm" is a rare term, used only here in Josephus, and most often associated in other literature with the compact Spartan way of speaking.	The Spartans detested lengthy speech and trained their young to speak, if at all, with extreme conciseness (Plu., *Lyc.* 19–20); collections of Laconian ("laconic") apophthegms circulated widely in antiquity.

BIBLIOGRAPHY

Adam, A.
    1972   *Antike Berichte über die Essener.* Berlin.
Bauer, W.
    1924   Essener. *PWRE Supplementband* 4:386–430.
Baumgarten, A. I.
    1984   Josephus and Hippolytus on the Pharisees. *HUCA* 55:1–25.
Baumgarten, J. M.
    1967   The Essene Avoidance of Oil and the Laws of Purity. *RevQ* 6:183–92.
Beall, T. S.
    1988   *Josephus' Description of the Essenes Illustrated by the Dead Sea Scrolls.* Cambridge.
Bergmeier, R.
    1993   *Die Essener-Berichte des Flavius Josephus: Quellenstudien zu den Essenertexten im Werk des judischen Historiographen.* Kampen.
Bilde, P.
    1988   *Flavius Josephus between Jerusalem and Rome: His Life, His Works and Their Importance.* Sheffield.
Black, M.
    1956   The Account of the Essenes in Hippolytus and Josephus. Pages 172–82 in *The Background of the New Testament and its Eschatology.* Edited by W. D. Davies and D. Daube. Cambridge.
Bloch, R. S.
    2002   *Antike Vorstellungen vom Judentum: der Judenexkurs des Tacitus im Rahmen der griechisch-römischen Ethnographie.* Stuttgart.
Boyle, A. J. and W. J. Dominik, eds.
    2003   *Flavian Rome: Culture, Image, Text.* Leiden.
Burchard, C.
    1962   Pline et les Esséniens. *RB* 69:533–69.
    1977   Die Essener bei Hippolyt: Hippolyt, REF. IX 18, 2–28, 2 und Josephus, Bell. 2, 119–161. *JSJ* 8:1–41.
Cansdale, L.
    1997   *Qumran and the Essenes: A Re-evaluation of the Evidence.* Tübingen.
Cartledge, P. and A. Spawforth
    1989   *Hellenistic and Roman Sparta: A Tale of Two Cities.* London.
Cody, J. M.
    2003   Conquerors and Conquered on Flavian Coins. Pages 103–23 in *Flavian Rome: Culture, Image, Text.* Edited by A. J. Boyle and W. J. Dominik. Leiden.
Corbeill, A.
    2004   *Nature Embodied: Gesture in Ancient Rome.* Princeton.
Cross, F. M.
    1961   *The Ancient Library of Qumran and Modern Biblical Studies.* New York.
Donceel, R.
    1997   Qumran. Pages 392–96 in vol. 4 of *The Oxford Encyclopaedia of Archaeology in the Near East.* Edited by E. M. Meyers. Oxford.
Droge, A. J. and J. D. Tabor.
    1992   *A Noble Death: Suicide and martyrdom among Christians and Jews in Antiquity.* San Francisco.
Dupont-Sommer, A.
    1961   *The Essene Writings from Qumran.* Cleveland.
Eckstein, A. M.
    1995   *Moral Vision in the Histories of Polybius.* Berkeley.
Edmondson, J., S. Mason, and J. Rives, eds.
    2005   *Flavius Josephus and Flavian Rome.* Oxford.

Farmer, W. R.
1973   *Maccabees, Zealots, and Josephus: An Inquiry into Jewish Nationalism in the Greco-Roman Period.* Westport.
Feldman, L. H.
1998   *Josephus's Interpretation of the Bible.* Berkeley.
2005   Parallel Lives of Two Lawgivers: Josephus' Moses and Plutarch's *Lycurgus.* Pages 209–42 in *Flavius Josephus and Flavian Rome.* Edited by J. Edmondson, S. Mason, and J. Rives. Oxford.
Ferguson, J.
1975   *Utopias of the Classical World.* London.
Gallivan, P.
1981   The Fasti for A.D. 70–96. *CQ* 31:186–220.
Garnsey, P.
1999   *Food and Society in Classical Antiquity: Key Themes in Ancient History.* Cambridge.
Gleason, M. W.
1995   *Making Men: Sophists and Self-Presentation in Ancient Rome.* Princeton.
Golb, N.
1995   *Who Wrote the Dead Sea Scrolls? The Search for the Secret of Qumran.* New York.
Goodman, M.
1987   *The Ruling Class of Judaea: The Origins of the Jewish Revolt against Rome AD 66–70.* Cambridge.
Grabbe, L. L.
1992   *Judaism from Cyrus to Hadrian.* 2 vols. Minneapolis.
Gray, R.
1993   *Prophetic Figures in late Second Temple Jewish Palestine: The Evidence from Josephus.* Oxford.
Hadot, P.
1998   *The Inner Citadel: The Meditations of Marcus Aurelius.* Cambridge.
Hengel, M.
1989   *The Zealots: Investigations into the Jewish Freedom Movement in the Period from Herod I until 70 A.D.* Edinburgh.
Hirschfeld, Y.
2004   *Qumran in Context: Reassessing the Archaeological Evidence.* Peabody.
Hölscher, G.
1916   Josephus. *PWRE* 18:1934–2000.
Isaac, B. H.
2004   *The Invention of Racism in Classical Antiquity.* Princeton.
Isaac, B. H. and I. Roll
1976   A Milestone of A.D. 69 from Judaea: The Elder Trajan and Vespasian. *JRS* 66:15–19.
Jaeger, W.
1973   *Paideia: The Ideals of Greek Culture.* Oxford.
Kennedy, G. A.
1994   *A New History of Classical Rhetoric.* Princeton.
Kohler, K.
1901–1906   Essenes. Pages 224–32 in vol. 5 of *Jewish Encyclopaedia.* Edited by I. Singer et al. New York.
Laqueur, R.
1970   *Der jüdische Historiker Flavius Josephus: Ein biographischer Versuch auf neuer quellenkritischer Grundlage.* 1920. Repr. Darmstadt.
Levick, B.
1999   *Vespasian.* London.

Mader, G.
    2000   *Josephus and the Politics of Historiography: Apologetic and Impression Management in the Bellum Judaicum.* Leiden.
Mason, S.
    1988   Priesthood in Josephus and the 'Pharisaic Revolution.' *JBL* 107:657–61.
    1991   *Flavius Josephus on the Pharisees: A Composition-Critical Study.* Leiden.
    1994   Josephus, Daniel, and the Flavian House. Pages 161–91 in *Josephus and the History of the Greco-Roman Period: Essays in Memory of Morton Smith.* Edited by F. Parente and J. Sievers. Leiden.
    2001   *Life of Josephus.* Vol. 9 of *Flavius Josephus: Translation and Commentary.* Series edited by S. Mason. Leiden.
    2005   Figured Speech and Irony in the Works of T. Flavius Josephus. Pages 243–88 in *Flavius Josephus and Flavian Rome.* Edited by J. Edmondson, S. Mason, and J. Rives. Oxford.
Mattern, S. P.
    1999   *Rome and the Enemy: Imperial Strategy in the Principate.* Berkeley.
Matthews, S.
    2001   *First Converts: Rich Pagan Women and the Rhetoric of Mission in Early Judaism and Christianity.* Stanford.
May, J. M.
    1988   *Trials of Character: The Eloquence of Ciceronian Ethos.* Chapel Hill.
Mayer-Schärtel, B.
    1995   *Das Frauenbild des Josephus: Eine sozialgeschichtliche und kulturanthropologische Untersuchung.* Stuttgart.
Mellor, R.
    2003   The New Aristocracy of Power. Pages 69–91 in *Flavian Rome: Culture, Image, Text.* Edited by A. J. Boyle and W. J. Dominik. Leiden.
Meshorer, Y. A.
    1982   *Ancient Jewish Coinage.* 2 vols. New York.
Parente, F. and J. Sievers, eds.
    1994   *Josephus and the History of the Greco-Roman Period: Essays in Memory of Morton Smith.* Leiden.
Price, J. J.
    1992   *Jerusalem under Siege: The Collapse of the Jewish State, 66–70 C.E.* Leiden.
Rajak, T.
    1983   *Josephus: The Historian and his Society.* London.
    1994   Ciò Che Flavio Giuseppe Vide: Josephus and the Essenes. Pages 141–60 in *Josephus and the History of the Greco-Roman Period: Essays in Memory of Morton Smith.* Edited by F. Parente and J. Sievers. Leiden.
Sanders, E. P.
    1992   *Judaism, Practice and Belief, 63 BCE–66 CE.* London.
Schaefer, P. and M. R. Cohen
    1998   *Toward the Millennium: Messianic Expectations from the Bible to Waco.* Leiden.
Schneider, R. M.
    1998   Die Faszination des Feindes: Bilder der Parther und des Orients in Rom. Pages 95–146 in *Das Partherreich und seine Zeugnisse.* Edited by J. Wiesehöfer. Stuttgart.
Schwartz, S.
    1990   *Josephus and Judaean Politics.* Leiden.
Smith, M.
    1958   The Description of the Essenes in Josephus and the Philosophoumena. *HUCA* 35:273–93.

Stegemann, H.
    1992   The Qumran Essenes—Local Members of the Main Jewish Union
                    in Late Second Temple Times. Pages 83–166 in *The Madrid Qumran
                    Congress: Proceedings of the International Congress on the Dead Sea Scrolls,
                    Madrid 18–21 March 1991*. Edited by J. T. Berrerra and L. V.
                    Montaner. Leiden.
Stern, M.
    1974–1984   *Greek and Latin Authors on Jews and Judaism: Edited with Introductions,
                    Translations and Commentary*. 3 vols. Jerusalem.
Tabor, J. D. and E. V. Gallagher
    1995   *Why Waco? Cults and the Battle for Religious Freedom in America*. Berkeley.
Thackeray, H. St. J.
    1967   *Josephus: The Man and the Historian*. New York. (1929)
Tigerstedt, E. N.
    1974   *The Legend of Sparta in Classical Antiquity*. 2 vols. Stockholm.
Tyree, E. L. and E. Stefanoudaki.
    1996   The Olive Pit and Roman Oil Making. *BA* 59:171–78.
VanderKam, J. C.
    1994   *The Dead Sea Scrolls Today*. Grand Rapids.
Vermes, G.
    1995   *The Dead Sea Scrolls in English*. London.
Vermes, G. and M. D. Goodman, eds.
    1989   *The Essenes According to the Classical Sources*. Sheffield.
Wardman, A.
    2002   *Rome's Debt to Greece*. Bristol.
Weeber, K.-W.
    2003   *Luxus im alten Rom: Die Schwelgerei, das suesse Gift*. Darmstadt.
Williams, C. A.
    1999   *Roman Homosexuality: Ideologies of Masculinity in Classical Antiquity*.
                    Oxford.
Williams, D. S.
    1994   Josephus and the Authorship of *War* 2.119–161 (on the Essenes).
                    JSJ 25:207–21.
Ziolkowski, A.
    1993   Urbs Direpta, or How the Romans Sacked Cities. Pages 69–91
                    in *War and Society in the Roman World*. Edited by J. Rich and
                    G. Shipley. London.

WHAT DIFFERENCE DOES PHILOSOPHY MAKE? THE THREE SCHOOLS AS A RHETORICAL DEVICE IN JOSEPHUS

Gunnar Haaland

1. *Introduction*

With the possible exception of the *Testimonium Flavianum*, no other text from the writings of Josephus is more famous than his excursuses on the three schools of Jewish philosophy in *War* 2.119–166, and in *Antiquities* 13.171–173 and 18.11–22. Historians have scrutinized and debated these texts and their contexts almost endlessly in order to reconstruct history.[1] More recently, several scholars have argued that a closer analysis of the literary shape and function of these excursuses is a necessary prerequisite for any reconstructing of history.[2]

  This article will focus mainly upon the literary and historiographical perspectives, and deal with historical reconstruction only very briefly. I will examine the excursuses in their respective contexts in order to determine their function within Josephus' narrative argument.[3] My claim is that, rather than explaining the storyline, these excursuses are rhetorical devices that display authorial concerns on a more sophisticated level. They provide enhancement and ornamentation to the narrative and reveal important aspects of Josephus' strategy of persuasion. Particularly, I will pay attention to the excursuses as presentations of what we may call the "model Jews" of Josephus. His last work *Against Apion*, being without any presentation of the three schools of phi-

---

[1] Such discussions can be found in virtually every presentation of late Second Temple Judaism, and in much of the literature referred to below. For a comprehensive review of scholarship up until 1980, see Feldman 1984, 542–672. For more recent contributions, see e.g., Vermes and Goodman 1989; Saldarini 1988; Stemberger 1995; Baumgarten 1997.

[2] See e.g., Mason 1991; Rajak 1994; McLaren 2000.

[3] In line with much recent scholarship, I assume that, though Josephus was working with sources, he can be held accountable for the excursuses as we have them. See e.g., Mason 1991, 176–77, 210–11, 373; McLaren 2000, 42. A brief quotation from Marcus' footnote to *Ant.* 13.288 in the Loeb edition may serve as an example of the dominant approach some decades ago: "the style of most of the passages on the Jewish sects suggests the hand of Nicolas."

losophy, provides an interesting counterpoint and will be examined toward the end of the article. First, however, there is a need for a brief preamble about Josephus' excursuses in general and my approach to the three excursuses on the Jewish philosophies in particular.

2. *The Narrative and Rhetorical Function of Josephus' Excursuses*

Josephus equips his narratives with several types of excursuses, ranging from brief digressions to elaborate compositions. The narrative and rhetorical function of these excursuses vary in many respects. McLaren distinguishes between the *descriptive excursus* and the *analytical excursus*:[4]

> The first presents descriptive accounts that help provide detail and background information for the reader. The many geographical descriptions of regions and locations are the best examples. . . . They are normally introduced into the text when the region or location first becomes an important part of the narrative.
> The second type . . . is a careful mixture of what appears to be excursus and explicit commentary. The important point to note about these excursuses is that they are not used simply as an occasion to provide descriptive information. Their positioning in the text is generally dictated by authorial concerns other than a desire to present background information.

This distinction is clearly helpful since it alerts the reader to the importance of narrative context and authorial comments, and draws attention to the various narrative and rhetorical functions of the excursuses. In the context of the present investigation, however, it is important to note that no excursus—and arguably nothing else in a text—is purely descriptive. To stick to McLaren's example: The geographical excursuses are not "entirely descriptive," even though they "are not couched in any interpretative clothing." As McLaren correctly points out, they "display a concern to provide the reader with information that will encourage a sense of wonder at the feats performed and the splendour of the country."[5] In other words: These excursuses provide not just information and explanation, but also embellishment and rhetorical amplification.

Instead of assigning the excursuses on the philosophies to one of

---

[4] McLaren 2000, 32–33.
[5] McLaren 2000, 32. For examples of such geographical excursuses, see *War* 2.188–191 (on Ptolemais and its surroundings), 3.35–58 (on Galilee, Perea, Samaria and Judea), 3.158–160 (on Jotapata and its fortifications), 3.506–521 (on the Sea of Galilee, the sources of Jordan and the area around the lake), 4.452–485 (on Jericho,

two—or more—categories, I will examine a) to what extent the excursuses provide necessary, or at least relevant, background information that elucidates the storyline, and b) to what extent they are vehicles of other authorial concerns.[6]

The first point relates to the narrative on a very basic level, taking the interruption of the chronological record of events as a point of departure, and asking to what extent the excursus provides *explanation* of the storyline that it interrupts. This is a matter of understanding the narrative as narrative.

The second point relates to the interpretation of the narrative as *persuasion*. It aims at discovering how the introduction of an excursus enhances the narrative, reveals authorial strategies, hints at particular preferences, makes explicit certain judgments, etc. These are more intricate matters and invite for various suggestions and longer discussions. Accordingly, an amount of selectiveness is necessary when dealing with this latter point.

3. War *2.119–166*

The Narrative Context of the First Excursus

The presentation of the three schools of Jewish philosophy first appears in the second book of *War*. This book deals with the period from the death of Herod the Great to the early stage of the Jewish revolt. After recording the disturbances that broke out following Herod's death, the division of the country between his sons and the Roman takeover of Judea from Archelaus, we are introduced to Judas the Galilean:[7]

> (Judas) incited his countrymen to revolt, upbraiding them as cowards for consenting to pay tribute to the Romans and tolerating mortal masters, after having God for their lord. This man was a sophist who

---

the Jordan Valley, the Dead Sea and Sodom, interrupted by a brief narrative sequence in *War* 4.477), and *War* 5.184–247 (on the Jerusalem temple). For an example of the analytical excursus according to McLaren's categorization, see e.g., *War* 3.70–109 (on the Roman army).

[6] As far as I can see, McLaren's labeling of the *Antiquities* 13 excursus as descriptive and the two others as analytical, does not contribute significantly to an otherwise fruitful discussion. See McLaren 2000, 42. More important is the observation on p. 39 that the excursuses "are not placed when the groups are first mentioned in the narrative."

[7] The writings of Josephus are quoted from the translations of the Loeb Classical Library, unless otherwise indicated.

founded a school of his own (ἦν δ᾽ οὗτος σοφιστὴς ἰδίας αἱρέσεως),[8] having nothing in common with the others. Jewish philosophy, in fact, takes three forms. The followers of the first school are called Pharisees, of the second Sadducees, of the third Essenes. (*War* 2.118–119)

The extensive presentation of the Essenes comes next, followed by the much shorter presentations of the Pharisees and Sadducees.[9] At the end of this excursus, one would expect a return to Judas the Galilean and his call for revolt. This does not happen. Instead the narrative moves on to Philip and Antipas, their building projects, the accession of Tiberius and his commission of Pilate. Both Judas and the schools of philosophy are left behind.

The First Excursus as Explanation

At first look, the background information provided by the excursus on the philosophies appears rather unnecessary when it comes to understanding what is going on in the narrative. The extensive treatment of the Essenes seems particularly out of proportion. The excursus disturbs rather than supports the record of political leaders and popular insurrectionists. Most strikingly, we look in vain for the kind of information that would clearly have been most relevant, namely the position of the respective schools on the issue of Roman rule.[10]

However, upon closer examination, a certain amount of relevance can be detected. In connection with the removal of Archelaus by the Romans, Josephus narrates how Archelaus sent for "the soothsayers and some Chaldaeans" to have them interpret a dream and how this task was accomplished by "a certain Simon, of the sect

---

[8] Thackeray translates "sect" for αἵρεσις, while I prefer "school." Thackeray's description of Judas the Galilean as the *founder* of this αἵρεσις is an idiomatic translation that is justified by the context, and supported by the parallel in *Ant.* 18.9. See also the entry to σοφιστής in Rengstorf 1973–1983, as well as McLaren 2004, 98–99. Mason (1995, 162) translates "a sophist of his own private school."

[9] Several scholars have claimed that especially the account of the Essenes appears to be borrowed. See e.g., Moore 1929, 374. Smith (1958, 293) points to Gerasa, Philadelphia or another Hellenistic city in Transjordan as likely places of origin. However, Rajak insists that "the Jerusalem priestly establishment could hardly have afforded to be wholly ignorant of what radical Jewish sectarians a stone's throw from Jerusalem were thinking and doing," and reads the account mainly as reflecting Josephus' personal knowledge. See Rajak 1994, 144 (quotation), 155.

[10] See McLaren 2004, 99–100. Note that Mason (1991, 123) detects such information in the description of the loyalty of the Essenes toward authorities (*War* 2.140). However, Beall (1988, 80–81) convincingly argues that this is a matter of obedience toward the Essene leadership.

(γένος) of the Essenes" (*War* 2.112–113). One may argue that a further presentation of the Essenes would be proper in this context. In fact, the following excursus includes information on Essene soothsaying: "There are some among them who profess to foretell the future, being versed from their early years in holy books, various forms of purification and apophthegms of prophets; and seldom, if ever, do they err in their predictions" (*War* 2.159).

Nonetheless, the account of the Essenes (*War* 2.119–161) is far too extensive to be fully explained as an explanatory footnote to the record of Simon's interpretation of Archelaus' dream (*War* 2.112–113). Such a reading is also complicated by the substantial material between the two texts and would make the following presentation of the Pharisees and Sadducees (*War* 2.162–166) mostly irrelevant.

We may add that an Essene, even an Essene soothsayer, named Judas appears already in *War* 1.78–80. That account would have been a proper place for a further presentation of the Essenes or even for the inclusion of the extensive excursus, but this does not happen.[11] Quite different, however, is the presentation we find in *Antiquities* 15.371–379. In this passage, the comparison between the Essenes and the Pythagoreans, together with the record of a prophecy by Menahem the Essene, is clearly introduced in order to explain the narrative.

The first account of the Pharisees in *War*, describing their rise to power during the reign of Alexandra (*War* 1.110–113), contains a brief, informative and relevant description of the Pharisees as "a body of Jews with the reputation of excelling the rest of their nation in the observance of religion, and as exact exponents of the laws" (*War* 1.110). This account involves the Pharisaic movement as such, not only an individual as in the two accounts of Essene soothsayers in *War*.[12] It could therefore have been an even more suitable context for the excursus on the three schools, but Josephus does not seize that opportunity.[13]

---

[11] The same applies to the parallel accounts in *Antiquities* on Judas the Essene (*Ant.* 13.311–313) and Simon the Essene (*Ant.* 17.346–348).

[12] Different from the Pharisees and Sadducees, the Essenes as a collective never appear as main characters in Josephus' record of history. The closest they get is the description in *Ant.* 15.71–72, 78 of the favorable treatment they received from King Herod.

[13] This is probably a matter of deliberate rhetorical design. Since the Pharisees are the "bad guys" in *War* 1.110–113, the introduction of a laudatory excursus would not fit. See Mason 1991, 110–15. However, Josephus could have created a beautiful juxtaposition of the seemingly pious Pharisees and the truly pious Essenes. But again, he does not seize the opportunity.

It seems as if Josephus deliberately chooses to present an excursus on the three schools together, rather than distributing the information on the different schools to their proper places in the narrative. And instead of introducing the excursus at the first possible juncture, he apparently saves it for a particular occasion.

The conclusion must be that the excursus on the Jewish philosophies in *War* 2.119–166 makes little sense if we approach it as an extensive, explanatory footnote. It is not introduced to help us understand the storyline, but the inclusion of the excursus is nonetheless a deliberate authorial choice. The mentioning of Simon the Essene (*War* 2.113) and particularly of Judas the Galilean and his αἵρεσις (*War* 2.118) may have triggered the introduction of the excursus,[14] but its main purpose must be a different one.

We may even adopt the opposite approach, and ask: Why does Josephus lend a certain prestige to Judas by referring to him as a σοφιστής and the leader of a αἵρεσις?[15] Why not simply call him a στασιαστής ("rebel") or something similar? Since this school immediately disappears from the narrative never to return, one might suspect that the narrative is deliberately designed to accommodate the introduction of the excursus on the three noble schools. In other words: Could it be that the cause–effect pattern is the opposite from what is usually assumed? Could it be that the description of Judas is a product of the excursus, rather than a—more or less coincidental—trigger?

The First Excursus as Persuasion

If the excursus is not introduced in order to clarify the storyline, what other authorial concerns does it display? We may also include the more speculative assumption suggested at the end of the previous paragraph, and ask: If the narrative is deliberately designed to facilitate the inclusion of the excursus, what could be the reasons for such a move?

---

[14] This is the first time Josephus uses the word αἵρεσις with specific reference to a "school" or "faction." In the more general meaning of "choice," the term appears already in *War* 1.199.

[15] It is not clear to what extent the word σοφιστής is negatively loaded in this particular passage and from Josephus' pen in general. The word is always applied to troublemakers of some sort, but the preceeding presentation of the two σοφισταί (*War* 1.648–656, also referred to in *War* 2.10) is full of positive characteristics: They had "a reputation as profound experts in the laws of their country, who consequently

First, the inclusion of this excursus is completely in line with one of Josephus' major concerns in *War*: to acquit the Jewish nation from being collectively responsible for the revolt, by instead insisting that only a limited group of rebels were to be blamed from among the Jews.[16] The call for a revolt against the Romans by Judas the Galilean represents a critical development in the narrative, and therefore a proper occasion for the introduction of a laudatory account as some sort of counterpoint. As this Judas is presented as "a sophist who founded a school of his own," the presentation of three dignified schools of philosophy fits neatly, even if it is mostly irrelevant to the unfolding narrative, and even if the school of Judas has "nothing in common with the others" (*War* 2.118).

Secondly, my suggestion that this particular presentation of Judas the Galilean may be triggered by a desire to include the excursus makes it necessary to move our attention for a moment from the function of the excursus, in order to examine the function of the account on Judas. As we are not told anything about the fate of Judas, the nature of the revolt or the Roman response, the brief account of Judas represents a digression and not an integral part of the storyline. Smith accordingly considers the excursus to be "a digression from a digression from a digression," and elaborates as follows: "It was under Coponius—by the way—that Judas the Galilean started the revolt. This Judas—by the way—was a sophist who founded a sect of his own. For—by the way—there are three schools of philosophy among the Jews."[17]

Smith does not discuss the implications of this structure, but according to McLaren, this is one of the reasons for viewing the account

---

enjoyed the highest esteem of the whole nation" (*War* 1.648). Thackeray translates "doctors" in this account, while Feldman prefers "scholars" in his translation of the parallel account (*Ant.* 17.152, 155). Our passage, with its juxtaposition of the novel school of a single sophist and three established schools of philosophy, obviously points to the inferiority of the former. Note, however, the neutral translation in Mason (1991, 121): "This man represented a peculiar school of thought." As for the remaining occurrences, they are all parts of derogatory statements. This applies to the second reference to Judas the Galilean (*War* 2.433), the reference to his son Menahem (*War* 2.445), as well as the one occurrence in *Against Apion*. In the former case the ambiguous superlative δεινότατος ("most redoubtable") is attached, while the final occurrence is accompanied by heavy, negative qualifiers: "the Lysimachuses and Molons and other writers of that class, reprobate sophists and deceivers of youth" (*Apion* 2.236).

[16] See e.g., *War* 1.10–11, 27, along with Rajak 1983, 78–103; Bilde 1988, 74, 77; Mason 1991, 121–22; McLaren 2000, 44–45.

[17] Smith 1958, 276.

of Judas the Galilean as "a crafted and manipulated construction by Josephus."[18] My reading could be used as a further argument along this line.

Be this as it may, it remains obvious that Josephus could clearly have depicted Judas more harshly than he does. However, the effect of his description is that he gets a suitable occasion for introducing the three schools of philosophy as a presentation of Jewish culture at its best.

This brings us to a third point: The schools of philosophy, and particularly the Essenes, represent "model Jews."[19] Rajak notes: "Josephus wished to depict the Essenes to Romans as the quintessential Jews. Philo had acclimatized the subject to Greek literature and Pliny the Elder had alerted a Roman readership."[20] In other words, Josephus' presentation of the three schools is a piece of idealized, stereotyped ethnography. Typically enough, this presentation contains universal values as well as particular, ethnographic traits. The Essenes exhibit standard virtues such as temperance, rejection of pleasures, control over passions (*War* 2.12), endurance (*War* 2.138), and contempt of torture and death (*War* 2.151–153).[21] Such virtues were in antiquity attributed to all great men—philosophers, politicians or warlords, Romans, Greeks or barbarians regardless. At the same time these "model Jews" are coated in a very particular way, namely as "sages of the type the East was expected to produce."[22] Of the numerous examples of this tendency in the presentation of the Essenes, I will mention only two: the morning prayers to the sun (*War* 2.128)[23] and the skills in foretelling the future, which we have already touched upon (*War* 2.159).[24] In short, Josephus depicts the Essenes as exponents of standard manly virtues, dressed as barbarian ascetic sages.

---

[18] McLaren 2004, 90, cf. 93–94.

[19] Mason in this volume suggests that the exposition of Judean character, understood as an accentuation of Judean manliness, is the chief goal of *War*. This new and stirring approach highlights the importance of the first excursus as a presentation of Josephus' "model Jews."

[20] Rajak 1994. Rajak refers to Paul 1992 for this view.

[21] For an extensive presentation of these features, see Mason in this volume. Note that the account of the Essenes focuses mainly upon their lifestyle, while the brief records of the Pharisees and Sadducees address behavior, doctrine and comparative stance quite evenly, as noted by McLaren 2000, 36.

[22] Momigliano 1975, 86.

[23] See e.g., Beall 1988, 132; Förster 2005.

[24] Note that Simon the Essene is mentioned together with "some Chaldaeans" in *War* 2.112–113.

Of course, all attempts to reconstruct history must take into consideration that Josephus' accounts are modeled according to ethnographical ideals and stereotypes. Without entering into a further discussion at this point, which would be beyond the scope of this article, I simply subscribe to Rajak's position: "We are not dealing with an *either/or* as tends to be supposed (*either* ethnographic fiction *or* a realistic account), but with a *both/and*. Josephus' digression on the Essenes are texts which *both* conform to historiographical canons *and* draw upon the author's experience... The difficulty lies in understanding how the two elements interact."[25] As we return to the narrative and rhetorical perspectives rather than the historical, we may note the neat interaction between the characters displayed in the narrative and those of the excursus. The complex and often tragic family-business of the Herodian house (*War* 1.431–2.100) is juxtaposed with the abstinence from family life (*War* 2.120–121), the strict discipline (*War* 2.134–153), and the elected leadership (*War* 2.123) of the Essenes.[26] In effect, the virtues of the "model Jews" of the excursus provide a certain compensation for the vices of the main characters of the narrative.

Some more points could have been made at this stage, but we will have occasion to pick them up later on. It is therefore time to proceed to the briefer excursus in *Antiquities* 13.

4. Antiquities *13.171–173*

The Narrative Context of the Second Excursus

The thirteenth book of *Antiquities* covers roughly the Hasmonean period. In the first part of the book, we follow Jonathan through his changing fortunes. From *Antiquities* 13.145 and onwards, Demetrius II Nicanor is the main antagonist. After defeating him in Galilee (*Ant.* 13.158–162), Jonathan renews the friendship treaties with Rome and Sparta (*Ant.* 13.163–170). At this point, Josephus leaves his source, 1 Maccabees. Before proceeding to Jonathan's further victories over Demetrius, he introduces a brief excursus on the three Jewish schools. This excursus only deals with one topic, namely the position of the three schools on the question of "fate or free will."

---

[25] Rajak 1994, 145.
[26] See Mason in this volume.

The Function of the Second Excursus

The second excursus makes little sense if we view it as an explanatory footnote. Neither Pharisees, nor Sadducees nor Essenes play any part in this record of military events. The two former factions first appear in *Antiquities* 13.288–298, where it is reported how the favor of John Hyrcanus passes from the Pharisees to the Sadducees.[27] At the end of this account, the Essenes are briefly mentioned in a cross-reference to the *War* 2 excursus (*Ant.* 13.298), and shortly afterwards Judas the Essene appears on the stage (*Ant.* 13.311–313).

Daniel Schwartz notes that Josephus "justifies the insertion by introducing it by 'At this time,' but this need be no more than a convenient way of linking otherwise irrelevant sources."[28] Even if historians will appreciate such "a purely chronological notice,"[29] and even if we assume that Josephus' concern was simply to present Jewish philosophical schools and to date them in the early Hasmonean period,[30] the insertion of the excursus precisely in *Antiquities* 13.171–173 is indeed peculiar. Sievers suggests that it is occasioned simply by Josephus' need to fill in some vacant space in his manuscript.[31] McLaren claims that "the only possible connection between the narrative and the summary" is found in Jonathan's reflection upon how he is helped by the providence of God (πρόνοια θεοῦ, *Ant.* 13.163).[32] However, I will claim that another connection is more striking,

[27] In this connection, the different views of the Pharisees and the Sadducees concerning oral tradition is briefly explained (*Ant.* 13.297). This note provides the background for understanding what is going on when Hyrcanus abrogates and prohibits the νόμιμα ("regulations") of the Pharisees. The passage starts with a cross-reference to the excursus in *Ant.* 13.171–173, and ends with a cross-reference to the more extensive one in *War* 2.119–166. Note also that the Pharisees reappear in *Ant.* 13.401–423.

[28] Schwartz 1983, 161. Schwartz subscribes to the view that the excursus is borrowed from Nicolaus of Damascus. See also e.g., Moore 1929, 383–84. However, Williams (1997, 56–58) claims on the basis of stylometric analysis that Josephus was himself the final author of the account.

[29] Moore 1929, 372.

[30] See e.g., Mason 1991, 196–212. The antiquity of the philosophical schools is also stressed in *Ant.* 18.11.

[31] Sievers (2001) notices that the brief excursus apparently replaces 1 Macc 12:19–23 in Josephus' account, and that those missing verses have already been paraphrased in *Ant.* 12.226–227. His suggestion is that Josephus initially used these verses twice, but later attempted to improve his text by instead pasting the brief excursus in *Ant.* 13.171–173.

[32] McLaren 2000, 39, 42. See also Martin 1981, 135. The fact that the word εἱμαρμένη ("fate") is used in the excursus, and not πρόνοια ("providence"), makes

namely the mentioning of Rome and Sparta. As the narrative moves
to these prestigious locations, Josephus simply takes the opportunity
to put the Jewish nation on the map not only politically, but also
culturally and intellectually.[33]

This gives us occasion to address one of the points that we did
not touch upon above, and that has to do with Josephus' way of
doing ethnography. We have previously noticed how Josephus conforms
to preconceived, Greek conceptions of the Jews as representatives of
barbarian sages. At the same time, however, he takes a different tack:
By using what we may term a strategy of analogies, he wants his readers to recognize the similarity between the Jewish and Greek cultures.

This strategy appears explicitly already in the first excursus, as the
Essene doctrine on the afterlife is connected to Greek beliefs (*War*
2.155–156). McLaren points out that simply by using the words
"school" and "philosophy," Josephus encourages such analogies.[34]
The position of the three schools on "fate or free will"—which dominates the second excursus—is phrased in a language that is easily
intelligible to a Hellenistic-Roman reader, but alien as a biblical
idiom;[35] it is as if these schools were indeed Greek schools of philosophy.
Explicit equations appear twice, between Essenes and Pythagoreans
in *Antiquities* 15.371, as we have already noted, and between Pharisees
and Stoics in *Life* 12.[36]

As we will see at the end of the article, this strategy of analogies
was to a large extent abandoned by Josephus at a later point. So far

---

this suggestion less striking, but still worthy of consideration. The word πρόνοια,
which is introduced by Josephus in his rendering of 1 Macc 12:1, is used very frequently by Josephus, but he consistently prefers εἱμαρμένη in the school excursuses.
Cf. Mason 1991, 141–42, 397.

[33] See Martin 1981, 135. Mason (1991, 396–97) rightfully criticizes Martin's major
argument concerning an astrological rather than philosophical interpretation of
εἱμαρμένη, but I still think Martin's observations on the contextual links remain
valid.

[34] McLaren 2000, 39. He correctly points out that φιλοσοφία and cognates are
missing from the second excursus, while αἵρεσις lacks from the third, but this does
not affect his argument. Cf. Mason (1991, 128, 397) for similar points.

[35] "For Heimarmene in the definition of the schools there was no equivalent
word in Hebrew—and no corresponding conception." Moore 1929, 379. As for the
conceptual inadaptability, recent scholarship is much more careful. See e.g., Mason
1991, 133–42, 384–98.

[36] The commonly accepted emendation of *Ant.* 18.22 implies an analogy between
the Essenes and the Dacian Ctistae. However, this analogy represents the approach
we addressed above; it is not an analogy to Greek culture and philosophy, but to

we may conclude that the most obvious function of the excursus in *Antiquities* 13.171–173 is that of providing adornment to the narrative.

5. Antiquities *18.11–22*

The Narrative Context of the Third Excursus

The eighteenth book of *Antiquities* records the events from the deposition of Archelaus to the death of Gaius Caligula. The third excursus on the philosophies conforms to that in *War*, by being linked to the call for revolt by Judas the Galilean,[37] but this time he is aided by a Pharisee named Saddok. Josephus' presentation of their message (*Ant.* 18.4–5) is more expansive than in the first account (*War* 2.218), without being much more informative. He briefly notes that their call was positively received among the populace and adds an expansive lamentation (*Ant.* 18.6–10), of which I quote only parts:

> Here is a lesson that an innovation and reform in ancestral traditions weighs heavily in the scale in leading to the destruction of the congregation of the people. In this case certainly, Judas and Saddok started among us an intrusive fourth school of philosophy . . . planting the seeds of those troubles which subsequently overtook it, all because of the novelty of this hitherto unknown philosophy that I shall now describe. (*Ant.* 18.9)

The excursus on the three philosophies is followed by a similar account of the fourth philosophy (*Ant.* 18.23–25), before we return the census of Quirinius that occasioned the call for revolt by Judas and Saddok (*Ant.* 18.26 cf. 1–3). Again, we lack information about the outcome of the revolt. We may only guess that the removal of Joazar, the dovish high priest, was occasioned by the insurrection.

The Third Excursus as Explanation

Finally, we encounter an excursus that immediately makes good sense within its context! In this case Judas' faction is labeled the "fourth philosophy" and is described in connection with and comparison to

---

a different group of far-away barbarian ascetics. For a discussion of this text, see e.g., Beall 1988, 121–22.

[37] In *Ant.* 18.4 he is called "a Gaulanite from the city of Gamala," while he reappears as "Judas the Galilean" in *Ant.* 18.23.

the three noble ones. Josephus claims that the teaching of the fourth
philosophy is identical to that of the Pharisees, "except that they
have a passion for liberty that is almost unconquerable, since they
are convinced that God alone is their leader and master" (*Ant.* 18.23).
In this context, the presentation of the different teachings on destiny, afterlife and so on, really serves as relevant background information. We may nonetheless ask whether there is really any need
for a new presentation of the three schools. The answer is probably that the cross-reference in *Antiquities* 18.11 could have been
sufficient.

The Third Excursus as Persuasion

Of course, by bringing a more extensive account yet again, Josephus
is making the same point as he did in *War* 2: Jewish factions are
basically far from dangerous, but Judas represents the start of a
destructive trend of insurrection and separatist ideas. This point is
made even more strongly in *Antiquities* 18 than in *War* 2.[38] At the
same time, this fourth philosophy once again plays no part in the
continuation of the narrative, so we may still wonder why Judas is
presented as the founder of a philosophical school.

   In fact, this faction receives even more prestige in *Antiquities* 18
than in *War* 2, being lined up along with the others as the fourth
philosophy and explicitly linked to the Pharisees. On the other hand,
the prestige of the Pharisees arguably receives a blow.[39] How do we
explain this development? Daniel Schwartz points out that by the
time Josephus wrote *Antiquities* "the question of Jewish rebellion against
Rome was much more remote than it was when Josephus wrote *BJ*
in the seventies." Josephus was therefore less cautious in his editing
of problematic source material.[40] McLaren argues for the opposite case,
that the revised line of argument in *Antiquities* 18 demonstrates Josephus'

---

[38] See *Ant.* 18.9 (quoted above).
[39] "If intended as criticism of the Pharisees it is, as best, indirect." McLaren 2004,
107. As we will see below, the presentation of the Pharisees in *Ant.* 18.12–15 is
expanded and enhanced compared to the *War* 2 account. This change more than
compensates for the link to the fourth philosophy.
[40] Schwartz 1983, 169. Rajak (1994, 160) presents a similar approach when she
suggests that the presentation of the Essenes in *Antiquities* 18—being less authentic
and more dependent on Philo—indicates that his interest in the affairs of Judea
had declined since the composition of *War*. She concludes that "the Josephus of
the *Antiquities* lacked the communicative passion of the aspiring younger man."

sustained apologetic concern and his unrelenting pursuit of a convincing argument. His strategy in *War* 2 is to pass over Judas the Galilean as quickly as possible, and instead focus the attention of his readers toward the noble Essenes. In *Antiquities* 18 he makes a more direct attack on Judas, and admits the links between Judas and the Pharisees, because the former approach has proved unsuccessful.[41]

I would like to emphasize that no matter what reasons Josephus had to give Judas more space and relative prestige, his heavy and extensive denouncements in *Antiquities* 18.4–10 effectively counteract and compensate for the former move.[42]

Secondly, I will stress that as long as Judas is made the leader of a philosophical school, and as the description of three ancient schools is appended immediately afterwards, one would expect exactly what Josephus provides in *Antiquities* 18, namely a further description of Judas' school in relation to the others. The tailoring of the *War* 2 account—next to nothing about Judas' school and disproportionately much about the Essenes—therefore remains the most striking.

The excursus in *Antiquities* 18 is furthermore less peculiar when we focus specifically on the presentation of the three ancient philosophies. Unlike the *War* 2 account, but similar to that of *Antiquities* 13, there is a good balance between the presentations of the three schools and the Pharisees are described first. In addition, several important elements from the *War* 2 account of the Essenes are transferred to the *Antiquities* 18 account of the Pharisees. The most prominent example is the doctrine of the afterlife. This motif is presented elaborately and constitutes the climax of the first account of the Essenes (*War* 2.154–158), while it is only briefly mentioned in the accompanying account of the Pharisees (*War* 2.163). In the third excursus the tables are turned. The description of the Pharisaic doctrine of the afterlife has become the extensive one (*Ant.* 18.14–15) and its function, structure and vocabulary are also similar to that of the Essenes in the first excursus.[43] All this implies that the Essenes no

---

[41] See McLaren 2000, 43–44; McLaren 2004, 106–7.
[42] See Mason 1991, 283–84. Note also that Josephus blames the Romans in *Ant.* 18.25.
[43] See also the transfer of the term δίαιτα ("manner of living"), which is used five times with reference to the Essenes in the *War* 2 excursus and twice with reference to the Pharisees in the *Antiquities* 18 excursus, and the introduction of Pharisaic abstention from luxury (*Ant.* 18.12) along with the community of goods among the Essenes (*War* 2.122; *Ant.* 18.20).

longer play the role of "model Jews" alone, even if the presentation of them is still highly favorable. As the three schools are given a more even treatment, the emphasis of this three-part structure is stressed, and the "model Jew" stands as a member of a well-established and distinguished school of philosophy.[44]

As we will see toward the end of the article, the "model Jew" is redefined when we come to Josephus' last work, *Against Apion*.

6. *Two Supplementary Perspectives*

It appears from the examination of the three texts that these excursuses on the Jewish schools of philosophy are not primarily introduced to provide explanation and background information to the narrative. As we do not assume that these excursuses were included to inform modern scholars on the main trends of Jewish thought in the late Second Temple period, we have looked for other explanations, and these will be summarized at the end of the article. At this point we will add two supplementary perspectives. The first relates to the brief reference to the schools in *Life*, while the second relates to the number of schools in the scholarly reconstruction of history.

---

[44] There has been a vivid scholarly debate about Josephus' presentation of the Pharisees. Smith (1956, 74–78) claimed that Josephus in *Antiquities* exaggerates the importance of the Pharisees in order to promote their stance toward the Romans. This view has been supported by e.g., Neusner 1972; Cohen 1979, 237–38; Goodblatt 1989. D. Schwartz (1983) has argued that Pharisaic political involvement has been suppressed from *War*, while several anti-Pharisaic passages from Nicolaus of Damascus have slipped through Josephus' editing of *Antiquities*. In his opinion, the third excursus reflects the overall pro-Pharisaic tendency in *Antiquities*. S. Schwartz (1990, 170–208, 216 [quotations]) similarly noticed that the presentation of the Pharisees in *Antiquities* is far from unconditional flattery, and modified Smith's hypothesis accordingly, claiming that Josephus was promoting a group with "much in common with the Pharisees," namely "the Rabbis, or some group much like the Rabbis." Mason (1991) has altered the parameters of the discussion more radically, contesting the whole idea of a pro-Pharisaic tendency in *Antiquities* and claiming that Josephus is consistently lamenting the popularity and influence of the Pharisees throughout his writings. For an attempt to reconcile Josephus' claims about the great influence of the Pharisees with the sparse evidence for Pharisees being involved in political decision-making, see Goodman 1999b. For the purpose of our study, it is sufficient to note that the description of the Pharisees in the excursuses is basically favorable. Even if this bias is clearly determined by the overall function of the excursuses, namely to present Jewish culture at its best, these accounts are still relevant for our perception of Josephus' attitudes. Not only does he intentionally include the Pharisees in these laudatory accounts; in the first and third excursus he even clearly compares them favorably to the Sadducees.

Life *10*

The analogy between the Pharisees and the Stoics in *Life* 12 has already been commented upon. At this point we will only briefly examine the narrative and rhetorical function of the reference to the three schools in *Life* 10: "At about the age of sixteen I determined to gain personal experience of the schools among us.[45] These, as I have frequently mentioned, are three in number—the first that of the Pharisees, the second that of the Sadducees, and the third that of the Essenes." Since this is not an excursus, the question about the function of the text is therefore a different one. However, the passage is similar to the excursuses in two important ways: The three schools are mentioned together and they are not the focus of the narrative.[46] They are introduced here in the context of Josephus' education, which establishes him as a thoroughly capable politician. The function of *Life* 10 is therefore a rhetorical one, namely to boost Josephus' *ethos*.[47] Accordingly, this passage fits well with our reading of the excursuses.

How many Philosophies?

As mentioned above, Josephus obviously did not have the modern scholar in mind when he produced these excursuses. However, scholars tend to assume that these texts provide a fairly comprehensive picture of Judaism at the end of the Second Temple period. Rather unconsciously, the following equation is often presupposed: Pharisees + Sadducees + Essenes = Judaism. Thackeray's translation of *Life* 10 is but one example: "of the several sects into which our nation is divided" for τῶν παρ' ἡμῖν αἱρέσεων.[48] Similar biases appear frequently in the scholarly literature.[49]

---

[45] Thackeray translates "the several sects into which our nation is divided." As I will show shortly, Thackeray's translation reflects a common misperception.

[46] A prominent Pharisee, Simon, son of Gamaliel, plays an important role later on, in *Life* 189–203, 216, 309, but that does not affect the present reading of this passage.

[47] Josephus' education in philosophy as preparation for a public career conforms very well to Roman ideals. Some knowledge of philosophy was appreciated, be getting too deeply involved was discouraged, and a public career was to be prefered. See e.g., Tacitus' record of the education of Agricola (*Agricola* 4). This point has previously been made by several scholars. See e.g., Mason 2001, 20.

[48] Thackeray's translation of *War* 2.119 has a similar bias.

[49] McLaren (2000, 31, 39), for example, commends the approach of Goodman to which we will turn in a moment, but later drops his guard and claims that in *War* 2.119 "'philosophy' is used . . . to describe Jewish religion as a whole." Mason's

Against this approach, Goodman argues: "It seems certain that Josephus did not intend to encompass all varieties of contemporary Judaism in his set-piece description of the three *haireseis*."[50] As Josephus elsewhere refers to several other types of religious teachings within Judaism,[51] his excursuses could easily have included more than three factions. Goodman aptly notes that "his insistence on this three-fold division is bizarre when the whole point of describing the three philosophies in that context was to introduce to readers a novel Fourth Philosophy, on which he laid the blame for the outbreak of the war against Rome in 6 C.E."[52] When Josephus returns to the schools in *Life*, the fourth school is, of course, absent: "Thus he managed to combine his own assertion that there were four Jewish *haireseis* with the continuing assumption that there were really only three."[53]

Goodman's approach conforms well to my reading of the excursuses as deliberately designed, rhetorical products. However, I have suggested a different cause–effect pattern, namely that the whole point of presenting Judas as the head of a fourth school of philosophy might have been to introduce to his readers an excursus on the three established schools of philosophy.

I would also suggest pushing Goodman's perspective even further and insisting on a clear distinction between Josephus' αἱρέσεις on the one hand, and "Jewish religious groups" on the other. I suspect that the association of these two categories rests on one of the two following, questionable assumptions—one older and one more recent. The former is to perceive Josephus' language as an artificial "hellenization," that is to say: There were different religious groups among the Jews, and Josephus calls them αἱρέσεις or φιλοσοφίαι to make them comprehensible to a non-Jewish audience.[54] The latter approach is the totally opposite, namely to perceive first-century Judaism in all its variations as philosophy.[55] In both cases, the three-fold pattern of Josephus appears to be the result of deliberate selection.

---

description of the three schools as "mainstream Judaism" is similarly imprecise, while the label "recognized Judaism" fits Josephus' concern much better. See Mason 1991, 121–23.

[50] Goodman 1995, 164.

[51] Goodman mentions Banus, Philo, John the Baptist, and Jesus among numerous other proponents of distinct types of Judaism in the writings of Josephus.

[52] Goodman 2000, 3; cf. Goodman 1995, 163.

[53] Goodman 1995, 164.

[54] See e.g., Bousset 1926, 187.

[55] See e.g., Smith 1956, 79–81; Mason 1991, 186; Mason 1993, 12–18; Mason 1996, 41–46.

However, if we for the sake of the argument take Josephus' presentation in *Life* at face value, it must have been possible to be both a member of the priestly upper class and an acknowledged expert in the Jewish laws without really being familiar with the three αἱρέσεις. What Josephus claims to have done at the age of sixteen was to sign up for a quite particular type of Jewish education, separate from any "mainstream Judaism."[56] This corresponds well to the figures given by Josephus,[57] the limited importance of these factions within his narrative, and his restricted use of αἵρεσις, φιλοσοφία, and cognates of the latter in other contexts within *War*, *Antiquities*, and *Life*.[58]

This approach allows for a somewhat different historical reconstruction than that of Goodman: Even if there was a broad spectrum of different Jewish religious groups toward the end of the Second Temple period, there might still be some truth to Josephus' claim that there were basically three philosophical schools among the Jews. If that is the case, it is indeed remarkable that Josephus dresses Judas the Galilean as the leader of an additional school of philosophy.

No matter what, it is clear that the rhetorical strategy of the *War* 2 and *Antiquities* 18 excursuses is not to claim that Jews in general are peace-loving, virtuous and noble, but to insist that among the Jews there are certain philosophers who display perfect virtue. We will shortly see that in *Against Apion* Josephus extends his claims to the nation as such.

7. *A Complimentary Perspective:* Against Apion *2.145–296*

Compared to our findings so far, the question posed in the title of this article receives a quite different answer when we turn to Josephus' last work, *Against Apion*. The final part of this treatise contains an extensive and energetic presentation of the Jewish constitution, its laws and the way of life they prescribe (*Apion* 2.145–296). These

---

[56] "He meant no more than he said: like other cultured peoples, the Jews had their intellectuals (philosophers), and like other philosophers, they belonged to different 'schools' of opinion." Skarsaune 2002, 107.

[57] These figures are: "over six thousand" Pharisees (*Ant.* 17.42), "but few" Sadducees—"men of the highest standing" (*Ant.* 18.17), and "more than four thousand" Essenes (*Ant.* 18.20).

[58] Apart from references to the three schools and that of Judas the Galilean, αἵρεσις only occurs twice with the restricted meaning of "party" or "faction" (*Ant.* 7.347; 15.6). See Mason 1991, 125–28. Similarly, φιλοσοφία and its cognates only reappear in *War* 3.361; *Ant.* 1.25; 8.44; 12.37, 99, 101; 16.398; 18.259.

pages are full of "model Jews," but no presentation of different schools of Jewish philosophy appears. In fact, *Against Apion* is interesting to our discussion exactly because there is no such presentation.

In this treatise, total unity and harmony exist among the Jews:

> To this cause above all we owe our admirable harmony (ὁμόνοια). Unity and identity of religious belief, perfect uniformity in habits and customs, produce a very beautiful concord in human character. Among us alone will be heard no contradictory statements about God, such as are common among other nations...even boldly propounded by philosophers.... Among us alone will be seen no difference in the conduct of our lives. With us all act alike, all profess the same doctrine about God. (*Apion* 2.179–181)

Within such a framework there is clearly no room for three different schools of Jewish philosophy. At the same time, and this is more surprising, descriptions of the Jews and their way of life in terms of "philosophy" and "wisdom" disappear almost completely.[59] However, the noble character and admirable lifestyle of the Jewish philosophers—particularly the Essenes, of course—prevail in a different coating. The "model Jew" of *Against Apion* is pious, virtuous, and willing to die for the sake of the laws. Thus, he resembles the Essene, as well as the Pharisee, in several manners.[60] But he is not any more a member of such an elite faction. He has become a common citizen—an active member of society, not an ascetic and not a philosopher. The ideal community of the few has been replaced by the ideal society of the many.[61]

This shift is all the more peculiar when we consider some source-critical issues. The account of the Essenes in *Antiquities* 18.18–22 is clearly related to that of Philo in *Quod omnis probus liber sit* 75–91,

---

[59] For details on the restrained use of philosophical vocabulary in *Against Apion*, see Haaland 1999, 288–99. A more thorough treatment is in progress.

[60] See e.g., *Apion* 2.145–146, 193–208, 293–294. The parallels between the Essenes of *War* 2 and the Jews of *Against Apion* 2.145–296 span from general traits such as piety, virtue and contempt of death, to very particular features such as having sex only for the sake of procreation. See the thorough presentation by Mason in this volume. Note also the parallel between the ὁμόνοια of the Pharisees in *War* 2.166 (to which we will shortly return) and that of the Jews in *Against Apion*.

[61] The Jewish nation as a whole is in focus throughout this account. Josephus presents Moses as the lawgiver and educator of the people—women and children included (*Apion* 2.145–183), maps out a social hierarchy with the high priest and the priesthood at the top (*Apion* 2.184–194), records laws on cult and purity, marriage and family, birth and funeral, education of children and respect for elders, friendship and treatment of foreigners, describes the punishments for transgression

either by direct dependence or a common source,[62] and the same applies to *Apion* 2.145–219 in relation to Philo's *Hypothetica* 7.[63] *Hypothetica* 11 contains Philo's second account of the Essenes. It is therefore not unlikely that Josephus had access even to that account while composing *Against Apion*. We recognize the traits of the Essenes, but these Jewish philosophers are not allowed to appear on the stage.[64]

In *Against Apion* the strategy of analogies is replaced by a strategy of outbidding: Jewish culture is superior to that of the Greeks.[65] This is clearly evident in the treatment of Greek philosophy. The most distinguished Greek philosophers are presented as students of Moses, but inferior to him in many respects: less accurate in their perceptions, less strict in their moral standards and less successful in conveying their teaching to the masses.[66] This strategy of outbidding is

---

and the rewards for obedience to the laws (*Apion* 2.195–219), and compares different aspects of the Jewish culture to those of the Greeks and other nations (*Apion* 2.154–178, 220–286). While Greek philosophy is addressed to the few, and while religious, moral and legal education in most cultures is done insufficiently, Moses succeeded in creating a national mass movement of piety, virtue and law-abidance (*Apion* 2.169–178).

[62] See e.g., Rajak (1994, 147) who opts for direct dependence, and Smith (1958, 279) who argues for a common source.

[63] Quite a lot has been written on the source-critical relationship between these two texts, as well as the sentences of Pseudo-Phocylides. For two recent approaches, of which the latter is clearly to be preferred, see Carras 1993; Gerber 1997, 42–49, 100–18.

[64] Gerber (1997, 101) claims that the account of the Essenes in *Hypothetica* 11 displays no proximity to *Apion* 2.145–296. However, there are plenty of overlaps in motifs and terminology, e.g., the prominence and recurrence of κοινωνία and cognates (3 occurrences of both κοινωνία and κοινός in *Hypoth.* 11 against 7 and 8 respectively in *Apion* 2.145–296, etc.), the presentation of κοινωνία as a principle laid down by "our lawgiver" (ὁ ἡμέτερος νομοθέτης in *Hypoth.* 11.1 and ὁ νομοθετήσας ἡμῖν in *Apion* 2.145–146), the promotion of a life (βίος, e.g., *Hypoth.* 11.4, 18 and *Apion* 2.156, 181, 210) characterized by supreme holiness (ὁσιότης in *Hypoth.* 11.1 and ὁσιώτατος in *Apion* 2.192), virtue (ἀρετή, *Hypoth.* 11.2 and a dozen occurrences in *Apion* 2.145–296), humanity (φιλανθρωπία, *Hypoth.* 11.2 and *Apion* 2.146, 213, 261), moderation (*Hypoth.* 11.11 and e.g., *Apion* 2.204), etc. The closest parallel is probably found in *Hypoth.* 11.1–2 and *Apion* 2.210. The former text explains that the Essenes live together (οἰκέω) on the basis of shared vocation (προαίρεσις) rather than descent (γένος), and the latter justifies the acceptance of converts because "it is not family ties (γένος) alone which constitute relationship (οἰκειότης), but agreement (προαίρεσις) in the principles of conduct."

[65] This strategy is used from the very beginning of the treatise (*Apion* 1.6–72), and permeates the final part of it (*Apion* 2.145–296). We have encountered this kind of rhetoric already in *Antiquities*, and significantly, it was in a reference to the Essenes (*Ant.* 18.20). Cf. also e.g., *Ant.* 1.22–23.

[66] See e.g., *Apion* 1.165, 175–182; 2.164–178, 220–224, 255–257, 281.

also applied in relation to Sparta: "the Lacedaemonians thought good strictly to observe their laws only so long as they retained their liberty and independence, but when they met with reverses of fortune forgot well-nigh all of them. We, on the contrary, . . . never even in the direst extremity proved traitors to our laws" (*Apion* 2.227–228).

The Spartans were highly admired by philosophers for their manly virtues and, accordingly, the presentation of the Essene philosophers in *War* 2 is replete with Spartan themes.[67] In *Against Apion*, however, the Spartans are juxtaposed with the Jews and loose the battle.[68]

How do we account for these differences between *Against Apion* and the earlier writings of Josephus? Partly, they may be explained as a matter of genre. Josephus could hardly have written *War*, *Antiquities*, and *Life* without any records of disagreement, disputes and conflicts between Jews. It would be impossible to recount the biblical narrative and later Jewish history without such elements. His sources demand it, and the historiographical genre encourages it.[69] Accordingly his claim is that Jewish culture at its best displays a civilized interaction between well established and highly respectable factions.[70] *Against Apion*, on the other hand, allows ideals to materialize without restraints. Consequently, Josephus is much more daring, and paints a picture of total harmony and unity.[71]

However, there are no formal reasons why the three schools could not have enhanced and colored the presentation of the Jewish way

---

[67] See Mason in this volume.

[68] See the extensive juxtaposition in *Apion* 2.225–235, from which the quotation above is taken. Among several examples of the utilization of this strategy, those most relevant to the present investigation have been mentioned.

[69] Accordingly, no bold claims about Jewish ὁμόνοια are ever made in *War*, *Antiquities*, or *Life*. The description of the Pharisees in *War* 2.166 is the closest we get, while the only forceful and programmatic statement regarding the nation as a whole is a negative one, namely that the Jews had preferred "sedition to concord" (ἀντὶ μὲν ὁμονοίας στάσιν, *War* 6.216). Similarly, the programmatic usages of ὁμονοέω ("be harmonious") in *Apion* 2.294, ἡμερότης ("friendliness") in *Apion* 2.151, 213, κοινωνία ("community") in *Apion* 2.146, 151, 196, 208, 291, and συμφωνία ("harmony") in *Apion* 2.170 are without parallels in *War*, *Antiquities*, and *Life*. In these works, unity and harmony are ideals that are fully materialized only by the Pharisees and the Essenes, most strongly expressed in the *War* 2 excursus.

[70] McLaren (2000, 39) points out that by using words like "philosophy" and "school," Josephus "conveys the impression that Jews were legitimately engaged in dialogue about issues within their religion."

[71] See *Apion* 2.170, 179–181 (quoted above), 283, and Haaland 1999, 292. Note the inclusion of συμφωνία ("harmony"), apparently at the expense of φρόνησις ("prudence," "intelligence"), in the list of cardinal virtues in *Apion* 2.170.

of life in *Against Apion*. Why could the Jews of *Against Apion* not be "legitimately engaged in dialogue about issues within their religion?"[72] This is hardly a matter of genre. Similarly, a reference to genre does not explain the absence in *Against Apion* of "Jewish philosophy" and "Jewish wisdom."[73] Finally, I see no reason why the genre of *Against Apion* should prevent Josephus from making links to Pythagoreans and Stoics as he does in *Antiquities* and *Life*.

The genre of the work does not prevent such descriptions, but the apologetic and rhetorical strategy of the work does. One of the main motives in *Against Apion* is namely the contrast between Jewish culture and Greek culture. As a major expression of this contrast, Jewish unity is set up against Greek discord.[74] Accordingly, there is no room for a spectrum of different Jewish schools of philosophy. The reluctance to speak about "Jewish philosophy" and "Jewish wisdom" is probably also a by-product of this overall anti-Greek strategy, since "philosophy" was such a prominent feature of Greek culture.

In other words, in *War* and *Antiquities*, Josephus needs some sort of division in order to prove that only a limited group of rebels are to blame for the Jewish revolt, while in *Against Apion* he chooses unity in order to demonstrate the excellence and superiority of the Jewish culture.

The stress on Jewish unity is but one example of how Josephus in *Against Apion* carefully adopts Roman ideals and values in his presentation of Jewish culture.[75] The Jews of *Against Apion* "are, if you will, *Judaei togati*."[76]

In a recent article,[77] I suggest that this shift in apologetic and rhetorical strategy may have been occasioned by certain historical events in Rome. In the autumn of 93 c.e., Domitian killed the leading figures of the so-called "Stoic opposition" and expelled other philosophers—among them Epictetus—from the capital. These events

---

[72] Cf. McLaren 2000, 39.
[73] The Essenes of *War* 2 "irresistibly attract all who have once tasted their wisdom (σοφία)" (*War* 2.158). The attraction of the Jewish way of life to outsiders is described in many ways in *Against Apion*, but never in terms of σοφία. See e.g., *Apion* 2.281–286.
[74] See e.g., Haaland 1999, 291–92; Goodman 2000, 41.
[75] See e.g., Goodman 1994; Goodman 1999a; Haaland 1999; Barclay 2000; Barclay 2004.
[76] Barclay 2000, 232.
[77] Haaland 2005.

concur more or less with the release of *Antiquities* and *Life*. It would, then, make sense to understand the absence of "Jewish philosophy" as an adoption by Josephus to a changed climate in Rome. As he wrote *Against Apion*, neither Pythagorean-looking Essenes nor Stoic-looking Pharisees were anything to brag about.

8. *What Difference Does Philosophy Make?*

Regarding the *War* 2 excursus, Neusner makes the following claim: "The section is complete as it stands and could have been placed just as well in any other part of the narrative. It neither illuminates, nor is illuminated by, its setting."[78] Schwartz presents a similar statement with reference to the *Antiquities* 13 excursus: "As it stands, the function of this passage is incomprehensible."[79]

By reading the excursuses not only as explanatory footnotes, but as vehicles of authorial concerns on a more sophisticated level, we have seen that particularly the first of these claims must be modified. It appears that the three excursuses on the schools of philosophy—even including that of *Antiquities* 18—are not introduced in order to ease the reading of the narrative, but in order to control and direct it.

Most obviously, the excursuses represent straightforward adornments of the narrative, as presentations of Jewish culture at its best. They provide opportunities for Josephus to present his "model Jews" as displaying manly virtues such as endurance, self-control and contempt of death. These "model Jews" are dressed according to common preconceptions of barbarian sages[80] and presented through analogies with Greek philosophical schools.

At the same time, the excursuses in *War* 2 and *Antiquities* 18 demonstrate Josephus' ongoing concern to acquit the Jewish people in general from any responsibility for the revolt.

I have argued that there may be a more subtle relationship between the account of Judas the Galilean and the *War* 2 excursus than

---

[78] Neusner 1972, 231.
[79] Schwartz 1983, 161.
[80] "Undoubtedly he was catering to the interests of Roman readers, with whom ascetic philosophers in out-of-the-way countries enjoyed a long popularity." Smith 1956, 75. Note that Josephus utilizes the image of the barbarian priestly sages in his argument for the great antiquity of the Jews in the first part of *Against Apion* (*Apion* 1.28–43).

usually admitted. Instead of reading the account of Judas as triggering the inclusion of the excursus, I suggest the opposite cause–effect pattern. Apparently, the presentation of Judas is deliberatively designed to allow for the introduction of the three traditional schools.

In *Antiquities* 18 Josephus follows a similar path, but includes a more elaborate presentation of Judas' faction as the fourth philosophy. This implies that Josephus was willing to make some serious concessions in order to deliver an important point: Even though internal strife and separation between the Jews have caused disaster, Jewish culture at its best displays a civilized interaction between noble factions.

As for the *Antiquities* 13 excursus, a narrative and rhetorical function beyond that of adornment is more difficult to discern. My modest contribution has been to point out—along with Martin—the mentioning of Sparta and Rome as a suitable context for a presentation of the Jewish schools of philosophy.

The overall analysis clearly indicates that Josephus considered the material on the three schools of philosophy a trump card, which he played carefully, but still eagerly, both in *War* and *Antiquities*, and even in *Life*. In *Against Apion* he chooses differently, and I have suggested some reasons for this development. It is clearly a product of the overall apologetic and rhetorical strategy of *Against Apion*, but it may also be a result of specific political developments in Rome.

Finally, the character of Josephus' "model Jew" remains the same in many respects, but the dressing is submitted to change. In the *War* excursus we encounter the Essene ascetic, a typical representative of "barbarian sages." In the *Antiquities* excursuses we meet philosophers of a more Greek flavor. Finally, in *Against Apion* 2.145–296 the "model Jew" is no longer a philosopher. He appears as a respectable citizen, clearly and thoroughly romanized. My speculation is that this transition to some extent reflects a development in the way Josephus perceived himself as a Jew in Rome.

BIBLIOGRAPHY

Barclay, J. M. G.
    2000   Judaism in Roman Dress: Josephus' Tactics in the *Contra Apionem*. Pages 231–45 in *Internationales Josephus-Kolloquium Aarhus 1999*. Edited by J. U. Kalms. Münster.
    2004   The Politics of Contempt: Judaeans and Egyptians in Josephus's *Against Apion*. Pages 109–27 in *Negotiating Diaspora: Jewish Strategies in the Roman Empire*. Edited by J. M. G. Barclay. London. Preliminary version pages 327–58 in *SBL Seminar Papers, 2000*. Atlanta.

Baumgarten, A. I.
    1997   *The Flourishing of Jewish Sects in the Maccabean Era: An Interpretation.* Leiden.
Beall, T. S.
    1988   *Josephus' Description of the Essenes Illustrated by the Dead Sea Scrolls.* Cambridge.
Bilde, P.
    1988   *Flavius Josephus between Jerusalem and Rome: His Life, His Works, and Their Importance.* Sheffield.
Bousset, D. W.
    1926   *Die Religion des Judentums im späthellenistischen Zeitalter.* Edited by Hugo Gressmann. Tübingen. Repr. 1966.
Carras, G. P.
    1993   Dependence and Common Tradition in Philo *Hypothetica* VIII 6.10–7.20 and Josephus *Contra Apionem* 2.190–219. *Studia Philonica Annual* 5:22–47.
Cohen, S. J. D.
    1979   *Josephus in Galilee and Rome: His Vita and Development as a Historian.* Leiden.
Feldman, L. H.
    1984   *Josephus and Modern Scholarship (1937–1980).* Berlin.
Förster, N.
    2005   Some Observations on Josephus' Description of the Essenian Morning Prayer. Pages 245–53 in *Josephus and Jewish History in Flavian Rome and Beyond.* Edited by J. Sievers and G. Lembi. Leiden.
Gerber, C.
    1997   *Ein Bild des Judentums für Nichtjuden von Flavius Josephus: Untersuchungen zu seiner Schrift Contra Apionem.* Leiden.
Goodblatt, D.
    1989   The Place of the Pharisees in First Century Judaism: The State of the Debate. *JSJ* 20:12–30.
Goodman, M.
    1994   Josephus as Roman Citizen. Pages 99–106 in *Josephus and the History of the Greco-Roman Period: Essays in Memory of Morton Smith.* Edited by F. Parente and J. Sievers. Leiden.
    1995   A Note on the Qumran Sectarians, the Essenes and Josephus. *JJS* 46:161–66.
    1999a   Josephus' Treatise *Against Apion.* Pages 45–58 in *Apologetics in the Roman Empire: Pagans, Jews, and Christians.* Edited by M. Edwards, M. Goodman and S. Price. Oxford.
    1999b   A Note on Josephus, the Pharisees and Ancestral Tradition. *JJS* 50:17–20.
    2000   *Josephus and Variety in First-Century Judaism.* PIASH 7:1–13.
Haaland, G.
    1999   Jewish Laws for a Roman Audience: Toward an Understanding of *Contra Apionem.* Pages 282–304 in *Internationales Josephus-Kolloquium Brüssel 1998.* Edited by J. U. Kalms and F. Siegert. Münster.
    2005   Josephus and the Philosophers of Rome: Does *Contra Apionem* Mirror Domitian's Crushing of the 'Stoic Opposition'? Pages 297–316 in *Josephus and Jewish History in Flavian Rome and Beyond.* Edited by J. Sievers and G. Lembi. Leiden.
Martin, L. H.
    1981   Josephus' Use of *Heimarmene* in the *Jewish Anitquities* XIII, 171–3. *Numen* 28:127–37.
Mason, S.
    1991   *Flavius Josephus on the Pharisees: A Composition-Critical Study.* Leiden.
    1993   Greco-Roman, Jewish, and Christian Philosophies. Pages 1–28 in *Religious and Theological Studies.* Edited by J. Neusner. Vol. 4 of *Approaches to Ancient Judaism: New Series.* Edited by J. Neusner. Atlanta.

1995   Chief Priests, Sadducees, Pharisees and Sanhedrin in Acts. Pages 115–77 in *The Book of Acts in Its Palestinian Setting*. Edited by R. Bauckham. Vol. 4 of *The Book of Acts in Its First Century Setting*. Edited by B. W. Winter. Grand Rapids.

1996   *Philosophiai*: Graeco-Roman, Judean and Christian. Pages 31–58 in *Voluntary Associations in the Graeco-Roman World*. Edited by J. S. Kloppenborg and S. G. Wilson. London.

2001   *Life of Josephus*. Vol. 9 of *Flavius Josephus: Translation and Commentary*. Edited by S. Mason. Leiden.

McLaren, J. S.

2000   Josephus's Summary Statements regarding Essenes, Pharisees and Sadducees. *ABR* 48:31–46.

2004   Constructing Judaean History in the Diaspora: Josephus's Accounts of Judas. Pages 90–108 in *Negotiating Diaspora: Jewish Strategies in the Roman Empire*. Edited by J. M. G. Barclay. London.

Momigliano, A.

1975   *Alien Wisdom: The Limits of Hellenization*. Cambridge.

Moore, G. F.

1929   Fate and Free Will in the Jewish Philosophies according to Josephus. *HTR* 22:371–89.

Neusner, J.

1972   Josephus' Pharisees. Pages 224–44 in *Ex Orbe Religionum: Studia Geo Widengren Oblata 1*. Edited by J. Bergman, K. Drynjeff and H. Ringgren. Leiden. Several reprints, e.g., Josephus' Pharisees: A Complete Repertoire. Pages 274–92 in *Josephus, Judaism and Christianity*. Edited by L. H. Feldman and G. Hata. Leiden, 1987.

Paul, A.

1992   Flavius Josèphe et les Esséniens. Pages 126–38 in *The Dead Sea Scrolls: Forty Years of Research*. Edited by D. Dimant and U. Rappaport. Leiden.

Rajak, T.

1983   *Josephus: The Historian and His Society*. London.

1994   *Ciò che Flavio Guiseppe vide*: Josephus and the Essenes. Pages 141–60 in *Josephus and the History of the Greco-Roman Period: Essays in Memory of Morton Smith*. Edited by F. Parente and J. Sievers. Leiden.

Rengstorf, K. H., ed.

1973–1983 *A Complete Concordance to Flavius Josephus*. 4 vols. and 1 suppl. Leiden. Repr. in 2 vols., Leiden, 2002.

Saldarini, A. J.

1988   *Pharisees, Scribes and Sadducees in Palestinian Society*. Wilmington. Repr., Grand Rapids, 2001.

Schwartz, D. R.

1983   Josephus and Nicolaus on the Pharisees. *JSJ* 14:157–71.

Schwartz, S.

1990   *Josephus and Judaean Politics*. Leiden.

Sievers, J.

2001   Josephus, First Maccabees, Sparta, the Three *haireseis*—and Cicero. *JSJ* 32:241–51.

Skarsaune, O.

2002   *In the Shadow of the Temple: Jewish Influences on Early Christianity*. Downers Grove.

Smith, M.

1956   Palestinian Judaism in the First Century. Pages 67–81 in *Israel: Its Role in Civilization*. Edited by M. Davis. New York. Repr. pages 183–97 in *Essays in Greco-Roman and Related Talmudic Literature*. Edited by H. A. Fischel. New York, 1977.

    1958   The Description of the Essenes in Josephus and the Philosophoumena.
            HUCA 29:273–313.
Stemberger, G.
    1995   *Jewish Contemporaries of Jesus: Pharisees, Sadducees, Essenes.* Translated by
            A. W. Mahnke. Minneapolis.
Vermes, G. and M. D. Goodman.
    1989   *The Essenes: According to the Classical Sources.* Sheffield.
Williams, D. S.
    1997   Josephus or Nicolaus on the Pharisees? *REJ* 156:43–58.

JOSEPHUS AND ANTIPAS: A CASE STUDY OF JOSEPHUS' NARRATIVES ON HEROD ANTIPAS

Morten Hørning Jensen

Galilean Studies and Herod Antipas

The last three decades have seen a highly interesting debate on first-century Galilee, with inputs from several fields of scholarship such as historical Jesus research, archaeology, rabbinic studies, and Josephus studies. It is possible to trace how the discussion of the various issues has moved from the initial stage marked by rather presumptuous statements based on a thin corpus of material to a stage characterized by more precision in what material to bring in and what to exclude. Gross descriptions of Galilee "as Hellenized as anywhere else in the Roman world" have proved to be unwarranted as more and more archaeological material has been made available. Instead a new and refined focus has been on what *then* went on in early first-century Galilee. With the advent of Herod Antipas as the first indigenous ruler in many years, Galilee experienced some, perhaps even radical, changes manifested in large building projects such as Sepphoris and Tiberias. This way Antipas is perceived as the key to a broad understanding of the socio-economic conditions of first-century Galilee.[1]

However, it is still highly debated what impact the reign of Antipas had on the socio-economic conditions of his area. As pointed out by Halvor Moxnes,[2] two pictures have evolved. *Either* Antipas is viewed as a buffer against direct Roman rule and exploitation, thereby

---

[1] The intensified focus on Antipas within Galilean research can be seen in many places. The works of Sean Freyne provide an interesting example. In his early works, he depicted Antipas as a buffer against direct Roman influence, who secured stability (Freyne 1988, 136–43; 1994, 85–86). In his later works, he depicts Antipas as the most important factor for a socio-economic reorientation of Galilee, who increases debt and tenancy (Freyne 2000; see also Freyne 2001a, 2001b, and 2002). Other important works with special emphasis on Antipas include: Horsley 1999, 62–65; Silberman 1997; Horsley and Draper 1999; Horsley 2001, 2003; Fiensy 1997; Sawicki 2000; Arnal 2000; Reed 2000, 83–89, 218–20; Crossan and Reed 2001; Moxnes 2003.

[2] Cf. Moxnes 1998, 2001.

providing a good basis for trade and mutual enrichment of both
urban and rural areas (a "picture of harmony"), *or* Antipas is depicted
as a typical tyrant extracting heavy taxes from his region for the
financing of his building programme, which resulted in economic
upheaval with increasing indebtedness and tenancy (a "picture of
conflict"). An example of this last position could be Reed and Crossan's
study, *Excavating Jesus*, in which Antipas is presented as the provok-
ing reason for the two messianic figures from his regions, John the
Baptist and Jesus.[3]

Test Case

How can this deadlock be explained? It seems to have to do with
two things: On the one hand, our sources on Antipas and his impact
on Galilee are not overwhelming and they leave many questions
unanswered that we find important. This gives room for interpretation to "fill in the gaps." On the other hand, it is clear that nearly
all defenders of the picture of conflict utilize models from cross-cultural
anthropology or socio-scientific criticism, while the opposite is true
for the defenders of a picture of harmony.[4]

One way out of this impasse is to outline the available source
material and treat it thoroughly on its own premises instead of going
back and forth between the different groups of material, as is often
done in the discussion. A comprehensive approach including utilization of models is warranted only on the basis of well-argued presentations of each corpus of material. It is the aim of this article to
make a step in that direction by presenting the material about Antipas
in the writings of Josephus and to evaluate it within its own context.

The case to investigate concerns what kind of picture we have of
Antipas in the writings of Josephus. Is it incoherent and incomplete?
Or is clear-cut and aimed? Only after such a literary analysis can
a historical synthetic approach proceed.[5]

---

[3] Cf. Crossan and Reed 2001, xviii, 113 and other places. For similar views, see
also e.g., Horsley 1995, 226; 1999, 62, and Arnal 2000, 10–11.
[4] This is not the place for a full demonstration of this statement, but again the
work of Freyne provides a good example. The shift in the evaluation of the impact
of Antipas' reign was prompted by utilization of the socio-economic model of
T. F. Carney (cf. Freyne 2000).
[5] A study of Antipas within Josephus' writings from a literary perspective is not
thoroughly covered in earlier research, in which the main focus has been on historical

Josephus and History

The need for such an approach is highlighted by the present state of studies in Josephus as a writer of history. Though this entire volume bears witness to the fact that this debate is far from settled, important recent studies by Steve Mason, for example, make a strong case for the intelligent and creative structure of the writings of Josephus.[6] In particular the many editorial remarks in the *Antiquities* must be emphasized.[7] Compared to the *War*, Josephus constantly comments on the stories he renders by inserting his own personal statements, thus providing the reader with a "divine scale of reference," a divine judgment. By paying attention to the many comments and evaluations, we will get an idea about why he narrated the way he did. It is thus more fruitful to read the narratives by Josephus with a method of "Tendenzkritik" than with a method of "contradiction" as often done. Though careful attention should be given not to define Josephus' tendencies beforehand and so risk conflating the picture, it holds good prospects to read the individual stories from the larger perspective. Therefore, to get a sense of Josephus' intentions, we need to arrive at his description of Antipas through a close reading of his description of other members of the Herodian house. Such a survey promises to provide an understanding of Josephus' description of Antipas from within his own horizon and delivers a point of departure for a broad historical inquiry including all other sources available.

Josephus on the Herodian House

The Foundation of the Herodian House

The Herodian house is introduced with Antipater, the father of Herod the Great. In the *War* he is described as an old enemy of Aristobulus and as a wealthy Idumean, a principal of his nation (πρωτεύων τοῦ ἔθνους, 1.123), who at a certain point courageously

---

chronological questions often treating Antipas only in connection with a general study of Herod the Great or the Herodian house (cf. Brann 1873; Schürer 1901, 431–49; Schürer 1973–1987, 1:340–53; Otto 1913; Jones 1938; Harlow 1954; Perowne 1958; Bruce 1963; Hoehner 1972; Kokkinos 1998; Richardson 1999).

[6] Cf. Mason 2003a, 2003b, 2005a, and 2005b. Another important study for the topic under investigation here is Krieger 1994.

[7] Cf. Mason 2003b, 588.

aided Caesar's campaign in Egypt, for which he was generously
rewarded with Roman citizenship, exemption from taxes and other
honours and marks of friendship (τιμῆς καὶ φιλοφρονήσεως, 1.194).
Upon Antipater's death by poison, Josephus describes him as an
energetic man (δραστήριος ἀνὴρ, 1.226). In the *Antiquities*, the picture of Antipater is different. He is called a rebel (στασιαστὴς, 14.8),
who looked jealously at Aristobulus (ὑφοραω, 14.11), and therefore
constantly levelled accusations and brought charges against him before
Hyrcanus (ἑκάστης ἡμέρας πλαττόμενος καὶ διαβάλλων, 14.14). We
are, however, still informed of Antipater's military aid to Caesar in
Egypt and the way he is rewarded for this (14.133–139) and when
he dies, Josephus evaluates him as a man distinguished for piety and
justice (εὐσεβείᾳ τε καὶ δικαιοσύνῃ διενεγκὼν) and committed to his
country (περὶ τὴν πατρίδα σπουδῆ, *Ant.* 14.283). A description using
the words εὐσέβεια and δικαιοσύνη is highly noteworthy since his
son Herod is accused of lacking these things.

A development from the *War* to the *Antiquities* is then traced, though
not in an unequivocal manner. The appearance of the Herodian house
is clearly in itself ambiguous for Josephus. On the one hand, it was
an aid to Hyrcanus and helped to keep the Jewish nation on good
terms with Rome. It even contained good rulers like Phasael, who in
the *War* as well as in the *Antiquities* is described as a mild and fair
ruler of Jerusalem (*War* 1.206–207; *Ant.* 14.161–162). On the other
hand, problems evolve around Herod, as we shall now see.[8]

Herod the Great

The description of Herod the Great is the longest sequence on a
single person in Josephus (*War* 1.204–673 and *Ant.* 14.158–17.199).
From *War* to *Antiquities*, Josephus changes his narrative on at least
two points. First, the structure is changed from being thematic in
the *War* to being chronological in the *Antiquities*. In the *War*, the surrounding political history is concentrated into one section (going from
1.204 to 1.400), then follows the story of Herod's building activities
(1.401–428) after which, upon a minor digression on Herod's physical
constitution (1.429–434), Herod's family tragedies are presented

---

[8] In an interesting analysis, Mason explains the double-sided description of most
of Josephus' characters, including Herod the Great, as an expression of Josephus'
wish to imitate the "hallmark of Roman historiography" (Mason 2003b, 571), namely
such rounded double-sided descriptions.

(1.435–664). Second and most notable is the fact that Josephus is more judgmental in the *Antiquities*. Through several editorial asides (cf. e.g., Ant. 14.274; 15.266–267, 328; 16.150–159; 17.180–181, 191–192; 18.127–129), he advances a negative judgement of Herod. In an article from 2002, Gideon Fuks points to altogether six instances in which Herod is judged by Josephus for his attitude towards the Jewish religion.[9] Fuks' list could be increased to at least eighteen incidents in which Josephus, either directly by himself or indirectly through some pious Jews, accuses Herod of being a transgressor of the law (παρανομία, e.g., *Ant.* 14.167; 15.243, 266, 328; 16.4; 17.150, 304), a transgressor of the ancestral traditions (πάτριος, e.g., *Ant.* 15.277, 281), customs and practices (ἔθος, e.g., *Ant.* 15.267, 268, 274, 288, 328, 365), of being impious (ἀσέβεια/ἀσεβὲς, e.g., *Ant.* 15.275; 16.402; 17.1; cf. also *Ant.* 15.182, 267, 288, 365), and of being a cruel (ὠμότης, e.g., *War* 1.534; *Ant.* 17.191) tyrant (τυραννικός τυραννίς, e.g., *War* 2.84; *Ant.* 14.165; 16.4; 17.304).[10]

Thus Herod offends in a three-fold way: First, in his relations to his Hasmonean family-in-law. Second, by being too *philoromaios*, i.e., too friendly towards the Roman establishment through games and lavishly built temples, and in this way he transgressed the ancestral laws by innovations foreign and destructive to Jewish practices and customs. Third and finally, by being a cruel tyrant who lacked any kind of moderation. In two passages, Josephus advances his view of Herod, blaming him even further for being part of the reason for the ultimate destruction of Jerusalem and the temple (cf. 15.267 and 15.281). These things taken together prove to Josephus that Herod was an innovator who inflicted things on the Jews that were not known previously.[11]

First, Herod' relations to his Hasmonean family-in-law deteriorate quickly after the joyful engagement (*War* 1.240–241; *Ant.* 14.299) and later marriage to Mariamme (*War* 1.344; *Ant.* 14.467), peaking

---

[9] Fuks 2002.

[10] A full and more detailed analysis of this material will be provided in my forthcoming PhD dissertation, Jensen 2006.

[11] Mason has pointed out how the perseverance of aristocratic conservative traditions was a major issue for Josephus (Mason 2003b, 577–81), and points to the speech of Sentius in the Senate (*Ant.* 19.167–184). It can be added that the accusations of Sentius against the Roman *princeps* are exactly the same as those leveled against both Herod and the fourth philosophy, namely for departing from the law by the introduction of new practices, behaving tyrannically, and thus being the ultimate reason for the destruction of the city.

with the executions of the young Aristobulus, Hyrcanus, Mariamme, her mother Alexandra and, finally, his two sons by Mariamme, Aristobulus and Alexander. It is highly interesting to note how each of these killings is harshly commented on in the *Antiquities* whereas, in the *War*, they are simply just described. One example could be the execution of Hyrcanus. Josephus describes him as the only one left of royal rank (ἀξιώματος βασιλικοῦ) and more worthy of the kingdom than Herod (ἄνδρα τυχεῖν τῆς βασιλείας ἀξιώτερον, 15.164), whereas Herod is clearly the one to blame. Hyrcanus was gentle and moderate (ἐπιεικὴς καὶ μέτριος), whereas the acts of Herod were neither just nor pious (οὔτε δίκαιον οὔτ᾿ εὐσεβὲς, 15.182). Herod is thus contrasted with the Hasmonean family and accused by Josephus of being impious, unjust, and having one of the typical characteristics of tyranny: Lack of moderation. Another example is found in *Ant.* 15.266, where Josephus summarizes the consequences of Herod's execution of Mariamme (15.202–239), her mother Alexandra (15.251), and the sons of Baba (15.263) by saying that no one was now left alive from the family of Hyrcanus, and *therefore* no one was left to prevent his unlawful acts (μηδενὸς ὄντος ἐπ᾿ ἀξιώματος ἐμποδὼν ἵστασθαι τοῖς παρανομουμένοις, 15.266). Again a clear distinction is made between Herod and the Hasmonean royal lineage. When Herod finally had his two sons by Mariamme killed, it is said to be the "demonstrative proof of his impiety impossible to punish" (ἀσεβείας τεκμήριον ἀνυποτιμήτου, 16.402).

Second, Josephus clearly connects the actions against the Hasmonean family with the lack of obedience of the law. In one of the highly important editorial remarks, *Ant.* 15.267, Josephus summarizes his view of Herod in three points: (a) because of the executions (διὰ τοῦτο), Herod forsook even more the customs of the fathers (μᾶλλον ἐξέβαινεν τῶν πατρίων ἐθῶν); (b) with foreign practices he changed the ancient way of living that had been inviolable (ξενικοῖς ἐπιτηδεύμασιν ὑποδιέφθειρεν τὴν πάλαι κατάστασιν ἀπαρεγχείρητον οὖσαν); and (c) therefore, by these means, no little evil wrongdoing happened at a later time (ἐξ ὧν οὐ μικρὰ καὶ πρὸς τὸν αὖθις χρόνον ἠδικήθημεν) because what had earlier brought about piety in the people was neglected (ἀμεληθέντων ὅσα πρότερον ἐπὶ τὴν εὐσέβειαν ἦγεν τοὺς ὄχλους). In a profound way, Josephus directly connects the reign of Herod to the fall of the temple, as he also does with the fourth philosophy (*Ant.* 18.1–10, cf. below). The next paragraphs exemplify this statement by Josephus. Herod is accused both of setting

up athletic contests, and of building a theatre and an amphitheatre
in Jerusalem. Both are said to be foreign according to Jewish practice (κατὰ τοὺς᾽ Ἰουδαίους ἔθους ἀλλότρια, *Ant.* 15.268). Again it is
important to note the different flavour of the *War*. In *War* 1.404
Herod's building of the temple at Paneion is mentioned without any
comments. Likewise, in *War* 1.415 the games in Caesarea are mentioned without any negative remarks, and *War* 1.426–428 even praises
Herod as a saviour of the Olympic Games in Greece. In the *Antiquities*,
however, Josephus clearly condemns both the games and the buildings. In *Ant.* 15.274–276 games involving wild animals and gladiators are judged as a dissolution of the customs held in esteem by
the Jews (κατάλυσις τῶν τιμωμένων παρ᾽ αὐτοῖς ἐθῶν), and as impiety (ἀσεβὲς) exemplified in the display of trophies (τρόπαια) thought
to bear images (ἐικόνες) forbidden by the custom of the fathers
(πάτριος). With admiration Josephus tells us how the Jews of Jerusalem
accused Herod of this and how some of them as a sacred act from
God (ὅσιος, 15.281) even tried to kill Herod with daggers for his
breaking of habits (ἔθος, 15.274), his impiety/godlessness (ἀσεβὲς,
15.275), and his violation of the custom of the fathers (πάτριος,
15.276, τὰ πάτρια, 15.281).[12]

Finally, Josephus accuses Herod of being a cruel tyrant, which is
also seen as an expression of his lawlessness. The accusation is found
in both the *War* and the *Antiquities*, though stated more clearly in
the latter. *Antiquities* 16 opens with the accusation that Herod introduced a law without any precedent (νόμον οὐδὲν ἐοικότα τοῖς πρώτοις,
16.1), which in its harshness proved to be an act "not of a royal
person but of a despotic ruler" (οὐ βασιλικῶς ἀλλὰ τυραννικῶς, 16.4).
In another important editorial remark with a direct evaluation of
Herod (*Ant.* 16.150–159), this time with an outspoken "I" (ἐγὼ, 16.152,
μοι, 16.159), Josephus delves into the double-sided nature of Herod
both being beneficent (εὐεργεσία, 16.150) and unjust in his harsh
punishments (τὰς τιμωρίας καὶ ἀδικίας, 16.151), and a stranger to
all kind of moderation (πάσης μετριότητος ἀλλότριον, 16.151). Josephus
finds an explanation in Herod's love of honour (φιλότιμος, 16.153).
Anything he did was based on his desire to be famous. But, as
Josephus finally states, "the Jewish nation is by law alienated by such

---

[12] It is worth noticing how Josephus in *Ant.* 19.335–337 praises Agrippa I for
building a theatre and an amphitheatre, as well as for entertaining the people with
gladiators and the killing of criminal men.

things and habituated to love what is rightful more than what leads to honour" (τό γε μὴν᾽ Ἰουδαίων ἔθνος ἠλλοτρίωται νόμῳ πρὸς πάντα τὰ τοιαῦτα καὶ συνείθισται τὸ δίκαιον ἀντὶ τοῦ πρὸς δόξαν ἠγαπηκέναι, 16.158). When Herod finally dies, Josephus inserts another editorial aside in the *Antiquities*, evaluating Herod in a harsh way saying that he was "a man cruel to all on equal basis" (ἀνὴρ ὠμὸς εἰς πάντας ὁμοίως) and was "easy to anger but above justice" (ὀργῆς μὲν ἥσσων κρείσσων δὲ τοῦ δικαίου, 17.191). In the parallel passage of the *War*, we find no accusation of either cruelty or impiety, just a notion of him being unlucky in his private life (1.665).[13]

Thus, though Josephus along the way also notes some positive things about Herod (cf. e.g., *Ant.* 15.299–316; 380–425; 16.58–65), he is accused of at least three interwoven crimes: (a) of his violation of the law and habits, with the executions of his Hasmonean family members; (b) of his attitude towards foreign religion; and (c) of his cruelty. Taken together, Herod introduced new traditions alien to Jewish practice and he was, in the eyes of Josephus, one of the reasons for the disaster that ultimately led to the destruction of the temple (cf. *Ant.* 15.267; 281).

Archelaus

These verdicts are cast upon Archelaus as well. He is accused of being impious, of acting against the law and of being a cruel tyrant. Actually, the two accounts of Josephus more or less follow the same scheme and contain the same view on Archelaus but the *Antiquities* is slightly more outspoken with its final comment by Josephus clearly accusing Archelaus of transgressing the law (17.341).

Before going to Rome for the trial over Herod's wills, Archelaus became engaged in an upheaval in the temple resulting in a massacre of pilgrims. Even though Josephus in both accounts paints a picture of a fairly patient Archelaus, who initially tried to give in to the demands of the masses (*War* 2.4–11; *Ant.* 17.204–212), he is rebuked by both the party of Antipas and later by the Jewish delegation, who wanted direct Roman rule. The allegations include cruelty (ὠμότης, *War* 2.31, 88–89; *Ant.* 17.230, 313), a tyrannical nature (τῆς φύσει

---

[13] With the death of Herod, Josephus is not quite done with accusing him. Later occasions count charges brought forward by a Jewish delegation in Rome (*War* 2.84–92; *Ant.* 17.299–310) and comments in connection with the introduction of Agrippa I (*Ant.* 18.127–129).

τυραννίδος, *Ant.* 17.237), impiety and lawbreaking (παρανομηθεῖσιν, *War* 2.32, δυσσέβεια; *Ant.* 17.237, 313), as well as an accusation of making himself king (*War* 2.26–30; *Ant.* 17.230). He has shown himself to be a true son of his father (*War* 2.89; *Ant.* 17.312).

Instead of providing any actual events from the reign of Archelaus, Josephus spends time on the remarkable story of the Alexander fake, who just by having the look of Mariamme's son was able to stir up Jews in the Diaspora (*War* 2.101–110; *Ant.* 17.324–338). This insertion is important for the overall narrative, and bolsters Josephus' picture of how the true royal heritage is found in the Hasmonean remnants of Mariamme.

Following this rather peculiar insertion, Josephus explains how the reign of Archelaus came to an end. Both accounts include the story of how a group of leading Samaritans and Jews, united for the occasion, travelled to Rome to accuse Archelaus of governing with cruelty and tyranny (τὴν ὠμότητα αὐτοῦ καὶ τυραννίδα, *Ant.* 17.342; cf. *War* 2.111). The *Antiquities* further adds an accusation that Archelaus broke the law (τοῦ πατρίου παράβασιν, 17.341) by marrying Glaphyra, since she had already been married to his half-brother, Alexander, the son of Mariamme. Finally, in both the *War* and the *Antiquities*, the downfall of Archelaus is bolstered by the dreams he and his wife Glaphyra had just before they went to Rome to receive their banishment. As pointed out by J. W. van Henten (2003), the two dreams function as divine verdicts over Archelaus' ungodly way of life and prepare the reader for a new era in Judea without Herodian rule by the will of God.

The Fourth Philosophy

The downfall of Archelaus and the inauguration of direct Roman rule in Judea bring about a rebellion led by Judas of Gamala (*Ant.* 18.4) or the Galilean (*War* 2.118). Josephus' account of this event in *Antiquities* 18.1–10 has some very important additions compared to the *War* 2.118, in which Josephus in a profound way accuses Judas and his companions of being the ultimate reason for the *War*.[14]

---

[14] The importance of these comments is highlighted by the fact that the presentation of the fourth philosophy is both historically questionable (cf. McLaren 2001) and not internally coherent, since 18.23–24 seems to describe Judas and his followers in a positive manner as being almost identical with the Pharisees (cf. Krieger 1994, 20–28).

We are introduced to the two basic options of response to the Roman takeover of Palestine: One is represented by the high priest Joazar, who is able to calm down some of the Jewish resistance to foreign rule including the census in connection with taxation (18.3) while another is represented by Judas from Gamala and his helper Saddok the Pharisee. At first hand, Josephus seems to describe their programme in a straightforward manner, namely that they initiated a rebellion (ἀπόστασις) because the census and the taxation (ἀποτίμησις) was unacceptable, since it would lead to slavery, and that the deity (τὸ θεῖον) would honour such goals and be a helper in the unavoidable rebellion and bloodshed to come (*Ant.* 18.4–5 = *War* 2.118). However, the *Antiquities* adds some highly important paragraphs (18.6–10), that form an editorial aside and present his own interpretation of the party: (a) they were responsible for every kind of misery since "there was no evil that did not come forward from these men" (κακόν τε οὐκ ἔστιν, οὗ μὴ φυέντος ἐκ τῶνδε τῶν ἀνδρῶν, 18.6);[15] (b) they were the ultimate reason for famine, for the war, and not least for the fall of the temple (κατασκαφαί, μέχρι δὴ καὶ τὸ ἱερὸν τοῦ θεοῦ ἐνείματο πυρὶ τῶν πολεμίων ἥδε ἡ στάσις, 18.8b); (c) all of this was nothing but an innovation, neglecting the tradition of the fathers (τῶν πατρίων καίνισις, 18.9), introducing ideas unknown to Judaism at an earlier time.

Thus the evaluation of the fourth philosophy is just as harsh as that of Herod. Interestingly enough, there is an obvious point that unites them further. Both the Herodian house and the fourth philosophy represented the introduction of practices and ideas unknown to Judaism at in an earlier state. What divides is the attitude towards Rome, but according to Josephus it brought about the same result, whether to be too insensitive towards the Jewish religion and its practices, and too friendly towards Rome, or the opposite. Both attitudes eventually led to the ultimate disaster, the destruction of the temple.

Philip the Tetrarch

Within the line of bad Herodian rulers—Antipater, Herod, and Archelaus—Philip the tetrarch is presented as a notable exception. Not much is told about him apart from two texts summarising his building activity (*War* 2.167–168; *Ant.* 18.27–28), and Josephus just

---

[15] This notion is further defined by four instrumental datives in *Ant.* 18.7.

provides detail on his reign in a final obituary (*Ant.* 18.106–108). Three important things are noted: First, Philip is described as "μέτρι-ος" and "ἀπράγμων," moderate and easy-going. Second, he devoted all his time to his area. Finally, he is pictured as a righteous ruler ready to set up his court on the roadside if so needed to free those unjustly convicted (τοὺς ἀδίκως ἐν ἐγκλήμασι γενομένους, 18.107).

Furthermore it is worth noticing how Josephus contrasts the good reign of Philip to that of Antipas. According to Krieger, the next section (18.108–126) describes Antipas in an ambiguous and rather negative way: "Vor allem aber ist Philippos—und dies führt Josephus breit aus—ein gerechter und beflissener Richter für seine Untertanen und steht auch hier im Kontrast zu Herodes Antipas, der den „guten Mann" Johannes den Täufer hinrichten lässt."[16] Likewise, while Philip stays in his area satisfied with his allotment, Antipas twice travels to Rome to improve his situation.

Agrippa I

Next to Herod the King, Agrippa I—or Agrippa the Great—as he is called by Josephus, is the Herodian ruler that Josephus is most informative about. Again there is a noticeable difference between the *War* and the *Antiquities*. Not only is the latter much longer, but it also contains some very important statements by Josephus in several editorial remarks, which function as hermeneutic keys to his overall narrative. In short the following may be noted.

First, by way of introduction, Josephus shows with a genealogical table how Agrippa descends from the real royal Hasmonean line through Mariamme (*Ant.* 18.127–142). Josephus frankly states that the genealogy is "proper for the history" (διὰ τὸ ἀνήκειν τῇ ἱστορίᾳ), and aimed at Herod the Great he claims that no advantage can outdo piety towards the divine (πρὸς τὸ θεῖον εὐσεβειῶν, 18.127), proven by the fact that within a century almost all his lineage had perished with the exception of Agrippa. He, on the other hand, "advanced to the greatest honour and power" (ἐπὶ μέγιστον ἀξιώματός τε ἅμα προκόψειεν καὶ δυνάμεως, 18.142).

Second, through an extravagant life in Rome, Agrippa ran up huge debts and, finally landed in prison in Rome after openly wishing

---

[16] Krieger 1994, 51.

Gaius to be emperor instead of Tiberius. In this, the greatest peril
resembling, for example, the situation of Joseph and Israel in Egypt
and presently Josephus and the Jewish nation, a couple of prophecies make it clear to Agrippa that he will recover through "divine
providence" (τοῦ θείου τὴν πρόνοιαν, *Ant.* 18.197). Later in an editorial remark, Josephus states how the whole story of Agrippa's fall
and exaltation by the will of God is "a proof of how God sometimes lets fall what is great, and how he raises what has fallen (ἵν'
ᾖ δεῖγμα καὶ τοῦ τὰ μεγάλα δύνασθαί ποτε πεσεῖν καὶ τοῦ τὸν θεὸν
ἐγείρειν τὰ πεπτωκότα, 19.294).[17]

Third, Josephus clearly points out how Agrippa answered this
Divine providence by an exemplary rule, including courageous stands
against the religious oppression of the Jews (cf. *Ant.* 18.289–301;
19.278–291; 300–311) and heartfelt religious practice as "he fulfilled
sacrifices not neglecting anything demanded by the law" (ἐξεπλήρωσε
θυσίας οὐδὲν τῶν κατὰ νόμον παραλιπών, *Ant.* 19.293).

Finally, this picture is bolstered even further in Josephus' final
summarising statement on Agrippa (19.328–334). Josephus contrasts
him to Herod, saying that "he was not resembling in his way of life
the Herod who had reigned before him" (κατ' οὐδὲν Ἡρώδῃ τῷ πρὸ
ἑαυτοῦ βασιλεῖ τὸν τρόπον συμφερόμενος, 19.328). Herod was evil
(πονηρός) and relentless (ἀπότομος) in his punishments and more gentle to the Greeks than to the Jews (19.329). Agrippa, on the other
hand, is praised by Josephus for his mild, beneficent and benevolent nature (πρᾳὺς . . . εὐεργετικὸς . . . φιλάνθρωπος, 19.330) towards
all alike. "He stayed continuously in Jerusalem" (συνεχὴς ἐν τοῖς
Ἱεροσολύμοις ἦν) and "he kept the tradition of the fathers spotlessly"
(τὰ πάτρια καθαρῶς ἐτήρει). "He therefore kept himself entirely pure,
and no day went by for him without the sacrifices ascribed by the
law" (διὰ πάσης γοῦν αὐτὸν ἦγεν ἁγνείας οὐδ' ἡμέρα τις παρώδευεν
αὐτῷ τὰ νόμιμα χηρεύουσα θυσίας, 19.331). None of this in included
in the *War*.[18]

---

[17] The same thing is stated in Josephus' editorial remark on Gaius in *Ant.* 19.15–16.
The downfall of Gaius is said to provide "a proof of the power of God" (πίστιν
τοῦ θεοῦ τῆς δυνάμεως) that will "comfort those who lie in destiny (i.e., bad)" (καὶ
παραμυθίαν τοῖς ἐν τύχαις κειμένοις), as well as teach anyone else to conduct one's
life according to virtue (ἀρετῇ, 19.16).

[18] Again it is interesting to note how Josephus includes contrasting stories, this
time of negative sort, e.g., *Ant.* 19.332, 345–346, 352.

Preliminary Conclusion

This short survey has dealt with Josephus' fundamental struggle to solve the complex question of how the temple could be destroyed and how the former gracious situation can be restored. In this connection, two seemingly opposite stands are one and the same thing for Josephus. Both the Herodians' insensitive and hostile stand against the Jewish tradition, law and religion and that of the fourth philosophy towards Rome ultimately led to the destruction of the temple (cf. esp. *Ant.* 15.167, 281; 18.8).

The right balance was achieved by Agrippa I, and the way Josephus alters his story in the *Antiquities* is extremely important when it comes to understanding Josephus' overall aim with his narrative. It is not that Josephus found him blameless and, as a matter of fact, he represents one of many examples of what Mason has pointed out to be a deliberate way of imitating Roman historiography through double-sided portraits (cf. Mason 2003b, 570–71). What really matters, though, is how Josephus in several editorial remarks presents the story of Agrippa as the key to understanding the post-seventy situation of the Jews. Agrippa is a sign of hope. If the people and the Roman authorities act according to the old rules and traditions, then the Deity will reverse the fortune of the pious and righteous (cf. *Ant.* 18.197 and 19.294) and punish the hubris of the impious as done before in the cases of, for example, Herod the Great and Gaius (cf. e.g., *Ant.* 19.15–16).

Josephus on Antipas

Turning to Josephus' description of Antipas, the question is how such a broader view of the literary structure of Josephus' narrative creates a background for evaluating his account of the reign of Antipas. It will be argued that though the narrative on Antipas is comparably short,[19]

---

[19] The material on Antipas can be divided into three parts: (a) Material concerning the youth of Antipas and the trial of the will of Herod in Rome (*Ant.* 17.20, 188, 224–318; *War* 1.646, 2.20–95). (b) Material concerning the founding of Sepphoris (*Ant.* 18.27) and Tiberias (*War* 2.167–168; *Ant.* 18.36–38; *Life* 64–69). (c) Material concerning events during the reign of Antipas in *Ant.* 18.36–38, 101–125, 240–255 and *War* 2.178–183. This part contains the actual narratives on Antipas with *Ant.* 18.101–125 as the central block with stories centered on Antipas not found in the *War*. Altogether, eight episodes are provided: (1) the founding of Tiberias

it is precise and significant in the light of Josephus' general editorial intentions in his description of the Herodian house. Once again
it is possible to trace a mutually connected two-fold concern of
Josephus. Antipas is evaluated in the light of, on the one hand, his
relationship to Rome and, on the other hand, Jewish law, practice
and religion, though in a less pronounced way than in the cases
seen above.

Antipas and Rome

The passages Josephus has included on Antipas mostly concerns the
period under Tiberius, and it is clearly explained how Antipas managed to establish a good relationship with Tiberius. This is demonstrated in four texts:

First, *Ant.* 18.36–38 tells about the founding of Tiberias and opens
with the remark that "Herod the tetrarch, because he had advanced
much before Tiberius in regard to friendship, had a city built and
named it" after him Tiberias (Ἡρώδης δὲ ὁ τετράρχης, ἐπὶ μέγα γὰρ
ἦν τῷ Τιβερίῳ φιλίας προελθών, οἰκοδομεῖται πόλιν ἐπώνυμον αὐτῷ
Τιβεριάδα, *Ant.* 18.36). It should be noted that Feldman in his Loeb
translation renders this rather freely: Antipas "advanced much *among
the friends of Tiberius*" (my italics). However, the text does not read
"φιλίους"/friends but φιλίας (from φιλία/friendship). The idea of
Feldman's translation must be to take φιλίας as an accusative plural.
But then it should in a narrow sense be translated to mean "among
the friendships before Tiberias." A more straightforward reading
would be to take φιλίας as a genitive singular and translate it as
"before Tiberius in regard to friendship." This would underline even
more what is also implied in the wider translation by Feldman that
Antipas received the highest degree of political position as a formal
"friend of Rome."[20]

Second, the good relationship with Tiberius also appears in *War*
2.178, in which Josephus notes how Tiberius turned down Agrippa

---

(*Ant.* 18.36–38), particularly the decoration of the palace, *Life* 64–67; (2) the peace
treaty with Parthia on the Euphrates (*Ant.* 18.101–105); (3) Antipas' marriage to
Herodias (*Ant.* 18.109–112); (4) the war with Aretas (*Ant.* 18.113–115); (5) Antipas
and John the Baptist (*Ant.* 18.116–119); (6) Vitellius' and Antipas' preparations for
war against Aretas (*Ant.* 18.120–125); (7) Antipas' employment of Agrippa (*Ant.*
18.148–150; *War* 2.178); (8) Antipas' plea for kingship and his subsequent banishment
(*Ant.* 18.240–256; *War* 2.181–183).
    [20] Cf. Braund 1984, 23–27.

when he came to Rome to accuse Antipas. It is not said what he is accused of, but perhaps the passage could be connected with *Ant.* 18.149–150 describing how Antipas having placed the indebted Agrippa in the office by Antipas as *agonoramos* of Tiberias, reproached him for his poverty. This infuriated Agrippa and he left Tiberias eventually ending up in Rome, where he became a friend of Gaius. Even so, Agrippa obviously did not have the luck to shake Tiberius' trust in Antipas.

Third, Antipas' high status is further highlighted by the role he was given in the top-level political meeting between Rome and Parthia under Tiberius (*Ant.* 18.101–105).[21] The eastern border of Parthia constituted a recurring problem for Rome as outlined by Josephus in the preceding paragraphs (18.96–100). With the mission to negotiate a peace treaty, the legate of Syria, Vitellius, was sent to meet Artabanus, who had just recaptured the throne. They met, flanked by their bodyguards, on a bridge on the Euphrates and were able to work out an arrangement after which Antipas entertained them in a luxurious tent in the middle of the bridge (18.102). Though it is not said exactly what role Antipas played during the negotiations, Antipas was able to write a letter to Tiberius so precise (ἀκριβῶς) and detailed that nothing was left for the proconsul to tell. When Vitellius later did so, Tiberius downplayed his report since the matters had already been made clear (δῆλος) by Antipas (18.104–105). This made Vitellius upset, but he hid his anger for a later opportunity.

Finally, Antipas' good relationship with Tiberius was demonstrated when he was attacked by Aretas and his army was destroyed. Though seemingly only hearing the story from the point of view of Antipas, Tiberius took his side in this quarrel and "looked in anger the attempt of Aretas and wrote to Vitellius to carry out war and if he caught him alive to lead him up in chains or if he killed him to have his head sent to him" (ὁ δὲ ὀργῇ φέρων τὴν Ἀρέτα ἐπιχείρησιν γράφει πρὸς Οὐιτέλλιον πόλεμον ἐξενεγκεῖν καὶ ἤτοι ζωὸν ἑλόντα ἀναγαγεῖν δεδεμένον ἢ κτεινομένου πέμπειν τὴν κεφαλὴν ἐπ' αὐτόν, *Ant.* 18.115).

---

[21] It should be noted that there is a chronological issue tied to this meeting. Suetonius and Dio Cassius place it after the death of Tiberius. Hoehner (1972, 253–54) discusses the problem in detail and follows Täubler, who favoured the chronology of Josephus since both Suetonius and Dio Cassius were hostile towards Tiberius and therefore had an motive to deprive him of this success.

Antipas and the Jewish Nation and Religion

Antipas' relations to his Jewish subjects were a different story according to Josephus. A picture with substantial problems is revealed:

First, Antipas' foundation of Tiberias in honour of Tiberius (*Ant.* 18.36–38) created a dual problem: (a) for one thing, the city was inhabited by a highly questionable mob of people, a "promiscuous rabble" as Feldman translates σύγκλυδες in the Loeb edition. Though some are said to be magistrates or men in office (ἐν τέλει, 18.37), it appears from the description that most were former slaves who had just been freed (μηδὲ σαφῶς ἐλευθέρους, 18.38) or the poor people in need (ἄνδρας ἀπόρους, 18.37), who were brought in from all over (πανταχόθεν, 18.37). Some were dragged there forcibly (πρὸς βίαν, 18.37). However, they are said to be "from the land subject to him" (ἐκ τῆς ὑπ᾽ αὐτῷ, 18.37). This could be understood as if they were already tenants and therefore would not really have much to complain about at least from an economic point of view. Antipas further freed them in great numbers and showed himself as a benefactor (κἀπὶ πολλοῖς ἠλευθέρωσεν καὶ εὐηργέτησεν, 18.38) by building houses "to the end," i.e., fully equipped, and adding plots of land of his own (κατασκευαῖς τε οἰκήσεων τέλεσι τοῖς αὐτοῦ καὶ γῆς ἐπιδόσει, 18.38). All of this on the single condition that they were not to leave the city again (ἀνάγκασμα τοῦ μὴ ἀπολείψειν τὴν πόλιν ἐπιθείς, 18.38); (b) the second problem concerned that fact that Antipas "knew the foundation of the city to be against the law and contrary to the Jewish ancestral tradition because it was placed on graves" (εἰδὼς παράνομον τὸν οἰκισμὸν ὄντα καὶ ἀπὸ τοῦ Ιουδαίος πατρίου διὰ τὸ ἐπὶ μνήμασιν, 18.38). They became uprooted in great numbers when Tiberias was founded, and with an implied reference to Num 19.11,16, Josephus says that "the settlers are unclean for seven days, as the law proclaims for us" (μιαροὺς δὲ ἐπὶ ἑπτὰ ἡμέρας εἶναι τοὺς οἰκήτορας ἀγορεύει ἡμῖν τὸ νόμιμον, *Ant.* 18.38).[22] What can we learn from this story? For one thing, Antipas is described as a benefactor who, first freed a lot of people, built them fully equipped houses, and even allotted them plots of his own land. The foundation of Tiberias seems to have been a great economic investment by Antipas. For another

---

[22] Also *Life* 65 describes how Antipas decorated the interior of his palace with images of living animals (ζῴων μορφὰς). For a historical discussion of this matter, see e.g., Roth 1956; Levine 1997, 11; Vogel 1999.

thing, Josephus is clearly focused on the implied transgression of the law and explicitly states how Antipas in this case showed himself to be a transgressor of Jewish religion just like his father. In a fine analysis, Krieger goes even further and sees the story as slanderous polemics against Antipas. He is the only active person, which Josephus underlines by telling how even people of very low and poor status had to be bought to live there.[23]

The second instance in which Herod Antipas falls short is in his marriage to Herodias, the wife of his half-brother Herod, according to Josephus:[24] (a) the story (*Ant.* 18.109–115) is placed right after the praise of the now deceased Philip. At some occasion Antipas visited his half-brother Herod and fell in love with his wife Herodias (ἐρασθεὶς δε Ἡρωδιάδος, 18.110), the sister of Agrippa the Great; (b) Antipas asked her to marry him and she accepted on the condition that his present wife, the daughter of the Nabatean king, Aretas, would be expelled (ἐν ταῖς συνθήκαις ὥστε καὶ τοῦ Ἀρέτα τὴν θυγατέρα ἐκβαλεῖν, 18.110); (c) again the deeds and doings of Antipas are described as having a twofold problem: For one thing, this escapade turned out to be politically fatal. In the following paragraphs it is described how Aretas made war on Antipas, who suffered a severe blow having his entire army destroyed (διεφθάρη πᾶς ὅ Ηρῴδου στρατὸς, 18.114). For another, the marriage is condemned as contravening the law (τῶν πατρίων, 18.136). As a matter of fact, Josephus constructs a parallel to Archelaus. Also his second marriage to Glaphyra is deemed unholy and held against him.

The third case that shows how Antipas dealt with the Jewish law follows immediately after this, namely the episode of the death of John the Baptist. This narrative is extremely telling when it comes to understanding Josephus' view of Antipas: (a) the story is a digression prompted by the destruction of Herod Antipas' army. Without any further definition we are told that "some of the Jews thought

---

[23] Cf. Krieger 1994, 29–31.

[24] Kokkinos (1998, 264–71) has advanced an interesting hypothesis on how to interpret the sources on Antipas' second marriage to Herodias, and on how to understand his trip to Gaius to obtain the rank of king, in which the episodes are not seen as erotically motivated, but as a daring political attempt to obtain the tetrarchy of the deceased Philip, whose widow was Herodias. For the traditional view, see Krieger 1994; Hoehner 1972, 150–68, 257–65.

that the destruction of the army was an act of God" (τισὶ δὲ τῶν
Ἰουδαίων ἐδόκει ὀλωλέναι τὸν Ἡρώδου στρατὸν ὑπὸ τοῦ θεοῦ, 18.116),
which further was thought to be both "very much just" (μάλα δικαίως,
18.116) as revenge for what Antipas had done against John the so-
called Baptist; (b) in the following paragraph, Josephus gives a description of John the Baptist substantiating this judgement. He is said to
be a good man (ἀγαθὸν ἄνδρα, 18.117), urging people to seek virtue
(ἀρετή) and to practice justice (δικαιοσύνη) towards each other and
piety (εὐσέβεια) towards God. In other words, he is described in
exactly opposite terms to those used about Herod the Great and
Archelaus; (c) in *Ant.* 18.118 Josephus then explains the situation that
forced Antipas to have John killed. The mob rallied and Herod
feared that John's great arguments over the people should lead to
some kind of rebellion (ἐπὶ ἀποστάσει τινὶ φέροι) since it seemed that
they would follow every council of his (πάντα γὰρ ἐῴκεσαν συμβουλῇ
τῇ ἐκείνου πράξοντες). So Antipas held it to be much better (πολὺ
κρεῖττον ἡγεῖται) to act in advance and execute him (προλαβὼν
ἀνελεῖν), instead of later regretting the consequences (τοῦ μεταβολῆς
γενομένης μή εἰς πράγματα ἐμπεσὼν μετανοεῖν). From all we know of
ancient bandits and messianic figures, Antipas' action is just what
one may expect from a client king or local ruler; (d) but in the
following paragraph, Josephus judges the incident through the eyes
of the Jews (this time without the qualifying "some of"). Due to
Herod's ὑποψία, his "suspicion" or perhaps "jealous watch" (Liddell-
Scott, II), John is brought to Machaerus and killed. The Jews had
the opinion (τοῖς δὲ Ιουδαίοις δόξαν) that as "punishment for this the
destruction of the army had happened as an act of God, who wanted
to maltreat Herod"; (ἐπὶ τιμωρίᾳ τῇ ἐκείνου τὸν ὄλεθρον ἐπὶ τῷ
στρατεύματι γενέσθαι τοῦ θεοῦ κακῶσαι Ηρώδην θέλοντος, 18.119).
Thus, Josephus clearly condemns the action of Antipas as unjust,
ungodly and perhaps also an act of tyranny, although this verdict is
not presented in a direct way with a personal "I-statement" as in
many other cases.

Finally, however, a small notice in *Ant.* 18.122 balances this negative judgment of Antipas' feeling for the Jewish religion and tradition. Josephus tells how Vitellius, on his way to punish Aretas yielded
to the wishes of the Jews not to march through Judea with his army
since they found the images to be against the law (18.120–121).
Instead, he "himself together with Herod the tetrarch and his friends

went up to Jerusalem to sacrifice to God in the traditional feasts of the Jews present there" (αὐτὸς μετὰ Ἡρώδου τοῦ τετράρχου καὶ τῶν φίλων εἰς Ἱεροσόλυμα ἀνῄει θύσων τῷ θεῷ ἑορτῆς πατρίου τοῖς Ἰουδαίοις ἐνεστηκυίας). It would, naturally, have been of great interest if Josephus had elaborated on Antipas' religious role and function in Jerusalem after the removal of Archelaus. Since he does not do so, it is difficult to derive firm descriptions from this small notice.

Preliminary Conclusion

To sum up, Antipas is described as having close connections with the Roman emperor Tiberius and, as with Herod the Great, this Roman preference is coupled with an insensitive attitude towards the Jewish religion. In three cases, the foundation of Tiberias, the marriage to Herodias, and the killing of John the Baptist, Antipas is judged as a violator of the law and tradition. In particular, *Ant.* 18.101–129 is narrated as a chain of incidents, which taken together clearly build up an argument: (a) Antipas is a political fool who loses the good relationship with his nearest Roman protector, Vitellius, when informing Tiberius about the peace treaty with Parthia (18.101–105); (b) in contrast, his brother Philip is a just, moderate and easy-going ruler (18.106–108); (c) but Antipas gave in to his feelings and divorced the daughter of the neighbouring king, Aretas, which got him involved in the fatal war where he lost his army (18.109–115; (d) this is presented as a just revenge from God because Antipas had killed a good (ἀγαθός) man who was filled with ἀρετή, δικαιοσύνη, and εὐσέβεια (116–119); (e) finally, Antipas was caught in the events. When Tiberius died, Vitellius refused to wage war against Aretas (18.120–125); (f) added to this, when the narratives about Antipas come to an end, his counterpart is presented, Agrippa the Great, who is magnificently introduced and directly contrasted to Herod the Great and the rest of his lineage (18.125–129).

However, deliberately or not, this picture cracks in a couple of places. In one place Josephus lets us know how Antipas went to Jerusalem to sacrifice during the Passover (18.122). Likewise it is not clearly stated whether or not Josephus also viewed Antipas as a τύραννος. One could argue, as Krieger does, that the forceful resettlement of people to Tiberias as well as the insensitive and jealousy-motivated killing of John the Baptist, are typical signs of tyranny.[25] However, in both cases Josephus does not state it directly, but rather softens the picture of a tyrant by letting us know, in the case of Tiberias, how Antipas took care of the resettled people (18.36–38) and, in the case of John, how he had to take action against him to prevent a possible uprising (18.118).

Thus, the picture of Antipas is more nuanced than that of other members of the Herodian house. Nevertheless, in the light of what has been established above, through a general survey of Josephus' treatment of the Herodian house, it becomes clear how Josephus wants to present Antipas as another example of bad Herodian rule, who was not able to safeguard the ancient and stable Jewish way of life. Antipas eventually comes to serve as a warning of how the Deity punishes those not living in accordance with the law. This is stated indirectly in the case of John the Baptist through "some Jews" (*Ant.* 18.116) or just "the Jews" (18.119), and directly by Josephus himself in the story of Antipas' downfall. Driven by Herodias, Antipas asked Gaius to be ranked as king, but was removed as tetrarch instead. In a final editorial remark on Antipas, Josephus comments: "But God inflicted this punishment on Herodias for the envy against her brother and on Herod for listening to women's light talk" (Ἡρωδιάδι μὲν δὴ φθόνου τοῦ πρὸς τὸν ἀδελφὸν καὶ Ἡρώδῃ γυναικείων ἀκροασαμένῳ κουφολογιῶν δίκην ταύτην ἐπετίμησεν ὁ θεός *Ant.* 18.255, not found in *War* 2.181–183).

Conclusion

This article has attempted to examine Josephus' description of Antipas within its context. Instead of reading the stories as isolated incidents, we can gain a feeling of Josephus' aims and intentions embedded in the way he presents his stories. The main question was whether Josephus' description is incoherent and incomplete, or whether it is clear and telling. Although we could have wished for more stories to be included, it has been argued that Josephus uses Antipas in a clear and distinct way as a part of what he intends to demonstrate.

---

[25] Cf. Krieger 1994, 53, esp. n. 8.

As shown in modern research,[26] many intentions merge in the writings of Josephus. Among the most important are: (a) on a profound theological level to come to terms with how the temple could have been destroyed; (b) on a national-religious level to revive Jewish self-identity; and (c) on a political level to find a way to re-establish the former good relationship between Rome and the Jewish nation by pointing to the narrow balance between Jewish and Roman considerations. Thus Josephus is constantly providing examples of good and bad and is fairly easy to follow by his intensive and consistent use of catch-words e.g., παράνομος, ἔθος, πάτριος, ἀσεβὲς, εὐσεβὲς, ἀσέβεια, τυραννίς, τυραννικός, μέτριος, ὠμότης. On the background of this, the following three points may be concluded.

First, in the context of Josephus' description of the Herodian house, Antipas is presented as one of the "tragic stories." Though perhaps not as tragic as other members because of the lack of outspoken despotic cruelty, he is, from a Josephan-Jewish perspective, one of the rulers who were too friendly with the Romans and too insensitive towards Jewish law, practice and religion. Where does this take us? My first conclusion is that though we do not have an extensive description of Antipas, we have a clear one. Measured by Josephus' overall aims, he tells us what we need to know.

Second, does this help us to answer the questions raised by modern research? Sadly enough, Josephus does not seem to ask questions "from below." Josephus is mainly focused on the ruling class, relations with Rome, and the high priests and the temple. Not much is said about the economic conditions of the lower classes. The only economic element is a positive one indicating how Antipas provided fully equipped houses together with plots of land for the forcefully re-housed settlers. This is my second conclusion: Josephus does not intend to answer our set of questions.[27]

Third, my final conclusion is, however, that if we counterbalance the picture Josephus gives of Antipas with his own disclosed intentions, we might—stretching the material to the limits—say the following: *Antipas was by no measure remarkable either in deeds or misdeeds.* In the *War* he is only mentioned in occasional updates. In the *Antiquities* we find a little more. But if Josephus' intentions are taken into

---

[26] Cf. e.g., Bilde 1979; Krieger 1994; Mason 2003b.
[27] Cf. also Mason 2003a, 55.

account, the picture of Antipas still turns out to be rather non-remarkable: (a) the foundation of Tiberias seemed to be an economic benefit for the tenant population, and the religious transgression was not decisive—Josephus could freely enter the city during the *War* as we read in the *Life*; (b) the killing of John the Baptist might have shocked those who followed him, but was only to be expected from a local client ruler who wanted to restore calm and is exactly what Josephus approves of in other instances; (c) the marriage to Herodias certainly seems to have been expensive, but only for Antipas himself without any known consequences for the population; (d) finally, Josephus is not able to come up with any real examples of cruelty. This is, however, an argument from silence.

Finally, when returning to the two basic pictures of Galilee, a full historical inquiry will have to await analyses of all other available material. In the interval the preceding analysis may justly conclude that a substantiation of either picture is not possible if we argue strictly on the basis of what Josephus says, since his focus is somewhere else rather than on Antipas' influence on rural peasant life in Galilee. If, however, we include Josephus' intentions, the way he discloses himself in the stories of Antipas and what he does not say on Antipas that could have bolstered his line of arguments, *then* a picture of Galilee on the brink of meltdown in the first half of the first century can hardly be substantiated by the narratives of Josephus.

BIBLIOGRAPHY

Arnal, W.
   2000   *Jesus and the Village Scribes: Galilean Conflicts and the Setting of Q.* Minneapolis.
Bilde, P.
   1979   The Causes of the Jewish War According to Josephus. *JSJ* 10:179–202.
Brann, M.
   1873   Die Söhne des Herodes. Eine biographische Skizze. 2. Antipas. *Monatsschrift Für Geschichte Und Wissenschaft Des Judentums* 22:305–44, 407–20, 459–74.
Braund, D.
   1984   *Rome and the Friendly King: The Character of the Client Kingship.* London.
Bruce, F. F.
   1963   Herod Antipas, Tetrarch of Galilee and Peraea. *ALUOS* 5:6–23.
Crossan, J. D., and J. L. Reed
   2001   *Excavating Jesus: Beneath the Stones, Behind the Texts.* New York.
Fiensy, D. A.
   1997   Jesus' Socioeconomic Background. Pages 225–55 in *Hillel and Jesus: Comparative Studies of Two Major Religious Leaders.* Edited by J. H. Charlesworth, and L. L. Johns. Minneapolis.

Freyne, S.
  1988   *Galilee, Jesus and the Gospels: Literary Approaches and Historical Investigations.*
          Philadelphia.
  1994   The Geography, Politics, and Economics of Galilee and the Quest for
          the Historical Jesus. Pages 75–122 in *Studying the Historical Jesus: Evaluations
          of the State of the Current Research.* Edited by B. Chilton, and C. A. Evans.
          Leiden.
  2000   Herodian Economics in Galilee. Searching for a Suitable Model. Pages
          86–113 in *Galilee and Gospel: Collected Essays.* Tübingen: Mohr Siebeck.
          (First published in *Modelling Early Christianity: Social-Scientific Studies of the
          New Testament in Its Context* [1995]: 23–46.) London.
  2001a   A Galilean Messiah? *ST* 55:198–218.
  2001b   The Geography of Restoration: Galilee-Jerusalem Relations in Early
          Jewish and Christian Experience. *NTS* 47:289–311.
  2002   The Revolt From a Regional Perspective. Pages 43–56 in *The First
          Jewish Revolt: Archaeology, History, and Ideology.* Edited by. A. M. Berlin
          and J. A. Overman. London.
Fuks, G.
  2002   Josephus on Herod's Attitude Towards Jewish Religion: The Darker
          Side. *JJS* 53:238–45.
Hanson, K. C.
  1997   The Galilean Fishing Economy and the Jesus Tradition. *BTB* 27:
          99–11.
Hanson, K. C., and D. E. Oakman
  1998   *Palestine in the Time of Jesus: Social Structures and Social Conflicts.* Minneapolis.
Harlow, V. E.
  1954   *The Destroyer of Jesus: The Story of Herod Antipas Tetrarch of Galilee.* Oklahoma
          City.
Henten, J. W. van
  2003   The Two Dreams At the End of Book 17 of Josephus' *Antiquities.* Pages
          78–93 in *Internationales Josephus-Kolloquium Dortmund 2002.* Edited by J. U.
          Kalms, and F. Siegert. Münster.
Hoehner, H. W.
  1972   *Herod Antipas.* London.
Horsley, R. A.
  1995   Archaeology of Galilee and the Historical Context of Jesus. *Neot*
          29:211–29.
  1999   Jesus and Galilee: The Contingencies of a Renewal Movement. Pages
          57–74 in *Galilee Through the Centuries: Confluence of Cultures.* Edited by
          E. M. Meyers. Winona Lake.
  2001   *Hearing the Whole Story: The Politics of Plot in Mark's Gospel.* Louisville.
  2003   *Jesus and Empire: The Kingdom of God and the New World Disorder.* Minneapolis.
Horsley, R. A., and J. A. Draper
  1999   *Whoever Hears You Hears Me: Prophets, Perfomance, and Tradition in Q.*
          Harrisburg.
Horsley, R. A., and N. A. Silberman
  1997   *The Message and the Kingdom: How Jesus and Paul Ignited a Revolution and
          Transformed the Ancient World.* Minneapolis.
Jensen, M. H.
  2006   Herod Antipas in Galilee. Tübingen.
Jones, A. H. M.
  1938   *The Herods of Judaea.* Oxford.
Kokkinos, N.
  1998   *The Herodian Dynasty: Origins, Role in Society and Eclipse.* Sheffield.

Krieger, K.
    1994   *Geschichtsschreibung Als Apologetik Bei Flavius Josephus.* Tübingen.
Levine, L. I.
    1997   Archaeology and the Religious Ethos of Pre-70 Palestine. Pages
                110–20 in *Hillel and Jesus: Comparative Studies of Two Major Religious
                Leaders.* Edited by J. H. Charlesworth and L. L. Johns. Minneapolis.
Mason, S.
    2003a   Contradiction or Counterpoint? Josephus and Historical Method.
                RRJ 6(2–3):145–88.
    2003b   Flavius Josephus in Flavian Rome: Reading On and Between the
                Lines. Pages 559–89 in *Flavian Rome: Culture, Image, Text.* Edited by
                A. J. Boyle, and W. J. Dominik. Leiden.
    2005a   Figured Speech and Irony in T. Flavius Josephus. Pages 243–88 in
                Flavius Josephus and Flavian Rome. Edited by J. Edmondson, S. Mason,
                and J. Rives. Oxford.
    2005b   Of Audience and Meaning: Reading Josephus' *Bellum Iudaicum* in
                the Context of a Flavian Audience. Pages 70–100 in *Josephus and
                Jewish History in Flavian Rome and Beyond.* Edited by Joseph Sievers
                and Gaia Lembi. Leiden.
McLaren, J. S.
    2001   "Would the Real Judas Please Stand Up?" [cited 2001]. Online:
                http://www.josephus.yorku.ca/pdf/mclaren2001.pdf.
Moxnes, H.
    1998   Jesus' galilæiske kontekst: Den historiske Jesus i forhold til hus,
                landsbyog by. Pages 103–36 in *Den historiske Jesus og hans betydning.*
                Edited by T. Engberg-Pedersen. København.
    2001   The Construction of Galilee As a Place for the Historical Jesus—
                Part 2. *BTB* 31:64–77.
    2003   *Putting Jesus in His Place: A Radical Vision of Household and Kingdom.*
                Louisville.
Otto, W.
    1913   "Herodes Antipas." Pages 167–91 in *PW, Supplementband II.* Edited
                by Georg Wissowa. Stuttgart.
Perowne, S.
    1958   *The Later Herods: The Political Background of The New Testament.* London.
Reed, J. L.
    2000   *Archaeology and the Galilean Jesus: A Re-Examination of the Evidence.*
                Harrisburg.
Richardson, P.
    1999   *Herod: King of the Jews and Friend of the Romans.* 1996. Reprint.
                Minneapolis.
Roth, C.
    1956   An Ordinance Against Images in Jerusalem, A.D. 66. *HTR* 49:169–77.
Sawicki, M.
    2000   *Crossing Galilee: Architectures of Contact in the Occupied Land of Jesus.*
                Harrisburg.
Schürer, E.
    1901   *Geschichte des jüdischen Volkes im Zeitalter Jesu Christi—Erster Band.* 3 ed.
                Leipzig.
    1973–1987   *The History of the Jewish People in the Age of Jesus Christ (175 B.C.–A.D.
                135): A New English Version.* Revised and edited by G. Vermes, F.
                Millar, and M. Goodman. 3 vols. in 4. Edinburgh.
Vogel, M.
    1999   Vita 64–69, Das Bilderverbot und die Galiläapolitik des Josephus.
                JSJ 30:65–79.

JOSEPHUS AND THE *PSALMS OF SOLOMON* ON HEROD'S MESSIANIC ASPIRATIONS: AN INTERPRETATION

Samuel Rocca

1. *Introduction*

For various reasons Josephus was biased against Herod. Thus Josephus probably underplayed Herod's successful rule and popularity as King of Judea in the eyes of his Jewish subjects. One of the results of Josephus' bias was that King Herod was denied any ruling ideology or any political program.

It seems to me that the ruling ideology of King Herod, or how he presented himself towards his Jewish subjects, which is very important for understanding his long and peaceful rule, can indeed be reconstructed using both literary and numismatic evidence, which obviously includes Josephus, in spite of himself.

2. *Herod and King Solomon*

Herod was recognized as king of Judea by the Roman Senate in 40 B.C.E. For the Romans he was therefore Herod, king of the Jews, *rex Iudaeorum*, for the Greeks in the East, he was βασιλεὺς τῶν ᾽Ιουδαίων, but he was also for the Jews, the vast majority of his subjects no less than מלך היהודים.

For the Jews, the word *melek* (king) was associated with a glorious ancient past, known to the vast majority: the ancient monarchy of the First Temple period. I therefore suggest that Herod wanted to be seen by his Jewish subjects as the successor of the glorious kings of the house of David who once ruled Israel,[1] and in particular King Solomon.

---

[1] Schalit (1962, 232–34; 2001, 471–4) emphasized Herod's messianic ideology. According to Schalit, as the Pharisees saw that the throne of Israel belonged to the legitimate house of David and not to the Hasmoneans or Herod, the latter, influenced by Pollio (identified by Schalit as Hillel), developed his messianic ideology, centered on the building of the temple.

This article is based on my PhD thesis written at Bar Ilan University under the supervision of Prof. Albert Baumgarten.

Moreover, this association with the ancient Jewish past was even more necessary for Herod, since he could not inherit the earlier Hasmonean ideology of rule.[2] Of course, as Herod was a commoner, and not part of the Jewish priestly aristocracy, he could not in any way share in the Hasmonean ruling ideology vis-à-vis the Jews.

Herod's innovation is thus to present himself to his Jewish subjects as the successor of the Israelite kings. However, like the Hasmoneans before him, King Herod continued to present himself vis-à-vis his Gentile subjects as a *basileus*, following the Macedonian tradition of rule and that of the surrounding Hellenistic world.

As the successor of the Israelite kings of Judah, Herod could present to his Jewish subjects renewed images of ancient glory, never forgotten by the Jews. This tradition was very much alive, as Jewish historians rewrote their ancient history in the Hellenistic period for both a Jewish and Gentile public.[3] In fact the Jews considered the period of David and Solomon as the most glorious in their history. In the distant past King David had dominated a huge empire that stretched from the Sinai to southern Syria, and King Solomon, his son, had built the first temple. Both were celebrated in the Bible and by Jewish Hellenistic writers, who boasted of this glorious past.

There was an element of prestige that could connect Herod to Kings David and Solomon in the eyes of his Jewish subjects: the extension of the Herodian kingdom, which more or less covered the borders of the legendary Kingdom of David and Solomon, as described in the 2 Samuel.[4] Thus as ruler of a great empire, Herod could present himself to his Jewish subjects as the successor of King David.

Still it is a mistake to attribute to Herod an ideal tie with King David only, whose legendary glamour had already been exploited

---

[2] The ruling ideology of the Hasmoneans consisted in presenting to foreign Greek powers an all-powerful Greek *basileus*, in the Macedonian tradition, and to Jewish subjects the lawful high priest, head of the *Hever Hayehudim*.

[3] Although in the Herodian period the Bible was not yet canonized because various books were still disputed, the Books of Samuel and Kings were well known to the vast Jewish public at this time. These books were translated into Greek sometime in the Hellenistic period. Moreover, various Hellenistic-Jewish writers, mainly in Alexandria, but also in the land of Israel, composed various books of history, following the Greek method of historiography, dedicated to the ancient and glorious past of the Jews. Thus it is right to say that the ancient Jewish kings had become well-known, both in Jewish-Hellenistic circles, and in the wider Hellenistic world.

[4] See 2 Sam 3:3; 5:11; 8:6; 10, 14; 10:19; 13:37; 16:27; 1 Kgs 5:4; 1 Chr 19:1.

by the Hasmoneans.[5] Of all the successful rulers of Judah, as Solomon, Hezekiah, and Josiah, Herod chose as his paradigm the most magnificent one and of course the most well-known: King Solomon.

The golden age of King Solomon's reign was still seen as the highest point by the Jews in the Hellenistic-Roman Period. The Jews knew Solomon through the Bible as the temple builder[6] and as the ruler who, after King David's war of conquest, brought a long era of peace and prosperity to his huge empire. Solomon was also known as the paradigm of a just ruler,[7] who ensured his subjects a fair trial. Furthermore Solomon was considered a sage[8] and perhaps the most learned of his age.[9] If to his father David were attributed the Psalms, to Solomon were attributed the Song of Songs, Ecclesiastes, and the Book of Proverbs.

On the other side, there were less admired deeds. Solomon's court had a reputation of magnificence but also of luxury, with his many wives and concubines.[10] Solomon was also accused in the last years of his reign of introducing pagan cults to Jerusalem to satisfy his foreign wives.[11] Deuteronomy commands a king not to multiply horses and wives,[12] yet Solomon did the opposite.[13] But first and foremost Solomon was known as an absolute ruler, a quality that Herod could only admire.

Thus there was no better paradigm for Herod than Solomon. Herod could not only present himself as the successor of Solomon, but could also "correct" the various mistakes and errors attributed to the legendary Israelite king and, in fact, surpass him in all deeds.

---

[5] The Hasmoneans had already chosen King David as their model. See Gruen 1998, 138–41.

[6] See 1 Kgs 6:1–38 and 7:13–50.

[7] On the well-known judgment of Solomon, see 1 Kgs 3:15–28.

[8] See 1 Kgs 3:5–14 on the dream of Solomon when the young king asked G-d for an "understanding heart." On Solomon's universal reputation for wisdom, see 1 Kgs 5:9–14.

[9] For the historical figure of Solomon, see Miller and Hayes 1986, 189–217; the provocative book of Finkelstein and Silberman 2001, 123–49; and for a more traditional interpretation from the archaeological viewpoint, Mazar 1990, 368–403.

[10] Solomon built various palaces for himself, for his court, and for his most important wife, Pharaoh's daughter (1 Kgs 7:1–12). On Solomon's marriages to foreign women and the impressive list of his wives and concubines, see 1 Kgs 11:1–4.

[11] 1 Kgs 11:5–10.

[12] Deut 17:16–17.

[13] On Solomon's horses and chariots, see 1 Kgs 10:2, and on his fortifications at Jerusalem, Hazor, Megiddo, and Gezer, see 1 Kgs 9:15. It seems to me that the biblical historian wishes to underline that the primary task of Solomon's army is to suppress possible revolts among his subjects, much oppressed by taxes and levies.

Herod thus rebuilt the temple; but his temple was bigger than the one built by Solomon. Herod, like Solomon, entertained a luxurious court, which was also a center of learning. Furthermore like Solomon, Herod had many wives. Last but not least, Herod strove to bring to his subjects a long era of peace and prosperity, again as Solomon had done.

Moreover, the figure of King Solomon was also very popular among Hellenized Jews; thus, by choosing Solomon as his paradigm, Herod could endear himself to the Jewish upper class of the Greek-speaking Diaspora, Greek Gentile intellectuals, as well as the ruling class of Roman Phoenicia. Utilizing the paradigm of Solomon, Herod chose from the Jewish past a figure that was characterized by the qualities of the ideal Hellenistic king, as depicted by the Jewish Hellenistic historians Eupolemus, Theophilus, Dios, Menander, and Josephus.[14]

Eupolemus, probably from Hasmonean Judea, in his book "On the Kings of Judea," depicted Solomon not only as the temple builder, but also as a shrewd diplomat. The Solomon of Eupolemus had a good relationship with both Egypt and Tyre, the two other powers that dominated the ancient Near East, and furthermore he held the military-political balance. Thus Eupolemus underlines Solomon's wide international connections, the respect with which he was regarded, and also how he exercised tight command over his expanded homeland.

Only fragments remain of Eupolemus' book. One of these describes the epistolary relationship between Solomon and Vaphres, King of Egypt, and Souron, the ruler of Tyre, Sidon, and Phoenicia. Souron is depicted as "subordinate" to Solomon.[15]

Other historians, such as Theophilus, Dios, and Menander, depicted Solomon as a tolerant figure vis-à-vis the various pagan cults in foreign lands. Thus according to Theophilus, the King of Tyre employed the gold of Solomon to erect a statue of his daughter.[16]

---

[14] The real contemporary rulers of Solomon were Shishak, Pharaoh of Egypt, and Hiram, King of Phoenician Tyre. See Gruen 1998, 141–46.

[15] See Fallon 1985, 861–72. In Eupolemus there are various references to the contemporary period; for example, there is a clear reference to Leontopolis among the places listed by Vaphres, as the site of the temple of Onias IV. This is clearly a polemic against the Zadokite priesthood, which abandoned Jerusalem to build a new temple in Egypt. The wishful thinking of Solomon is that the Ptolemaic rulers, moved by the proud heritage of the Egyptian Jews, their faithful subjects, would support Judah Maccabaeus in his struggle against the Seleucids, the traditional adversaries of the Ptolemies. See Gruen 1998, 142.

[16] Gruen 1998, 146 n. 32. Theophilus is mentioned by Eusebius, *Praep. ev.* 9.34.19. According to the largely unknown historians Dios and Menander, the King of Tyre

Other books connected with Solomon, such as Sirach, the Wisdom of Solomon, and the *Testament of Solomon*, will not be considered here.[17]

3. *Josephus as Evidence for Herod's Ruling Ideology*

How is Herod's ruling ideology reflected in both the literary sources and the material evidence?

Although Josephus was biased against Herod, he mentions him at least twice in direct connection with the house of David and King Solomon, and more than once indirectly.

The most striking example is Herod's speech before rebuilding the Temple Mount. In this speech the connection between Herod and King Solomon is emphasized. The first challenge that Herod faced, and of course the most important one, was the rebuilding of the temple as a worthy successor to that built by King Solomon.

In this case Josephus has no choice but to link these two rulers, Solomon and Herod. In a speech before the beginning of the work, which Josephus attributes to Herod but probably originated with Nicolaus, Herod compares himself with Solomon. For both rulers obviously the temple was their most important achievement. Herod thus says that, since the exiles from Babylon had not rebuilt a temple to compare with the one erected by Solomon, he will do so.[18]

In Herod's speech and elsewhere[19] there is also an implicit criticism of his Hasmonean predecessors. Although the Hasmonean rulers were independent, and had the power to act as they wished, they had not rebuilt the temple, nor gathered in the exiles.

In fact, Herod not only rebuilt the temple more splendidly than the one built by Solomon, but Herod's temple played a much larger role in contemporary Jewish society. While the purpose of Solomon's

---

used the gold provided by Solomon to decorate the temple of Zeus (at Heliopolis?) with a golden column. Dios and Menander are mentioned by Josephus in *Apion* 1.112–120. Josephus' narration of Solomon's reign is dealt with below.

[17] The Wisdom of Solomon as well as Sirach are apocryphal and inspired by the legendary wisdom of Solomon, but Solomon himself is not the protagonist. On the *Testament of Solomon*, see Duling 1985, 935–88. Solomon is the main character but this depiction of him as master of the demons is not helpful in recovering the historical figure.

[18] *Ant.* 15.385.

[19] When Herod was dying and defending his record he explicitly criticized the Hasmoneans for not having rebuilt the temple to its proper dimensions (*Ant.* 17.162).

temple was to meet the needs of the royal court, as a sort of "Royal Chapel,"[20] Herod built a real "House for all the Nations."

Moreover as a successor to the house of David, Herod claimed his right to dominate the Temple Mount. Solomon had done the same, but from the beginning of the Second Temple period this had been the prerogative of the high priest.

This problem did not trouble the Hasmonean ruler, who was both king and high priest, and as high priest rather than king, dominated the Temple Mount. Yet Herod wanted to dominate the Temple Mount as king, and so he did. Of course only the successor to the house of David could claim possession of the Temple Mount. Herod could dominate the Temple Mount through his monumental rebuilding, but could not take upon himself any ritual duty as the Davidic kings had done (as heirs of Melchizedek).[21] These duties had been clearly defined at the beginning of the Second Temple period as the exclusive right of the high priest. With regard to this the Hasmonean rulers had an advantage. However, Herod dominated the high priesthood because he appointed and dismissed the high priests. Thus without taking the ritual duties upon himself, Herod succeeded in administering them.

Moreover, according to Josephus, like King Solomon, Herod offered sacrifices—clearly a prerogative of the priests in the Second Temple period—during the first Nabatean war, outside Jerusalem.[22] It is important to stress that in the First Temple period the Davidic king arrogated to himself the prerogative to offer sacrifices in place of the priests. The best known example is of course Solomon's inauguration of the first temple at Sukkoth, when he, and not the high priest, performed sacrifices.[23] Thus Herod once again consciously imitates Solomon, making sacrifices in front of the army.

There is another important point that probably led Herod to choose Solomon as his model, and that is the messianic nature of

---

[20] According to Miller and Hayes (1986, 202), Solomon built the temple as a royal chapel for the king and senior priests.

[21] The Davidic king took upon himself important ritual duties. Solomon blessed the congregation of Israel, offered up sacrifices, and dedicated the temple, according to Ps 110:4–5. David's house inherited the right to rule from Melchizedek, "king of Salem, priest of G-d Most High, Creator of heaven and earth." The Davidic kings are thus heirs of Melchizedek, the king who blessed Abraham, progenitor of the Israelite people. See Mazar 1992, 65–66.

[22] *Ant.* 15.147 and *War* 1.380. It is also probable that the Hasmonean high priests would have done the same thing but then they were actually priests!

[23] On the inauguration of the first temple, see 1 Kgs 8:1–64. Another prerogative of the priests that Solomon assumes is the blessing of the people.

the depictions of Solomon that had developed during the centuries.[24] However, the messianic aspect of King Herod's ideology is difficult to define. There are acts that can be interpreted not only to symbolize Herod's ties with Solomon, but also his messianic aspirations. In other words, both facets of the ideology overlap.

Thus the wish of King Herod to be seen as "successor" of Solomon was expressed tangibly vis-à-vis his Jewish subjects in the coronation ceremony. This ceremony probably had a certain messianic connotation. It seems to me that Herod revived the suggestive crowning ceremony of the kings of Judah to underline his link with the Davidic dynasty. The coronation ceremony at the beginning of the Israelite monarchy consisted only in the sacramental rite of anointing the ruler with oil on his accession to the throne.[25] It seems that only with Solomon the anointing developed into a complicated crowning ceremony, performed in front of the temple. 2 Kings describes this ceremony twice, with Solomon and Joash. The two rites are similar.[26]

The ceremony began when the high priest invested the king with the insignias of royalty, which were the *netzer* and the *eduth*.[27] The next and most important step was the anointing. This act was also performed by the high priest. Anointing has a religious connotation since it is accompanied by the arrival of G-d's presence (Shekinah)

---

[24] Although in Kings there is no trace of messianism in the description of the house of David, Isaiah presents the Davidic ruler as the Messiah. In Isa 6:12–13, the Messiah, the pure child Immanuel, will refuse evil and choose good. Isa 9:4 predicts that the Messiah will bring justice, peace, and prosperity. The figure of the Messiah in Isaiah, shaped the development of Jewish messianism in later periods. Isaiah was well known in the Second Temple period and the entire book was found on a scroll in the Qumran library. Matthew presents the child Jesus as the Messiah because he is the scion of David, as Isaiah predicted. The Messiah, the Son of David, came to be identified as Solomon, as in the *Psalms of Solomon*, because this king was associated with peace.

[25] In Israel this function was performed by the prophet or by the priest, acting on behalf of the G-d of Israel. The main ritual act took place when the priest or the prophet, as Messenger of the L-rd, poured oil on the head of the one about to be crowned and consecrated him as the chosen one of G-d. See Mazar 1992, 55–67 esp. 59.

[26] The crowning ceremony of Solomon is described in the 1 Kgs 1:32–38 and that of Joash in 2 Kgs 11:12–20. Solomon was consecrated at Gihon, the spring of Jerusalem. Joash, however, was consecrated in the temple precinct (2 Kgs 11:14). See de Vaux 1961, 100–113.

[27] The *netzer* was the royal diadem or crown. The *eduth*, testimony or solemn law, could have been the bracelets or the Book of the Covenant. According to 2 Kgs 11:12, the priest Jehoiada gave to Joash the *nezer* and the *eduth*. These two items do not appear in the crowning of Solomon.

for every act and decision of the future king. Once a king is anointed
he shares in the holiness of G-d and he is thus inviolable.[28] Then
the new sovereign was acclaimed, the shofar was sounded, and the
people shouted, "Long live the king!"[29] After the acclamation, everyone left the sanctuary and entered the palace, where the new king
sat on his throne.[30] This was an act of acknowledgment by the people
of the ruler's new status as king. The throne is the symbol of royal
power.[31] Psalms praising the new ruler were also sung.[32]

At first glance there is no inference in Josephus that Herod was
crowned according to the ancient Israelite custom, here outlined.
Josephus describes the crowning ceremony of Herod's son, Archelaus,
after the seven days of mourning for his father Herod, as prescribed
by Jewish law.[33] Archelaus, after distributing gifts to the people, went
up to the Temple Mount. There, in front of the temple the crowning ceremony was performed. Archelaus, then praised (by whom, by
the high priest?), is enthroned on a throne of gold. After the enthronement the people acclaim him. The ceremony described by Josephus
presents a striking similarity with the one described in the Bible and
so very different from those of the Hellenistic kings. There are only
two notable exceptions to the biblical ceremony: Archelaus is neither
anointed nor crowned. Is this Josephus' lapse or perhaps an implied
censure? Neither I think. More likely, Archelaus was not anointed
as this would have been considered no less binding than the crown
itself and so would have angered Augustus.

---

[28] Sam 9:16; 10:1, for the anointing of Saul. According to de Vaux (1961, 103–05),
this act confers grace.

[29] See 1 Kgs 1:34 et al. According to De Vaux (1961, 104), this acclamation
does not mean that the people chose the king, but that the people accepted the
choice made by the L-rd.

[30] On Solomon, see 1 Kgs 1:46 and on Joash, 2 Kgs 11:19.

[31] The throne as symbol of royal power appears in Ps 45:7. As the L-rd is the
true king of Israel, the royal throne is called "the Throne of G-d" (1 Chr 2:23).
The D-vine throne, according to Psalms 89:15 and 97:2 was supported by justice
and right. The same goes for the earthly throne of the Judean king, which was
firmly established on justice (Prov 16:12; 25:5; 29:14 and Ps 72:1–2). See de Vaux
1961, 106.

[32] 1 Kgs 1:40 and 2 Kgs 11:13–14. It is possible that Pss 2 and 110 were sung
as they allude to the rites of enthronement. See de Vaux 1961, 108–9.

[33] *Ant.* 17.200 and *War* 2.1–2. Josephus does not describe Agrippa I's crowning
ceremony. He states, however, that when the king arrived in Jerusalem, he brought
sacrifices to the temple, the Nazirites had their heads shorn, and he dedicated his
gold chain, given him by Gaius (*Ant.* 19.293–295). It is possible that Agrippa I was
crowned some time after his triumphal entrance in Jerusalem.

Archelaus is also not crowned, although this, like anointing, was clearly part of the original ceremony. Josephus clearly states that Archelaus refused the crown and asked to wait for "Caesar." Of course Archelaus, as a client king of Rome, had to wait for the formal investiture as king of Judea by Augustus. Archelaus could not allow himself to antagonize the Roman ruler by performing a ceremony that needed the express authorization of Rome. In the end, poor ruthless Archelaus was appointed ethnarch and not king of Judea.

That the ceremony performed in Jerusalem is really the ancient Jewish practice is confirmed by another episode. Archelaus refused the diadem offered him by the soldiers at Jericho and in so doing refused the Hellenistic investiture by the army, the custom of Macedonian rulers. He wanted to be crowned as a Jewish, not a Macedonian, king.

Josephus describes this ceremony as nothing new. The Hasmonean kings were probably crowned following the Macedonian custom. Thus the only person that could be crowned according to the ancient Israelite custom was Herod. When? Herod began his career as king in heathen Samaria. It is possible that Herod was anointed and crowned king of the Jews after his conquest of Jerusalem but then the city was devastated after a long siege and not all the new subjects of King Herod would have been in the mood to appreciate a crowning ceremony. It is thus probable that this ceremony was performed only after the completion of the Temple Mount, or maybe at its inauguration in the last years of Herod's rule, around 15 B.C.E. It is interesting that the high priest in 15 B.C.E. was none other than Boethus, Herod's future father-in-law, an Egyptian Jew from Alexandria, and so removed from Judean politics. Boethus was a figure who could have anointed and crowned Herod without creating any political or religious problem.[34]

Moreover there is other evidence, from material culture, that corroborates Josephus' story. A coin minted by Herod in Jerusalem depicts on the obverse the royal diadem with the Greek letter "chi," inside, while the reverse depicts a table. According to Meshorer the obverse can be interpreted in light of a Talmudic passage: "In anointing kings one draws the figure of a crown and with priests in the shape of the letter chi. Rav Menashiah said, like a Greek chi"

---

[34] See Richardson 1996, 243–44.

(b. Kerithot 5b). Thus Herod wished to stress the cooperation between kingship, symbolized by the diadem, and the priesthood, symbolized by the *chi*. Herod was anointed king, in the fashion of the kings of Judah in the First Temple period by the high priest. Therefore the obverse can only be a reference to the Israelite king's crowning ceremony, adopted by Herod. The reverse probably depicts a tripod, a vessel in the classical world associated with the temple.[35]

Although Josephus is biased against King Herod, it is still possible to use the information he provides, critically of course, to link him with Solomon. According to Josephus, when Herod needed funds, he opened the tombs of David and Solomon but did not find any money. He did find golden furniture, however, which he took away, probably to melt it. He then searched for the bodies of the two kings. But "a flame burst upon the two guards sent to search the bodies" and they were killed. Herod built a propitiatory monument on the spot.[36] Josephus writes that Nicolaus of Damascus also mentions this monument, but not the attempted tomb robbery. Josephus' report of tomb robbery is a literary *topos* of slander. In the classical world, it is tyrants who sack tombs and temples, as did Hiero of Syracuse, and of course Caligula, who plundered the tomb of Alexander the Great.

First of all it is doubtful both that Herod wished to sack the tomb, as Josephus claims, and that he found objects of gold inside it. If these had been deposited, no doubt some tomb-thief would already have stolen them after more than eight hundred years. Nicolaus does not mention these objects. It is probable that Herod beautified the so-called tombs of David and Solomon to highlight his connection with the house of David, and with Solomon, his model. Herod's deed was not uncommon in the Mediterranean world. Rebuilding the venerable tombs of heroes and historical personalities was a recognized way to assert legitimate leadership.[37]

---

[35] On the diadem and the *chi*, see also Meshorer 1982, 24–25. The *chi* possibly stands for the word *christos* or anointed. On the tripod, see *m. Sheqalim* 6:4 and Meshorer 1982, 23–24; 2001, 65–66.

[36] *Ant.* 16.179–184.

[37] There are many examples. The first is Alexander the Great, who laid a wreath on the tomb of Achilles when he landed in Asia Minor. His friend Hephaistion did the same with the Tomb of Patroclus. See Arrian, *Anabasis* 1:12. See Lane Fox 1987, 113. Augustus erected in the Roman Forum a shrine to his adoptive father Julius Caesar—Divus Caesar. See *Res Gestae Divi Augusti*, 4:19; also Cassius Dio 51:22, 2–3. See also Zanker 1989, 39, 86. Another good example is Apollonius of

A critical view of Herod's building projects outside Judea confirms this connection with Solomon, for Herod's *euergetism* imitates that of his ancient model. Just as the Solomon depicted by Eupolemus and the other Hellenistic Jewish historians was a generous benefactor towards Phoenician cities and colonies, so also was Herod. He erected many monuments in the Phoenician cities of Ascalon, Ptolemais, Berytus, Byblos, Sidon, Tripolis, and of course Tyre, the city of biblical Hiram (Eupolemus' Souron).[38] As successor to Solomon, he repaid the *euergetism* of King Hiram. I consider the *euergetism* shown by King Herod to the hellenized Phoenician cities rather different from that displayed to the Greek cities of Syria, Asia Minor, and continental Greece. In the first instance Herod behaved as the successor of Solomon while in the second he acted as a Macedonian king, the successor of Alexander the Great.

Finally, it is interesting to analyze the figure of King Solomon himself as portrayed by Josephus in his *Antiquities*. At first reading it seems that Josephus' Solomon mirrors his counterpart in 1 Kings. However, some passages possibly reflect an imaginary Solomon who mirrors King Herod. Some of Solomon's feats in Josephus' narrative were probably inspired by King Herod. These include the rebuilding of Jerusalem's walls (*Ant.* 8.21, 150) Solomon's sacrifice in Hebron (8.22–25; not mentioned in the Bible though Herod built a structure there, known today as "Haram El Khalil"), the building of the temple (8.61–129), and of a royal palace in Jerusalem (8.130–140). The last two structures, the temple and the palace, were dominant features of Herodian Jerusalem. It seems therefore that Josephus' depiction of Solomon in Herodian terms reflects Herod's attempt to associate himself with Solomon.

It is important to stress that Josephus' *Antiquities* was written more than ninety years after King Herod's death. Thus it easy to understand

---

Tyana, who renewed the tombs of the Eretrians, deported in Media by the Persians. See Philostratus, *Vit. Apoll.* 1:24; also Anderson 1994, 104. From Judea come other examples. Herod rebuilt the Tomb of the Patriarchs at Hebron (Lightstone 1984, 70–71). According to Matthew, the Pharisees rebuilt the tombs of the prophets as an act of self-glorification (Matt 23:29–30).

[38] According to *War* 1.422, Herod built gymnasia at Tripolis and Ptolemais; a city wall around Byblos; stoas, agoras, and temples at Berytus and Tyre; a theatre at Sidon; and bathhouse, fountains, agora, and basilica at Ascalon. Eupolemus (34: 16) notes, "As for Souron, he [Solomon] sent to Tyre the golden column, which is set up in Tyre in the Temple of Zeus." See Fallon 1985, 871.

that *post facto* the figures of the two kings merged into each other.[39] Josephus may not have been conscious of the fact!

4. *The* Psalms of Solomon *as External Contemporary Evidence of Herod's Ruling Ideology*

Interesting evidence of King Herod's ideology of rule comes from the *Psalms of Solomon*. Moreover it is external evidence, in the sense that it is not attributable to King Herod, and does not come from Josephus. The *Psalms of Solomon* expressed the wishful thinking of one of Herod's Jewish subjects. I concur with the view that the so-called *Psalms of Solomon*, written in Hebrew in Herodian Jerusalem, make Solomon the paradigm for Herodian rule, and that behind the mask of the Messiah is the figure of Herod himself.[40]

Pss. Sol. 17 is the most telling. The author hopes that at the end the reign of the Davidic Messiah will replace the illegitimate rulers (17:1, 5, 23–51; 18:6–10), the Hasmoneans, and bring about the establishment of an independent Jewish kingdom, after the expulsion of foreign influence. Similarities between Solomon and the messianic figure in *Pss. Sol.* 17 include the following: each is a Son of David, who extends the boundaries of the kingdom, restores and beautifies Jerusalem, and defends the worship of G-d. Both received tribute from foreign monarchs and rose above all other kings in wisdom and justice. However, although Solomon sinned by multiplying silver and gold, horses, chariots, and ships, and was guilty of pride and oppression, the Messiah will not commit such transgressions (*Pss. Sol.* 17:33).

Like the biblical commentaries from Qumran (e.g., 4Q169),[41] at least three of the psalms (*Pss. Sol.* 2, 8, and 17) refer to contemporary historical events, such as the capture of Jerusalem by Pompey.[42]

---

[39] *Ant.* 8.1–211. My thanks to Professor Daniel Schwartz of the Hebrew University of Jerusalem for his helpful suggestions.

[40] The *Pss. Sol.* is a collection of eighteen psalms preserved in Greek, probably composed in the second part of the first century B.C.E. See Wright 1985, 640–41; also Schürer 1973–1987, III.1 192–95.

[41] The attribution of the *Psalms* to Solomon is later. It was the similarity between *Pss. Sol.* 17, and the canonical Ps 72, which had traditionally been attributed to Solomon, that established the link between this collection and Solomon. See Schürer 1973–1987, III.1 430–32 (on Nahum). For the translation see Vermes 1987, 231–35.

[42] The central event described in most of the *Psalms of Solomon* is the capture of Jerusalem by Pompey in 63 B.C.E. The Hasmoneans, who seized David's throne,

There are various likely references to Herod in the *Psalms*. It is possible that *Pss. Sol.* 11:4 reflects the building of the Temple Mount itself. Thus I believe that the verse "He flattened high mountains into level grounds for them" (see Isa 40:4) clearly refers to the erection of the southern part of the Temple Mount esplanade by Herod. Indeed the enlargement of the surface of the Temple Mount and the building of huge superimposed arches would surely have excited the fantasy of the local population. Moreover the verse "Temple worshipping and pilgrims coming from east and west, north and the far distant islands" (*Pss. Sol.* 11:4) reflects the new status of the temple rebuilt by Herod and the pilgrimage to this temple from the Diaspora. However, it is *Pss. Sol.* 17 that contains most of the references to Herod.

Verses 21 to 46 describe the messianic kingdom of the Son of David. The Messiah, Son of David, "will destroy the unrighteous rulers" (*Pss. Sol.* 17:22). If the Hasmoneans were these unrighteous rulers, Herod had them exterminated.[43] The Messiah, Son of David, will also "purge Jerusalem from Gentiles" (*Pss. Sol.* 17:22). It seems strange to think that Herod, so open to foreign culture and influence, could have been imagined as the ruler that purged the Holy City of Gentiles. The truth of this boast is that Herod limited Gentile visitors to the Outer Court or Gentile Court of the Temple Mount.

Antiochus III had published a decree that threatened punishment by a fine for any foreigner coming within the limits of the temple (*Ant.* 12.145–146). However, by Herodian times the penalty for any transgressor was not merely a fine, but death, as reported by Josephus

---

behave disgracefully and desecrated the temple, bring as D-vine retribution the violent conquest of Jerusalem, the defilement of the temple, and the captivity of part of the population. *Pss. Sol.* 2, 8 and, 17 describe the conquest of Jerusalem and the defilement of the temple (*Pss. Sol.* 2:1–6) (*Pss. Sol.* 8:14–19), the captivity, the rape etc. (*Pss. Sol.* 2:7–15) (*Pss. Sol.* 8:30–23), but also the death of Pompey (*Pss. Sol.* 2:26–29). See Abel 1947, 243–55. Three groups of people are described: the Gentiles or the Romans of Pompey, the Sinners or the Hasmoneans and the Sadducees, and the devout or pious, probably the Pharisees or, according to Dupont-Sommer, the Essenes (Wright 1985, 642). Efron (1987, 219–86) does not accept this thesis, since for him the *Pss. Sol.* do not describe the end of the Hasmonean dynasty, nor any recognizable period, but are the product of a Hellenistic Jew removed from the reality of late first-century B.C.E. Judea.

[43] Herod had Antigonus, the last Hasmonean ruler, beheaded after the conquest of Jerusalem. Moreover, Herod arranged for the drowning at Jericho of Aristobulus, the young high priestly son of Hyrcanus II. He also had his beloved wife, Mariamme, executed.

and as we know from an inscription in Greek and Latin that divided
the Outer from the Inner Courts. Herod's decree was confirmed by
Augustus and continued even after Judea became a Roman province
in 6 c.e. This explains why the anonymous psalmist wrote that Herod
purged Jerusalem of Gentiles.[44]

In *Pss. Sol.* 17:30–31, the Messiah "will purge Jerusalem [and make
it] holy as it was even from the beginning, for nations to come from
the end of the earth to see his glory, to bring as gifts her children
who had been driven out, and to see the Glory of the L-rd, with
which G-d had glorified her." Here the concept of purity, very important for the author and highlighted earlier, (*Pss. Sol.* 17:22) is this
time given an ecumenical meaning. The new purified temple will be
visited by nations coming from the ends of the earth. This time the
Gentile visitors, like M. Vipsanius Agrippa,[45] and not the Jewish pilgrims, are tied to the sanctity and purity of the temple.

Jerusalem is called holy from the beginning, as Herod, according
to the psalmist, brought back to Jerusalem the glory of Solomon's
golden age.

The author finds also the occasion to underline that the Messiah
will "drive out the sinners from the inheritance" (*Pss. Sol.* 17:23).
Herod indeed, as we shall see, did curb the Sadducees' domination
of temple worship, "their inheritance," in favor of the Pharisees.

The anonymous psalmist is very appreciative of Herod's foreign
policy. When he writes, "he [the Messiah] will have Gentile nations
serving under his yoke" (*Pss. Sol.* 17:30), he clearly refers to Herod's
rule over Iturea, Batanea, and Gaulanitis, where nomads dwelled,
and also over the Greek cities of the coast and the Decapolis.

Moreover, when he writes that "he will not rely on horse and
rider and bow, nor he will collect gold and silver for war" (*Pss. Sol.*

---

[44] The penalty is a fine, and quite an expensive one! Josephus, in *Ant.* 15.417
and *War* 5.194, reports the well-known inscription. The decree survives in two
forms, one fragment in the Rockefeller Museum of Jerusalem and the other at the
Archaeological Museum of Istanbul. According to Bickerman (1947, 387–405), a
pagan visitor would have not seen any reason to be offended by being excluded
from holy ground. Other inscriptions from the Hellenistic East forbid the uniniti-
ated to enter a pagan *temenos*. See also Rabello (2000, IIIa–IIIb), who stresses that
this law dated from Herod's reign and not, as thought by other scholars, from the
successive Roman rule.

[45] Among the distinguished Gentile visitors was Agrippa, the friend and chosen
successor of Augustus, who visited the kingdom of Herod in 15 b.c.e. and offered
various expensive sacrifices in the temple (*Ant.* 16.14).

17:33–34), the psalmist highlights that Herod received from Augustus all these territories without waging war. Furthermore, his reign was quite peaceful and Herod, most of the time, remitted the taxes of his Jewish subjects.

The psalmist is mainly concerned, however, with the Messiah's justice (*Pss. Sol.* 17:26; 35:43). Herod's swift justice was probably one of the characteristics of his rule. Similarly, as noted above, Solomon's justice was widely renowned and also exploited in Hellenistic Jewish literature.

It is possible that the author of the *Psalms of Solomon* was a Pharisee,[46] in which case it would attest to both the popularity of Solomon and to the of Herodian family's popularity in some Pharisean circles.

In conclusion, it is interesting to compare my analysis of Herod's messianic ideology with E. P. Sanders' view of Jewish messianic ideals in the late Second Temple period, which he thinks were shared by most Jews. According to Sanders, with the coming of the Messiah the whole of Israel will be reassembled, the Gentiles will convert to Judaism or submit to Jewish rule, the temple will be renewed in a more glorious way; the kingdom will be reestablished and worship will be purified. Sanders brings various examples from the Apocrypha to show that this messianism is common to all Jews, including those who produced the *Psalms of Solomon*. Herod, as we have seen, realized in his time a common messianic expectation.[47]

No less interesting is to compare Herod's messianic ideals with the talmudic sages' ideals of kingship and messianism. Once more Herod's messianic propaganda of kingship is corroborated by later texts.[48]

---

[46] The *Psalms of Solomon* are imbued with a traditionalist spirit of piety and insist on the fulfilling of the commandments in the Decalogue (*Pss. Sol.* 14:2). Obedience to the law, together with a clear belief in free will (*Pss. Sol.* 9:4) and future life or damnation (*Pss. Sol.* 3:16; 13:9–11, 14, and 15), are all characteristics of Pharisean doctrine. In *Pss. Sol.* 10:7 it is said that, "the synagogues of Israel will glorify the L-rd's name." However the synagogue was an institution not necessarily connected with the Pharisees. The term "synagogue" in the *Psalms of Solomon* appears both as συναγωγή (*Pss. Sol.* 10:8; 17:18, 48 and 50) and as προσευχή (*Pss. Sol.* 6:5). The first term refers to the community of believers, the second probably to the building itself.

[47] Sanders 1992, 291–94.

[48] See Maimonides, *Hilchot Melachim and Milchamotteihem (The Laws of Kings and Their Wars)*. In *Hilchot Melachim* 1.4 Maimonides treats the appointments of kings, but does not require the king to come from the house of David (cf., *t. Yevamot* 102a, *b. Qiddushin* 76b), while he also deals with the crowning ceremony, which includes the anointing (*Hilchot Melachim* 1.7); (cf., *b. Kerithot* 5b and *Pirqe Rabbi Eliezer* 17). Later (*Hilchot Melachim* 1.10) Maimonides notes that when a non-Davidic king is

5. *Herod and the Hellenistic Tradition of Rule in the East:*
A Comparison with the Hasmoneans and Other Macedonian Rulers

Finally it is worth comparing Herod's ideology of rule with that of his predecessors, the Hasmoneans, and with other Hellenistic dynasts of the East.

King Alexander Jannaeus probably presents the best example of Hasmonean ruling ideology. He governed as both high priest and king. Moreover, it is clear from his coins that the title of king has no Jewish meaning. Jannaeus does not want to restore the splendors of the house of David, even if his kingdom reaches the same borders as his famed predecessors. His royal title has a purely Greek-Macedonian meaning.[49] Thus for his Jewish subjects this royal title could have had no real value, since it did not reference any ancestral symbolism of royalty. On the contrary, it seems that the title of king was the fruit of international recognition in the Hellenistic world for which the Hasmonean rulers, Aristobulus and Alexander Jannaeus, strove. This legitimacy of rule, however, had value only for the external Greco-Macedonian world. For the Jews, Alexander Jannaeus was simply the high priest.[50]

anointed it is with balsam oil; he further states that although David has acquired kingship for him and his male descendants forever, his acquisition of the monarchy was conditional, applying only to the righteous among his descendants. In *Hilchot Melachim* 1.8 it is maintained that a prophet can appoint a king from any tribe of Israel, and that if he follows the path of the Torah and *mitzvot* and fights the wars of G-d, he is considered a king and all the commandments associated with the monarchy apply to him (cf., *y. Horayot* 3:2). Regarding the messianic king, who will renew the Davidic dynasty (though no blood ties between the Messiah and the David dynasty are stressed), Maimonides adds that he will rebuild the temple as King Herod did (*Hilchot Melachim* 11.1). Maimonides (*Hilchot Melachim* 11.3) also stresses the human distinctiveness of the Messiah: "One must not presume that the Messiah King must work miracles and wonders."

[49] On his coins Alexander Jannaeus is named "King Alexander," clearly the successor of Alexander the Great, whom the rash Hasmonean king tried to imitate with various degrees of success. A strong and powerful army supported his rule, and thus his ideology and the organization of his court clearly imitates the splendors of the Macedonian monarchy. It is not clear whether this *imitatio Alexandri* actually disguised in some way the conquest and destruction of various Greek cities by a Jewish ruler. The fact that part of his army was composed of Greek mercenaries, and that a Greek power like the Ptolemies recognized his rule, probably meant that in the eyes of most of the Greeks Alexander Jannaeus was indeed considered a legitimate Greek ruler. His ideology of royalty was thus rooted in the Hellenistic conception of rule, not in the Jewish one.

[50] According to Schalit (2001, 474–76), the Pharisean leadership could not accept that one who was not from the house of David could sit on Judea's throne. However it seems to me that the Pharisees contested Alexander Jannaeus' position as high

Moreover, it is possible to see through the coins of Jannaeus that his Macedonian vision of monarchic rule based on Alexander's model, embraced the idea of Jewish leadership, but rooted in the figure of the high priest. This dichotomy is apparent in his coinage: on the obverse of the coins there is the inscription in Greek ΑΛΕΧΑΝΔΡΟΥ ΒΑΣΙΛΕΩΣ. Clearly, Jannaeus wanted to show that he considered himself part of the royal heritage of eastern Hellenistic rulers. It would probably have been difficult for him to resist the temptation to associate his Greek name, the same as that of Alexander the Great, with the title of his glorious predecessor: βασιλεύς.[51] To make his message even more explicit, Jannaeus minted another denomination with the inscription "King Alexander" in Aramaic, the language spoken by the lower strata of the neighboring populations.[52] On the reverse this often appears inside a wreath, sometimes ivy, in paleo-Hebrew script: "יהונתן הכהן הגדל וחבר היהודים" (Jehonathan the High Priest and the Council of the Jews)[53]—as on the coins of his father. Jannaeus wants to present himself to the Greek Hellenistic world as one of the *Diadochi* of Alexander the Great. To his Jewish subjects, however, he is first and foremost the high priest. He is not an absolute ruler, but must consult and respect the decisions of the Council of the Jews. He thus shows to his Jewish subjects that he is ready to share his authority with the Council. The wreath, a symbol of authority in the Hellenistic world, symbolically crowns both him and the Council of the Jews.

---

priest, not his royal title. For them, as for the rest of the Jews, his royalty was just one title as good as another. Schwartz (1992, 44–56) notes that the Pharisees did not oppose the Hasmoneans as high priests but as kings, since they resisted the linkage of religion and state, which would have brought the former down with the latter! Schwartz bases his theory on various talmudic texts such as *b. Qiddushin* 66a, a well known *baraita* in which the Pharisees ask King Alexander Jannaeus to keep the king's crown but to abdicate the priesthood. Schwartz sees in this source the opposite: the Pharisees wish him to abdicate as king, not as high priest. Another source is *b. Horayot* 13a (see also *t. Horayot* 13a, 2:8, *y. Horayot* 3:9–48b), where it is written that a sage takes precedence over a king of Israel, since when the sage dies there is no replacement, but when a king dies all of Israel is fit for his succession. Obviously, for the Pharisees there was no problem that a common Jew, not from the stock of David, should rule as king of Israel, whether he was a Hasmonean or Herod! In *b. Avodah Zarah* 8b (also *b. Shabbat* 15a, R. Jose writes that the wicked kingdom took over Israel 180 years before the temple was destroyed. Schwartz stresses that the wicked kingdom referred to the Hasmoneans, not the Romans of Pompey!

[51] Meshorer 1982, 118.
[52] Meshorer 1982, 79–80.
[53] Meshorer 1982, 63–66, 69–76.

It is important to note the use of this paleo-Hebrew script instead
of square writing on the coins of Jannaeus, since this script had
begun to fade from use long before his time. The use of such a
script in this late period therefore has an ideological meaning. Jannaeus
wanted to show his ties with the biblical past (not necessarily with
King David's house) and perhaps the continuity of rule with the earlier Oniad high priests.[54]

Herod's "propaganda" for his Jewish subjects, presenting him as
successor to the house of David, reflected a policy followed by other
Hellenistic rulers in the East. The Macedonian rulers of Egypt and
Syria assumed the titles of ancient Near Eastern rulers. The Ptolemies
of Egypt became pharaohs,[55] and the Seleucids of Syria, although
to a lesser degree, presented themselves as the successors of the Great
King or the rulers of Babylon.[56]

Herod thus tries to imitate a very ancient tradition of kingship,
common to most peoples of the ancient Near East. It must be clearly
understood that what Herod is doing is nothing new. The only
difference between Herod and the Macedonian kings is that Herod
was a native.

---

[54] See Naveh 1987, 112–24 and Rappaport 1991, 481–90.

[55] From the beginning the Ptolemies assumed the title of pharaoh, as Alexander
had done before, to ensure the allegiance of the natives, still much attached to their
traditions. Moreover, differing from the Seleucid reign, where many Greek cities
were founded, the only Greek city in Egypt was the metropolis of Alexandria. Most
of the Greek and Macedonian settlers did not dwell in the city, but in the country, side by side with the natives. The first Ptolemies had restored and erected temples to the Egyptian native gods, the best example being the Temple of Edfu.
Moreover in Alexandria, where the Ptolemies resided, the main city gods were not
Greek but the Egyptian Serapis and Isis. There was a clear dichotomy in the royal
iconography of the Ptolemies: on the coins and statues in the royal palace of
Alexandria and outside Egypt, they were depicted as Macedonian rulers, with their
own characteristic attributes such as the diadem. However, on the walls of the
Egyptian temples, reliefs made for the natives depicted the Ptolemaic ruler as the
pharaoh of Egypt, descendant of Osiris, sometimes with the double crown, sometimes with the blue crown. The Ptolemaic queen was depicted as Isis. On Ptolemaic
Egypt and this dichotomy, see Grimm 1998, 94–98; Charron 1998a, 170–80,
Charron 1998b, 192–201; Chaveau 1998, 187–92; Bowman (1986, 121–203) on the
relationship between Greeks and natives and on the temples. Preaux (1997, 192–95,
241–59, 264–65) gives a general description of the phenomenon in the Hellenistic
world.

[56] The Seleucid Empire is still relatively unknown. Sherwin-White and Kuhrt
(1993) remains the best reference work on the relationship between the various
native peoples, including the Jews, and the Seleucid rulers. On the ideology of kingship, see 129–32. On Babylonia, see 149–61. See also Sherwin-White and Kuhrt
(1990).

Appendix
Messianism in Judea and Rome

It might be interesting to speculate on whether the concept of a messianism that highlighted peace might have influenced, or been influenced by the tone of Augustan propaganda. There is a certain similarity between Jewish messianism, which emphasized peace as its main ideal, and those ideals expressed by Virgil in the *Fourth Eclogue*. The *eclogue* was dedicated to Asinius Pollio, in whose household Herod's sons, Alexander and Aristobulus, stayed when Herod sent them to Rome to be educated.[57] Virgil might have had occasion to meet them. They arrived in 23 B.C.E. and Virgil died in 19 B.C.E., and it is known that he frequented Pollio's house. Could Virgil have picked up the mysticism of the *4 Eclogue* from the entourage of the Judean princes? Probably not, since *Ecl.* 4 was composed many years before, around 40 B.C.E.[58] The *4 Eclogue*, although partially expressing Augustan ideals, was mainly a private matter for the consulship of Asinius Pollio.[59]

BIBLIOGRAPHY

Abel, F. M.
    1947 Le siège de Jérusalem par Pompée. *RB* 54:243–55.
Anderson, G.
    1994 *Sage, Saint and Sophist: Holy Men and their Associates in the Early Roman Empire.* London.
Bickerman, E.
    1947 The Warning Inscription of Herod's Temple. *JQR* 37:387–405.

---

[57] *Ant.* 15.343.

[58] See La Penna 1983, xlix–li.

[59] On Virgil, *Ecl.* 4, see Galinsky (1996, 91–93), who points out that although this composition evokes the return to the Golden Age of Saturn, the effort and pursuit so typical of the Augustan ethos is absent. Galinsky also notes the variety of traditions, eastern and western, from which Virgil draws. On Asinius Pollio, Herod, and Herod's sons, see Feldman 1996, 37–45 and 52–56. Feldman argues that Pollio could not have ignored the Jews in Rome, nor their history and religion, for he was associated with Timagenes of Alexandria, who in his *Universal History* included a detailed and favorable treatment of Jews, and Alexander Polyhistor, who also wrote on Jews in a positive way. Asinius Pollio not only knew Herod, but as consul in 40 B.C.E. he was instrumental in helping Antony and Octavian in having Herod made king. Feldman argues that the contact with Herod and his retinue influenced *Ecl.* 4. Yet Herod in 40 B.C.E. had much more serious political issues on his agenda, to say the least. If there is any Jewish influence on the *Ecl.* 4, it does not come from Herod.

Bowman, A. K.
      1986   *Egypt after the Pharaohs 332 B.C.–A.D. 642.* London.
Charlesworth, J. H., ed.
      1985   *The Old Testament Pseudepigrapha II.* New York.
Charron, A.
      1998a   La sculpture en Égypte à l'époque ptolémaique. Pages 170–80 in *La
                gloire d'Alexandrie: 7 Mai–26 Juillet 1998.* Paris.
      1998b   Les Ptolémées et les animaux sacrés. Pages 192–201 in *La gloire
                d'Alexandrie: 7 Mai–26 Juillet 1998.* Paris.
Chauveau, M.
      1998   Clergé et temples: rites, richesse et savoir. Pages 189–92 in *La gloire
                d'Alexandrie: 7 Mai–26 Juillet 1998.* Paris.
De Vaux, R.
      1961   *The Institutions of the Old Testament, Vol. I—Social Institutions.* New York.
Ephron, J.
      1987   *The Psalms of Solomon, The Hasmonean Decline and Christianity.* Leiden.
Feldman, L. H.
      1996   *Studies in Hellenistic Judaism.* Leiden.
Finkelstein, I., and Silberman, N. A.
      2001   *The Bible Unearthed: Archaeology's New Vision of Ancient Israel and the Origin
                of its Sacred Texts.* London.
Galinsky, K.
      1996   *Augustan Culture.* Princeton.
Gloire d'Alexandrie, [La]: 7 Mai–26 Juillet 1998.
      1998   Association Paris Musâees. Paris.
Grimm, G.
      1998   *Le Sérapéion.* Pages 94–98 in *La gloire d'Alexandrie: 7 Mai–26 Juillet 1998.*
                Paris.
Gruen, E. S.
      1998   *Heritage and Hellenism: The Reinvention of Jewish Tradition.* Berkeley.
La Penna, A.
      1983   *Introduzione in Virgilio: Bucoliche.* Milan.
Lightstone, J.
      1984   *The Commerce of the Sacred: Mediation of the Divine among Jews in the Graeco-
                Roman Diaspora.* California.
Maxwell Miller, J., and Hayes, J. H.
      1986   *A History of Ancient Israel and Judah.* Philadelphia.
Mazar, A.
      1990   *Archaeology of the Land of the Bible 10,000–586 B.C.E.* New York.
Mazar, B.
      1992   *Kingship in Ancient Israel, Biblical Israel, State and People.* Jerusalem.
Meshorer, Y. A.
      1982   *Ancient Jewish Coinage.* 2 vols. New York.
Naveh, J.
      1987   *Early History of the Alphabet.* Jerusalem.
Preaux, C.
      1997   *Le Monde Hellenistique* I. Paris.
Schwartz, D.
      1992   *Studies in the Jewish Background of Christianity.* Tübingen.
Rabello, A. M.
      2000   *The Jews in the Roman Empire: Legal Problems From Herod to Justinian.* Aldershot.
Rappaport, U.
      1991   The Hasmonean State and Hellenism. *Tarbiz* 60:481–90.

Richardson, P.
   1996   *Herod King of the Jews and Friend of the Romans*. Columbia.
Sanders, E. P.
   1992   *Judaism, Practice and Belief, 63 B.C.E.–66 C.E.* London.
Schürer, E.
   1973–1987   *The History of the Jewish People in the Age of Jesus Christ (175 B.C.–A.D.
                 135): A New English Version*. Revised and edited by G. Vermes,
                 F. Millar, and M. Goodman. 3 vols. in 4. Edinburgh.
Shalit, A.
   1962   *King Herod: Portrait of a Ruler*. Jerusalem.
   2001   *König Herodes. Der Mann und Sein Werk*. Berlin.
Sherwin-White, S., and Kuhrt, A.
   1990   *Hellenism in the East: The Interaction of Greek and Non-Greek Civilizations
                 from Syria to Central Asia after Alexander*. Berkeley.
   1993   *From Samarkhand to Sardis. A New Approach to the Seleucid Empire*.
                 Berkeley.
Vermes, G.
   1987   *The Dead Sea Scrolls in English*. Harmondsworth.

JOSEPHUS AS A SOURCE FOR ECONOMIC HISTORY: PROBLEMS AND APPROACHES

Jack Pastor

Introduction

At the outset we must point out that no one today would take seriously research on a historical period that does not have at least some presentation and discussion of the economic milieu. Can you imagine a history of modern Ireland without a discussion of the potato famine or the developments in industrialization? Even without a slavish and no longer fashionable dedication to the Marxist approach to history, one still recognizes the importance of the economic background to a better understanding of most if not all historical problems.[1]

However when we come to presenting a history of the Second Temple period we are faced with the unpalatable truth that the sources for economic history so handily available to our colleagues who deal with modern or even medieval history are for us very few and disparate.[2]

True we have an inscription here, a papyrus there, and coins everywhere, but that is nowhere near the wealth of material that stands waiting for the historian of later periods.

We lack the mountains of data, the census, the tax rolls, the pay records, and the legal records of permits and litigation that serve the historians of other periods so well.

What we have is Josephus.

Josephus is certainly our most important source for the history of Second Temple Judea.[3] Without Josephus one might reasonably claim that we do not have a history of the period. He is the primary source for the political history of the era, providing detailed information

---

[1] For an example of an historian who presented Second Temple Judea in a Marxist light see the writings of H. Kreissig, and especially Kreissig 1989, 265–77.

[2] An example of an influential historical survey which includes a sub-chapter on the economy is Lewis 1995.

[3] See the extensive bibliographies such as Feldman 1984, Schreckenberg 1997, and most recently the on-line bibliography at http://pace.cns.yorku.ca.

on governments, leaders, wars and revolutions. We use him to fill in gaps in our knowledge of Roman History, Hellenistic History, and even the history of the Parthian Kingdom.

In addition he serves as a most enlightening source for the religious and cultural history of the time. We fill in the picture presented by rabbinic sources with knowledge gleaned from Josephus. He even tells us about religious developments in the pagan world. These and more, his usefulness to archaeology and historical geography are beyond question. What would we know of Masada, Gamla, Herodion, Caesarea, Jerusalem, and so many more famous sites if we did not have Josephus to explain the history behind the material culture now found in excavations?

These aspects of Josephus have been known and utilized by generations of scholars. But, also scattered throughout Josephus' compositions is a plethora of information on economy and economic matters. This information is almost never developed into well-elucidated narratives, but remains anecdotal. Much of this information is difficult to analyze, and even more difficult to confirm. Can we rely on this information in order to draw useful conclusions and gain insights into historical questions having economic aspects? Can we use Josephus for economic history?

Regarding this question the comments made in a recent review of a book dealing with questions of economic history present us with one answer: I quote with excisions and emendations, the italics are mine:

> Extracting piecemeal information . . . from the *extant textual sources* the author's approach comes at the expense of general theoretical issues . . . and archaeological evidence . . .
> Unfortunately, the *limited nature of written sources* . . . makes his approach rather unsatisfying. His arguments are often ad hoc, and he is frequently reduced to wringing information on the agricultural economy from *literary works* . . . that were *never intended for such purposes*.
> (He) is not clear and convincing in answering these questions because of *limited focus on textual sources* . . .[4]

We think the major thrust of this writer can be summed up in his words "wringing information on the agricultural economy from literary works never intended for such purposes."

---

[4] Harrison 1999.

Well, that is one way of looking at it; yet there are other points of view:

For example Shimon Applebaum's article "Josephus and the Economic Causes of the Jewish War" relies on Josephus to present the contribution of economic factors to the Great Revolt of 66 C.E.[5]

In a different vein, but also relying greatly on information gleaned from Josephus we have Sean Freyne's chapter "Economic Realities and Social Stratification" in his book *Galilee from Alexander the Great to Hadrian*.[6]

An earlier work that tried to describe the economic life of Judea and also relied heavily on Josephus was *Jerusalem in the Time of Jesus* by Jeremias.[7]

There are also those historians who choose to use vignettes from Josephus in order to better base their view of a problem or to describe a situation.

Examples of this sort of use of Josephus are many; just to name a few: Smallwood turns to Josephus to explain the dismissal of Archelaus, stressing economic aspects of his reign that led to his failure.[8] Sanders uses Josephus to describe the background of ordinary life to the practice of Judaism in Roman and Herodian Judea. For Sanders ordinary life is very similar to what others would call economic life.[9] Martin Goodman credits economic disequilibrium as a major contributor to the outbreak of the Great Revolt.[10] All these scholars, and many more have, quarried in Josephus despite the literary nature of the source or the fact that Josephus, just like all the rest of the ancient historians did not write economic history *per se*.[11]

So despite the obvious problems of using a literary text not intended for economic history we propose that the nuggets of economic information found in Josephus can be exploited to learn something about the economic life of the period of the Second Temple and illuminate other historical questions such as political and religious history.

---

[5] Applebaum 1989.
[6] Freyne 1980, 155–207.
[7] Jeremias 1969.
[8] Smallwood 1981, 115.
[9] Sanders 1992, 119–21, and passim.
[10] Goodman 1987.
[11] Finley 1985. The debate on whether Finley exaggerated his position on the ancient economy or not still flares up from time to time, yet no one claims he was wrong on this point: ancient historians did not write economic history.

But first we must start out by defining what economic information is. When is an historical fact an economic historical fact?

This basic question is often neglected when writing history based on Josephus. For example one historian wrote: ". . . when Cestius Gallus and later Vespasian were compelled to destroy the villages of the territory of Antipatris . . . they were depriving the city's inhabitants of their food supply."[12]

By this token one could claim that the suicide of the Jewish rebels on Masada was an economic fact because it decreased the consumer base of the Dead Sea area. Continuing this approach would make all historical evidence economic history, an obvious absurdity. So we must first decide when is evidence economic evidence.

Economics is that part of human society that describes the way which society produces goods and services and how it distributes them. It is the way resources are managed. Economic history or economic historical facts include agriculture, manufacturing, construction, settlement, prices, taxes, and markets, to mention only a few general topics.

If Josephus provides us with evidence that can be *directly* related to the economic activity of the period then it enters our field of study.

Approaches

How should we approach the raw material that Josephus provides?

Although much depends on what we are trying to study, and may change our approach, we suggest that a two-phased method is most useful.

First we must realize that much of the material in Josephus can be classified according to subjects. Some of these topics include a surprisingly large amount of material. In a sense quantity can sometimes be quality, and the more Josephus mentions a topic the easier it is to get a feel for his reliability, the easier it is to confirm or dismiss his evidence. By the same token a one-time mention of a topic creates all sorts of doubts as to its provenance and accuracy.

This brings us to the next framework for organizing and utilizing the economic evidence in Josephus: what we will call "detail type." We suggest that all of the economic evidence in Josephus can be organized according to groups classified by the amount of particular

---

[12] Applebaum 1989, 237.

detail, expressly: items of explicit detail, items of general detail, and specific organized narratives of a situation or occurrence.

An item of explicit detail is one that presents us with quantifiable facts. Prices, tax rates, sizes, and numbers of people, beasts, ships, etc. are examples of detailed information.

Items of general detail are statements that while particularized in some respects still remain unquantified and are difficult to value. These general descriptions are the very many unquantified and undetailed statements Josephus makes without any specific reference to prices or quantities They would include the glowing claims that areas such as the Galilee are fertile and well-watered or the assertion that the Jews in Caesarea draw confidence from their wealth (*Ant.* 20.175) and some of them had large sums of money (*Ant.* 20.177). Mention of estates, statements about the high value of certain crops are further examples of general details (e.g., *Ant.* 15.96; *War* 1.362).

Specific organized narratives are the recounting of situations or occurrences that include several detailed pieces of information and are more susceptible to analysis both in comparison to the rest of the source and in comparison to other sources. An outstanding example of this would be the long and relatively detailed account of the famine during Herod's reign (*Ant.* 15.299–316).

What should be our methodology? Unsurprisingly, one must treat Josephus' economic evidence using exactly the generally accepted approaches toward any literary historical source: internal and external analysis. We should ask if the information contradicts other aspects of the internal evidence; whether the material has corroboration from independent sources; and what purpose the information serves in the greater scheme of Josephus' composition.

After having adopted or adapted Josephus' evidence we still have the problem of using it to create an accurate historical picture. Once again, the strictures of research methodology must be observed.

For example one historian dealt with the tax income from Herod's kingdom, he quite correctly tried to compare the per capita payment of Judea to that of a neighboring country, Egypt. But then he came to the conclusion that the total figure presented by Josephus must be wrong because this scholar multiplied the per capita tax of Egypt by three million. His error was accepting that totally impossible figure for the population of Judea at that time.[13] And of course,

---

[13] For a summary of the various approaches and conclusions regarding the population of Judea see Pastor 1997, 6–8.

he failed to demonstrate that Egypt's per capita tax was the same
as Judea's.[14]

Upon completion of the historical analysis we find ourselves with
a body of economic information that can illuminate other historical
questions.

A Food Crisis

At this juncture I would like to present an example of how economic information in Josephus can be approached.

First a question of bread prices:

In a recent translation and commentary of Josephus' *Antiquities* the
following account was treated in this fashion.

> . . . shortly before the recent war, when Claudius was ruler of the
> Romans and Ismaelos was high priest among us, and when famine
> gripped our land so that an *assaron* was sold for four drachmas, when
> wheat-flour was brought in during the festival of unleavened bread,
> amounting to seventy *kors*—these are thirty-one Sicilian or forty one
> Attic medimnoi—not one of the priest dared to eat a crumb, although
> such great want gripped the land . . .[15]

The commentator explains the sizes of an *assaron* and the *medimnos*,
noting that Josephus is inconsistent regarding the size of the *kor*;
however regarding the famine he writes "We have no other information about this famine."[16] And he goes on to deal with the chronological problems presented by the source. Neither the prices and
their fluctuations, nor the famine itself draw any comment.

Returning to the source; we are told an *assaron* sold for four drachmas. An *assaron* is 1/100 of a *kor*, that is, it equals 3.95–4.65 liter.[17]
We are therefore dealing with about one drachma per liter. The

---

[14] Applebaum 1989, 241.
[15] Feldman 2000 on *Ant.* 3.320–321.
[16] Feldman 2000, 329, n. 960.
[17] In *Ant.* 3.321 Josephus writes that 70 *kors* equal 31 Sicilian or 41 Attic medimni. Thackeray rightly points out (p. 475 n. c) that in *Ant.* 15.314 Josephus wrote
that 1 *kor* equals 10 Attic *medimini*. The Attic *medimni* according to Thackeray equals
"a bushel and a half," i.e., at 35.238 liters to the bushel the *medimni* equals 52.857
liters. This would mean that the kor is 30.96 liters. However Marcus in his note
to *Ant.* 15.314 (Josephus LCL, vol. VIII, 150, n. a) states that the *kor* equals 7 attic
medimnoi which at the scale noted equals c. 370 liters. Yet there are many other
suggestions: 394 liter according to Jeremias (1969, 129 n. 17) based on 30 *seah* of
13 liters almost the 395 liters suggested by Oakman (1986, 85 n. 70), and also

"normal" non-famine price was about one drachma per 4.3 liters; hence the famine price is about four times the regular price.[18]

Of course one could at the outset claim that this is an unsubstantiated tale whose only purpose is to demonstrate the piety of the priests.

But, in another place and in greater detail we have shown that in all probability the famine occurred.[19] And there is supporting testimony from other sources.[20]

Josephus is opening up a window onto wider economic questions that in turn pose questions of both political and social history. Why or how did the famine occur? In fact how often were there famines?

How did price fluctuation affect the society? What were the ramifications of the rise in prices for those who could pay, and also for those who could not? How did the famine relief, or lack of it, affect the political and social fabric of Judean society and its perception of Roman rule? These questions are sometimes answered in part by Josephus himself, or can be answered by the same tools we would use in any other Josephean problem—internal and external criticism.

This was just a short anecdote; a good example of a long narrative that contains economic material is the account of the famine during Herod's reign.

Famine in Herod's Day

The narrative appears in *Ant.* 15.299–316, although we will deal with only some portions of it here.

This narrative is a fairly complete account of a famine that includes many of the aspects inexorably tied in with the famine phenomenon. In summary here are the details as presented by Josephus:

> In the 13th year of Herod there was a great famine. (299)
> The Famine was caused by continual droughts. (300)
> Even the wild plants did not grow.

Hamel 1990, 244. The values published in research can reach to a high of 465 liters per *kor* which can be calculated by using Milik's value of the *seah*, Milik 1959, 151 n. 1. See also *IDB* 4.828–839 and *DJD* II, 97 note a; 214.

[18] Jeremias (1969, 123) obtains the "normal price" from *m. Pe'ah* 8:7, and confirms it by comparison to Mark 6:37,44, and Cicero, 2 *Verr.* III 81, no. 188–189. Oakman (1986, 60) accepts the same reckoning.

[19] Pastor 1997, 151–56.

[20] *Ant.* 3.320–321; 20.51–53; Acts 11:27–31; Eusebius *Hist. eccl.* II.12; Schoene 1967, 152; Orosius VII 6.9–17.

There was an outbreak of plague caused and exacerbated by the famine. (300–301)

The populace was demoralized and totally enervated by the situation. (301)

The populace had no grain left. The stores had been eaten. (302)

There was no seed left and no new crop of seeds. (302)

The drought lasted at least two years. (302)

The populace turned to alternate livelihoods. (303)

The treasury was empty because there was no revenue from agriculture. (303)

Herod had no reserves because of his building policy. (303)

Neighboring countries had no grain. (305)

Even small quantities at high prices were unavailable. (305)

Herod converted his treasures into coin. (306)

He tried to buy grain from Egypt. (307)

The Prefect of Egypt was the deciding factor on who would get grain, how much, and when. (307)

The grain was transported by ship. (307)

The king distributed the food, carefully. (309)

Many could not prepare food for themselves as they usually did. (309)

Food was prepared by bakers operated by the government. (309)

It was winter and many people had no clothing. (310)

The populace had no flocks of beasts left because they had been destroyed and consumed. (310)

Herod also aided neighboring cities and Provincia Syria. (311)

The next harvest was successful. (311)

To bring in the harvest Herod operated a force of 50,000 men. (312)

Herod imported 90,000 *kors* of grain to Judea, 80,000 intended just for Judea, the rest for neighboring countries. (314)

If we check this narrative from the two aspects of internal and external evidence, and check the external evidence according to details we come to the conclusion that this story in great part is true. There are some exaggerations, but the aggregate of the story is authentic. Moreover we learn something about economic interrelationships characteristic of Herod's kingdom. To check the story one must compare its parts with material drawn from climate studies, anthropological and archaeological material, historical sources of different kinds, and also famine studies. Here are a few points to consider.

Josephus blames a drought for the famine. To anyone with the slightest familiarity with the climate of Judea, Syria, Lebanon, and Jordan, this will come as no surprise.[21] The surprise is that drought

---

[21] Baly 1957, 50.52; Hamel 1990, 102–108; My own examination of the rainfall record of Jerusalem for the period 1846/7–1959/60 indicates that the total annual precipitation fell below the minimum level necessary for wheat nine times in those 113 years.

does not cause famine more often. By checking both the historical record in Josephus and drought records we learn that only if there is a two year drought is there also a famine. For the period between the mid-nineteenth century till the onset of the recent period of global warming, one finds that on the whole there were two years of successive drought only once every twenty-five years.[22]

Josephus account is very accurate as to behavior of the society regarding, crops, planting, harvesting, storage.

Planting of grains is in the fall, after the first winter rains have prepared the soil. The crops are harvested in the spring.[23] If there was drought that season, there is no crop. However the Mediterranean farmer always has at least one year's reserve of grain stored.[24] Hence he makes it through the next season and plants again. If this time there is a drought, now the second consecutive year, he has finished his reserves.[25] At this point a food crisis occurs, but there is one last source of grain for food, the seeds that were being kept for planting. But now there is no reserve with which to plant. The seed grains are consumed as food, and the farmer has no seeds to plant even if the drought breaks.

Every famine study demonstrates that as the famine gets worse there is a concomitant increase in infectious diseases.[26] That the spread of disease is in of itself one more contributory to the famine, decreasing the number of people who can effectively work to overcome the situation, and of course increasing the risk of more infections through corpses.

The disappearance of grain stores is not only a function of the actual consumption, but is accelerated by market forces. Those, those lucky few, who have some grain beyond their needs hoard it. Hoarding is not merely done as self-protection, but in the expectation of selling at peak price.[27]

[22] Scott *IDB* 3:625; Orni and Efrat 1971, 148–49.
[23] Feliks 1963, 142.
[24] Clark and Haswell 1970, 58–62; on the practice of storing two years supply as hedge against crisis: Varro, *Rust.* 1.57,3; *t. Avodah Zarah* 4:1; *t. Demai* 1:13–14.
[25] As a subsistence-farming society approaches harvest time a pre-harvest hunger occurs as the stocks of food from the previous harvests dwindle. The society is dependent on the new crop to increase the amount of food available for consumption. The failure of the new crop causes a food crisis at the very least, and depending upon the availability and efficiency of famine protection institutions, the situation can deteriorate into famine. See Clark and Haswell 1970, 22–23.
[26] Garnsey 1988, 26, 28; Garnsey 1999, 34–61; Brunt 1971, 135; Sen 1981, 20–26; Livi-Bacci 1985, 100.
[27] Garnsey 1988, 77; Sen 1981, 76, 80.

People who no longer can earn a livelihood in agriculture look for alternate sources of income, especially if the work carries with it "entitlements." This could be the military, or dependent labor of some kind.

Ostensibly the drought-famine situation cut deeply into Herod's revenue indicating the relative importance of the agricultural sector to the state's prosperity.[28] What we know of the tax structure in Hellenistic and Roman times supports this contention. Moreover, the account before us is one of the few sources that acknowledge that Herod's building program was a major drain on revenue.

The claim that except for Egypt neighboring countries also had no grain helps to validate the authenticity of the narrative. For drought to be real and not a literary creation it must meet certain physical criteria. One of these is that drought either is in all southern Greater Syria or it is not a drought. Either everyone in the area has rain, or no one has rain. This of course excludes Egypt that benefits from an entirely different source of precipitation. The agriculture of Egypt and Palestine are dependent on two separate and different patterns of precipitation. Egypt is watered by the Nile, Israel by western winter cyclones. That is why Egypt can have plenty while Syria starves. As a result Egypt was called on to sell grain to the disparate people of Syria, but there the market was not free, but a government controlled market. The Roman governor decided who would buy, at what price, and in which quantities on the basis of criteria having almost nothing to do with market forces.

Grain was transported by ship if at all possible. Seaborne commerce was significantly cheaper and faster than transportation of cargoes by land, it still is. Ships could carry larger burdens than pack animals or wagons could, and they made better time.[29] This came as an advantage to Palestine whose lengthy sea coast provides many landing opportunities for those who would supply her by sea. Stretched all along her Mediterranean sea-board were cities, large and small, with landing facilities of some nature. Some of these were barely usable (Shiqmona) others were major ports (Acco-Ptolemais). They all offered the possibility of a gateway into the hinterland for those who would wish to import grain.

---

[28] Jones 1964, 464–66 suggested up to 95% of the revenue of the later Roman Empire was drawn from agriculture, although a maximalist view this illustrates the contribution of agriculture to the state revenue.
[29] D'Arms and Kopff 1980; Hopkins 1983.

Herod had to move about 28,000–33,000 tons. Ships of 150 tons
were common in Hellenistic times, while the standard grain-ships on
the Alexandria-Italy line were 340 tons.[30] Using ships of 150 tons,
anywhere from 180 to 220 shiploads would be a perfectly reasonable task. Egypt supposedly provided Rome with 135,000 tons annually.[31] It has been shown that Rome imported the bulk of the 250,000
tons of grain a year she needed.[32] One scholar stated that it was
not impossible that Rome shipped in as much as 400,000 tons of
grain annually.[33] In summary, the amount of grain that Herod had
to move was not extraordinary, and if we take into account that
Petronius allegedly arranged for the shipping, the transport problem
was easily surmountable because the Alexandrian grain fleet shipped
far larger quantities than Herod's.

The claim that there were no flocks left, and that people had no
cloth or wool to make new clothing fits perfectly with what we know
of famine dynamics. As the price of grain soars people sell their
finished goods, anything and everything that can be converted into
money or traded for grain goes to that end. Then there is a massive slaughter of flocks; but not to eat the meat, rather to eliminate
the animals as competitors for grain. Meat is a very inefficient way
of getting calories when compared to eating the grain directly.
Mediterranean herds were not kept for the meat; they were kept for
the wool and the dairy products.[34]

Up to this point Josephus' famine narrative has stood up well.
Where are the problems? We cannot know about the 50,000 agricultural workers. We cannot confirm that Herod organized the baking
of bread, although this would stand to reason. It fits the approach
to famine relief from other places.

To sum up. This was just one instance of history with an economic slant that can be found in Josephus' writings. The historian
who delves into Josephus' writings should do justice to this aspect
of his work.

---

[30] White 1984, 145.
[31] Casson 1984, 96–97.
[32] Rickman 1980, 263, 267.
[33] Garnsey 1983, 118.
[34] Garnsey 1999, 18.

BIBLIOGRAPHY

Applebaum, S.
  1989   Josephus and the Economic Causes of the Jewish War. Pages 237–64 in *Josephus, the Bible and History*. Edited by. L. H. Feldman and G. Hata. Detroit.
Baly, D.
  1957   *The Geography of the Bible.* New York.
Benoit, P., J. T. Milik, and R. de Vaux
  1961   *Les grottes de Murabba'at.* Oxford.
Brunt, P. A.
  1971   *Italian Manpower.* Oxford.
Buttrick, G. A. ed.
  1982   *The Interpreters Dictionary of the Bible.* 5 vols. Nashville.
Casson, L.
  1984   The Role of the State in Rome's Grain Trade. Pages 96–116 in *Ancient Trade and Society*. Detroit.
Clark, C. and M. Haswell
  1970   *The Economics of Subsistence Agriculture.* London.
D'Arms, J. H. and E. C. Kopff, ed.
  1980   *Roman Seaborne Commerce. Memoirs of the American Academy in Rome*, vol. 36. Rome.
Feldman, Louis H.
  1984   *Josephus and Modern Scholarship (1937–1980).* Berlin.
  2000   *Judean Antiquities 1–4.* Vol. 3 of *Flavius Josephus: Translation and Commentary*. Translation and Commentary by L. H. Feldman. Edited by S. Mason, Leiden.
Feliks, J.
  1963   *Agriculture in Palestine in the Period of the Mishna and Talmud.* Jerusalem. [Hebrew]
Finley, M. I.
  1973   *The Ancient Economy.* Berkeley. Repr., 1985.
Freyne, S.
  1980   *Galilee From Alexander the Great to Hadrian.* Wilmington. Repr., Edinburgh, 1998.
Garnsey, P.
  1983   Grain for Rome. Pages 118–38 in *Trade in the Ancient Economy*. Edited by P. Garnsey, K. Hopkins, and C. R. Whittaker. Berkeley.
  1988   *Famine and Food Supply in the Graeco-Roman World.* Cambridge.
  1999   *Food and Society in Classical Antiquity.* Cambridge.
Goodman, M.
  1987   *The Ruling Class of Judaea.* Cambridge
Hamel, G.
  1990   *Poverty and Charity in Roman Palestine: First Three Centuries C.E.* Berkeley.
Harrison, T. P.
  1999   Review of J. Pastor, *Land and Economy in Ancient Palestine. Near Eastern Archaeology* 62:56–57.
Hopkins, K.
  1983   Models, Ships, and Staples. Pages 92–105 in *Trade and Famine in Classical Antiquity*. Edited by P. Garnsey and C. R. Whittaker. Cambridge.
Jeremias, J.
  1969   *Jerusalem in the Time of Jesus.* London: SCM Press.
Jones, A. H. M.
  1964   *Later Roman Empire.* Oxford.

Kreissig, H.
    1989   A Marxist View of Josephus' Account of the Jewish War. Pages 265–77
            in *Josephus, the Bible and History*. Edited by L. H. Feldman and G. Hata.
            Detroit.

Lewis, B.
    1995   *The Middle East: 2000 Years of History From the Rise of Christianity to the*
            Present Day. London.

Livi-Bacci, M.
    1985   The Nutrition–Mortality Link in Past Times. Pages 95–100 in *Hunger*
            and History. Edited by R. I. Rotberg and T. K. Rabb. Cambridge

Mason, S. ed.
    2000   *Judean Antiquities 1–4*. Vol. 3 of *Flavius Josephus: Translation and Commentary*.
            Translation and Commentary by L. H. Feldman. Edited by S. Mason.
            Leiden.

Milik, J. T.
    1959   *Ten Years of Discovery in the Wilderness of Judaea*. London.

Oakman, D. E.
    1985   *Jesus and the Economic Questions of His Day*. Lewiston.

Orni, E., and E. Efrat
    1971   *Geography of Israel*. Jerusalem.

Rickman, G. E.
    1980   The Grain Trade Under the Roman Empire. Pages 261–75 in *Roman*
            Seaborne Commerce. (*Memoirs of the American Academy in Rome*, vol. 36.) Edited
            by J. H. D'Arms and E. C. Kopff. Rome.

Pastor, J.
    1997   *Land and Economy in Ancient Palestine*. London.

Sanders, E. P.
    1992   *Judaism: Practice and Belief 63, B.C.E.–66 C.E.* London.

Schoene, A. ed.
    1967   Eusebius, Chronicorum Canonum. Dublin.

Schreckenberg, H.
    1997   *Bibiliographie Zu Flavius Josephus*. Leiden.

Sen, A.
    1981   *Poverty and Famines: An Essay On Entitlement and Deprivation*. Oxford.

Smallwood, E.
    1981   *The Jews Under Roman Rule*. Leiden.

White, K. D.
    1984   *Greek and Roman Technology*. Ithaca, New York.

Zangemeister, C., ed.
    1882   Orosius *CSEL, Pauli Orosii Historiarum Adversus Pagano*. Vindobonae.

PART FOUR

JOSEPHUS AND ARCHAEOLOGY

NOBLE DEATHS AT GAMLA AND MASADA?
A CRITICAL ASSESSMENT OF JOSEPHUS' ACCOUNTS
OF JEWISH RESISTANCE IN LIGHT
OF ARCHAEOLOGICAL DISCOVERIES

Kenneth Atkinson

The sieges of Gamla and Masada were crucial episodes in the First Revolt. Gamla's capitulation to the Romans in 67 C.E. was one of the first major battles in this conflict while Masada's 73 C.E. downfall marked the terminus of the hostilities. Contemporary readers of Josephus' *War* cannot help but be moved by his dramatic accounts of the *Sicarii's* final hours atop Masada and the immense suffering of Gamla's inhabitants. Unfortunately, virtually all of our knowledge about what transpired atop Masada's summit and in Gamla's streets comes from Josephus. If we did not have Josephus' *War*, we would not even know about the noble deaths at Masada or Gamla. The question facing all Josephus scholars regarding these accounts of noble death, as well as other stories in the *War*, is whether they are true?

Although we lack other accounts of the First Revolt that could corroborate Josephus' narratives, we do have a slightly more impartial witness to these battles. Archaeology provides independent evidence that can sometimes be used to verify or refute Josephus' *War*. Unfortunately, the material culture obtained from archaeology is not mute but, like a written text, requires interpretation. Nevertheless, the basic facts provided by archaeology are not in dispute. Archaeology reveals that Jews at Masada and Gamla were besieged by Roman troops during the mid-first century C.E. If we only had archaeology, what would we conclude about these two sieges? Does archaeology have anything to tell us about what actually took place during these two battles? For students of the First Revolt, the central question is whether the archaeological evidence supports Josephus' accounts of noble death at Masada and Gamla?

This study will look into this issue by first summarizing Josephus' accounts of each battle before reviewing the results of the archaeological excavations. For each site, I will focus on what archaeology alone tells us about the sieges of Masada and Gamla. I will then briefly compare this evidence with Josephus' *War* to see if the material culture derived from archaeology supports his narrative. The conclusion will make some comments on Josephus' use of noble death as a theme in the *War*.

Josephus and Masada

The story of Masada is undoubtedly the most well known episode in Josephus' *War* (7.252–406). First seized by Menahem the Galilean at the outbreak of the First Revolt sometime in the midsummer of 66 C.E., the fortress of Masada later fell into the hands of his relative Eleazar ben Yair, a leader of the *Sicarii*.[1] The capture of Masada provided these insurgents with ample arms, many of which they used against the Romans in Jerusalem. The *Sicarii* occupying Masada raided neighboring settlements, such as Ein Gedi where they killed 700 Jews (*War* 4.399–409). Flavius Silva, commander of the Tenth Legion, laid siege to Masada. The *Sicarii* unsuccessfully attempted to halt the Roman onslaught with the construction of a wooden wall, which the Romans set on fire. In the final hours of the siege, Eleazar delivered two speeches inciting his fellow *Sicarii* to commit suicide rather than be captured by the Romans. Ten men were chosen by lot to slaughter all the others. When Silva's troops stormed Masada they found the bodies of 960 men, women, and children. Only two women, who had hidden below ground, survived to report the tragic story of Masada's final hours. Is this story true? Is Josephus a faithful chronicler of historical events, or something more akin to a historical novelist, who uses historical events as a departure point to frame a good story? Or, is Josephus a liar?

Archaeology and Masada

What does archaeology have to tell us about the siege of Masada? The fortress of Masada is among the world's best preserved Roman

---

[1] Josephus frequently states that Masada was held by the *Sicarii* (*War* 4.399–400, 516; 7.253, 275, 297, 311). I accept the view that the *Sicarii* and *Zealots* were different groups that were often opposed to one another. See further Hayward 1986, 598–606. See also Cotton and Geiger 1989, 4–7.

siege sites. Because of its remote location, Masada's siege works have survived relatively intact. This has led many to assume that the Romans expended an unprecedented amount of military effort to capture Masada.[2] Is this assumption correct? Was the siege of Masada unique, or was it a routine military engagement?

Masada's eight Roman camps contain numerous rows of stone-built *triclinia*, each of which supported a single tent that housed a *contubernium*: a group of eight men who ate and slept together. By calculating the number of these sleeping units, we can come up with a fairly reliable estimate as to the number of Roman troops at Masada. Because of erosion and other factors that have disturbed these camps, estimates of their living capacity vary between 7,000–9,000 men.[3] Archaeology provides us with a reasonably accurate estimate concerning the number of Roman troops at Masada. The next issue is to determine what archaeology can tell us about the composition of these troops? In other words, did the Romans commit an excessive number of soldiers to the siege of Masada?

A Roman legion of the first century C.E. on paper had the strength of 4,800 soldiers.[4] Masada's two largest camps, B and F, are of

---

[2] Determining the length of Masada's siege is complicated by the fact that Josephus does not give the date when it began or the year when it ended. See Roth 1995, 88, 109 n. 155. Eck (1969, 282–89) used two inscriptions that record the career of L. Flavius Silva to place Masada's fall in 74 C.E. This date may be supported by papyri discovered during the Masada excavations (Locus 1039). See further Campbell 1988, 156–58; Cotton 1989, 157–62; Cotton and Geiger 1989, 21–23, 62–67.

[3] Richmond (1962, 152) estimated that Masada's camps held about 7,200 soldiers while Yadin (1966, 218) believed that they could house 9,000 troops. Shulten's estimate falls in the middle at 8,000 men. Shulten (1933, 83–86) proposed the following distribution: 4,000 infantry from the Tenth Legion occupied Camps B and F; two military cohorts of 1,000 each resided in Camps C and E; four quingenarian infantry cohorts (500 each) resided in the remaining camps (A, D, G, and H). Neither Roth nor Shatzman sought to determine which units occupied each camp, but the former estimated that approximately 8,000 soldiers were at Masada while the latter placed the figure between 7,000 and 8,000. Both concluded that a single legion with 6 auxiliaries lived in the camps. Roth 1995, 92–93; Shatzman 1997, 123. The estimated size of the legionary force at Masada cited in this study must be considered only approximate. Roman legions, like contemporary military forces, were never at full strength due to deaths, injuries, discharges, and temporary gaps in the arrival of replacements. See further Bennet 1986, 707–16; Davison 1989, 1:12–16, 124–27, 176–80; Johnson 1983, 166–75; Pseudo-Hyginus, *De munitionibus castrorum* 1.

[4] This is based on the following standard figures given in Roman texts: ten squads (*contubernia*) of eight men each make up a century (80 men); six centuries a cohort (480 men); and ten cohorts a legion (4,800 men). These figures do not include

sufficient size to have accommodated this number. The auxiliaries, who were largely of Syrian origin, would have inhabited the other camps.[5] Written evidence from military diplomas show that a provincial auxiliary garrison in 86 C.E. consisted of two *alae* (cavalry) and four cohorts (infantry), with an ostensible strength of 2,240 infantry, 1,152 cavalry, for a total of roughly 3,392 men.[6] If we adopt these figures for Masada it would bring the total number of Roman soldiers to approximately 8,000. Masada's eight camps could have held precisely this number of men. Based on literary texts, we can estimate that around 2,000 military slaves and 3,000 corvée laborers would have accompanied this army. The walled camp near the siege ramp, and the 30 *canabae* near camps E and F, could have accommodated this number.[7] The archaeological remains from Masada suggest that approximately 13,000 men, both soldiers and camp followers, were on the Roman side. This number matches remarkably well the literary evidence for the size of a first-century C.E. legion and its followers. Archaeology, when compared with Roman documents, shows that a single legionary force besieged Masada.

Archaeology does not provide sufficient evidence to determine the number of people atop Masada who opposed the Romans. It does reveal that Masada was a difficult site to occupy. The excessive number of storage facilities, cisterns, defensive walls, and two palaces, combined with Masada's location, reveal that it was built as a royal fortress. Inscriptions and other archaeological evidence show that the majority of Masada's extant structures were constructed during the reign of Herod the Great. The Latin papyri discovered at Masada indicate that it was occupied by a Roman garrison after 70 C.E.[8]

the auxiliary units consisting of *alae* (cavalry) and infantry discussed below. For the archaeological and literary evidence upon which these figures are based, see further Roth 1994, 346–62; Webster 1985, 96–166.

[5] Syria was the primary recruiting ground for archers during the late Roman Republic and remained an important source of troops during later periods. See further Caesar, *Bell. Afr.* 20.1; *idem, Bellum civ.* 1.51; 3.4; Kennedy 1989, 235–46; Davies 1977, 260–62. Josephus mentioned a centurion named Gallus in the siege of Gamla who, along with his companions, was a Syrian (*War* 4.37–38). See also *War* 2.268; 3.67, 211; 4.38; 5.42, 550–552, 556; 6.54–55.

[6] *CIL*, 16.33; Cotton and Geiger 1989, 14–15; Kennedy 1985, 253–63. Auxiliary strength based on the figures in Roth 1995, 91–92.

[7] Estimates based on Roth 1995, 94–95. For the labor camp and *canabae*, see further Richmond 1962, 151; Yadin 1966, 220. Shatzman (1997, 121) identifies approximately thirty shops south of Camp F and west of Camp E.

[8] The Latin papyri, all found in Locus 1039, can be dated on internal grounds from after 70 C.E. (no. 72) to around 73 C.E. (no. 724). See Cotton and Geiger 1989, 27.

The remains of squatter's residences, ovens, and gendered objects such as spindle whorls, indicate that families occupied Masada while it was under siege.[9] The discovery of several *miqva'ot*, stone vessels, a synagogue, numerous objects bearing Jewish names, as well as Jewish religious texts, show that these occupants were Jewish. The archaeological remains, coupled with Masada's limited dwelling space, suggest that there were insufficient occupants living atop the site during the siege to have posed any serious threat to the 7,000–8,000 Roman soldiers encamped below. Based on archaeology, we would conclude that a single Roman legion besieged a fairly small number of Jews, including families, who had for some reason sought refuge atop this desert fortress.

Archaeology alone cannot tell us the precise length of Masada's siege. It suggests that it was perhaps shorter than commonly assumed. Masada's eight camps lack ditches, which either indicate that the legions did not expect to stay long or that these camps were built after the abatement of the winter rains.[10] The ceramics in Masada's camps consist almost entirely of locally made storage jars that would have been used for transporting and storing food and liquids and not for cooking. In contrast, the Tenth Legion's base at Binyanei Ha'uma in Jerusalem contains a kiln and the full ceramic repertoire of cooking vessels and kitchenware indicative of a long-term settlement.[11] The Romans at Masada used the metal cooking vessels that were part of their mess-kits, which all soldiers carried in the field. The lack of cooking vessels from Masada's camps suggests that they were occupied for a relatively short period of time.

Masada's siege wall is among the most impressive features at the site. It is approximately 4,500 meters in length with an average width

---

[9] See further Reich 2001, 149–62. For photographs of some of these objects, including baskets, cosmetic pallets, and a woman's plaited hair, see Yadin 1966, 140–63, 193–99.

[10] Richmond 1962, 146–48. Schulten (1933, 91, 164) notes that magazines and ditches were present in Roman camps at Numantia in Spain, which was besieged during the winter of 134/33 B.C.E. For the typical features found in Roman camps, whether constructed of turf or stone, and tents, see further Vegetius, *Epitoma rei militaris*, 1.22; Polybius, 7.26–42; Webster 1985, 169–74, 167–230; Gilliver 1993, 49–54; Johnson 1983, 45–52; Goldsworthy 2003, 171–72.

[11] Magness 2002, 189–212; 1996, 181. Magness notes that the fine painted table wares and Nabataean bowls found in Masada's camps come primarily from the officers' living quarters.

of 1.65 meters. It stood about 3 meters high.[12] These dimensions are rather deceptive. Based on the estimated number of troops housed in Masada's camps, it would have taken approximately two weeks to construct the camps and siege wall, with an additional week required for the supply roads.[13] While this may sound rather implausible, Josephus witnessed Vespasian's four legions encircle the entire city of Jerusalem with a stone siege wall, and build thirteen forts, in only three days. He also wrote that a detachment of infantry and cavalry constructed a 10-kilometer road from Gabara to Jotapata in four days.[14] Perhaps the most surprising feature of Masada's siege wall is not that it was constructed fairly quickly, but that it was unnecessary. A single Roman legion possessed more than sufficient troops to literally surround Masada and prevent any sorties or escape attempts. Jonathan Roth has proposed that Masada's circumvallation wall was constructed primarily as "busy work" for the army.[15] Given the number of troops at Masada, and the fact that the Jews atop the citadel were essentially trapped, Roth's thesis is not as foolish as it may sound: it has been the job of army officers of all ages to keep their soldiers busy in the field in order to instill discipline, train them for battle, and keep them out of trouble.

Masada's siege ramp is undoubtedly the most controversial feature at the site. Dan Gil's geological study of Masada's ramp suggests that it was built upon a natural spur. This issue is still debated

---

[12] The walls that surround Masada contain approximately 38,000 cubic meters of stone (calculation based on Roth 1995, 99). Webster (1985, 172) estimates the wall at 4,296 meters long with a height of 1.2 meters and a thickness of 0.6 meters while Shatzman (1997, 123–24) places its total length at 3,000 meters. Shatzman also comments that the eastern section of this wall included at least fourteen towers placed at intervals of 80 to 100 meters. Towers were not necessary in the western section since this wall extended to the cliffs. Similar figures for these towers are offered by Richmond 1962, 153.

[13] Richmond 1962, 153; Roth 1995, 98–101, 109; Shatzman 1997, 125.

[14] *War* 5.508–509 (Jerusalem); 3.141–142 (Jotapata road). Vespasian used the fifth, tenth, and the fifteenth legions during his northern campaign (*War* 3.64–65). The twelfth legion, which was disgraced due to its loss in battle at the beginning of the revolt (*War* 2.499–555), later fought in Jerusalem and helped to build its siege works (*War* 5.466–472). Titus also had 1,000 men from each of Egypt's two legions as well as 3,000 troops from the Euphrates (*War* 5.44), likely from the IV Scythica and VI Ferrata, that replaced some of the troops that Vespasian had sent with Mucianus to Italy (*War* 4.632; 5.43). The fifth, tenth, and fifteenth legions fought at Gamla along with additional forces supplied by Agrippa (*War* 4.11–16). For Roman construction methods and the speed at which legions were able to build roads and related structures, see further, Johnson 1983, 71–77.

[15] Roth 1995, 101.

since it is difficult to determine the ramp's original dimensions. Gil's thesis is supported by Josephus' statement that one path to the fortress of Masada was apparently located atop a "white" (λευκὴν) spur (*War* 7.306).[16] Based on the estimate of the amount of earth in the ramp, Roth has suggested that it would have taken a force of only 2,400 men working around the clock, in three shifts of 800 men each, less than 16 days to construct Masada's siege ramp.[17] While this figure is likely in need of some adjustment, and it probably took a bit longer to construct the ramp, Roth's calculations are supported by Josephus' *War*. According to Josephus, the average time for the construction of a typical siege ramp during the First Revolt was only 20 days while facing armed resistance. In comparison, during the Gallic War the army of Julius Caesar built a ramp 23.5 meters in height, 97 meters in length, and 50 meters in width that held two siege towers, in only 25 days despite heavy rains and an opposing force of 40,000 Gauls.[18] Masada's siege ramp, while an impressive achievement, was not unprecedented by Roman military standards.

It is unlikely that the defenders atop Masada could have posed much resistance. The Romans could have easily countered any attempts to block construction of the siege ramp by stationing artillery on the white spur or atop a siege tower. The archaeological evidence suggests that this is exactly what happened. Numerous ballista stones were discovered atop Masada. Roman ballista had a range of between 366–457 meters (400–500 yards).[19] Camp F was 360 meters from Masada while camp E was approximately 220 meters. Because these two camps were within the range of any artillery mounted on Masada's walls, it is unlikely that the Romans would have built them so close to the site unless they were certain that the occupants of Masada had none.[20] This suggests that the

---

[16] Gill 1993, 569–70; 1984, 22–31, 56–57.

[17] Roth (1995, 101–5) bases his estimate on a figure of approximately 37,500 cubic meters of earth and timber in the ramp. Gill estimated the ramp's total volume at around 663,000 cubic feet and proposed that it took about one month to build. For a slightly different reconstruction, see Shatzman 1997, 126–28.

[18] Caesar, *Bell. gall.* 7.22–24, 28. While fighting Vercingetorix at Gergovia, Caesar's two legions connected his two camps with a double trench twelve feet wide overnight. *Bell. gall.* 7.36.

[19] Marsden 1969, 91. See further Webster 1985, 240–45 and plates XXVII–XXIX.

[20] For evidence in support of this thesis, see the figures in Roth 1995, 95–98; Holley 1994, 360–62. Shatzman (1989, 474–75) is slightly more cautious and suggests that artillery engines had different ranges and that there is no way of knowing what

defenders of Masada had no artillery, and that the ballista stones
found inside the fortress were shot there by the Romans. The discovery of numerous ballista stones strewn around the breach suggest
that the Romans used a continuous volley of suppressing fire to keep
Masada's defenders away from its walls. We can assume that the
combination of siege machinery and Roman archers made resistance
nearly impossible for Masada's occupants. There is no conclusive
archaeological evidence that the people atop Masada hindered the
Roman siege.

What does archaeology tell us about Masada's defenders? Yigael
Yadin found skeletons of men, women, and children in two locations: the bathhouse in the northern palace (3 skeletons) and the
southern cave (25 skeletons). Many show signs of teeth marks suggesting that they had been disinterred by animals. This is evident
by the disarray of these skeletons and their broken long bones, which
were apparently cracked open by hyenas or jackals to extract their
marrow. Although Yadin discovered the remains of 25 people in the
southern cave (Locus 2001), he only found 220 bones. An adult
skeleton contains 206 bones. Scavengers removed ninety six percent
of the skeletal material. The skeletons in the bathhouse, which included
the remains of a woman's plaited hair, were likely transported there
by animals. While archaeology does show that Jews were at Masada,
the presence of pig bones intermingled with these skeletons—a feature common to Roman burials—suggests that they are the remains
of pagans.[21] The absence of mass graves leads to the conclusion that

type may have been stored at Masada before its capture. In light of the locations
of camps E and F, it may be significant, as Roth comments, that Josephus does
not mention any artillery among Herod's stores at Masada (*War* 7.295–298). It is
unlikely that the Jewish defenders of Masada would have brought artillery to the
site, or that such equipment, if it was already there, would have been fit for use
after approximately 70 years in storage. There is no evidence to support Netzer's
theory for the existence of a tower with one or more ballistae mounted on it in
casemate Locus 1038. Netzer is correct that the wood in this room was likely used
for the construction of the wooden wall mentioned by Josephus to block the Roman
battering ram (*War* 7.311–315). The ballista stones in this structure, however, were
merely thrown in by Roman soldiers during their cleaning operation as evident by
the extensive debris in this region. The Romans likely projected a heavy volley of
suppressing fire at this section of the casemate wall since it jutted out and provided
a spot for archers to shoot at the Roman siege engines. The large stones designed
for rolling were primarily found near the Snake Path and casemate Locus 1039.
See further Netzer 1991, 26–31; 1989, 311–20; Holley 1994, 353–55; 360–61.
   [21] See further, Zias, Segal, and Carmi 1994, 366–67; Zias 2000,732–38; 1998,
40–45, 64–66. See also Yadin 1966, 54–58, 192–99.

the Romans likely captured the majority of Masada's defenders. Archaeology provides no evidence to support Josephus' account of noble death at Masada.

Archaeology, Masada, and Josephus

Does archaeology verify or refute Josephus' account of Masada's siege? In asking this question we must remember that neither Josephus nor his patrons Vespasian and Titus were at Masada when it was besieged.[22] Based on archaeology alone, we would conclude that the siege at Masada was typical by Roman standards. The size of the legionary force encamped around Masada show that the Romans considered this campaign to be a fairly routine military engagement that would not keep them in the field for a protracted period of time. This evidence matches Josephus' *War*, which states that a single legionary force besieged Masada. In some respects Josephus adds to our understanding of what likely transpired during the battle. His account of the *Sicarii's* construction of a wall to impede the Roman battering ram may be supported by the absence of wood from several of Masada's structures.

Does archaeology provide any evidence to support Josephus' account of noble death at Masada? While some Jews may have killed themselves during the siege, seeing no hope as their fortress was about to succumb to the Romans, there is no archaeological evidence that Masada's defenders committed mass suicide. The absence of mass graves, combined with the lack of living quarters atop Masada, may even suggest that there were far fewer than 960 people atop Masada. Archaeology provides no definitive evidence that Masada's defenders were able to pose much resistance, which suggests that most were likely captured by the Romans.

Archaeology does indicate that Josephus has perhaps not told us the full story of what actually transpired atop Masada. A reused

---

[22] Yadin's excavations revealed that Josephus' description of Masada is mistaken in many respects. For example, Josephus mentions only the northern palace, which he calls the western palace (*War* 7.287), and 37 towers whereas 27 were found. This suggests that Josephus never actually climbed atop Masada since it is unlikely that he would have omitted the presence of two palaces. At most, he perhaps saw it from a distance, possibly during his three-year sojourn with Bannus (*Life* 11). See further Bilde 1988, 58–59; Broshi 1982, 379–84; Yadin 1966, 41–73. 117–63.

Herodian jar found at Masada bears an inscription, which its final
editor Joseph Naveh translates, "Ananias the high priest and Aqaviah
his son" (ה[נ]נ[י]ה כהנא רבא עקביא בריה).[23] Ananias bar Nedebaeus
served as high priest from 48–59 C.E. Although his son Aqaviah was
previously unknown, according to Josephus (*War* 2.409), it was Ananias'
son Eleazar who refused to offer sacrifices on behalf of the Emperor
that precipitated the First Revolt. If we did not have Josephus'
account, we would likely use this inscription to suggest that Masada's
leaders were priests.[24] Since Josephus for the most part places the
blame for the atrocities and mass suicides during revolt upon the
Sicarii and other rebels, and not on the priestly elite, it is very possible that Josephus' account of Masada is even more fictitious than
we realized. Josephus likely obscured the participation of priests at
Masada, and possibly in the First Revolt, since he himself was a
priest living comfortably in Rome. Based on archaeology alone, we
would simply conclude that the defenders of Masada succumbed to
the same fate as their fellow countrymen who opposed the Romans,
namely slavery and, if they were unfortunate, death in the arena.

Josephus and Gamla

Gamla presents us with a valuable site for verifying the accuracy of
Josephus' narrative regarding Masada. Unlike Masada, Josephus was
at Gamla for the entire thirty-days during which it was besieged by
three Roman legions (*War* 4.83). Josephus had been taken prisoner
a few months earlier at Jotapata (Yodefat). According to Josephus'
own testimony, he fortified Gamla, knew its inhabitants, and watched
the siege from the Roman camp. Vespasian, Titus and Agrippa were
also at Gamla and, therefore, could testify to the accuracy of Josephus'
account. According to Josephus, Gamla was first loyal to the Romans
and then, due to the arrival of rebels, opposed Agrippa and joined

---

[23] Yadin, Naveh, and Meshorer 1989, 37–38, plate 30. For a discussion of possible priestly involvement in the events at Masada, see further Wise 1994, 52–102.
For a different perspective, see VanderKam 2004, 455–63.

[24] A Paleo-Hebrew papyrus fragment found at Masada likely contains a Samaritan
prayer, which could indicate the presence of some Samaritans at the site. See further Talmon 1997, 220–32. I am grateful to M. Mor for this reference. The finding
of a fragment of the "Songs of the Sabbath Sacrifice" may also suggest that some
members of the Qumran community were at Masada.

the revolt. In preparation for the Roman onslaught, Agrippa block-aded the roads leading from the Galilee to the Golan, especially those that supplied Gamla. Agrippa attempted to convince Gamla's occupants to surrender and then unsuccessfully besieged the town for seven months.[25]

When Vespasian and Titus, with the fifth, tenth, and fifteenth legions, supported by Agrippa's forces, reached Gamla the town housed over 9,000 people (*War* 4.80–81). According to Josephus' account, the Romans succeeded in breaching Gamla's wall with bat-tering rams (*War* 4.20). Vespasian led the charge and became trapped in the city. He barely escaped with his life by interlocking his shield with those of his comrades. Later, three soldiers from the fifteenth legion crept up to Gamla's tower at night. They toppled it by remov-ing some of its foundation stones (*War* 4.62–69). Vespasian's son Titus led the final assault into the city. As the fighting became fierce, Gamla's inhabitants retreated to the town's citadel. A change in the wind favored the Romans, who continued to fire a volley of arrows at the unfortunate inhabitants (*War* 4.75–77). At this point, the men, women, and children of Gamla, according to Josephus, "plunged headlong with their wives and children into the ravine which had been excavated to a vast depth below the citadel" (*War* 4.79–80). Five thousand people committed suicide while four thousand were killed by Roman swords. There were no survivors, with the excep-tion of two women. Gamla, after first being besieged for seven months by Agrippa's forces, succumbed to the Romans after a thirty-day siege (*War* 4.80–83).[26]

Archaeology and Gamla

The archaeological evidence from Gamla suggests that the siege that occurred there was considerably shorter than the siege of Masada.[27]

---

[25] For these events, see *War* 2.574; 4.1–83; *Life* 59–61, 114, 177, 179–87, 186, 398. According to *Life* 114, Agrippa's siege of Gamla was under the command of Aequus Modius. Agrippa had a large cavalry force that he recruited from his king-dom (*War* 2.421). See further Gracey 1986, 319–21.

[26] According to Josephus, these two women were nieces, on their mother's side, of Philip, son of Jacimus, who was King Agrippa's lieutenant. *War* 2.421, 556; 4.81; *Life* 46.

[27] I accept the identification of es-Salam (es-Sanam) as Gamla, which was exca-vated by the late Shmarya Gutman (1909–1996). See further, Syon 1995, 3–24.

Conventional Roman tactics dictated that if a town or city could not be overcome after an initial assault, or convinced to surrender, then it would be surrounded with a circumvallation wall such as the one constructed at Masada. There are no remains of Roman camps at Gamla or on the plateau to its north and south. While it is possible that wooden structures existed, the absence of pottery indicating the location of such camps is telling.[28] There are no remains of a circumvallation wall or any Roman structures at Gamla. The archaeological evidence suggests that the Romans did not expect to be at Gamla very long. It also shows that the Romans were confident that there was no danger of being attacked since they did not need to construct any fortified tactical camps.

From a tactical viewpoint, Gamla was a perfect site for a Roman legion to assault. It was not a fortress like Masada, but an ordinary town with a unique location. Gamla was in a canyon. Because of the steepness of the ridge upon which Gamla is situated, the town was built only on its southern slope. The deep canyons on all but one of its sides formed natural protective barriers. For this reason, Gamla had only a single wall that guarded the saddle that connected the town with the plateau above. Because Gamla was naturally isolated, there was no need to construct siege walls. The steep chasms that surround Gamla on all but one of its sides formed natural siege walls. Soldiers positioned atop the ravine to Gamla's south could have looked down inside the city and signaled the best locations for placing the siege equipment.

See also Avi-Yonah 1976, 58; Bar-Kochva 1976, 54–71. There is as yet no official report of the Gamla excavations. For preliminary results of the archaeological excavations of Gamla, from which the findings mentioned in this section were obtained, see Gutman 1994. My appreciation to D. Syon, the current director of the Gamla excavations, for providing additional information about the site to be published in the final report. Although I spent two seasons excavating with Gutman and Syon at Gamla, none of the views expressed in this study should be attributed to them.

[28] Gutman failed to find any trace of camps at Gamla or on the surrounding plateaus. It should be pointed out that Gutman excavated and restored Camp A at Masada. See further, Gutman 1964, 88–123. The absence of a circumvallation wall or siege ramp at Gamla is especially surprising since they are both present at the site of Khirbet el-Hamam, which Zertal (1995) identifies as Narbata. This town was likely besieged in 66 C.E. by Gallus. The camps at Khirbet el-Hamam are small and should be considered tactical bases rather than living-quarters. They are similar to those found at Machaerus which, like Masada and Khirbet el-Hamam, also contains a circumvallation wall. See further Stroebel 1974, 128–84.

Gamla's single wall would not have posed much of an obstacle to a besieging force. It bulges, zigzags, projects, and retracts. Gamla's round tower, situated at the highest point on the wall, was poorly constructed. It lacks a foundation and simply abuts the wall. Some locations, such as the "study room" adjacent to the famous synagogue, were filled in with stones to strengthen Gamla's wall. Gamla's poorly constructed wall suggests that it was hastily completed just prior to the Roman siege. In fact, Gamla had no defensive wall prior to the siege.[29]

The numerous weapons and armament found at Gamla testify to the ferocity of the Roman siege that took place there. Some 2,000 basalt ballista stones, 1,600 iron arrowheads, 100 catapult bolts, and other weapons, as well pieces of Roman armor, have been uncovered.[30] The number of arrowheads and ballista stones discovered at Gamla are unsurpassed from any other site in the Roman Empire. Unlike Masada, projectile points of the type that would have been shot by legionaries from torsion bows were found at numerous locations.[31] If we simply compared the archaeological evidence from Gamla with the finds from Masada, we would have to conclude that the Roman siege of Gamla was much more intense and violent than the siege of Masada.

The archaeological remains and weapons discovered during Shmarya Gutman's excavation allow us to reconstruct what took place during Gamla's siege. Gutman discovered a breach in Gamla's wall, which is located at its weakest point where it is only two meters wide. Just to the south of this breach the wall reaches a width of four meters. This provides additional evidence that the Romans across the ravine used signals to guide the battering ram to the wall's most vulnerable section. The distribution of the weapons, which are concentrated at the breach and two other locations where portions of the wall are missing, suggest that battering rams were placed at multiple locations. Most weapons were discovered within a band of approximately 50 meters along the wall, which implies that most of

---

[29] The thickness of the wall at the time of the siege was only 2.05 meters while some sections were increased to four meters. Syon 2002, 136–37. The techniques used to strengthen Gamla's wall, as well as some other features undertaken to counter Roman siege tactics, are similar to those discovered at Yodefat (Jotapata). See Adan-Bayewitz and Aviam 1997, 131–65; Aviam 2002, 121–33; 2004, 110–22.

[30] Syon 2002, 141–45.

[31] Magness 1992, 58–67.

the fighting took place in a fairly narrow zone. The furthermost ballista stones were found some 60 meters inside the city. Since ballistae have a range of 366–457 meters (400–500 yards), the Romans likely placed their siege equipment approximately 300 or more meters from Gamla's walls. This calculation is confirmed by the accidental discovery of a pile of ballista stones 300 meters outside Gamla's wall, which was likely the location of a ballista emplacement.

Archaeology, Gamla, and Josephus

Does archaeology support Josephus' description of Gamla's siege? Josephus' narrative of the final battle for Gamla closely parallels his account of Masada: a crowded city, overwhelming Roman forces, a great wind during the final battle, and a mass suicide. According to Josephus, Gamla's inhabitants jumped into an artificial ravine (*War* 4.79). This description does not match Gamla's peak, which displays no discernable signs of any buildings or trenches. Gamla's summit, although it has undoubtedly changed a little over time due to earthquakes and erosion, could not have held many people, perhaps a few hundred at the most. Although it does overlook a deep natural ravine, it would have been physically impossible for many people to have jumped from it to their deaths. While it is likely that some people did commit suicide by jumping from Gamla's peak, most were probably pushed down Gamla's steep slope in the ensuing panic. Josephus' statement that 9,000 people perished at Gamla is certainly a gross exaggeration.

The lack of any human bones with the exception of a single lower jawbone, or burials from Gamla, despite fourteen seasons of excavation, suggest that few people actually died at the site. Moreover, Josephus hints that this was so. He tells us that during the siege many escaped by walking down Gamla's supposedly impenetrable ravines and through its tunnels, leaving behind only the weak and starving (*War* 4.53, 62–69). Josephus mentions that he built tunnels at Gamla (*War* 4.9, 51). There is no evidence for the existence of tunnels at Gamla. An underground hideout of this type of was discovered at Jotapata.[32]

---

[32] Aviam 2002, 125. See also Aviam 2004, 123–32.

According to Josephus, Gamla's fortifications were so great that "its occupants felt greater confidence in the nature of their site than did those of Jotapata, though far inferior to them in the number of combatants" (*War* 4.10). Josephus likely assumed that the residents at Gamla would have fortified their town in the same manner as he had strengthened Jotapata, since both shared a similar topography and were naturally protected on three sides. Josephus merely combined his first-hand knowledge of Jotapata with what he saw from Vespasian's camp during the battle of Gamla to write his narrative of Gamla's siege. This would account for his statement that Gamla's inhabitants were more confident in their fortifications than those of Jotapata. It also explains Josephus' inaccuracies regarding Gamla's typography and fortifications, which are inexplicable if he had supervised the construction of its defenses and had been placed in command of the Galilee and Golan.

Despite Josephus' inaccuracies, his account of Vespasian's siege of Gamla is a valuable eyewitness description of Roman battle tactics. His description of Titus' use of cavalry at Gamla in conjunction with infantry, while it may seem unlikely, is an accurate portrayal of Roman warfare from this time.[33] Likewise, Josephus' account of Vespasian's near death at Gamla is undoubtedly true. Vespasian's troops flawlessly executed a *testudo*, in which soldiers interlock their shields giving the appearance of a tortoise shell.[34] It was the Romans' training that permitted Vespasian and his soldiers to perform this complicated maneuver and successfully retreat while under attack. In his speech following this incident, Vespasian acknowledged this fact when he compared the Romans with the rebels inside Gamla. Unlike the incautious and impetuous barbarians inside Gamla, Vespasian told his legions that the Romans owed their success to their skill and discipline (*War* 4.45–46).

---

[33] Cavalry normally served as a secondary force with the infantry comprising the main fighting body. When cavalry were weak, or conditions dictated, they were strengthened with lightly armed foot soldiers. Caesar combined cavalry with foot soldiers against Ariovistus during his Gallic campaign. *Bell. gall.* 1.48. Cavalry and infantry were also combined at Jerusalem (*War* 5.331), Beth Nimra (*War* 4.421–436), Mt. Tabor (*War* 4.57), and Jotapata (*War* 3.254). Cavalry were also used to isolate besieged populations (*War* 3.144, 310; 4.87; 5.446). See further, Webster 1985, 231–32; Davies 1989, 141–51.

[34] *War* 4.33–35. This maneuver was also used at Jerusalem (*War* 2.537) and Jotapata (*War* 3.270). Julius Caesar's army successfully used this tactic against Vercingetorix (*Bell. gall.* 7.85). See also *Bell. gall.* 2.6.

As in the case of Masada, the archaeological evidence perhaps betrays a more sinister motivation behind Josephus' account of Gamla's siege. If Josephus knew Gamla as well as he claimed, then perhaps he is hiding his own involvement in the Roman siege. The Romans breached Gamla's wall precisely at its weakest point, and positioned their artillery at the best location. According to Josephus, three soldiers from the fifteenth legion knew that a few men could collapse Gamla's tower simply by removing a few of its stones. How could the Romans have known that this tower lacked a foundation? Who could have provided this valuable information to the Romans? Josephus? If so, Josephus may have hid the fact that he betrayed Gamla's inhabitants, as he later betrayed his fellow Jews in Jerusalem, in order to ingratiate himself with Vespasian, and save his own life.

If Josephus' *War* is credible, and Josephus did fortify Gamla and train its army, then perhaps his account conceals something else. The archaeological evidence suggests that Gamla's residents did not put up much of a fight and succumbed to Vespasian's forces rather quickly. Gamla's fortifications were rather meager and could not have held out for very long. If Josephus was a general, archaeology suggests that he was a failure as a military leader. His own *War* implies that he never had firm control over Gamla's rebels, if indeed he ever held any leadership position at all.[35]

A close reading of Josephus' *War*, especially when it is compared with his *Life*, suggests that Gamla's downfall was precipitated by an internal civil war. Josephus mentions that Gamla was at first loyal to the Romans and then joined the revolt (*Life* 46–61).[36] Agrippa's blockade hastened Gamla's demise by depriving the town of food and supplies. In his *Life* (185–186), Josephus mentions that when the rebels arrived at Gamla to urge its inhabitants to join the revolt, these outsiders murdered many of Gamla's leaders. This infighting clearly weakened the town prior to Vespasian's arrival. This desperate situation was compounded with the flight of many of Gamla's fighters who, according to the *War*, simply abandoned their starving countrymen during their hour of need. These men simply climbed

---

[35] For this possibility, see further Rappaport 1994, 279–89; 1992, 95–114. For a related study that focuses on Josephus' character, see Mason 1997, 31–77.
[36] For the discrepancies between Josephus' accounts of Gamla, especially in relation to the activities of Philip son of Jacimus, see further Cohen 1979, 160–69; Mason 2003, 49–56.

down Gamla's supposedly impenetrable chasms. They likely escaped through the rivers and steep ravines that led to the Sea of Galilee. A close reading of his narrative even suggests that Gamla's downfall was perhaps more tragic than Masada's since many of its fighters proved to be cowards and simply ran away.

Noble Deaths at Masada and Gamla

There is no archaeological evidence to support Josephus' accounts of mass suicides at Masada and Gamla.[37] The similarities between his accounts of the battles of Gamla and Masada are remarkable: mass deaths and women survivors. They suggest that these stories function as literary devices to praise Jew and Roman alike.[38] By presenting his readers with fictional stories of noble deaths at Gamla and Masada, Josephus demonstrates the bravery and obstinacy of the Jewish population to account for difficulties that the Romans experienced in ending this revolt. At the same time, he highlights the superiority of the Roman legions, who had to overcome formidable military and typographical obstacles to crush this rebellion.

For Josephus, suicide praises both victor and vanquished alike and also serves as a moral lesson. Victory and defeat are traditionally measured by the greatness of one's opponents. The tenacity of the Jews, who were unique because of their willingness to die for their religion and land, explains the length and difficulty that the Romans experienced suppressing the First Revolt. Suicide also lends nobility to what were likely two disgraceful defeats. Josephus' stories gave the defenders of Masada and Gamla some dignity in the face of overwhelming might, but nevertheless allowed him to blame their defeat upon God. The Romans were invincible, and fortune sided with them, because God had willed it so. Josephus makes this clear when he has Eleazar say in his dramatic speech atop Masada: "Do not attach the blame to yourselves, nor the credit to the Romans, that this war with them has been the ruin of us all; for it was not

---

[37] For an earlier study that also doubted the veracity of Josephus' account of noble death at Masada, see Cohen 1982, 385–405. For this issue, see further Klassen 2000, 456–73; Ladouceur 1980, 245–60; 1987, 95–113.

[38] For the importance of noble death in Josephus' writings, see further van Henten 1999, 123–41 and this volume; Weitzman 2004, 230–45.

their might that brought these things to pass, but the intervention of some more powerful cause has afforded them the semblance of victory" (*War* 7.360). For Josephus, the internal Jewish war led God to abandon the Jewish people and use the Romans as a divine instrument of punishment. It was this infighting that led many of Gamla's soldiers to abandon their fellow citizens during Vespasian's siege.

Josephus' accounts of mass suicide at Gamla and Masada also served another purpose: they were intended to prevent further insurrection. For Josephus, both his *War* and *Antiquities* emphasize the theme that the masses need direction since they are often swayed, as they were at Gamla, by "what anyone said" (*Ant.* 4.37).[39] The First Revolt largely broke out when Jews waged war against their fellow Jews. Josephus makes it clear in his introduction to the *War* that it was only a few Jews who ultimately brought destruction upon themselves and the nation (*War* 1.10). Consequently, Josephus sought to distinguish these rabble-rousers from the majority of Jews whom they had led astray. It was these troublemakers who had convinced Gamla's occupants to oppose the Romans. This rabble was also responsible for the tragedy of Masada. For Josephus' Roman audience, the message of Gamla and Masada is that the masses, if not led by legitimate leaders, will select demagogues from their own numbers, who will ultimately lead the populace to their own destruction.

For Josephus, suicide that was deliberate, defiant, and vengeful elicited his admiration, such as the cases of Samson (*Ant.* 5.316–317), Herod's brother Phasael (*Ant.* 14.367–369; 15:13), and the Roman soldier Longus (*War* 6.186–187).[40] Those who committed suicide for the wrong motives, such as Herod the Great when he fled from his enemies near Masada (*Ant.* 14.355–358), were looked upon with contempt. The anticipatory suicide of the defenders at Masada was similar to this type of suicide since Josephus portrayed it as God's retribution. The mass suicide at Gamla was of a similar kind since the defenders of the site foolishly opposed the overwhelming military might of the Roman Empire. The defenders of Gamla and Masada were doomed since they were not simply fighting the Romans, but because they failed to realize that they were actually opposing God. Josephus learned this lesson at Jotapata and, like the biblical

---

[39] Mason 1997, 46–48. See also Sterling 2000, 147–48.
[40] Hankoff 1977, 1986–92.

Jeremiah, unsuccessfully attempted to warn his fellow Jews to submit to God's chosen agents of destruction.

Despite its apologetic proclivities, Josephus' *War* is an important historical work. No comprehensive eyewitness account of Roman legions in action survives between the writing of various Commentaries containing the records of Julius Caesar's campaigns and Josephus' *War*.[41] Nevertheless, based on the archaeological discoveries from Gamla and Masada, we should not only question the accuracy of Josephus' accounts of noble death, but also perhaps read his *War* with a greater degree of skepticism than we have become accustomed. It is clearly a work of historical propaganda that was intended to praise both Jew and Roman alike, as well as its author. The acceptance of Josephus' *War* by archaeologists and historians as a reliable record of the First Revolt testifies to his success as a writer of historical fiction. Josephus not only fooled many in antiquity, but the archaeological evidence from Gamla and Masada suggests that he continues to deceive many today.

BIBLIOGRAPHY

Adan-Bayewitz, D. and M. Aviam
    1997 Iotapata, Josephus, and the Siege of 67: Preliminary Report on the 1992–94
            Seasons. *JRA* 10:131–65.
Aviam, M.
    2002 Yodefat/Jotapata: The Archaeology of the First Battle. Pages 121–33 in
            The First Revolt: Archaeology, History, and Ideology. Edited by A. M. Berlin
            and J. Overman. London.
    2004 *Jews, Pagans and Christians in the Galilee.* Rochester.
Avi-Yonah, M.
    1976 *Gazetteer of Roman Palestine.* Jerusalem.
Bar-Kochva, B.
    1976 Gamla in Gaulanitis. *ZDPV* 92:54–71.
Bennet, J.
    1986 Fort Sizes as a Guide to Garrison Type: A Preliminary Study of Selected
            Forts in the European Provinces. Pages 7–16 in *Studien zu den Militärgrenzen
            Roms III.* Edited by C. Unz. Stuttgart.
Bilde, P.
    1988 *Flavius Josephus Between Jerusalem and Rome.* Sheffield.
Broshi, M.
    1982 The Credibility of Josephus. *JJS* 33:379–84.
Campbell, D.
    1988 Dating the Siege of Masada. *ZPE* 73:156–58.

---

[41] Gichon 1986, 287–323.

Cohen, S. J. D.
    1982   Masada: Literary Tradition, Archaeological Remains, and the Credibility
           of Josephus. *JJS* 33:385–405.
    1979   *Josephus in Galilee and Rome: His Vita and Development as a Historian.* Leiden.
Cotton, H. M.
    1989   The Date of the Fall of Masada: The Evidence of the Masada Papyri.
           ZPE 78:157–62.
Cotton, H. M. and J. Geiger
    1989   *Masada II: The Yigael Yadin Excavations: 1963–65, Final Reports. The Latin and
           Greek Documents.* Jerusalem.
Davies, J. L.
    1977   Roman Arrowheads from Dinorben and the *Sagittarii* of the Roman Army.
           Britannia 8:260–62.
Davies, R.
    1989   *Service in the Roman Army.* Edinburgh.
Davison, D. P.
    1989   *The Barracks of the Roman Army from the 1st to 3rd Centuries A.D.: A Comparative
           Study of the Barracks from Fortresses, Forts and Fortlets with an Analysis of Building
           Types and Construction, Stabling and Garrisons.* 2 vols. Oxford.
Eck, W.
    1969   Die Eroberung von Masada und eine neue Inschrift L. Flavius Silva
           Nonius Bassus. *ZNTW* 60:282–89.
Gichon, M.
    1986   Aspects of a Roman Army in War According to the *Bellum Judaicum* of
           Josephus. Pages 311–23 in *The Defence of the Roman and Byzantine East.*
           Edited by P. Freeman and D. Kennedy. Oxford.
Gill, D. A.
    1993   Natural Spur at Masada. *Nature* 364:569–70.
    1984   It's a Natural: Masada Ramp was not a Roman Engineering Miracle.
           BAR 27:22–31, 56–57.
Gilliver, C. M.
    1993   Hedgehogs, Caltrops and Palisade Stakes. *JRMES* 4:49–54.
Goldsworthy, A.
    2003   *The Complete Roman Army.* London.
Gracey, J.
    1986   The Armies of the Judaean Client Kings. Pages 311–23 in *The Defence of
           the Roman and Byzantine East.* Edited by P. Freeman and D. Kennedy.
           Oxford.
Gutman, S.
    1964   *With Masada.* Tel Aviv. [Hebrew]
    1994   *Gamla—A City in Rebellion.* Tel Aviv. [Hebrew]
Hankoff, L. D.
    1977   Flavius Josephus: First-Century A.D. View of Suicide. *New York State Journal
           of Medicine.* October: 1986–1992.
Hayward, C. T. R.
    1986   Appendix B: The Fourth Philosophy: Sicarii and Zealots. Pages 598–606
           in vol. 2 of E. Schürer, *The History of the Jewish People in the Age of Jesus
           Christ (175 B.C.–A.D. 135): A New English Version.* Revised and edited by
           G. Vermes, F. Millar, and M. Goodman. 3 vols. in 4. Edinburgh.
Henten, J. W. van
    1999   Martyrion and Martyrdom: Some Remarks about Noble Death in Josephus.
           Pages 123–41 in *Internationales Josephus-Kolloquium Brüssel 1998.* Edited by
           J. U. Kalms and F. Siegert. Münster.

Holley, A. E.
1994 The Ballista Balls from Masada. Pages 349–65 in *Masada IV: The Yigael Yadin Excavations: 1963–65, Final Reports. Lamps, Textiles, Basketry, Cordage and Related Artifacts, Wood Remains, and Ballista Balls.* Edited by J. Aviram, et al. Jerusalem.

Johnson, A.
1983 *Roman Forts of the 1st and 2nd centuries A.D. in Britain and the German Provinces.* New York.

Kennedy, D.
1985 Military Cohorts: The Evidence of Josephus, BJ, III.4.2(67) and of Epigraphy. *ZPE* 61:253–63.
1989 The Military Contribution of Syria to the Roman Imperial Army. Pages 1235–46 in *The Eastern Frontier of the Roman Empire.* Edited by D. H. French and C. S. Lightfoot. Ankara.

Klassen, W.
2000 The Archaeological Artifacts of Masada and the Credibility of Josephus. Pages 456–73 in *Text and Artifact in the Religions of Mediterranean Antiquity: Essays in Honour of Peter Richardson.* Edited by S. G. Wilson and M. Desjardins. Waterloo.

Ladouceur, D. J.
1980 Masada: A Consideration of the Literary Evidence. *GRBS* 21:245–60.
1987 Josephus and Masada. Pages 95–113 in *Josephus, Judaism, and Christianity.* Edited by L. H. Feldman and G. Hata. Detroit.

Magness. J.
1992 Masada—Arms and the Men. *BAR* 18:58–67.
1996 Masada 1995: Discoveries at Camp F. *BA* 59:181.
2002 In the Footsteps of the Tenth Roman Legion in Judea. Pages 189–212 in *The First Revolt: Archaeology, History, and Ideology.* Edited by A. M. Berlin and J. Overman. London.

Marsden, E. W.
1969 *Greek and Roman Artillery: Historical Development.* Oxford.

Mason, S.
1997 An Essay on Character: The Aim and Audience of Josephus' Vita. Pages 31–77 in *Internationales Josephus-Kolloquium Münster 1997.* Edited by J. U. Kalms. Münster.
2001 *Life of Josephus.* Vol. 9 of *Flavius Josephus: Translation and Commentary.* Edited by S. Mason. Leiden.

Netzer, E.
1991 The Last Days and Hours at Masada. *BAR* 17:26–31.
1992 How Anti-Roman was Galilee? Pages 95–114 in *The Galilee in Late Antiquity.* Edited by L. I. Levine. New York.
1994 Where Was Josephus Lying—In His *Life* Or In The *War?* Pages 279–89 in *Josephus and the History of the Greco-Roman Period.* Edited by F. Parente and J. Sievers. Leiden.

Rappaport, U.
1989 The Process of Masada's Destruction. *ErIsr* 20:311–20. [Hebrew]

Reich, R.
2001 Women and Men at Masada: Some Anthropological Observations Based on the Small Finds (Coins, Spindles). *ZDPV* 117:149–62.

Richmond, I. A.
1962 The Roman Siege-Works of Masada, Israel. *JRS* 54:142–55.

Roth, J.
    1995   The Length of the Siege of Masada. *SCI* 14:87–109.
    1994   The Size and Organization of the Roman Imperial Legion. *Historia* 43:346–62.
Schulten, A.
    1933   Masada. Die Burg des Herodes und die römischen Lager. *ZDPV* 56:1–185.
Shatzman, I.
    1989   Artillery in Judaea from Hasmonean to Roman Times. Pages 461–83 in *The Eastern Frontier of the Roman Empire.* Edited by D. H. French and C. S. Lightfoot. Ankara.
    1997   The Roman Siege of Masada. Pages 109–30 in *The Story of Masada: Discoveries from the Excavation.* Edited by G. Hurvitz. Provo.
Sterling, G. E.
    2000   Explaining Defeat: Polybius and Josephus on the Wars with Rome. Pages 135–51 in *Internationales Josephus-Kolloquium Aarhus 1999.* Edited by J. U. Kalms. Münster: Lit.
Stroebel, A.
    1974   Das römische Belagerungswerk um Machärus. Topographische Untersuchungen. *ZDPV* 90:128–84.
Syon, D.
    1995   The Identification of Gamla—Through the Sources and by Results of the Excavations. *Cathedra* 78:3–24.
    2002   Gamla: City of Refuge. Pages 143–53 in *The First Jewish Revolt: Archaeology, History, and Ideology.* Edited by A. M. Berlin and J. A. Overman. London.
Talmon, S.
    1997   Masada Fragment of Samaritan Origin. *IEJ* 47:220–32.
VanderKam, J. C.
    2004   *From Joshua to Caiaphas: High Priests After the Exile.* Minneapolis.
Webster, G.
    1985   *The Roman Imperial Army of the First and Second Centuries A.D.*, 3rd ed. Totowa.
Weitzman, S.
    2004   Josephus on How to Survive Martyrdom. *JJS* 40:230–45.
Wise, M. O.
    1994   *Thunder in Gemini: And Other Essays on the History, Language and Literature of Second Temple Palestine.* Sheffield.
Yadin, Y.
    1966   *Masada: Herod's Fortress and the Zealots' Last Stand.* Tel Aviv.
Yadin, Y., J. Naveh, and Y. Meshorer
    1989   *Masada I: The Yigael Yadin Excavations: 1963–65, Final Reports: The Aramaic and Hebrew Ostraca and Jar Inscriptions, The Coins of Masada.* Jerusalem.
Zertal, A.
    1995   The Roman Siege System at Khirbet al-Hamam (Narbata). Pages 71–94 in *The Roman and Byzantine Near East: Some Recent Archaeological Research.* Edited by J. H. Humphrey. Ann Arbor.
Zias, J.
    1998   Whose Bones?: Were They Really Jewish Defenders? Did Yadin Deliberately Obfuscate? *BAR* 24:40–45, 64–66.
    2000   Human Skeletal Remains from the Southern Cave at Masada and the Question of Ethnicity. Pages 732–38 in *The Dead Sea Scrolls: Fifty Years After Their Discovery.* Edited by L. H. Schiffman, E. Tov, and J. C. VanderKam. Jerusalem.

Zias, J., D. Segal, and I. Carmi
  1994   Addendum: The Human Skeletal Remains From the Northern Cave at Masada—A Second Look. Pages 366–67 in *Masada IV: The Yigael Yadin Excavations: 1963–65, Final Reports. Lamps, Textiles, Basketry, Cordage and Related Artifacts, Wood Remains, and Ballista Balls.* Edited by J. Aviram, et al. Jerusalem.

THE ARCHAEOLOGICAL ILLUMINATION OF JOSEPHUS' NARRATIVE OF THE BATTLES AT YODEFAT AND GAMLA

Mordechai Aviam

There are four detailed narratives in the *Jewish War* of the sieges and battles at Yodefat (*War* 3.145–288, 316–339), Gamla (*War* 4.11–53, 62–83), Jerusalem (*War* 5.67–228), and Masada (*War* 7.304–406). The longest and most detailed siege narratives are Yodefat and Jerusalem, followed by Gamla and Masada. Josephus was probably an eye-witness for the battles at Jerusalem, and because of the importance of the city as the capital of Jewish life and the core of the revolt, Josephus gave a full, long and detailed narrative of the horrors of the siege and its end. Yodefat was the first battle between Jews and Romans in the revolt, and the fact that Josephus was its commander, explains the length and detail of the description. The two other narratives are much shorter although they include some very detailed episodes. Since Yodefat and Gamla were abandoned after their destruction (and then largely excavated), the scene was frozen in the summer of 67 and autumn of 68 C.E. and this can provide us with an unusual perspective for investigating a main problem in the field of Josephan studies: how accurate were his narratives?

Out of the 19 fortified sites prepared by Josephus in the Galilee and Golan (*War* 2.573–576, *Life* 187–188) to confront the Romans, only five stood and fought against the legions: Yodefat, Yapha (*War* 3.289–306), Migdal (*War* 3.462–504), Gamla and Mount Tabor (*War* 4.54–61).

At the two of these sites that were besieged, conquered, and destroyed by Vespasian's army, large-scale excavations took place: at Gamla (by Shemaryahu Gutman for the Department of Antiquities), from 1976 to 1998 and 2000 when almost 300 squares (about 7.5 dunnams out of 140 dunnams, about 5% of the site) were excavated (Gutman 1994). At Yodefat (myself for the University of Rochester and Israel Antiquities Authority) excavations took place from 1992 to 1998 and 2000, when a hundred squares (2.5 dunnams, out of 47, about 5% as well) were excavated. An analysis and comparison of the finds allow us to review Josephus' detailed narratives in the

light of the scientific, modern excavations according to their preliminary reports.

Geographical Descriptions

Gamla

The accuracy of Josephus' geographical descriptions was discussed
by many scholars[1] and then confirmed with the discovery and
identification of Gamla in 1968. The resemblance between the hill
named "es-Salem" in Arabic and Josephus' description of Gamla is
startling. No wonder Yizhaki Gal, the surveyor who first found the
site, said that when he stood for the first time in the summer of
1968 on the platform to the north-east of the site, the only thought
he had in mind was Josephus' description of Gamla. The shape of
the hill just like a camel's hump, the houses built on the steep south-
eastern slope, the steeper north-western slope, and even the problematic eye connection with Tarichaea-Migdal are all described by
Josephus and can be identified on the site.

Yodefat

There are four geographical components described by Josephus that
are clearly visible at the field: 1) The hill is hidden between high
peaks (*War* 3.160); 2) The accessible side is from the saddle in the
north (*War* 3.158–159); 3) The steep slopes on three sides, especially
to the east (*War* 3.158); 4) The lack of any natural source of water
in the town (*War* 3.181–183).

Josephus' Fortification Project

Gamla

Gamla is mentioned in Josephus' list of the sites fortified by him
during the revolt (*War* 2.574). The topographical situation at Gamla
is very different from the one at Yodefat. The steep ravines from
the west, east, and south precluded the need to build a wall around

---

[1] E.g., Safrai 1982.

the town from these sides. The wall was built along the northern saddle. It was constructed by blocking the original gaps between existing houses, filling up the rooms with stones, destroying houses that were in the way of the new "wall line," and probably reusing their stones to reinforce the outer walls of other houses. As yet there is no final report of Gamla, but according to Danny Sion, (I am grateful for the information), the houses that were destroyed and left out of the wall, are clearly dated to the early Roman period.

Yodefat

According to the list of sites fortified by Josephus (*War* 2.573, *Life* 188), the town appears twice but he does not supply us with further details about the wall. There are some scholars who suspect that Josephus' list of fortified sites was a matter of fiction while other scholars suspect that the remains seen on surface at the site might not even belong to this project.[2] Our excavations concentrated on the northern side, as well as other soundings along the perimeter of the wall.[3] In the north, we discovered that the early phase of the wall is late Hellenistic-Hasmonean, dated to the beginning of the first century B.C.E., and it surrounded only the summit of the hill. Above the northern part of the Hasmonean remains, a casemate wall was built in the early Roman period, while a solid line of an inner fortification was added to the south of it. It seems as if some segments of the Hasmonean wall were still standing and were reused (with some rebuilding) at the time of the war, while in other parts the early wall was already missing and the gap was closed with a new casemate wall.

At the western side of the northern fortification an early Roman period wall buts the Hasmonean one, and from this point down to the southern plateau, the early Roman period wall surrounds the entire parameter of the town, enforced with a few square towers. This wall was built in part as a solid wall, and in part as a casemate wall. In my opinion the reason for this type of construction was the space that was left between the margin of the town and the steep slopes. The goal was probably to erect a casemate wall but if

---

[2] Meyers 1977.
[3] Adan-Bayewitz and Aviam 1997; Aviam 2004.

there was not enough space, a solid wall was built instead. On one spot, along the western wall of the southern plateau, the wall was built by using as a foundation the western wall of a private house. Two rooms of this house were forfeited to give space to the new defending wall. The house was dated according to the pottery in the fill to the early Roman period. South of this point two casemates were uncovered, one is large, and the other is much smaller. They were both founded on bedrock, and in the small room a rock-cut pit was identified. While excavating it, a shaft was discovered, 1 m. deep leading to a tunnel of 2.5 m. long with a gabled roof that opened into two rock-cut rooms on one level, and another in a lower level reached through a short shaft. The fact that the entrance to this hiding complex is in the center of this small casemate shows that the underground shelter was designed together with the wall, to be used in case the wall failed to protect the town.

Along the eastern side of the plateau, the wall was exposed along more than 50 m. In one place a pottery kiln was discovered, superimposed by the wall. The excavation proved that the kiln produced the same type of jars as those discovered on the floors of the destroyed houses within the town, dated by the coins of Nero to the second half of the first century c.e., and they were found together with arrowheads and ballista stones. This provides substantial proof that the erection of the wall was for the purpose of the war that finally destroyed the town.

The Assault Ramp

Gamla

According to Josephus, the XV and the V legions constructed assault ramps in front of the town's wall to advance the battering rams (*War* 4.13–14). The topography of Gamla does not necessarily require ramps to bring the machines closer to the wall, but according to the narrative, the citizens of Gamla dug "trenches" or a moat in front of the wall that, according to Josephus, were filled up by the soldiers of the X legion. The excavations never investigated this area, but on the surface it seems that there are remains of a moat, and the perpendicular pile of soil could be the remains of a low ramp. In front of the round tower there is a large pile of soil that was also not checked.

Yodefat

Josephus' narrative concerning the ramp is one of the more detailed (*War* 3.161–165), and he describes how stones, soil, and wood were collected by the Romans and piled on the northern slope. By the end of the operation, the level of the ramp reached to the upper parts of the wall. In a long discussion with Duncan Campbell, who is writing a book on Roman siege wars, we tried to analyze the size of the ramp according to the topography of Yodefat's northern saddle, and I hope that this study will come out soon in a reconstructed drawing. Our excavation on the northern slope revealed two layers that seem to me to be a part of the ramp. The lower level, which is about 1 m. thick, included stones and soil, while the upper one, about 0.4 m. thick, was made of strong white cement that was mixed with crushed pottery and stones. In both layers bow arrowheads were found, while in the lower level, a catapult arrowhead as well as two caligae nails were found. All along the northern slope, small revetment walls are visible, supporting the layers of soil and cement. The excavated cement and the small horizontal supporting walls were not found elsewhere along the slopes of Yodefat's hill.

Roman Artillery

Gamla

About 100 catapult arrowheads were found at Gamla, as well as 1,500 ballista stones weighing from 2 kg. to 20 kg., and in caliber from 10 to 33 cm., all made of local basalt. Most of these finds were collected from the uncovering of the length of the wall and about 50 m. inside the wall. This is completely different from the finds at Yodefat where such objects were found all over the site. The explanation lies in the topographical difference between the two sites. At Gamla the only possible location for the machines was on the platform to the northeast, a place that allowed them to shoot on the wall and into the town, but not very far away from the wall.

Yodefat

Both catapult arrowheads and ballista stones were found at the site. The ballista-stones collected at the site, weigh from 1 kg. to 2 kg.

They are all round, made of local limestone, and carry chisel marks. They were discovered mainly along the northern wall, but also in the residential area and one was even found in the fill of a cistern. The distribution of the stones throughout the town matches Josephus' description of the shooting of the machines "with the effect not only of driving the Jews from the ramparts, but of rendering untenable all the space behind them which came within range of the missiles" (*War* 3.167–168 [Thackeray, LCL]). According to him there were 160 machines around the town, a number that matches the common information about the Roman army artillery force, a light "carro-ballistae" to each century, and a heavy one to each cohort. The fact that all of the ballista stones found at the site are of the small caliber hints to the fact that the artillery power used in the siege was based mainly on the 120 carroballistae of the three legions besieging Yodefat.

In this case, Josephus' description of the heavy stones (up to 30 kg.) was not verified by the archaeological finds (*War* 3.167). About 10 iron catapult-arrowheads were found in the upper level along the northern wall, an area named by Josephus as the "fire line." We have to keep in mind that the remains along the northern wall, being the highest point of the site, are poor as most of the area was heavily eroded. Some were found on the northern slope, in the remains of the ramp. About 10 catapult arrowheads were discovered in the residential areas, and two or three of them were directly on the floors of the houses. They are all of the same type with a pyramidal point and hole for the shaft at the bottom, 8 cm. to 15 cm. long and weigh between 20 gr. to 30 gr. These arrows were able to penetrate the defenders shield.

Roman Army Equipment

Gamla

The report on the Roman army equipment will be published by Guy Stieble, and he was kind enough to inform me that there are about 200 different artifacts identified as remains from Roman army equipment. In a narrow alley, near the breach in the wall, parts of Roman army armor and a part of a helmet were found, as well as bronze scales of another type of armor. Three bronze plaques with the names of soldiers were recovered, and these were probably used as nametags that were most likely attached to the helmets or other part of equipment, and a bronze tip of a sheath was also found.

Yodefat

As mentioned above two caligae nails were found in the ramp, while another one or two were found in the town. The tip of what could be a Roman sword was discovered in the residential area on the eastern slope. Very few other bronze elements could be associated with Roman army equipment but not even one armor scale was unearthed.

Breaching the Walls

In the case of Gamla and Yodefat the narrative is very similar. The ramming machines were brought to the wall and after a period of time (at Yodefat the description includes the destruction of one of the battering rams) the wall was breached but the attack through the breach failed.

Gamla (War 4.20–21)

During the uncovering of the wall, a slightly different type of collapse was identified, which looks like, and was suggested by the excavator, to be a breach in the wall. Its level of preservation above the ground supports its identification as a man-made breach, probably the result of the activity of a battering ram. Nearby hundreds of ballista stones and arrowheads were found.

Yodefat (War 3.213–221)

Josephus describes the attack of the battering rams on the northern walls and how it was breached. The remains of the early Roman wall in this area were poorly preserved. The excavations uncovered only one casemate preserved above the foundations. The western corner of this room was filled with stones from the floor level to the modern surface. The side of the fill along the wall was built of larger boulders, arranged as headers. While digging the stone-fill in the corner, a ballista stone was found inside, proof that it was constructed during the actual battle itself. It was probably placed at this specific spot against one of the ramming machines.

Face-to-Face Battles

Gamla (War *4.20–29*)

As the wall was breached, the Roman troops invaded the town, encountering face-to-face battle with Jewish warriors in the houses and on the street. The Romans were defeated according to Josephus because they were fighting from an inferior position, from the bottom of the town up to the top of it. When the Jews attacked them from above, they defended themselves from the roofs but the heavy weight on these roofs caused their collapse. The destroyed houses created a domino affect and a large part of the town, in the invaded area, collapsed killing many Roman soldiers. This is probably reflected in the discovery of the Roman officer equipment mentioned above, as well as the rest of other Roman pieces of military equipment.

Yodefat (War *3.265–270*)

The only face-to-face battle took place on the breach itself according to Josephus' narrative, and the Romans did not succeed in breaking into the town. As the northern wall was preserved mostly below the foundations, there was almost no chance of finding any remains of this heavy fighting.

The Final Conquest

Gamla (War *4.62–81*)

In a night-time undermining some Roman soldiers succeeded in destroying the high tower of the wall, probably the round tower discovered at the north upper part of the wall. The morning after the Roman army invaded the town and slowly pushed the besieged inhabitants up the hill. As in many of the battle narratives, this battle was also subject to interference by heavenly forces that favored the Romans. In this case it was a strong eastern wind that pushed away the Jewish arrows and helped the Roman arrows reach up the hill. The only way to avoid the Roman soldiers, who were climbing up the hill, was to try to escape through the extremely steep and rocky north-western slope, a situation that is probably described by Josephus when he says, "while those who flung themselves over the cliff were found to exceed five thousand" (*War* 4.80–81 [Thackeray, LCL]).

Yodefat (War *3.323–339*)

According to Josephus' narrative, the town was conquered by a "commando" attack. After the armies entered the town, and here also there was heavenly aid since heavy fog prevented the besieged from identifying what had happened, the Romans conquered the summit and pushed the defenders and the crowd down the steep eastern slope. According to his description men, women, and children were slaughtered in the streets. The day after the conquest Roman soldiers searched the hiding places and killed those who had sought shelter in the underground cavities.

During our excavations from the first season we found human bones in every house and cistern. In a large cistern, behind a small, poorly built wall, a large heap of gathered human bones was discovered. This included bones of more than 20 individuals, men, women, and children from the age of 5 to 16 years old. Our anthropologist identified cut marks from a heavy sharp tool on two of the skulls. The date of this group of gathered bones, as well as the other group of a man, woman, and child found on the floor of another cistern also surrounded by a low wall, and the bones found on the floors of the destroyed houses were precisely fixed to the second half of the first century C.E.

Conclusion

Against the background of this archaeological data, I would like to suggest some conclusions:

1) Josephus' descriptions of the two sites are very accurate. Many scholars have reflected on the accuracy of his geographical descriptions in the cases of Masada, the Dead Sea, the Jordan River, and more.
2) In few of the sites appearing in the list of the 19 fortified settlements that I discussed recently,[4] there are some remains of walls, discovered by a survey and minor excavations (Beer Sheba, Arbel, Mt. Nitai, and Mt. Tabor) that hint at a fortifying operation. It is clear now from both Gamla (the destroyed houses out of the wall line, the filled rooms along the wall, such as the study room adjacent to

---

[4] Aviam 2004, 92–105.

the synagogue, and the blocking of gaps between the houses) and Yodefat (casemate on the northern fortification, the house buried by the wall on the west, the underground shelter under the casemate floor, and the cancellation of the pottery kiln on the east) that the walls were built in a hurry, reusing remains of earlier fortifications and houses, sometimes with very poor foundations. It points to a period of stress, shortage of time, and probably little financial investment as well. This corresponds with Josephus' story about the projects he undertook shortly after he arrived in the Galilee.

3) Although the remains of the assault ramp at Gamla were not excavated at all, the field signs suggest that an earthwork was conducted in front of the round tower, and at least in one place along the wall. At Yodefat, however, the signs are much clearer. Along the northern slope, the only excisable side of the town, small retaining walls, layers of soil, stones, and cement were identified in which arrowheads, of both bows and catapults, were found, as well as a few caligae nails. All these finds suggest that the ramparts were built only along the northern side, where the main battle took place, as described by Josephus. From his description it is clear that the entire town was walled but the battle was centered along the northern slope. The archaeological finds suggest exactly the same.

4) In both sites there are remains of the Roman artillery attack. At Gamla a couple of thousands of ballista stones were found, mainly along the wall. The heaviest are about 20 kg., which is close to Josephus' description of Yodefat. Most of the stones are about 2 kg. to 6 kg., and in caliber of about 10 cm. to 16 cm., the same size as most of the stones at Yodefat. The difference in weight has to do with the fact that at Gamla they were all chiseled from local heavy basalt stone, while at Yodefat they are made of local limestone. The range from which they were shot at Gamla was closer (about 200 m. or less, the distance between the natural ramp on the north-east and the wall), but the weight of the stones was heavier. At Yodefat the Romans could shoot into the town from all sides, as described by Josephus, and the range was about 250 m. to 300 m., while the stones were of the small caliber and weight (about 2 kg). The fact that so many stones were found at Gamla has to do with the topography and the location of the breaching attacks. Here the breaching took place at a lower and moderate point of the site, while at Yodefat it was at the highest place.

The hundreds of stones shot at the breaching spot at Yodefat were all washed downhill while at Gamla they were trapped by the collapse of the wall and the houses behind it. The large number of machines mentioned by Josephus correspond with the known number in the Roman units, and there was enough space around Yodefat to place and use all of them, while at Gamla numbers are not mentioned and there is a space for only a few of them.

5) There is no doubt that the Roman army, especially in battles that they won, never left any of the bodies of soldiers. The remains of Roman army equipment at Gamla show that during the fighting in the town, after the wall was breached, some Roman soldiers were killed or lost parts of their equipment like swords, helmets shields, and armor. This is exactly as Josephus describes the battle. While at Gamla the Roman army was trapped in the town, at Yodefat it was defeated on the wall and the remains were collected by the Romans later or washed down during the subsequent years. According to Josephus' narrative, the final conquest of Yodefat was accomplished with only one loss for the Romans, a fact that is illuminated by an almost complete lack of Roman army equipment.

6) In the two narratives, Josephus tells us about the breaching of the wall by battering rams. At Gamla, the state of preservation displays the only known breach of a wall from antiquity that corresponds with Josephus' description. At Yodefat the finds from the fill in the corner of the casemate, placed there during the actual war, suggest a reinforcing of the wall against a battering ram on the northern slope, the location of the assault ramp.

7) The descriptions of the face-to-face battles correspond very well to the topographical description and the actual topography of both sites. When the Romans breached the wall at Gamla, in one or two places at the central part of the wall, the battle was on the streets, inside the houses, and on the roofs with the Roman soldiers chasing the defenders up the hill, while the Jews took shelter on the rocks on the crest. At Yodefat the "fire line" or the actual war, took place at the highest point of the hill. The face-to-face battle was near the wall and on the attack-bridges, which were laid by the Romans on the wall. The early morning attack and the incursion into the town took place at the same spot as well, and from this point the Roman troops conquered the town from the top of the slopes to the east and south.

8) In more than 250 excavated squares at Gamla, only one human jaw was identified. A large number of remains from Roman army equipment were found such as parts of helmets, different kinds of armors, some name-tags of soldiers, decorations for horses, shields, and more. These finds completely correspond with Josephus' description that Roman soldiers were trapped in the collapsing houses. Their bodies were probably rescued after the conquest of the town, but the remains of their equipment point to serious damage to the troops. During the second attack, most of the Jews fled to the upper parts of the town, but these areas were poorly preserved and barely excavated. Josephus' narrative switches here to the "glorious death" of the Jews by suggesting that they jumped over the cliff and 5,000 of them were killed in this way, while "only" 4,000 were killed by the Romans. The small amount of human remains suggests that if there was a massacre in the conquered town, it happened on the summit and not in the main parts of the town. At Yodefat human remains were identified everywhere, in every excavated cistern, in the weight-pit of the olive oil cave, on the floors of the houses and in the fill above the floors, a fill that is a result of the destruction of the town. There are at least three examples of arm bones (men and women) that show perpendicular cut marks from sharp tools. These are the typical marks on victims' bones resulting from protecting their faces from the beating of a sword attack. Two skulls from the large cistern are carrying cut-marks of sharp tools that probably were the cause of death. At Yodefat, differently from any other site of the First Revolt excavated so far, the evidence is crystal clear. Hundreds or even thousands of human beings, men, women, and children, died or were massacred in the houses, streets, and hiding places, and their bodies were left there for a long time. It was only after a year or more, when Jews came back to the disserted town, that they dug for the remains and buried them in open caves and cisterns. This massacre and the rage of the Roman troops are clearly visualized in Josephus' narrative.

Step-by-step, argument after argument, the architecture and artifacts unearthed at Yodefat and Gamla illuminate Josephus' narratives of these battles. Although there is no doubt that Josephus used a common literary style of writing, copied geographical descriptions from earlier authors, and used the Roman army commentary to describe the entire war, I think that the excavations of Gamla and Yodefat, as well as the survey of Josephus' fortified sites, prove that Josephus was an eye-witness and took some part in the actual organizing of the Galilee. There is no reason to suspect that he was the commander of the Galilee or initiated the erection of the fortifications in the cities, towns, and villages, but his very detailed narrative of the battle at Yodefat, illuminated by the archaeological finds, strongly suggests that he was there, and probably commanded that battle.

BIBLIOGRAPHY

Adan-Bayewitz, D. and M. Aviam
   1997   Iotapata, Josephus and the Siege of 67: Preliminary Report on the 1992–
           1994 Seasons. *JRA* 10:131–65.
Aviam, M.
   2004   *Jews, Pagans and Christians in the Galilee.* Rochester.
Gutman, S., and Y. Rapel
   1994   *Gamla—A City in Rebelion.* Tel Aviv. [Hebrew]
Meyers, E.
   1977   Survey in Galilee. *Explore* 3:7–17.
Safrai, Z.
   1982   The Description of Eretz Israel in Josephus' works. Pages 91–115 in
           Josephus Flavius: Historian of Eretz-Israel in the Hellenistic-Roman Period. Edited
           by U. Rappaport. Jerusalem. [Hebrew]

JOSEPHUS AND ARCHAEOLOGY ON THE CITIES OF THE GALILEE

Zeev Weiss

Two cities are known in the Lower Galilee of the first century C.E. Sepphoris, the capital of the Galilee, has a long history that can be traced back to the Persian period, whereas Tiberias, which governed the region for several decades, was newly founded in the early first century C.E. by Herod Antipas. Josephus, historian and commander of the Galilee during the first Jewish revolt against Rome, provides valuable information about these two cities, their populations, and the major events that transpired there prior to and during the revolt.

Josephus remarks that Sepphoris and Tiberias were the two largest cities in the Galilee (*Life* 346). Modern scholarship often considers them to have been of equal standing;[1] each was autonomous and had its own territory (χώρα),[2] each had a majority Jewish population—although it is assumed that pagans also lived in both locales[3]—and each was decorated with public buildings to serve the needs of its local inhabitants. It is generally acknowledged that both cities, influenced by Greco-Roman culture in the first century C.E., underwent major developments, for the most part, during the reign of Herod Antipas.[4] Unlike Pliny or Pausanias, Josephus does not provide a proper description of the urban topography, nor does he mention the monumental buildings constructed by Herod Antipas either in Sepphoris or his new capital. Nevertheless, from his description of the events in the Galilee during the first revolt, we learn about several public institutions in Tiberias whose construction most scholars attribute to this Tetrarch. It is also assumed that Herod Antipas would have established a capital commensurate to his status as a

---

[1] On this approach in modern scholarship, see Smallwood 1976, 183–84; Rappaport 1988, 20–23; Freyne 1992, 75–91; Roller 1998, 240–42; Horsley 1996, 49–60.

[2] Avi-Yonah 1984, 131–42. In contrast to a Greek *polis*, Tiberias did not have a true *chora*, according to Hoehner (1972, 100).

[3] Meyers 1997, 63–64. On the pagan population in the Galilean cities, see Freyne 1998, 167–75.

[4] On Herod Antipas's rule over the Galilee, see Hoehner 1972, 43–110; Horsley 1995, 64–67.

Roman "client king" and that Sepphoris was the obvious site for his agenda.[5]

When mapping Josephus's references to the two cities in *War, Life*, and even *Antiquities*, one comes to the realization that the author provides more information about the physical, institutional, and governmental entities of Tiberias than those of Sepphoris. *Life* furnishes the most details, with parallels in *War* and less in *Antiquities*.[6] However, the disparity between the number of references, as well as in the degree of detail Josephus provides, at first glance seems to create a disproportionate picture.

Josephus visited Sepphoris more than once, but the Sepphoreans (Σεπφωρῖται; *Life* 373)—acting independently during the revolt— opposed the rebels, closed the city gates, and joined the Romans. In contrast, Josephus's focus of attention and activity was in Tiberias, where various factions in the city debated amongst themselves whether to join or oppose the commander of the Galilee. Trying to convince the Tiberians to join him, Josephus maintained an active presence within the city, visiting some of its buildings and meeting with the inhabitants or the local municipal leadership. Josephus's motivation to describe the nature of events and his role as the commander of the Galilee during the first Jewish revolt may explain, on the one hand, why the information about Sepphoris is meager compared to that of Tiberias. The two cities indeed had much in common, both in architectural appearance and municipal governance. On the other hand, can it be proven that first-century Sepphoris and Tiberias were equally endowed with municipal institutions and monumental buildings, presumably established by or following Herod Antipas' rule in the Galilee, or did the picture drawn by Josephus impart a different reality in each of these cities? What, then, does Josephus's description infer regarding Tiberias and Sepphoris on the eve of the revolt and how does it help us in reconstructing the urban landscape of the two cities that rivaled for supremacy in the Galilee in the course of the first century c.e.?[7]

---

[5] Horsley 1996l, 49–51.

[6] See the references below to the various subjects relating to Tiberias and Sepphoris.

[7] According to Miller (1987, 1–24), the rivalry between the two cities characterizes the pre-revolt period even though rabbinic literature offers no evidence for any type of competition between them. Goodman (1983, 133–34) and Levine (1978, 175–78) argue that the tension between Tiberias and Sepphoris did not disappear entirely in the first centuries following the destruction of the temple.

In an attempt to reconstruct the urban topography of Sepphoris and Tiberias, we will focus on the literary sources concerning both cities and analyze the textual information in light of what we know from the archaeological finds unearthed at these sites in recent years. Our investigation will move from Tiberias to Sepphoris; the information culled from our detailed discussion will allow us to determine the nature of these cities and answer the questions at the core of this inquiry. What was the physical appearance of these Galilean cities in the first century C.E. and what type of governance structure did they have? Our discussion and conclusions have many implications for elucidating the early history of Tiberias and Sepphoris, and, most importantly, touch upon the major questions with which scholars of both Jewish and Christian history are grappling. They relate to the nature of the local population in first-century Galilee, the impact of Hellenism and Roman culture in the Galilee, the urban-rural relationship (center and periphery), Jesus's activity in the Galilee, and the physical backdrop of the New Testament accounts.

Tiberias

Located on the western shore of the Sea of Galilee, Tiberias was founded in 19 C.E. by Herod Antipas, who made it his capital.[8] Josephus briefly describes its territory, specifying the problems Antipas faced in populating the city (*Ant.* 18.36–38; *War* 2.614–615). However, unlike his description of the building projects undertaken by Antipas's father, Herod the Great, in Caesarea (*War* 1.408–416; *Ant.* 15.331–341),[9] the historian offers no information regarding Tiberias's architectural appearance or public buildings. Only when recounting the events on the eve of the revolt does he relate to Tiberias. Like the Greco-Roman *polis*, the city summoned assemblies of the citizens (*War* 2.618) and had a council (βουλή) of six hundred members headed by an *archon* (ἄρχων) and a committee of ten people

---

[8] According to Avi-Yonah (1950, 167–69), Tiberias was founded in 18 C.E.; according to Hoehner (1972, 94–95), it was in 23 C.E.; based on an analysis of the coins, the city was founded in 19 B.C.E.; see Meshorer 2001, 81–82.

[9] For further information about the Herodian buildings unearthed in Caesarea, see Raban and Holum 1996; see also Frova 1961, 167–74; Kahn 1998, 123–42; Gleason 1998, 23–52; Holum et al. 1999, 13–27. On the architectural layout of Caesarea from its foundation throughout the Byzantine period, see Patrich 2001b, 77–110.

(δέκα πρῶτοι).[10] Josephus also mentions two officials in Tiberias—the ὕπαρχος, who supervised the city's affairs, and an ἀγορανόμος, who oversaw the local markets (*War* 2.615; *Life* 134; *Ant.* 18.149). Two lead weights found in the city specify several *agoranomoi*: Gaius Julius (fig. 1) held the office in Herod Antipas's 34th year (29/30 C.E.), and two others, Iaesaias son of Mathias and Ainimos son of Monimos, during the reign of Agrippa II (61/62 C.E.).[11] Among the buildings and institutions that stood in Tiberias, Josephus mentions a stadium (*War* 2.618; 3.539; *Life* 92, 331)[12] near the seashore and a *proseuche* (*Life* 277, 280), both of which accommodated a large number of people. The city boasted a royal bank as well as archives, which were restituted to Sepphoris in 61 C.E., after Nero transferred Tiberias to Agrippa II (*Life* 38).[13] Herod Antipas built a magnificent palace, which was decorated with figural designs and palatial furnishings (*Life* 65–69). John of Gischala wished to visit the Τιβεριάδι θερμοῖς, referring to the hot baths in nearby Hammat. This complex was most probably under the jurisdiction of Tiberias since Josephus ordered the city's *hyparchoi* to extend hospitality to him (*War* 2.614–15; *Life* 85–86). Tiberias was also fortified with a wall constructed either at the time of its foundation or on the eve of the revolt.[14]

Despite the scanty remains that have been excavated in Tiberias, the existence of two massive buildings in the city offers a glimpse into its architectural appearance in the first century. A monumental gate with a round projecting tower on either side of the entrance, as well as the beginning of a northbound paved road, were uncovered south of Tiberias (fig. 2). The gate, not far from the city's infrastructure, marks the city limits.[15] Similar freestanding gates on the outskirts

[10] *boule*: *War* 2.639–640; *Life* 64, 169, 284, 300, 313, 381; *archon*: *War* 2.599; *Life* 134, 271, 278, 294; *deka protoi*: *War* 2.639–640; *Life* 64–65, 69, 296.

[11] Qedar 1986–87, 29–35. On the *agoranomos* in talmudic literature, see Sperber 1977, 227–43.

[12] The stadium is mentioned also in *y. 'Erub.* 5.1.22b, indicating its continual use, at least up to the early third century C.E.

[13] See also Freyne 1980, 130; Kasher 1988, 11.

[14] Josephus notes (*Life* 186) that he repaired Tiberias's walls, thus allowing us to believe that they were built by Herod Antipas. In effect, Josephus emphasizes elsewhere (*War* 2.573; *Life* 155–156) that he himself was responsible for their construction. Accordingly, Avi-Yonah (1950, 163–64) maintains that the wall was constructed in Tiberias on the eve of the revolt, whereas Hoehner (1972, 95) argues that Herod Antipas fortified Tiberias with a massive wall.

[15] Foerster 1977, 87–91; Stacy 2004, 23–28. For the reconstruction of the gate, see Hirschfeld and Reich 1988, 114–15.

Fig. 1   Lead Weight from the time of Herod Antipas inscribed with the name Gaius Iulius, an *agoranomos* in Tiberias (after: Qedar 1986–87, 30, Fig. 1).

Fig. 2   Gate with two round towers discovered south of Tiberias, at the beginning of the stone-paved road leading to the city center (after: Foerster 1977, 88).

of the city are known elsewhere in ancient Palestine, but the best parallel, at least in terms of its architecture, comes from Gadara, where the gate was aligned with the *decumanus maximus* and led toward the city's center.[16]

The location of the stadium mentioned by Josephus has been debated by scholars in past years;[17] evidence of its remains appears to have been found in the salvage excavations conducted by Dr. Moshe Hartal of the Israel Antiquities Authority in the summer of 2002.[18] Part of a semicircular structure measuring 39 m. in diameter was exposed on the shore of the Sea of Galilee, 200 m. north of the city's center. More than 10 m. were unearthed of a massive ashlar wall running north to south and curving westward, measuring 9 m. wide and preserved to a height of 3 m. An analysis of the finds and their comparison with similar structures at other sites indicate that these remains are part of the semicircular southern end (*sphendone*) of a stadium (fig. 3). The location of the structure along the seashore certainly corroborates Josephus's account, which describes how he fled from his enemies gathered at the stadium, to the beach, and into a boat that took him to the middle of the lake (i.e., the Sea of Galilee) (*War* 6:18–19; *Life* 92–96).

Herod the Great's hippodrome/stadium in Caesarea Maritima lends further support to the suggested identification.[19] Herod Antipas, who supposedly built the stadium in Tiberias, followed in the footsteps of his father, who constructed the hippodrome/stadium in his own city, Caesarea. The structures in both cities are located along the seashore and aligned on a north-south axis, with the *sphendone* at the southern end. In addition, similar building methods were applied at both locations; the rows of seats were constructed against a massive 9 m. wall. The total width of the building in Tiberias (39 m.) is narrower than the one in Caesarea (70 m.), and therefore its conjectured

---

[16] Weber 1991, 123–26; 2002, 326–30. Another city gate with two rounded towers dated to the first century C.E. was unearthed at Susita (Hippos); see Segal 2003, 16–17.

[17] Avi-Yonah (1974, 29) places the stadium inside the city. According to Harris (1972, 25), it was located south of the city though near it; Lämmer (1976, 49), in contrast, places the stadium north of the city. For further information regarding its location in light of *y. 'Erub.* 5.1.22b, see Lieberman 1932, 207–9; Schwabe 1949, 238–42.

[18] Hartal 2002, 22–24.

[19] Porath 1995 15–27; Patrich 2001a, 268–83; Porath 2003, 31–33. Clarifications regarding the name of the building in light of the terminology used by Josephus and archaeological finds, see Humphrey 1996, 121–29.

Fig. 3 View of the semicircular southern wall (*sphendone*) of the stadium in Tiberias. The parallel walls above this curved one belong to a vaulted structure from the Byzantine period that continued to be used in the Umayyad period (Courtesy of M. Hartal, Israel Antiquities Authority).

measurements may indicate that the former was used only for athletic contests while the latter was a multipurpose structure for chariot races, athletic contests, and gladiatorial combats.[20] Further excavations will certainly provide more information about the lost stadium, even though the question regarding its location now seems to be resolved.

The coins minted by Herod Antipas in Tiberias add another facet that complements the Roman-civic character of the city. Tiberias

---

[20] The width of the track in the stadium, according to Humphrey, usually ranges between 10 and 33 m., which is much narrower than the width of the smallest hippodrome or circus; see Humphrey 1986, 525–28. For a discussion of Herodian hippodromes and stadia in our region, see Weiss 1999, 34–35.

Fig. 4   Coin of Herod Antipas, 19 c.e. (after: Meshorer 2001, 301, Fig. 75).

was granted the right to issue coins and to reckon its era.[21] Its first coins were minted with the foundation of the city in the year 19 (Λ ΚΔ) and bears the name TIBERIAC on the obverse; the reverse depicts a reed with the date and the Greek inscription ΗΡΩΔΟΥ ΤΕΤΡΑΡΧΟΥ (fig. 4). This issue was followed by four additional mintings in 29/30, 30/31, 33/34, and 39 c.e. All the coins bear floral motifs: the reed, palm branch, palm tree, and date cluster.[22] According to Meshorer, similar city coins were minted in 53/54, but the inscription on their obverse reads "of the Emperor Claudius."[23]

Sepphoris

Josephus mentions several events connected with the early history of Sepphoris that are important to our discussion. Herod the Great owned a royal palace in the city, and it is from there that Judas son of Ezechias confiscated arms after the king's demise (*War* 2.56; *Ant.* 17.271). Herod Antipas made Sepphoris his capital until he founded Tiberias. Josephus briefly indicates that Antipas "fortified Sepphoris to be the ornament of all Galilee, and called it Autocratoris" (Σέπφωριν τειχίσας πρόσχημα τοῦ Γαλιλαίου παντὸς ἠγόρευεν αὐτὴν

---

[21] Avi-Yonah 1950, 166; Meshorer 1988, 96–98.
[22] Meshorer 2001, 81–85.
[23] Meshorer 2001, 177.

Αὐτοκρατορίδα—*Ant.* 18.27). Although it is difficult to determine the exact meaning of Αὐτοκρατορίς—a reference honoring Augustus, conveying the idea of an Imperial or capital city, or simply that Sepphoris was granted autonomy[24]—most scholars believe that Herod Antipas fortified Sepphoris and rebuilt it after the city was captured and burnt by Varus, the governor of Syria, and that he also established various public buildings in the city that are often found in Roman towns, such as the theater (see below).[25] Antipas's monumental building achievements transformed Sepphoris into what Josephus called "the ornament of all Galilee."

Reading Josephus's works carefully, one realizes that the author describes only one building project conducted in the city: after being fortified by Herod Antipas, Josephus tells us that Sepphoris was considered πρόσχημα τοῦ Γαλιλαίου (*Ant.* 18.27). This phrase describes, as Stuart Miller suggests, "the town's capability to serve as a bulwark to fend off hostile incursions" due to its geographical position and massive walls, however it makes no reference to other building projects that Herod Antipas may have initiated by in the city.[26] Sepphoris was renowned for its defensive features, as mentioned elsewhere by Josephus who, on the eve of the revolt, authorized the Sepphoreans to build, or as I would assume, to renovate the existing walls (*War* 2.574).[27] The fortifications at Sepphoris, "the largest city of Galilee, a fortress in an exceptionally strong position," and the difficulty in conquering it because of this fact, moved Vespasian— according to Josephus—to help the Sepphoreans who came before him at Ptolemais (Akko) by sending them a garrison of cavalry and infantry to assure their protection and to "repel invasions in the event of the Jews causing trouble" (*War* 3.31–34). The rabbis, too, who were also acquainted with the nature of the city's defenses,

[24] Schürer 1979, 2.174 n. 485; Hoehner 1972, 86. According to Kokkinos (1998, 234), the city's new name is attributed to the celebrations held in 6 c.e. in honor of Augustus, and prior to 9 c.e., after Antipas's return from Rome.

[25] Hoehner 1972, 86–87; Smallwood 1976, 118–19; Freyne 1998, 137–38; Horsley 1996, 49–60. The construction of additional buildings is attributed by some scholars to Herod Antipas; see here as well as below, Strange 1992, 23–59; Reed 2000, 62–96. Chancey (2001, 127–45), on the contrary, argues that there is not enough evidence to support the assumption that Greco-Roman culture influenced Sepphoris by the first century c.e.

[26] Miller 1984, 56–57; 2001, 454.

[27] On the relationship between the various references to Josephus concerning the construction of the city wall at Sepphoris, see Cohen 1979, 215–16, 245–48.

used the term *castra* (קצטרא שבציפורי) when referring to the fortified acropolis (e.g., *m. Arak.* 9:6; *t. Šabb.* 13.9 [Lieberman 1962: 60]; Sifra, Be'har 4:1 [I. H. Weiss 1946: 73]).[28]

Later on, after Sepphoris regained its status as the capital of the Galilee, the royal bank and archives were restored to the city (*Life* 38–39). We know very little about the city's municipal institutions in the first century C.E. Josephus frequently mentions the Σεπφωρῖται (*Life* 373, 380, 394, 411),[29] but nowhere does he specify any of the functioning officials in Sepphoris, nor does he elaborate who the public leaders of the city were (*War* 2.574, 645; *Life* 373, 394, 411).[30] The old *archei* (ἀρχή = ἀρχεῖον?) of Sepphoris mentioned in talmudic sources may also indicate some governmental institution that functioned there in earlier days, however there is nothing in the texts other than the former existence of the Jewish court to imply the city's municipality (*m. Qidd.* 4:5).[31] Among the public buildings gracing Sepphoris we hear only about the *agora*, the marketplace where Josephus met Jesus and asked him to show repentance and be loyal to him (*Life*, 104–107). The *agora* in Sepphoris, as in any other Hellenistic town, was an open area, at times lined with buildings nearby, where merchants gathered to sell their goods.[32]

Coins were not minted in Sepphoris in the first half of the first century C.E., neither by Herod Antipas nor the city government.[33] Therefore, Sepphoris lacked yet another feature characterizing autonomous cities at the time. Only in 67/68 C.E., at wartime, were coins first minted in the city (fig. 5). The inscription on the obverse reads: "Year 14 of the Emperor Nero Claudius" (ΛΔΙ/ΝΕΡΩΝΟ/ΚΛΑΥ-ΔΙΟΥ/ΚΑΙCΑΡΟ/C) and that on the reverse: "In the days of Vespasian of the people of Neronias-Sepphoris, city of peace" (ΝΕΡΩΝΙΑ CΕΠΦΩ

---

[28] See also Miller 1984, 15–30. Sepphoris is also mentioned among the walled cities; on the physical layout of these cities, see Adan-Bayewitz 1997, 449–70.

[29] Some of the city's inhabitants who participated in the discussions of the rabbis are called ציפוראי in Talmudic literature; see, for example, *y. Maʿaś.* 1.4.49a; *y. Šabb.* 4.2.7a. For further discussion of this name, see Miller 1990, 15–22; 1992, 175–200; 1999, 543–73. Miller 1992, 175–200.

[30] See also Freyne 1980, 124.

[31] See also Kohut 1878–92, 1.287; Jastrow 1950, 121; Sperber 1984, 62–63.

[32] On the Hellenistic agora and adjacent buildings, see Coulton 1976, 62–65; Chamoux 2003, 272–76.

[33] For a discussion of the coins minted in Sepphoris, see Meshorer 1979, 159–71, esp. 159–63.

Fig. 5   Coin from Sepphoris, minted during the Great Revolt againts Rome (67/68 C.E.). Obverse: "Year 14 of the Emperor Nero Claudius"; reverse: pair of cornucopiae and a caduceus; "In the days of Vespasian of the people of Neronias-Sepphoris, city of peace" (after: Meshorer 2001, 95).

ΕΠΙ/ΟΥΕCΠΑCΙΑΝΟΥ ΕΙΡΗΝΟΠΟΙ).[34] Naming the city "Eirenopolis, Neronias-Sepphoris" corroborates Josephus's account of the city's behavior in opposing the revolt (*War* 3.30–34).[35] Do these new names imply that Sepphoris was awarded a new rank after opening its gates to the Romans? Or is it possible that Sepphoris's submission to Rome afforded it a new political status as well as the right to mint coins on which the city expressed servility to its Roman master? An evaluation of the information discussed so far, together with the archaeological finds presented below, validates our assumption that Sepphoris, in the course of events following the revolt, moved into a new era by becoming a Roman *polis*, which entirely influenced the city's architectural composition.

The archaeological remains unearthed at Sepphoris in recent years are far richer and varied compared to those from Tiberias, shedding new light on the architectural, cultural, and physical appearance and development of the city from the late Hellenistic period through the Byzantine era. Sepphoris in the Hellenistic period stretched across the hill and its slopes (fig. 6).[36] Excavations conducted on the

---

[34] Meshorer 2001, 102–5.
[35] See also discussion of the city's behavior during the revolt: Meyers 2002, 110–19.
[36] Meyers 1998: 343–55.

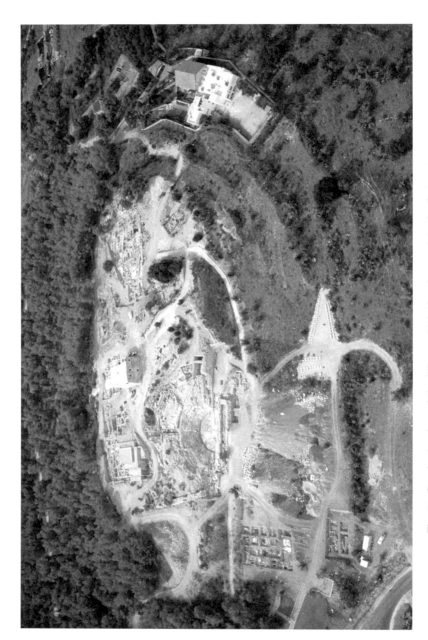

Fig. 6 Sepphoris, view of the hill on which the city stood in the first century c.e.

plateau east of the hill indicate that later on the city expanded in this direction, boasting an impressive grid of streets, with a colonnaded *cardo* and *decumanus* intersecting at its center. Some of the new streets east of the acropolis were supposedly linked to already existing ones on the hill itself and continued to run beyond the city limits, connecting Sepphoris with its agricultural hinterland and interurban roads. Various public and private buildings were erected throughout the Roman city; among those public buildings known today are a forum, bathhouses, a theater, and a monumental building identified as a library or an archive.[37]

None of the Roman-style public buildings unearthed at the site so far is dated to the early first century C.E.; they seem to have been constructed when the city was expanded and completely remodeled as a Roman *polis* at the end of the first or early second century C.E., when the city's infrastructure in Lower Sepphoris was well established. In the discussion that follows we will focus on a number of structures that helped us form a different perception, which was reached after years of excavation and an analysis of the finds unearthed at the site.

Colonnaded Streets

In the middle of the Lower City, which served as Sepphoris's urban center, two colonnaded streets were discovered—the *cardo* on a north-south axis and the *decumanus* on an east-west axis (fig. 7). The latter functioned as the main artery by which one entered the city from the east.[38] It crossed the breadth of the Lower City, reaching the foot of the hill. The streets were paved with hard limestone, whereas the sidewalks lining both sides of the streets were covered with mosaic floors. The stone slabs in the *cardo* are marked with ruts made by carriage or wagon wheels that passed over this thoroughfare for many years. The small shops along the colonnaded streets seem to have been part of Sepphoris's lower marketplace, where the hub of work

---

[37] For further discussion of the archaeological remains at Sepphoris, see Netzer and Weiss 1994; Weiss and Netzer 1997, 2–21; Meyers 1992, 321–38; Nagy et al. 1996; Weiss and Netzer 1997, 117–30. On the relationship between private and public building in ancient Sepphoris, see Weiss, in press.

[38] The *decumanus* may be linked at its eastern end with the road running from Tiberias to Sepphoris, as mentioned in Talmudic sources; see, for example, *Lev. Rab.* 16.1 (Margulies 1953–60, 348).

Fig. 7 Sepphoris, view of the colonnaded streets built on the saddle east of the hill, next to which public buildings and private dwellings were built in the Roman period.

and commercial life in the city was undoubtedly centered and which we read about in talmudic literature.[39] Early second-century potsherds, as well as a coin dated to the time of Trajan (98–117 C.E., Locus 77.1375), were found sealed in two probes conducted beneath the pavement of the main thoroughfares in Lower Sepphoris—one in the *cardo* and the other in the *decumanus*—and provide a *terminus post quem* for the construction of this street network.[40]

A Monumental Building adjacent to the Intersection in the Lower City

A large structure (40 × 60 m.) occupying an entire *insula* was excavated by the University of South Florida expedition near the intersection of the *cardo* and the *decumanus* in the Lower City.[41] The building, identified by the excavator as a basilical hall, had a peristyle court-

---

[39] "It was said of R. Eleazar that he sat and studied Torah in the lower market of Sepphoris while his linen cloak lay in the upper market of the town . . ." (*b. ʿErub.* 54b).

[40] These finds are based on the unpublished excavations of the Hebrew University excavation team. Two additional probes, more limited in scope, were conducted by the University of South Florida expedition, under the direction of J. Strange, in a small section at the northern end of the *cardo*. In one probe (Square 77), two stone slabs from the street were removed, and in another (Square 59), only four stone slabs; see McCollough and Edwards 1997, 135–42. The chalk layer found by the University of South Florida expedition, 30–50 cm. beneath the *cardo*, is indicative, they believe, of the early route of the road, connected, perhaps, to the entire street network whose construction they attribute to Herod Antipas. This is based on the material finds and on a coin of Herod Archelaus that was found in Square 77. This conclusion is interesting but not entirely proven by the finds; by the limited scope of the probe, it would be prudent to exercise great caution before drawing conclusions. The plaster layers in the two probes made by the South Florida expedition can be explained in a number of ways, but there is no reason to connect them to the route of the *cardo* that, it is believed, was laid and built by Herod Antipas. The chalk layer was not detected in the probes conducted in the areas of the Hebrew University team. It may be assumed that the remains of the plaster layer found beneath the northern part of the *cardo* belong to an early route, perhaps one that led from the fields and cemetery in the east, through the saddle westward, and to the city on the hill. Alternatively, this level may have been a remnant of the floor from an unknown building or agricultural installation (threshing floor?) that stood on the site before the street network of the Lower City was laid by the end of the first century or early second century C.E. However, we do not have enough data to prove that this complicated network was built in the early first century C.E. On the basis of the remains found by the Hebrew University excavation team, and on the fact that this level was not found in the probes conducted in their areas, it seems more likely that, for some reason, the plaster layer was intended to reinforce the street in the same spot. Perhaps the difference in heights and the topography required a solution at this specific spot before the building of the *cardo* and the street network at the end of the first or beginning of the second century C.E.

[41] Strange et al. 1993, 29–30; 1996, 117–21; 1999, 122–28.

yard surrounded by rooms of various sizes and decorated with colorful mosaic floors. Based on the published material, it can be identified as a forum—a freestanding edifice linked to the street network, similar to those found in other provincial cities.[42] The "Herodian stones" (characterized by their defined margins) incorporated into the building's southern and eastern foundation walls led the excavator to assume that the construction of the edifice may have begun under Herod Antipas, however the suggested date seems unconvincing for various reasons. For one, stones with defined margins are not necessarily indicative of a Herodian date, as this construction method, evident elsewhere in Sepphoris, was still being used in the late first and early second centuries c.e.[43] The earliest mosaics from three phases unearthed in the building are dated to the Severan era, according to Roussin,[44] however no other floors inside the building predate these mosaics and point to an earlier stage with a Herodian date. Moreover, the building's boundaries align perfectly with the adjacent early second-century street grid and could by no means have an earlier date. Nor can it be assumed that the building was constructed prior to the street network and only later on influenced the orientation of the latter; rather, the opposite it true: it is the existing adjacent thoroughfares that dictated the building's boundaries.

The Theater

The construction of the theater, the last building to be discussed in this context, is attributed by many scholars to Herod Antipas. The theater was built on the northern side of the hill, whose natural slope sustained the building's lower cavea, measuring ca. 74 m. in diameter and containing some 4,500 seats (fig. 8).[45] The layout of the theater, its construction methods, and architectural ornamentation follow well-known Roman patterns in other theaters in the region and beyond. Waterman's expedition, which in 1931 excavated one

---

[42] Cf., e.g., the buildings in Velleia, Italy and Nicopolis ad Istrum, Bulgaria; Ward-Perkins 1981, 175–76; 249–50; see also Owens 1992, 150.

[43] Stones with defined margins were incorporated in the building identified either as a library or an archive unearthed on the eastern slope, see Weiss 2000, 25–26; 2001, 29.

[44] Roussin 1994, 221–30; 1996, 123–25; 1999, 171–75.

[45] Waterman 1937, 6–12; Netzer and Weiss 1994, 14–17; Weiss and Netzer 1997, 7–8.

Fig. 8 View of the theater that was built on the northern slope of the hill in Sepphoris.

trench inside the theater, dated its construction to the Herodian period based on historical data, attributing it either to Herod the Great or his son, Herod Antipas.[46] The University of South Florida expedition excavated the northwestern corner of the theater between 1985 and 1987, identifying two phases inside the building based on the debris that covered it.[47] The first, according to McCollough, is dated to the first half of the first century C.E. on the basis of the pottery remains, thereby attributing its construction to Herod Antipas. In contrast, the Hebrew University team, which has excavated almost the entire theater since 1985, including reexamining those sections uncovered by the other expeditions, argues that the theater was constructed in a single phase in the late first or early second century C.E.[48] Many scholars, for various reasons, have adopted the earlier date for the building, i.e., that it was constructed by Herod Antipas, who beautified Sepphoris with an array of monuments (not yet found) and made it "the ornament of all Galilee."[49] Such an assumption, however, ignores the evidence at hand.

The later date of the theater established by the Hebrew University team relies on a range of archaeological factors: material culture, building construction, building plan, architectural ornamentation, and—looking at the broader picture—how the theater fits into Sepphoris's new urban infrastructure.

A sealed assemblage of ceramic vessels—jars, jugs, and cooking ware from the second half of the first century (70–80 C.E.)—was found in a cistern located beneath the semicircular outer wall of the theater and thus antedates the building's construction (fig. 9). The location of the cistern in relation to the theater wall clearly indicates that it was earlier and was canceled with the development of the theater. Thus, the material finds sealed beneath the theater, under a very thick layer of fill, serve as a *terminus post quem* for the construction of this monumental building. Finds uncovered in several additional

---

[46] The members of the expedition did not agree on the dating. Yeivin (1937, 29–30) thought the theater was constructed by Herod Antipas, whereas Waterman (1937, 29 n. 51) attributed the building to his father, Herod the Great.

[47] Strange et al. 1985, 298–99; 1987, 280; 1988, 189–90. The excavation results were recently analyzed and published in a short report, see McCollough 2003, 9–10.

[48] E. M. Meyers et al. 1987, 277–88; 1990, 220–22; Weiss and Netzer 1994, 41; 1997, 7–8; 1998, 23, 25.

[49] Segal 1995, 4–5, 41–43; Horsley 1996, 52–56; Roller 1998, 242; Kokkinos 1998, 234.

Fig. 9   Cistern and the sealed assemblage of ceramic vessels discovered inside it when building the theater in Sepphoris. The vault and ashlars wall above the cistern belong to the outer wall of the theater.

soundings inside the theater point to the same date. The construction of the lower cavea on the natural slope and support of the
upper cavea with vaults are both building methods employed in theaters erected throughout Syro-Palestine from the late first century
C.E. onwards.[50] The design of various parts of the Sepphoris theater,
such as the *proscaenium*, whose façade is decorated with alternating
square and semicircular niches, follows patterns found in other buildings constructed in the second century C.E.[51] An analysis of the architectural decoration as well points to a later date for the theater.
Several dressed stones found in the debris around the stage and
belonging to the *scaenae frons*, such as Corinthian capitals, friezes, and
cornices, were molded with patterns comparable to Late Roman
architecture known elsewhere.[52] Finally, the construction of a monumental theater is compatible with the city's massive development
in the late first and early second centuries C.E., with the expansion
of the inhabited area eastward and the construction of the civic center in Lower Sepphoris. Enhancing Sepphoris's urban landscape with
a theater amidst other Roman-style public buildings by the late first
or early second century C.E. is consistent with the urbanization process
of cities in ancient Palestine following the suppression of the Great
Revolt.[53] It thus seems unreasonable to attribute it to Herod Antipas,
when the city was confined to the hill and its slopes.

Archaeological Evidence for First-Century Sepphoris

After eliminating the possibility that Sepphoris was monumentally
built by Herod Antipas, what archaeological evidence do we have
for first-century Sepphoris and what do we know about the city's
architectural appearance on the eve of the revolt? Based on the
archaeological excavations conducted so far at the site, it seems that
Sepphoris in the Second Temple period was constructed, as men-

[50] Weiss 1995a, 60–70; 1995b, 4–6.
[51] Weiss 1995a, 75–77. The *proscaenium* of the Herodian theater at Caesarea
Maritima was shaped differently than the one at Sepphoris and was also decorated
with a wall painting or paintings; see Frova 1961, 95–96, 112–14, 167–68.
[52] Weiss 1995a, 80–84. On the architectural decoration in Roman public buildings during this period, see Lyttelton 1974, 11–15.
[53] Gerasa was immensely developed with the construction of the street network
and several public buildings by the late first century C.E., see Kraeling 1938, 45–56;
Seigne 1992, 331–41. Several first-century public buildings are known at Bet Shean,
but it was during the second century C.E. that the city was fully developed, with

tioned earlier, on the hill and its slope. The city featured simple buildings that lacked an air of monumentality. In addition to the road leading to the city, as well as some agricultural implements that complete the rural appearance of the immediate vicinity, only a few buildings, if any, would have been noticeable in Lower Sepphoris. Except for a military complex or fortress unearthed by the Sepphoris Regional Project on the western acropolis, no evidence of the city's walls has been found so far at the site. This building, with its massive walls, identified by the excavator as the *castra*, was constructed ca. 100 B.C.E. and was buried intentionally some time before 68 C.E.[54]

In addition, remains of some houses dating to the early Roman period were found in several areas on the acropolis, indicating that private homes were built on the hill and slopes of the early city (fig. 10). The style and plan of these houses were typical of contemporary Galilean construction. The houses that continued to be used by the local inhabitants in the first centuries C.E. did not have a fixed plan and even incorporated changes throughout the period. Some of these structures, built with indigenous fieldstones and cut stones and having plaster-paved floors, also contained ritual baths (fig. 11), cisterns, and storage rooms in their basements.[55]

No remains have been recovered of the palatial building, which according to Josephus stood in Sepphoris in the days of Herod the Great or where his son resided when in the city (*War* 2.56; *Ant.* 17.271). Nevertheless, fragments of frescoes from fills beneath the House of Dionysos suggest that such a palatial structure could have stood not far from here. These plaster fragments were adorned with floral patterns in several shades on a gray-black background, reminiscent of the third Pompeian style.[56] Even if we cannot link these sherds

---

the construction of the major thoroughfare in the Lower City as well as the various public buildings comprising the new civic center there; see Tsafrir and Foerster 1994, 92–104; Mazor and Bar-Nathan 1994, 117–21; Tsafrir and Foerster 1997, 85–99.

[54] Meyers 1998, 343–55; 1999, 109–22.

[55] Private homes were found on the western acropolis, see Meyers et al. 1995, 68–71; 1997, 265–68; 1998, 278–81; Weiss and Netzer 1997, 8. Remains of other dwellings were uncovered on the eastern acropolis beneath the House of Dionysos, which was constructed ca. 200 C.E., see Talgam and Weiss 2004, 27. For further discussion of the private homes at Sepphoris and their comparison to other similar structures in the Galilee and beyond, see Hoglund and E. M. Meyers 1996, 39–43; Rutgers 1998, 179–95.

[56] Talgam and Weiss 2004, 27. A comprehensive analysis of the decorative plaster fragments from Sepphoris was carried out by Vilozny, in her Masters thesis

Fig. 10   Remains of dwellings discovered on the western side of the acropolis. Some of the houses were built at the end of the Hellenistic period and continued to be used in the first century C.E.

Fig. 11   Ritual bath (*miqweh*) discovered beneath the remains of the House of Dionysos, on the eastern side of the hill in Sepphoris.

to the palatial building in Sepphoris, it should be assumed that they decorated some other prominent structure that stood on the hill in the first century C.E.—as was the case in Gamla or nearby Yodfat.[57] The *agora*, the local marketplace of the early city mentioned by Josephus and of which remains have not been found to date, was in all probability located in the center of the hill or slightly east of it. Access to the top of the hill was most probably from the east, where the path on the slope was easier to climb; this road, how- ever, has not yet been exposed in the excavations.

Tiberias and Sepphoris in the First Century C.E.—An Architectural Image of Antithetical Neighbors

After reviewing the evidence for both Galilean cities, one may con- clude, based on an analysis of the textual data against the archae- ological finds known to date from Tiberias and Sepphoris, that each locale was indeed forged differently in the first century. Tiberias had the internal organization and political independence of a *polis* while, hypothetically, Sepphoris could have been organized as such, although the meager evidence cannot support such an assumption. Architecturally speaking, each city had a distinct look. Tiberias, constructed by Herod Antipas, embraced a monumental appearance and boasted several public buildings from the outset, as did his father's building projects and as known in other Roman cities of the early empire. In contrast, Sepphoris on the eve of the Great Revolt had a rural semblance, less impressive than its counterpart and lacking most of the Roman-style public buildings. Large areas of the city were occu- pied by private dwellings, whereas the palatial residence, fortress, agora, and some other buildings that filled the needs of its inhabi- tants, such as an archive and treasury, were most probably located on the summit. The lack of Roman-style public buildings in first- century Sepphoris is evident not only from the archaeological finds but is also confirmed by Josephus's testimony. The author neither ignores the buildings in Sepphoris nor refrains from mentioning them,

---

(2004, 51–56). Her conclusions will be published in a separate article. The patterns that decorated Herod Antipas's palace in Tiberias, unlike those from Sepphoris, also contained figures of animals; see *Life* 65–69.

[57] Syon and Yavor 2000, 13–15; Aviam 1999, 98.

but rather faithfully describes the reality of his era, wherein the city lacked a monumental appearance—in contrast to its counterpart Tiberias.

A similar situation, in which two neighboring cities had a diverse architectural appearance, is known in two Pisidian cities, Sagalassus and Cremna in Asia Minor.[58] Roman-style buildings were introduced into Sagalassus from the mid-first century C.E., changing its architectural landscape to resemble other cities in the empire.[59] Cremna, on the other hand, refounded as an Augustan colony, retained its indigenous appearance whereas Roman public buildings were not constructed in the city until the reign of Hadrian.[60] Pausanias's description of Panopaeus in Phocaea reflects, too, a similar phenomenon in the mid-second century C.E. Although Panopaeus maintained its urban political status, it is to be distinguished from its neighboring cities because—as attested by Pausanias—it had no public buildings, "no gymnasium, no theater, no market and no water coming down to a fountain. . . ."[61] It would not be surprising, then, if Tiberias and Sepphoris, too, each bore distinct physical appearances in the first century C.E. The processes of Hellenization and Romanization were not completed in one day, just as it should not be assumed that the local inhabitants in both cities absorbed this new culture all at once. Rather, their exposure was probably gradual and proceeded at a different pace in each locale.

Conclusion

The urban topography of Tiberias and Sepphoris in the first century C.E. was different in each city, in some way resembling the situation at Sagalassus and Cremna or Panopaeus and the other Phocaean cities. Tiberias, founded by Herod Antipas as the new capital of the Galilee, had a monumental appearance, whereas Sepphoris on the eve of the revolt had a simple, rural semblance. Herod Antipas

---

[58] Perkins and Nevett 2000, 218–27.
[59] Waelkens 1993, 37–81; Vandeput 1997, 14–24.
[60] Mitchell 1995, 53–77.
[61] Pausanias, *Descr.* 10.4.1–4. On the architectural topography of the Greek cities in Roman times, see Alcock 1996, 129–71. On Pausanias's work in describing the cities in Greece, see Habicht 1998, 28–63. According to Strabo (*Geogr.* 9.2.5), additional settlements were lacking urban color and looked like villages in every respect.

indeed contributed to Sepphoris and refurbished its wall, however the bulk of his resources and attention were invested in the building of Tiberias, which he adorned with monumental structures, as would befit a Roman city that was to serve as the capital of the entire Galilee. Only years later, after the suppression of the revolt, did Sepphoris—owing to its pro-Roman stance—make great strides in its transformation from a Galilean town into a prominent Roman *polis*. In the ensuing years of the Roman era, both of these Galilean cities resembled each other in their governing institutions, public edifices, and cultural patterns. Their urban landscape, too, was not very different from other cities that flourished in ancient Palestine in the first centuries C.E.

BIBLIOGRAPHY

Adan-Bayewitz, D.
 1997   The Tannaitic list of "Walled Cities" and the Archaeological-Historical Evidence from Iotapata and Gamla. *Tarbiz* 66:449–70. [Hebrew]
Alcock, S. E.
 1996   *Graecia Capta: The Landscapes of Roman Greece.* Cambridge.
Aviam, M.
 1999   Yodfat—Uncovering a Jewish City in the Galilee from the Second Temple Period and the Time of the Great Revolt. *Qadmoniot* 118:98. [Hebrew]
Avi-Yonah, M.
 1950   The Foundation of Tiberias. *IEJ* 1:167–9.
 1974   *Atlas Carta for the Second Temple, Mishnaic and Talmudic Periods.* Jerusalem. [Hebrew]
 1984   *Historical Geography of Palestine: From the End of the Babylonian Exile up to the Arab Conquest.* [Hebrew]
Chamoux, F.
 2003   *Hellenistic Civilization.* Oxford.
Chancey, M.
 2001   The Cultural Milieu of Ancient Sepphoris. *NTS* 47:127–45.
Cohen, S. J. D.
 1979   *Josephus in Galilee and Rome: His Vita and Development as a Historian.* Leiden.
Coulton, J. J.
 1976   *The Architectural Development of the Greek Stoa.* Oxford.
Foerster, G.
 1977   The Excavations at Tiberias. *Qadmoniot* 10:87–91. [Hebrew]
Freyne, S.
 1980   *Galilee from Alexander the Great to Hadrian 323 B.C.E to 135 C.E.* Wilmington.
 1992   Urban-Rural Relations in First-Century Galilee: Some Suggestions from the Literary Sources. Pages 75–91 in *The Galilee in Late Antiquity.* Edited by L. I. Levine. New York.
 1998   *Galilee, Jesus and the Gospels, Literary Approaches and Historical Investigations.* Philadelphia.
Frova, A.
 1961   *Scavi di Caesarea Maritima.* Rome.

Gleason, K. L.
    1998   The Promontory Palace at Caesarea Maritima: Preliminary Evidence
                    for Herod's Praetorium. *JRA* 11:23–52.
Goodman, M.
    1983   *State and Society in Roman Galilee, A.D. 132–212.* Totowa.
Habicht, C.
    1998   *Pausanias' Guide to Ancient Greece.* Berkeley.
Harris, H. A.
    1972   *Greek Athletics and the Jews.* Tel Aviv.
Hartal, M.
    2002   The Stadium of Tiberias. *Etmol* 28:22–4. [Hebrew]
Hirschfeld, Y. and R. Reich
    1988.   The City Plan of Tiberias in the Roman-Byzantine Period. Pages
                    111–18 in *Tiberias: From Foundation to the Muslim Conquest.* Edited
                    by Y. Hirschfeld. Jerusalem.
Hoehner, H. W.
    1972   *Herod Antipas.* Cambridge.
Hoglund, K. G. and E. M. Meyers
    1996   The Residential Quarter on the Western Summit. Pages 39–43
                    in *Sepphoris in Galilee: Crosscurrents of Culture.* Edited by R. M. Nagy
                    et al. Raleigh.
Holum, K. G. et al., eds.
    1999   The Temple Platform: Progress Report on the Excavations. In
                    Caesarea Papers 2.12–34. Portsmouth.
Horsley, R. A.
    1995   *Galilee: History, Politics, People.* Valley Forge.
    1996   *Archaeology, History and the Society in Galilee: The Social Context of Jesus
                    and the Rabbis.* Valley Forge.
Humphrey, J. H.
    1986   *Roman Circuses: Arena for Chariot Racing.* London.
    1996   "Amphitheatrical" Hippo-Stadia. In *Caesarea Maritima—Retrospective
                    after Two Millennia,* ed. A. Raban and K. G. Holum, 121–9. Leiden.
Jastrow, M.
    1950   *A Dictionary of the Targumim, The Talmud Babli and Yerushalmi, and the
                    Midrashic Literature.* New York.
Kahn, L. C.
    1998   King Herod's Temple to Roma and Augustus at Caesarea Maritima.
                    Pages 123–42 in *Hellenic and Jewish Arts.* Edited by A. Ovadiah.
                    Tel Aviv.
Kasher, A.
    1988   The Founding of Tiberias and Its Role as the Capital of the
                    Galilee. Pages 3–11 in *Tiberias: From Foundation to the Muslim Conquest.*
                    Edited by Y. Hirschfeld, 3–11. Jerusalem. [Hebrew]
Kohut, A. (ed.)
    1878–1892   *Aruch Completum.* Vienna.
Kokkinos, N.
    1998   *The Herodian Dynasty, Origins, Role in Society and Eclipse.* Sheffield.
Kraeling, C. H.
    1938   *Gerasa: City of the Decapolis.* New Haven.
Lämmer, M.
    1976   Griechische Wettkämpfe in Galiläa unter der Herrschaft des Herodes
                    Antipas. *Kölner Beiträge zur Sportwissenschaft* 5:37–67.
Levine, L.
    1978   R. Simeon b. Yohai and the Purification of Tiberias: History and
                    Tradition. *HUCA* 49:143–85.

Lieberman, S.
    1932   Emendations on the Jerushalmi (c). *Tarbiz* 2:207–9. [Hebrew].
    1962   (ed.) *Tosefta, Mo'ed.* New York. [Hebrew]
Lyttelton, M. L.
    1974   *Baroque Architecture in Classical Antiquity.* London.
Margulies, M.
    1953–1960 *Leviticus Rabbah.* Jerusalem. [Hebrew]
Mazor, G. and R. Bar-Nathan
    1994   Scythopolis: Capital of *Palestina Secunda. Qadmoniot* 27/107–108: 117–37. [Hebrew]
McCollough, C. T.
    2003   The Theater at Sepphoris: From Herodian Theater to Municipal Theater Complex. *ASOR Newsletter* 53:9–10.
McCollough, C. T. and Edwards, D. R.
    1997   Transformations of Space: The Roman Road at Sepphoris. Pages 135–42 in *Archaeology and the Galilee: Texts and Contexts in the Greco-Roman and Byzantine aperiods.* Edited by D. R. Edwards and C. T. McCullough. Atlanta.
Meshorer, Y.
    1979   Sepphoris and Rome. Pages 159–71 in *Greek Numismatics and Archaeology, Essays in Honor of Margaret Thompson.* Edited by Mørkholm and N. M. Waggoner. Wetteren.
    1988   The Coins of Tiberias. Pages 96–102 in *Tiberias: From Foundation to the Muslim Conquest.* Edited by Y. Hirschfeld, 96–102. Jerusalem. [Hebrew]
    2001   *A Treasury of Jewish Coins from the Persian Period to Bar Kokhba.* Jerusalem.
Meyers, E. M.
    1992   Roman Sepphoris in Light of New Archeological Evidence and Recent Research. Pages 321–38 in *The Galilee in Late Antiquity.* Edited by L. I. Levine. New York.
    1997   Jesus and His Galilean Context. Pages 57–66 in *Archaeology and the Galilee: Texts and Contexts in the Greco-Roman and Byzantine Periods.* Edited by D. R. Edwards and C. T. McCollough. Atlanta.
    1998   The Early Roman Period at Sepphoris: Chronological, Archaeological, Literary and Social Considerations. Pages 345–55 in *Hesed Ve-Emet, Studies in Honor of Ernest S. Frerichs.* Edited by J. Magness and S. Gitin. Atlanta.
    1999   Sepphoris on the Eve of the Great Revolt (67–68 C.E.): Archaeology and Josephus. Pages 109–22 in *Galilee through the Centuries: Confluence of Cultures.* Edited by E. M. Meyers. Winona Lake.
    2002   Sepphoris, City of Peace. Pages 110–19 in *The First Jewish Revolt: Archaeology, History and Ideology.* Edited by A. M. Berlin and J. A. Overman. London.
Meyers E. M. et al.
    1987   Sepphoris (Sippori), 1986 (I)—Joint Sepphoris Project. *IEJ* 37:275–88.
    1990   Sepphoris (Sippori), 1987–1988. *IEJ* 40:219–22.
    1995   Sepphoris (Sippori), 1994. *IEJ* 45:68–71.
    1997   Sepphoris (Sippori), 1996. *IEJ* 47:264–68.
    1998   Sepphoris (Sippori), 1997. *IEJ* 48:278–81.
Miller, S. S.
    1984   *Studies in the History and Tradition of Sepphoris.* Leiden.
    1992   R. Hanina bar Hama at Sepphoris. Pages 175–200 in *The Galilee in Late Antiquity.* Edited by L. I. Levine. New York.
    1987   Intercity Relations in Roman Palestine: The Case of Sepphoris and Tiberias. *AJS Review* 12:1–24.

1990   Zippor'aei, Tibera'ei and Deroma'ei: Their Origins, Interests and
              Relationship. Pages 15–22 in *Proceedings of the Tenth World Congress
              of Jewish Studies*, B II. Jerusalem.
1999   Those Cantankerous Sepphoreans Revisited. Pages 543–73 in *Ki
              Baruch Hu: Ancient Near Eastern, Biblical and Judaic Studies in Honor of
              Baruch A. Levine*. Edited by R. Chazan et al. Winona Lake.
2001   Josephus on the Cities of Galilee: Factions, Rivalries and Alliances
              in the First Jewish Revolt. *Historia* 50/4:453–67.

Mitchell, S.
1995   *Cremna in Pisidia: An Ancient City in Peace and in War*. London.
Nagy, R. M. et al., eds.
1996   *Sepphoris in Galilee: Crosscurrents of Culture*. Raleigh.
Netzer, E. and Z. Weiss.
1994   *Zippori*. Jerusalem.
Owens, E. J.
1992   *The City in the Greek and Roman World*. London.
Patrich, J.
2001a   The *Carceres* of the Herodian Hippodrome/Stadium at Caesarea
              Maritima and the Connection with the Circus Maximus. *JRS*
              14:268–83.
2001b   "Urban Space in Caesarea Maritima, Israel," pages 77–110 in
              Urban Centers and Rural Contexts in Late Antiquity. Edited by T. S.
              Burns and J. W. Eadie. East Lansing.
Perkins, P. and L. Nevett
2000   Urbanism and Urbanization in the Roman World. Pages 218–27
              in *Experiencing Rome: Culture, Identity and Power in the Roman World*.
              Edited by J. Huskinson. London.
Porath, Y.
1995   Herod's "Amphitheater" at Caesarea: A Multipurpose Entertain-
              ment Building. Pages 15–27 in *The Roman and Byzantine Near East:
              Some Recent Archaeological Research*. Edited by J. H. Humphrey. Ann
              Arbor.
2003   Theatre, Racing and Athletic Installations in Caesarea. *Qadmoniot*
              125:25–42. [Hebrew]
Qedar, S.
1986–1987   Two Lead Weights of Herod Antipas and Agrippa II and the
              Early History of Tiberias. *INJ* 9:29–35.
Raban, A. and K. G. Holum, eds.
1996   *Caesarea Maritima—Retrospective after Two Millennia*. Leiden.
Rappaport, U.
1988   Tiberias and Its Place in the Great Revolt. Pages 12–23 in *Tiberias—
              From Foundation to the Muslim Conquest*. Edited by. Y. Hirschfeld.
              Jerusalem. [Hebrew]
Reed, J. L.
2000   *Archaeology and the Galilean Jesus*. Harrisburg.
Roller, D. W.
1998   *The Building Program of Herod the Great*. Berkeley.
Roussin, L.
1994   A New Mosaic from Sepphoris in Galilee. Pages 221–30 in *VI
              Coloquio Internacional sobre Mosaico Antiguo, Palencia-Mérida Octubre 1990*.
              Edited by C. M. Batalla. Guadalajara.
1996   The Birds and Fishes Mosaic. Pages 123–25 in *Sepphoris in Galilee:
              Crosscurrents of Culture*. Edited by R. M. Nagy et al. Raleigh.

1999   Spheres of Influence in the Mosaics of Sepphoris. Pages 171–75
            in *La mosaïque gréco-romaine VII*. 1. Edited by M. Ennaïfer and
            A. Rebourg. Tunis.
Rutgers, L. V.
1998   Some Reflections on the Archaeological Finds from the Domestic
            Quarter on the Acropolis of Sepphoris. Pages 179–95 in *Religious
            and Ethnic Communities in Later Roman Palestine*. Edited by H. Lapin.
            Bethesda.
Schürer, E.
1973–1987   *The History of the Jewish People in the Age of Jesus Christ (175 B.C.–A.D. 135):
            A New English Version*. Revised and edited by G. Vermes, F. Millar,
            and M. Goodman. 3 vols. in 4. Edinburgh.
Schwabe, M.
1949   The History of Tiberias. Pages 238–42 in *Johanan Levy Volume*.
            Edited by M. Schwabe and J. Gutmann. Jerusalem. [Hebrew]
Segal, A.
1995   *Theaters in Roman Palestine and Provincia Arabia*. Leiden.
2003   Horvat Susita. *Hadashot Arkheologiyot* 115:16–17.
Seigne, J.
1992   Jérash romaine et byzantine: développement urbain d'une ville
            provinciale orientale. Pages 331–41 in *Studies in the History and
            Archaeology of Jordan*. IV. Edited by G. Bisheh. Amman.
Smallwood, E. M.
1976   *The Jews under Roman Rule, From Pompey to Diocletian*. Leiden.
Sperber, D.
1977   On the Office of the *agoranomus* in Roman Palestine. *ZDMG*
            127:227–43.
1984   *A Dictionary of Greek and Latin Legal Texts in Rabbinic Literature*. Ramat
            Gan.
Stacy, D.
2004   *Excavations at Tiberias, 1973–1974: The Early Islamic Periods*. Jerusalem.
Strange, J. F.
1992   Some Implications of Archaeology for New Testament Studies.
            Pages 23–59 in *What Has Archaeology to do with Faith?* Edited by
            J. Charlesworth and W. Weaver. Valley Forge.
Strange, J. F. et al.
1985   Sepphoris (Sippori), 1985 II. *IEJ* 35:297–99.
1987   Sepphoris (Sippori), 1986 II. *IEJ* 37:278–80.
1988   Sepphoris (Sippori), 1987. *IEJ* 38:188–90.
1993   Zippori 1991. *ESI* 13:29–30.
1996   The Eastern Basilical Building. Pages 117–21 in *Sepphoris in Galilee:
            Crosscurrents of Culture*. Edited by R. M. Nagy et al. Raleigh.
1999   Sepphoris. *IEJ* 49:122–8.
Syon, D. and Z. Yavor.
2000   Gamla—Old and New. *Qadmoniot* 121:2–33. [Hebrew]
Talgam, R. and Z. Weiss.
2004   *The Mosaics in the House of Dionysos at Sepphoris: Excavated by E. M.
            Meyers, E. Netzer and C. L. Meyer*. Qedem 44. Jerusalem.
Tsafrir, Y. and G. Foerster
1994   The Hebrew University Excavations at Beth-Shean, 1980–1994.
            Qadmoniot 27/107–108:92–104. [Hebrew]
1997   Urbanism at Scythopolis—Beth Shean in the Fourth to the Seventh
            Centuries. *DOP* 51:85–99.

Vandeput, L.
    1997   *The Archaeological Decoration in Roman Asia Minor, Sagalassos: A Case Study.* Turnhout.
Vilozny, N.
    2004   The Sepphoris Wall Paintings as a Mirror of Artistic Painting throughout the Roman Empire in the Second and Third Centuries C.E. Masters thesis, Hebrew University of Jerusalem. [Hebrew]
Waelkens, M.
    1993   *Sagalassos I, First General Report on the Survey (1986–1989) and Excavations (1990–1991).* Leuven.
Ward-Perkins, J. B.
    1981   *Roman Imperial Architecture.* Harmondsworth.
Waterman, L.
    1937   *Preliminary Report of the University of Michigan Excavations at Sepphoris, Palestine in 1931.* Ann Arbor.
Weber, T. M.
    1991   Gadara of the Decapolis: Tiberias Gate, Qanawat el-Far'oun and Beit Rusan: Achievements in Excavation and Restoration at Umm Qais. Pages 123–26 in *The Near East in Antiquity.* II. Edited by S. Kerner. Amman.
    2002   *Gadara-Umm Qēs.* I. Wiesbaden.
Weiss, I. H. ed.
    1946   *Sifra.* New York. [Hebrew]
Weiss, Z.
    1995a   Games and Spectacles in Roman Palestine and their Reflection in Talmudic Literature. Ph.D. Dissertation, Hebrew University of Jerusalem. [Hebrew]
    1995b   Roman Leisure Culture and Its Influence upon the Jewish Population in the Land of Israel. *Qadmoniot* 109:2–19. [Hebrew]
    1999   Adopting a Novelty: The Jews and the Roman Games in Palestine. Pages 23–49 in *The Roman and Byzantine Near East: Recent Archaeological Research.* II. Edited by J. H. Humphrey. Portsmouth.
    2000   Zippori—1999. *Hadashot Arkheologiyot* 112:25–6. [Hebrew]
    2001   Zippori—2000. *Hadashot Arkheologiyot* 113:29. [Hebrew]
    Forthcoming   Private Architecture in the Public Sphere: Urban Dwellings in Roman and Byzantine Sepphoris. In *From Antioch to Alexandria: Studies in Domestic Architecture during the Roman and Byzantine Periods.* Edited by K. Galor and T. Waliszewski. Providence.
Weiss, Z. and E. Netzer
    1994   Zippori—1992–1993. *ESI* 14:40–6.
    1997   Architectural Development of Sepphoris during the Roman and Byzantine Periods. Pages 117–30 in *Archaeology and the Galilee: Texts and Contexts in the Greco-Roman and Byzantine Periods.* Edited by D. R. Edwards and C. T. McCollough. Atlanta.
    1997   The Hebrew University Excavations at Sepphoris. *Qadmoniot* 113:2–21. [Hebrew]
    1998   Zippori—1994–1995. *ESI* 18:22–27.
Yeivin, S.
    1937   Historical and Archaeological Notes. Pages 17–34 in *Preliminary Report of the University of Michigan Excavations at Sepphoris.* Ann Arbor.

A SPECIAL LECTURE TO MARK THE HOSTING OF THE
INTERNATIONAL JOSEPHUS COLLOQUIUM IN TRINITY
COLLEGE DUBLIN

ROBERT TRAILL: THE FIRST IRISH CRITIC OF WILLIAM WHISTON'S TRANSLATION OF JOSEPHUS[1] (A SPECIAL LECTURE TO MARK THE HOSTING OF THE *INTERNATIONAL JOSEPHUS COLLOQUIUM* IN TRINITY COLLEGE DUBLIN)

Gohei Hata

Every student of Josephus knows the name of William Whiston (1667–1752) and his translation of Josephus, but I presume, very few scholars know the name of Robert Traill, a graduate of this Trinity College in Dublin, who became the first Irish translator of Josephus as well as the first critic of William Whiston's translation. So, on this special occasion for the International Colloquium on Josephus held here in Dublin, I would like to share my great respect for Robert Traill with you, by placing him in the translation history of Josephus in the English-speaking world.

English Translations of Josephus in the Seventeenth Century

We do not know who the first English translator of Josephus was. Two of the English translators of Josephus in the 17th century did refer to the name of Morisyn as the first English translator. In his "Advertisement to the Reader" in 1733, John Court speaks of this person by saying: "The first English version of Josephus, was that done by Morisyn: 'tis of a very old standing, and its phrase is grown

[1] I am grateful to Dr. Zuleika Rodgers for her kindness in giving me an opportunity for my talk in the colloquium. I am also grateful to Prof. Honora H. Chapman for her reading this paper and checking my English. In the first international colloquium on Flavius Josephus in memory of the late Prof. Morton Smith held at San Miniato, 2–5 November, 1992, I made a proposal to the participants that we should collect any modern translations of Josephus. I have tried to be faithful to my word and I have already written two papers in Japanese: Hata 2001, 89–104, 2002, 65–84. On this occasion I would like to propose that all available translations in all modern languages, at least, English, French, German, and Italian, should be gathered together in one center. For English translations, I presume that one of the colleges in the University of Oxford may be a good candidate, and I have already discussed with Profs. Martin Goodman and Tessa Rajak the possibility of donating my collection on Josephus to Oxford.

now almost obsolete, tho' in the main it comes as near the Greek, as any that have succeeded it." In his 1692 edition, Roger L'Estrange also makes a brief comment on this person by saying: ". . . and even our Old English Translation of that book by P. Morisyn hath this paragraph [= a paragraph on Jesus] at large." In the first discourse attached to the 1732 edition of H. Jackson's Josephus is also found the similar remark on Morisyn: "Baronius mentions an old Hebrew copy of Josephus, in which this passage appear'd to have been inserted, but was erased; and even our old English translation of that book by P. Morysin hath this paragraph at large." It is now clear that Morisyn's translation of Josephus was still available before 1692 or even in 1732 or in 1733, but we do not know exactly when it was published. Prof. Louis H. Feldman, one of the most distinguished bibliographers of Josephus, in our private correspondence, expressed his hesitation to attribute the honor of the first English translator to this person.[2] Prof. Feldman's hesitation is evidently derived from a lack of evidence. I have so far visited the British Library, the library of the universities of Oxford and Cambridge, Marsh's Library and Trinity College's Library in Dublin, but with no good result. A friend of mine recently advised me to check one of the libraries in Italy. I will go and try in the very near future. If I could find it, I would say to you, "Eureka, eureka, and eureka." These three words of Archimedes would be more than enough to express my joy.

If Morisyn was not the first translator, then the honor will be given to Thomas Lodge whose Josephus appeared in 1602. The title page reads: "The famous and memorable works of Josephus, a man of much honour and learning among the Jews. Faithfully translated

---

[2] In his recent letter (dated 28 Nov., 2004) to the author, Prof. Feldman again expressed his view on this person. He made the following suggestion in the letter: "Morisyn is Peter Morvvne, whose name is variously spelled as Morwyng, Morvvyn, and Morwyn, who in 1558 translated into English the work known as *Josippon*, which is, as you know, a very free paraphrase of Josephus's *Jewish War* and whose translation went through as many editions between the mid-sixteenth and mid-seventeenth centuries, twenty-one, as did Whiston's translation of Josephus into English in the eighteenth century. Indeed, so popular was *Josippon* that the translation by Morvvyn dated 1718 in Boston is the first book of Jewish authorship printed in America, though it was not actually issued in 1722. It is true that Morryn is not the same as Morisyn but it is pretty close, since the first three letters are the same and the last two letters are the same. Since it was published in 1558 it was earlier than the translation of Josephus by Thomas Lodge, which was published in 1602." See also Feldman's (1984, 61) for further discussion.

out of the Latin, and French by Thomas Lodge, Doctor in Physics."
This translation is dedicated to Charles Lord Howard, a cousin of
Elizabeth I (1558–1603). Lodge does not explain in any place which
Latin text or which French translation he used. The title page of
the *Jewish War* reads: "The Lamentable and Tragical History of the
Wars and Utter Ruin of the Jews." The phrase in this title, "Utter
Ruin of the Jews" may suggest the existence of anti-Jewish elements,
but we could point out that throughout his translation, there are no
anti-Jewish remarks or sentiment at all. However, as we will see, in
its revised edition or in its abridged edition, this title page functions
as a base for transmitting an anti-Jewish message to the audience
because this title page was to be printed in large characters for the
sake of emphasis. According to Heinz Schrekenberg, Lodge's translation was reprinted once almost every ten years in the seventeenth
century.[3] Milton (1608–1674) read this translation; Shakespeare
(1564–1616), I do not know.[4]

In 1676, Lodge's translation was revised on the basis of Arnauld
D'Andilly's translation published in France in 1667. The name of
this reviser is not given anywhere in the translation. "Advertisements
concerning the works of Josephus" are written in a very Christian
spirit, in other words, in a very anti-Jewish spirit. Let me quote some
parts of the work.

> It may be boldly affirmed, That never was seen a greater example
> thereof, than the ruin of that ungrateful Nation, of that proud City,
> and of that venerable Temple; since although the Romans were Masters
> of the World, and that this Siege was the work of one of the great-
> est Princes they glory to have had for Emperors, the power of this
> victorious people and the heroic valor of Titus would have in vain
> undertaken this design, if God had not chosen them to be the exe-
> cutioners of his justice. The blood of his Son shed, the most horrid
> of all crimes, was the only true cause of the ruin of that unhappy
> City. The heavy hand of God upon that wretched people caused that
> how terrible soever the War was that assaulted them without, it was
> yet much more dreadful within, by the cruelty of those unnatural Jews,
> who more like Devils than men, destroyed by the Sword and the
> Famine, of which they were the Authors, 1,100,000 persons; and
> reduced the remainder to that pass, that they could hope for no safety
> but from their Enemies, by casting themselves into the arms of the

---

[3] Schreckenberg 1968, 21.
[4] See Feldman 1984, 861–63.

Romans. Such prodigious effects of vengeance for the death of a God, might pass for incredible with those who have not the happiness to be enlightened with the light of the Gospel, if they were not related by a Man of that very same Nation, as considerable as Josephus was, for his Birth, for his quality of Priest and for his Virtue. And methinks 'tis visible, that God minding to make use of his testimony to authorize such important truths, preserved him by a miracle, when after the taking of Josaphat [Jotapata?], of forty which were retired with him into a Cave, the lot being cast so often to know who should be slain first, he only and one other remained alive. This shows that this Historian is to be considered with a different respect from all others, since whereas they relate only humane Events, although dependent on the orders of the Supreme Providence, it appears that God cast his eye upon him to make him subservient to the greatest of his designs.

Here we could read a very strong anti-Jewish message supported by the theological vandalism of the Christianity of the day. This message seems to be equal in kind to that of Eusebius. The author in the advertisements further adds the following remarks in terms of the fulfillment of the prophecy of Josephus:

For we must not only consider the destruction of the Jews as the most dreadful effect that ever was Gods [God's?] justice, and as the most dismal image of the vengeance which he will exercise at the last day against the Reprobate: we must also behold it as one of the most illustrious proofs which it hath pleased him to give the men of the Divinity of his Son; inasmuch as this prodigious Event had been foretold by our Saviour in precise and intelligible terms. He had said to his Disciples, shewing them the Temple of Jerusalem, That all those goodly buildings should be so destroyed, that there should not be left one stone upon another, s. Matth 24. ver. 2. s. Mark 13. ver. 2. s. Luke 19. v. 44. And also, That when they should see Jerusalem encompassed by the Armies, they should know that its desolation was at hand, s. Luke 21. ver. 20.

He had mentioned particularly the dreadful circumstances of this desolation. He had said to them, Woe to those that shall be with child or give suck in those days; for there shall be great distress in the land, and wrath upon this people. And they shall fall by the edge of the sword, and shall be led away captive into all Nations, and Jerusalem shall be trodden down by the Gentiles, s. Luke 31. ver. 23, 24.

And lastly he had declared that the accomplishment of these prophecies was ready to come to pass; That the time was drawing nigh that their house should be left unto them desolate: and that even such as were then living should see it, Verily I say unto you, All these things shall come upon this generation, s. Matth. 23. ver. 38, & 39.

All these things had been foretold by our Saviour, and written by the Evangelists before the revolt of the Jews, and at a time when there was not yet the least appearance of so strange a Revolution.

Now inasmuch as Prophecy is the greatest of Miracles, and the most powerful way whereby God Almighty authorizes his doctrine; this Prophecy of Jesus Christ, to which no other is comparable, may be justly accounted the chief and most irrefragable evidence to mankind of his Divine Birth and Mission. For as no other Prophecy was ever more clear, so neither was any more punctually accomplished. Jerusalem was destroy'd to the ground by the first Army that besieged it; there remained not the least footstep of that proud Temple, the wonder of the Universe, and the object of the Jews vanity; and the calamities which ruined them, answered precisely to the dreadful Prediction of our Saviour. . . .

Prophecy is the greatest of miracles. The fall of the temple in the year 70 C.E. occurred according to the prophecy of Jesus Christ. Therefore, this guarantees the divinity of Jesus Christ. This syllogism sounds very strange. Although today's New Testament scholarship would regard all the words of Jesus cited here as the ones the gospel writers put into the mouth of Jesus after the war against the Romans, in the seventeenth century when all the words of Jesus were believed to have come directly from his mouth and, therefore, they were thought to be authentic, this kind of theological vandalism could stride a main street of Christian theology and disseminate anti-Jewish germs everywhere, if not, at least among the readers of the works of Josephus in the English translation. Not only in the advertisements, but also in the layout of the title page of the *Jewish War* that is quite different from that of Lodge's translation, we see a very strong anti-Jewish message.

In 1692, Sir Roger L'Estrange's translation was published in London. Under the title page is written: "All carefully revised and compared with the original Greek." That this translation is from Greek is emphasized because the previous translations were made from the Latin text with the help of a French translation. However, L'Estrange does not clarify which Greek text he used for his English translation, though he mentions in the preface that Dr. Hudson, chief keeper of the Bodleian Library (of the University of Oxford) was pleased to take on comparing the translation with the Greek.

On the left side of the title page is depicted the portraits of Vespasian, Titus, Josephus, and L'Estrange. Josephus wears a turban, with a staff is in his right hand.

Attached to this translation are two discourses written by Dr. Wills. The first one examines the life and religion of Josephus and then discusses the so-called testimony of Josephus on Christ in Book 18 of the *Jewish Antiquities*. L'Estrange seems to have included this discourse because by this time many learned men began to argue against the authenticity of this famous passage.[5]

Also attached to this translation is a list of subscribers' names. According to it, four hundred and thirty-eight people promised to purchase the translation upon publication and eight hundred and thirty-four copies were made for sale. There is one interesting fact that this list suggests. It is the fact that the purchasers of this translation were no longer restricted to church-related people such as baxters, preachers of the gospel, and ministers of the gospel. People like writers, weavers, maltmen, smiths, shoemakers, masons, skinners, store-masters, inn-keepers, barbers, farmers, sadlers, and bakers gave their names as subscribers and each purchased at least one copy of the translation. If you were interested in a sociological analysis of the readers of Josephus, a list of subscribers and their professions often attached to the seventeenth and eighteenth century editions of Josephus would be very helpful, I presume.

L'Estrange (1616–1704), the royalist, was very active in the world of politics. He was sentenced to death in 1644 on suspicion of espionage. Though he fled, he was caught and imprisoned at New Gate. Four years later, he escaped from the prison and was given pardon by Cromwell. In 1688 when the Glorious Revolution took place, he was in favor of James II and wrote many pamphlets against Milton in opposition to the revolution. He is also known to have published *The Public Intelligence* and *The Observer* and he was knighted in 1685. When James II was dethroned, L'Estrange suffered the loss of all publicly important positions. How could he sustain his family? He did so by translating some of the classics into English.[6] According to Schreckenberg, his Josephus was printed not only in London but also in some other places of England fifteen times in the eighteenth century and in the years 1773–1775, it was also printed in Philadelphia and New York on the New Continent.[7]

---

[5] See the discussions in Feldman 1984, 679–703 and Whealey, 2003.
[6] L'Estrange's life could be easily learned from the *Dictionary of National Biography*.
[7] Schreckenberg 1968, 29.

In 1699, an abridged edition of Josephus was published. The title page reads: "The works of the learned and valiant Josephus, epitomized from the Greek original." The anti-Jewish preface is written on the basis of the advertisement attached to Thomas Lodge's revised edition. Comparison between the two in terms of the use of the same or similar phraseologies or sentence structures suggests that the author was the same. This abridged edition did not sell well. It was printed again in 1702 and disappeared from the market.

Daniel Defoe, author of *Robinson Crusoe*, also wrote *A Journal of the Plague Year* which depicted the plague of London in 1665. In this book, a man who appeared in London in the very midst of the plague and predicted its fall is compared to a man who appeared in Jerusalem at the very end of the war against the Romans and predicted its fall.[8] Daniel Defoe knew the *Jewish War* of Josephus very well, or I should say boldly that because he was very familiar with the *Jewish War*, he was induced to depict the plague of London. His Josephus might have been Thomas Lodge's translation or its revised edition, L'Estrange's translation, or Dandilly's French translation.

Josephus in the Eighteenth Century

In 1732, H. Jackson's Josephus was published in London. The title of this edition is: "A complete collection of the genuine works of Flavius Josephus, faithfully translated from the original Greek." This edition is a copy of L'Estrange's Josephus, with two discourses attached to it. This Josephus was printed again in 1736 and then disappeared.[9] It has now become a rare book.

In 1733, John Court's Josephus was published in London. The title of this book is: "The works of Flavius Josephus, translated from the original Greek, according to Dr. Hudson's edition." The title of Book 1 of the *Jewish War* is: "Flavius Josephus of the *Jewish War*; and The Destruction of Hierosoluma [i.e., Jerusalem]." Book 2, Book 4, Book 5, Book 6, and Book 7 read respectively: "Flavius Josephus of the *Jewish War*: or the Jewish History of the Fall" and Book 3 reads: "Flavius Josephus of The *Jewish War*: or the Jewish History

---

[8] *War* 6.300–309.
[9] Schreckenberg 1968, 39.

of the Destruction." Under the repetition of these similar titles is
hidden an anti-Jewish message.

In 1737, that famous English translation of William Whiston was
published in London. I presume that many scholars came to know
Josephus first through Whiston's translation in modern dress. The
title page reads: "The genuine works of Flavius Josephus, the Jewish
historian. Translated from the original Greek, according to Havercamp's
accurate edition." The title of each of the seven books of the *Jewish
War* is written in all capital letters: "Flavius Josephus of the *Jewish
War*: or his History of the Destruction of Jerusalem." Since this title
is to be repeated seven times, the visual impact of its anti-Jewish
message upon the readers would have been great.

Attached to this translation were eight dissertations written by
Whiston himself. Each of them is filled with his strong Christian passion. The first dissertation is: "The testimonies of Josephus concerning
Jesus Christ, John the Baptist, and James the Just, vindicated." As
the title suggests, by this time the number of those intellectuals who
attempted to deny or at least doubt the authenticity of the testimony
of Josephus on Jesus Christ was on the sharp increase. Whiston, in
his own way, tried to defend its authenticity. In this same dissertation, Whiston mentions that "though Josephus did not declare himself to be openly a Christian, he was one of the Jewish Nazarens or
Ebionites who believed Jesus of Nazareth to be the true Messiah."
I presume the idea of ascribing Josephus to the Ebionite Christian
sect comes from Eusebius.[10] According to him, Ebionite Christians
held Jesus "to be a plain and ordinary man who had achieved right-
eousness merely by the progress of his character and had been born
naturally from Mary and her husband." For those interested in, for
example, James Ussher's chronological studies in the seventeenth century, or in Newton's *Chronology of Ancient Kingdoms Amended*, I advise
you to read another of Whiston's dissertations entitled: "A large
Enquiry into the true Chronology of Josephus." I am sure you will
find how biblical chronology was used to determine the beginning
of the world as well as its end.

Whiston inserted a large number of footnotes into his translation.
Some of them are strongly anti-Jewish. Let me quote one example.
In the preface to the *Jewish War*, Josephus says (in Whiston's translation):

---

[10] Eusebius, *Hist. eccl.* 3. 27.

"Accordingly it appears to me, that the misfortunes of all men, from the beginning of the world, if they be compared to these of the Jews are not so considerable as they were." Whiston gives a footnote to the phraseology of "these of the Jews." Whiston thus comments:

> That these calamities of the Jews, who were our Saviour's murderers, were to be the greatest that had ever been since the beginning of the world, as our Saviour had directly foretold, Matt. xxiv. 21, Mar. xiii. 19, Luc. xxi. 23, 24, and that they proved to be such accordingly, as Josephus is there a most authentic witness.[11]

The label such as "Saviour's murderers" in this citation could be easily found in the *Ecclesiastical History* of the 4th century Eusebius.[12] Whiston makes similar anti-Jewish comments throughout his translation. The idea of Josephus' being eventually an Ebionite Christian is repeatedly expressed in his dissertations[13] and in the footnotes of both the *Jewish War* and *Jewish Antiquities*.[14] In one of his footnotes in Book 20 of the *Jewish Antiquities*, Whiston claims that the Queen of Adiabene, who came to Jerusalem during a famine in the time of Claudius Caesar and provided the Jews with food, was a Christian,[15] and in his footnote in *Life*, Whiston states that there is a great possibility that a man named Banus (or Bannus), under whom Josephus claimed to have trained himself in the wilderness in his early years, was a follower of John the Baptist.[16] These footnotes are evidently derived from his Christian passion or ambition for linking any passage in Josephus, if possible, with the New Testament, but this kind of manipulation of sources baffles us today. Book 6 of the *Jewish War* depicts the burning down of the temple in Jerusalem,[17] and Whiston makes several outrageous interpretations based on Christian vandalism. It was only in 1921 that these eccentric footnotes were to be removed by Margoliouth when he edited Whiston's translation in his own way.

---

[11] Whiston, Vol. 2, 691.

[12] Concerning the labels Eusebius used against the Jewish people, see my article, 2001.

[13] See dissertation I on "The Testimonies of Josephus Vindicated" and dissertation II on "The copy of the Old Testament made use of by Josephus, proved to be that which was collected by Nehemiah." These dissertations are attached to the beginning of Volume II.

[14] Vol. I, 22, 664, and Vol. II, 800, 1011. Whiston also says in Vol. II, 755 that Josephus became a "Catholic(k) Christian."

[15] Vol. I, 634.

[16] Vol. I, 656.

[17] See, for example, Vol. II, 906.

William Whiston studied at the University of Cambridge. In 1696, he published a book entitled *A New Theory of the Earth* and dedicated it to his master, Isaac Newton. Whiston claims in this book that the story of the flood in Genesis had an historical foundation and that he could scientifically demonstrate it from the collision of comets. In 1701 Whiston was invited to come back to Cambridge by Newton as his substitute and taught mathematics there, and two years later, he taught both mathematics and natural philosophy as successor to Newton. He is said to have made a great contribution in spreading Newton's theories. During this period, Whiston became interested in the study of theology, and in 1708 he published a paper in which he claimed that the doctrine of the trinity was wrong. This paper suggested Whiston's sympathy with Arius of the fourth century who denied the divinity of Christ. After its publication, a rumor spread immediately that Whiston came to support the doctrine of Arius. As a result, he was labeled a heretic and expelled from Cambridge in 1710 on a charge of having taught a doctrine contrary to that of the Anglican Church. He was forty-three years old then. Expulsion from Cambridge became the turning point of his life. He left the Anglican Church and joined the Baptist Church, which guaranteed him the freedom of faith. He became enthusiastic about the revival movement of primitive Christianity and kept saying that the prophecy of the Bible would soon be realized. In 1726 Whiston became more fanatical, and with a portable temple of Ezekiel in hand, he visited towns and villages throughout England and preached that the Jews would soon return to Palestine and that the real temple would be built upon Mount Zion when the Messiah comes. Some people listened to him, but many frowned on his Christian fanaticism and refused to believe him. Every time he was in a coffee house in the City (that is London), people left to avoid any involvement with him.[18]

---

[18] There are many articles on William Whiston, including the one in the *Dictionary of National Biography* and they can be easily found them on the web. Force (1985) is a must-see book for those who want to know Whiston better. Metzger (1983, 523) refers in his article to "Whiston's interpretation of the significance of the rumor, circulating in 1726, that an illiterate farm woman of Surrey, named Mary Toft, had given birth to a litter of rabbits. To the torrent of pamphlets and editorials for and against the truth of the story, Whiston added his impassioned defense—for he was convinced that here was a signal of the fulfillment of Ezra's prophecy that at the end of the age "the women shall bring forth monsters" (Ezra 5:8). Whiston's portraits can be seen in the National Portrait Museum in London.

When did Whiston start his translation work of Josephus? According to his own statement in the second volume of his complete Josephus,[19] Whiston started on 9th December, 1734 at the age of sixty-seven and finished it on 6th January, 1736 at the age of seventy. This suggests that he spent only a little more than two years for the completion of his translation. Marvelous speed indeed![20] Because Whiston was a successor to Newton, because he translated Josephus from the original Greek, not from the Latin and French, and because he guaranteed the authenticity of the testimony of Josephus on Jesus Christ, people came to look upon Whiston's translation as being completely free from any error and placed it in the highest rank tantamount to that of King James Version. This was the birth of what I call the "Whiston Myth." Although there are many defects in Whiston's Greek text, many errors in his own translation, and many irrelevant footnotes in the text itself, once the "Whiston Myth" was born, no one tried to examine the quality of his translation any longer. A myth is a smoke screen to hide the truth. Myth is something that induces people to intellectual sloth.

Whiston's translation was printed in several cities of England. In London alone, it was printed four times in the eighteenth century and twenty-six times in the next century. Whiston's translation was brought to the New Continent toward the end of the eighteenth century and won a large number of readers. Thomas Jefferson (1743–1826), the third President of the United States, was one of them.

In 1740, that is, three years after the publication of Whiston's Josephus, James Wilson's edition of Josephus was published in London. This was actually Jackson's Josephus, which I have already mentioned. We know nothing of this James Wilson. Because his Josephus disappeared from the market soon after its publication, it is now almost impossible to find it, and Heinz Schreckenberg failed to register it in his *Bibliographie*. This rare book is now owned by a collector of early printed editions of Josephus in Kansas City.[21]

---

[19] Vol. II, 1023 (no page number).

[20] See also "A Compleat(e) Chronological Catalogue of Mr. Whiston's Writings" attached at the very end of Vol. II. He did publish sixty-two books as of July 8th 1737.

[21] Prof. Steve Mason kindly introduced her to me several years ago, and finally last fall after the SBL conference in Atlanta, my wife and I flew to Kansas and had the privilege of seeing this Wilson's Josephus, together with some other precious texts of Josephus, including incunabula. A marvelous collection, indeed. I am very grateful to Prof. Mason for introducing this collector to me.

Although Wilson mentions nowhere the name of William Whiston, the use of the phrase of "a fair and just Translation" in his preface seems to suggest at first sight that he had Whiston's translation in mind. However, as we have already pointed out, this Wilson's Josephus is completely based upon Jackson's translation and the preface itself is from that edition!

Five more different versions of Josephus were to be published in the second half of the eighteenth century. The edition of Thompson and Price was published in London in 1777. "The works of Flavius Josephus" is its title. Very simple, indeed. The title page reads: "The whole newly translated from the original Greek by Ebenezer Thompson, D. D. and William Charles Price, L. L. D." Although this title page emphasizes that this new translation is based on the Greek text, it does not mention which Greek text they used or how they divided labor in their translation effort.

Under the frontispiece of volume one is written: "Let every Christian, while his bosom glows, think of our pious Jew." With the phrase "our pious Jew," Josephus maybe Christianized here. Although in this edition many illustrations and maps are inserted, some of them have nothing to do with the text itself. Two examples: illustrations of "Mary Magdalen (Magdalene?) admiring the wisdom and goodness of Jesus"[22] and of Peter's vision in the Acts 10:9–23.[23] Both Thompson and Price seem to have had the intention of Christianizing their readers through Josephus.

Let us have a look at the first part of the preface. It says:

> The sacred Scriptures excepted, there are no writings extant of equal authority with those of Flavius Josephus; nor any which exhibit such incontestable evidence in favour of the Truths of Christianity. An instance, perhaps, cannot be produced, wherein the most obstinate Disbelievers have not been struck with, at least, a temporary conviction, on perusal of our ancient and learned historian; and when people begin to doubt on the important article of religion, they will deliberately examine into the foundation of their principles, and carefully separate truth from falsehood: whence it may be inferred, that the work in question has caused more converts to the doctrines of the Old and New Testament than the united labours of every other profane writer.

---

[22] Vol. II, inserted between 8 and 9.
[23] Vol. II, inserted between 524 and 525.
[24] Schreckenberg 1968, 57–58.

The "most obstinate Disbelievers" referred to in the larger case are the Jews or the Jewish nation.

In 1785, Charles Clarke's Josephus was published in London. Its title is very simple: "The whole works of Flavius Josephus translated from the original Greek." According to this title page, Clarke is "Professor of languages, and teacher of the Greek, Latin and Hebrew." The footnotes to this edition were made by the Reverend Mr. Yorke of Oxford, but there are no anti-Jewish elements in them. This edition was reprinted in London in 1794 and in Manchester in 1813.

In 1789, when the French Revolution took place, George Henry Maynard's Josephus was published in London. Its title was: "The Works of Flavius Josephus, the celebrated warlike, learned and authentic Jewish historian." The title page proudly states that this edition is from the original Greek, but as Schreckenberg has pointed out correctly,[24] this is entirely based on Clarke's Josephus. In the frontispiece are depicted the three figures of Moses, Aaron, and Josephus and the picture of the fall of Jerusalem is seen between Moses and Josephus. It has the following explanation: "In the distance, the Roman army destroying the City of Jerusalem, over which are Thunder and Lightning to denote its being through the vengeance of heaven, and behind the Setting Sun signifying the total destruction of the Jewish Empire."

I believe the value of Maynard's Josephus as an antiquarian book is highly enhanced thanks to the insertion in *Jewish Antiquities* of three illustrations made by William Blake. They are the parting of Lot and Abraham, the battle of Ain and the destruction of the city by the army of Joshua, and the fugitive Shechemites.[25]

In the translator's address to the reader, Maynard presupposes that his readers are "those who are curious in searching into ancient history." He then introduces Josephus to his readers, and claims that, "there is good reason to believe that the author, at that time he wrote it, was more than almost persuaded to be a Christian himself." Maynard, like William Whiston, seems to have a firm belief that Josephus had to be a Christian:

Maynard further says:

> That famous passage, introduced in the 4th Chap. of the 18th Book of his *Antiquities*, concerning our blessed Saviour, and which some superficial judges have pretended is spurious, will certainly appear, if

---

[25] Maynard, 12, 64, and 76.
[26] Maynard, 644.

fairly, and even critically examined, to be evidently such a plain and
simple narration of an historical fact, as any Jew, in his situation, might
have written to the Heathens; especially if we recollect that Josephus
frequently tells his readers that he relates facts as he finds them; and,
in his account of the opinions of the Pharisees, and the Sadducees or
Essenes, he gives them as he found them in their books. Why then
should he not be supposed to give us, with the same candour, though
he does it in so respectful a manner, and a plain relation of what he
saw and heard concerning the Christians, and the opinion of their
blessed master: especially as the Christians were then very numerous,
and the general topic of discourse both among Jews and Romans?

Maynard's Josephus provides his readers with a book-length account
of the "Continuation of the history of the Jews, from the time of
Flavius Josephus. Including a period of upwards of 1700 years." This
contains an account of the dispersion of the Jewish people into the
various parts of Europe, Asia, Africa, and America, their different
persecutions, transactions, and present state throughout the known
world.

One of the questions Christians may have entertained concerning
the Jewish people was unfortunately this: why are they still allowed
to exist on earth after they have committed such a crime against
Christ? Is there any providential meaning for their existence? Indeed,
in England where people had such a sentiment, though the Jewish
people had the experience of being expelled from there in the time
of Edward I in 1290, they were not yet extinguished. Thus, Maynard
attempts to answer this question, and in doing so refers to important events in their history such as: their synagogues destroyed by
the Christians during the reign of Theodosius, Justinian's edicts against
the Jews, the cruel massacre by the crusaders, persecution by Henry
III, king of Castile, protection by the Popes Innocent II and Alexander
III, persecution and massacre by the Inquisition, heavy taxation under
Henry III of England, expulsion from England by King Edward,
persecutions in Germany, Pope Pius IV's edicts against the Jews,
expulsion of the Jews by Pope Pius V, the reception of the Jews in
Bohemia, Hungary, Moravia, Hamburg, and Holland. Each of these
events is described in a fairly objective manner.

To the eyes of those pious Christians who believed everything in
the Bible as true, divine prophecies were the kind that must be
fulfilled in history and are being fulfilled in the present on-going
time. Because of this belief, fundamentalist Christians attempted to
read ancient literature and examined various events therein and

claimed that divine prophecies were fulfilled. Maynard was one of them. In his "Illustration of the predictions of the principal prophets, whose names are mentioned in the works of Flavius Josephus," Maynard picks up the prophecy of Noah, the prophecies concerning Ishmael, the prophecies of Jacob, the prophecies of Moses, Jeremiah, Isaiah, the prophecies of Nineveh, Babylon, Tyre, the prophecy of Egypt, and the prophecies and visions of Daniel, and then refers the previous interpretations of these prophecies and visions, and tries to see their fulfillment in history. One example is this. Deuteronomy 28:29 says that "for the rest of your life, people will beat and rob you, and no one will be able to stop them." Maynard sees the fulfillment of this prophecy in this passage in the time of Henry III, who laid a heavy tax on the Jewish people or in the time of Edward I, who expelled the Jews from England. On the fate of the Jewish people, Maynard states that, "Ever since the Jews have absolutely rejected the gospel, and been no longer the people of God, there have not been any visible manifestations of a Divine interpretation in their favour. As a punishment for their infidelity they have, for ages past, been dispersed all over the world without having either a temporal or spiritual protector. They are despised in all parts where they inhabit, and are the general scoff and ridicule of the people of all kingdoms."[26] This same Maynard also says that,

> . . . it must be allowed, that the Jews are exceeding blamable for still persisting in their infidelity, after so many means have been taken to bring them to a sense of conviction: but this does not authorize us to proscribe, abuse, injure and oppress them, as Christians of more zeal than either knowledge or charity have, in all ages been inclined to do. 'Charity is greater than faith' and it is worse in us to be cruel and uncharitable, than it is in them to be obstinate and unbelieving.[27]

Some of you may recall the remarks of ancient Christian writers who, in terms of providential care, attempted to explain the continued existence of the Jewish people on earth. What did St. Augustine say about it? You could compare his remarks with Maynard's.

Thomas Bradshaw's Josephus was published in London somewhere between 1795 and 1800. This is not registered in Schreckenberg's *Bibliographie*. Its title was: "The whole Genuine and Complete Works

---

[27] Maynard, 647.

of Flavius Josephus, the learned and authentic Jewish historian and
celebrated warrior." This Josephus was now available in the quarto
size, not in the folio size. It thus became easier for readers to carry
Josephus and read him anywhere. This edition borrows from Maynard
the account of the history of the Jews, but its title was changed into
"The History of the Jews: Continued from the time of Josephus to
the present, including a space of many centuries" and the original
lengthy account is simplified. The concluding remarks are:

> From the entire history of the Jews, taken in all its parts, it is beyond
> a doubt that unbelief has been the source of all their calamities. A
> view of the remarkable events which took place in the earliest ages,
> exhibits a striking display of the divine mercy and justice, as well as
> the certain effects of incredulity and impenitence. Disobedience suc-
> ceeded calamity, and calamity deliverance: obedience met its reward,
> and disobedience its punishment. . . . In the succeeding times, their
> conduct seems invariable; and to this day they appear bent on their
> own destruction, by continuing in obstinacy and unbelief. God grant
> that the scales of ignorance may speedily fall from their eyes; and that
> they may, as individuals and as a nation, be brought to behold the
> light of the knowledge of the glory of God, as it shines in the person
> and face of Jesus Christ![28]

Josephus in the Nineteenth Century

We are now entering the nineteenth century. This century finally
saw the appearance of our hero, Robert Traill, who became the first
Irish translator of Josephus as well as the first critic of William
Whiston's translation.

Robert Traill was born in 1793 as the third son of the Rev.
Anthony Traill, Archdeacon of Connor and of Agnes, daughter of
William Watts Gayer.[29] He entered Trinity College Dublin in 1814
and after graduation he was ordained by the Bishop of Gloucester
and worked for his diocese in England. Robert Traill then succeeded
to the parish of Schull, County Cork in 1830. The parish of Schull,
at the extreme southwest point of Ireland, was very populous. He

---

[28] Bradshow, 693.
[29] Biographical details of Robert Traill come mainly from the editor's preface
written by Isaac Taylor (1862, xix–xxiv).

found the population in a state of deplorable destitution, especially during the years of the great famine. This horrible situation might be comparable to that in Jerusalem as depicted by Josephus, though of course the causes of the famines were totally different between the two. During the time of this great famine, Robert Traill used up his private fortune to save his parish people. Not only that, he kept travelling from house to house, from hovel to hovel, in his parish to console and encourage those people who were just waiting for death. Only death could relieve them from agony, as it was 2,000 years ago in Jerusalem. In one of his letters addressed to his friend, Robert Traill says: "Death by famine, and then by pestilence, will sweep this country of a third of its people." The Irish population is said to have been drastically reduced from eight million before the famine and the pestilence to six million after them.

Robert Traill himself became a victim of the pestilence in 1846. In the light of our translation history, we could say that Robert Traill followed in the steps of his predecessor, Thomas Lodge, who also became a victim of famine and pestilence in the year 1625.

Robert Traill's fondness for Greek literature directed his attention to the writings of Josephus at an early age, and led him to have an ambition of translating Josephus into English anew because he was beginning to be sure that Whiston's translation was full of defects. We do not know exactly when Robert Traill started his work of translating Josephus into English, but we do know that he completed the translation of the *Jewish War* and *Life* just before he succumbed to the pestilence. After his death, Robert Traill's translation was immediately edited by Isaac Taylor and published in two volumes in 1847 and 1851. Attached to the first volume are the two prefaces, that is, the translator's preface and the editor's preface. In his preface, Robert Traill speaks of Whiston's translation:

> The present translator of Josephus does not propose to invite attention to his own labours by aiming to disparage those of his predecessors in the same line. On the contrary, he readily admits that the several English versions of the Jewish Historian have had their merit; it seems to be generally agreed also, that they have now had their day. As to the last of these translations, few competent persons, if any, would profess to think that there is no room to wish for anything more exact as a rendering of the Greek or more fluent and agreeable as to style, than Whiston's translation. Nevertheless, the invidious task of

proving that, in places innumerable, Whiston's version is faulty [according to Hata's judgment, this "innumerable places" must have meant more than several thousand] as well as the very superfluous endeavour to show that, as a literary composition, it is crabbed and repulsive, the present translator declines.[30]

I will not add anything to Robert Traill's own comment. As we have seen, Josephus has been read in modern English translations since the beginning of the seventeenth century, and Josephus has been widely read since the appearance of Whiston's translation in 1737 because of the "Whiston Myth."

It is an act of faithfulness to scholarship to doubt a myth, but it is an act of courage to challenge the myth openly. Robert Traill, though he himself did not improve Whiston's translation, challenged the "Whiston Myth" and made an openly critical remark on his translation. Thanks to his scholarship and his courage, some of the scholars in the succeeding generations came to realize that they had to improve Whiston's translation because of his great influence upon the readers. So, Arthur Richard Shilleto, sometime scholar of Trinity College in the University of Cambridge and translator of Plutarch's works, who also noticed the "strange and erratic" understanding of Christianity in Whiston, attempted to improve his translation on the basis of *Flavii Iosephi opera, graece et latine*, edited by G. Dindorfs and published in Paris in 1845–1846. Shilleto's edition was published in the series of the Bohn's Libraries in the year of 1889–1890. As for Whiston's footnotes, Shilleto was most critical. He pointed out that some of them had nothing to do with the text itself. Thus, although some of Whiston's footnotes are retained as they were, most of them were either truncated or erased. Topographical notes are made by Sir C. W. Wilson. This edition was printed five times in London.[31] It was also printed in America. And after Shilleto, D. S. Margoliouth, in 1921, further improved the text of Whiston, and finally deleted the dissertations and footnotes that were "antiquated in matter, and still more in spirit."[32] The spirit referred to herein is undoubtedly the one derived from, in Shilleto's words, a "strange and erratic" understanding of Christianity in Whiston, which is evidently anti-Jewish.[33]

---

[30] The translator's Preface, xv.
[31] Schreckenberg 1968, 45.
[32] See the editor's preface on p. vii in the 1906 edition of *Works of Flavius Josephus*, published in London by George Routledge & Sons.
[33] As to the quality of the revisions made by Shilleto and Margoliouth, Feldman (1984, 29) expresses his disappointment

Concluding Remarks

On the special occasion of the International Josephus Colloquium in Trinity College Dublin, I have attempted to talk about Robert Traill, a proud product of this College against the background of the translation history of Josephus in the seventeenth and eighteenth centuries. In doing so, I have paid special attention to anti-Jewish remarks made by the translators of Josephus because I wanted to show you how Josephus was abused and misused by Christians not only in antiquity but also in modern times. As everyone knows, and as we have shown, William Whiston was the most influential in the translation history of Josephus at least in the English-speaking world.

Robert Traill was the first critic of Whiston's translation of Josephus, which was full of errors, erratic Christian interpretations, as well as anti-Jewish sentiments. I have not yet examined in full how much Traill was sensitive to the anti-Judaism of Whiston, his predecessors and his successors up to his time in the nineteenth century, but I am beginning to feel that because he was sensitive to the anti-Jewish statements of Whiston, he began to show his special attention to the quality of Whiston's translation. In any case, it is evident that he was the first critic of Whiston's translation. I respect him very much, and I hope you share with me my respect for him.

BIBLIOGRAPHY

Feldman, L. H.
    1984   *Josephus and Modern Scholarship* (1937–1980). Berlin.
Force, J. E.
    1985   *William Whiston: Honest Newtonian*. London.
Hata, G.
    2001   Eusebius and Josephus: The way Eusebius Misused and Abused Josephus. Pages 49–66 in *Patristica*. Supplementary vol. 1.
    2001   English translations of Josephus in the 17th and 18th Centuries (Part 1). *Tama Bijyutu University Bulletin*. 16:89–104.
    2002   English translations of Josephus in the 18th and 19th Centuries (Part 2). *Tama Bijyutsu University Bulletin*. 17:65–84.
Metzgter, B. M.
    1983   The Fourth Book of Ezra. Pages 517–559 in The *Old Testament Pseudepigrapha*, Vol. 1. Edited by J. H. Charlesworth. Garden City.
Schreckenberg, H.
    1969   *Bibliographie zu Flavius Josephus*. Arbeiten zur Literatur und Geschichte des hellenistischen Judentums 1. Leiden.
Taylor, I.
    1862   *The Jewish War of Flavius Josephus: A New Translation*. London.
Whealey, A.
    2003   *Josephus on Jesus: The Testimonium Flavianum Controversy from Late Antiquity to Modern Times*. New York.

INDEX OF ANCIENT SOURCES

Hebrew Bible/Old Testament

New Testament

New Testament Apocrypha

Rabbinic Literature

OTHER RABBINIC WORKS

CHRISTIAN WRITERS

INSCRIPTIONS AND PAPYRI

GENERAL INDEX

INDEX OF MODERN AUTHORS